ZAGATSURVEY®
25TH ANNIVERSARY

U.S. FAMILY
TRAVEL GUIDE

**Editors: Donna Marino, Betsy Andrews
& Caren Weiner Campbell**

**Published and distributed by
ZAGAT SURVEY, LLC
4 Columbus Circle
New York, New York 10019
Tel: 212 977 6000
E-mail: familytravel@zagat.com
Web site: www.zagat.com**

Acknowledgments

We thank Kevin Arnovitz, Nikki Buchanan, Rona Gindin, Meesha Halm, Carolyn Heller, Jeanette Foster, Michael Klein, Rochelle Koff, Rita Kyriakides, William McGee, Lori Midson, Cynthia Nims, Shelley Skiles Sawyer, Mary Stagaman and Tanya Wenman Steel; and our staff, especially Michael Gitter and Kelly Sinanis, as well as Reni Chin, Larry Cohn, Carol Diuguid, Ann Duggal, Griff Foxley, Schuyler Frazier, Jeff Freier, Shelley Gallagher, Curt Gathje, Randi Gollin, Katherine Harris, Natalie Lebert, Mike Liao, Dave Makulec, Laura Mitchell, Rob Poole, Benjamin Schmerler, Troy Segal, Robert Seixas, Daniel Simmons, Yoji Yamaguchi and Sharon Yates.

We are especially grateful to *Parenting* magazine, which provided the Travel Tips on page 8 and enabled us to survey so many travel-savvy parents for this guide.

Contents

About This Survey

Since 1979, Zagat Survey has reported on the shared experiences of people like you. What started 25 years ago as a hobby involving 200 friends has come a long way. Today we have more than 250,000 surveyors. Now we've teamed up with *Parenting* magazine to bring you our first *Survey* designed specifically with children in mind and focusing on the leading family-oriented attractions, hotels and restaurants across the United States.

Rating Attractions: What's truly different about this family-travel survey is that the attractions are rated by more than 11,000 avid travelers (61% female) on both Child Appeal and Adult Appeal. As any traveling parent knows, often the two are quite different. And since kids' ages make a difference, we've used icons to point out places that are especially suited to toddlers, younger and older children. Our reviewers have also given each attraction a score for its Public Facilities (i.e. consumer-friendly amenities such as on-site restaurants, restrooms and parking) and one for Service (whether you'll find friendly, available staffers).

Lodging and Dining: To further help family travelers we've included listings and reviews of hotels and restaurants near each attraction. You may notice that some get different ratings than in other Zagat Surveys and that we've included a new Family Appeal score. That's because the family travelers we surveyed have different needs than adult singles and couples. Since Zagat publishes restaurant guides for numerous individual cities, we've added some of the best family-friendly places that you won't want to miss (these additions appear without scores).

Best Bets: To help you find the best attractions for your family, we've prepared a number of lists – see Most Popular (page 15) and Top Ratings (pages 16–24) – as well as 80+ handy indexes. (See Table of Contents).

Other Zagat Guides: Many of our other guides are perfect companions to this one, including our city restaurant guides, *Top U.S. Hotels, Resorts & Spas* and *America's Top Golf Courses.* Our restaurant *Surveys* are also available by subscription at zagat.com.

To join this or any of our upcoming *Surveys*, just register at zagat.com. Each participant will receive a free copy of the resulting guide when published. Your comments and even criticisms of this guide are also solicited. You can contact us at familytravel@zagat.com. We look forward to hearing from you.

New York, NY
May 18, 2004

Nina and Tim Zagat

Getting a Good Deal

Avoid the Rack Race: After several slow years, travel is picking up around the U.S. As a result, room rates are again on the rise. But you can still get great values if you live by the motto "ask and you shall receive." There are always empty hotel rooms to fill – and hoteliers ready to deal – especially during off-peak times. Published or quoted rates are just a starting point: Don't be afraid to negotiate and be sure to ask about special promotions and room upgrades. And remember, it's the reservationist at the hotel who is authorized to bargain, not the toll-free operator.

Make it Suite: Certain hotels especially cater to parents with children, via both special rates and facilities. Among the best are all-suite hotels that let kids stay with their parents for free and include kitchens, which can save you on restaurant bills.

Net Savvy: You'll often find the best bargains on the Web, particularly for last-minute trips. To get excess inventory that's substantially marked down, book online via individual hotels or larger integrated sites such as Expedia, Hotels.com, Priceline, Travelocity and Orbitz. (See "Useful Web Sites & Telephone Numbers", page 12).

You've Got a Friend: Travel agents offer experience, and their on-property contacts can often be invaluable. The key is finding the right travel counselor who both understands your family's needs and will work with you. With such a professional you will save both time and money.

Buyer Beware: There's a tremendous difference in room type, so ask where yours is located, whether it has a view, etc. Be sure to ask about specific amenities that are meaningful to you. If you don't like the room when you arrive ask for another.

Hidden Costs: Sometimes a deal isn't a deal – ask in advance about taxes and charges (such as phone or parking fees). In fact, you're always better off using your own cell phone to avoid outrageous phone fees.

Family-Friendly Features: Depending on your needs, check out our Special Features indexes for hotels with swimming pools for kids, arcade/game rooms or playgrounds, and for restaurants that offer crayons/games at the table and many other amenities. Indexes start on page 270.

Oil for Those Squeaky Wheels: If you're dissatisfied with any element of your trip, don't be afraid to speak up. Any good hotel or restaurant will do as much as it can to rectify problems. And if you don't get a satisfactory response on-site, send a letter to the property's general manager or parent company when you return home, with a CC to "Zagat Survey, Customer Satisfaction."

Parenting Magazine's Travel Tips

Since you're a parent, you probably *already* know to expect the unexpected. Here are some mom-tested ideas for making the most of any family vacation, surprises and all:

The Early Bird: Driving? Know that no matter what time you aim to leave, it'll be at least an hour later before you're on your way. Plan accordingly. Flying? Shoot for the earliest flight of the day (less chance for delays). That means you may be up at 4 AM, but it beats sitting in a crowded airport with a cranky toddler. If that's not doable, try for a flight that coincides with naptime.

Get Packing: You really don't have to bring a different outfit for every single day (for you *or* your kids). Mix and match, and live with some mustard stains. If your child's a pack rat, give her one (small) backpack she can fill with whatever she wants, and you're in charge of the rest. For a baby, a car seat is a must – you can use it on the plane, in a restaurant, even on the beach.

Secure for Sure: If your child can walk, he's going to have to go through security alone. Practice before you leave so it seems like a game, and warn him that he's going to have to be separated from a beloved blankie for a few seconds. Sneakers are a pretty safe bet for security machines since most don't have metal. And be sure to check that you leave the area with all your belongings.

Time Stands Still: "Are we there yet?" Probably not, so bring along some new, small toys to dole out as surprises along the way (Silly Putty and Mad Libs are good choices). Other options for the easily amused: a roll of tape, magnets, sketch pads and an old, nonworking cell phone. When driving, make frequent stops to stretch your legs and see some quirkier sights.

Tire the Tots: If your kids are ready for a nap before you board a flight, all the better. Sure, the airlines will let passengers with small children board first, but consider skipping this perk to let them run around and burn off a little more energy. If you're flying with more than one child, give each one a turn in the window seat. Avoid seats over the wings if you're hoping the view will entertain for a little while. Some parents swear by bulkhead rows (the first row behind the wall that separates economy from first class) because there's more room, but you'll have to stash all your carry-ons overhead. And make sure you get pool or ocean water out of little ears before the return flight.

Home Sweet Hotel: Many properties will childproof your room if you call ahead – but it can't hurt to take some extra electrical-outlet covers, corner bumpers and a night-light. You can also ask the hotel to remove all the items from the minibar (or hide the key when you arrive) – those $7 cans of peanuts can add up. To kids, motels are as much fun as fancier places. Many have in-room fridges – the best place to stock up on snacks.

Amusing Moments: The No. 1 rule at amusement parks: Don't try to do it all – you'll wind up with a hot, cranky, tired and disappointed crew. Think about what makes sense for the ages and interests of your kids (this guide should help) and then check a map to find the rides or shows you want to see – and all the bathrooms nearby. Buy tickets ahead of time if you can, and take advantage of express passes or other benefits of staying at an affiliated resort. And when you get inside, go left since most people veer to the right, then make a beeline for the back of the park and work your way forward.

Meltdown Madness: Maybe this'll be the trip when no one cries, sulks or falls to the floor in a fit. Or maybe not. Escape the scene of a tantrum if you have to (you may miss the hayride, but it wasn't going to be fun with a shrieking child anyway). One smart way to avoid too many meltdowns is to plan no more than two major activities per day.

Snack Attack: Have healthy snacks on hand in case it's hunger that's causing a temper tantrum. Make lunch the main meal of the day, when everyone's still feeling chipper, and keep munchies and fruit in your room for late-night options. If you're tired by nightfall, order in room service or call for a pizza delivery.

Staying on Schedule: If your child always has a nap after lunch, arrange your day so there's time for one during your vacation too. Or if you allow dessert only after a certain number of green items are eaten, stick to it. (A bellyful of ice cream is a terrible thing to mix with a jostling ride on a kiddie coaster.) Little ones are comforted by routines, and the more they know what to expect, the more fun you'll all have.

Tot-Free Time: You planned this fantastic family trip – you deserve a little break. As much fun as it is to see your child's face light up when he spots a dolphin, you could undoubtedly use some time away. Utilize kids' clubs and babysitting services to take advantage of the spa or a fine-dining meal of your own. Spend at least 15 minutes with your kids and the caregiver before you leave them, however, to make sure they're comfortable.

Ratings & Symbols

Name, Address, Phone Number & Web Site

Age Appropriateness, Hours & Credit Cards

Zagat Ratings

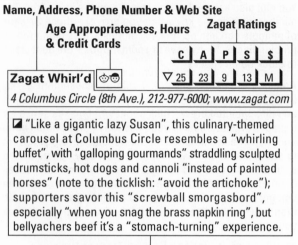

	C	A	P	S	$
Zagat Whirl'd ☺☻	▽ 25	23	9	13	M

4 Columbus Circle (8th Ave.), 212-977-6000; www.zagat.com

☑ "Like a gigantic lazy Susan", this culinary-themed carousel at Columbus Circle resembles a "whirling buffet", with "galloping gourmands" straddling sculpted drumsticks, hot dogs and cannoli "instead of painted horses" (note to the ticklish: "avoid the artichoke"); supporters savor this "screwball smorgasbord", especially "when you snag the brass napkin ring", but bellyachers beef it's a "stomach-turning" experience.

Review, with surveyors' comments in quotes

The ratings scale is as follows:

0–9 poor to fair	**20–25** very good to excellent
10–15 fair to good	**26–30** extraordinary to perfection
16–19 good to very good	▽ low response/less reliable

A spot listed without ratings is a **write-in** or **newcomer**.

Places with top ratings and greatest importance are shown in **CAPITAL LETTERS**. Before reviews a symbol indicates whether responses were uniform ■ or mixed ◪.

Attractions Ratings & Icons

C Child Appeal
A Adult Appeal
P Public Facilities
S Service

C	A	P	S	$
25	23	9	13	M

Public Facilities include consumer amenities such as restrooms, on-site restaurants and ease of getting around.

Service ratings are for the friendliness and availability of tour guides, rangers, docents and other personnel.

The **Cost ($)** column reflects the attraction's high-season price range for one Young Child (4–7) and one Adult.

$0 Free	**E** $31–$60
I $15 or less	**VE** $61 or more
M $16–$30	

Age Appropriateness:
☺ = Best for Toddlers (3 & under)
☺ = Best for Young Children (4–7)
☺ = Best for Preteens (8–12)
No icon means appropriate for all ages.

Hotel Ratings

FA Family Appeal
R Rooms
S Service
P Public Facilities

FA	R	S	P	$
25	23	9	13	$200

The **Cost ($)** column reflects the hotel's high-season rack rate, i.e. its asking price, for a standard double room. Be sure to ask if this is the best rate or if there are family packages available.

For Hotel Chains, cost is shown below. Prices vary significantly by season.

I Inexpensive, below $100   **E** Expensive, $201–$349
M Moderate, $100–$200   **VE** Very Expensive, $350 or more

Restaurant Ratings & Icons

FA Family Appeal
F Food
D Decor
S Service

FA	F	D	S	$
25	23	9	13	E

The **Cost ($)** column reflects our surveryors' estimate of the price of dinner including one drink and tip. Depending on their ages your kids may be able to eat for as much as 50 percent less. The price range is indicated as follows:

I $15 and below   **E** $31–$50
M $16–$30   **VE** $51 or more

Hours:
🌑 = serves after 11PM
☒ = closed on Sunday

Credit Cards:
⊘ = no credit cards accepted

Useful Web Sites & Telephone Numbers

HOTEL CHAIN	WEB SITE	PHONE
Adam's Mark	adamsmark.com	800-444-2326
Amanresorts	amanresorts.com	800-477-9180
Amerisuites	amerisuites.com	800-477-9180
Best Western	bestwestern.com	800-528-1234
Caesars	caesars.com	800-223-7277
Clarion	clarionhotel.com	800-252-7466
Comfort Inn	comfortinn.com	800-252-7466
Courtyard by Marriott	courtyard.com	800-321-2211
Crowne Plaza	crowneplaza.com	800-227-6963
Days Inn	daysinn.com	800-325-2525
DoubleTree	doubletree.com	800-222-8733
Embassy Suites	embassysuites.com	800-362-2779
Fairfield Inn	fairfieldinn.com	800-228-2800
Fairmont	fairmont.com	800-441-1414
Four Points	fourpoints.com	888-625-5144
Four Seasons	fourseasons.com	800-332-3442
Grand Hyatt	hyatt.com	800-233-1234
Hampton Inn	hamptoninn.com	800-426-7866
Harrah's	harrahs.com	800-427-7247
Hilton	hilton.com	800-774-1500
Hilton Garden Inn	hiltongardeninn.com	800-774-1500
Holiday Inn	holiday-inn.com	800-465-4329
Homewood Suites	homewood-suites.com	800-225-5466
Howard Johnson	hojo.com	800-406-1411
Hyatt	hyatt.com	800-233-1234
Hyatt Regency	hyatt.com	800-233-1234
InterContinental	interconti.com	800-327-0200
Joie de Vivre	jdvhospitality.com	800-738-7477
Kimpton Group	kimptongroup.com	800-546-7866
La Quinta	laquinta.com	800-531-5900
Leading Hotels	lhw.com	800-223-6800
Le Méridien	lemeridien.com	800-543-4300
Loews	loewshotels.com	800-235-6397
Luxury Collection	luxurycollection.com	800-325-3589
MainStay Suites	mainstaysuites.com	800-660-6246
Mandarin Oriental	mandarin-oriental.com	866-526-6567
Marriott	marriott.com	800-228-9290
Millennium Hotels	millenniumhotels.com	866-866-6455
Nikko	nikkohotels.com	800-645-5687
Omni	omnihotels.com	800-843-6664
Pan Pacific	panpac.com	800-327-8585
Park Hyatt	hyatt.com	800-233-1234
Peninsula	peninsula.com	800-262-9467
Preferred Hotels	preferredhotels.com	800-323-7500
Radisson	radisson.com	800-333-3333

Ramada	ramada.com	800-272-6232
Red Lion	redlion.com	800-733-5466
Regal Hotels	regalhotel.com	800-222-8888
Regent	regenthotels.com	800-545-4000
Relais & Châteaux	relaischateaux.com	800-735-2478
Renaissance	renaissancehotels.com	800-468-3571
Residence Inn	residenceinn.com	800-331-3131
Ritz-Carlton	ritzcarlton.com	800-241-3333
Rosewood	rosewoodhotels.com	888-767-3966
Sheraton	sheraton.com	800-325-3535
Shoney's Inn	shoneysinn.com	800-552-4667
Small Luxury Hotels	slh.com	800-525-4800
Sonesta	sonesta.com	800-766-3782
St. Regis	stregis.com	877-787-2447
Swissôtel	swissotel.com	888-737-9477
Travelodge	travelodge.com	800-578-7878
Westin	westin.com	800-937-8461
W Hotels	whotels.com	877-946-8357
Wingate Inns	wingateinns.com	800-228-1000
Wyndham	wyndham.com	800-822-4200

AIRLINE

AirTran	airtran.com	800-247-8726
Alaska Airlines	alaskaair.com	800-426-0333
Aloha Airlines	alohaair.com	800-367-5250
American	americanair.com	800-433-7300
America West	americawest.com	800-235-9292
Continental	continental.com	800-525-0280
Delta	delta.com	800-221-1212
Frontier	frontierairlines.com	800-432-1359
Hawaiian Airlines	hawaiianair.com	800-367-5320
JetBlue	jetblue.com	800-538-2583
Midwest Airlines	midwestairlines.com	800-452-2022
Northwest	nwa.com	800-225-2525
Song	flysong.com	800-359-7664
Southwest	southwest.com	800-435-9792
Spirit Airlines	spiritair.com	800-772-7117
Sun Country	suncountry.com	800-241-6522
United	united.com	800-241-6522
US Airways	usair.com	800-428-4322

CAR RENTAL

Alamo	alamo.com	800-327-9633
Avis	avis.com	800-230-4898
Budget	budget.com	800-527-0700
Dollar	dollar.com	800-800-4000
Enterprise	enterprise.com	800-736-8222
Hertz	hertz.com	800-654-3131
National	nationalcar.com	800-227-7368
Payless	paylesscar.com	800-729-5377
Thrifty	thrifty.com	800-367-2277

RAILROAD/BUS

| Amtrak | amtrak.com | 800-872-7245 |
| Greyhound | greyhound.com | 800-231-2222 |

VISITORS' BUREAU

Atlanta	atlanta.net	800-285-2682
Baltimore	baltimore.org	800-282-6632
Boston/Cape Cod	bostonusa.com	800-888-5515
Chicago	chicago.il.org	877-244-2246
Cincinnati	cincyusa.com	800-246-2987
Dallas	dallascvb.com	800-232-5527
Ft. Worth	fortworth.com	800-433-5747
Denver	denver.org	800-233-6837
Hawaii	gohawaii.com	800-464-2924
Houston	houston-guide.com	800-446-8786
Las Vegas	lvcva.com	877-847-4858
Los Angeles	lacvb.com	800-228-2452
Miami	miamiandbeaches.com	888-766-4264
New Orleans	neworleanscvb.com	800-672-6124
New York City	nycvisit.com	212-484-1222
Orlando	orlandoinfo.com	866-696-7526
Philadelphia	pcvb.org	800-225-5745
Phoenix/Scottsdale	arizonaguide.com	866-275-5816
San Diego	sandiego.org	619-236-1212
San Francisco	sfvisitor.org	888-782-9673
Seattle	seeseattle.org	206-461-5840
St. Louis	explorestlouis.com	800-916-8938
Washington, DC	washington.org	800-422-8644

WEB SITE/TRAVEL AGENCY

AAA	aaa.com	800-272-2155
American Express	travel.americanexpress.com	800-346-3607
Carlson Wagonlit	carlsonwagonlit.com	763-212-1000
CheapTickets	cheaptickets.com	888-922-8849
11th Hour Vacations	11thhourvacations.com	864-331-1140
Expedia	expedia.com	800-397-3342
Hotels.com	hotels.com	800-246-8357
Hotwire	hotwire.com	877-468-9473
International Tours	itcruises.com	800-928-8888
Liberty Travel	libertytravel.com	888-271-1584
OneTravel	onetravel.com	800-929-2523
Orbitz	orbitz.com	888-656-4546
Priceline	priceline.com	866-925-5373
Quikbook	quikbook.com	800-789-9887
Site 59	site59.com	800-845-0192
The-Hotels.com	the-hotels.com	800-297-0144
Travelocity	travelocity.com	800-249-4302
Travelweb	travelweb.com	866-437-8132
TravelWorm	travelworm.com	888-700-8342
Uniglobe	uniglobetravel.com	800-999-8000
USA Hotels	1800usahotels.com	800-872-4683
VacationKids.com	vacationkids.com	610-681-7360
Virtuoso	virtuoso.com	800-401-4274

Most Popular Attractions

These are our surveyors' 50 favorite attractions, in order:

1. Magic Kingdom, *Orlando*
2. Epcot, *Orlando*
3. American Museum of Natural History, *New York City*
4. Disneyland, *Los Angeles*
5. Central Park, *New York City*
6. Disney-MGM Studios, *Orlando*
7. Metropolitan Museum of Art, *New York City*
8. Disney's Animal Kingdom, *Orlando*
9. Bronx Zoo, *New York City*
10. Yosemite National Park, *Yosemite National Park, CA**
11. Grand Canyon National Park, *Grand Canyon, AZ**
12. San Diego Zoo, *San Diego*
13. Fountains of Bellagio, *Las Vegas*
14. National Air & Space Museum, *Washington, DC*
15. Yellowstone National Park, *West Yellowstone, MT**
16. Alcatraz Island, *San Francisco*
17. Islands of Adventure, *Orlando*
18. Universal Studios, *Orlando*
19. Golden Gate Bridge, *San Francisco*
20. SeaWorld Orlando, *Orlando*
21. Yankee Stadium, *New York City*
22. Times Square, *New York City*
23. Fenway Park, *Boston*
24. Museum of Science, *Boston*
25. San Diego Wild Animal Park, *San Diego*†
26. Central Park Wildlife Center, *New York City*
27. SeaWorld, *San Diego*
28. Disney's California Adventure, *Los Angeles*
29. Exploratorium, *San Francisco*
30. Statue of Liberty, *New York City*
31. Getty Center, *Los Angeles*
32. Fisherman's Wharf, *San Francisco*
33. Pike Place Market, *Seattle*
34. Haleakala National Park, *Hawaii*
35. Muir Woods National Monument, *San Francisco*†
36. Faneuil Hall/Quincy Mkt., *Boston*
37. Grand Teton National Park, *Moose, WY**†
38. U.S. Holocaust Memorial Museum, *Washington, DC*
39. Hoover Dam, *Las Vegas*
40. Niagara Falls, *Niagara Falls, NY**†
41. Art Institute of Chicago, *Chicago*
42. Empire State Building, *New York City*
43. Kaanapali Beach, *Hawaii*
44. National Aquarium, *Baltimore*†
45. Rockefeller Center, *New York City*
46. Balboa Park, *San Diego*
47. Franklin Institute Science Museum, *Philadelphia*
48. Audubon Zoo, *New Orleans*
49. New England Aquarium, *Boston*
50. Legoland California, *San Diego*

---

* See review in Other Notable Attractions section, page 249.

† Indicates a tie with attraction directly above.

50 Top-Rated Attractions

Rated by average of combined scores for Child Appeal, Adult Appeal, Facilities and Service.

27 Magic Kingdom, *Orlando*
Discovery Cove, *Orlando*
Monterey Bay Aquarium, *Monterey**
St. Louis Zoo, *St. Louis*
26 Disneyland, *Los Angeles*
Cedar Point, *Sandusky, OH**
Grant's Farm, *St. Louis*
San Diego Zoo, *San Diego*
National Air & Space Museum, *Washington, DC*
Disney's Typhoon Lagoon, *Orlando*
San Diego Wild Animal Park, *San Diego*
Disney-MGM Studios, *Orlando*
Cincinnati Zoo/Botanical Garden, *Cincinnati*
SBC Park, *San Francisco*
Blizzard Beach, *Orlando*
Museum of Science, *Boston*
Denver Museum of Nature & Science, *Denver*
National Aquarium, *Baltimore*
Fort Worth Zoo, *Dallas/Ft. Worth*
Safeco Field, *Seattle*
Audubon Aquarium of the Americas, *New Orleans*
Hersheypark, *Philadelphia/Lancaster*
Disney's Animal Kingdom, *Orlando*
SeaWorld, *San Diego*
Newport Aquarium, *Cincinnati*
Epcot, *Orlando*
Paramount's Kings Island, *Cincinnati*
25 Camden Yards, *Baltimore*
Islands of Adventure, *Orlando*
Museum of Science & Industry, *Chicago*
John G. Shedd Aquarium, *Chicago*
St. Louis Science Center, *St. Louis*
SeaWorld Orlando, *Orlando*
Houston Museum of Natural Science, *Houston*
Louisiana Children's Museum, *New Orleans*
Great American Ball Park, *Cincinnati*
Colonial Williamsburg, *Williamsburg**
National Museum of Natural History, *Washington, DC*
Yosemite National Park, *Yosemite National Park, CA**
Pacific Science Center, *Seattle*
Fort Worth Museum of Science and History, *Dallas/Ft. Worth*
Yellowstone National Park, *West Yellowstone, MT**
National Constitution Center, *Philadelphia*
Magic House, *St. Louis*
Ballpark in Arlington, *Dallas/Ft. Worth*
Busch Gardens, *Williamsburg**
Woodland Park Zoo, *Seattle*
Maui Ocean Center, *Hawaii*
Museum of Natural History & Science, *Cincinnati*
Franklin Institute Science Museum, *Philadelphia*

Top-Rated Attractions by Type

Amusement Parks
26 Cedar Point, *Sandusky, OH**
Paramount's Kings Island, *Cincinnati*
25 Busch Gardens, *Williamsburg**
23 Six Flags Georgia, *Atlanta*
Six Flags St. Louis, *St. Louis*
22 Hines Carousel Gardens, *New Orleans*

Aquariums
27 Monterey Bay Aquarium, *Monterey**
26 National Aquarium, *Baltimore*
Audubon Aquarium, *New Orleans*
Newport Aquarium, *Cincinnati*
25 John G. Shedd Aquarium, *Chicago*
SeaWorld, *Orlando*

Ballparks
26 SBC Park, *San Francisco*
Safeco Field, *Seattle*
25 Camden Yards, *Baltimore*
Great American Ball Park, *Cincinnati*
Ballpark in Arlington, *Dallas/Ft. Worth*
Minute Maid Park, *Houston*

Government Buildings
23 White House, *Washington, DC*
United States Capitol, *Washington, DC*
21 Bureau of Engraving, *Washington, DC*
20 National Archives, *Washington, DC*
Denver U.S. Mint, *Denver*
19 Supreme Court, *Washington, DC*

Historical Interest
25 Colonial Williamsburg, *Williamsburg**
George Ranch Park, *Houston*
24 Mount Vernon, *Washington, DC*
23 USS Constitution, *Boston*
Museum of Westward Expansion, *St. Louis*
Independence National Historical Park, *Philadelphia*

Malls/Shopping
22 Newport on the Levee, *Cincinnati*
Toys "R" Us, *New York City*
21 Prudential Center/Skywalk, *Boston*
Faneuil Hall/Quincy Mkt., *Boston*
20 Pike Place Market, *Seattle*
Arundel Mills, *Baltimore*

Museums: Art
24 Modern Art Museum/Fort Worth, *Dallas/Ft. Worth*
Metropolitan Museum of Art, *New York City*
Cincinnati Art Museum, *Cincinnati*
Kimbell Art Museum, *Dallas/Ft. Worth*
Art Institute of Chicago, *Chicago*
23 Getty Center, *Los Angeles*

Museums: Children's

25 Louisiana Children's Museum, *New Orleans*
Magic House, *St. Louis*
Center for Puppetry Arts, *Atlanta*
City Museum, *St. Louis*
24 Children's Museum, *Houston*
Children's Museum, *Boston*

Museums: Natural History/Science

26 National Air & Space Museum, *Washington, DC*
Museum of Science, *Boston*
Denver Museum of Nature & Science, *Denver*
25 Museum of Science & Industry, *Chicago*
St. Louis Science Center, *St. Louis*
Houston Museum of Natural Science, *Houston*

National Monuments/Memorials

24 U.S. Holocaust Museum, *Washington, DC*
23 USS Arizona Memorial, *Hawaii*
Battleship Missouri Memorial, *Hawaii*
22 USS Pampanito, *San Francisco*
Muir Woods National Monument, *San Francisco*
21 Holocaust Memorial, *Miami*

National Parks

25 Yosemite, *Yosemite National Park, CA**
Yellowstone, *West Yellowstone, MT**
24 Grand Canyon, *Grand Canyon, AZ**
23 Independence, *Philadelphia*
Grand Teton, *Moose, WY**
22 Olympic, *Seattle*

Theme Parks

27 Magic Kingdom, *Orlando*
26 Disneyland, *Los Angeles*
Disney-MGM Studios, *Orlando*
Hersheypark, *Philadelphia/Lancaster*
Epcot, *Orlando*
25 Islands of Adventure, *Orlando*

Water Parks

27 Discovery Cove, *Orlando*
26 Disney's Typhoon Lagoon, *Orlando*
Blizzard Beach, *Orlando*
23 Venetian Pool, *Miami*
Wet 'n Wild, *Orlando*
22 Splashtown, *Houston*

Zoos/Animal Parks

27 St. Louis Zoo, *St. Louis*
26 Grant's Farm, *St. Louis*
San Diego Zoo, *San Diego*
San Diego Wild Animal Park, *San Diego*
Cincinnati Zoo/Botanical Garden, *Cincinnati*
Fort Worth Zoo, *Dallas/Ft. Worth*

Top-Rated Attractions by City

Atlanta
25 Fernbank
Center for Puppetry Arts
Turner Field
24 World of Coca-Cola Pavillion
Zoo Atlanta
23 Chattahoochee Nature Center
Stone Mountain Park
Six Flags Over Georgia
Atlanta History Center
22 Atlanta Botanical Garden

Baltimore
26 National Aquarium
25 Camden Yards
24 Maryland Science Center
23 Baltimore Zoo
22 American Visionary Art Museum
Walters Art Museum
Baltimore Museum of Art
Port Discovery
21 Assateague Island National Seashore
U.S. Naval Academy

Boston/Cape Cod
26 Museum of Science
24 New England Aquarium
Children's Museum
New England Aquarium: Whale Watch
23 USS Constitution Museum
Museum of Fine Arts
John F. Kennedy Library & Museum
Peabody Museum
Fenway Park
22 Flying Horses Carousel

Chicago
25 Museum of Science & Industry
John G. Shedd Aquarium
Field Museum of Natural History
Brookfield Zoo
24 Lincoln Park Zoo
Chicago Botanic Garden
Chicago Children's Museum
Art Institute of Chicago
Wrigley Field
23 Adler Planetarium & Astronomy Museum

Cincinnati
26 Cincinnati Zoo & Botanical Garden
Newport Aquarium
Paramount's Kings Island
25 Great American Ball Park
Museum of Natural History & Science
24 Kentucky Horse Park
Cincinnati Art Museum
Krohn Conservatory

Dallas/Ft. Worth

26 Fort Worth Zoo
25 Fort Worth Museum of Science & History
   Ballpark in Arlington
24 Modern Art Museum of Fort Worth
   American Airlines Center
   Bass Performance Hall
   Science Place
   Dallas Arboretum & Botanical Garden
   Morton H. Meyerson Symphony Center
   Kimbell Art Museum

Denver

26 Denver Museum of Nature & Science
25 Coors Field
24 Children's Museum of Denver
   Denver Zoo
22 Denver Botanic Gardens
   Denver Art Museum
21 Ocean's Journey
20 Denver U.S. Mint
   Six Flags Elitch Gardens
18 16th Street Mall

Hawaii

25 Maui Ocean Center
24 Old Lahaina Luau
   Polynesian Cultural Center
23 Hanauma Bay Nature Preserve
   Kaanapali Beach
   Bishop Museum
   USS Arizona Memorial
   Battleship Missouri Memorial
22 Sea Life Park
   Waikiki Aquarium

Houston

25 Houston Museum of Natural Science
   George Ranch Historical Park
   Minute Maid Park
24 Children's Museum of Houston
   Space Center Houston
   Houston Zoo
   John P. McGovern Museum of Health
23 Museum of Fine Arts
22 Hermann Park
   Splashtown Houston

Las Vegas

24 Shark Reef
   Siegfried & Roy's Secret Garden/Dolphin Habitat
22 Fountains of Bellagio
   Mystic Falls
   Star Trek: The Experience
   Flamingo Wildlife Habitat
   Wet 'n Wild Water Park
   Gondola Rides at the Grand Canal
21 Lion Habitat
   Hoover Dam

Los Angeles

26 Disneyland
25 Long Beach Aquarium of the Pacific
24 Universal Studios Hollywood
California Science Center
Museum of Tolerance
Disney's California Adventure
23 Getty Center
Warner Bros. Studios
Knott's Berry Farm
22 Huntington Library

Miami

24 Miami Metro Zoo
Miami Museum of Science & Planetarium
23 Venetian Pool
22 Everglades National Park
21 Vizcaya Museum & Gardens
Matheson Hammock Park
Pro Player Stadium
Holocaust Memorial
Bill Baggs Cape Florida Recreational Area
Fairchild Tropical Garden

New Orleans

26 Audubon Aquarium of the Americas
25 Louisiana Children's Museum
Audubon Zoo
24 National D-Day Museum
22 Hines Carousel Gardens
New Orleans Museum of Art
New Orleans Botanical Garden
21 Six Flags New Orleans
Audubon Park
Hermann-Grima House

New York City

25 American Museum of Natural History
24 Bronx Zoo
Metropolitan Museum of Art
Radio City Music Hall
23 Chelsea Piers
Madame Tussaud's New York
Museum of Television & Radio
22 Intrepid Sea, Air & Space Museum
Brooklyn Children's Museum
Toys "R" Us

Orlando

27 Magic Kingdom
Discovery Cove
26 Disney's Typhoon Lagoon Park
Disney-MGM Studios
Blizzard Beach
Disney's Animal Kingdom
Epcot
25 Islands of Adventure
SeaWorld Orlando
Universal Studios

Philadelphia/Lancaster

26 Hersheypark
25 National Constitution Center
Franklin Institute Science Museum
23 Winterthur & Enchanted Woods
Longwood Gardens
Crayola Factory
Wachovia Center
Philadelphia Museum of Art
Independence National Historical Park
Philadelphia Zoo

Phoenix/Scottsdale

24 Bank One Ballpark
Arizona Science Center
Phoenix Zoo
23 McCormick-Stillman Railroad Park
Heard Museum
22 Desert Botanical Garden
21 Scottsdale Museum/Contemporary Art
20 America West Arena
18 Casa Grande Ruins National Monument
Old Town Scottsdale

San Diego

26 San Diego Zoo
San Diego Wild Animal Park
SeaWorld
25 Reuben H. Fleet Science Center
Legoland California
24 Birch Aquarium at Scripps
23 Balboa Park
Maritime Museum
22 San Diego Aerospace Museum
19 Old Town San Diego State Historic Park

San Francisco

26 SBC Park
25 Exploratorium
24 Chabot Space & Science Center
23 Lawrence Hall of Science
22 San Francisco Zoo
USS Pampanito
Muir Woods National Monument
San Francisco Museum of Modern Art
Golden Gate Park
Six Flags Marine World

Seattle

26 Safeco Field
25 Pacific Science Center
Woodland Park Zoo
24 Museum of Flight
23 Seattle Aquarium
Experience Music Project
Children's Museum
22 Olympic National Park
Space Needle
21 Klondike Gold Rush National Park

St. Louis

27 St. Louis Zoo
26 Grant's Farm
25 St. Louis Science Center
Magic House
City Museum
Silver Dollar City
24 Butterfly House
Missouri Botanical Garden
23 Museum of Westward Expansion
Gateway Arch

Washington, DC

26 National Air & Space Museum
25 National Museum of Natural History
24 National Museum of American History
International Spy Museum
Mount Vernon
U.S. Holocaust Memorial Museum
23 National Zoological Park
White House
United States Capitol
National Gallery of Art

50 Top Attractions by Child Appeal

Rated by Child Appeal scores alone.

30 Magic House, *St. Louis*
29 Disneyland, *Los Angeles*
Magic Kingdom, *Orlando*
Paramount's Kings Island, *Cincinnati*
Toys "R" Us, *New York City*
Sesame Place, *Philadelphia/Lancaster*
Children's Museum, *Boston*
Hersheypark, *Philadelphia/Lancaster*
Please Touch Museum, *Philadelphia*
Bronx Zoo, *New York City*
St. Louis Zoo, *St. Louis*
Exploratorium, *San Francisco*
Louisiana Children's Museum, *New Orleans*
Pacific Science Center, *Seattle*
Legoland California, *San Diego*
Fort Worth Museum/Science & History, *Dallas/Ft. Worth*
Monterey Bay Aquarium, *Monterey**
Children's Museum, *Denver*
McCormick-Stillman Railroad Park, *Phoenix/Scottsdale*
San Diego Zoo, *San Diego*
Woodland Park Zoo, *Seattle*
Fort Worth Zoo, *Dallas/Ft. Worth*
Children's Museum, *Houston*
28 Lincoln Park Zoo, *Chicago*
National Aquarium, *Baltimore*
SeaWorld, *San Diego*
National Zoological Park, *Washington, DC*
Center for Puppetry Arts, *Atlanta*
Newport Aquarium, *Cincinnati*
Flying Horses Carousel, *Boston*
Audubon Aquarium of the Americas, *New Orleans*
Denver Zoo, *Denver*
Crayola Factory, *Philadelphia/Lancaster*
Cincinnati Zoo & Botanical Garden, *Cincinnati*
City Museum, *St. Louis*
National Air/Space Museum, *Washington, DC*
Brookfield Zoo, *Chicago*
Blizzard Beach, *Orlando*
Six Flags Marine World, *San Francisco*
San Diego Wild Animal Park, *San Diego*
Six Flags Over Georgia, *Atlanta*
Philadelphia Zoo, *Philadelphia*
New England Aquarium, *Boston*
Museum of Science, *Boston*
Houston Zoo, *Houston*
Splashtown, *Houston*
Zoo Atlanta, *Atlanta*
Audubon Zoo, *New Orleans*
Disney's Typhoon Lagoon Park, *Orlando*
California Science Center, *Los Angeles*

Family Travel Directory

ATTRACTIONS
HOTELS
RESTAURANTS

Atlanta

Though it's romantically remembered for its role in Gone with the Wind turmoil, nowadays Atlanta is thriving and widely considered the capital of the New South. Home of the Braves, Falcons and Hawks, the sports-loving city received special attention as the site of the 1996 Summer Olympics. It's blessed with relatively mild weather year-round (summer temps average around 90 degrees, winters the low 40s), and even the August humidity is survivable with an occasional AC break. Downtown is easy to navigate, with plenty of attractions within a few-block radius. On the west side reside CNN Center, Centennial Olympic Park and the Children's Museum. Not far to the east of the business district are the State Capitol, the World of Coca-Cola and various Martin Luther King–related attractions; just to the north, Midtown offers the Botanical Gardens, Piedmont Park and the Center for Puppetry Arts. All are accessible by MARTA, Atlanta's user-friendly public transportation system ($1.75 a ride; unlimited weekly passes for $13), but you'll need a car to hit kid fave Six Flags Over Georgia or nearby destinations such as Savannah or Charleston, S.C.

ATTRACTIONS

Ratings: Child Appeal, Adult Appeal, Public Facilities, Service, Cost

	C	A	P	S	$

Atlanta Botanical Garden ☺

| 17 | 26 | 25 | 22 | I |

1345 Piedmont Ave., NE (bet. 14th St. & Monroe Dr.); 404-876-5859; www.atlantabotanicalgarden.org

☑ For a "lovely" few hours' respite "from the hustle and bustle", try this "accessible", "soothing oasis" "surrounded by a beautiful park" in Midtown; while "older kids don't find much appeal" beyond the "colorful" "poison dart frogs", younger ones "love" the "incredible children's garden" where they can splash in the fountains, visit multiple themed areas like the Beehive Meadow and enjoy "performances at the little amphitheater"; with light bites on-site and "plenty of room to run wild" or "push a stroller", even mom and dad should find this relaxing.

Atlanta Cyclorama & Civil War Museum ☺

| 17 | 26 | 22 | 21 | I |

Grant Park, 800 Cherokee Ave., SE (Grant Park Pl.); 404-658-7625; www.bcaatlanta.com

☑ This veteran attraction "brings to life" the "history of Atlanta's Civil War experience" in a "theaterlike setting" located in Grant Park; while there's "zero appeal for small children", it's "enjoyable" for "war buffs", "school-age" kids and teens who "will learn something" in a "pretty cool" way; open since 1893 it houses the historic locomotive *Texas*, and is possibly the longest-running show in the U.S., plus it's a "great break from the heat" and located "right next to Zoo Atlanta."

Atlanta History Center ☺

| 17 | 25 | 25 | 23 | M |

130 W. Paces Ferry Rd. (Andrews Dr.); 404-814-4000; www.atlhist.org

☑ "See history come alive" at this "terrific museum" in the heart of Buckhead where kids can "wander around" the "hands-on historic" Tulley Smith Farm featuring live animals and "period crafts" (they actually shear sheep and "weave wool each spring"); both "permanent and temporary" exhibits are a "perfect" blend of education and entertainment, and a tour of the adjacent circa-1800s Swan House by a "pleasant" staff "recalls the best and worst of the antebellum South" for older kids, teenagers and adults; N.B. if you need a break, there's an old-fashioned tearoom on the property.

Centennial Olympic Park | 21 | 19 | 18 | 14 | $0 |

bordered by Baker and Marietta Sts., Park Ave. W. and Centennial Olympic Park Dr.; 404-222-7275; www.centennialpark.com
■ You can practically hear the theme music at this "lovely reminder of the 1996 Olympic Games" – a "refreshing change from the Downtown high-rise scenery"; "ultraconvenient", this 21-acre park earns pint-size praise for the "fabulous" fountain water rings "shooting out of the sidewalks" ("bring swimsuits"); also appealing are the "free concerts", fireworks, "spectacular lights" and "ice-skating in December"; P.S. "CNN Center is right across the street."

Center for Puppetry Arts | 28 | 23 | 23 | 25 | M |

1404 Spring St. (18th St.); 404-873-3391; www.puppet.org
■ A "magical world awaits" at this "treasure" in Midtown, rated No. 1 for Child Appeal in Atlanta, where the "excellent" shows will "transfix" even a six-month-old; "make-your-own puppet workshops", "full-length plays" and an "interactive museum" ("hands on? my five-year-old couldn't keep her hands off!") add up to an "undeniably cool" attraction presided over by a professional staff; though there are some "innovative" "adult-oriented shows", preteens "might get bored"; N.B. to avoid paying full price, go to dress rehearsals.

Chattahoochee Nature Center | 26 | 24 | 22 | 22 | I |

9135 Willeo Rd. (bet. Azalea Dr. & Timber Ridge Rd.), Roswell; 770-992-2055; www.chattnaturecenter.com
■ Pack a picnic and trek to Roswell for a "perfect family outing" at this "huge nature area" with "something for everyone", be it "beautiful" wooded walks, an "animal-rescue program, displays", guided canoe trips and a 127-acre natural classroom; it's "hard to find the first time", but once you arrive, there are "wonderful docents" who point out wildlife and flora "at its best."

CNN Center ☺ | 15 | 24 | 24 | 22 | M |

1 CNN Ctr. (Marietta St.); 404-827-2300; 877-426-6868; www.cnn.com/studiotour
■ "Talk about being newsworthy", this "interesting" attraction gives "preteens, teens and adults" "an insiders' view on how the world gets its news" from the 24-hour cable giant; you can "see yourself on TV", run into "your favorite anchors", ride the "fascinating multistory escalator" and be led by "charming guides" on the "interactive tours" before heading to the "enormous food court" and the Cartoon Network store; it takes about 45 minutes to view, but the "lines on Saturdays can be daunting" and "reservations are recommended."

Ebenezer Baptist Church ☺ | 12 | 25 | 20 | 20 | $0 |

407 Auburn Ave., NE (Jackson St.); 404-688-7263; www.historicebenezer.org
◪ "Stand in the footprint of history" at this Downtown church where you can "sit in the pews and feel the electricity" as you gaze at the "pulpit where Martin Luther King preached"; besides taking an "interesting tour" given by an "extremely well-spoken staff", consider attending one of the Sunday services where "lively music" and "social-justice sermons" are "quite moving"; while all this is a "good history lesson for older kids", younger ones may daydream.

Fernbank Museum of Natural History/Science Center | 26 | 25 | 26 | 24 | M |

767 Clifton Rd., NE (Ponce de Leon Ave.); 404-929-6300; www.fernbank.edu
■ This "beautiful" facility, rated the city's top attraction, is in "one of Atlanta's most historic" sections not far from Downtown and focuses on the natural sciences; "interactive children's areas" "delight",

and the atrium's dinosaur is a "favorite for all ages"; there's "easy elevator access for strollers", and adults can enjoy their own "fun-filled Friday night" with martini and IMAX movie events that "rock"; across the parking lot at the Science Center there's a "wonderful planetarium" and an adjacent forest.

Georgia State Capitol ☺ | 13 | 20 | 20 | 19 | $0 |
Washington St., SW (Capitol Sq.); 404-656-2844;
www.sos.state.ga.us/state_capitol
☑ With its "total renovation" recently completed, Downtown's "Gold Dome" is a "much better" place to get "a good sense of the state" with "well-informed" free tours that are best for budding politicians, older kids and teens; it may not score too high for Child Appeal but the Georgia Capitol museum with two-headed creatures and other "freak animals" will perk up the pint-sized set.

Imagine It! | _ | _ | _ | _ | M |
The Children's Museum of Atlanta ☺☺
275 Centennial Olympic Park Dr., NW (Baker St.); 404-659-5437;
www.childrensmuseumatl.org
There's no such thing as "don't touch" at this brand-new Downtown kiddie fantasy where little ones can discover, explore, pretend and dance their way around interactive exhibits including an underground garden, a water station (raincoats and galoshes provided), tree house and TV studio; there are plenty of places for parents to perch, along with a full-service restaurant and gift shop with cute toys, and it's right next to Centennial Olympic Park and CNN so older kids (eight and above) can do that instead.

King Center, The | 16 | 25 | 20 | 20 | $0 |
(MLK National Historic Site) ☺
449 Auburn Ave., NE (bet. Boulevard & Jackson St.); 404-526-8900;
www.thekingcenter.org
☑ Even though there's "not much to hold a younger child's attention", this attraction "should be on every person's itinerary when visiting Atlanta", especially if they're "interested in learning about the legacy of Martin Luther King Jr."; besides exhibits about Reverend King's life and good works, there are an "inspiring reflecting pool", "peaceful fountains" and "the eternal flame at MLK's tomb"; though it's a "wonderful tribute", some surveyors report that the center itself is a "tad dusty" and "run-down."

Martin Luther King Jr.   ▽ | 11 | 21 | 21 | 22 | $0 |
Birth Home ☺
501 Auburn Ave., NE (Hogue St.); 404-331-3920;
www.nps.gov/malu
☑ Older children, teenagers and adults gain "insight into the man who became a hero" on this "interesting tour of Dr. King's" "well-preserved" home; "excellent guides" give a "unique perspective" on the famous Civil Rights leader's formative childhood, so even if little ones' attentions wane, it's a worthwhile stop for a 30-minute visit; N.B. tours begin every hour on the hour, and every half hour during the summer, but be prepared to wait a bit.

Michael C. Carlos Museum | 14 | 25 | 25 | 24 | I |
Emory University, 571 S. Kilgo Circle (Dowman Dr.); 404-727-4282;
www.carlos.emory.edu
☑ The kids are bound to like the mummy and other "ancient treasures" found at this "relatively small" but "very impressive" museum on the Emory campus; visitors say the "varied" collections are "beautifully displayed", and though it's more engaging for adults, the "helpful" staff and children's concerts increase its appeal to kids.

Piedmont Park

| 22 | 24 | 18 | 13 | $0 |

1071 Piedmont Ave., NE (12th St.); 404-875-7275;
www.piedmontpark.org

☑ "Atlanta's" "own mini–Central Park" (also designed by Frederick Law Olmsted) is a "beautiful oasis in Midtown" that's "great for pets, kids and families" thanks to lakes, playgrounds, arts festivals, concerts and "lots of space to run", "throw a Frisbee", "people-watch" or picnic; "parking is a hassle" and it's "not safe at night", but improvements have made it "cleaner" than ever; N.B. naturalist-led programs for kids are held three Saturdays per month.

SciTrek ☻

| 26 | 19 | 20 | 19 | M |

395 Piedmont Ave., NE (bet. Pine St. & Ralph McGill Blvd.);
404-522-5500; www.scitrek.org

☑ You can "keep little hands busy" for an hour or two at this "way-cool" Downtown "science museum" where more than 120 interactive "toys and exhibits" are "ever-changing" and "entertaining for all ages"; adults don't have as much fun as kids and a few find the facility "really run-down" (some "exhibits do not function properly"), but at least "the staff is wonderful."

Six Flags Over Georgia ☺

| 28 | 23 | 21 | 18 | VE |

7561 Six Flags Rd. (off I-20), Austell; 770-948-9290; www.sixflags.com

☑ "Oriented toward teenagers and young adults", this amusement park, which just added its 10th roller coaster and four other rides for 2004, is "one of the best Six Flags in the U.S." say fans who find plenty of "thrills", shows and concerts, as well as "ridiculously long lines" that prompt them to "visit on a weekday"; party-poopers deem it a "way-too-expensive" "redneck alternative to Disney" where they "don't cater to parents with small children"; to avoid the "less-than-exciting food", "bring your own picnic."

Southern Museum of Civil War and Locomotive History ☻☻

| ▽ 18 | 25 | 23 | 23 | I |

2829 Cherokee St. (Main St.), Kennesaw; 770-427-2117;
www.southernmuseum.org

☑ Considered by some to be "the best site in the Metro area for history buffs", this "fascinating" Kennesaw venue, 30 minutes from Downtown, attracts "big and little kids" with a Civil War museum that offers changing exhibits; families also enjoy "rewarding" outdoor hiking paths up the mountain where "you can find old bullets and arrowheads" – in fact, some say the "true attraction" is the climb and the "beautiful view"; the reproduction of a turn-of-the-century locomotive factory is an extra bonus.

Stone Mountain Park

| 24 | 25 | 23 | 21 | E |

US 78, exit 8, Stone Mountain; 770-498-5690; 800-317-2006;
www.stonemountainpark.com

■ "More than just a mountain", this "huge" "theme park and history lesson rolled into one" boasts "lots of attractions for young and old" including themed events, a museum village, paddle boats, petting zoo, train ride, "above-average golf courses", a mini zoo and much more (it "has to be seen to be believed"); "the real deal" is the "exhilarating" climb (or tram ride) to the top for "breathtaking views" from this "Mt. Rushmore of the South"; "give it a full day", or even a weekend, since there are camping options and on-site hotels.

Turner Field

| 25 | 27 | 26 | 21 | E |

755 Hank Aaron Dr., SE (bet. Bill Lucas Dr. & Fulton St.); 404-522-7630;
www.atlantabraves.com

☑ "If you like baseball", then you and your kids "will love" this "beautiful" "new ballpark with an old-time feel" where there's "lots to do behind the scenes" like "free interactive games" (including a "super-cool", "virtual-reality" "batting cage") and a "fabulous stadium tour" – better yet, if you're there for a Braves game, there's "not a bad seat in the house"; the "grounds are always sparkling clean", and there are "varied and ample concessions", although the food is a bit "overpriced"; P.S. budget-watchers can bring a soft-sided cooler (check in advance for restrictions), and bargain for "standing-room-only tickets."

Underground Atlanta

| 12 | 16 | 14 | 14 | $0 |

50 Upper Alabama St. (bet. Central & Peachtree Sts.); 404-523-2311; www.underatl.com

☑ Paved with cobblestones and lined with vintage storefronts, this sunken Downtown shopping area "fascinates" some with its "historical and architectural aspects"; first-timers flock because the city's "tourist center is located here" (with a "helpful staff at the info desk"), as is a half-price ticket booth; boosters boast about "neat little shops", "activities and arcades" and say the sheltered site is a "nice reprieve" from the hot sun; however, a larger contingent of critics complain that "locals don't go" to this "nondescript" venue and call it an "overrated", "dark and unappealing" "tourist trap" that may be unsafe – "bring Kevlar."

World of Coca-Cola Pavillion

| 24 | 23 | 25 | 23 | M |

55 Martin Luther King Jr. Dr., SW (Central Ave.); 404-676-5151; www.coca-cola.com

■ This "pop culture" shrine is a "symbol of Atlanta that should be on everyone's list" thanks to its "surprisingly entertaining" interactive displays that "appeal to all ages" (even adults who take a "journey down memory lane"); "the best part" for kids is the "all-you-can-drink" "cascading sodas" and samples from around the world "ranging from delicious to downright awful"; still, for the "ultimate sugar buzz" and a "fun" "couple of hours", you can't do better for less.

Zoo Atlanta

| 28 | 24 | 22 | 21 | M |

Grant Park, 800 Cherokee Ave., SE (Grant Park Pl.); 404-624-5600; www.zooatlanta.org

■ "Big enough to spend an afternoon" but "not so big that you have to skip features to avoid kiddie meltdowns", this "easy-to-navigate" zoo situated not far from Downtown appeals to kids of all ages; there are plenty of "healthy well-displayed animals" (the "pandas are a must") in "carefully crafted habitats," and a train ride, carousel and playground area are "huge hits for toddlers", who can also "play in the (adjacent) park."

HOTELS

Ratings: Family Appeal, Rooms, Service, Public Facilities, Cost

| FA | R | S | P | $ |

Four Seasons

| 19 | 27 | 28 | 28 | $275 |

75 14th St.; 404-881-9898; 800-332-3442; www.fourseasons.com; 226 rooms, 18 suites

☑ "Don't stay anywhere else if you can afford it", say those who find that this upscaler, a five-minute walk from Piedmont Park, "aims to welcome families – particularly on weekends"; the service, as always, is "outstanding", and there are childproof rooms available, as well as cribs and babysitting services; while the hotel may "not be the most appealing for kids", it is within five miles of both the World of Coca-Cola and the Fernbank Museum of Natural History, and the "great concierge has good recommendations" for appropriate activities.

JW Marriott Hotel Lenox

| 21 | 24 | 23 | 23 | $225 |

3300 Lenox Rd., NE; 404-262-3344; 800-228-9290; www.marriott.com; 367 rooms, 4 suites

■ Parents like the location of this Buckhead hotel since it's "attached to the Lenox Mall" where "teens can shop on their own" and there's a "food court for easy meals"; a "friendly atmosphere", "well-maintained, secure" facilities, child-care services, an indoor pool, an on-site restaurant and in-room high-speed Internet access further the family appeal; it's eight miles from the Atlanta Zoo and 13 miles from Six Flags Over Georgia, so a few wish it were closer to Downtown.

Ritz-Carlton Buckhead

| 18 | 25 | 27 | 26 | $379 |

3434 Peachtree Rd., NE; 404-237-2700; 800-241-3333; www.ritzcarlton.com; 524 rooms, 29 suites

☑ It's "nice to have your child greeted upon arrival and presented with a logo stuffed animal" say pleased parents who patronize this "top-of-the-line" Buckhead facility that exhibits "first-class service" from a "very cordial and warm staff"; the ritzy location near the city's top shopping and dining places it "between two malls" for convenient buying expeditions; although some say it's "not suitable" for very young children, there are babysitting services upon request, an indoor pool and a "fabulous Sunday tea for girls and their moms."

Sheraton Buckhead

| ▽ 21 | 19 | 20 | 22 | $179 |

3405 Lenox Rd., NE; 404-261-9250; 800-325-3535; www.sheraton.com; 360 rooms, 9 suites

■ If you're looking for Buckhead lodging that's easy on the wallet, head to this "lovely" choice "across a busy street" from the Lenox Mall; kids can splash about in the outdoor pool, parents enjoy the fitness center and there's "easy public transportation to Downtown" for visiting popular attractions such as the Imagine It! Children's Museum and SciTrek, a tot-friendly science and technology center.

Westin Peachtree Plaza

| 19 | 24 | 22 | 23 | $385 |

210 Peachtree St., NW; 404-659-1400; 800-937-8461; www.westin.com; 1028 rooms, 40 suites

■ Plan to "spend hours on the glass elevators" when you take the kids to this Downtown property, 'cause they "love going to the top to enjoy the view of the city"; there's "loads of seating in the massive lobby", and the staff "makes traveling with little ones easier", offering rollaway beds; since it's near the CNN Center and Centennial Olympic Park, you'll have plenty to do before returning for a swim in the indoor/outdoor pool (it has a retractable roof).

Top Family-Friendly Hotel Chains in the Area:

Embassy Suites   Hyatt
Hampton Inn   Marriott
Holiday Inn   Residence Inn
Homewood Suites

See Hotel Chain reviews, starting on page 256.

RESTAURANTS

Ratings: Family Appeal, Food, Decor, Service, Cost

| FA | F | D | S | $ |

American Roadhouse

| 24 | 17 | 16 | 17 | I |

842 N. Highland Ave. (bet. Drewry St. & Greenwood Ave.); 404-872-2822

☑ For "dependable" American treats, head to this "super place" in Va-Highlands, where burger-weary parents praise the "healthy choices"; while some roadies rail that the eats are just "average", at least there's "something to please" every finicky eater in tow, and the "young staff with a high energy level" ensures plenty of "tasty love."

Buckhead Diner ❽

| – | – | – | – | E |

3073 Piedmont Rd., NE (E. Paces Ferry Rd.); 404-262-3336; www.buckheadrestaurants.com

"A diner for people who wouldn't normally be caught dead in one", this "upscale" Buckhead production is "no Mel's", offering a "gourmet yet grounded" all-day menu of New American "classics" that "never disappoint" in a "streamlined", "stainless-steel" space; there's "something for everybody", from "families" with young kids to "out-of-towners" like "Elton John" – including "excessive waits" (though "lunch is a lot less busy"); while a few feel it's "not what it used to be", loyalists insist it's still "holding its own."

Fogo de Chão

| – | – | – | – | E |

3101 Piedmont Rd., NE (bet. E. Paces Ferry & Peachtree Rds.); 404-995-9982; www.fogodechao.com

"Welcome to Atkinsville" crow carnivores at this "all-you-can-eat" churrascaria that sets the "gold standard" for Brazilian steakhouses with an "endless" "smorgasbord of good grub", including a salad bar that's one of the "best in the city"; kids will love being served "tender, juicy" "meat on a stick" by "gauchos" who deliver "dedicated, determined and dependable" service in a setting so "macho" "you can almost see the haze of testosterone in the room"; N.B. a recent expansion carved out a snazzy new bar and waiting area.

Jalisco ⊠

| ∇ 27 | 22 | 14 | 25 | I |

Peachtree Battle Shopping Ctr., 2337 Peachtree Rd., NE (bet. Lindbergh Dr. & Peachtree Hills Ave.); 404-233-9244

■ "They know how to cater to families" ("fast service for anxious kids") at this Peachtree Battle Shopping Center classic just a short minivan jaunt up from Downtown/Midtown, where the "tolerant, nice" staff delivers "delicious" Tex-Mex meals in a decidedly "casual" atmosphere; should the "authentic" eats prove too hot for tender little taste buds, cool relief can be found at the "Baskin-Robbins next door."

Mick's

| 20 | 18 | 17 | 17 | M |

Lenox Sq., 3393 Peachtree Rd., NE (Lenox Rd.); 404-262-6425
557 Peachtree St., NE (North Ave.); 404-875-6425
2110 Peachtree Rd., NW (Bennett St.); 404-351-6425
Underground Atlanta, 75 Upper Alabama St., SW (Peachtree St.); 404-525-2825

☑ "You can always count on" this local, seemingly "omnipresent" American network (the branches are independently owned) for a "bright", "noisy atmosphere" and a quite "decent" kids' menu of burgers, fries and sandwiches; the "grown-up food is nothing special" – "although children of all ages are sure to love" the signature Oreo cheesecake – and several scold "the slow service", but it's "still yummy after all these years" say sentimental sorts who "grew up eating here."

Nuevo Laredo Cantina ⊠

| 20 | 27 | 16 | 20 | M |

1495 Chattahoochee Ave., NW (bet. Collier & Howell Mill Rds.); 404-352-9009; www.nuevolaredocantina.com

■ "Like a homey roadside eatery in Mexico", this "out-of-the-way" Westside ethnic "with a buzz" may not be "much to look at", but its "cheap and delicious food" (the "best in Atlanta" amigos attest) makes it *mucho simpatico* "for a big family meal" – "except maybe on weekend nights" when grown-ups gather for "excellent drinks" and people-watching.

Pappadeaux Seafood Kitchen | 21 | 24 | 21 | 23 | M |

10795 Davis Dr. (Mansell Rd.), Alpharetta; 770-992-5566
2830 Windy Hill Rd. (I-75), Marietta; 770-984-8899
www.pappadeaux.com

☑ At this "N'Awlins-type" seafood chain, "shockingly" "huge", shareable helpings of "rich, delicious" Cajun-Creole fin fare, including "hauntingly good" crawfish bisque and "anything fried you can imagine", are served by a "friendly" staff in "large, breezy" "family-oriented" spaces that can get "rowdy"; razzers rename it "Pappadon'ts" for "bland", "mass-market" eats, "slow" service and an atmosphere of "chaos."

Trader Vic's ☒ | _ | _ | _ | _ | E |

Hilton Atlanta, 255 Courtland St., NE (Baker St.); 404-221-6339;
www.tradervicsatlanta.com

"Tourists", "conventioneers" and wide-eyed youngsters "love the tacky tiki", "faux-island charm" of this Downtown Asian-Continental with a "Polynesian" twist where "bowlfuls" of "tropical drinks" may send you "hulaing into the Hilton" and make the "so-so" food seem "good enough"; but a "tired" scene and "less-than-professional" service convince critics to "stay away."

Varsity ⇄ | 25 | 16 | 17 | 20 | I |

1085 Lindbergh Dr. (Cheshire Bridge Rd.); 404-261-8843
61 North Ave., NE (Peachtree St.); 404-881-1706 ☾
11556 Rainwater Dr. (Haynes Bridge Rd.), Alpharetta;
770-777-4004
2790 Town Center Dr. (Mall Blvd.), Kennesaw; 770-795-0802
www.thevarsity.com

■ Every family with children both "little and overgrown" "needs to visit" this 1928 Downtown "landmark" off Peachtree Street (with newer suburban siblings) "at least once" for a "true pre-McDonald's experience"; the "famous frosted orange" drink washes down onion rings, "hamburgers and hot dogs galore" – all "heavy on the grease" though, so "bring the antacids"; "easy to spot with bright colors and pennants", the interior boasts TVs and a "loud atmosphere where shenanigans wouldn't even be noticed", but since it's also a "real drive-in", "if the kids misbehave you can eat in the car"; P.S. while it's "always packed", the "lines move quickly."

Zesto Drive In | ▽ 23 | 17 | 16 | 18 | I |

1181 E. Confederate Ave. (Moreland Ave.); 404-622-4254 ⇄
377 Moreland Ave., NE (McLendon Ave., NE); 404-523-1973
544 Ponce de Leon Ave., NE (Monroe Dr., NE); 404-607-1118
151 Forest Pkwy. (Old Dixie Hwy.), Forest Park; 404-366-0564 ☾⇄

■ This locally owned chain is "perfect for families and screaming kids" in search of "tasty" hamburgers, hot dogs, Tater Tots and some Greek-inspired dishes, to be topped off with "appealing ice-cream treats"; all offer "fast" service and retro '50s drive-in decor, and at the Forest Park outlet, you can get breakfast as early as 6AM.

RESTAURANT CHAINS

See reviews, starting on page 262.

Ratings: Family Appeal, Food, Decor, Service, Cost

| FA | F | D | S | $ |

Applebee's | 21 | 16 | 17 | 17 | M |

11070 Alpharetta Hwy. (bet. Mansell Rd. & Sun Valley Dr.), Roswell;
770-992-3423

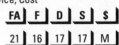

Benihana   23 | 20 | 18 | 22 | E
Peachtree Ctr., 229 Peachtree St. (International Blvd.); 404-522-9627
2143 Peachtree Rd. (Bennett St., NW); 404-355-8565

California Pizza Kitchen ⊠   21 | 21 | 16 | 19 | M
3393 Peachtree Rd. (Lenox Rd.); 404-262-9221
4600 Ashford-Dunwoody Rd. (Perimeter Ctr., N); 770-393-0390

Cheesecake Factory   21 | 23 | 21 | 20 | M
3024 Peachtree Rd. (Pharr Rd.); 404-816-2555
Perimeter Mall, 4400 Ashford Dunwoody Rd. (Abernathy Rd.);
678-320-0201

Chili's Grill & Bar ⊠   21 | 19 | 18 | 19 | M
Atlanta Hartsfield Int'l, Concourse A; 404-530-7513
Atlanta Hartsfield Int'l, North Terminal; 404-530-7544
2133 Lavista Rd., NE (bet. Druid Hills Rd. & Merry Ln.); 404-325-8680
2075 Cooledge Rd. (Rte. 9), Tucker; 770-493-1779

Chuck E. Cheese's ⊠   26 | 10 | 17 | 13 | I
2990 Cumberland Blvd., SE (Cumberland Pkwy.); 770-435-9036

Dave & Buster's ⊠   26 | 16 | 21 | 17 | I
2215 D & B Dr. (Delk Rd.), Marietta; 770-951-5554

Don Pablo's ⊠   20 | 19 | 18 | 18 | I
3131 Cobb Pkwy., SE (Cumberland Pkwy.); 770-955-5929

Fuddrucker's ⊠   24 | 20 | 15 | 16 | I
Perimeter Mall, 240 Perimeter Ctr. Pkwy. (bet. Hammond Dr. &
Perimeter Center Way); 770-399-6641
815 Sidney Marcus Blvd. (Rte. 400); 404-264-0079
11000 Alpharetta Hwy. (bet. Mansell Rd. & Sun Valley Dr.), Roswell;
678-352-3290

Hard Rock Cafe   22 | 16 | 26 | 18 | M
215 Peachtree St., NE (International Blvd.); 404-688-7625

Joe's Crab Shack ⊠   23 | 17 | 21 | 19 | M
3013 Peachtree Rd. (Pharr Rd.); 404-869-0500
4300 Stone Mountain Hwy. (Ross Rd.), Lilburn; 770-736-2900

Johnny Rockets   25 | 17 | 20 | 18 | I
Phipps Plaza, 3500 Peachtree Rd. (Oak Valley Rd.); 404-233-9867 ⊠
6510 Roswell Rd., NE (bet. Abernathy & Johnson Ferry Rds.);
404-257-0677
Underground, 50 Upper Alabama St., SW (Pryor St.); 404-525-7117 ⊠
5 West Paces Ferry Rd. (Peachtree Rd.); 404-231-5555 ⊠

LongHorn Steakhouse   21 | 21 | 19 | 21 | M
2151 Peachtree Rd. (Collier Rd.); 404-351-6086
6390 Roswell Rd. (Abernathy Rd.); 404-843-1215
900 Mansell Rd. (Alpharetta Hwy.), Roswell; 770-642-8588
1420 Towne Lake Pkwy. (I-575, exit 8), Woodstock; 770-924-5494

Maggiano's Little Italy   22 | 22 | 21 | 22 | M
Perimeter Mall, 4400 Ashford Dunwoody Rd. (I-285, exit 29);
770-804-3313
3368 Peachtree St., NE (Hwy. 400); 404-816-9650

Max & Erma's ⊠   22 | 20 | 19 | 21 | I
1155 Mount Vernon Hwy. (Mt. Vernon Blvd.); 770-551-0055

Old Spaghetti Factory, The ☒ | 25 | 20 | 22 | 20 | I
249 Ponce de Leon Ave. (Penn Ave.); 404-872-2841

Olive Garden ☒ | 20 | 19 | 18 | 19 | M
905 Holcomb Bridge Rd. (Warsaw Rd.), Roswell; 770-642-0395

**On the Border
Mexican Grill & Cantina** | 20 | 19 | 19 | 18 | M
Buckhead Station, 1 Buckhead Loop (bet. Lenox & Peachtree Rds.);
404-816-3171

Outback Steakhouse | 20 | 22 | 18 | 20 | M
Buckhead Court Shopping Ctr., 3850 Roswell Rd., NE (Piedmont Rd.);
404-266-8000

Roadhouse Grill ☒ | 20 | 18 | 16 | 18 | M
2810 East-West Connector (Austell Rd.), Austell; 770-222-0749

T.G.I. Friday's ☒ | 21 | 17 | 18 | 17 | M
2841 Greenbriar Pkwy. (Headland Dr., SW); 404-344-4342
2061 Peachtree Rd., NE (bet. Bennett St. & Montclair Dr.);
404-350-0199
1925 Powers Ferry Rd. (Windy Hill Rd., SE); 770-951-0821

Baltimore

"Oh, say can you see" – everything from history to nature to science to baseball? You can in Baltimore, birthplace of "The Star-Spangled Banner." This harbor city on the Chesapeake Bay is best to visit in the spring and fall (when temps hover in the mid-50s), since summers can be hot (mid-80s and up) and humid. Still, even the sultriest months are made pleasurable by War of 1812 reenactments at Fort McHenry, ball games at Camden Yards and steamed blue crabs alfresco at Harborplace. Probably most famous as a visitor destination is the Inner Harbor, site of the National Aquarium and brimming with shops, restaurants, museums and hotels. Water taxis from Inner Harbor travel to 11 landings at reasonable all-day rates. Additional attractions and the historical neighborhoods of Federal Hill and Fell's Point can be reached on foot from the waterfront. Washington, DC, 35 miles south, is easily reached via Amtrak or the less-pricey local MARC train. If you're venturing down to Annapolis or across the bay to St. Michael's or the Eastern Shore, you'll want a car – but during the peak months of July and August, be ready for crowds.

ATTRACTIONS

Ratings: Child Appeal, Adult Appeal, Public Facilities, Service, Cost

	C	A	P	S	$

American Visionary Art Museum ☺ | 14 | 27 | 25 | 23 | I
800 Key Hwy. (Covington St.); 410-244-1900; www.avam.org
☑ "A breath of fresh air" blows in from this "small", "off-the-wall" Harborplace museum "dedicated to self-taught artists"; featuring "unusual" rotating exhibits, it's "understandably uneven in quality but quite interesting to explore", at least with older kids and teens who like art; the organic restaurant is "great" and the on-site gift shop is brimming with "cute trinkets" – just check ahead since some shows are "adult-themed", and note that the open riser staircase "is a parent's nightmare."

Arundel Mills 😊😊 | 18 | 23 | 22 | 18 | $0 |

7000 Arundel Mills Circle (Ridge Rd.), Hanover; 410-540-5100; www.arundelmillsmall.com

☑ "If you keep walking, you'll end up where you started" at this "carnival-like mall" 20 minutes out on Rte. 295 South with more than 200 stores and outlets configured in a "big loop"; you could stall, though, at "Jillian's arcade for fun and games", CrayolaWorks for "activities to keep kids busy" or at the "terrific Egyptian-themed" 24-plex; refuel at the "huge food court" or at Medieval Times, but "watch out for weekends" unless you're 12 to 18 years old, and note that parking mirrors the stroll, i.e. "you'll circle for a while."

Assateague Island National Seashore | 25 | 26 | 17 | 17 | I |

7206 Nat'l Seashore Ln. (off Rte. 611), Berlin; 410-641-1441; www.nps.gov/asis

☑ "Wild horses couldn't drag me away" say nature lovers "retreating from Ocean City's chaos" and heading south "over the bridge" to these "beautiful, unspoiled" barrier islands where the "ponies and deer roam free" through "marshes, forest trails" and "beaches that stretch for miles"; "get there early", "stay for knowledgeable ranger talks" and even reserve ahead for "rustic" but "wonderful camping"; while it rates high for both Child and Adult Appeal, just be forewarned that summer brings "herds of wandering SUVs" and "mosquitos to test one's spirit."

Babe Ruth Birthplace and Museum 😊😊 | 19 | 24 | 19 | 18 | I |

216 Emory St. (bet. Portland & W. Pratt Sts.); 410-727-1539; www.baberuthmuseum.com

■ "Love the Babe or hate the Babe", this "important shrine for baseball fans", "a stone's throw from Camden Yards" in South Baltimore, hits "a home run" for "a good pre-game stop" with "five-year-olds and up who have an interest" in America's pastime; the museum "gives a transcendant sense of the Bambino" that's "fun for sports historians" and "interesting even for non-fans", but the legend's childhood "row house is a tight squeeze", so it's "not the place for strollers or active toddlers."

Baltimore Museum of Art 😊 | 13 | 27 | 24 | 22 | I |

10 Art Museum Dr. (N. Charles St.); 410-396-7100; www.artbma.org

☑ You'll find a "stupendous collection" of Impressionist works at this "lovely" Charles Street museum; while the art "from all over the world" is most likely to appeal to adults and teens, there are "special exhibits and programs designed for children"; still, parents enjoy it more since they can even get an upscale bite at "the terrific restaurant" "overlooking the sculpture garden."

Baltimore Museum of Industry 😊 | ▽ 21 | 25 | 23 | 24 | I |

1415 Key Hwy. (bet. Lawrence & Webster Sts.); 410-727-4808; www.thebmi.org

■ "This place worships the past", and what a "fantastic way" it has of "showing young people what things looked like, smelled like, were like" during the Industrial Revolution; with "every exhibit meant to be touched", this "unique" museum "on the water Downtown", includes a walk-through 1886 bank, a replica of the 1910 Bunting Pharmacy where Noxzema was invented and an exhibit "kids love" where they "allow you to become part of a mock oyster cannery" circa 1865.

Baltimore Zoo | 27 | 23 | 21 | 19 | M |

Druid Hill Park, Druid Park Lake Dr. (Eutaw Pl.); 410-366-5466; www.baltimorezoo.org

■ "You feel like you're in the country", but this "perfect adventure" is "in the heart" of the city's Druid Hill Park; from the "stellar bird and rain forest" to the "new Arctic Watch polar bear area" where you "get right next to" the big guys, most of the critters are "close together", and the "lush" "grounds are just large enough to spend a day without feeling overwhelmed", despite "hills"; the kids' rides, petting zoo and "enthusiastic staff enhance the visit" for the toddler set.

CAMDEN YARDS ☺
| 25 | 28 | 27 | 23 | E |

(aka Oriole Park)

333 W. Camden St. (S. Eutaw St.); 410-685-9800; www.theorioles.com
■ Fans sing "Take Me Out to the Ball Game" "a few blocks from the harbor" at the "place that initiated the retro-stadium craze", the Orioles' "squeaky-clean" home, where "they dust your seat before you sit" – and anywhere you do, it's a "treat" because there's "an interesting sight line from every one"; kids "love the walkway behind the outfield" with "plaques scattered" "where home-run balls have landed", parking is "unbelievably convenient" and if "the crab cakes are pricey", hey, at least the food is "not your typical beer and dogs."

Fort McHenry ☺☺
| 19 | 25 | 19 | 19 | I |

Fort Ave. (off I-95); 410-962-4290; www.nps.gov/fomc
■ "The rockets' red glare comes to life" at this "piece of American history"; after the free, "short video" in the "great visitors' center", take the "awe-inspiring", self-guided tour to learn about "how our flag was still there" – "you can just imagine the raging battle" that "inspired Francis Scott Key to write 'The Star-Spangled Banner'"; little tots will be bored, but "helpful" rangers and reenactors "teach the whole family about the War of 1812", and active kids "enjoy climbing the many cannons" amid the "breathtaking waterside" setting.

Gettysburg National Military Park ☺
| – | – | – | – | $0 |

97 Taneytown Rd. (bet. Hunt & Steinwehr Aves.), Gettysburg; 717-334-1124; www.nps.gov/gett
President Lincoln may not have believed that his speech on this battlefield would long be remembered, but his famous address is one reason so many march to this 6,000-acre National Park 50 miles northwest of Baltimore; families can spend a few hours touring the site of the Civil War's largest battle (on their own or with a guide), appreciate 1,400 markers and monuments, walk 26 miles of paved trails, enjoy summertime events at its amphitheater, pay their respects at the National Soldiers' Cemetery, picnic on the grounds and take a gander at the Cyclorama, a 360-ft.-long circular oil painting depicting the climactic fight; best for history-minded preteens and teens, it has an on-site campground open from mid-May to October.

Harborplace
| 20 | 24 | 22 | 19 | $0 |

200 E. Pratt St. (bet. South & S. Calvert Sts.); 410-332-4191; 800-427-2671; www.harborplace.com
☑ "There's always something going on" at this slightly "cheesy" but "still attractive multilevel mall in a vibrant Inner Harbor setting" with lots of facilities for fun; "walk around with your family", check out the "street performers", "watch the small boats coming and going", tour "historic sailing and Naval vessels", visit "great museums nearby", go in for some shopping in "a few nice, little touristy stores" and "don't pass up those crab cakes" at the many "kid-friendly" indoor/outdoor eateries; just don't get "crushed" by summer's "milling millions."

Maryland Science Center
| 27 | 23 | 23 | 22 | M |

601 Light St. (bet. E. Lee St. & Key Hwy.); 410-685-5225; www.mdsci.org
■ "Tons of interactive exhibits" bring out the Einstein in every tyke for an afternoon at this "refreshingly open" science museum across the harbor from the National Aquarium; there's a "great kids' room" for

the littlest geniuses, "everyone can appreciate the awesome IMAX", and in May 2004, budding paleontologists will thrill at the new addition's "hands-on" meet-and-greet with the dinosaurs while young physicists will take a quantum leap in Newton's Alley; "children have so much fun, they'll forget that they're learning" here.

NATIONAL AQUARIUM   28 | 27 | 25 | 22 | M

501 E. Pratt St. (S. Gay St.); 410-576-3800; www.aqua.org

■ "Herds" of kids stare "spellbound" at the "wonderful assortment of sea creatures" in this "jewel" (rated the city's No. 1 attraction as well as its top spot for Child Appeal); located on Baltimore's Inner Harbor, it's a "gorgeous multilevel aquarium that gives you a scuba diver's perspective without getting you wet"; "with tons to do" – from the "outstanding dolphin show" to the "walk-through rain forest" to the "impressive shark tank" viewed from "spiral walkways" – you'd best "plan for a whole day"; sure, it can get "jammed" and there's "annoying timed ticketing" and a no-stroller policy, but they're expanding, with a 12-story glass cube under construction.

Port Discovery   27 | 18 | 21 | 19 | M

35 Market Pl. (E. Lombard St.); 410-727-8120; www.portdiscovery.org

◪ An "incredible place to let kids loose" at Harborplace is this "amazing children's museum" where all ages get "really hands-on", staffing a TV studio, discovering a lost pharaoh's tomb and playing ace detectives, problem-solving their way through a mystery house; though much of the "wonderful place" is "geared for ages five and up", "there is a small area for infants and toddlers", and special programs are a rip-roaring good time for the whole family.

US Naval Academy ☺   16 | 25 | 22 | 21 | I

121 Blake Rd. (Maryland Ave.), Annapolis; 410-263-6933; www.navyonline.com

■ "It brings a lump to one's throat to see the middies marching en masse" on the "beautiful grounds" of this tradition-steeped Annapolis college; it appeals mostly to preteens and teens, and you "can't go wrong" on the guided tour where you'll see "sailboats, a view of the bay", "interesting architecture", a "fabulous chapel" and "a bit of Naval history"; the visitors' center "contains model ships and other kid-friendly exhibits" so it's enough to make your whole family "swell with patriotic pride" – just "leave your bags" in the car and "don't forget your picture ID in these times of heightened alert."

USS Constellation ☺   22 | 24 | 17 | 19 | I

Pier 1, 301 E. Pratt St. (South St.); 410-539-1797; www.constellation.org

■ "Could our early sailors really have fought wars in such a tiny space?" – aye-aye, and your crew can learn how on this masted sloop docked at Pier 1 "for a peek at what Naval service was like", as "volunteer reenactors" provide "a realistic look" at the life of seamen "during this ship's active tour of duty" in the Civil War era; it's all hands on deck for interactive activities like turning the capstan and bracing the yards on a self-guided tour that's "interesting for school-aged kids", especially if you're "there when they fire the cannon."

Walters Art Museum ☺   12 | 27 | 24 | 24 | I

600 N. Charles St. (Centre St.); 410-547-9000; www.thewalters.org

◪ Everyone can "turn into a kid imagining they're a knight", especially in the armor room, at this Mt. Vernon museum displaying "an eclectic mix of art and artifacts" and "great visiting exhibits", including "occasional family-oriented" shows; older kids and adults find it "exciting to stroll" in the "gorgeous, classic" building "through many eras" of creations, followed by a "terrific Sunday brunch" in the restaurant, but it has to be regarded as more of an adult-friendly than a child-friendly experience.

HOTELS

Ratings: Family Appeal, Rooms, Service, Public Facilities, Cost

FA	R	S	P	$

Harbor Court Hotel

| 19 | 26 | 25 | 25 | $330 |

550 Light St.; 410-234-0550; 800-824-0076; www.harborcourt.com; 174 rooms, 22 suites

■ A "nice alternative to the chains", this "beautiful" hotel is "best for older children" say parents, since it's "within easy walking distance of the Science Museum, Aquarium and waterfront"; the "nighttime view of the harbor is wonderful", and if you're a sports-minded bunch, Camden Yards, home of the Baltimore Orioles, is just a few blocks up the street; the on-site "pool provides a nice diversion" and "the staff is friendly toward kids" so even if there are "less expensive" spots to stay, this is one of the favorites.

Hyatt Regency

| 21 | 22 | 21 | 22 | $270 |

300 Light St.; 410-528-1234; 800-233-1234; www.hyatt.com; 461 rooms, 25 suites

☑ The "convenient location" within walking distance of most main attractions is the biggest appeal of this chain outpost that's got an open skywalk to the Harborplace and "lovely views"; though generally "more of a road warrior's hotel" with "run-of-the-mill rooms", there's a "nice pool" and it's "across the street from Morton's Steakhouse" so it works for some.

Marriott Waterfront Baltimore

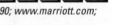

| – | – | – | – | $325 |

700 Aliceanna St.; 410-385-3000; 800-228-9290; www.marriott.com; 728 rooms, 22 suites

Kids enjoy the indoor pool and the water taxi ride to the Inner Harbor from this newcomer located across the water from Downtown Baltimore, which means close proximity to ESPN Zone, the Gallery Shops, the Port Discovery Children's Museum, the National Aquarium and Maryland Science Center; parents appreciate the babysitting and child-care services, the no-smoking rooms and the valet parking.

Renaissance Harborplace

| 20 | 23 | 22 | 23 | $249 |

202 E. Pratt St.; 410-547-1200; 800-535-1201; www.renaissancehotels.com; 582 rooms, 40 suites

☑ "Location is everything" say fans of this Marriott-managed "standout" in the "center of activity" at the Harborplace; "teenage mall rats rejoice" over its proximity to the Gallery (it's connected), and while it may seem "fancy for kids", there's an indoor pool, "huge rooms" and the restaurant makes its own ice cream; so even though some say "the most easily amused child would be bored in a matter of minutes" here, others report they'd "definitely go again."

Sheraton Inner Harbor

| 18 | 20 | 20 | 20 | $279 |

300 S. Charles St.; 410-962-8300; 800-325-3535; www.sheraton.com; 317 rooms, 20 suites

☑ A "great place from which to start your Baltimore adventure", this hotel "within walking distance to the Harborplace and Camden Yards" is a "good choice for families" since there's "lots to do in the area"; though spoilsports snap that it could use a spruce-up, at least "the kids love the pool" and parents like the hassle-free proximity to major attractions.

Top Family-Friendly Hotel Chains in the Area:

Embassy Suites   Homewood Suites
Hampton Inn   Residence Inn
Holiday Inn

See Hotel Chain reviews, starting on page 256.

RESTAURANTS

Ratings: Family Appeal, Food, Decor, Service, Cost

	FA	F	D	S	$

Baugher's

	27	20	13	22	I

289 W. Main St. (Rte. 31), Westminster; 410-848-7413

■ "An old-fashioned soda fountain greets you as you enter" this "casual" country homestead, for over 50 years "a good, safe stop when you're in the area" around Westminster; with "fresh ingredients" provided by its nearby orchard and fields, its "farmstand-simple", "homestyle" American cooking "won't scare the kiddies away."

Cafe Hon

	22	17	21	22	M

1002 W. 36th St. (bet. Falls Rd. & Roland Ave.); 410-243-1230

■ A "noisy" "neighborhood star", this Hampden Hon-ey "epitomizes Old Baltimore" with "satisfying" American "diner food" – "try the meatloaf" – served by "really friendly" waitresses "with spunk" and beehive hairdos in a "quirky", "casual setting" (though "fairly tight, the space is sufficient for toddlers and children").

Chick & Ruth's Delly

	20	20	14	19	I

165 Main St. (Conduit St.), Annapolis; 410-269-6737; www.chickandruths.com

☑ "Politicians mix with Naval Academy plebes" and "kids of all ages" at this Downtown "Annapolis institution" famed for its "fun" atmosphere, "plentiful" deli sandwiches and "the best milkshakes"; it does get "cramped", and apparently "the decor hasn't been updated since it opened" in '65, but that "adds to its charm" declare devotees who've dated, mated and now bring their own kids here.

City Cafe

	▽ 15	21	22	20	M

1001 Cathedral St. (Eager St.); 410-539-4252

☑ A convenient location near the Baltimore Washington Memorial makes this sunlit, "hip, urban cafe" "great for a quick lunch" before or after a patriotic pilgrimage; the "trendy" New American menu offers basics like burgers and carrot cake, but some warn that while "older kids would be fine here, little ones don't fit in with the PIB (people in black)" scene.

Friendly Farm

	27	20	18	23	M

17434 Foreston Rd. (Mount Carmel Rd.), Upperco; 410-239-7400; www.friendlyfarm.net

☑ "A ride through the country, gaggles of geese and doughnut holes – what more could a four-year-old ask for?" not much, and that's why folks "have been going for years" to this "family-style", family-run restaurant set on a 200-acre Upperco farm; "kids love the animals that roam" around (petting is encouraged), and afterwards "all will enjoy" the hearty American eats.

Joy America Cafe

	–	–	–	–	E

American Visionary Art Museum, 800 Key Hwy. (Covington St.); 410-244-6500; www.spikeandcharlies.com

"Especially in the summer when you can sit outside on the terrace" "near the fanciful whirligig sculpture", or inside at a seat by the "giant moon window" for "the best view of the harbor", it's just as "fun" to eat at as it is to visit the American Visionary Art Museum where this "exciting, original" "rooftop" Pan-Latin puts out "delightful" "works of art" to match the "wondrous" collection beneath it; kids enjoy watching "gaucamole be prepared tableside" as they joyously nosh from the children's menu.

L.P. Steamers   – | – | – | – | M

1100 E. Fort Ave. (Woodall St.); 410-576-9294; www.lpsteamers.com
So what if it's a "total dive"? – ignore the decor, grab a "picnic table" on the "roof deck" for "great views" of the skyline and dig into some of the "best crabs" in town at this "classic", convenient to Ft. McHenry and the South Baltimore Little League action across the street; just prepare to get pinched by the prices, as the scarce crustacean supply "these days" means a family meal can get "expensive fast"; N.B. if your kids aren't claw crackers, you can order burgers or chicken tenders.

Phillips   – | – | – | – | M

Harborplace Light Street Pavilion, 301 Light St. (Pratt St.); 410-685-6600
12 Dock St. (Randall St.), Annapolis; 410-990-9888
www.phillipsfoods.com
When the kid gets crabby, sit her down, ply her with chowder crackers and teach her how to crack a claw at these convenient crustacean stations at Harborplace and new to Annapolis; wherever the seafood is reasonably priced and plentiful, and there's outdoor seating along the water, you'll find hordes of other tourists, but look on the bright side – your youngster might meet another little oystercatcher in the crowd to play with; N.B. there are also three locations in Ocean City en route to Assateague, but not all of them abut the briny blue.

Sabatino's   – | – | – | – | M

901 Fawn St. (High St.); 410-727-9414; www.sabatinos.com
Even "tourists" feel they've "come home" at this "classic, classic, classic" Little Italy "original", a "Baltimore tradition" predicated on "large portions, prodigious use of garlic and a way with vegetables" peddled by "rude"-"friendly" "grandmother waitresses" till 3 AM weekends; as your "children run around", dig in: "you can always count on the Bookmaker salad to be delicious" and you "can't go wrong" with the baked shells, even if "locals" gripe that it's "not as good as" back when it was their "favorite as a kid."

Samos ⊠⊅   – | – | – | – | M

600 S. Oldham St. (Fleet St.); 410-675-5292
Join "cops, politicos, locals and suburban Greeks", all honorary members of "the large family get-together" at this "spectacular" yet "unpretentious" Aegean eatery in Greektown; "zesty" eats "Zorba would rave" about come in such "cheap", "gargantuan portions" that the all-cash, BYO "hole-in-the-wall" offers "possibly the East Coast's finest value"; note to parents of fidgeters: "no reservations and wild popularity" equal "long weekend waits", but "the turnover's pretty good", so those hungry little mouths get fed fast.

RESTAURANT CHAINS

See reviews, starting on page 262.

Ratings: Family Appeal, Food, Decor, Service, Cost

	FA	F	D	S	$
Applebee's	21	16	17	17	M

Reisterstown Road Plaza, 6798 Reisterstown Rd. (Brookhill Rd.); 410-358-4468
Annapolis Mall, 2141 Generals Hwy. (Defense Hwy.), Annapolis; 410-573-0078

Baja Fresh Mexican Grill 🅂   20 | 22 | 14 | 18 | I
2512-A Solomons Island Rd. (Old Solomons Island Rd.), Annapolis;
410-897-0090

Bertucci's 🅂   23 | 20 | 17 | 19 | M
2207 Forest Dr. (Rte. 2), Annapolis; 410-266-5800

California Pizza Kitchen 🅂   21 | 21 | 16 | 19 | M
201 E. Pratt St. (bet. Calvert & South Sts.); 410-783-9339
1870 Annapolis Mall (Bestgate Rd.), Annapolis; 410-573-2060

Chevys Fresh Mex 🅂   23 | 19 | 18 | 18 | M
2436 Solomons Island Rd. (Neal St.), Annapolis; 410-573-4932
Arundel Mills Mall, 7000 Arundel Mills Circle (off Hwy. 100), Hanover;
410-799-1505

Chuck E. Cheese's 🅂   26 | 10 | 17 | 13 | I
5912 Baltimore Nat'l Pike (off Hwy. 695); 410-719-8850
8354 Eastern Ave. (Diamond Point Rd.); 410-288-9393

Don Pablo's 🅂   20 | 19 | 18 | 18 | I
8161 Honeygo Blvd. (Campell Blvd.); 410-931-7966

Fuddrucker's 🅂   24 | 20 | 15 | 16 | I
125 Market Pl. (bet. Lombard & Pratt Sts.); 410-625-0995
175 Jennifer Rd. (West St.), Annapolis; 410-266-8030

Hard Rock Cafe 🅂   22 | 16 | 26 | 18 | M
601 E. Pratt St. (bet. Gay St. & Market Pl.); 410-347-7625

Johnny Rockets 🅂   25 | 17 | 20 | 18 | I
1084 Annapolis Mall (Commerce Pike Dr.), Annapolis; 410-897-0717

Outback Steakhouse 🅂   20 | 22 | 18 | 20 | M
2400 Boston St. (Hudson St.); 410-522-7757
4215 Ebenezer Rd. (Belair Rd.); 410-529-7200
2207 Forest Dr. (Solomons Island Rd.), Annapolis; 410-266-7229
12471 Ocean Gateway (Waterview Dr.), Ocean City; 410-213-2595

Red Robin 🅂   25 | 20 | 19 | 20 | M
1073 Annapolis Mall (Bestgate Rd.), Annapolis; 410-573-1155

Romano's Macaroni Grill 🅂   21 | 21 | 19 | 21 | M
178 Jennifer Rd. (West St.), Annapolis; 410-573-1717

Uno Chicago Grill 🅂   20 | 18 | 15 | 16 | M
Harborplace, 201 E. Pratt St. (bet. Calvert & South Sts.); 410-625-5900

Boston/Cape Cod Area

*Crucible of liberty, center of learning and one of the country's most
compact cities, Boston is wonderful for walkers, even young ones.
Start at Boston Common and stroll the Freedom Trail in the footsteps
of Paul Revere and John Adams; you'll soon pass dignified Beacon
Hill and the fun Faneuil Hall waterfront marketplace. When you get to
lantern-lit Old North Church, you're in the North End, home to the
city's best Italian restaurants. Surrounding that neighborhood, the Big
Dig highway revamp – nearly a done deal at $13 billion-plus – has
streamlined auto traffic, but it's still pretty dismal for drivers Downtown,
so hop on the subway (locally known as the "T") if you're making for*

Fenway Park or elegant Back Bay, or crossing the Charles River to Cambridge's Harvard Square and its surrounding namesake university. Autumn is the city's liveliest season, with crisp nights, colorful foliage and lots of football weekends – but if you visit in summer you can hear the Boston Pops playing on the Esplanade on July 4, or head north to the Maine coast or southeast to Cape Cod, Martha's Vineyard and Nantucket. For full flexibility in exploring these venues, you'll need a car.

ATTRACTIONS

Ratings: Child Appeal, Adult Appeal, Public Facilities, Service, Cost

C	A	P	S	$

Arnold Arboretum ☺

17	26	16	14	$0

125 Arborway (Centre St.), Jamaica Plain; 617-524-1718; www.arboretum.harvard.edu

☑ "If you're nuts about trees", head for this "magical" (and "free") "urban oasis", an outdoor "museum" of "exotic and familiar" plants, where "you feel smart" just "walking around" (it's operated by Harvard); "don't miss Lilac Sunday in May", but in "all seasons" "kids can run", bike or fly kites while adults "sniff the flowers" or examine the "bonsai collection"; the older folks like this better than their offspring (getting "bored" preteens "interested in" shrubs "ain't gonna happen") and it "isn't convenient to other city attractions", but it's a good break for flora fanatics.

Black Heritage Trail ☺

16	22	15	18	$0

46 Joy St. (bet. Cambridge & Myrtle Sts.), Boston; 617-725-0022; www.afroammuseum.org

■ Although "overshadowed by the Freedom Trail", this "rewarding tour of Boston's original African-American community" showcases an oft-"neglected part of our country's history"; start this "free self-guided" walk at the Museum of Afro-American History, then check out the "cool" African Meeting House next door; parents of preschoolers point out, however, that "children under six may not appreciate" this stroll through the past.

Boston Common

19	22	16	12	$0

bordered by Beacon, Boylston, Charles, Park & Tremont Sts., Boston; 617-426-3115

■ "Cows used to graze" on this centuries-old "swath of lawn in the middle of the city" that many call a "mini–Central Park"; "play Frisbee" or "break out the picnic basket" while spying on the "colorful local characters", or head for "the Frog Pond" – wading "for toddlers" "in the summer" and "ice skating for everyone in winter" – with an "exceptional playground" nearby; in warm weather, take in "free plays", movies and festivals, but "don't linger" "after dark", and beware that both service and "bathrooms are scarce."

Boston Public Garden

23	25	17	14	$0

bordered by Arlington, Beacon, Boylston & Charles Sts., Boston; 617-426-3115

■ These "idyllic" "formal gardens" are a "nice breather" for the whole family; "don't miss the Swan Boats", an "old-fashioned treat" that "everybody loves" whether "you're four, 14 or 44" (though teens might not "want their friends to catch them enjoying themselves"); travelers with toddlers should "read *Make Way for Ducklings* beforehand", then visit the sculpture of Mrs. Mallard and her eight hatchlings (the city's "No. 1 photo op for kids"); "if there were bathrooms", this "quintessential" "oasis" between Back Bay and Beacon Hill "would be perfect."

Boston Public Library 😊😊

| 13 | 25 | 23 | 22 | $0 |

700 Boylston St. (Exeter St.), Boston; 617-536-5400; www.bpl.org

☑ "Stunning architecture, great murals" by John Singer Sargent, a "scrumptious", "new on-site restaurant" "and, oh, books too" make this "imposing" Copley Square "landmark" "worth a look"; even if "not too many kids are crazy about libraries", this one has a "well-equipped children's room", and the "grand" edifice "should please the adults" (you can "stop in to check your e-mail" or read "newspapers from all over the world"); P.S. the "hidden courtyard" "makes you feel miles away" from the Back Bay's "hubbub."

Bud's Go-Karts 😊

| ▽ 27 | 20 | 16 | 16 | I |

9 Sisson Rd. (Main St.), Harwich Port; 508-432-4964

■ "Generations of families have zipped around the track" at this Harwich "tradition" that's a welcome "diversion from the beach" and a "treat your kids will not forget" (young 'uns under seven have to "eagerly await the day that they're tall enough to ride alone"); the staff "keeps the go-karts in great condition and makes everyone aware of the rules", so even though "lines can be long at peak hours" and some adults merely tolerate the trip, it's an overall terrific "vacation night out."

Bunker Hill Monument 😊

| 15 | 21 | 14 | 13 | $0 |

Monument Ave. (Hioh St.), Boston; 617-242-5641

☑ "It's a long way up" the 294 steps to the pinnacle of this 221-ft. granite obelisk at "the end of the Freedom Trail" in Charlestown – but as a tribute to one of the American Revolution's first battles it's "a must-see for patriotic tourists" (not to mention a handy "way to tire out the kids"), and the reward for the "climb to the top" is a "great view on a clear day"; however, unless you're "a history buff", revolutionaries retort "why bother" with this "poor man's Washington Monument"?

Cape Cod Children's Museum 😊 ▽

| ▽ 23 | 14 | 15 | 16 | I |

577 Great Neck Rd. S. (bet. Ockway Bay Rd. & Old Dock Ln.), Mashpee; 508-539-8788; www.capecodchildrensmuseum.pair.com

☑ "When it rains on the Cape" and "you need something to do with your kids", this modest Mashpee museum has plenty to occupy the little ones "for an afternoon"; "best for those under age five", it's a "small place" run by a pleasing staff and offers all "the standard activities", from a pirate ship to a puppet theater; the facility is "a little worn", though, and on bad-weather days, it can be "incredibly overcrowded and hectic" so the sacrifice is all on the parents for this outing.

Cape Cod Museum of Natural History

| – | – | – | – | I |

869 Rte. 6A (bet. Lower Rd. & Pine Hill Dr.), Brewster; 508-896-3867; www.ccmnh.org

This Brewster museum is particularly worthwhile for first-time visitors to Cape Cod, thanks to plenty of please-touch exhibits about local flora and fauna (whales, sea birds), three nature trails through the woods and salt marsh, and a variety of naturalist-led family field walks; kids have special ocean-themed activities downstairs, or can join staffers to feed the resident fish, lobsters, frogs and turtles; the museum is open year-round, but winter hours and activities are more limited; N.B. nature tours to other areas of the Cape are offered as well.

Cape Cod National Seashore

| – | – | – | – | $0 |

Salt Pond Visitor Ctr., Nauset Rd. (Rte. 6), Eastham; 508-255-3421; www.nps.gov/caco

Stretching nearly 40 miles from Chatham to Provincetown along the peninsula's outer shore, the Cape's prime recreation area has more than 43,600 acres of dune-filled beaches, crashing surf, and cycling and hiking paths; in summer, rangers lead an assortment of walks, canoe trips and nature programs, but at any time of year you can enjoy the place by strolling along the shoreline and dipping your toes into the Atlantic; N.B. two of its beaches – Coast Guard in Eastham and Herring Cove in Provincetown – stock wheelchairs that can travel over sand.

Cape Poge Wildlife Refuge

–	–	–	–	I

Dike Rd. (off Chappaquiddick Rd.), Chappaquiddick Island; 508-627-7689; www.thetrustees.org

On the eastern edge of Chappaquiddick Island, part of Martha's Vineyard, this secluded seven-mile-long barrier beach and wildlife refuge contains salt marshes, wind-sculpted cedars and nesting shorebirds; it's crisscrossed with trails for nature walks, plus guides lead canoe trips for birdwatching, over-sand vehicle excursions to the best sites for surf-fishing and tours of the area, including the Cape Poge Lighthouse, built in 1893; N.B. no mountain biking allowed.

Children's Museum, The ☺

29	21	24	23	M

300 Congress St. (bet. Atlantic Ave. & Sleeper St.), Boston; 617-426-6500; www.bostonkids.org

■ "Everybody will have a blast" at this "awesome", "high-energy" "family favorite" on the waterfront, voted Boston's No. 1 for Child Appeal in this *Survey* and pretty appealing for 'rents as well, thanks to its "imaginative", "thoughtfully put-together", "hands-on exhibits" involving "art and science, plus clean and messy play"; just "allow plenty of time" – "kids can spend hours and hours here", since there's "tons of stuff for even the littlest ones to do" – and be prepared for a "hectic", "riotous" scene (it's "crowded on school holidays"); P.S. on Fridays from 5–9 PM, "admission is $1" – "what a deal!"

Faneuil Hall/Quincy Market

19	24	21	20	$0

bordered by Chatham, Clinton, Commercial & Congress Sts., Boston; 617-635-1887; www.faneuilhallmarketplace.com

☑ "You'll see everything from comedians to clowns to magicians" at this "festive" urban marketplace, a "teeming" "carnival" of "street performers", "chain stores" and "outdoor vendors" encompassing three renovated 19th-century buildings; meanwhile, "even the fussiest eaters will find something they like" ("from gelati to a five-course meal") in the "massive food court" or numerous restaurants – still critics call this little more than "a glorified mall" with "inadequate seating"; P.S. "historic" Faneuil Hall next door is where the Sons of Liberty persuaded Colonial Bostonians to revolt.

FENWAY PARK ☺

25	28	18	19	E

4 Yawkey Way (Brookline Ave.), Boston; 617-236-6666; www.bostonredsox.com

☑ The national pastime "doesn't get better than this" declare devotees of the Red Sox' "classic" "all-American ball park" where "you're so close to the players, you can almost touch them"; worshipers at this "shrine" should also "take the tour" so "your Nomar wanna-be can run the bases", "touch the Green Monster" and "sit in the dugout"; sure, seats are "cramped" but when the Yankees come to town, you won't notice because the crowd is standing most of the time at this "temple of baseball."

FleetCenter ☺☺

20	22	24	19	E

1 FleetCenter Pl. (Causeway St.), Boston; 617-624-1000; www.fleetcenter.com

☑ This "comfortable", "wonderfully modern" facility at North Station hosts "lots of family-oriented" entertainment, from "the circus to ice shows to sporting events" (it's home to the NBA Celtics and NHL Bruins, plus an on-site sports museum), and views are "great no matter where you sit"; aesthetes assail it, though, as an "antiseptic"

"K-Mart of an arena" ("none of the historic, nostalgic appeal of the old Boston Garden"), and penny-pinchers pout "you'll need to take out a second mortgage" to afford admission.

Flying Horses Carousel ☺

| 28 | 22 | 19 | 18 | I |

33 Oak Bluffs Ave. (Seaview Ave.), Oak Bluffs; 508-693-9481
■ "You can't help but smile" when you're riding this Martha's Vineyard "landmark" that's "one of the oldest carousels in the nation"; "kids have been enjoying" this "utterly magical" experience "for generations", and trying to "catch the brass ring is the extra that keeps them coming back"; this "charming" "slice of American history" "fits right into the ambiance of Victorian Oak Bluffs", so "you almost don't mind waiting in the inevitable line."

Franklin Park Zoo

| 25 | 19 | 17 | 18 | I |

1 Franklin Park Rd. (Blue Hill Ave.), Dorchester; 617-541-5466; www.zoonewengland.com
☑ "Always fun for the kids", this "up-and-coming" zoo in a Frederick Law Olmsted–designed park in Dorchester allows visitors to "see a wide variety of species" and "get close to the animals", "yet it's not so big that it takes all day"; rooters "recommend the butterfly garden" ("the monarchs come right up to you"), a "neat bird area" and an "excellent climbing structure for little ones", but some say this "underfunded" facility "in a tough part of town" "isn't in the same league" with other menageries, while the "poor service" makes the "potential gem" a "bit of a disappointment."

Freedom Trail ☺☺

| 18 | 26 | 16 | 14 | $0 |

Start at Boston Common, Boston; 888-733-2678; www.thefreedomtrail.org
■ "Walk through our country's early history" when you "follow the red-brick line", a two-and-a-half-mile self-guided tour with 16 stops between Boston Common and Charlestown; "wear comfortable shoes" and "carry a guidebook" – or "pick up the trail randomly and see what adventures you'll find" – then sit down in the North End "with a tasty Italian lunch"; "it would be un-American to miss this" stroll "back in time", but "half the trail" in one day may be plenty "for little legs" and wandering minds; tender tootsies tell us trolleys traverse this trail too.

Harvard Square

| – | – | – | – | $0 |

JFK St. (Massachusetts Ave.), Cambridge; 617-491-3434; www.harvardsquare.com
You don't have to be a college student to find the environs of Harvard University stimulating – the whole family can find several hours' worth of fun here, punctuated by meals that can range from pepperoni pizza to roast duck (not to mention ice cream, a local obsession); the littlest ones can frolic in wide-open JFK Park near the Charles, while older kids and teens can shop for underground comic books, video games, sporting goods or funky beads; meanwhile, street musicians, magicians and other buskers provide free open-air entertainment; if you have academic interests, stroll through the campus and dormitories of the oldest American university.

John F. Kennedy Library and Museum ☺

| 14 | 28 | 27 | 24 | I |

Columbia Pt. (off I-93), Dorchester; 617-514-1600; 866-535-1960; www.jfklibrary.org
☑ "Worth a visit even for Republicans", this "well-designed" "collection of all things Kennedy" presents "modern American political history" "in an accessible yet sophisticated manner"; little girls will adore this year's exhibit of Caroline's international doll collection, but overall the museum's "touching tribute to JFK, Jackie and family" is best "for

older children" or baby boomers who remember "the magic that was Camelot"; while the "breathtaking I.M. Pei building" may be "a bit out of the way" in Dorchester, "gorgeous" "views of Boston Harbor" make up for it.

Jump On Us
Trampoline Fun House ☻☺

▽ | 28 | 14 | 18 | 17 | I |

260 Rte. 28 (bet. Cozy Home Terr. & Standish Way), West Yarmouth; 508-775-3304

■ "They jump, they sleep, you smile" thanks to this West Yarmouth attraction, where "kids get a workout and parents get a break"; it's "a great energy burner", particularly "on a cloudy day" or when you've had too much of the beach; even if some adults "would love to drive" right by according to its ratings for Adult Appeal, young children "love to go here" – "just don't take them right after a meal."

Minute Man
National Historical Park ☺

| – | – | – | – | $0 |

174 Liberty St. (Estabrook Rd.), Concord; 978-369-6993; www.nps.gov/mima

To see where that shot heard round the world was actually fired, head west to Lexington and Concord, to this 900-acre national park; it encompasses the North Bridge battle site, part of Paul Revere's route (including the spot where the British captured him), and two helpful visitors' centers; the multimedia presentation "The Road to Revolution" elucidates the 1775 events, and at Hartwell Tavern, rangers in period dress demonstrate musket firing, open-hearth cooking and other aspects of Colonial life; N.B. reconstruction of the North Bridge is scheduled for 2004.

Museum of Fine Arts ☺

| 15 | 28 | 27 | 24 | M |

Avenue of the Arts, 465 Huntington Ave. (bet. Forsyth Way & Louis Prang St.), Boston; 617-267-9300; www.mfa.org

■ According to mommies, "kids love the mummies" at this "impressive" "world-class institution" in the Fenway where it "would require several days" to see all the "amazing art and artifacts", from the Egyptian room to the Impressionists to the Asian collections; to keep children from getting restless, pick up a "terrific activity kit", check out the "well-run kids' programs", or visit the "cheap and tasty cafe downstairs"; P.S. embarking on an extensive expansion, the MFA will be "under renovation over the next few years" – call before visiting.

MUSEUM OF SCIENCE

| 28 | 26 | 25 | 24 | M |

Science Park at the Charles River Dam (off Rte. 28), Boston; 617-723-2500; www.mos.org

■ Even with so many competing attractions in Boston, respondents rave that this "venerable" yet "exciting" institution is worth a half-day, since it really "makes science fun" (even for adults) and they've voted it the top overall attraction in the city; explore such "eye-catching", "hands-on" exhibits as "interactive" "musical piano steps", "sensational kinetic sculptures", an "immersive digital fish tank" and a "neat" domed Omni theater; in addition, "enthusiastic staffers" present "great demos" ("watch lightning being created!"), while an "ample food court" serves up both "first-rate views of the Charles River" and food; although a fraction frets about "out-of-hand" admission prices, this "favorite family place" remains "world-class."

New England Aquarium

| 28 | 25 | 23 | 22 | M |

Central Wharf, Milk St. (Atlantic Ave.), Boston; 617-973-5200; www.neaq.org

◪ "Like the Guggenheim with a fish tank", this "mesmerizing" multi-level "circular" aquarium on the waterfront is a "must-see", housing "every known species of aquatic life" and garnering high ratings for both Child and Adult Appeal; you can "press your face against the glass until a shark swims by", watch "penguins galore" or a "funny" sea lion show, or scope out the "cool" 3-D IMAX; toddlers are tickled by the Activity Center's games and stories, while older children "enjoy the marine hospital" where ocean creatures get some TLsea; P.S. this "great escape" is often "very crowded."

New England Aquarium: Whale Watch ☺☺

| 25 | 26 | 20 | 24 | E |

Central Wharf, Milk St. (Atlantic Ave.), Boston; 617-973-5206; www.neaq.org

■ Seeing "a giant whale racing next to your boat will take your breath away", say satisfied seafarers after this three- to five-hour excursion, one of several cetacean-sighting cruises departing from the waterfront; the "kind and helpful on-board staff" imparts "fascinating" history and makes you feel like "you're in *National Geographic*" – a benefit, "since it takes time to get to the viewing areas"; pass it up "if things are gray and choppy", unless you don't mind a "long ride with vomiting children"; N.B. no kids under three allowed.

New England Fire and History Museum ☺☺

| ▽ 21 | 22 | 19 | 22 | I |

1439 Main St. (bet. Brier Ln. & Swamp Rd.), Brewster; 508-896-5711

☑ "Enthusiastic volunteers" "who clearly enjoy their work" "keep this small museum alive"; "toddlers enjoy playing on the trucks" outdoors, while older children "absorb more of the history of firefighting" and appreciate the "meticulously maintained antique engines"; there's "no technology" here, "just good old-fashioned fire stuff", so for younger kids or the inferno-indifferent, it may well be a "yawn, even on a rainy day."

Old North Church, The ☺

| 15 | 24 | 19 | 19 | I |

193 Salem St. (bet. Charter & Hull Sts.), Boston; 617-523-6676; www.oldnorth.com

☑ "Step back to the 1700s" in this "important historic site", where a pair of lanterns hung in the steeple launched Paul Revere's famous ride; it "makes one feel quite patriotic" to pause at this "stop on the Freedom Trail" that's "in mint condition", and it's worth bringing kids who are "old enough for *Johnny Tremain*" (they'll appreciate the "informative guides"); besides, the North End location is just "a short walk to some of the best Italian restaurants on this side of the pond."

Paul Revere House ☺

| 19 | 24 | 19 | 20 | I |

19 North Sq. (Prince St.), Boston; 617-523-2338; www.paulreverehouse.org

■ "One if by land, two a must-see" say surveyors who've sought out the "famous home of one of the fathers of our country" that's also the "oldest house" still standing "in Boston"; for an "approachable and low-key illustration of Colonial life", kids can "take part in activities" or watch demonstrations (silversmithing, cabinetmaking); they'll "love" how this "picturesque" cottage is "just their size", though parents may wonder how Revere (father of 16) "fit all those children into this tiny" dwelling.

Peabody Museum ☺☺

| 20 | 26 | 22 | 22 | I |

11 Divinity Ave. (Kirkland St.), Cambridge; 617-496-1027; www.peabody.harvard.edu

■ Harvard's "old-fashioned museum" of anthropology boasts an "eclectic collection", from "African masks and Native American items" to "dinosaur bones"; the same ticket gets you into the neighboring Museum of Natural History, which houses the "amazing glass flower" collection, rock and mineral exhibits, and other "unusual artifacts"; just outside of Harvard Square, it makes "a great stop on any tour of Cambridge"; N.B. it's free on Sunday mornings.

Plimoth Plantation ☺

| – | – | – | – | E |

137 Warren Ave. (Plimoth Plantation Hwy.), Plymouth; 508-746-1622;
www.plimoth.org

Forty miles south of Boston, this living history village has 'pilgrims'
going about their work – cheesemaking, blacksmithing, herb-growing –
as if it were still the 17th century (they'll act appropriately clueless if
the kids ask them about TVs or other modern conveniences); also on the
property are re-created Native American huts, and nearby is Downtown
Plymouth, with a seaworthy replica of the 1620s *Mayflower.*

Prudential Center & Skywalk ☺☺

| 20 | 23 | 22 | 20 | $0 |

800 Boylston St. (Fairfield St.), Boston; 617-859-0648; 800-746-7778;
www.prudentialcenter.com

☑ "On a clear day", from the 50th floor of this Back Bay office tower
and shopping center, families enjoy the "fantastic panoramic views"
"of the city and far beyond", and "kids love the elevator ride up",
"picking out famous sights"; back at ground level, "protected from
the weather", are "typical stores and souvenir shops", a "large food
court" and several restaurants.

USS Constitution Museum ☺

| 24 | 26 | 21 | 22 | $0 |

Charleston Navy Yard, 55 Constitution Rd. (N. Washington St.),
Boston; 617-426-1812; www.ussconstitutionmuseum.org

☑ Here's a chance to "step back in time" to "see how sailors of the
18th century lived"; known as Old Ironsides, "this lovingly preserved"
vessel in the Charlestown Navy Yard is "the U.S. Navy's oldest actively
commissioned ship"; with "real sailors as your guides", "history comes
alive" on this "200-year-old icon", which is "educational", "fun" and
free, but with tight security in effect, lines can be "long."

Zooquarium

| 22 | 15 | 15 | 17 | M |

674 Rte. 28 (Courtland Way), West Yarmouth; 508-775-8883;
www.zooquariumcapecod.net

☑ On a rainy day or when "sun-weary", this "homegrown" aquarium/
zoo "fulfills its purpose" – and it's compact enough to be "manageable
for young kids"; some visitors vaunt the "sea lion exhibit and show" and
the touch-me tidal pools that little ones "love", though the disgruntled
declare that some creatures "don't look too happy to be here" and
deem the experience "overpriced", since there's "not much to see."

HOTELS

Ratings: Family Appeal, Rooms, Service, Public Facilities, Cost

| FA | R | S | P | $ |

Boston Harbor Hotel

| 20 | 26 | 25 | 25 | $305 |

70 Rowes Wharf, Boston; 617-439-7000; 800-752-7077; www.bhh.com;
204 rooms, 26 suites

■ It may "look very fancy" but they "handle a toddler tantrum with a
smile" at this "waterfront" property with "large rooms" and proximity
to the New England Aquarium (two blocks away), as well as Faneuil
Hall (a three-block walk); there's an "excellent Sunday brunch", a
restaurant that offers "half-portions that work well for children" and
views of the ships, so even if some say it's "expensive" and "very
upscale", it's generally "worth it."

Chatham Bars Inn

| 23 | 22 | 24 | 26 | $320 |

297 Shore Rd., Chatham; 508-945-0096; 800-527-4884;
www.chathambarsinn.com; 163 rooms, 42 suites

■ "The cottages are great for families" at this "respite on the Cape"
that's "perfect for a week in the summer", especially when you stay in a

"beach house with a large front porch and rocking chairs overlooking the ocean"; it has the "best kids' camp ever" (they'll "talk about the activities years later"), "child-sized Victorian furniture", a "not-to-be-missed Sunday brunch" and a "wonderful kiddie pool" and playground; sure, it's "expensive, but most find there's "something for everyone."

Four Seasons

| 20 | 27 | 29 | 26 | $425 |

200 Boylston St., Boston; 617-338-4400; 800-332-3442;
www.fourseasons.com; 202 rooms, 72 suites

■ "It's a pleasure to bring a child here" fawn fans of this "impeccable" hotel where little ones are "just as important as any other client", receiving "welcome gifts" at check-in, swim toys in the pool, crayons at dinner (there's "a good menu selection" for smaller appetites, too) and "full cribs with their own bedding", plus complimentary milk and cookies in the "childproofed rooms"; then there's the "magnificent Boston Public Garden location" (yes, the staff provides food to feed the ducks) "overlooking Boston Common."

Harbor View Hotel

| ∇ 23 | 18 | 20 | 21 | $330 |

131 N. Water St., Edgartown; 508-627-7000; 800-225-6005;
www.harbor-view.com; 118 rooms, 9 suites, 2 townhouses

■ Head to this "magical" Martha's Vineyard hotel (circa 1891) for "spectacular views of Edgartown Harbor" and proximity to many of the 63 miles of beaches in the area; the "easy walk" to the charming, brick-paved town "makes it worthwhile to stay here", and families find the two-bedroom townhouses a "more spacious option", while "kids love to swim in the outdoor pool after a day" on the sand; some say the "food is above average" at the on-site waterview Coach House restaurant, but there are plenty of additional dining spots nearby.

Marriott Copley Place

| 22 | 20 | 20 | 22 | $359 |

110 Huntington Ave., Boston; 617-236-5800; 888-236-2427;
www.marriott.com; 1100 rooms, 47 suites

■ Located in the "heart of the Back Bay area" with a "sightseeing trolley that stops in front", this chain outpost is especially "worth staying in during winter" or a scorching summer since it's attached via covered skywalk to Prudential Center mall (which parents find "safe enough" to feel secure about letting teens shop on their own); although the hotel can be "somewhat impersonal", the "indoor pool is lots of fun", there are "nice cribs" should you need one and it's less than a mile to Fenway Park and Boston Common.

Millennium Bostonian Hotel

| 19 | 20 | 20 | 19 | $249 |

26 North St., Boston; 617-523-3600; 866-866-8086;
www.millennium-hotels.com; 193 rooms, 8 suites

☑ If you want "close proximity to Faneuil Hall", "you can't beat the location" of this hotel that's also "steps from Quincy Market, great restaurants and shopping", easing the burden of traveling around with tots; the property has an "innlike" feel, and "can be a good value for the money", though a few fume over a "noisy location" and complain they could have more going on for kids.

Ocean Edge Resort

| 25 | 22 | 21 | 25 | $378 |

2907 Main St., Brewster; 508-896-9000; 800-343-6074;
www.oceanedge.com; 90 rooms, 245 villas

☑ "Close to quaint Brewster" in a "lovely part of the Cape", this resort is "perfect for families", particularly in the summer when the daily 'Ocean Edgeventures' program, featuring turtle tracking and tidal walks, is a big hit with youngsters; "some units are better than others" advise regulars, but there's "great access to a bike path", a pool with a snack bar, "golf galore", "many dining options including carryout" and a "fantastic beach", so be prepared for a "crowded" scene.

Westin Copley Place

| 21 | 23 | 22 | 23 | $429 |

10 Huntington Ave., Boston; 617-262-9600; 800-937-8461;
www.westin.com; 754 rooms, 49 suites

☑ "Heavenly cribs help everyone sleep better" at this Back Bay hotel "in the center of everything" with an indoor attached skywalk to Copley Place and the Prudential Center malls (especially good in winter "if you have toddlers" since you avoid all that bundling up, and good for "moms who can sneak out to shop while dad babysits"); the "riverfront view is extraordinary", and family packages include buffet breakfasts, trolley tours and milk and cookies; even if it "seems sterile and too busy" to a few, most believe it "accommodates families well."

Top Family-Friendly Hotel Chains in the Area:

Embassy Suites	Hyatt
Hampton Inn	Residence Inn
Holiday Inn	Ritz-Carlton
Homewood Suites	

See Hotel Chain reviews, starting on page 256.

RESTAURANTS

Ratings: Family Appeal, Food, Decor, Service, Cost

| FA | F | D | S | $ |

Artu

| 20 | 19 | 15 | 17 | M |

6 Prince St. (bet. Hanover St. & North Sq.), Boston; 617-742-4336
89 Charles St. (bet. Mt. Vernon & Pinckney Sts.), Boston; 617-227-9023

■ "A reasonable price for reasonable food" – all the Italian classics, from antipasti to pastas to sorbetto – is the ticket at this pair of "informal" trattorias "conveniently" located in the North End and on Beacon Hill (the latter in a "small", cozy basement); though they don't cater to kids specifically, the staff is reasonably "child-friendly."

Betty's Wok & Noodle Diner

| – | – | – | – | M |

250 Huntington Ave. (Mass. Ave.), Boston; 617-424-1950;
www.bettyswokandnoodle.com

"Mix and match" "your own noodles, toppings and sauces" to come up with a customized bowl at this "funky" diner where Pan-Asian cuisine meets Nuevo Latino; it's a "fun concept" for wee ones and couples alike that "adds a creative element to a meal "before the theater, symphony" or family outing; design divas defend the "cool retro-chic" decor (think '50s LA), still, dissenters dismiss the "generic" eats as "all gimmick" while wondering "where, oh, where is the staff?"

Black Dog Tavern

| 25 | 19 | 22 | 20 | M |

21 Beach St. ext. (Vineyard Haven Harbor), Vineyard Haven; 508-693-9223;
www.theblackdog.com

☑ "This place is [practically] a cult", so "be prepared to wait" for "one of the ultimate Martha's Vineyard experiences": "great views of the harbor", "hearty", "family-friendly" American eats and a "low-key atmosphere" (i.e. "no one's going to give you a dirty look if your three-year-old gums a hamburger roll"); some hounds howl "the food's just ok", but most maintain this "well-known stop" is "worth it"; oh, and "when you leave, stop by the store" to "pick up a T-shirt" or kiddie sweatshirt.

Cap'n Frosty's ⌧

| – | – | – | – | I |

219 Rte. 6A (S. Yarmouth Rd.), Dennis; 508-385-8548

Fish 'n' chips and soft-serve ice cream – what more could you want from a summer-only Cape Cod eatery? – this popular order-at-the-counter spot run by a friendly crew on Route 6A in Dennis serves all the standards in fried seafood; if the super-casual dining room is too cramped, get yours to go, and head back to the beach.

Chatham Squire | 22 | 19 | 19 | 21 | M |

487 Main St. (bet. Chatham Bars Ave. & Seaview St.), Chatham; 508-945-0945; www.thesquire.com

■ The feel is pure "old Cape Cod" at this "funky local place with the required fishy decor", an "affordable" all-American "favorite" for "New England summertime meals" with plenty of seafood on the menu (and "kid-friendly" choices, too); so, as long as you're "willing to wait for a table", strap on your sandals and head for this "casual", "comfortable" Chatham corner.

China Pearl | 22 | 22 | 15 | 17 | M |

9 Tyler St. (Beach St.), Boston; 617-426-4338
288 Mishawum Rd. (Ryan Rd.), Woburn; 781-932-0031

■ "Yum yum, dim sum" – that's the verdict on this "popular" "Chinatown landmark" where "everyone can sample different" small dishes; it's "big and noisy", and "you might have to wait" on weekends (arrive before 11 AM to beat the crowds), but "children from toddlers on up will be happy" with "the variety of goodies"; just "don't expect handholding service from the cart-pushers."

Durgin Park | 21 | 18 | 14 | 14 | M |

Faneuil Hall Mktpl., 340 N. Market St. (Congress St.), Boston; 617-227-2038; www.durgin-park.com

☑ "No one notices kid noise" at this "rambunctious" "quintessential family restaurant", a "historic" Faneuil Hall "institution" (it opened in 1827) where the "crusty" "waitresses are a hoot" and "pushy service is part of its charm"; nostalgists love sharing the communal tables, and little ones will enjoy "chowing down" on "simple", "wholesome" New England fare; but unsentimental crabs snap that with such "bland" "tourist" dishes, "no wonder the Colonialists had such a short life expectancy."

Fire & Ice | 23 | 19 | 20 | 17 | M |

205 Berkeley St. (St. James Ave.), Boston; 617-482-3473
50 Church St. (bet. Brattle & Palmer Sts.), Cambridge; 617-547-9007 ●

☑ "It's a rare child who wouldn't love" "choosing his own" Eclectic ingredients, then "watching the chefs flip and sizzle the dinner" "on a giant grill" at this "fast-paced", "all-you-can-eat" Mongolian BBQ-style duo in the Back Bay and Harvard Square; fire-eaters find it "loads of fun" and "even the pickiest kids will have something to sample"; however, others icily note "the novelty wears off quickly" and warn the "self-serve" and stand-in-line "format can be difficult to navigate" with toddlers.

Full Moon | – | – | – | – | M |

138 Mass. Ave. (Milton St.), Arlington; 781-646-1404
344 Huron Ave. (bet. Chilton & Fayerweather Sts.), Cambridge; 617-354-6699
www.fullmoonrestaurant.com

"Where Chardonnay and BRIO train sets are both readily available", these "kiddie-centric" "restaurants designed for families" in Arlington and Fresh Pond serve food "like you'd make at home – if you had the energy" and talent; rugrats relish the colorful play area, while grown-ups are grateful for the "decent" New American cooking; however, some peace-loving parents suggest "skip it if you have no baby on board" because the chattering, "whining" and chaos can be too overwhelming.

Legal Sea Foods
| 18 | 24 | 19 | 21 | M |

Copley Pl., 100 Huntington Ave. (bet. Dartmouth & Exeter Sts.), Boston;
617-266-7775
Long Wharf, 255 State St. (Atlantic Ave.), Boston; 617-227-3115
26 Park Plaza (Columbus Ave.), Boston; 617-426-4444
20 University Rd. (Eliot St.), Cambridge; 617-491-9400
www.legalseafoods.com

☑ When you're looking for finny fare prepared "just the way you want it", this "quintessential Boston seafood experience" "won't let you down"; whether you're "taking out-of-town visitors", "mom and dad" or a boatload of kids, you can "depend" on this "solid performer"; sure, it's a chain, but if you can "ignore all the tourists" and "wade through" the sea of "crowds" to "catch a table", you'll get "good, fresh fish – enough said."

Mr. & Mrs. Bartley's
Burger Cottage ⊠⇗
| – | – | – | – | I |

1246 Mass. Ave. (Plympton St.), Cambridge; 617-354-6559;
www.mrbartleys.com

"If your inner carnivore is raging" and your hungry brood is too, feed them "amazing hamburgers" prepared "any way you want" (including junior-sized, if you're a kid, that is) at this "cheesy", "retro" "dive" that's "still the undisputed champ" of a patty on a bun (don't miss the "out-of-this-world onion rings"); decorated "like a freshman dorm room" and worked by a "plucky" staff, it can be a total "madhouse", but since 1961 this "kitschy" "institution" has been "where Harvard Square 'meats'" – "long may it grill."

Union Oyster House
| 17 | 21 | 20 | 19 | E |

41 Union St. (bet. W. Hanover & North Sts.), Boston; 617-227-2750;
www.unionoysterhouse.com

■ "A fine choice for family dining" offering "a real fish and chowder-house experience", this "touristy" Faneuil Hall "Boston pleaser" dating back to 1826 has an "authentic" tavern "ambiance that cannot be beat"; "older kids will appreciate the history" – the oyster bar, where Daniel Webster dined, is said to be the oldest continuous restaurant in America – while "younger kids will appreciate the cornbread" and other "basic", "satisfying" seaworthy fare.

Upper Crust
| 22 | 25 | 15 | 17 | I |

20 Charles St. (Beacon St.), Boston; 617-723-9600
286 Harvard St. (Beacon St.), Brookline; 617-739-8518
www.theuppercrustpizzeria.com

☑ With "every combination of topping imaginable" at these Beacon Hill and Brookline pie parlors, the "thin-crust" "designer pizzas" "may even get your kids to eat their veggies"; despite "tight quarters", it's an "easygoing" place, though "by the time your food arrives", youngsters may be "under the table" (order "by the slice" if you can't wait); N.B. the suburban location specializes in children's parties pre- or post-shows at the nearby Coolidge Corner Theatre, an art deco movie palace.

RESTAURANT CHAINS

See reviews, starting on page 262.

Ratings: Family Appeal, Food, Decor, Service, Cost

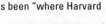

| FA | F | D | S | $ |

Baja Fresh Mexican Grill ⊠
| 20 | 22 | 14 | 18 | I |

Faneuil Hall Mktpl., Commercial St. (bet. Chatham & Clinton Sts.), Boston; 617-557-5111

Bertucci's   23 | 20 | 17 | 19 | M
Faneuil Hall Mktpl., 22 Merchants Row (State St.), Boston; 617-227-7889
Kenmore Sq., 533 Commonwealth Ave. (Beacon St.), Boston; 617-236-1030 🖥
39-45 Stanhope St. (bet. Berkeley & Clarendon Sts.), Boston; 617-247-6161 🖥
21 Brattle St. (Church St.), Cambridge; 617-864-4748

California Pizza Kitchen   21 | 21 | 16 | 19 | M
City Place, 137 Stuart St. (bet. S. Charles & Tremont Sts.), Boston; 617-720-0999
Prudential Ctr., 800 Boylston St. (Ring Rd.), Boston; 617-247-0888
*Cambridgeside Galleria, 100 Cambridgeside Pl. (bet. 1st St. & Land Blvd.),
Cambridge; 617-225-2772*

Cheesecake Factory 🖥   21 | 23 | 21 | 20 | M
*The Shops at Prudential Center, 115 Huntington Ave. (Garrison St.),
Boston; 617-399-7777*

Chili's Grill & Bar 🖥   21 | 19 | 18 | 19 | M
Copley Place, 100 Huntington Ave. (off I-90), Boston; 617-859-0134
114 Mt. Auburn St. (Dunster St.), Cambridge; 617-876-8990

Hard Rock Cafe 🖥   22 | 16 | 26 | 18 | M
131 Clarendon St. (bet. Columbus Ave. & Stuart St.), Boston; 617-424-7625

LongHorn Steakhouse 🖥   21 | 21 | 19 | 21 | M
401 Park Dr. (Brookline Ave.), Boston; 617-247-9199

Maggiano's Little Italy   22 | 22 | 21 | 22 | M
4 Columbus Ave. (Church St.), Boston; 617-542-3456

Olive Garden 🖥   20 | 19 | 18 | 19 | M
1095 Iyanough Rd. (Bearses Way), Hyannis; 508-775-9896

Outback Steakhouse 🖥   20 | 22 | 18 | 20 | M
1070 Iyannough Rd. (Bearses Way), Hyannis; 508-778-8787

T.G.I. Friday's 🖥   21 | 17 | 18 | 17 | M
149 Staniford St. (Merrimac St.), Boston; 617-557-4575
26 Exeter St. (Newbury St.), Boston; 617-266-9040

Uno Chicago Grill   20 | 18 | 15 | 16 | M
731 Boylston St. (bet. Exeter & Fairfield Sts.), Boston; 617-267-8554 ◗
1 Brookline Ave. (Kenmore Sq.), Boston; 617-262-4911 ◗
Faneuil Hall Mktpl., 22 Clinton St. (North St.), Boston; 617-523-5722
280 Huntington Ave. (Gainsborough St.), Boston; 617-424-1697

Chicago

*Look out from the Hancock Observatory or the even-higher Sears
Tower, and you'll see that Chicago is a city with a capital C – and that's
not just for convention center. From the Field Museum, Art Institute
and Shedd Aquarium in Grant Park to baseball and American Girl
Place to deep-dish pizza and hot dogs, the Midwest's main metropolis
makes for a fun family foray. Windy City winters tend to be tough, so
the busy (if hot and humid) summer is when Navy Pier's Ferris wheel
springs to life and home runs thrill crowds at U.S. Cellular and Wrigley
Fields. The best times to visit, though, are spring and autumn, which
are both cooler (with average temps in the 40s and 50s) and less
crowded. The Loop, Chicago's Downtown, is bounded to the east by
Lake Michigan, where many attractions await. Just to its north is the
main shopping street, Michigan Avenue, aka the "Magnificent Mile,"*

highlighted by Water Tower Place, Marshall Field's and Neiman Marcus. Though you can get around on foot Downtown, the El, subway, local bus (all $1.75 for adults) or metered taxis can take you north to the Lincoln Park Zoo or south to Hyde Park for the Museum of Science and Industry. If you're traveling farther – to Lisle's Morton Arboretum or up to Milwaukee – it's easiest to drive.

ATTRACTIONS

Ratings: Child Appeal, Adult Appeal, Public Facilities, Service, Cost

C	A	P	S	$
24	25	23	22	M

Adler Planetarium and Astronomy Museum
1300 S. Lake Shore Dr. (McFetridge Dr.); 312-922-7827; www.adlerplanetarium.org

■ "Stars and planets, who can beat it?" ask astro-philes of this "top-notch" museum and planetarium – the nation's first – which enables space cadets to spend "a few hours" "playing in the solar system" and "exploring the universe"; it's a "wonderful educational opportunity" thanks to "great facilities" and service and "lots of interactive things for children" in "amazing exhibits" that "appeal to all but the youngest" (the "dark theaters" "can be scary to toddlers"); P.S. the lakefront location makes it "a great spot for pics of the skyline."

–	–	–	–	$0

American Girl Place ☺
111 E. Chicago Ave. (bet. Michigan & Rush Sts.); 877-247-5223; www.americangirlplace.com

If your daughters have been swept up in the American Girl trend, they'll go wild at this store–cum–tourist attraction just off Michigan Avenue; naturally, you can drop a serious wad of cash on the historically themed dolls and their clothes, furniture and accessories (not to mention matching outfits for your kid!), but there's more: you can watch a doll-centric musical, have your doll's hair done or treat yourselves – and your doll – to tea; special events include a "Date with Dad", a reading circle or a hands-on cooking class.

15	29	27	23	M

Art Institute of Chicago ☺
111 S. Michigan Ave. (bet. Jackson & Monroe Sts.); 312-443-3600; www.artic.edu

■ "On the A-list" of "premier museums in the U.S.", this adult must-see "world-class" "mecca" is "one of the jewels of Chicago" and "more user-friendly than other traditional art houses"; "from Warhol to Miro, Renoir and Chagall", there's a "jaw-dropping" "cornucopia" of "treasures", especially the "oh-my-gosh" Impressionist collection that will "wow" "anyone out of diapers"; parents point out it's "a perfect place to give kids their first crack at real art" – the "great miniature rooms" and medieval weapons are "big hits with little ones", and weekends feature "superb children's programs"; better yet, it's "close to the Loop and easy to get to"; N.B. free admission on Tuesdays.

28	26	23	21	I

Brookfield Zoo
8400 W. 31st St. (Golf Rd.), Brookfield; 708-485-0263; www.brookfieldzoo.org

■ "For a day of sheer joy", it's "worth the trip" 14 miles out to suburban Brookfield, because this "year-round favorite" managed by a "friendly staff" is simply "fantastic"; "check out the Hamill Family Play Zoo" ("pet some animals, do a craft") and "don't miss the dolphin show"; "even in winter", there are "indoor exhibits worth visiting" (plus "the animals are typically more active" in "cooler weather"); sure, it's "a haul from the Loop", but at least there's "parking", though there's an additional charge for the children's and family play zoos.

Chicago Botanic Garden
| 19 | 28 | 25 | 23 | $0 |

1000 Lake Cook Rd. (off I-41), Glencoe; 847-835-5440;
www.chicago-botanic.org

■ "If you're into gardens", branch out and see this "serene", "gorgeous" 385-acre "oasis" in Glencoe (25 miles north of the city) that's home to two million plants; its "totally awesome aviary" and "model railroad will thrill" the kids, and "fun demonstrations" showcase a staff that earns high ratings; from April to October a 45-minute "tram ride provides an overview" of this "vast area", but if the little ones just "enjoy running around", you "can spend all day walking" here; best of all, there are "no weeds to pull."

Chicago Children's Museum ☺
| 28 | 21 | 24 | 22 | I |

700 E. Grand Ave. (Navy Pier); 312-527-1000; www.chichildrensmuseum.org

■ Preschool paleontologists "can never dig up a dinosaur too many times", grin grown-ups who've watched their kids "play, explore and learn" at this "fun" "hands-on" museum "right Downtown at Navy Pier"; "best for younger children" who "have a blast" (the Waterways exhibit is a particular "highlight"), it's "worth visiting over and over", and even "adults are encouraged to participate" – so who cares if it's "crowded" and "parking is a pain"?

Chicago Cultural Center ☺
| 12 | 23 | 23 | 21 | $0 |

78 E. Washington St. (bet. Garland Ct. & Michigan Ave.); 312-346-3278;
www.chicagoculturalcenter.org

■ With hundreds of "fantastic free programs" every year, there's plenty to do in this "historical Downtown setting", a "beautiful" 1897 beaux arts palace that hosts special exhibits, "lunchtime concerts", plays, dance performances and more; adults, who appreciate this attraction much more than their kids do, should take notice of the "incredible mosaics" on floors and walls and then "look up at one of the loveliest ceilings anywhere"; the appeal to children definitely "depends on the exhibition" or event, however.

Chicago Historical Society ☺
| 16 | 25 | 23 | 24 | I |

1601 N. Clark St. (North Blvd.); 312-642-4600; www.chicagohs.org

■ "The Chicago fire! Abraham Lincoln! the stockyards! now this is fun!" rhapsodize reviewers of this "underappreciated and overlooked" "sleeper" in Lincoln Park, a "gutsy history" museum that's "small" and "manageable for kids" "10 or older"; "tours are exceptionally well-done", as are the reenactments with actors portraying area notables, and visitors who are "surprised and pleased" with the curators' "wit and ingenuity" declare "if you like" the City of Big Shoulders, "you'll love it" here; N.B. the on-site American restaurant offers a $3 children's menu.

Field Museum of Natural History ☺
| 26 | 27 | 25 | 23 | I |

1400 S. Lake Shore Dr. (McFetridge Dr.); 312-922-9410; www.fmnh.org

■ There's "almost too much to see" in this "classic" "palace of a museum" "on the lake" that's "one of the best stops in Chicago" for families; "kids will love" "spectacular" Sue, "the world's most famous T. Rex", plus other "accessible, readable" and "extraordinary displays" like the "Egyptian section, with mummies and relics from the pyramids"; "it can be overwhelming", so "look at the Web site ahead of time to let everyone choose the exhibits they want to see" and "plan on spending the day", 'cause "this place rocks."

Grant Park
| 19 | 22 | 18 | 14 | $0 |

331 E. Randolph St. (Columbus Dr.); 312-742-7648;
www.chicagoparkdistrict.com

■ Known as 'Chicago's front yard', this "neighborly" "green haven" that embraces three fine museums (the Art Institute, the Field Museum and the Shedd Aquarium) is an "island of calm" amid the metropolis; "don't miss" the "fantastic" nightly "light show" at the 1927 Buckingham Fountain, a spouting extravaganza that "shoots water up into the sky", and watch for other "wonderful special events" (July's Taste of Chicago, free concerts); given the "gorgeous views of the lake", it's also "real nice to walk" here or just enjoy the "wide-open space."

Hancock Observatory
| 23 | 25 | 22 | 20 | M |

John Hancock Ctr., 875 N. Michigan Ave. (bet. Chestnut & Delaware Sts.); 312-751-3681; 888-875-8439; www.hancock-observatory.com

■ Gaze out at "four states by day, a billion lights by night" from the 94th floor of this 1969 skyscraper that has "fabulous views, even in the ladies' room"; the elevator ride up is "amazing", and "when the skies are clear", not only can you "see across the lake", but "all of Chicagoland" is "spread before you" – plus "kids love the outdoor walkway" ("don't worry, it's encased with wire"); it may be only "the third-tallest building" in town, but it's certainly "nothing to scoff at."

Harold Washington Library Center
| 18 | 24 | 27 | 25 | $0 |

400 S. State St. (bet. Congress Pkwy. & Van Buren St.); 312-747-4300; www.chipublib.org

■ "You want a book? guess who has it", bubble bibliophiles of this "impressive" behemoth, a "stunning" 1991 building that "mixes classic and modern architecture" and houses "everything from DVDs to a foreign-language lab"; earning our reviewers' praise for its facilities and staff, it's a "great place" to learn about "Chicago history or genealogy", and the children's collection is the city's most complete; N.B. take a look at the Storybook Dollhouse, decked out with dozens of allusions to kids' stories, poems and nursery rhymes.

JOHN G. SHEDD AQUARIUM
| 28 | 27 | 25 | 22 | E |

1200 S. Lake Shore Dr. (McFetridge Dr.); 312-939-2438; www.sheddnet.org

■ The "rainbow of colorful fish", the "enchanting" dolphins and beluga whales, a shark reef and other "aquatic treasures" "will keep kids of all ages oohing and aahing for hours" at this "top-notch" "treasure", the world's largest indoor aquarium, located in Grant Park "on the shores of Lake Michigan"; "arrive early to avoid the lines" and "make sure you're there for feeding time", recommend fans swept away by the sea-nery, but a few crabs carp that "at $21 per person, you really have to like fish."

Lincoln Park Zoo
| 28 | 26 | 22 | 21 | $0 |

2200 N. Cannon Dr. (bet. Fullerton Pkwy. & Lake Shore Dr.); 312-742-2000; www.lpzoo.com

■ "Many childhood memories" are made at this "manageably sized" "urban zoo" that surveyors voted No. 1 for Child Appeal in Chicago in this *Survey*; younger ones "love the train rides and the petting zoo", and school-agers are "fascinated by the variety of species to see", while parents appreciate the "convenient" Lincoln Park location and "walkable", well-designed layout; there's space "to run around" and a cafeteria that will "please picky" eaters, but best of all, surveyors "can't believe" that this "terrific" "old-fashioned" attraction is "free!"

Millennium Park
| ▽ 18 | 20 | 19 | 14 | $0 |

55 Michigan Ave. (bet. Madison & Washington Sts.); 312-742-5222

☑ Under development in Grant Park's northwest corner, this 24-acre green space is "getting better every month"; skaters are already enjoying the ice rink, and at press time a Frank Gehry–designed band shell was nearing completion; another soon-to-be-added amenity that will likely raise its Child Appeal rating is a Ferris wheel, while art lovers will like the 60-ft.-long polished-steel sculpture by artist Anish Kapoor and the 1,500-seat concert hall; it may be "only a matter of time" before this becomes Chicago's "crown jewel", though the impatient importune "in which millennium will this park open?"

Morton Arboretum

∇ 16	25	23	23	I

4100 Rte. 53 (off I-88), Lisle; 630-719-2400; www.mortonarb.org

■ Chicagoans consider this "fine display of nature" 25 miles west of Downtown a retreat for all seasons: in spring or summer it's "a great place for picnics" or to "listen to a ball game under a shady tree", in the fall "the flora is sheer joy" as is "making a snowman in winter"; throughout its 1,700 acres – encompassing a marsh, a conifer forest, a 100,000-daffodil glade and a tallgrass prairie – families can hike trails, "go for a pleasant drive" or take the hour-long tram tour; though it's a bit outside the city, it's just the ticket when you need a break.

MUSEUM OF SCIENCE AND INDUSTRY ☺

28	27	25	23	I

5700 S. Lake Shore Dr. (57th St.); 773-684-1414; www.msichicago.org

■ Voted the city's No. 1 overall attraction in this *Survey*, "the coolest museum in a world-class museum city" "never ceases to amaze, amuse and educate"; "dive in a U-boat, go down into a coal mine, fly in an airplane" and "touch and explore" "whazzits and wazzoos that would spin anyone's head" (with young children, "make sure to visit the Idea Factory"); since it's in Hyde Park, "getting there" can be "a stretch", but it's "highly worth it" because "unlike your high school chemistry teacher", this "venerable" institution "makes science accessible and fun."

Navy Pier ☺☺

23	22	21	19	$0

600 E. Grand Ave. (off Lake Shore Dr.); 312-595-7437; 800-595-7437; www.navypier.com

■ If you get "bored" at this "entertaining" "amusement park on the water", "check if you have a pulse"; with "lots of rides", "IMAX showings", "awesome fireworks", mini golf, an outdoor stage and plenty of "big-time hustle and bustle", there's "always something to do"; "the Ferris wheel is a thrill" for kids ("parents will appreciate the view" of the skyline), and there's "plenty to keep teens interested" (just "bring lots of money"); however, "the food is nothing to salute", unfortunately, and "few locals admit" to visiting this "honky-tonky" place.

Peggy Notebaert Nature Museum

∇ 25	24	23	22	I

2430 N. Cannon Dr. (Fullerton Pkwy.); 773-755-5100; www.chias.org

■ "Interactive, friendly and fun", this eco-themed Lincoln Park nature museum is a "wonderful place for children and adults"; the Butterfly Haven (stocked with flutterers from around the world) is "fabulous", and in the Extreme Green House, kids get a "good introduction to energy conservation" too; there's even a "nice cafeteria" tucked among the many "hands-on exhibits", so admirers are adamant you "won't want to leave"; N.B. admission is free on Thursdays.

Sears Tower ☺

22	25	22	19	M

233 S. Wacker Dr. (bet. Adams St. & Jackson Blvd.); 312-875-9696; www.sears-tower.com

☑ "Get higher than you've ever been" at the Western Hemisphere's tallest building, where the "astounding" "views of the Windy City" from the 103rd-floor observation deck make you feel like you're on "top of the world"; the "cool" "high-speed elevators appeal to kids", and "at each vantage point", "buildings are labeled for easy identification"; just "beware if you fear heights" (it's "not for small children"), plus penny-pinchers protest the price for this experience is "steep" – "if it's overcast", save your cash and "go for pizza instead."

Soldier Field ☺ | 16 | 23 | 21 | 19 | E |

425 E. McFetridge Dr. (Columbus Dr.); 312-235-7000; www.soldierfield.net
☑ "A must for any Bears fan", this 1924 "landmark football field" was "totally overhauled and redesigned in 2003"; the result, some say, is a "superb job of remodeling a historic structure" – a "classic" "place to watch" NFL and Major League soccer teams and "be proud of your home" club; while "inside, it's great", a vocal minority vents that the exterior "looks like a spaceship" ("an embarrassment to the city"), and since it lacks spaces for children to play or rest, the stadium is "not that kid-friendly" either.

Spertus Museum ☺   ∇ | 14 | 23 | 22 | 25 | I |

618 S. Michigan Ave. (Harrison St.); 312-322-1747; www.spertus.edu
■ The few who've found this "excellent small museum of Judaica" admire the collection of art that illustrates Jewish history and life from biblical times to more recent days; the adult programs, including lectures and films, are first-rate, and "the kids' area is great", too – a hands-on re-creation of an archeological dig in Israel, where youngsters can excavate replicas of ancient artifacts; N.B. free admission on Fridays; closed Saturdays.

Symphony Center ☺☺ | 13 | 25 | 24 | 23 | I |

220 S. Michigan Ave. (Adams St.); 312-294-3000; 800-223-7114; www.cso.org
■ Adults find the "world-class acoustics" help make this HQ of the Chicago Symphony Orchestra "one of the great concert halls" (you "have to experience" this "terrific" building "at least once", since "every seat is excellent"); children over eight are welcome at regular performances – "just make sure your kids know how to behave in a concert" – but you can bring younger ones to the Family Matinees, for ages five to eight, that are offered three times a year; N.B. no jeans.

Union Station ☺ | 14 | 20 | 18 | 18 | $0 |

210 S. Canal St. (bet. Adams St. & Jackson Blvd.); 312-322-4269
☑ "The ghosts of the era of the cross-country pleasure train" are alive and well in this "classic station", a "big", "beautiful" Downtown depot serving 50,000 commuters a day that's "one of the few" of its type "left in the U.S."; it's decidedly an adult dalliance, where some savor sitting in the "impressive" marble-clad Great Hall for prime "people-watching" – "everyone and their mother passes through" – but they admit there's "not a lot here for kids" unless you plan to "actually take" the railroad.

U.S. Cellular Field ☺ | 19 | 19 | 17 | 15 | E |

333 W. 35th St. (Shields Ave.); 312-674-1000; www.whitesox.com
☑ Athletic supporters assert this post-Comiskey "home of the White Sox" "is the best for kids" of "any stadium in Chicago", thanks to such "nice facilities" as a free Fundamentals area where junior jocks can bat and run bases, and a Rain Room that diffuses cooling mist onto overheated fans; however, rooters "don't recommend the steep upper-deck seats" (though ongoing renovations may improve the situation), and regard the 1991 complex's "sterile" "concrete-and-plastic style" as "an insult to the baseball gods"; N.B. once a month, kids get in for $1.

Wrigley Field ☺ | 24 | 28 | 21 | 21 | E |

1060 W. Addison St. (bet. Clark St. & Sheffield Ave.); 773-404-2827; www.chicagocubs.com
■ Even "New Yorkers" cheer for this "baseball fans' heaven", because what the "ancient but intimate" ballpark "lacks in modern amenities, it more than makes up in historic charm" via "ivy-covered outfield walls", a "manual scoreboard" and, of course, "the lovable Cubs"; "parking is nearly impossible" but it's "easily reached on the local trains", and the 90-minute tours are "great for the whole family"; for

"lots of local color", hit adjacent Wrigleyville, where the "friendly" "neighborhood has embraced" the team "like the bleacher bums have embraced beer."

HOTELS

Ratings: Family Appeal, Rooms, Service, Public Facilities, Cost

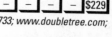

	FA	R	S	P	$

DoubleTree Guest Suites

| – | – | – | – | $229 |

198 E. Delaware Pl.; 312-664-1100; 800-222-8733; www.doubletree.com; 345 suites

Remodeled in 2003, this all-suite property is a good value for families since rooms have separate living areas, a sleeper sofa, complimentary coffee and tea, and high-speed Internet access; there's an on-site pool, babysitting services, cribs and playpens available and high chairs and children's menus in the restaurant; N.B. the Hancock Observatory is across the street and the Chicago Children's Museum is one mile south.

Embassy Suites Lakefront

| – | – | – | – | $280 |

511 N. Columbus Dr.; 312-836-5900; 800-362-2779; www.embassysuites.com; 455 suites

Within walking distance of Navy Pier (there's a free trolley there as well), this all-suite spot features spacious units with separate living rooms, refrigerators, microwaves and SONY Playstations and offers complimentary cooked-to-order breakfasts each morning; an indoor swimming pool keeps kids happy on rainy days, and cribs and high chairs ease the burden of toddler-toting parents.

Four Seasons

| 21 | 28 | 29 | 27 | $535 |

120 E. Delaware Pl.; 312-280-8800; 800-332-3442; www.fourseasons.com; 175 rooms, 168 suites

■ You can't beat the "outstanding" indoor pool – "great for all ages" year-round – at this "big and heavenly" hotel that offers "unbelievable amenities for children"; the "top-of-the-line treatment" for tots includes bath toys, "milk and cookies at bedtime and happy-face waffles at Sunday brunch"; oh, and there are "family rates on connecting rooms" and it's just a five-minute walk to the Hancock Observatory for a sweeping view of Lake Michigan and the city, so "if you're willing to pay the rent", this one's "simply the best."

House of Blues Hotel

| 21 | 23 | 22 | 22 | $359 |

333 N. Dearborn St.; 312-245-0333; 877-569-3742; www.loewshotels.com; 347 rooms, 20 suites

◩ Teens and preteens will "love this ultracool place" with a "fun and lively environment", "lots of noise", good dining options (including a Smith & Wollensky Steakhouse) and an on-site concert hall – a "great place to see shows"; it's "not for young kids", but for those who want to "hang with the 'in' crowd" and be a few minutes' walk to the Navy Pier and the Magnificent Mile, this one hits all the right notes.

Omni Chicago

| ▽ 20 | 24 | 25 | 24 | $349 |

676 N. Michigan Ave.; 312-944-6664; 800-843-6664; www.omnihotels.com; 347 suites

■ "Cribs and roll-away beds are gladly provided" at this all-suite hotel on bustling Michigan Avenue, a "great location for the Navy Pier" and Magnificent Mile; the "child-friendly staff" makes a stay "easy and enjoyable", the young 'uns like the Omni Kids program (they get their own activity bag) and it's just three blocks from both ESPN Zone and the Lakefront.

Park Hyatt

| 19 | 24 | 26 | 23 | $425 |

800 N. Michigan Ave.; 312-335-1234; 800-778-7477; www.hyatt.com; 196 rooms, 8 suites

☑ Parents have mixed opinions over this high-end property across from the Water Tower that's "best suited for business travelers": a few happily report their "kids would not get out of the bath" (they have oversized tubs and flat-screen LCD TVs), the "spacious" quarters mean there's plenty of square footage to stretch out and the "American Girl [doll] shop is directly across the street", providing hours of delight for young fans, but a few fussbudgets find this upscaler just "a bit stiff" for the little ones.

Peninsula

| 20 | 28 | 28 | 28 | $445 |

108 E. Superior St.; 312-337-2888; 866-288-8889; www.peninsula.com; 256 rooms, 83 suites

☑ The "best new kid on the block" is a pleasant surprise for kids themselves, say parents floored by this "fabulous" high-end hotel; sure, it's "definitely a splurge", but "what a staff – ask for anything and it will find a way" to deliver, while "large rooms make it quite comfortable for families"; an "awesome pool", great games and movies for children and a special menu for tots are further reasons why moms and dads say this property appeals to more than just the traveling business brigade.

Ritz-Carlton (A Four Seasons Hotel)

| 20 | 28 | 28 | 26 | $435 |

160 E. Pearson St.; 312-266-1000; 800-621-6906; www.fourseasons.com; 344 rooms, 91 suites

■ Sure, it's a bit high-end for young ones, but the "top-notch" service at this property in Water Tower Place means the "staff is quite solicitous" to all ages, offering "special kids' meals and amenities" including a welcome box with homemade cookies, child-sized robes, toiletries and, upon request, childproofed rooms, games, books, in-room Playstations, cribs, roll-away beds, baby tubs, strollers and other infant accessories; with a playground right across the street and sightseeing boat tours just a 15-minute walk away, kids can't help having a "great", "luxurious" time.

Sheraton Chicago Hotel & Towers

| 19 | 19 | 21 | 21 | $299 |

301 E. North Water St.; 312-464-1000; 877-242-2558; www.sheraton.com; 1176 rooms, 33 suites

☑ Choose this "excellent value" for "location, location, location" since it's "right across the street from Navy Pier" with "many great activities" for traveling tots, including an IMAX movie theater; just be prepared for a "large, rambling" facility with a business vibe, and "nothing too exciting" for kids beyond the indoor pool.

Westin River North

| 18 | 23 | 22 | 21 | $499 |

320 N. Dearborn Ave.; 312-744-1900; 877-866-9216; www.westinchicago.com; 407 rooms, 17 suites

☑ "Diverse enough to have family appeal", this hotel within walking distance of Michigan Avenue's restaurants and shopping offers cribs and roll-away beds for tots, in-room Nintendo game systems and lovely views of the city skyline or the lake; but it's all about the central location for most guests, who can easily get to the theater district, Navy Pier and other attractions.

Top Family-Friendly Hotel Chains in the Area:

Hampton Inn	Hyatt
Holiday Inn	Marriott
Homewood Suites	Residence Inn

See Hotel Chain reviews, starting on page 256.

RESTAURANTS

Ratings: Family Appeal, Food, Decor, Service, Cost

	FA	F	D	S	$

American Girl Place Cafe
	27	20	26	24	M

American Girl Pl., 111 E. Chicago Ave. (N. Michigan Ave.); 312-943-9400; www.americangirl.com

■ "Delivering the all-American fantasy for girls", this "special-occasion spot" within the wildly popular toy store/museum/theater is "a true delight", particularly "for mothers and daughters"; "decorated in black-and-white with vibrant pink", it's a "magical zone" "off Michigan Avenue" (opposite the Water Tower), where the "friendly staff" "caters to children", treating them "like little princesses", "with high chairs and tea sets for their dolls" as well; whether for a prix fixe brunch, lunch, dinner or (especially recommended) afternoon tea, it's "worth the splurge" – just "don't make a boy" tag along.

Ann Sather
	–	–	–	–	I

3411 N. Broadway (W. Roscoe St.); 773-305-0024
1448 N. Milwaukee Ave. (North Ave.); 773-394-1812
3416 N. Southport Ave. (W. Roscoe St.); 773-404-4475
929 W. Belmont Ave. (Sheffield Ave.); 773-348-2378
www.annsather.com

A "Chicago institution", these "friendly", "stroller-accommodating" Traditional American–Swedish restaurants and cafes "remain a guilty pleasure" for families on the lookout for "an unrestrained calorie" and "comfort food" "splurge", "especially at breakfast" given their "legendary cinnamon rolls"; while locations vary from "homey" to "cramped", there's always "plenty of character and characters" on hand – including more than a few "screaming kids and harried moms"; N.B. bring your own liquor to the Wrigleyville and Lakeview locations.

Berghoff, The
	16	22	21	19	M

17 W. Adams St. (bet. Dearborn & State Sts.); 312-427-3170 🗷
O'Hare Int'l Airport, Concourse C; 773-601-9180
www.berghoff.com

🖬 "Kids like the link to the past" (it's "exactly the same as when Father was a boy") and "the simple, good bread, wursts" and Wiener schnitzel served in the "old-world" "wood-paneled rooms" at the Loop location of this German-American "Chicago classic"; it's "not really a family spot", however, so while *der kinder* are welcome, "they'll need to behave", lest they incur the wrath of the "brusque" but "professional waiters"; N.B. quicker, more casual bites are available at the new underground cafe and the O'Hare branch.

Flat Top Grill
	24	23	19	20	M

3200 N. Southport Ave. (Belmont Ave.); 773-665-8100
319 W. North Ave. (Orleans St.); 773-787-7676
1000 W. Washington Blvd. (Carpenter St.); 312-829-4800
726 Lake St. (Oak Park Ave.), Oak Park; 708-358-8200
www.flattopgrill.com

■ "Even the pickiest eaters have no cause to complain" at these "all-you-can-eat" Asian-American stir-fry joints, since "the vast array of ingredients" chosen from the buffet ensures that "all ages are bound to find something they like"; furthermore, the "children will be captivated by the culinary action" as they "watch their food prepared" before their eyes by the grill chefs; fans flatly declare this is a "great place to fill up" on soup, salad or moo shu pancakes in a "casual environment."

foodlife | 21 | 20 | 19 | 17 | M |

Water Tower Pl., 835 N. Michigan Ave. (bet. Chestnut & Pearson Sts.); 312-335-3663; www.leye.com
■ Like a "food court on steroids", this Eclectic eatery with a "marketplace concept" and decor at Water Tower Place ("good when shopping") "keeps everyone happy" with the equivalent of "multiple restaurants under one roof"; given the "unbelievable variety", "each family member can get what they're hankering for" – from burgers to Thai to Mexican – though when it's "busy", the "serve-yourself" setup can make it "hard to keep track of the kids."

Gold Coast Dogs | 22 | 21 | 9 | 15 | I |

2415 N. Clark St. (Fullerton St.); 773-770-3555
159 N. Wabash Ave. (bet. Lake & Randolph Sts.); 312-917-1677
17 S. Wabash Ave. (Monroe St.); 312-578-1133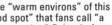
1429 W. Montrose Ave. (Clark St.); 773-472-3600
www.goldcoastdogs.net
 "A kid's dream" – and "a cardiologist's nightmare" – this chain of "classic Chicago" hot dog joints (that serves char-burgers and cheddar fries, too) makes a "satisfying" stop for children's "favorite foods"; they're "not much to look at", but you can chow down at "inexpensive" rates, despite doubters who yap that "there are better dogs barking around this city."

John's Place | – | – | – | – | M |

1200 W. Webster Ave. (Racine Ave.); 773-525-6670
"When pushing a stroller", stroll on into the "warm environs" of this "reliable", "friendly" DePaul "neighborhood spot" that fans call "a great family place" thanks to "somewhat creative" Eclectic fare (including a "great brunch") made from lots of "natural ingredients"; still, some former regulars rue the rugrats "running rampant" in this "kiddie central" (there must be a "zillion babies") and report "standard fare", "long waits" and "slow service."

Leona's | ▽ 23 | 23 | 18 | 19 | M |

1419 W. Taylor St. (bet. Bishop & Loomis Sts.); 312-850-2222; www.leonas.com
 Serving up everything from pasta to pizza to chicken to ribs, this popular Southern Italian–American in Little Italy is "a great family choice"; the food is "always good" and kids appreciate that there are "no surprises" on the thick tomes masquerading as menus; "plus, they deliver (a must in winter)"; N. B. there are many other locations of this chain throughout the city.

Lou Mitchell's ⌐ | ▽ 19 | 21 | 14 | 17 | M |

565 W. Jackson Blvd. (Jefferson St.); 312-939-3111
O'Hare Int'l Airport, Terminal 5; 773-601-8989
■ Since the Roaring '20s, this "American classic" coffee shop has been serving "good, old-fashioned breakfast" (lunch, too) to the West Loop, with Milk Duds–studded offerings to satiate the small fry; "at peak hours" this "favorite" gets quite "crowded", but once seated you'll be "in and out quick" (indeed, "you might get the bum's rush if you dally"); N.B. the takeout-only O'Hare outlet is open 24 hours.

Pizzeria Uno/Due | 24 | 22 | 17 | 18 | M |

619 N. Wabash Ave. (bet. Ohio & Ontario Sts.); 312-943-2400
29 E. Ohio St. (Wabash Ave.); 312-321-1000
866-600-8667; www.unos.com
■ They may "be a national [chain] now", but "it all started here" on the North Side at these two "original Chicago" pie shops that still have supporters swooning over the "deep-dish delights"; partisans proclaim that these "perfect pizzas" are "the one and only", especially when you "top 'em off with the chocolate peanut butter cup dessert";

certainly, they "keep the family happy", so "you can't leave the city without visiting" one – just "expect a wait at key dining times."

Potbelly Sandwich Works　　　| 21 | 22 | 17 | 19 | I |

One Illinois Center, 111 E. Wacker Dr. (Michigan Ave.); 312-861-0013 🖾
190 N. State St. (Lake St.); 312-683-1234
The Shops at North Bridge, 520 N. Michigan Ave. (Grand Ave.); 312-644-1008
55 W. Monroe St. (Dearborn St.); 312-577-0070 🖾
www.potbelly.com

■ "When you want relatively healthy fast food", this counter-service deli chain's "extremely affordable", toasted, "crusty sandwiches are irresistible"; "all the locations are always packed" ("a little crowded for strollers"), but "the line moves quickly", and "older kids" "love watching the [subs] go into the oven and come out yummy"; P.S. the Lincoln Park original boasts "funky" decor "sprinkled with" "antique doodads."

R.J. Grunts　　　| 24 | 22 | 23 | 22 | M |

2056 N. Lincoln Park W. (Dickens Ave.); 773-929-5363; www.leye.com

■ "Convenient for lunch after a morning at the zoo", this Lincoln Park all-American "is a fun family place"; "the menu offers lots of kid-friendly comfort food" (what child "doesn't love a hamburger" or would "pass up the cookie–ice cream dessert"?), while grown-ups settle into the "classic" '70s scene and gorge on the groaning salad bar ("rumor has it invented here"), fajitas or chili; sole caveat is that "the tables are packed tightly together, which can make high-chair placement tricky."

RESTAURANT CHAINS

See reviews, starting on page 262.

Ratings: Family Appeal, Food, Decor, Service, Cost

	FA	F	D	S	$
Applebee's	21	16	17	17	M
6656 W. Grand Ave. (Normandy Ave.); 773-836-7696					
Baja Fresh Mexican Grill 🖾	20	22	14	18	I
180 N. Michigan Ave. (bet. Lake & Randolph Sts.); 312-223-1113					
Benihana	23	20	18	22	E
Fitzpatrick Hotel, 166 E. Superior St. (Michigan Ave.); 312-664-9643					
Bubba Gump Shrimp Co. 🖾	24	18	23	20	M
Navy Pier, 700 E. Grand Ave. (Lake Shore Dr.); 312-252-4867					
Buca di Beppo 🖾	24	19	22	21	M
2941 N. Clark St. (bet. Oakdale & Wellington Sts.); 773-348-7673					
521 N. Rush St. (bet. Grand Ave. & Illinois St.); 312-396-0001					
California Pizza Kitchen	21	21	16	19	M
52 E. Ohio St. (bet. Rush St. & Wabash Ave.); 312-787-6075					
North Ave. Collections, 939 W. North Ave. (Sheffield Ave.); 312-337-1281					
Water Tower Pl. Shopping Ctr., 835 N. Michigan Ave., 7th fl. (bet. Chestnut & Pearson Sts.); 312-787-7300					
Cheesecake Factory	21	23	21	20	M
John Hancock Ctr., 875 N. Michigan Ave. (bet. Chestnut & Delaware Sts.); 312-337-1101					
Chili's Grill & Bar 🖾	21	19	18	19	M
2 E. Ontario St. (State St.); 312-943-1510					

Chuck E. Cheese's ⑤ | 26 | 10 | 17 | 13 | I |
5030 S. Kedzie Ave. (51st St.); 773-476-0500
1830 W. Fullerton Ave. (bet. Clybourn & Damen Aves.);
773-871-2484

Dave & Buster's | 26 | 16 | 21 | 17 | M |
1030 N. Clark St. (bet. Maple & Oak Sts.); 312-943-5151

Hard Rock Cafe | 22 | 16 | 26 | 18 | M |
63 W. Ontario St. (bet. Clark & Dearborn Sts.); 312-943-2252

Joe's Crab Shack ⑤ | 23 | 17 | 21 | 19 | M |
745 N. Wells St. (bet. Chicago Ave. & Superior St.); 312-664-2722

Johnny Rockets ⑤ | 25 | 17 | 20 | 18 | I |
901 N. Rush St. (Wabash Ave.); 312-337-3900

Maggiano's Little Italy | 22 | 22 | 21 | 22 | M |
516 N. Clark St. (Grand Ave.); 312-644-7700

Original Pancake House, The | 24 | 22 | 12 | 17 | I |
22 E. Bellvue Pl. (Rush St.); 312-642-7917 ⑤
22 E. Bellvue Pl. (bet. Michigan Ave. & Rush St.); 312-642-7917 ⑤
1517 E. Hyde Park Blvd. (Lake Park Ave.); 773-288-2322 ⑤
2020 N. Lincoln Park West (Clark St.); 773-929-8130 ⑤
10437 S. Western Ave. (bet. 104th & 105th Sts.); 773-445-6100 ⑤

Outback Steakhouse ⑤ | 20 | 22 | 18 | 20 | M |
8101 W. Higgins Rd. (bet. Linden & Newton Aves.); 773-380-0818

Rainforest Cafe | 27 | 16 | 27 | 18 | M |
605 N. Clark St. (bet. Ohio & Ontario Sts.); 312-787-1501

T.G.I. Friday's ⑤ | 21 | 17 | 18 | 17 | M |
153 E. Erie St. (bet. N. Michigan Ave. & N. St. Clair St.);
312-664-9820

Cincinnati

Sixty percent of Americans live within 500 miles of Cincinnati, aka the Queen City, which sits regally on a river bend overlooking the conjunction of Ohio, Kentucky and Indiana. Her Highness combines impressive family attractions (a first-rate zoo and world-class aquarium) with a down-to-earth Midwestern sensibility for a relaxed, friendly and, for the most part, inexpensive vacation. To get your bearings Downtown, start at lively, centrally located Fountain Square, where this heavily German-inflected city throws its annual Oktoberfest; and then head southeast to the 22-acre riverfront park, Bicentennial Commons. Eden Park, home of the Cincinnati Art Museum, is to the northeast, just east of I-71; the renovated 1933 Union Terminal, now known as the Cincinnati Museum Center, lies northwest, just beyond I-75. You can take the convenient $1 Southbank Shuttle through Downtown and past the Great American Ball Park, then across the river to Newport on the Levee. In general, though, a car is crucial for getting around, especially if you want to see surrounding sites like Louisville, central Kentucky's Daniel Boone territory or the Native American ruins of Ohio. Try to schedule a visit in the crystalline days of June, before the summer humidity sets in.

ATTRACTIONS

Ratings: Child Appeal, Adult Appeal, Public Facilities, Service, Cost

C	A	P	S	$

Beach, The ☺

▽ 27	23	23	21	E

2590 Waterpark Dr. (off Kings Mill Rd.), Mason; 513-398-7946; 800-886-7946; www.thebeachwaterpark.com

■ Water babies bob and bounce at these 35 acres of wet, wonderful fun, one of the nation's best water parks for a "day in the sun with the whole family" or 'dive-in movies' on Saturday nights; wee ones can wade in the children's pool on Splash Mountain, while their sibs try tubing a 1,200-ft. river, running rapids in a natural stream, or descending a five-story-high slide; meanwhile, grown-ups can chill in the 85-degree spa pool or just "have a glass of wine and relax."

Cincinnati Art Museum ☺☺

15	27	27	26	$0

Eden Park, 953 Eden Park Dr. (off Martin Dr.); 513-721-5204; www.cincinnatiartmuseum.org

■ "One of the more sophisticated museums in the country" houses "appealingly displayed" art in light-filled galleries where future collectors can "roar at the [Greek] funerary lions" or "crow at Chagall's rooster"; this newly expanded, "spacious" museum is "very welcoming" say parents who clearly find a higher Adult Appeal than Child Appeal, though it does "cater to the little ones" with special tours, family Saturdays and an education center with a changing array of hands-on activities; even better, it's "always free", so "if tots have a meltdown at the Monet, you can exit knowing you can come back anytime"; P.S. the cafe has a "terrific children's menu."

Cincinnati History Museum ☺

▽ 24	28	28	25	I

Cincinnati Museum Ctr., 1301 Western Ave. (Hopkins St.); 513-287-7000; 800-733-2077; www.cincymuseum.org

■ Your "entire family, including grandparents" will find "lots to do" in the "very nice exhibits" that tell the city's history from its frontier-post beginnings through the early 1900s; guided by costumed storytellers (the service gets high marks from reviewers), river rats can board a 94-ft. sidewheel steamboat, ride on a pint-size flatboat that comes apart to build a cabin or explore a "great scale model of the city" – and thanks to this gallery's location in the "amazing", restored art deco train station that is Museum Center, it's a "wonderful way to spend the day."

CINCINNATI ZOO AND BOTANICAL GARDEN

28	27	25	24	M

3400 Vine St. (Erkenbrecher Ave.); 513-281-4700; 800-944-4776; www.cincinnatizoo.org

■ "The perfect size for a family outing", this "beautifully laid out" and "easy-to-navigate" site with "lush botanical gardens" is big enough to have "something captivating around every manicured corner" but "small enough to be manageable in a day"; its "wide array of exhibits" allows visitors to "come face-to-face with underwater polar bears", "spooky vampire bats", elephants, white tigers, [Madagascar] hissing cockroaches and other "unique animals"; surveyors' pick for the city's No. 1 attraction, it's also "one of the oldest zoos in the country" and a National Historic Landmark.

Cinergy Children's Museum

–	–	–	–	I

Cincinnati Museum Ctr., 1301 Western Ave. (Hopkins St.); 513-287-7000; 800-733-2077; www.cincymuseum.org

At this surefire family spot in the Union Terminal's Museum Center, a nine-part exploration extravaganza, kids can learn as they splash and spray (hydraulics), climb and peek (nature and ecology), plan and build (engineering) or bounce a ball (physics); a global gallery introduces them to the lives of children in other countries (Tanzania, Russia), while, at Little Sprouts Farm, the tiniest tots can roll and toddle – plus hear stories every Wednesday; N.B. discounts are available on combo tickets to more than one Museum Center attraction.

Coney Island

▽ 26 | 21 | 20 | 20 | E

6201 Kellogg Ave. (Sutton Rd.); 513-232-8230; www.coneyislandpark.com
■ All the "other attractions are just accessories" to the "really spectacular", "humongous" Sunlite Pool, where "lifeguards need boats to get to the center" of the three-million-gallon "largest recirculating pool in the world"; the sun decks, waterslides and six diving boards are "a blast" for the younger crowd (if not so much for parents), as are the retro rides that include a painted carousel, Dodgem Cars and bumper boats; the Famous Fairways miniature-golf course and several picnic areas overlooking the Ohio River round out this nostalgic park that's been part of Cincinnati summers since 1867; N.B. admission prices go way down at 4 PM.

Great American Ball Park ☺

24 | 28 | 27 | 22 | I

100 Main St. (Broadway St.); 513-765-7000; www.cincinnatireds.com
☑ There's "not a bad seat in the house" in this "very family-friendly" new stadium, home to the Cincinnati Reds, baseball's oldest club; at this "terrific venue" (a "huge improvement" over now-demolished Cinergy Field), little leaguers can watch the grass-field action while downing the local chow from bratwursts to goetta (ground-meat-and-oatmeal) dogs; there are "few amenities" for kids, though, so if the game's slow, divert them with the whiz-bang, state-of-the-art scoreboard and the fireworks after each home-team home run; N.B. a year-round team museum will open in September.

Kentucky Horse Park ☺☺

24 | 26 | 25 | 23 | E

4089 Iron Works Pike (bet. I-75 & Newton Pike), Lexington, KY; 859-233-4303; 800-678-8813; www.kyhorsepark.com
■ "One of a kind in the nation", this "heaven for horse lovers" in the "rolling bluegrass region" near Lexington, Kentucky (about 80 miles from Cincinnati), "shouldn't be missed" by friends of Flicka or curious city folk; the 1,200-acre working farm is home to some 50 "lively" breeds – from Clydesdale to Miniature Donkey – and two interactive museums whose "educational" films and exhibits on breeding, racing and history ensure "hours of fascination"; also among the mane events are trail and pony rides, polo and steeplechase competitions and biannual shows of equine art.

Krohn Conservatory ☺☺

22 | 26 | 24 | 22 | $0

Eden Park, 950 Eden Park Dr. (off Martin Dr.); 513-421-4086
■ Botanophiles blossom in Eden Park's "gorgeous" "old-school" greenhouse, a free five-part mega-terrarium filled with "exotic plants from all over the world" (rain forests, deserts, the tropics); it feels like a "hidden gem", especially "on a cold winter's day" or in late spring at the "unforgettable", "spectacular" annual Butterfly Show ("kids really enjoy" holding out orange slices for the insects to "land all over them"); fortunately, the "manageable size" means the permanent displays "can be done in an hour or less."

Museum of
Natural History & Science ☺

26 | 25 | 25 | 24 | I

Cincinnati Museum Ctr., 1301 Western Ave. (Hopkins St.); 513-287-7000; 800-733-2077; www.cincymuseum.org
■ "Kids love this place", one of three museums in national landmark Union Terminal; sometime spelunkers will be "impressed" by the "very

realistic" simulated limestone cave that has 500 feet of passageways, underground streams and waterfalls, and a live brown-bat colony that takes flight once a day; back up in the light, tomorrow's scientists can wander the crevasses of a glacial ice cavern or scout the Ohio River valley of 17,000 B.C. before investigating the workings of the human body or watching staffers work to preserve newly collected fossils.

NEWPORT AQUARIUM
| 28 | 26 | 25 | 23 | M |

Newport on the Levee, 1 Aquarium Way (bet. Columbia & Monmouth Sts.), Newport, KY; 859-491-3467; 800-406-3474; www.newportaquarium.com

☑ Across the Ohio River from downtown Cincinnati, this "surprisingly good aquarium" adjacent to Newport on the Levee is a "well-designed" facility that's "stimulating for all ages"; "walk-through" displays include an "excellent jellyfish exhibit", a "neat hands-on area" where little folk can "touch turtles, starfish, etc." and an "entrancing shark tunnel"; a few do "not enjoy the no-stroller policy" on "crowded" days, but luckily, "backpacks are provided" to tote "small children."

Newport on the Levee
| 18 | 25 | 25 | 21 | $0 |

1 Levee Way (E. 3rd St.), Newport, KY; 859-291-0550; 866-538-3359; www.newportonthelevee.com

☑ This sprawling entertainment and shopping complex with a "great, stadium-style movie theater" may be "the best place to people-watch" in the Cincinnati area; though it's "mostly focused on dining and late-night bar entertainment" (in "terrific" restaurants offering "snacks to gourmet dining"), a scoop of "delicious ice cream" paired with Mrs. Fields cookies can be a sweet ending to a visit to the adjacent Newport Aquarium or a walk across the Purple People Bridge that spans the Ohio River from Cincinnati to Newport.

Ohio Renaissance Festival ☺☺
| ▽ 22 | 25 | 18 | 20 | M |

Renaissance Park, Rte. 73 (off I-71), Harveysburg; 513-897-7000; www.renfestival.com

■ At Harveyburg's authentically recreated 16th-century village (about an hour from Cincinnati), fantasy fans "get pulled into the story every time"; nine themed weekends draw "people of all ages" (including a "heavy-metal contingent") to watch jousting and swordplay plus 12 stagefuls of family entertainment (stunts, comedy, music) and demos of blacksmithing, glassblowing, cobbling and armor-making; the Harry Potter set will love a "chance to get muddy" and eat steak-on-a-stake, making this a "great way to spend an autumn afternoon"; N.B. runs August 28 – October 24, 2004.

PARAMOUNT'S KINGS ISLAND
| 29 | 26 | 25 | 22 | VE |

6300 Kings Island Dr. (off I-71), Mason; 513-754-5700; 800-288-0808; www.pki.com

■ "Scooby dooby doo!" says it all when it comes to this "stupendous", "well-run" theme park that kids "beg to go back" to (it's got the highest Child Appeal score in Cincinnati); amid "clean", "beautiful surroundings" are "old-fashioned thrills and cutting-edge rides", and the "variety of things to do", from "the water park to hanging out with the Rugrats" will make the day zoom by; don't miss the roller coasters (from "rickety wooden to whisper-fast") and the "soak zone", but bring a "change of clothes for the ride home."

Robert D. Lindner Family OMNIMAX Theater
| ▽ 22 | 27 | 24 | 21 | I |

Cincinnati Museum Ctr., 1301 Western Ave. (Hopkins St.); 513-287-7000; 800-733-2077; www.cincymuseum.org

■ "One of the best" of its ilk, this "nice facility" has drawn 4.5 million visitors (since 1990) for its repertoire of eye-popping films that capture the power of the great sharks, the soaring peaks of Mt. Everest or the heat of a NASCAR race; the five-story (by 72-ft.) domed screen, combined with a 15,000-watt digital sound system, may make the experience too intense for those prone to motion sickness – whether young or old – but the rest of the Museum Center, located in historic Union Terminal, is suitable for all audiences.

HOTELS

Ratings: Family Appeal, Rooms, Service, Public Facilities, Cost

FA	R	S	P	$
–	–	–	–	$189

Embassy Suites Cincinnati Rivercenter
10 E. River Center Blvd., Covington, KY; 859-261-8400; 800-362-2779; www.embassysuites.com; 226 suites
Nab a weekend special and head to this chainster on the banks of the Ohio overlooking downtown Cincinnati, where baseball boosters will be close to the Great American Ballpark and directly on the Southbank Shuttle route for access to kid pleasers like the Newport Aquarium (there are hotel packages that include tickets); suites have full-size sleeper sofas, living areas, microwaves and fridges, and rates include cooked-to-order breakfasts.

–	–	–	–	$230

Hilton Cincinnati Netherland Plaza
35 W. Fifth St.; 513-421-9100; 800-774-1500; www.hilton.com; 619 rooms, 15 suites
Parents will appreciate this art deco landmark, listed on the National Register of Historic Places, because it's part of the Carew Tower complex of shops and restaurants where there's plenty to please families; the property is also within easy walking distance of the Great American Ball Park and just two miles south of the Newport Aquarium; cribs and high chairs are available on request, there's a fitness center on-site and the contemporary American restaurant is fine for tots.

▽	22	23	24	21	$275

Westin
21 E. Fifth St.; 513-621-7700; 888-625-5144; www.westin.com; 432 rooms, 18 suites
☑ With a "great Fountain Square location", just two blocks from the Great American Ballpark and a mile from the Cinergy Children's Museum, this "good all-around" hotel offers a signature 'heavenly crib' for tots under two, a dog bed for the family pet, rollaway beds and high-speed Internet access; there's an on-site restaurant with casual all-day dining that's appealing to families, as well.

Top Family-Friendly Hotel Chains in the Area:

Hampton Inn
Holiday Inn
Hyatt

Marriott
Residence Inn

See Hotel Chain reviews, starting on page 256.

RESTAURANTS

Ratings: Family Appeal, Food, Decor, Service, Cost

FA	F	D	S	$
24	25	21	24	M

Dewey's Pizza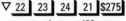
265 Hosea Rd. (Clifton Ave.); 513-221-0400; www.deweyspizza.com
■ It's "fun for all" at these popular gourmet pizzerias with a hip, contemporary feel that makes them "nothing like your typical chain";

foodies-in-training can "watch the pizza being made" in glass-enclosed kitchens, and adults will appreciate the "great salads."

La Rosa's

| 26 | 21 | 17 | 21 | I |

2684 Madison Rd. (Edwards Rd.); 513-347-1111
527 Sycamore St. (bet. 5th & 6th Sts.); 513-347-1111
2717 Vine St. (Charlton St.); 513-347-1111
1250 W. Eighth St. (Dalton Ave.); 513-347-1111
www.larosas.com

■ "Kids adore this chain", aka the "ultimate family pizza place", both for its "informal, fun" ambiance and its "hometown pie" that has a "taste like no other" (the red sauce is slightly "sugary"); in addition, "they serve a wide variety of food" (spaghetti, antipasti, subs) so "there is something for everyone" – even for finicky half-pints.

Montgomery Inn

| 22 | 27 | 22 | 24 | M |

925 Eastern Ave. (off I-471); 513-721-7427
9440 Montgomery Rd. (bet. Cooper & Remington Rds.), Montgomery; 513-791-3482 🖂

www.montgomeryinn.com

■ Known for "the ribs, the ribs, the ribs", this "local treasure" has "done well for over a generation" by offering "fantastic" barbecue and familial service ("no matter how old you are, the waitresses still call you 'hon'"); with a decor full of "sports stuff", "the Downtown location has the better atmosphere for families", while the Boathouse, with its "great views of the Ohio River", is "a little more fancy."

Palomino

| – | – | – | – | M |

Fountain Pl., 505 Vine St. (5th St.); 513-381-1300; www.palomino.com
It may be "best for older kids", but well-mannered youngsters of all ages can practice their white-tablecloth skills at this New American–Mediterranean, part of a national "classy chain", with a "great view of Fountain Square" (the city's gathering place for celebrations); inside, the open kitchen provides live entertainment, the staff is solicitous and there are "good children's selections" among the rotisserie meats.

Skyline Chili 🖂

| 23 | 20 | 13 | 21 | I |

254 E. Fourth St. (Sycamore St.); 513-241-4848
643 Vine St. (7th St.); 513-241-2020
1007 Vine St. (Court St.); 513-721-4715
580 Walnut St. (6th St.); 513-684-9600
www.skylinechili.com

■ "It's an acquired taste for sure, but once you acquire it, you'll always come back" to this "classic" known for "totally unique" chili that's purportedly made with cinnamon and served over spaghetti; "a step above fast food", it offers "table service that's always quick" and counter service that's quicker; even if the kids deem the dish "a little odd", grown-ups agree "the price is right."

RESTAURANT CHAINS

See reviews, starting on page 262.

Ratings: Family Appeal, Food, Decor, Service, Cost

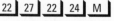

| FA | F | D | S | $ |

Applebee's

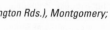

| 21 | 16 | 17 | 17 | M |

7920 Beechmont Ave. (Witt Rd.); 513-474-6605
9595 Colerain Ave. (Springdale Dr.); 513-385-0400
5050 Crookshank Rd. (Glenway Ave.); 513-451-3015
8565 Winton Rd. (Hempstead Dr.); 513-729-2400

Benihana 🚫 | 23 | 20 | 18 | 22 | E |
126 E. Sixth St. (bet. Main & Walnut Sts.); 513-421-1688
50 Tri-County Pkwy. (Princeton Pike); 513-772-4800

Cheesecake Factory 🚫 | 21 | 23 | 21 | 20 | M |
Kenwood Towne Centre, 7875 Montgomery Rd. (off Hwy. 71);
513-984-6911

Chili's Grill & Bar 🚫 | 21 | 19 | 18 | 19 | M |
11329 Montgomery Rd. (Kemper Rd.); 513-469-9888

Chuck E. Cheese's 🚫 | 26 | 10 | 17 | 13 | I |
8801 Colerain Ave. (Joseph Rd.); 513-385-1438
4394 Eastgate Square Dr. (Hwy. 32); 513-752-8188

Dave & Buster's 🚫 | 26 | 16 | 21 | 17 | M |
11775 Commons Dr. (E. Kemper Rd.), Springdale; 513-671-5501

Don Pablo's 🚫 | 20 | 19 | 18 | 18 | I |
9455 Colerain Ave. (Rte. 27); 513-741-0477
2692 Madison Rd. (Edwards Rd.); 513-631-1356
11363 Montgomery Rd. (Kemper Rd.); 513-489-8600
401 Riverboat Row (off I-471), Newport, KY; 859-261-7100

Johnny Rockets 🚫 | 25 | 17 | 20 | 18 | I |
7800 Montgomery Rd. (Kenwood Rd.); 513-791-5606

LongHorn Steakhouse 🚫 | 21 | 21 | 19 | 21 | M |
2692 Madison Rd. (Edwards Rd.); 513-351-4040
6620 Harrison Ave. (bet. Hearne & Rybolt Rds.); 513-574-6100
853 Eastgate North Dr. (off Hwy. 32); 513-947-8882

Max & Erma's 🚫 | 22 | 20 | 19 | 21 | I |
805 Eastgate North Dr. (off Hwy. 32); 513-752-6222
Sycamore Plaza, 7800 Montgomery Rd. (Kenwood Rd.); 513-794-0100

O'Charley's 🚫 | 22 | 21 | 18 | 18 | I |
5075 Crookshank Rd. (Glenway Ave.); 513-347-3200
4531 Eastgate Blvd. (Old State Hwy. 171); 513-753-6266
5262 Fields Ertel Rd. (Mason Montgomery Rd.); 513-469-0022

Olive Garden 🚫 | 20 | 19 | 18 | 19 | M |
475 Ohio Pike (bet. Hamblen & McClean Drs.); 513-528-4075
9654 Colerain Ave. (Springdale Rd.); 513-385-6300

Outback Steakhouse 🚫 | 20 | 22 | 18 | 20 | M |
9880 Colerain Ave. (Redskin Dr.); 513-245-0900
7731 Five Mile Rd. (Beechmont Ave.); 513-624-8181
6168 Glenway Ave. (bet. Parkcrest Ln. & Werk Rd.); 513-662-4900
8240 Montgomery Rd. (bet. Galbraith & Kugler Mill Rds.); 513-793-5566

Roadhouse Grill 🚫 | 20 | 18 | 16 | 18 | M |
4639 Ridge Ave. (Madison Rd.); 513-351-4333

T.G.I. Friday's 🚫 | 21 | 17 | 18 | 17 | M |
3780 Paxton Ave. (Ferdinand Pl.); 513-321-5121
6320 Glenway Ave. (Lawrence Rd.); 513-662-5555
8150 Montgomery Rd. (E. Galbraith Rd.); 513-891-0223
9141 Fields Ertel Rd. (Waterstone Blvd.); 513-683-6400

Tony Roma's 🚫 | 20 | 21 | 16 | 19 | M |
4022 Mt. Carmel Tobasco Rd. (Beechmont Ave.); 513-528-0290

Uno Chicago Grill ☒ | 20 | 18 | 15 | 16 | M |

342 Ludlow Ave. (bet. Middleton Ave. & Telford St.); 513-281-8667
627 Walnut St. (7th St.); 513-621-8667
7500 Beechmont Ave. (Five Mile Rd.); 513-231-8667

Dallas/Ft. Worth

Linked by Interstate 30, conjoined cities Dallas and Ft. Worth seem to have split personalities. Skyscrapered "Big D" caters to sophisticates with lavish shopping (at the West End Market Place, Uptown's chic McKinney Avenue and the immense Galleria mall, with an ice rink open even during the area's stifling summers) and high-brow arts districts; yet each fall, museum-stuffed, art deco–style Fair Park, to the east, also hosts the Texas State Fair. (Ride Uptown for free via the vintage, volunteer-run McKinney Ave. Trolley.) Mellower Ft. Worth has elegant museums, first-class cultural venues (e.g. Bass Performance Hall) and a top-notch zoo, but embraces its cow-town origins as well. The attractions corralled within its Stockyard District include twice-daily authentic cattle drives, weekly rodeos, the Texas Cowboy Hall of Fame and a small Western-themed amusement park. You can mosey from museum to concert hall to city park on the trolleys (T buses, costing $1.25, let bikers tote their two-wheelers for no extra charge), but driving is really the easiest way to see both cities and the welcoming, wide-open ranches beyond. Be careful, though: Folks here often call highways by names instead of numbers. U.S. 75 is Central Expressway, I-635 is the LBJ and I-35 may be either Stemmons or R.L. Thornton.

ATTRACTIONS

Ratings: Child Appeal, Adult Appeal, Public Facilities, Service, Cost

	C	A	P	S	$

Age of Steam
Railroad Museum 😊☺ | ▽ 24 | 23 | 21 | 21 | I |

Fair Park, 1105 Washington St. (bet. Fitzhugh & Parry Aves.), Dallas; 214-428-0101; www.dallasrailwaymuseum.com
■ Though it's geared "especially for the railroad enthusiast", this "very cool" Fair Park choo-choo cluster is "great fun for the entire family"; Thomas the Tank Engine aficionados can climb aboard "beautiful" restored pufferbellies, mid-century locomotives, Pullman sleepers and cabooses, inspect actual railway equipment, and stroll into a century-old depot or track down info about the iron horse and its role in American history; N.B. no restrooms available.

American Airlines Center ☺ | 19 | 27 | 27 | 24 | E |

2500 Victory Ave. (Wichita St.), Dallas; 214-222-3687; www.americanairlinescenter.com
■ "There's not a bad seat in the house" at this "huge" glass-walled "jewel" of an arena (home to the NBA Mavericks and the NHL Stars) that's a "first-class facility" for games, concerts, circuses, wrestling matches or rodeos; the Adult Appeal rating is understandably higher than the Child Appeal, but youngsters appreciate "kid-friendly food" (including BBQ in gut-busting "Texas-size portions"), the south lobby's "high-flying" aeronautical models and photos, and the soda shop modeled after a vintage Dr. Pepper bottling plant; "quick service" and 20 unisex 'family restrooms' please all, just "be prepared to spend a bundle."

Amon Carter Museum 😊😊

| 15 | 26 | 26 | 24 | I |

3501 Camp Bowie Blvd. (bet. Clifton & Montgomery Sts.), Ft. Worth; 817-332-8451; www.cartermuseum.org

■ "Texas to the core", this "fabulous" museum named after a Ft. Worth publisher and philanthropist has an "amazing collection of Western art" (Remington, O'Keeffe) along with other "great American" works (Hudson River School), so it's "fun" for little buckaroos who want to see "lots of cowboy stuff"; furthermore, since it's set in a "gorgeous, green park" and "there's no admission fee", "restless kids" can take periodic outdoor breaks; N.B. free children's programs on the first Sunday of every month.

Ballpark in Arlington 😊😊

| 25 | 27 | 26 | 23 | M |

1000 Ballpark Way (Randol Mill Rd.), Arlington; 817-273-5100; www.texasrangers.com

■ Everything "you see, hear or smell screams baseball" – from the "ball-shaped lights to the wonderful hot dogs" – at this "exceptionally designed stadium" that "pays homage to great parks of the past"; Little Leaguers will "love the interactive games behind center field", the "kid-sized cafe", the "great" tours (including dugout, press box and owner's suite) and the three-story museum of memorabilia; to cope with 100-degree summer heat "walk to TGI Friday's in the outfield" for "air-conditioning and food"; N.B. look for special 10th-anniversary events this year.

Bass Performance Hall 😊

| 14 | 28 | 29 | 25 | VE |

525 Commerce St. (bet. Houston & Market Sts.), Ft. Worth; 817-212-4325; 877-212-4280; www.basshall.com

■ "Angels look down on you" from the "baroque interior" of this "absolutely stunning" facility in Ft. Worth's Sundance Square, and its "amazing acoustics" ("you can hear every guitar pluck") make it "fantastic" for the classical arts (symphony, opera, ballet) and "the biggest country-music stars" – plus there's even "comfortable seating"; there's not a whole lot to impress kids, but they're certain to enjoy the Broadway musicals presented here by the city's Casa Mañana theater company.

Dallas Aquarium 😊😊

| 25 | 22 | 19 | 17 | I |

Fair Park, 1462 First Ave. (MLK Blvd.), Dallas; 214-670-8443; www.dallaszoo.com

☑ The offspring may be awestruck by the 135-pound snapping turtle, five-ft. electric eel or six-ft. pike at this "inviting retreat", a "hot and humid" home to some 6,000 "fascinating" fish, reptiles, amphibians and invertebrates; boosters bubble that this facility makes "excellent use of limited space" and "can just as easily be enjoyed in 30 minutes or three hours"; however, critics carp that the layout could be "more family-friendly" and call admission prices "high" for such a "small aquarium."

Dallas Arboretum and Botanical Garden

| 21 | 28 | 25 | 21 | I |

8525 Garland Rd. (bet. Lakeland Dr. & Whittier Ave.), Dallas; 214-515-6500; www.dallasarboretum.org

■ Stop and smell the roses at this "flowery retreat in the middle of the busy city", a "beautiful" 66-acre "picnic spot" of "well-manicured grounds", sculptures and fountains; it's "especially nice in the spring" when 2,400 azalea varieties bloom and toddlers take part in Mommy & Me Mondays (music, petting zoo, wagon rides); meanwhile, older kids may dig the hands-on horticulture at the new Trammell Crow Pavilion; veterans caution "wear a baby backpack" to manage the terrain and "don't expect services" – even with the Crow's Cafe, "concessions are scarce."

Dallas Museum of Art ☺☺

15	25	25	23	I

1717 N. Harwood St. (Ross Ave.), Dallas; 214-922-1200;
www.dallasmuseumofart.org

■ "Bring your walking shoes" to explore this century-old "medium-size gallery with a wide range" of "worthwhile exhibits" ("excellent Indonesian collection", "fabulous Mesoamerican pieces"); artsies assert it's a "great afternoon stop" "for any family" thanks to the "excellent children's areas", "helpful and informative" docents and family-friendly activities such as weekend sketching, late-night stories, hands-on projects; though a smattering of skeptics scowl "if you're planning on spending more than an hour, leave the kids at home", others find a visit here enjoyable.

Dallas Museum of Natural History

▽ 25	22	18	17	I

Fair Park, 3535 Grand Ave. (bet. 1st & 2nd Aves.), Dallas; 214-421-3466;
www.dallasdino.org

☑ Another of Fair Park's cluster of museums, this dino-mite art deco depository boasts "terrific dinosaurs" and other "wonderful interactive exhibits" that "make you feel like you are looking at the animals up close"; "children will enjoy" special events such as family festival days when they can bite into crunchy chocolate-covered crickets or touch toads, snakes and lizards; a faction of faultfinders frets that the facility "needs a facelift" – which is why plans are underway for a new 200,000-sq.-ft. building downtown.

Dallas Zoo

25	20	17	16	I

650 S. R.L. Thornton Frwy. (bet. Ewing & Marsalis Aves.), Dallas;
214-670-5656; www.dallaszoo.com

☑ At this 95-acre menagerie in Fair Park, the oldest zoo in Texas (1888), "kids will love" the new interactive children's area (petting zoo/farm, trading post, habitats to explore and the toddler-friendly Tot Spot) and "entertaining" annual events such as May's Safari Day (live music, crafts and touchable animals); overall, the facility "keeps improving" – witness its "natural-feel" Wilds of Africa section, which has a monorail and a "great viewing area" – but some spoilsports still find it "unimpressive" and "dingy", explaining it "needs a bit of financial support, fast."

Fair Park

21	21	16	14	$0

1300 Robert B. Cullum Blvd. (Grand Ave.), Dallas; 214-421-9600;
www.fairparkdallas.com

☑ Art deco aficionados "love just walking around" admiring the architecture at this 277-acre complex in downtown Dallas, a National Historic Landmark with the U.S.'s largest collection of 1930s expo edifices; among them are nine museums and six performance venues, including the "first-rate" Music Hall ("great summer musicals"), the Cotton Bowl stadium and the fairgrounds, home to the "awesome Texas state fair" (where "kids will have a blast"); that said, correspondents comment this place "needs a dose of urban renewal" and caution "the only time to go is during the day."

Fort Worth Botanic Garden

19	27	25	21	I

3220 Botanic Garden Blvd. (University Dr.), Ft. Worth; 817-871-7686;
www.fwbg.org

■ A "beautiful setting with statues and flowers galore", these beds of botanical bouquets are "worthy of family pictures" and picnics; "don't miss" the "peaceful and soothing Japanese gardens", "ideal for preschoolers and older children" who "love to explore the steps, trails and bridges" and watch "koi stampede across the pond" to be fed; also on hand are "exceptional" rose plantings, an aromatic fragrance plot and a popular collection of perennials ("catch the Herb Festival in May").

Fort Worth Museum of Science and History

| 29 | 25 | 24 | 23 | M |

1501 Montgomery St. (bet. Camp Bowie Blvd. & Crestline Rd.), Ft. Worth; 817-255-9300; www.fwmuseum.org

■ "You and the kids will want to stay all day" at this "A+" attraction, voted the city's No. 1 attraction for Child Appeal in this *Survey*; the ExploraZone is "a great place to learn", thanks to "hands-on science projects that delight children and adults alike"; "older ones will love" taking in the "fun IMAX theater", digging for fossils and speculating at the hands-on lab, while shorties 6 and under can head to Kidspace to shop at a miniature market, paint each other's faces, create computerized paintings or experiment with water.

FORT WORTH ZOO

| 29 | 26 | 26 | 23 | M |

Forest Park, 1989 Colonial Pkwy. (bet. Park Place Ave. & University Dr.), Ft. Worth; 817-759-7555; www.fortworthzoo.org

■ "Entertainment for all" can be found at the city's No. 1 overall attraction, a "world-class" menagerie that's a "better option" for a half day than "its counterpart" in Dallas; you feel "like you're on safari" as you stroll through the "gorgeous layout", viewing a "large variety of animals" in natural-looking settings, and the "train is fun for the kiddies" as it transports visitors to the "interactive Texas Wild!" attraction, an eight-acre exhibit with "an old-fashioned town"; P.S. toddlers are tickled that "the movie *Barney at the Zoo* was filmed here."

Grapevine Vintage Railroad

| 25 | 21 | 20 | 21 | M |

140 E. Exchange Ave. (Main St.), Ft. Worth; 817-625-7245; www.grapevinesteamrailroad.com

■ Also known as the 'Tarantula Train' because its track map resembles an enormous spider, this "well-restored" 1896 steam locomotive that pulls turn-of-the-century Victorian coaches and open-air touring cars is "a nice way to get to the stockyards" from the town of Grapevine (19 miles northeast of Fort Worth); another route follows the Chisholm Trail and the Trinity River on high trestles; pleased passengers profess it's a "fun" "outing for all ages", perhaps "a little pricey but worth it."

Kimbell Art Museum ☺

| 14 | 28 | 27 | 25 | $0 |

3333 Camp Bowie Blvd. (Arch Adams St.), Ft. Worth; 817-332-8451; www.kimbellart.org

■ "Small but mighty", rave reviewers who revere this "popular" "light-filled" Cultural District building that is "as worthy as" its "world-class" collection"; its "fantastic architecture" encases an "eclectic collection" ("one of everything", a "perfect introduction to art") plus "amazing traveling exhibits" that are bound to "excite and engage" older kids, teen art-lovers and their grown-ups; furthermore, "the cafe has a nice menu, a perfect garden setting" and a liquor license – though the "limited gallery space" is "packed on weekends", which often necessitates a ban on strollers.

Modern Art Museum of Fort Worth ☺

| 14 | 28 | 30 | 26 | I |

3200 Darnell St. (bet. Arch Adams St. & University Dr.), Ft. Worth; 817-738-9215; 866-824-5566; www.mamfw.org

■ "The architecture alone could warrant a visit", effervesce fans of this "stunning addition" to Ft. Worth's Cultural District, a "celebrated new building" (five "airy" pavilions set amid a "super-shallow" reflecting pool) that's "as wondrous as the art"; rated the top art museum in this *Survey*, its "accessible collection" of international postwar art ranges from "'my-kid-could-have-painted-that' to awe-inspiring", plus a "great restaurant on the premises" offers "excellent dining" and a "waterside view" – so even though parents may have to put up with some whining, they'll find it's worth it.

Morton H. Meyerson Symphony Center ☺

| 13 | 27 | 28 | 25 | E |

2301 Flora St. (bet. Leonard & Pearl Sts.), Dallas; 214-692-0203; www.dallassymphony.com

■ "For those with discerning tastes in music", the "state-of-the-art acoustics" in this "gorgeous" I.M. Pei hall make for a "first-class" evening with the Dallas Symphony Orchestra or touring genre bands; while ratings indicate adults are much more enamored than their offspring, "children enjoy" such events as the Family Concert Series on Sunday afternoons and "wonderful" hourlong programs ('The Lost Elephant', 'The Haunted Symphony') suitable for youngsters aged 6 or older; "take a guided tour if you can", and catch a free demonstration of the C.B. Fisk Opus 100 mechanical-action organ.

Movie Studios at Las Colinas, The ☺☺

| ▽ 20 | 19 | 20 | 19 | M |

(fka The Studios at Las Colinas)

6301 N. O'Connor Rd. (bet. Northwest Hwy. & Royal Ln.), Irving; 972-869-3456; www.studiosatlascolinas.com

■ This "really cool" Irving soundstage complex provides a touch of "Hollywood in Dallas" (and not just for horse operas – *Silkwood*, *RoboCop* and *JFK* were filmed here); visitors can "see how movies are made" via a "terrific, informative" behind-the-scenes tour, experiment with visual and sound effects, and examine classic memorabilia (Dorothy's blue dress from *The Wizard of Oz*, the Von Trapp family's matching outfits and Forrest Gump's bench); still, detractors deem it "overpriced" and query "what is it doing *here*?"

Old City Park ☺☺

| 23 | 22 | 20 | 22 | I |

1717 Gano St. (Ervay St.), Dallas; 214-421-5141; www.oldcitypark.org

■ You'll "feel like you've gone back in time" at this "great outdoor museum", a 13-acre historic village with Texan artifacts that date from 1840 to 1910 within "wonderful" structures like a working farm, Victorian homes, a traditional Jewish household, a school and a church; hourlong guided tours and multilingual audio tours are available at any time – plus on Saturdays kids can meet costumed reenactors, try crafts or help out with the chores; N.B. a two-hour campfire 'extravaganza' with hayride may be booked in advance.

Reunion Tower Observation Deck ☺

| 20 | 23 | 19 | 19 | I |

Hyatt Regency, 300 Reunion Blvd. (bet. Houston St. & Stemmons Frwy.), Dallas; 214-712-7145; 800-233-1234; www.hyatt.com

■ Hit the heights and take in the sights from this rotating lookout 50 stories above the city atop the Hyatt Regency's Reunion Tower; "everything's so flat you can see for miles", so it's "fun" for most – especially on the Fourth of July, when the tower-top restaurant, Antares, offers a "superb view" of the fireworks; however, wayfarers warn "anxiety-ridden travelers" to "beware: the elevator is usually packed" and the wait "too long", while other critics call the revolving repast "just another fancy", "overpriced" meal.

Science Place

| 28 | 24 | 22 | 22 | M |

Fair Park, 1318 Second Ave. (bet. Grand Ave. & MLK Blvd.), Dallas; 214-428-5555; www.scienceplace.org

■ Not just a "fun family outing", a trip to this "educational" edifice has attractions for all ages: "adults and teens will probably like the IMAX best"; youngsters "up to age 13" hail "hands-on science experiments" in physics, zoology, medicine and more, while sub-sevens can learn about numbers, senses and buildings in the Kids Place; still, as with many of its Fair Park neighbors, this institution that "in its heyday was a great place to entertain the kids" is now "in need of a facelift."

Sixth Floor Museum at Dealey Plaza ☺

| 11 | 26 | 21 | 19 | M |

411 Elm St. (Houston St.), Dallas; 214-747-6660; 888-485-4854; www.jfk.org

■ Peering out the windows to "see the same view Lee Harvey Oswald had" when he "shot President Kennedy (or did he?)" "brings a national tragedy to vivid life" at this "not-to-be-missed site" "for history buffs"; its "informative" and "tasteful" film clips plus an "excellent chronology and wonderful narrative" of the 1963 assassination are "sobering" yet "gripping" and therefore most appropriate and "appealing to older kids and teens" – it's certainly "not for toddlers", who will be "tugging on your pant leg" asking to leave.

Stockyards Collection Museum ☺ ▽

| 21 | 23 | 21 | 21 | $0 |

Livestock Exchange Bldg., 131 E. Exchange Ave. (Main St.), Ft. Worth; 817-625-5082; www.nfwhs.org

◩ For longhorn lovers interested in Fort Worth's cowtown origins, this museum in the historic Livestock Exchange Building is a "neat place to explore"; vintage photos and artifacts illustrate the history of the local stockyards, meatpacking plants and railroads that intertwined to create the area's cattle industry, while also commemorating the people who lived and worked here; as a result, surveyors say, it's "really interesting for adults" but likely to bore "wee little ones."

Texas Stadium ☺

| 19 | 22 | 16 | 15 | E |

Texas Stadium, 2401 E. Airport Frwy. (Walton Walker Blvd.), Irving; 972-785-5000; www.dallascowboys.com

◩ "And on the eighth day God created" this "sports wonderland", declare Cowboy devotees who dig the "open dome"; "the tour of the stadium and locker room is great for fans", who can "bring a football to toss" or "test their skill at field-goal kicking"; still, one reviewer's "one-of-a-kind" classic is another's "outdated" relic, and plenty of people "wish it were enclosed" – "it's hot in the summer and cold in the winter – advising "save your money and head to a sports bar instead."

Water Gardens Park ☺

| 24 | 24 | 20 | 12 | $0 |

bordered by Commerce, Houston, W. 13th & 15th Sts., Ft. Worth; 817-871-7275

■ "You will get wet" at Downtown's 5.4-acre "man-made marvel", a canyon-esque "interactive water monument" "to climb and explore"; "kids will have fun dipping in and climbing" and "adults will find it soothing" to "walk through hand in hand", so "allow enough time to go all the way down and back up"; however, do "be careful" – the rocks may be slippery – and since there are 19,000 gallons of H_2O splashing around you, "be sure you go to the bathroom" beforehand.

West End MarketPlace ☺

| 14 | 21 | 18 | 18 | $0 |

603 Munger Ave. (bet. Lamar & Record Sts.), Dallas; 214-748-4801; www.dallaswestend.org

■ Among the West End's converted turn-of-the-century warehouses (now shops and eateries) sits this former candy factory, a five-story emporium full of "great restaurant choices, fun sculptures and an arcade"; given the neighborhood's festivals, parades and open-air events, the market remains "crowded" and especially "popular with tourists", though a few fret it's "a little clichéd."

White Rock Lake Park

| 23 | 25 | 17 | 11 | $0 |

8300 E. Lawther Dr. (Buckner Blvd.), Dallas; 214-670-8283; www.dallascityhall.com

■ "If you like to walk, Rollerblade, bicycle", canoe or bird-watch – and what kid doesn't? – head to this 1,873-acre "natural gem", a

 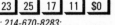

"delightful respite from city life" even though it's just 10 minutes from downtown Dallas; surrounding the lake – a former reservoir recently designated an Urban Wildlife Sanctuary – are 11 miles of trails, six playgrounds, a dog park and picnic grounds plus "lots of wildlife and wooded spaces"; N.B. anglers will need an up-to-date fishing license.

Women's Museum ☺

| 12 | 23 | 24 | 22 | I |

Fair Park, 3800 Parry Ave. (Commerce St.), Dallas; 214-915-0860; www.thewomensmuseum.org

■ "Bring your daughters" to this "fantastic" four-year-old Fair Park facility, a Smithsonian affiliate that focuses on female contributions to American society; amid "stunning architecture", "knowledgeable guides" explain the "contemporary", "entertaining and educational" interactive exhibits (on artists, writers, comedians, religious figures, athletes, activists), and "world-class visiting shows" pass through regularly as well; as "one of only a handful of museums devoted to women's history", it's "hard to beat" as a "good conversation starter."

HOTELS

Ratings: Family Appeal, Rooms, Service, Public Facilities, Cost

	FA	R	S	P	$

Four Seasons at Las Colinas

| 24 | 27 | 27 | 29 | $340 |

4150 N. MacArthur Blvd., Irving; 972-717-0700; 800-332-3442; www.fourseasons.com; 345 rooms, 12 suites

■ The report card reads "A+" for this "first-class" resort surrounded by 400 "sprawling" acres in the North Texas hills that's a "great spot for families to unwind and enjoy luxury" yet be just "minutes from Dallas"; with on-site golf, tennis and a spa for adults, and a "great pool" and welcome amenities for children (along with the supervised Kids for all Seasons program), "everyone's a winner" here and it's all accomplished "without being too stuffy."

Omni Mandalay Hotel

| ∇ 20 | 22 | 21 | 24 | $249 |

221 E. Las Colinas Blvd., Irving; 972-556-0800; 800-843-6664; www.omnihotels.com; 325 rooms, 96 suites

■ The Burmese design draws visitors to this "gorgeous hotel" outside Dallas, where "top-notch" service includes the Omni Kids program with special gifts for little ones; fitness-focused families can rent bikes to ride the trail around the property and stay in special 'Get Fit' rooms with treadmills and healthy snacks; there's a heated lakeside swimming pool and scheduled feedings of the two resident black swans in a "well-fenced area" to keep youngsters safe; N.B. it's just three miles from Texas Stadium, home of the Rangers baseball team.

Renaissance Worthington

| ∇ 21 | 25 | 26 | 26 | $225 |

200 Main St., Ft. Worth; 817-870-1000; 800-468-3571; www.renaissancehotels.com; 444 rooms, 30 suites

■ Who knew this hotel that "doesn't especially cater to families" would be so "very supportive" of their needs?; those with tots in tow appreciate the staff at this Sundance Square spot, feel "comfortable taking the baby to the restaurants" and report "the pool is a big hit"; it's also right in downtown surrounded by "lots of shops, movies and eateries" and three miles from the Ft. Worth Botanical Garden.

Westin Galleria

| 22 | 20 | 19 | 21 | $295 |

13340 Dallas Pkwy., Dallas; 972-934-9494; 888-625-5144; www.westin.com; 411 rooms, 21 suites

☑ "If you have children who like to ice-skate or hang out in the mall", this hotel connected to the Galleria is the location for you since there are so "many dining and shopping options at your doorstep" (Nordstrom, Tiffany, movie theaters, etc.) – all "great for keeping the family entertained"; infants sleep tight in those heavenly cribs and you can even bring the family dog, but snippy sorts say "other than being near" the stores it's a bit "sub-par" and a dozen miles to most major sights.

Westin Stonebriar Resort

22	24	21	25	$319

1549 Legacy Dr., Frisco; 972-668-8000; 888-627-8441; www.westinstonebriar.com; 288 rooms, 13 suites

☑ There's "plenty to do for the entire family" at this Westin "far out in Frisco" if you want a resort experience outside of Dallas (it's 22 miles from downtown); there's a "fun" outdoor pool, a "new minor-league ballpark" nearby and a mall within a few miles, and duffers appreciate the Tom Fazio–designed golf course; but city slickers snip that it's "in the middle of nowhere", even if it ends up "exceeding expectations."

Top Family-Friendly Hotel Chains in the Area:

Embassy Suites   Hyatt
Holiday Inn   Marriott
Homewood Suites   Residence Inn

See Hotel Chain reviews, starting on page 256.

RESTAURANTS

Ratings: Family Appeal, Food, Decor, Service, Cost

FA	F	D	S	$

EZ's

24	19	17	20	I

6833 W. Northwest Hwy. (Hillcrest Ave.), Dallas; 214-750-6677; www.ezsrestaurants.com

■ "Browsing all the selections" at this "casual", "loud" diner-style eatery in North Dallas could take all day but it offers "more interesting food than the standard kid-friendly place"; "from chili to fish to pizza", the American menu accommodates "picky eaters", and there are "healthy options as well"; just "don't leave without a delicious creamy milkshake" (the youngsters "can afford those calories"); N.B. children eat free on Wednesday nights.

Highland Park Pharmacy

23	19	18	20	I

3229 Knox St. (Travis St.), Dallas; 214-521-2126

■ A Highland Park "flashback", this "ice-cream parlor and sandwich shop in a real pharmacy" lets petite eaters "see how it was done in the old days" – going "belly up to the soda counter" to dig into such classic American fare as "pimento-cheese sandwiches" ("like your mom made") and "milkshakes to die for."

Joe T. Garcia's ⊭

23	22	20	21	M

2201 N. Commerce St. (22nd St.), Ft. Worth; 817-626-4356; www.joets.com

☑ There's plenty of space to "let the kids run around" this "old-style" Northside Mexican that takes up an entire city block "with swimming pools" – "don't let them fall in" – and "beautiful gardens"; amigos advise "don't even think about reading the menu – just order the family-style enchilada" dinner; unfortunately, while "the quality is consistent, the crowds are too", but "you can't beat the service, once you get it."

Kincaid's Hamburgers ⊠⊭

24	27	13	19	I

4901 Camp Bowie Blvd. (Eldridge St.), Ft. Worth; 817-732-2881

■ Since 1946, this institution in a "converted grocery" has been serving up "the best hamburgers in the whole wide world"; fans packing the "long tables" flip for the simply "delicious" patties, and it's always "busy enough that your loud-voiced child can't be heard"; so when wandering Ft. Worth, this is definitely a "don't-miss."

La Duni Latin Café

| – | – | – | – | M |

4620 McKinney Ave. (Knox St.), Dallas; 214-520-7300; www.laduni.com

You and your kinfolk "won't believe how little it costs to treat your taste buds" at this "cute", "lively" Pan-Latin American entry where the "super" dishes entice everyone in the family; grown-ups also appreciate the "imaginative cocktails" and "the best collection of South American wines in the Metroplex", sometimes poured by "owners who hang around and chat"; as regulars can attest, the "first-rate", "lip-smacking desserts" are also "not to be missed" (particularly the "to-die-for" *quatro leches* cake) and neither is the "novel Sunday brunch."

La Familia ⊠

| – | – | – | – | I |

2720 W. Seventh St. (Carroll St.), Ft. Worth; 817-870-2002

"What a joy to be greeted with the familiar handshake of Al" Cavazos, "the owner at the door" of this West Side "classic" where a "fast, friendly" staff serves up "fresh, reasonably priced" fare that fills the bill for flocks of families who fly here for "to-die-for fajitas", "wonderful beef tacos", "spicy, garlicky salsa" and "charra bean soup like mama would have made (if mama had been Mexican)"; P.S. try "the truly wonderful flaming flan for desert" (sure to widen some kids' eyes), but remember to "ask for it early" or you may "miss out" on this creative confection.

Lucile's Stateside Bistro

| – | – | – | – | M |

4700 Camp Bowie Blvd. (Hulen St.), Ft. Worth; 817-738-4761

"Appropriate for every occasion from Mother's Day brunch" with the whole clan "to a Friday night out", this "cheery" American eatery on the West Side's main drag is a "popular place for all ages", from tiny tots on up, getting high marks for "great breakfasts" and "casual lunches and dinners" thanks to a "wonderful variety" of dishes (folks "love their pastas, steaks, wood-oven pizzas" and "great desserts"), "reasonable prices and a helpful, courteous staff – what more could you ask for?"; P.S. September's popular "annual Lobsterama [event] is fabulous" too.

Purple Cow

| 28 | 16 | 21 | 19 | I |

110 Preston Royal Shopping Ctr. (Royal Ln.), Dallas; 214-373-0037
4601 W. Freeway (Rte. 30), Ft. Worth; 817-737-7177

☑ It's really "a diner, nothing more", but the "cool" color scheme and train circling the ceiling makes it seem "so different" at this "cute" spot in the Preston Royal Shopping Center; "young children love" the "purple ice cream" and "soda-fountain food", even though parents proclaim the "average" American chow is "not very adult-friendly"; on the other hand, elder sorts "can have a shot of their favorite liqueur with their shake", so "both young and old" end up "enjoying" the "upbeat atmosphere."

S & D Oyster Company ⊠

| – | – | – | – | M |

2701 McKinney Ave. (Boll St.), Dallas; 214-880-0111

The "line of Dallasites out the door verifies" the "longtime" "institution" status of this New Orleans–style seafood "classic" where throngs of hungry families "gorge on all manner of fried sea creatures" (like the "best shrimp" and "oysters in town"), not to mention "wonderfully consistent gumbo", "famous coleslaw", "great hushpuppies" and "to-die-for lemon pie" – all served by "the same familiar, old-style waiters" they've known "for years"; P.S. "be sure to let them make your cocktail sauce" "from scratch at your table."

Sonny Bryan's Smokehouse　　22 | 23 | 16 | 19 | I

2202 Inwood Rd. (Harry Hines Blvd.), Dallas; 214-357-7120 🖾
302 N. Market St. (Pacific Ave.), Dallas; 214-744-1610
Republic Towers, 325 N. St. Paul St. (bet. Bryan St. & Pacific Ave.),
Dallas; 214-979-0102 🖾
Alliance Ctr., 2421 Westport Pkwy. (Heritage Pkwy.), Ft. Worth; 817-224-9191
www.sonnybryansbbq.com
■ For "authentic seven-napkin Texas BBQ", "you can't go wrong
with" this "no-frills" chain that admirers insist belongs among "the
hallowed halls of" 'cue; besides the tasty meats, it makes "great pies
and cobbler", served by a "friendly" crew; all in all, a perfect place for
"kids who like to get their fingers messy."

Trail Dust Steak House　　27 | 19 | 22 | 22 | M

10841 Composite Dr. (Walnut Hill Ln.), Dallas; 214-357-3862;
www.traildust.com
■ "Bring the young 'uns and the boots cuz the whole family is gonna
have a good time" at this "loud" "country steakhouse" in North Dallas,
where the two-story indoor slide "keeps the kids occupied while you
wait for your hunk of meat" cooked over mesquite or "dance to the
country music" played by a live band Wednesday-Saturday; it's a real
"down-home" experience, so don't wear "nothing fancy" – especially
since "they cut off neckties and tack them to the wall."

RESTAURANT CHAINS

See reviews, starting on page 262.

Ratings: Family Appeal, Food, Decor, Service, Cost

	FA	F	D	S	$

Applebee's　　21 | 16 | 17 | 17 | M

5030 S. Hulen St. (Overton Ridge Blvd.), Ft. Worth; 817-423-8138
6600 West Frwy. (Lands End Blvd.), Ft. Worth; 817-732-8862
7855 Las Colinas Ridge (Karahan Pkwy.), Irving; 972-869-3690
1901 N. Beltline Rd. (bet. Willow Creek Dr. & W. Irving Blvd.), Irving;
972-313-0081

Baja Fresh Mexican Grill 🖾　　20 | 22 | 14 | 18 | I

3003 Knox St. (bet. Hwy. 75 & McKinney Ave.), Dallas; 214-219-8724
7601 N. MacArthur Blvd. (Las Colinas Blvd.), Irving; 469-420-9400

Benihana 🖾　　23 | 20 | 18 | 22 | E

7775 Banner Dr. (Merit Dr.), Dallas; 972-387-4404
3848 Oak Lawn Ave. (bet. Blackburn St. & Irving Ave.), Dallas; 214-559-3450

Buca di Beppo 🖾　　24 | 19 | 22 | 21 | M

7843 Park Ln. (N. Central Expwy.), Dallas; 214-361-8462

California Pizza Kitchen 🖾　　21 | 21 | 16 | 19 | M

8411 Preston Rd. (off Northwest Hwy.), Dallas; 214-750-7067

Cheesecake Factory 🖾　　21 | 23 | 21 | 20 | M

7700 W. Northwest Hwy. (bet. Boedeker St. & Hwy. 75), Dallas;
214-373-4844

Chili's Grill & Bar 🖾　　21 | 19 | 18 | 19 | M

246 Casa Linda Plaza (N. Buckner Blvd.), Dallas; 214-321-9485
7567 Greenville Ave. (bet. Meadow Rd. & Walnut Hill Ln.), Dallas; 214-361-4371
3230 Knox St. (Cole Ave.), Dallas; 214-520-1555
2222 W. Northwest Hwy. (off I-35e & Hwy. 12), Dallas; 214-358-5274

Chuck E. Cheese's 🗷   26 | 10 | 17 | 13 | I
Valley View Mall, 13364 Montfort Dr. (bet. James Temple Dr. & Perterson Ln.), Dallas; 972-392-1944
7110 S. Westmoreland Rd. (Camp Wisdom Rd.), Dallas; 972-298-7973

Dave & Buster's 🗷   26 | 16 | 21 | 17 | M
8021 Walnut Hill Ln. (N. Central Expwy.), Dallas; 214-353-0620
2601 Preston Rd. (bet. Rte. 121 & Warren Pkwy.), Frisco; 214-387-0915

Don Pablo's 🗷   20 | 19 | 18 | 18 | I
7050 Ridgmar Meadow Rd. (Altamere Dr.), Ft. Worth; 817-731-0497
5601 S. Hulen St. (Oakmeadow Dr.), Ft. Worth; 817-346-3787

Fuddrucker's 🗷   24 | 20 | 15 | 16 | I
4520 Frankford Rd. (Dallas Pkwy.), Dallas; 972-818-3833
5500 Greenville Ave. (Lovers Ln.), Dallas; 214-360-9390
5601 SW Loop 820 (Bryant Irvin Rd.), Ft. Worth; 817-263-0996

Hard Rock Cafe 🗷   22 | 16 | 26 | 18 | M
2601 McKinney Ave. (Routh St.), Dallas; 214-855-0007

Joe's Crab Shack 🗷   23 | 17 | 21 | 19 | M
10250 E. Technology Blvd. (off Northwest Hwy.), Dallas; 214-654-0909
2001 N. Lamar St. (Munger Ave.), Dallas; 214-220-0404

Johnny Rockets 🗷   25 | 17 | 20 | 18 | I
The Parks at Arlington Mall, 3811 S. Cooper St. (W. Arbrook Blvd.), Arlington; 817-419-0022

Maggiano's Little Italy 🗷   22 | 22 | 21 | 22 | M
205 Northpark Ctr. (Northwest Hwy.), Dallas; 214-360-0707

Medieval Times 🗷   29 | 14 | 25 | 19 | E
2021 N. Stemmons Frwy. (off I-35E), Dallas; 800-229-9900

Mimi's Cafe 🗷   23 | 21 | 22 | 20 | M
5858 SW Loop 820 (Bryant Irvin Rd.), Ft. Worth; 817-731-9644

Olive Garden 🗷   20 | 19 | 18 | 19 | M
10280 E. Technology Blvd. (Northwest Hwy.), Dallas; 214-902-8163
9079 Vantage Point Dr. (Greenville Ave.), Dallas; 972-234-3292
925 Alta Mere Dr. (Ridgmar Meadow Rd.), Ft. Worth; 817-732-0618
4700 SW Loop 820 (Hulen St.), Ft. Worth; 817-377-8091

On the Border   20 | 19 | 19 | 18 | M
Mexican Grill & Cantina 🗷
3130 Knox St. (bet. Cole & McKinney Aves.), Dallas; 214-528-5900
1801 N. Lamar St. (bet. Corbin & Hord Sts.), Dallas; 214-855-0296
Irving Mall, 2400 N. Beltline Rd. (off Rte. 183), Irving; 972-570-5032
1220 Market Pl. (MacArthur Blvd.), Irving; 214-574-8900

Original Pancake House, The 🗷   24 | 22 | 12 | 17 | I
5100 Beltline Rd. (Dallas Pkwy.), Dallas; 972-385-6468
2900 Lemmon Ave. (Oak Grove Ave.), Dallas; 214-528-7215
4343 W. Northwest Hwy. (Midway Rd.), Dallas; 214-351-2012

Outback Steakhouse 🗷   20 | 22 | 18 | 20 | M
2225 Connector Dr. (Technology Blvd.), Dallas; 214-956-8999
9049 Vantage Point Dr. (Greenville Ave.), Dallas; 972-783-0397
2102 N. Collins St. (Harwell Dr.), Arlington; 817-265-9381
1151 W. I-20 (bet. Cooper St. & Matlock Rd.), Arlington; 817-557-5959
4608 Bryant Irvin Rd. (off Hwy. 20), Ft. Worth; 817-370-7800

Romano's Macaroni Grill ⊠ | 21 | 21 | 19 | 21 | M |
5858 W. Northwest Hwy. (Douglas Ave.), Dallas; 214-265-0770
4535 Beltline Rd. (bet. Addison & Midway Rds.), Addison; 972-386-3831
2019 Brinker Ct. (off Ballpark Way), Arlington; 817-261-6676

T.G.I. Friday's ⊠ | 21 | 17 | 18 | 17 | M |
5100 Belt Line Rd. (Dallas Pkwy.), Dallas; 972-386-5824
9100 N. Central Expwy. (Park Ln.), Dallas; 214-363-2217
1713 N. Market St. (Ross Ave.), Dallas; 214-744-2936
9560 Skillman St. (Forrest View St.), Dallas; 214-343-0116

Tony Roma's ⊠ | 20 | 21 | 16 | 19 | M |
10310 Lombardy Ln. (Northwest Hwy.), Dallas; 214-902-0443
310 N. Market St. (Ross Ave.), Dallas; 214-748-6959
1075 W. I-20 (bet. Cooper St. & Matlock Rd.), Arlington; 817-467-9797

Uno Chicago Grill ⊠ | 20 | 18 | 15 | 16 | M |
300 Houston St. (2nd St.), Ft. Worth; 817-885-8667

Denver

With some 300 days of sunshine, it's no wonder the "Mile High City" is famous for its outdoorsy appeal. Best is the fall, when the temperatures are mild (in the 50s and 60s) and it's still possible to enjoy spectacular views of the towering Rocky Mountains from one of the city's rooftop patios. The compact city center is entirely walker-friendly and the free 16th Street Mall shuttle, which runs Downtown's one-mile length, is convenient for touring the State Capitol, the renowned Mint, the Art Museum and Larimer Square. Lower Downtown, or LoDo, is home to Coors Field, while just to the west, the Central Platte Valley boasts a bunch of family attractions, such as the Children's Museum and Ocean Journey. Visitors adhering to a strict Downtown itinerary can get by on public transportation (buses and light rail at $1.25 a ride), but you'll need a car to enjoy nearby Rocky Mountain National Park, a ski resort (e.g. Aspen or Vail) or St. Elmo, the well-preserved ghost town 140 miles to the southwest.

ATTRACTIONS

Ratings: Child Appeal, Adult Appeal, Public Facilities, Service, Cost

C	A	P	S	$

Butterfly Pavilion ☺☻ | – | – | – | – | I |
6252 W. 104th Ave. (off US 36), Westminster; 303-469-5441; www.butterflies.org
Filled with thousands of fluttering butterflies, this domed tropical forest in suburban Westminster is fitting for families fascinated by these flitting, flirting winged creatures; it features other invertebrates too – kids can hold a tarantula or Madagascar Hissing Cockroach, or stroke a starfish – plus supplementary presentations by entomologists and other experts; meanwhile, at the just-opened "Shrunk" exhibit, humans live a bug's life, strolling among towering animatronic scorpions, carpenter ants and dragonflies; N.B. newly hatched butterflies are released daily at 12:30 and 3:30.

Children's Museum of Denver | 29 | 20 | 24 | 23 | I |
2121 Children's Museum Dr. (23rd Ave.); 303-433-7444; www.cmdenver.org
■ It's a "great way to spend a rainy afternoon", rave regulars who recommend this "sense-stimulating", "captivating" and "educational" activity emporium, ranked Denver's No. 1 for Child Appeal in this *Survey*;

"divided by age group", the museum has "engaging" nature and community exhibits ("from the fire-truck area to the grocery store") and "great activities in a safe environment"; a section specifically for infants and toddlers "is a treat for the young and a break for the old", while "theme days and learning experiences" make this Platte place "surprisingly adult-friendly"; N.B. available for birthday parties.

City Park

| 20 | 21 | 14 | 11 | $0 |

bordered by E. 17th & E. 26th Aves., Colorado Blvd. & York St.; 720-913-0696; www.denvergov.org

☑ This "spacious" 314-acre expanse that borders the Denver Zoo is "a great place to hang out", affirm festive folks who flock to the "lovely" grounds for "beautiful views of the city and mountains, "lots of amenities" like "good playgrounds", tennis courts, swimming pools, rentable paddleboats, a public golf course and ample "green space" "to picnic"; devotees also deem the "free!" Sunday-evening concerts "a must for any family", though reviewers don't rate the overall facilities and service too highly.

Colorado History Museum ☺☺

| ▽ 20 | 23 | 23 | 23 | I |

1300 Broadway (13th Ave.); 303-866-3682; www.coloradohistory.org

■ Culture vultures consider this Capitol Hill "gem of a museum" "a must for tourists" for its "well-done" and frequently-"changing exhibits" about cowboys, Indians, trappers, miners and pioneers, especially an "enormously detailed Denver diorama" that opens "a wonderful time warp" back to the 19th-century; it's easy to navigate and reminders of the state's more distant past include "enjoyable" displays of prehistoric "dinosaur bones and animals" that certainly "keep the kids' attention."

Coors Field ☺

| 23 | 27 | 26 | 22 | E |

2001 Blake St. (20th St.); 303-762-5437; www.coloradorockies.com

■ This "fabulous" retro-style yet "modern" ballpark sets a "new standard", swoon surveyors who flock to "hip" Lower Downtown to "spend a sunny afternoon" here; seats boast "breathtaking views of the Colorado Rockies", there are multiculti munchies (sushi, soft tacos, calzones) and an on-site brewery, and "almost every hit" is a homer "because of the thin air"; "if the kids get bored", try the playground and interactive area (virtual home-run derby, fantasy-broadcast booth); however, "prices for everything are outrageous", warn wallet-watchers who prefer the "fun, cheap" Rockpile section.

Denver Art Museum ☺☺

| 16 | 25 | 24 | 24 | I |

100 W. 14th Ave. Pkwy. (Bannock St.); 720-865-5000; www.denverartmuseum.org

■ Old Masters don't always appeal to young viewers, but this "wonderful" and "well-thought-out" Capitol Hill neighborhood museum with a "fine" permanent collection and "interesting tours" can be an "exciting family outing", enthuse aesthetes, because it's so "child-friendly"; the array of "amusing" pastimes for kids includes "lots of multimedia exhibits", themed "activity backpacks", "special" weekend programs and hands-on 'Discovery Libraries' – plus, point out partisans, the "excellent" restaurant, Palettes, has a "don't-miss" lunch menu; N.B. kids always get in free, but a printable family pass on the Web site admits grownups gratis.

Denver Botanic Gardens

| 17 | 27 | 24 | 22 | I |

1005 York St. (bet. 9th & 11th Aves.); 720-865-3500; www.botanicgardens.org

■ Of course it's a "beautiful spot to relax", but this "charming" 23-acre, 17,000-species bloomery just west of Cherry Creek aims to stimulate visitors too, with everything "from a tropical rain forest with hundreds of orchids to a rock Alpine garden to a Japanese garden complete with tea house"; families can "spend several hours" at this "fantastic facility", and even though adults may be more charmed, "kids love" the Children's Secret Path, with its tunnels and planting boxes, and "there's lots of space to picnic under the trees" (plus "convenient food kiosks"); N.B. "the summer concerts are not to be missed."

Denver Museum of Nature and Science 😊😊

| 28 | 27 | 25 | 24 | I |

2001 Colorado Blvd. (Montview Blvd.); 303-322-7009; 800-925-2250; www.dmns.org

■ "Eye-popping from the entry on in", this "first-class museum" (voted the city's top attraction in this *Survey*) is equally as appealing to parents as to children, with "so much" "to offer families" spending a few days in Denver en route to the Rockies; you can "go for hours and still only see a small portion" though the "terrific dinosaurs", especially the "colossal T-Rex", are the "main event" for many, there's a lot more to do – including "the wonderful Hall of Life", the Discovery Zone, a "great IMAX theater", a "new top-rated planetarium", the "interactive" Space Odyssey and a host of "always-changing" "special exhibits"; P.S. "knowledgeable guides help you get the most out of your visit."

Denver U.S. Mint 😊

| 20 | 23 | 18 | 19 | $0 |

320 W. Colfax Ave. (bet. Cherokee & Delaware Sts.); 303-405-4761; www.usmint.gov

■ "Show me the money", demand currency-curious correspondents who put in their two cents to call this 1906 plant near the Colorado State Capitol a "can't-miss" activity for kids and adults alike; "well-done" tours led by "great guides" provide "fascinating background" as well as "absolutely irresistible" close-up views of "shiny coins" "being created and pressed" and "streaming off the production lines"; now "if only they would give samples out of their product!"; N.B. no parking available and you must book at least three weeks in advance through your Congressional representative.

Denver Zoo

| 28 | 24 | 22 | 21 | M |

2300 Steele St. (23rd Ave.); 303-376-4800; www.denverzoo.org

■ "How can you go wrong with a zoo?" – it's always a "fun family outing", and at this "underrated gem" next to City Park "you could spend a whole day"; highlights include a new aquarium housing "much more than just fish", a "terrific polar-bear exhibit" and a "don't-miss" gorilla colony, and "children will also love" the carousel, "train rides and sea lion shows"; handily, everything's located within "easy-to-navigate" confines that "won't overwhelm or wear out the family"; P.S. because of ongoing "major construction" "getting around can be a bear."

Ocean's Journey

| 25 | 21 | 20 | 19 | M |

Qwest Park, 700 Water St. (bet. 7th St. & Speer Blvd.); 303-561-4450; www.oceanjourney.org

◪ This million-gallon, three-story aquarium with more than 500 types of "fascinating" "water-loving creatures" aims to "engage kids with the wonders of the ocean" – and supplements the sea stuff with exhibits featuring "playful Bengal tigers" and "flash floods in the mountains" (a "real treat"); devotees dig this "great addition to the downtown area" calling it a "wonderfully thought-out", "first-class" place "for all age groups"; doubters disagree, declaring there's "not enough variety" at this "overpriced" and "geographically inappropriate" fishery.

Rocky Mountain National Park

| – | – | – | – | I |

1000 US 36 (off US 34), Estes Park; 970-586-1206; www.nps.gov/romo
Stunning vistas, snow-capped peaks, glistening lakes and free-roaming 'megafauna' like elk, moose, bighorn sheep and bears await the

outward-bound at this wildly popular year-round destination just 70 miles northwest of Denver; the park offers fly-fishing, camping, cross-country skiing, rafting, hands-on ranger-led presentations for kids (e.g., "Skins and Skulls") and more than 300 miles of hiking trails (some suitable for even the tiniest tykes) – though footsore folks may find a leisurely drive along scenic Trail Ridge Road an easier route to a Rocky Mountain high.

Six Flags Elitch Gardens

27	19	18	16	E

2000 Elitch Circle (Speer Blvd.); 303-595-4386; www.sixflags.com

☑ Convenience is a big plus for this "compact", "mid-size amusement park right near downtown", so thrill-seekers think it's "worth a day's visit", since "kids will delight in" the rides (at the Looney Tunes area for under-54-inchers, "mine couldn't wait to ride the small roller-coaster with his arms in the air") and love the Island Kingdom water park, a real "extra on hot days"; still, grumblers grouse about untidiness and tickets that are "way overpriced" so most parents only grudgingly devote the day; P.S. "get a discount coupon" or save 10 percent by buying tix online to print in advance.

16th Street Mall ☺

12	22	20	19	$0

16th St., from Cleveland to Market Sts.; 303-534-8500;
www.downtowndenver.com

☑ Families who love to shop "can spend hours" roaming I.M. Pei's "funky" pedestrian-only "indoor/outdoor mall", an "urbanized" downtown space incorporating T-shirt and gift boutiques, well-known national retailers at the adjacent shopping and entertainment complex, Denver Pavilions, "some of the best dining" in the city and "horse-drawn carriages on the weekend"; tykes "will like the street performers" while parents in tow appreciate the "pleasant stroll" (and, when young ones fade, the "handy and swift free shuttle service"); those with tiny tots, however, tsk-tsk about the "street kids", "skateboarders and homeless" people who sometimes "make this area unattractive."

State Capitol ☺

14	21	19	16	$0

200 E. Colfax Ave. (Sherman St.); 303-866-2604; www.state.co.us

■ "Climb to the top" of the Capitol's cupola, urge viewfinders who vow it's "worth the trip" to "look out over Denver" and peek at peaks 50 miles away; inside the "beautiful and historic" edifice, modeled on the U.S. Capitol, "friendly docents" discuss its "fabulous" water-themed murals and the "cool rotunda"; in summer, the adjacent Civic Center Park hosts "fun concerts and events" such as the People's Fair ("a highlight"); the area's also "beautiful at Christmas time", since the neighboring City and County Building is always "heavily decorated" with a "great" lighting display.

HOTELS

Ratings: Family Appeal, Rooms, Service, Public Facilities, Cost

FA	R	S	P	$

Brown Palace Hotel

17	20	23	21	$225

321 17th St.; 303-297-3111; 800-321-2599; www.brownpalace.com;
190 rooms, 51 suites

☑ While "kids wouldn't recognize any of the thousands of famous people" who've stayed at this "nostalgic hotel", they'll appreciate that it's "surprisingly nice for families" with "all the amenities you could ask for including car seats and strollers", plus video games for rent, afternoon tea that young girls love and free historical tours on Wednesdays and Saturdays; there are "special events throughout the year for children, including a lavish breakfast with Santa" say holiday travelers, so even if some find it's "not suitable for noisy toddlers", this "legendary" locale still impresses.

Teatro, Hotel

| ▽ | 18 | 24 | 24 | 25 | $225 |

1100 14th St.; 303-228-1100; 888-727-1200; www.hotelteatro.com; 103 rooms, 8 suites

■ It's "a little more upscale and chic than you might imagine for a family vacation", but this "small" boutique across from the Denver Center for the Performing Arts offers some nice touches including a "teddy-bear turndown" with every request for a crib, "rubber-ducky bubble baths", a pet-friendly program and complimentary Range Rover transportation in the downtown area; theater buffs say all the artifacts from theatrical productions that decorate this "lovely hotel" "take you to another world", and the on-site concierge can help you plan a mountain hike or a quick ski trip to Vail.

Westin Tabor Center

| ▽ | 18 | 23 | 23 | 25 | $259 |

1672 Lawrence St.; 303-572-9100; 800-937-8461; www.westin.com; 421 rooms, 9 suites

☑ Adjacent to the 16th St. Mall complex of shops and restaurants, this "predictable" chainster has "several features" enjoyed by the pint-sized set, including its signature 'heavenly beds', in-room refrigerators and complimentary shuttles to area museums and attractions; though some say it's "more of a business hotel than a family" spot, the location means you can walk to Coors Field for a Colorado Rockies baseball game or take a few minutes' drive to Six Flags Elitch Gardens.

Top Family-Friendly Hotel Chains in the Area:

Embassy Suites	Hyatt
Hampton Inn	Residence Inn
Holiday Inn	

See Hotel Chain reviews, starting on page 256.

RESTAURANTS

Ratings: Family Appeal, Food, Decor, Service, Cost

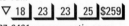

| FA | F | D | S | $ |

Annie's Cafe

| ▽ | 23 | 17 | 16 | 20 | I |

4012 E. Eighth Ave. (Colorado Blvd.); 303-355-8197

■ "One of Denver's best breakfasts" (served all day long) brings in believers to this retro American diner in Hilltop; "kids of all ages" and their chaperones can also slurp "thick milkshakes" and chow down on "don't-miss" chili burgers amid an appealingly "kitschy", "no-glitz" '50s-style atmosphere; a few fume over the "long waits for a table" (the "booths are prime real estate") and urge "get there early."

Casa Bonita

| – | – | – | – | I |

6715 W. Colfax Ave. (Pierce St.), Lakewood; 303-232-5115; www.casabonitadenver.com

Situated in a nondescript Lakewood mini-mall, this Pepto-Bismol-pink play palace draws throngs of kids and their reluctantly cooperative parents into its south-of-the-border-themed innards for cliff-diving theatrics, clowns, caves and caverns, cowboy shoot-outs, magicians and flame jugglers; the wholly average Mexican food is beside the point – although the sopapillas are surprisingly tasty.

Ristorante Piatti

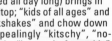

| ▽ | 20 | 24 | 25 | 21 | M |

190 St. Paul St. (2nd Ave.); 303-321-1919; www.piatti.com

■ For "fabulous" rustic food and decor, chic amici attend this "high-end" Cherry Creek Italian; "don't miss bread" accompanies a seasonally changing menu with "enough variation for everyone" (plus a few "surprises"); pizza-loving kids can make their own pies, while their adults can sip from more than 40 wines by the glass; P.S. "try the outdoor patio" in warm weather.

Saucy Noodle
▽ 22 | 20 | 18 | 22 | M

727 S. University Blvd. (Exposition Ave.); 303-733-6977; www.saucynoodle.com

■ "You have to love garlic to go here", say saucy sorts who salute this "family-oriented", "good ol' classic" Italian in upscale Bonnie Brae, where the proprietors "specialize in great" pasta of all shapes and sizes, with or without meat; in this convivial environment, pleased parents point out, it's "so loud" "you can't hear the toddlers scream" – but since "you might have to wait for a table", make sure to bring "back-up snacks" for "hungry kids."

Ted's Montana Grill
▽ 19 | 23 | 23 | 22 | M

1401 Larimer St. (14th St.); 303-893-0654; www.tedsmontanagrill.com

■ Surveyors stampede to media mogul Ted Turner's Larimer Square and Littleton chain links for buffalo – and lots of it; among the "excellent food" are "beautiful burgers" piled high with "enticing toppings", plus "great milkshakes"; it's also "fun for kids to look" around the tavern-like interiors.

White Fence Farm
– | – | – | – | M

6263 W. Jewell Ave. (bet. Sheridan & Wadsworth Blvds.), Lakewood; 303-935-5945; www.whitefencefarm.com

At this working farm-cum-country restaurant in Lakewood, Traditional American family-style poultry dinners are the specialty of the house, which means diners can have their chicken and pet it too – kids can get up close and personal with the animals in the 'O.K. Corral', take a horse-drawn carriage ride, feed the pond's fish or romp on the outdoor playground; during dinner, there's live bluegrass and country music in the Americana Barn; N.B. no reservations.

Zaidy's
▽ 25 | 23 | 18 | 23 | I

121 Adams St. (1st Ave.); 303-333-5336

■ The name means 'Grandpa's', so it's no surprise that this "great" Cherry Creek deli is a "perfect place for toddlers", with "friendly", "family-oriented" servers, crayons at the tables and a kid's menu; there's also a "large selection" of "very decent casual meals" for the older generation (the matzo ball soup is "a must" for cold sufferers); in general, it's "tough to beat", though aesthetes are apathetic about the "nothing-to-write-home-about atmosphere"; N.B dinner Wed.–Fri. only.

RESTAURANT CHAINS

See reviews, starting on page 262.

Ratings: Family Appeal, Food, Decor, Service, Cost

	FA	F	D	S	$
Applebee's 🖼	21	16	17	17	M
410 S. Colorado Blvd. (Virginia Ave.), Glendale; 303-333-0808					
Buca di Beppo 🖼	24	19	22	21	M
1400 Market St. (14th St.); 303-595-3287					
California Pizza Kitchen	21	21	16	19	M
Cherry Creek Mall, 3000 E. First Ave. (Steele St.); 303-388-5686					
Cheesecake Factory 🖼	21	23	21	20	M
Tabor Ctr., 1201 16th St. (Lawrence St.); 303-595-0333					

| 21 | 19 | 18 | 19 | M |

Chili's Grill & Bar ☒
951 16th St. (bet. Champa & Curtis Sts.); 720-904-8822
3625 S. Monaco Pkwy. (bet. E. Hampden Ave. & S. Narcissus Way);
303-691-2928

| 26 | 16 | 21 | 17 | M |

Dave & Buster's ☒
2000 S. Colorado Blvd. (I-25); 303-759-1515

| 22 | 16 | 26 | 18 | M |

Hard Rock Cafe ☒
500 16th St. (Glenarm Pl.); 303-623-3191

| 25 | 17 | 20 | 18 | I |

Johnny Rockets ☒
Cherry Creek Mall, 3000 E. First St. (Milwaukee St.); 303-399-5522
403 16th St. (Tremont Pl.); 303-623-3998

| 22 | 22 | 21 | 22 | M |

Maggiano's Little Italy
500 16th St. (Glenarm Pl.); 303-260-7707

| 25 | 20 | 22 | 20 | I |

Old Spaghetti Factory, The ☒
1215 18th St. (Lawrence St.); 303-295-1864

| 20 | 22 | 18 | 20 | M |

Outback Steakhouse ☒
16301 E. 40th Ave. (Chambers Rd.); 303-576-6633

| 21 | 21 | 19 | 21 | M |

Romano's Macaroni Grill ☒
Cherry Creek Mall, 2500 E. First Ave. (bet. Steele St. & University Blvd.);
303-399-6676

Hawaii

*Hawaii is paradise for kids and adults alike, with most families heading
to the six islands that attract tourism. Visit Oahu for Waikiki Beach
(full of restaurants, high-end shopping and kitsch – Don Ho is still
performing here) as well as Diamond Head Crater, Downtown Honolulu
and the funky surfer town of Waimea, then head to the neighbor
islands for some of the world's most beautiful beaches and other
outdoor adventures. The Big Island awes visitors with its handsome
hotels and still-erupting Kilauea; Maui entices with friendly resort
areas and miles of amazing oceanfront; Kauai is famed for its verdant
beauty plus kayaking, hiking and biking; on tiny Lanai, formerly home
to the world's largest (16,000-acre) pineapple plantation, you'll now
find an upscale haven with just two main luxury hotels, lots of solitude
and great snorkeling; and the least-developed Molokai is, to some, the
most Hawaiian of them all. You won't need a car in walkable Waikiki
(public buses are $2/ride and the tourist trolley offers unlimited use
for $20 per day), but you'll want to rent a vehicle to drive to the
Polynesian Cultural Center and SeaLife Park on Oahu's other side. On
the neighbor islands, a rental is a must.*

ATTRACTIONS

Ratings: Child Appeal, Adult Appeal, Public Facilities, Service, Cost

| C | A | P | S | $ |

| – | – | – | – | $0 |

Akaka Falls State Park
*end of Akaka Falls Rd. (off Mamalahoa Hwy.), Honomu, Big Island;
808-974-6200; www.state.hi.us/dlnr*
Eight miles north of Hilo, just outside of the tiny village of Honomu on the
Big Island, is one of the state's most scenic waterfalls, a free and easy

attraction for the entire family; the comfortable, mile-long, stroller-friendly loop through a rain forest – past bamboo and ginger – leads to the viewpoint, where all the water in the air from the 442-ft. Akaka and nearby Kahuna Falls means there'll probably be plenty of rainbows.

Ala Moana Beach Park

| 24 | 22 | 17 | 14 | $0 |

1201 Ala Moana Blvd. (Piikoi St.), Honolulu, Oahu; 800-464-2924; www.co.honolulu.hi.us

■ Away from the "noisy" part of Waikiki and not far from the Hilton Hawaii Village lies this "paradise" – "one of the best urban beaches in the U.S."; "shade trees", picnic tables, lifeguards and "gorgeous sunsets" delight kids and adults, who also find there are "usually no big waves" here and plenty of space for bike riding, rollerblading and sunbathing – and they can even shop at the Ala Moana Center across the street if they "go early in the day" to beat the "parking challenge."

Aloha Flea Market

| – | – | – | – | I |

Aloha Stadium, 99-500 Salt Lake Blvd. (Kamehameha Hwy.), Aiea, Oahu; 808-732-9611

Most kids are not fans of shopping, but this flea market is more of an outdoor bazaar and carnival, where you'll find a range of interesting food booths, unusual items for sale and old-fashioned barkers urging people to stop and look at their wares; located at the Aloha Stadium, a 30-minute drive from Waikiki, it offers such tempting goods, it's impossible to leave empty-handed, and for 50 cents it's the best two to three hours of entertainment in town, but it's only open on Wednesdays, Saturdays and Sundays, from 6 AM-3 PM.

Atlantis Submarine

| – | – | – | – | VE |

1600 Kapiolani Blvd. (Kaheka St.), Honolulu, Oahu; 808-356-1800
658 Front St. (bet. Dickenson & Prison Sts.), Lahaina, Maui; 808-356-1800
Kailua-Kona Pier (Alii Dr.), Kailua-Kona, Big Island; 808-356-1800
888-349-7888
www.atlantissubmarines.org

If snorkeling, or getting wet, is not your thing, you can still experience the underwater world – just hop aboard one of the submarines in this attraction's fleet, which will take you on an adventure below the surface in high-tech comfort; the trip is expertly narrated as you watch tropical fish and sunken ships, but children must be at least 36 inches tall to board, and claustrophobes may not want to.

Battleship Missouri Memorial ☺

| 18 | 27 | 23 | 23 | M |

Pearl Harbor, Battleship Row (off Kamehameha Hwy.), Honolulu, Oahu; 808-423-2263; www.ussmissouri.com

■ "Put your walking shoes on" for "lots of climbing up ladders" (don't "bring the little ones") at this "must-see", albeit "emotional", site: a 58,000-ton battleship where the "historic signing" of the Japanese surrender brought the end of World War II; "pay the extra money for the guided tour", and come early in the day, since reservations aren't accepted and it gets crowded later on; P.S. post 9-11 security is "much tighter", and backpacks are "no longer allowed."

Bishop Museum ☺

| 20 | 26 | 24 | 23 | M |

1525 Bernice St. (bet. Kalihi St. & Kapalama Ave.), Honolulu, Oahu; 808-847-3511; www.bishopmuseum.org

■ "Capes made of bird feathers" worn by Hawaiian kings, whale bones for "kids to ogle", an "extensive collection" of interesting Hawaiian artifacts, "hands-on" activities for children and plenty of "artistic" pieces to "enthrall" teens and adults "for hours" make this museum "enjoyable" for the "entire family"; a 20-minute drive from Waikiki, it's worth a "half-day visit" (especially on a rainy day), and "don't miss the hula" performances at 11 AM and 2 PM weekdays).

Diamond Head Crater ☺   16 | 24 | 14 | 12 | I
Diamond Head Rd. (18th Ave.), Honolulu, Oahu; 808-971-2525
■ It's worth climbing "endless steps" at Oahu's most famous landmark, because "once you're on top", the "incredible" views of Waikiki make you feel like a Hawaiian god; it's also a "great workout" say fit folks, who advise "wear good sneakers", "get there early" (it opens at 6 AM) to avoid the "humidity", "bring water" and pack a flashlight for the "underground tunnel"; P.S. it's "not stroller-friendly" and "too strenuous for small children."

Fort Derussy Park   23 | 24 | 21 | 19 | $0
Kalia Rd. (Kalakaua Ave.), Honolulu, Oahu; 800-464-2924
■ Believe it or not, there is a park in the middle of Waikiki with not only "a green spot of grass" on the world-famous beach where you can participate in a "potpourri of activities", but also a military family hotel (Hale Koa) and the U.S. Army Museum (plan to spend an hour perusing everything from ancient Hawaiian warfare items to modern-day, high-tech munitions); N.B. better still, you can see the Friday night fireworks over the Hilton Hawaiian Village from here after sundown.

Haleakala National Park ☺☺   18 | 27 | 16 | 17 | I
Park Headquarters Visitor Ctr., Hwy. 378 (off Hwy. 377), Makawao, Maui; 808-572-4400; www.nps.gov/hale
■ Where else can you ascend 10,000 feet "above the clouds" to the top of a dormant volcano?; you may not be able to pronounce it, but reviewers recommend seeing this "awe-inspiring" site, which last erupted in 1790, for "great family hiking" and for tours that take you up for an "unbelievable sunrise" ("frigid" winds and "temperatures in the 30s and 40s" are a shock) followed by a bike ride all the way down; you'll also want to visit the "breathtaking" Oheo Gulch, often mistakenly called Seven Sacred Pools, at the park's other end, accessible via the "winding" Hana Highway – it's got "nature's finest" scenery, but it's "not for the weak of stomach."

Hanauma Bay Nature Preserve ☺   27 | 28 | 21 | 18 | I
7455 Kalanianaole Hwy. (Rte. 72), Oahu; 808-396-4229; www.hanaumabayhawaii.org
■ For nature at its "finest", head to this "Disneyland of snorkeling" 15 minutes from Waikiki, a bay that's like a "fish tank without walls"; "go early" and spend a few hours to appreciate the "abundance of undersea life", "colorful creatures" and "warm water", since it can get hot and "extremely crowded" later on and it's hard to find parking (once the lot is full, you can't get in); keep in mind there's an "arduous walk" back up a "very, very steep" hill; N.B. it's closed on Tuesdays.

Hawaii Maritime Center ☺   – | – | – | – | I
Pier 7 (off Bishop St.), Honolulu, Oahu; 808-536-6373; www.bishopmuseum.org/hmc
Next door to Downtown "Honolulu's iconic Aloha Tower" (which our reviewers rave has "great shopping", "fun places" to eat and "beautiful" spots to "sit and watch the sunset") lies this museum of Hawaii's rich maritime past, with exhibits ranging from the Polynesians' journey to Hawaii 1,500 years ago to a flying mail boat display; plan to spend a couple of hours here, since the kids will love the skeleton of a humpback whale, as well as the Pacific islander sailing canoe moored next door alongside a four-masted schooner.

Hawaii Nature Center/'Iao Valley   17 | 23 | 16 | 12 | I
875 'Iao Valley Rd. (off Rte. 30), Wailuku, Maui; 808-244-6500; www.hawaiinaturecenter.org
■ This "picture-perfect" Maui park, two miles north of Wailuku, offers a "mist-shrouded" mountain jutting up 2,250 feet, "as if aliens placed it

there", a "crystal clear" stream and a thundering waterfall, along with "short, easy paved" trails that are "wheelchair and stroller friendly"; the "quiet" six-plus-acre valley is filled with "gorgeous natural scenery" and is next door to the "entertaining and educational" Hawaii Nature Center ($6 for adults/$4 for children), offering "hands-on" activities for kids.

Hawaii Volcanoes National Park ☺☺

| 22 | 27 | 17 | 18 | I |

Kilauea Visitor Ctr., Crater Rim Dr. (off Hwy. 11), Big Island; 808-985-6000; www.nps.gov/havo

■ A "unique spot on the planet", this park has one of the most popular "natural wonders" in the state: the bubbling, continuously erupting Kilauea volcano where you can see "lava flowing" ("wear good, close-toed shoes" or "they might melt"); going strong after 20 years, it offers a "glimpse into the formation" of the island that's not only "educational for a child" but "a marvel for an adult"; "allot most of the day" and come back after dark or by helicopter to "see the molten stuff pouring into the sea" in a billow of steam.

Honolulu Zoo

| 26 | 20 | 19 | 18 | I |

151 Kapahulu Ave. (Kalakaua Ave.), Honolulu, Oahu; 808-971-7171; www.honoluluzoo.org

■ Put this "excellent" zoo, "geared to the tropics", on the "to-do list", since little ones are "delighted" by the petting arena, the "great elephant encounters", the white monkeys and all the animals that are "so close" it's almost "as if you can touch them"; an "easy walk" from the center of Waikiki and right near Kapiolani Park, this "serene", "shady" spot allows families to wander "at their own pace"; P.S. "don't miss" the 'Zoo by Moonlight Tours' of nocturnal creatures during the full moon.

Iolani Palace ☺

| 12 | 26 | 23 | 23 | M |

King St. (Richard St.), Honolulu, Oahu; 808-522-0832; www.iolanipalace.org

☒ The "only royal palace" in America is something you won't see anywhere else, so take off your shoes (they'll give you soft slippers to protect the koa wood floors) and pad through this "unique slice" of Hawaiian history in Downtown Honolulu, the former home of the ruling Ali'i and the site of the overthrow of Queen Lili'uokalani by the U.S. government in 1893; just "keep a tight rein on the youngsters" because there are "major don't-touch rules" and "irreplaceable artifacts", so it's really "more for adults" and well-behaved preteens and teens.

Kaanapali Beach

| 25 | 26 | 22 | 20 | $0 |

Kaanapali Pkwy. (Nohea Kai Dr.), Kaanapali, Maui; 800-245-9229

☒ "Words can't describe how gorgeous it is" gush guests giddy over this "beautiful" beach fronting several "first-class hotels" (Maui Marriott, Hyatt Regency) as well as the Whaler's Village shopping complex; "turquoise waters", "delightful" white sand and "warm temperatures year round" mean it's "great for kids" and families, but adults may find it "a bit too crowded" and "too Waikiki-like" in high season, though it's very convenient to nearby Lahaina Town and the Sugar Cane Train.

Kauai Children's Discovery Museum

| – | – | – | – | I |

Kauai Village Shopping Ctr., 6458-B Kahuna Rd. (bet. Kawaihau Rd. & Waiakea Rd.), Kapaa, Kauai; 808-823-8222; www.kcdm.org

For rainy days, this enthralling, hands-on learning play center is the answer to every parent's prayers; located in Kapaa, the 7,000-sq.-ft. museum includes interactive exhibits that range from playing Hawaiian musical instruments to participating in virtual-reality television, and there's a toddler area for kids aged four and under; N.B. it's open Tuesday to Saturday (and Mondays during school breaks).

Lahaina-Kaanapali Sugar Cane Train ☺☺

| 23 | 16 | 17 | 19 | M |

975 Limahana Pl. (Honoapiilani Hwy.), Lahaina, Maui; 808-667-6851; 800-499-2307; www.sugarcanetrain.com

■ Preschoolers and train buffs "love" the "fun" 30-minute ride in this "beautifully restored" locomotive pulled by a steam engine, featuring open passenger cars; the 12-mile ride winds through former farms, but there's "no sugar cane along the route between Lahaina and Kaanapali now"; instead you get a conductor who sings and "plays the ukulele", calling out landmarks and making the trip "a hoot" for children, but if you're older than 8, it'll probably be "a real snoozer."

Manoa Falls ☺☺

| – | – | – | – | $0 |

Paradise Park, Manoa Rd., Honolulu, Oahu; 800-464-2924

For a serene setting away from the tourist hordes, this quiet rainforest 15 minutes from Waikiki offers a three-quarter-mile, well-marked (though often muddy) trail, which follows Waihi Stream and meanders through a tropical reserve, past guava trees, mountain apples and wild ginger to an idyllic waterfall; though it's a beautiful respite, the frequently moist and generally humid conditions make perfect breeding grounds for thirsty mosquitoes, so bring insect repellent and don't venture off the steep sides of the footpath.

Maui Ocean Center

| 28 | 25 | 25 | 23 | E |

192 Ma'alaea Rd. (Honoapiilani Hwy.), Ma'alaea, Maui; 808-270-7000; www.mauioceancenter.com

■ An "utterly fascinating", five-acre "kid-friendly" Maui facility, the top Hawaii attraction overall in this *Survey* also has the highest Child Appeal score; it gets parental points for "amazing" varieties of sea life in its Turtle Lagoon and Hammerhead Harbor, digital audio tours, "beautiful coral gardens" and a wonderful setting; plus it's a "great stop for parents with toddlers", so "allow at least a half day" to "enjoy it thoroughly"; P.S. there's an on-site restaurant.

Molokini ☺

| 21 | 27 | 16 | 18 | VE |

located 2½ miles off the southern coast of Maui, Molokini, Maui; 808-270-7383

◪ You'll be near "the tip of a volcano" in the middle of the ocean at this "snorkeling capital" a short boat trip from Maui, where the "unforgettable experience" includes observing an "array of sea life" such as whales, rays, eels, sharks, octopus, etc. – "wow"; but the "possibility of sea sickness" on the "often rough waters" getting to this crater basin dampens the spirits of some swimmers who are further brought down by the "extremely crowded" conditions; N.B. the cost reflects tour price.

Old Lahaina Luau

| 23 | 25 | 24 | 24 | VE |

1251 Front St. (bet. Kapunakea & Kenul Sts.), Lahaina, Maui; 808-661-9633; 800-248-5828; www.oldlahainaluau.com

■ You can't beat the "top-notch" oceanfront location on Maui of this "number one luau in Hawaii", which goes way beyond the "cheesy ones put on by most hotels", instead offering "excellent food", "awesome" entertainment and "authentic" traditional craft demonstrations; young and old enjoy the "grinding of the fresh poi" and the "unearthing of the pig", and better yet, there are "plenty of food options for picky kids" and "delicious" exotic drinks for mom and dad; P.S. it's just a few minutes' drive from the Kaanapali resort hotels, but you must "book well in advance."

Old Lahaina Town
| 17 | 24 | 20 | 19 | $0 |

648 Wharf St. (Canal St.), Lahaina, Maui; 808-667-9193; 888-310-1117;
www.visitlahaina.com

■ Visitors flock to this "delightful old seaport" that dates back to the "wild whaling days" of ancient Hawaii; it's a "charming" town populated with "quaint shops", "terrific restaurants" and "people of all ages" looking for a "fun day of browsing" and "people-watching"; it's just a short drive from Lahaina and parking can be "tough", but stick it out for all the "stuff to do", including visiting the huge "fairy-tale"-ish banyan tree with branches covering nearly an acre – kids will be "magnetized."

Polynesian Cultural Center ☺☺
| 24 | 24 | 24 | 24 | VE |

55-370 Kamehameha Hwy. (Laniloa St.), Laie, Oahu; 808-293-3333;
800-367-7060; www.polynesia.com

☑ "Ya gotta see" this "Epcot of the Pacific", "a living, hands-on" museum of "Polynesian culture" run by the Mormon Church and featuring various island villages, with "educational" demonstrations ("how to harvest and eat a coconut", "lei making") and high-diving performances providing "fun for the whole family"; "spend the entire day" because there's "so much to do" and it's a "long bus ride" or drive (over an hour) from Waikiki; a minority complains, however, that this "Disneyfied" spot is "overpriced."

Sea Life Park
| 27 | 21 | 21 | 21 | E |

41-202 Kalanianaole Hwy. (Makapuu Pt.), Honolulu, Oahu; 808-259-7933;
866-365-7446; www.sealifeparkhawaii.com

☑ "Sea World meets Hawaii" at this attraction that's "definitely geared toward kids" with "great entertainment" that includes performing dolphins and sea lions and "impressive exhibits" such as a sting ray lagoon, a 300,000-gallon aquarium, a seabird sanctuary and a sea turtle area; even the 45-minute "scenic ride" from Waikiki to get here is enjoyable, but a few foes feel it's a "small-scale, wanna-be Marine World" that's too "commercial" with its "trained seals" and "fish tanks."

USS Arizona Memorial ☺
| 16 | 28 | 25 | 24 | $0 |

Pearl Harbor, 1 Arizona Memorial Pl. (off Kamehameha Hwy.),
Honolulu, Oahu; 808-422-0561; www.nps.gov/usar

■ The top-ranked attraction for Adults in this *Survey* is a "poignant", "emotionally charged" "floating memorial" above the sunken battleship *USS Arizona*, bombed by the Japanese on December 7, 1941; first, you'll see a "stunning film", then take a "reflective" ferry ride to the "solemn, spiritual" platform where you "walk on sacred ground", feeling the "magnitude of that fateful day"; just "go early" suggest surveyors, since "lines are long", and keep in mind that any child "under 8 may get antsy and bored"; N.B. security precludes carrying anything onboard.

Waikiki Aquarium
| 25 | 23 | 20 | 21 | I |

2777 Kalakaua Ave. (Kapahulu Ave.), Honolulu, Oahu; 808-923-9741;
waquarium.otted.hawaii.edu

■ Fish fiends find this "hidden treasure" within a short walk of Waikiki's hotels a "comprehensive" collection of marine life "from the central Pacific" (children "love those cuttlefish", the "great jellyfish exhibit" and the monk seal habitat); it's "small" size makes it "easy to manage with kids" and good for a couple of hours' "break from beach activities"; take advantage of the "electronic guides" to make this an "informative", as well as "entertaining", inside view of ocean life.

Waikiki Beach
| – | – | – | – | $0 |

Kalakaua Ave. (bet. Saratoga Rd. & Kapahulu Ave.), Honolulu, Oahu;
877-525-6248

Hawaii's best-known beach, this one-and-a-half-mile crescent of imported white sand (from Molokai) is located at the foot of numerous famous high-rise hotels and attracts an astounding 5 million visitors from around the world each year; a sun-worshipers' mecca of surfing, outrigger canoeing, diving, sailing and snorkeling (all available for rent), it's also got showers, lifeguards, restrooms, historic signage, tiki torch lightings at sunset and, at the Kapiolani Park end, grills and picnic tables; N.B. if you're not staying in Waikiki, park near the Aquarium.

Waimea Canyon State Park

| – | – | – | – | $0 |

Waimea Canyon Dr. (off Hwy. 50), Lihue, Kauai; 808-274-3444
Kauai's version of the Grand Canyon, this great gaping gulch may be smaller – it's only a mile wide, 3,567 feet deep and 12 miles long – but it's equally impressive and a definite don't-miss stop while on the Garden Island; created when a massive earthquake sent all the streams flowing into a single river that carved out this picturesque ravine, Waimea can be viewed swooping in on a helicopter tour, up-close on a hike in the valley or from a roadside viewing area.

Wainapanapa State Park

| – | – | – | – | $0 |

Wainapanapa Rd. (off Hana Hwy.), Hana, Maui; 808-984-8109
Just outside of Hana, after a twisting, 50-mile, barely two-lane highway, sits one of the best nature preserves on Maui – 120 acres of beach park, with picnic tables, barbecue grills, restrooms, showers, an oceanfront trail and a black-sand shoreline; families will love the coastal hikes (mosquitoes are plentiful, so bring insect repellent) and picnicking, but swimming is generally unsafe due to powerful rip currents and strong waves; P.S. to have the place practically to yourself, go on a weekday.

HOTELS

Ratings: Family Appeal, Rooms, Service, Public Facilities, Cost

	FA	R	S	P	$

Fairmont Kea Lani

| 26 | 29 | 26 | 27 | $419 |

4100 Wailea Alanui Dr., Wailea, Maui; 808-875-4100; 800-441-1414; www.fairmont.com; 413 suites, 37 villas
■ This "breathtaking" Wailea all-suite resort gets "high marks across the board" from reviewers impressed with all the "fun activities for kids" (including a huge pool area with slides and bridges); guest quarters "easily accommodate two adults and three kids" and each has a small living room, microwave, refrigerator and DVD player; the oceanside walking path is "great for parents with strollers", there are "quite a few restaurants" to choose from, several world-class golf courses and a tennis center, and guests can arrange a day-trip to Lanai or a mountain bike ride down Haleakala.

Four Seasons Resort Hualalai

| 26 | 28 | 28 | 29 | $540 |

100 Ka'upulehu Dr., Kaupulehu-Kona, Big Island; 808-325-8000; 888-340-5662; www.fourseasons.com; 212 rooms, 30 suites, 1 villa
■ For "an out-of-this-world experience" (with prices to match) this "over-the-top" Big Island resort is "paradise" "for wealthy families", and there's "no better hotel to be a child" given its special programs, water sports, turtle and stingray feedings, kids-only pools and baby-proofed rooms; the quarters have "unbelievable views", the "great golf" pleases serious players and the on-site spa is "divine"; with so "many little extras" for tots, the "only downside is getting here."

Grand Wailea Resort

| 28 | 24 | 24 | 29 | $465 |

3850 Wailea Alanui Dr., Wailea, Maui; 808-875-1234; 800-888-6100; www.grandwailea.com; 728 rooms, 52 suites
■ "Everything is big" at this grand resort – from the "fabulous interconnected pools" with "amazing slides", built-in swim-up bars,

 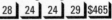

waterfalls and a water elevator to the "spa like no other" – no wonder "there are so many kids and families around"; "the beach, rooms, food and service are all incredible" too, gush guests, and there's "something for everyone" to do with onsite golf, tennis, "lots of restaurant choices" and proximity to tours of Haleakala and drives to Kula.

Hilton Hawaiian Village
26 | 21 | 21 | 25 | $299

2005 Kalia Rd., Honolulu, Oahu; 808-949-4321; 800-774-1500;
www.hilton.com; 2655 rooms, 345 suites

◪ A "city in itself", this "huge" resort, outside the frenetic part of Waikiki, has a "wealth of kids' activities" that makes them "always want to come back": penguin feedings, water sports, fireworks, live music, twilight torch lightings, numerous pools and a large stretch of white-sand beach; onsite shops include a link of the local Lappert's ice cream chain and an outlet of the ubiquitous Hawaii discount store ABC; but a few are "disappointed in the service" and recommend staying in its "superb" Alii or Kalia towers for better rooms.

Hilton Waikoloa Village
28 | 20 | 20 | 27 | $469

425 Waikoloa Beach Dr., Waikoloa, Big Island; 808-886-1234;
800-445-8667; www.hiltonwaikoloavillage.com; 1159 rooms, 57 suites,
25 cabanas

■ "From swimming with the dolphins to a tram ride around the grounds, this is a one-stop family adventure" that's a bit like a "Hawaiian-style Disneyworld"; there's "water, water everywhere", including pools with "slides that kids go nuts for" and lagoons with boats to carry guests from one end of the resort to the other; with nine restaurants, a spa and lots of nearby attractions like petroglyphs and helicopter tours of Hawaii Volcanoes National Park, "children of all ages will love it here."

Hyatt Regency
26 | 23 | 24 | 27 | $385

200 Nohea Kai Dr., Lahaina, Maui; 808-661-1234; 800-233-1234;
www.hyatt.com; 775 rooms, 31 suites

◪ Kids "love the endless pools, waterslides, flamingos and penguins" at this Kaanapali Beach resort just outside Lahaina Town (where they can board an Atlantis Submarine or hop aboard the Sugar Cane Train); there are "exotic animals in the lobby", a "nice beachside walkway with tiki torches that's great for nighttime strolls" and nearby shopping, golf and snorkeling; but a few nitpickers note the "average rooms" and just "adequate dining."

JW Marriott Ihilani Resort & Spa
24 | 27 | 26 | 28 | $354

92-1001 Olani St., Ko Olina, Kapolei, Oahu; 808-679-0079; 800-626-4446;
www.marriott.com; 351 rooms, 36 suites

◪ Get "away from Honolulu" at this "refined" property that's a half-hour drive from Waikiki in a "less familiar part of the island"; there's an "incredible marine program for kids" where they can hold rays and sea anemones, and "one of the best" luaus next door wins family praise, as do the on-site spa, the Ted Robinson–designed golf course and Azul restaurant; even if a few find this one "too far from most of the island's activities", the "sunsets are magical" and sometimes it's "nice to be removed from the hustle and bustle."

Kahala Mandarin Oriental
28 | 26 | 28 | 28 | $350

5000 Kahala Ave., Honolulu, Oahu; 808-739-8888; 800-367-2525;
www.mandarinoriental.com; 932 rooms, 33 suites

■ "Nothing beats the awesome dolphin lagoons" where children can watch the smiling creatures frolicking, and even swim with them, at this "fabulous paradise" just outside of Waikiki that's a "real kid pleaser"; a wading pool, a "beautiful beach", "extremely friendly service" and close proximity to Diamond Head are further draws, and adults looking for pampering can partake of the individual spa suites for luxurious treatments; in short, even at these prices, "what's not to love?"

Marriott Maui Resort & Ocean Club | 25 | 21 | 21 | 23 |$400|

100 Nohea Kai Dr., Lahaina, Maui; 808-667-1200; 800-763-1333; www.marriott.com; 269 rooms, 6 suites

☑ Folks with toddlers in tow find this Kaanapali Beach resort the "perfect destination", since the "kiddie pool has a sandy bottom so little ones can run around without falling on concrete" and there's an inexpensive self-service snack bar with all the essentials for hungry tots; though a few critics complain "rooms have no personality", others nod, sure, it's "not glitzy" here, but it *is* "comfortable and affordable", with a "good beach", a "nice staff" and close proximity to shopping.

Outrigger Waikiki | 23 | 18 | 19 | 20 |$290|

2335 Kalakaua Ave., Honolulu, Oahu; 808-923-0711; 800-688-7444; www.outrigger.com; 514 rooms, 16 suites

☑ The "cheerful family environment" of this hotel "conveniently located right in Waikiki" with "large rooms, beach access" and an "outstanding kids' program" pleases most budget-minded baby-toters who find it a "reasonably priced option" for family fun; but faultfinders fret over the "unappealing exterior", opting "to sleep here only and spend the day out"; N.B. have a meal at the lively Duke's oceanfront restaurant.

Waikoloa Beach Marriott ▽ | 24 | 15 | 21 | 23 |$325|
(an Outrigger Resort)

69-275 Waikoloa Beach Dr., Waikoloa, Big Island; 808-886-6789; 800-922-5533; www.waikoloabeachmarriott.com; 508 rooms, 17 suites, 20 cabanas

☑ Much "less glitzy than its ritzy neighbors", but "more manageable in size", this resort has a "wonderful ambiance" that's "perfect for families"; it has "one of the few swimming beaches on the Kohala Coast", landscaped walking paths, an ancient Hawaiian fishpond, a spa, 36 holes of oceanfront golf and a luau twice a week; but a few say the "nicely redone" rooms are "small."

Westin Maui | 26 | 21 | 22 | 24 |$350|

2365 Kaanapali Pkwy., Lahaina, Maui; 808-667-2525; 800-937-8461; www.westin.com; 731 rooms, 27 suites

☑ You'll have to drag your waterlogged kids out of the "awesome pool area" when it's time for a meal, since they'll clearly be in "heaven" among the "spectacular" slides, waterfalls and lagoons – a good thing, as the "beach is very short and the waves can be choppy"; though this Kaanapali Beach spot is "crowded with lots of tourists" and the rooms feel "cramped", parents can enroll children 5 to 12 years old in the Keiki Kamp for supervised Hawaiian activities; N.B. a brand-new spa debuts in spring 2004.

Top Family-Friendly Hotel Chains in the Area:
Holiday Inn
Ritz-Carlton
See Hotel Chain reviews, starting on page 256.

RESTAURANTS

Ratings: Family Appeal, Food, Decor, Service, Cost

FA	F	D	S	$
–	–	–	–	I

Big Island Grill ⌧

75-5702 Kuakini Hwy. (Hanama Pl.), Kailua-Kona, Big Island; 808-326-1153
Kailua-Kona families flock to this cheerful cafe serving American/local island cuisine, which is always packed from the first cup of coffee at

breakfast to the last bite of dessert at night, due to the great prices, fast service and delicious dishes (not to mention huge servings) of chef Bruce Goold's home cooking; this is *the* place to take the family for dinner for excellent fresh salmon, generous salads and the world's tastiest mashed potatoes.

Cheeseburger in Paradise

24 | 19 | 21 | 18 | M

811 Front St. (Lahainaluna Rd.), Lahaina, Maui; 808-661-4855; www.cheeseburgermaui.com

■ You "can't beat the front-row seat" on the ocean with the "spray on your face" at this spot in the "heart of the hottest town on Maui" (Lahaina) that's got "incredible burgers"; even though the view would be "worth it, even if the food weren't", "cute decor" in a "relaxing atmosphere", "old time" music and a staff that's "very friendly and eager to please" further pull families in; "small children might not like the lines to get in" though, but they can make a racket, since the "happiest customers wear earplugs."

Golden Dragon

20 | 24 | 23 | 25 | E

Hilton Hawaiian Vlg., 2005 Kalia Rd. (Ala Moana Blvd.), Honolulu, Oahu; 808-949-4321; www.hiltonhawaiianvillage.com

■ If you couldn't see Waikiki Beach, you'd swear you were in Hong Kong eating at the finest Chinese eatery say fans of this "yummy" restaurant at the Hilton Hawaii Village that's "quiet and removed from the bustle"; they "accommodate kids very nicely" and serve dishes "family-style", but with local residents celebrating special occasions, it's more of a "grown-up evening" place; P.S. bring your wallet, as prices are "high."

Haliimaile General Store

19 | 26 | 21 | 22 | E

900 Haliimaile Rd. (off Rte. 37), Makawao, Maui; 808-572-2666; www.haliimailegeneralstore.com

◩ "Our favorite spot on Maui" rave fans of this Pacific Rim eatery, the "best place" for a "great meal for the parents" and "low stress" atmosphere for "squirmy kids" (with a "keiki's menu" for the wee ones); off-the-beaten-track in the "remote location" of Haliimaile, it's worth a drive upcountry for the "first-rate" food, from the "freshest fruit" to "the most wonderful wines", but some warn it might be too sophisticated for youngsters.

Hula Grill

24 | 21 | 23 | 21 | I

2435 Kaanapali Pkwy. (off Honoapiilani Hwy.), Lahaina, Maui; 808-667-6636; www.hulagrill.com

■ If eating "on the beach, with shoes off and feet in the sand" sounds like every child's dream, this "casual and inexpensive" Hawaiian eatery in Kaanapali has everything: "great sunset views", "live music" (with an oceanside hula show) and "innovative" cuisine; the menu (everything from the "standard Maui-esque fare of seafood" to "first-class burgers") "caters to both young and old", and you must "save room" for the outstanding "hula pie" (with ice cream, macadamia nuts and chocolate cookie crumbs).

Mama's Fish House

20 | 28 | 25 | 25 | E

799 Poho Pl. (Hwy. 36), Kuau, Maui; 808-579-8488; www.mamasfishhouse.com

■ For the most "delicious Pacific Rim" cuisine (the "best fish I have ever put in my mouth"), it's worth the "search" for this Maui "hidden jewel" that's "not exactly in a convenient location"; penny-pinchers say it "may be too pricey for families" but with "first-class" service, "breathtaking" views of the ocean and a "stunning locale" in a "Hawaiian hut set back on the beach among the coconut trees", others find it an excellent choice.

Maui Tacos

| 22 | 20 | 10 | 16 | I |

275 Kaahumanu Ave. (bet. Kahului Beach Rd. & Wakea Ave.), Kahului, Maui;
808-871-7726
2411 S. Kihei Rd. (Alanui Ke Alii Rd.), Kihei, Maui; 808-879-5005
5095 Napilihau St. (Honoapiilani Hwy.), Lahaina, Maui;
808-665-0222
840 Wainee St. (Lahainaluna Rd.), Lahaina, Maui; 808-661-8883
www.mauitacos.com

■ For "yummy Mexican" food, that's "inexpensive", "healthy" and "fast", head to one of the numerous locations on Maui of chef Mark Ellman's "casual" chain eateries; there's a "kids' menu that kids will like", and adults appreciate the "no mess, no fuss" ("except for eating the taco") at these joints, which are barely more than a take-out counter (with limited eating space), but the "huge servings" keep the place hopping from 9 in the morning to 9 at night.

Merriman's Market Café

| – | – | – | – | M |

Kings Shops, 250 Waikoloa Beach Dr. (off Hwy. 19), Waikoloa, Big Island;
808-886-1700

Here's a lower-cost option to enjoy the Mediterranean cuisine of chef Peter Merriman (owner of Merriman's Restaurant in Waimea, on the Big Island, and Hula Grill on Maui) when you've got the kids in tow, since this boutique market cafe in the Kings' Shops at the Waikoloa Beach Resort has a casual atmosphere, outdoor dining where kids can wander around and plenty of fresh local produce, house-made sausages, artisan-style breads and great cheese and wines for lunch or a light dinner.

OnJin's Cafe 🖼

| – | – | – | – | M |

401 Kamakee St. (Queen St.), Honolulu, Oahu; 808-589-1666

The "secret" is starting to get out about this "lovely little" "boutique" bistro on the edge of Ala Moana that "deserves to be better known"; adults and kids "delight" in its "outstanding" "gourmet" take on traditional Hawaiian "plate lunches" ("the fanciest in town"), while evening eaters enjoy a "totally different dinner menu" of "creative", "delicious" Asian-French fare, all at family-friendly "bargain" prices; P.S. "attentive chef-owner" OnJin Kim is also a trained opera diva who's been known to sing during supper.

Pineapple Room

| 18 | 26 | 22 | 22 | E |

Macy's, Ala Moana Shopping Ctr., 1450 Ala Moana Blvd. (Atkinson Dr.),
Honolulu, Oahu; 808-945-8881; www.alanwongs.com

☑ Here's your chance to sample chef Alan Wong's "delicious" Pacific Rim cuisine, in a "casual" atmosphere that's "more conducive to younger children" than his "upscale" King Street site; located in Macy's in the Ala Moana mall, the "restaurant is beautiful", the "food excellent", and most important – "kids are welcome"; but a few naysayers claim it's not for "fussy eaters", since the "emphasis is on dining" and the "service is not rushed."

Roy's Kahana Bar & Grill 🖼

| 20 | 27 | 23 | 26 | E |

Kahana Gateway Shopping Ctr., 4405 Honoapiilani Hwy. (Hoohul Rd.),
Kahana, Maui; 808-669-6999

■ Not only "outstanding" Pacific Rim cuisine, but also "incredible" service that's "accommodating to toddlers" means it might be "the best meal you'll ever have without getting a babysitter" recount reviewers who relish chef Roy Yamaguchi's "elegant" Kahana location "overlooking the water"; "Key West" decor and "multiple-course kids' meals" that'll "keep them busy the entire time" (don't worry, they also have the "obligatory plain pasta and butter on hand") allow parents to "enjoy their dining experience" with "one of the West's best" cooks.

Sansei Seafood Restaurant & Sushi Bar

17	24	18	20	E

The Kapalua Shops, 115 Bay Dr. (Bay Rd.), Kapalua, Maui;
808-669-6286
Kihei Town Ctr., 1881 S. Kihei Rd. (Waimahainai St.), Kihei, Maui;
808-879-0004
Restaurant Row, 500 Ala Moana Blvd. (South St.), Honolulu, Oahu;
808-536-6286
www.sanseihawaii.com

■ "Fantastic sushi" and "amazing" Japanese food with "very kid-friendly" servers in a "comfortable" environment give chef D.K. Kodama's restaurants (two on Maui and one on Oahu) the "thumbs up"; they can be "a little pricey", so our readers recommend looking for early-bird discounts ("half-price" sushi), but be prepared to wait in line, and bring earplugs, since the music is "loud enough to muffle" even the loudest tantrum.

Side Street Inn

–	–	–	–	M

1225 Hopaka St. (Piikoi St.), Honolulu, Oahu; 808-591-0253

Though some say it's "more a bar than a restaurant", this laid-back Ala Moana "hole-in-the-wall" works for families because it's "known for" "simple", "out-of-this-world" Hawaiian "comfort food" at "bargain prices" and is "especially" "popular for its" "delicious" "fried pork chops", "the house specialty", as well as "very good blackened ahi" and "surprising chicken katsu"; you know you're avoiding the tourist scene when you come to this "always-busy favorite" of "in-the-know" "local folks", since it's also "frequented" by some of "Hawaii's greatest chefs", who "can be found" "hanging out" and "feasting" "when off-duty."

Zippy's

25	18	11	18	I

Kapalama Shopping Ctr., 1210 Dilingham Blvd. (Kohou St.), Honolulu, Oahu;
808-832-1750 🅢
666 N. Nimitz Hwy. (Pacific St.), Honolulu, Oahu; 808-532-4205
1725 S. King St. (bet. McCully & Punahou Sts.), Honolulu, Oahu; 808-973-0877
4134 Waialae Ave. (Hunakai St.), Honolulu, Oahu; 808-532-4205
www.zippys.com

■ The "Denny's of Hawaii", this "very popular family" restaurant chain, at a "multitude of locations" on Oahu, serves "sort-of-fast" "casual island food" at "decent prices" (and is a "local favorite" where you probably "won't see another tourist"); "perfect" for "kids of any size or age" and open "all hours", this is the place to go for a "fantastic value" on a "large selection" of items (chili, plate lunches, chocolate shakes).

RESTAURANT CHAINS

See reviews, starting on page 262.

Ratings: Family Appeal, Food, Decor, Service, Cost

	FA	F	D	S	$

Benihana 🅢

	FA	F	D	S	$
	23	20	18	22	E

Hilton Hawaiian Vlg., 2005 Kalia Rd. (Ala Moana Blvd.), Honolulu, Oahu;
808-955-5955

Bubba Gump Shrimp Co. 🅢

	FA	F	D	S	$
	24	18	23	20	M

75-5776 Alii Dr. (off Kuakini Hwy.), Kailua-Kona, Big Island; 808-331-8442
889 Front St. (Papalaua St.), Lahaina, Maui; 808-661-3111
Ala Moana Shopping Ctr., 1450 Ala Moana Blvd. (Piikoi St.), Honolulu, Oahu;
808-949-4867

Buca di Beppo 🅢   24 | 19 | 22 | 21 | M
1030 Auahi St. (Ward Ave.), Honolulu, Oahu; 808-591-0800

California Pizza Kitchen 🅢   21 | 21 | 16 | 19 | M
Pearlridge Center, 98-1005 Moanakea Loop (Rose Rd.), Aiea, Oahu; 808-487-7741
1450 Ala Moana Blvd. (bet. Atikinson Dr. & Piikoi St.), Honolulu, Oahu; 808-941-7715
Kahala Mall, 4211 Waialea Ave. (Kilauea Ave.), Honolulu, Oahu; 808-737-9446

Cheesecake Factory 🅢   21 | 23 | 21 | 20 | M
Royal Hawaiian Shopping Ctr., 2301 Kalakaua Ave. (Dukes Ln.), Honolulu, Oahu; 808-924-5001

Chili's Grill & Bar 🅢   21 | 19 | 18 | 19 | M
Pearl Ridge Mall, 98-130 Pali Momi St. (Rte. 99), Aiea, Oahu; 808-484-2900
2350 Kuhio Ave. (Walina St.), Honolulu, Oahu; 808-922-9697
4211 Waialae Ave. (Hunakai St.), Honolulu, Oahu; 808-738-5773

Chuck E. Cheese's 🅢   26 | 10 | 17 | 13 | I
820 W. Hind Dr. (Kalaianaole Hwy.), Honolulu, Oahu; 808-373-2151
850 Kam Hwy. (Waimano Home Rd.), Pearl City, Oahu; 808-455-1448

Hard Rock Cafe 🅢   22 | 16 | 26 | 18 | M
1837 Kapiolani Blvd. (Kalakaua Ave.), Honolulu, Oahu; 808-955-7383
900 Front St. (Papalaua St.), Lahaina, Maui; 808-667-7400

Old Spaghetti Factory, The 🅢   25 | 20 | 22 | 20 | I
1050 Ala Moana Blvd. (bet. Kamakee St. & Ward Ave.), Honolulu, Oahu; 808-591-2513

Original Pancake House, The 🅢   24 | 22 | 12 | 17 | I
1221 Kapiolani Blvd. (Pensacola St.), Honolulu, Oahu; 808-596-8213
1414 Dillingham Blvd. (Waiakamilo Rd.), Honolulu, Oahu; 808-847-1496

Outback Steakhouse 🅢   20 | 22 | 18 | 20 | M
Coconut Grove Mktpl., 75-5809 Alii Dr. (off. Hualalai Rd.), Kailua-Kona, Big Island; 808-326-2555
Kahana Gateway Shopping Ctr., 4405 Honoapiilani Hwy. (Hoohul Rd.), Kahana, Maui; 808-665-1822
1765 Ala Moana Blvd. (Hobron Ln.), Honolulu, Oahu; 808-951-6274
6650 Kalanianaole Hwy. (Portlock Rd.), Honolulu, Oahu; 808-396-7576

Planet Hollywood 🅢   24 | 13 | 24 | 16 | M
ANA Kalakaua Ctr., 2155 Kalakaua Ave. (Beach Walk), Honolulu, Oahu; 808-924-7877

Ruby's 🅢   24 | 19 | 20 | 19 | I
275 W. Ka'ahumanu Ave. (bet. Kahului Rd. & Wakea Ave.), Kahului, Maui; 808-248-7829

T.G.I. Friday's 🅢   21 | 17 | 18 | 17 | M
2058 Kuhio Ave. (bet. Namahana & Olohana Sts.), Honolulu, Oahu; 808-942-8443
950 Ward Ave. (S. King St.), Honolulu, Oahu; 808-524-8443

Tony Roma's 🅢   20 | 21 | 16 | 19 | M
1819 S. Kihei Rd. (Waimahaihai St.), Kihei, Maui; 808-875-1104
1972 Kalakaua Ave. (bet. Keoniana & Pau Sts.), Honolulu, Oahu; 808-942-2121
4230 Waialae Ave. (Hunakai St.), Honolulu, Oahu; 808-735-9595

Houston

If space is the final frontier, then it's fitting that expansive Houston, the nation's energy capital, is the powerhouse launching pad for NASA. Like Caesar's Gaul, the city is divided into three parts: Downtown, the Museum District south of Downtown and the thriving Galleria shopping and business center to the west. Free trolleys make frequent stops around Downtown; the MetroRail ($1/ride) cruises between Downtown and the Reliant Park sports venues via the Museum District (hop off here to blow kids' minds with the Menil Collection's Surrealist masterworks). Bus service, though difficult to navigate, is also available; however, this being Texas, a car makes the most sense: the Children's Museum, the Museum of Natural Science and the Hermann Park Zoo, Downtown's Minute Maid Park and theaters, and the Space Center to the south toward Galveston Bay are spread out all over. Many sites, such as George Ranch in Richmond, the San Jacinto Battleground and the USS Texas in La Porte, and Splashtown Houston in Spring are short drives out of town, as is Galveston, the Gulf of Mexico island, with its beaches, Victorian homes and historic port. Summers are hot and humid, but Gulf winds keep winters warm (around 50 degrees) for outdoor barbecue or Tex-Mex chowdowns.

ATTRACTIONS

Ratings: Child Appeal, Adult Appeal, Public Facilities, Service, Cost

C	A	P	S	$

Bayou Bend
Collection and Gardens 😊😊

12	26	25	22	I

1 Westcott St. (Memorial Dr.); 713-639-7750; www.mfah.org/bayoubend
🔲 The "historical home" of Houston's famed Hogg family, this stately, "splendid adjunct of the Museum of Fine Arts" in River Oaks gives a "true sense of the past in the South" via its 28 "beautiful" period rooms filled with antiques; it's a real "treat in the spring" when "azaleas are blooming" in the "immaculately kept", "gorgeous gardens"; while the only thing that "bored" young kids like is "the suspended walking bridge over the bayou" and the "wide-open lawn" to "run around in", adults get their half-day's worth; N.B. weekday tours require reservations.

Children's Museum of Houston

29	21	25	23	I

1500 Binz St. (La Branch St.); 713-522-1138; www.cmhouston.org
■ Respondents rhapsodize about this "fantastic", "entertaining and educational" museum, voted the city's No. 1 for Child Appeal in this *Survey*; its "plethora of hands-on activities" invite youngsters to "stay for hours" "exploring their creative side" while "experiencing history, culture and science"; "even the youngest babies can enjoy" the "brightly colored" Tot Spot (where "bigger kids aren't allowed"), and everyone loves the backyard's "water fountain complete with rubber ducks"; furthermore, the staff and "friendly volunteers" "do an amazing job"; the only flaw: it needs "more food options"; N.B. free admission on Thursday evenings.

Downtown Aquarium

–	–	–	–	I

410 Bagby St. (bet. Prairie & Preston Sts.); 713-223-3474; www.downtownaquarium.com
For an undersea adventure in the middle of Downtown, troll the waters at this small aquarium where the fishies adorn a mock oil rig, a faux sunken temple and a make-believe shipwreck; wanna-be divers dig man-handling manta rays in the hands-on section and boarding the little train that chugs safely through a glass tunnel in the shark den; after

ogling the Louisiana alligators and the Amazonian frogs, hook a bite at the restaurant surrounded by tanks chock-full of deep-sea denizens.

George Ranch Historical Park 😊😊 | 26 | 25 | 24 | 24 | I |

10215 FM 762 (Smithers Lake Rd.), Richmond; 281-343-0218; www.georgeranch.org

■ Kiddie cowpokes "can 'feel' the Old West" at this 'living history museum' 30 minutes southwest of Houston; among the "amazing" reenactments of "how early Texans lived and played" are "cowboys explaining how they herd cattle and why their horses are such an asset" and "people dressed in period clothing using period cooking materials" to prepare historically accurate food; if you ask questions, the "great staff" will "give you a lot of information", making a visit here a "wonderful way to spend a day."

Hermann Park | 25 | 24 | 22 | 17 | $0 |

Fannin St. (Hermann Dr.); 713-524-5876; www.hermannpark.org

■ "The city just spent a bundle to renovate" this mid-metropolis "oasis" and the results are "wonderful", so bring a picnic basket and "spend the day"; there's a "nice golf course", "romantic" McGovern Lake (kids under 12 can fish – bring your own pole), a $2 mini-train "that's a guaranteed winner for 3- to 6-year-olds", playgrounds with "age-appropriate jungle gyms", and "excellent operas, ballets" and concerts at the free outdoor theater; sadly, this "clean", "peaceful" park is often "underutilized", since it's "hot, hot, hot in the summer."

HOUSTON MUSEUM OF NATURAL SCIENCE 😊😊 | 26 | 27 | 26 | 22 | I |

Hermann Park, 1 Hermann Circle Dr. (San Jacinto St.); 713-639-4629; www.hmns.org

■ "Where else can mom gawk at diamonds, the kids chase butterflies and dad listen to rock music while staring at the stars?" – this Hermann Park heavyweight, which voters named Houston's No. 1 attraction in this *Survey*, exudes a "cool geek" vibe via its "top-notch planetarium", "world-class dinosaur exhibit", "captivating" hall of gems and minerals and immense IMAX; the "standout", however, is the "unbelievable" "greenhouse/tropical forest" that "captures the imagination" with its swarms of butterflies that will "land on your clothing"; naturally, weekends bring "longer lines and tons of people."

Houston Zoo, The 😊😊 | 28 | 25 | 23 | 21 | I |

Hermann Park, 1513 N. MacGregor Dr. (bet. Fannin St. & Holcombe Blvd.); 713-533-6500; www.houstonzoo.org

■ "Lions and tigers and bears, oh my"– at this "appealing" natural-habitat zoo in Hermann Park it's "easy to see the animals, who look happy in their homes"; the kids will have "a blast" at the "innovative" children's area, which "provides plenty of hands-on" activities and "close-up adventures"; meanwhile, practical parents point out, "the size is great" – "big enough to be interesting, small enough for a fun afternoon" – and "you can bring your own food and drinks, a big plus."

John P. McGovern Museum of Health & Medical Science, The 😊 | 25 | 23 | 24 | 23 | I |

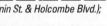

1515 Hermann Dr. (La Branch St.); 713-521-1515; www.mhms.org

■ "Learning biology was never so much fun" say surveyors smitten with this science pavilion, an affiliate of the Texas Medical Center and a "great place to spend a rainy day"; "larger-than-life-size" interactive displays that reveal all about the human body make anatomical adventures both "fun" and "educational", while a "kid-friendly" environment encourages youngsters to "become more familiar with their five senses"; proponents prescribe a visit to this "deserving" "real sleeper" to invigorate "the science geek in you."

Minute Maid Park 😊😊
| 23 | 26 | 27 | 22 | E |

501 Crawford St. (bet. Prairie St. & Texas Ave.); 713-259-8000; www.houstonastros.com

■ Formerly known as Enron Field (but rechristened two years ago), this home of the Astros is a "sparkling", "state-of-the-art" "showpiece"; its most "unbelievable modern marvel" is the retractable roof (a game can "start indoors on a hot summer day and end under the clear night sky"), but other "neat features" include an antique-style "train that goes back and forth" and a "top-notch children's play area"; wallet-watchers warn "eat before you go" – "concessions are a bit pricey"; N.B. kids 14 and under can get outfield seats for just $1.

Museum of Fine Arts 😊
| 13 | 28 | 27 | 23 | I |

1001 Bissonnet St. (Montrose Blvd.); 713-639-7300; www.mfah.org

■ There's "art for days" at this "newly renovated" Downtown complex, an "excellent facility" with a "fantastic", "widely varied" collection; it's "worth seeing", even for "children who tend to get bored", because the institution attracts "spectacular" traveling exhibits ("the one on the Impressionists was outstanding"); when paintings pale, take a "walk through the colorful and unusual tunnel" "between the buildings" – or come instead on Sundays, when families can make their own artworks; N.B. kids with a public library card get in gratis on weekends, while Thursdays are free for everyone.

Orange Show Center for Visionary Art 😊😊
| ▽ 26 | 22 | 17 | 15 | I |

2401 Munger St. (Gulf Fwy.); 713-926-6368; www.orangeshow.org

☑ Orange you glad this "quirky", "offbeat" installation of 'visionary art' is here? query connoisseurs who celebrate "eccentricity in Houston at last"; a visit to this "welded bunch of stuff" – folk artist Jeff McKissack's wacky, mazelike architectural tribute to his favorite fruit – allows you to "gaze on one man's passion"; "kids should love it", and even those who consider this "truly unique American experience" "weird" or "insane" have to marvel at "the things you can do with junk"; N.B. open weekends in spring and fall, plus Wednesday–Friday mornings in summer, and closed mid-December–mid-March.

Reliant Park
| – | – | – | – | M |

South Loop I-610 (bet. Fannin & Kirby Sts.); 832-667-1400; www.reliantpark.com

Houstonites and visitors alike rely on this multi-venue mega-park south of Downtown for rip-roaring good times of all kinds on a revolving round-up of sports and entertainment; from outdoor festivals in the Park to the Center's auto and gem shows, the Astrodome's marching-band battles, the circus and *Sesame Street Live* in the Arena, and Texan touchdowns or bucking rodeo broncos in the Stadium, the goings-on get big, big, bigger, and so does the fun; check the online calendar to see what's happening when you're in town.

San Jacinto Battleground State Historical Complex 😊
| 18 | 21 | 18 | 18 | $0 |

3523 Battleground Rd. (Monument Rd.), La Porte; 281-479-2431; www.tpwd.state.tx.us

■ "A great place for a picnic and a Texas history lesson", this state park east of Downtown commemorates a decisive 1836 battle against then-governing Mexico; "take the ride to the top of the monument", a stone column with an observation area 489 feet above ground, or check out the museum in its base for a 35-minute video about the event; occasional historical reenactments help bystanders "remember the Alamo" – or "kids can just run and play" and "enjoy the day"; N.B. the *U.S.S. Texas* battleship is a three-minute drive away.

Six Flags AstroWorld 😊😊

28	20	19	17	VE

9001 Kirby Dr. (W. Bellfort St.); 713-799-8404; www.sixflags.com

☑ With a "water park included in the admission price", summer-fun seekers willingly "cough up the dough" to cavort in this "standard Six Flags park", located "in the heart of the city"; "there's plenty for all to do" – a "great kids' area" (with an 1895 wooden carousel), "good live performances" and "some of the scariest roller coasters around"; still, veterans warn, "be prepared to walk a lot" and stand in lines that are often "unbearable" ("if you like to queue, this is the place for you").

Space Center Houston 😊

26	25	24	22	E

1601 NASA Rd. 1 (bet. Kings Park Ln. & Point Lookout Dr.); 281-244-2100; www.spacecenter.org

☑ "Calling all astronauts": Mission Control is the gravitational center of this "tourist highlight" where the "combination of interactive displays, movies and tours" offers "plenty to last the whole day"; over-the-moon boosters believe the site's "terrific" for "older children", who can "explore the various ships", "take a simulated flight, sample some space food", touch a moon rock and "try landing the shuttle" via video game; the alienated blast it as "nothing more than an overpriced theme park", so "commercialized" and "uninspired" it ends up being "kind of a letdown."

Splashtown Houston 😊😊

28	22	19	19	E

21300 I-45 N. (Louetta Rd.), Spring; 281-355-3300; www.sixflags.com

☑ This "standard water park" is a "can't-miss" "for a hot summer day"; naturally, "everyone else thinks so too", so you'll stand in line for the "nice rides", slides, chutes and floats ("some are pretty scary") that are "fun for all ages"; adults who have had their fill of "screaming kids" can "turn them (reasonably) loose, knowing they will be supervised" and then "go sit under a tree with an outrageously overpriced drink"; N.B. get a 10 percent discount when you buy tickets via the Web site.

USS Texas 😊

24	25	19	19	I

(aka Battleship Texas State Historic Site)

3527 Battleground Rd. (Monument Rd.), La Porte; 281-479-2431; www.tpwd.state.tx.us

■ "When visiting the San Jacinto Monument, take time to tour the Iron Lady" right nearby; "it is truly a learning experience" to explore this "great, historical" 34,000-ton battleship, which saw action in both world wars; if you plan to see the whole "wonderful" craft, prepare for a "workout" and be forewarned – it's "fun when the weather is nice", but in the August heat you may "feel like you're going to smother inside"; P.S. "off-limits areas" can be seen on a guided "hard-hat" outing for an extra fee.

HOTELS

Ratings: Family Appeal, Rooms, Service, Public Facilities, Cost

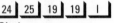

FA	R	S	P	$

Four Seasons

18	26	26	26	$330

1300 Lamar St.; 713-650-1300; 800-332-3442; www.fourseasons.com; 289 rooms, 115 suites

■ The "surprisingly family-friendly" vibe attracts parents with preteens to this luxury outpost close to the museum and theater districts, since the signature service means "they're very accommodating with everything from pull-out couches to cribs on rollers", and you can get a child-proof room, playpens, complimentary diapers, and use of toys, books and video games; it's a 15-minute drive to Hermann Park, the Zoological Gardens and Six Flags AstroWorld.

Houstonian, The
20 | 24 | 27 | 28 | $315

111 N. Post Oak Ln.; 713-680-2626; 800-231-2759; www.houstonian.com; 280 rooms, 8 suites

■ A "comfortable and relaxed" vacation can be had at this "high-service" resort in a wooded setting five miles from bustling Downtown; the lobby sports a 30-ft. hand-carved stone fireplace, and shoppers enjoy complimentary town car service to the Galleria (two miles away); with five tennis courts, two open-air pools, a full-service spa, a huge fitness facility, a climbing wall and access to the Red Stone Golf Club, "there are so many activities for each age" group, it'll be hard getting out to see area attractions.

JW Marriott
∇ 17 | 19 | 18 | 20 | $289

5150 Westheimer Rd.; 713-961-1500; 800-228-9290; www.marriott.com; 508 rooms, 6 suites

■ There's "easy access" to a host of attractions at this property "across from the Galleria", though you'll have to drive to most of them (the museum district is six miles from the hotel, while within eight miles are Minute Maid Park and Six Flags AstroWorld); there are indoor and outdoor pools, and some rooms have refrigerators and full kitchens available – "ideal for children" – plus, the property is one of several area Marriotts that offer packages including accommodations and tickets to the Space Center, 30 miles away.

Warwick, The
∇ 16 | 22 | 22 | 22 | $189

5701 Main St.; 713-526-1991; 800-298-6199; www.warwickhotelhouston.com; 234 rooms, 74 suites

◩ The location "adjacent to the entire museum district" – "within walking distance of Hermann Park, the Houston Zoo and the Museum of Natural Science" – makes this "nice old hotel" (built in 1925) a great option for families; "try to spend a day or two without a car" and stroll everywhere, or take the complimentary van to anything within a few miles, advise parents, who admit there's not a lot for kids within the hotel aside from impressive views.

Top Family-Friendly Hotel Chains in the Area:

Embassy Suites	Hyatt
Hampton Inn	Marriott
Holiday Inn	Residence Inn
Homewood Suites	Westin

See Hotel Chain reviews, starting on page 256.

RESTAURANTS

Ratings: Family Appeal, Food, Decor, Service, Cost

FA | F | D | S | $

Américas ⊠
– | – | – | – | E

The Pavilion, 1800 Post Oak Blvd. (bet. San Felipe St. & Westheimer Rd.); 713-961-1492; www.cordua.com

The South American menu at Michael Cordua's Galleria-area "crown jewel" has much in common with its "less pricey cousin, Churrascos" (including the "mouthwatering" steaks), but there's a high "wow factor" for both adults and children due to its "amazing decor" (like a "tree house in the middle" of a "rainforest on acid"); there's also "superior service" for young and old as well as "solid seafood" options (the "corn-crusted snapper is a must").

Aquarium
| 26 | 17 | 27 | 18 | M |

Downtown Aquarium, 410 Bagby St. (Preston St.); 713-223-3474; www.downtownaquarium.com

☑ "If your kids don't eat fish, they can eat *with* fish" at this "out-of-this-world", undersea "fantasyland" in the Downtown Aquarium complex where "the lights, colors and motion" from the "huge, mesmerizing tanks" "keep even the busiest youngster entertained"; you might not be amused by "crummy" surf-and-turf cuisine ferried by "well-meaning but unimpressive staff", but a "very special kid's dessert" will top off your "enthralled" small fry's "fun."

Azuma
| – | – | – | – | E |

5600 Kirby Dr. (Nottingham St.); 713-432-9649; www.azumajapanese.com

When you have a hankering for "hyper-fresh, delicious raw fish", "inventive rolls" and (perhaps more kid-pleasing) "authentic" robata dishes cooked over an open-fire grill, head to this Japanese spot near the Rice Village; growing teens will gravitate to "their specialty – the hot-rock beef" (kobe steak that "you cook" yourself "on what looks like a heated pet rock"); while the atmosphere within the "Asian-chic interior" is "fun" for all, some surveyors complain that "the service lags behind the food."

Café/Pâtisserie Descours ⧄
| – | – | – | – | M |

1330 Wirt Rd. (Westview Dr.); 713-681-8894

This "quaint" "neighborhood" Spring Branch spot manned by a "friendly, engaging staff" is actually two venues in one: the cafe serves "good French bistro cooking" for a "casual night out", while children prefer the "adjacent bakery" "specializing in desserts" that are "scrumptious", "dreamy" and "over-the-top" ("especially the scones, chocolate croissants" and "special orange rolls") – you can also grab a "tasty" sandwich here for one of the "best quick" lunches in town.

Daily Review Café
| – | – | – | – | M |

3412 W. Lamar St. (Dunlavy St.); 713-520-9217; www.dailyreviewcafe.com

"Hidden away on a River Oaks side street", this "stylish and clever" New American "gem" may be "hard to find", but "in-the-know" folks feel it's "worth the search" for a "creative", "ever-changing menu" of kid-friendly "chicken-pot-pie comfort food" that's "taken up a notch" to please adults as well; an "interesting wine list", a "pretty patio" and a "friendly staff" also help make it "a staple" for brunch, lunch or dinner.

Goode Co. Hamburgers & Taqueria
| 23 | 23 | 17 | 20 | I |

4902 Kirby Dr. (Westpark Dr.); 713-520-9153; www.goodecompany.com

■ "This ain't no fancy spot", but for "a great selection of Tex-Mex and burgers", plus "rich chocolate-cinnamon shakes", lead your posse into this West University "down-home" favorite where big folks slip bottles of "beer from iced tubs" "into their back jeans pockets" as they "stand in line to order", the counter "service is quick and efficient", "children love the courtyard" to "throw coins in the fountain" and if it's "rustic, hey, so are your kids" – one warning: your group will get "*muy gordo*" here.

Goode Co. Texas BBQ
| 24 | 27 | 21 | 20 | I |

8911 Katy Frwy. (Campbell Rd.); 713-464-1901
5109 Kirby Dr. (bet. Bissonnet St. & Westpark Dr.); 713-522-2530
www.goodecompany.com

■ "Go through the cafeteria line" at these "laid-back" joints, and you'll end up with "some of Houston's best barbecue"; the double-decker, colonnaded Katy Freeway facade is a might impressive, while West U is "basically a barn" with "picnic tables outside", but the "small" insides filled with "stuffed buffalo" are "soooo Texas", as are

 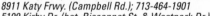

the "bargain prices" and "damn good" grub, including "out-of-this-world pecan pie" served lickety-split for an "ideal" meal for "rambunctious kids" "of all ages."

Mama Ninfa's
21	20	18	19	M

8353 Gulf Frwy. (Howard Dr.); 713-943-3183
3601 Kirby Dr. (Southwest Frwy.); 713-520-0203
2704 Navigation Blvd. (bet. Delano & Nagle Sts.); 713-228-1175
1650 Post Oak Blvd. (San Felipe St.); 713-623-6060
www.mamaninfas.com

☑ "*Delicioso*" declare amigos of this "Tex-Mex haven", a "happy" chain of cantinas dotting Houston where the "friendly staff" "provides crayons and place mats to color on" and tots "have fun looking at the walls" filled with Old West pictures; locals insist that Navigation Boulevard's "original is the real enchilada", though fajita fans feel all four locations convenient to tourist attractions are "decent" "for an easy meal with the kids" – "need a parent say more?"

Pico's Mex-Mex
∇ 19	24	18	18	M

5941 Bellaire Blvd. (Renwick Rd.), Bellaire; 713-662-8383;
www.picos.net

■ For "*fabuloso*" regional Mexican fare, such as *tikin xik* (snapper fillet char-broiled in banana leaves) and other specialties of the Yucatan, this long-standing Bellaire spot near the Galleria that's run by a "pleasant, courteous staff" is a popular local choice; "families enjoy" the casual ambiance, particularly outside near "the large fountain on the patio" or when the musicians strike up *la música*; N.B. on Mondays and Tuesdays, kids' plates are only 99 cents.

Tokyohana Grill & Sushi Bar
∇ 15	22	20	20	M

3239 Southwest Frwy. (Buffalo Spdwy.); 713-838-9560

■ Though adults may appreciate the "good sushi", it's the "chefs cooking at your table" Benihana-style who make this West U Japanese a "favorite" family experience; they're "extra friendly" to your small samurai, and while it's more "suitable for older kids than toddlers", it's "a great way to keep everyone entertained while dinner is being prepared."

Tony Mandola's Gulf Coast Kitchen
–	–	–	–	E

River Oaks Ctr., 1962 W. Gray St. (McDuffie St.); 713-528-3474;
www.tonymandolas.com

A "neighborhood favorite", this "casual, comfortable", "convivial Cajun-Italian" seafooder in River Oaks "inspires loyalty" with "incredibly fresh and beautifully prepared fish", "lovely oysters", "delicious crab" and "New Orleans–style po' boys" that kids'll love; the "attentive" and "knowledgeable" waiters treat everyone like "a member of the extended Mandola family" – in short, it's a "real Gulf Coast experience."

RESTAURANT CHAINS

See reviews, starting on page 262.

Ratings: Family Appeal, Food, Decor, Service, Cost

FA	F	D	S	$

Benihana ⊠
23	20	18	22	E

1318 Louisiana St. (Polk St.); 713-659-8231
Pinecroft Town Ctr., 1720 Lake Woodlands Dr. (Six Pines Dr.),
The Woodlands; 281-292-0061
9707 Westheimer Rd. (Gessner Rd.); 713-789-4962

California Pizza Kitchen ☒   21 | 21 | 16 | 19 | M
Memorial City Shopping Ctr., 303 Memorial City Way (off Katy Frwy.);
713-365-9473
1705-A Post Oak Blvd. (San Felipe St.); 713-963-9262

Cheesecake Factory ☒   21 | 23 | 21 | 20 | M
The Galleria, 5015 Westheimer Rd. (S. Post Oak Rd.); 713-840-0600

Chili's Grill & Bar ☒   21 | 19 | 18 | 19 | M
Galleria Shopping Ctr., 5015 Westheimer Rd. (S. Post Oak Rd.);
713-622-7924
10510 Northwest Frwy. (Magnum Rd.); 713-681-0582
3215 Southwest Frwy. (Buffalo Spdwy.); 713-592-5100
6121 Westheimer Rd. (bet. Briar Ridge & Potomac Drs.); 832-251-0454

Chuck E. Cheese's ☒   26 | 10 | 17 | 13 | I
6760 Antoine Dr. (W. Little York Rd.); 713-957-1230
600 Gulfgate Mall Center (Woodbridge Dr.); 713-645-5660
5535 Weslayan Ave. (Bissonnet St.); 713-666-9802

Dave & Buster's ☒   26 | 16 | 21 | 17 | M
6010 Richmond Ave. (Fountain View Rd.); 713-952-2233

Fuddrucker's ☒   24 | 20 | 15 | 16 | I
3100 Chimney Rock Rd. (Fairdale Ln.); 713-780-7080
403 Greens Rd. (Northchase Dr.); 281-876-2611
3929 Southwest Frwy. (Navajo St.); 713-621-8222
10500 Town & Country Way (Woodland Willows Dr.); 713-722-7440

Hard Rock Cafe ☒   22 | 16 | 26 | 18 | M
502 Texas Ave. (bet. Bagby & Smith Sts.); 713-227-1392

Joe's Crab Shack ☒   23 | 17 | 21 | 19 | M
2621 S. Loop Frwy. W. (bet. Buffalo Spdwy. & Kirby Dr.); 713-666-2150

Maggiano's Little Italy ☒   22 | 22 | 21 | 22 | M
2019 Post Oak Blvd. (bet. San Felipe St. & Westheimer Rd.); 713-961-2700

Olive Garden ☒   20 | 19 | 18 | 19 | M
12711 Gulf Frwy. (Fuqua St.); 281-922-1523
Memorial City Shopping Ctr., 1000 Memorial City (Gessner Rd.);
713-973-6287
10830 Northwest Frwy. (bet. 34th St. & Magnum Rd.); 713-682-1465
1010 Old Spanish Trail (Kirby Dr.); 713-665-6373

Outback Steakhouse ☒   20 | 22 | 18 | 20 | M
12130 Dickinson Rd. (off Hwy. 45); 281-464-8455
10001 Westheimer Rd. (Briarpark Dr.); 713-978-6283

Red Robin ☒   25 | 20 | 19 | 20 | M
7620 Katy Frwy. (Silber Rd.); 713-476-9096
10465 Richmond Ave. (Beltway 8); 713-783-0900

Romano's Macaroni Grill ☒   21 | 21 | 19 | 21 | M
10407 Katy Frwy. (Attingham Dr.); 713-973-6676
5802 Westheimer Rd. (bet. Chimney Rock Rd. & Fountain View Dr.);
713-789-5515
Willowbrook Mall, 7607 FM 1960 (Centerfield Blvd.); 281-955-1388

Ryan's Family Steakhouse ☒   24 | 17 | 12 | 16 | I
7211 Hwy. 6 S. (Rancho Mission Dr.); 281-498-0832
5601 W. 34th St. (bet. Antoine Dr. & Hwy. 290); 713-680-0665

T.G.I. Friday's ☒   21 | 17 | 18 | 17 | M
12150 Greenspoint Dr. (Benmar Dr.); 281-875-5185
12895 Gulf Frwy. (Kurland Dr.); 281-481-0932
12830 Northwest Frwy. (off Rte. 290); 713-460-1100
7728 W. FM 1960 (Tomball Pkwy.); 281-807-4243

Las Vegas

Las Vegas still lives up to its nickname, 'Sin City', with nightclubs, lavish floor shows and 24/7 gambling. But the infamous, neon-lit, four-mile Strip also offers plenty of options for vacationing families. You'll find indoor amusement parks, thrill rides, floating gondolas, big-cat habitats, an aviary, arcades, IMAX theaters, spectacular dancing fountains, kitschy museums, sky-high observation decks, replicas of the world's landmarks, over-the-top theme restaurants and belly-busting buffets. In addition, most hotels offer a full range of activities including swimming, tennis and golf. Some attractions are pricey, but overall family dining in Las Vegas is a bargain with discount coupons at many hotels. North of the Strip, the blinking billboard and shops of the Fremont Experience light up Downtown, while on the Arizona-Nevada border, a 45-minute drive east, the massive Hoover Dam offers a different kind of mind-bending experience. The best way to get around is by car, but a free monorail connects the Mandalay Bay with the Luxor and Excalibur, another joins the Bellagio with the Monte Carlo and a third runs between the MGM and Bally's. Kids will get a kick out of a classic streetcar replica called the Strip Trolley. If all else fails, hop a taxi outside your hotel – it's the only cab that can take you from NYC to Paris to Venice to Egypt in a quarter hour.

ATTRACTIONS

Ratings: Child Appeal, Adult Appeal, Public Facilities, Service, Cost

    C | A | P | S | $

Adventuredome   26 | 15 | 19 | 17 | E
Circus Circus, 2880 Las Vegas Blvd. S. (bet. Desert Inn Rd. & Sahara Ave.); 702-734-0410; 800-424-7287;
www.adventuredome.com
☑ "No parking issues, no weather issues" – if you're staying at "kid-friendly" Circus Circus, "you can't beat walking down an air-conditioned hallway into its indoor theme park" where "losing your shirt" can happen, not at the tables, but during a loop on the exciting roller coaster; "if you're an adult looking for a thrill", the "dated, crowded, noisy", "small setting" is "really not that much fun", but it is a "good place to lose the kids for a few hours" amid "laser tag, water rides and a miniature golf" course while you "check out the free show" on the midway.

Eiffel Tower Experience ☺☺   17 | 23 | 22 | 21 | M
Paris Las Vegas, 3655 Las Vegas Blvd. S. (bet. Flamingo Rd. & Harmon Ave.); 877-796-2096; www.caesars.com
☑ "Close your eyes, and you're in gay Paris", but keep 'em open because the "trés magnifique" ride up this "impeccable half-scale replica" of the Eiffel Tower has "the best seat in the house" to "watch the Bellagio fountains" and ogle the "amazing 360-degree view of the Strip"; it's "overcrowded", "a little dizzying" and the restaurant up top is "expensive for dinner", but adults, who like this more than their kids do, say "going for dessert only can be a wonderful treat", and even if the structure "looks phony", it's "cheaper" than flying to France.

Flamingo Wildlife Habitat ☺☺ | 22 | 22 | 23 | 20 | $0 |

Flamingo Las Vegas, 3555 Las Vegas Blvd. S. (bet. Flamingo Rd. & Sands Ave.); 702-733-3111; 800-732-2111; www.flamingolasvegas.com

☑ "When you need a sane moment away from the noise and lights", go in for a "calming stroll" by the fine pink-feathered namesakes at this "lush and lovely", if "old-style, zoo enclosure" "in the middle of the busy" Flamingo hotel; "combine it with the pretty good buffet" with a view, and "don't forget your camera" to capture the "beautiful landscape" teeming with "tropical birds" and (this being Vegas) Arctic flappers; in other words, "why penguins? why not."

FOUNTAINS OF BELLAGIO ☺☺ | 21 | 27 | 23 | 18 | $0 |

Bellagio, 3600 Las Vegas Blvd. S. (bet. Flamingo Rd. & Harmon Ave.); 702-693-7111; www.bellagiohotel.com

■ "The decadence of placing this much water in the middle of the desert and making it dance" "to an unseen orchestra" is typical Vegas, but – "ooh! aah!" – "who knew fountains could have such rhythm and personality?"; adults enjoy the "humorous music", and kids are "mesmerized" by the "best freebie in town" – besides, "on a hot day, the mist feels great"; it "gets crowded at night", so "get there early", or better yet, "dine across the street" for an "awesome" view.

Fremont Street Experience ☺ | 17 | 21 | 17 | 13 | $0 |

425 Fremont St. (bet. 4th St. & Las Vegas Blvd.); 702-678-5777; 800-249-3559; www.vegasexperience.com

☑ If your "kids can stay up", "trip off the Strip" to Downtown's "honky-tonk" for this "psychedelic", "jaw-dropping wonder" of a billboard that's "like a giant Lite Brite displaying moving graphics 50 feet in the air"; "kinda cheesy but pretty impressive at the same time", the "novelty" embodies "old Las Vegas tackiness"; "teens may like some of the music", and the adjacent mall's "cheap drinks" are "great for adults", but beware that the shady "cast of characters" and "seedy surroundings take away from the family appeal."

GameWorks ☺☺ | 27 | 18 | 21 | 16 | M |

3785 Las Vegas Blvd. S. (bet. Harmon & Tropicana Aves.); 702-432-4263; www.gameworks.com

☑ "Arcades of any sort are always good for the kiddies", and this "huge", "high-tech" one's "packed" with 'em, proving that "at least some of the machines in Vegas are not just for adults" and making for this *Survey's* top Child Appeal in town; though they'll require chaperones after 9 PM, in the mid-afternoon it's a "very cool" "place to let 'em run wild" and "rock climb too", so "drop off the older tykes with some dough and relax" – "the games will babysit for you all day" and you don't have to participate.

Gondola Rides at the Grand Canal | 18 | 22 | 23 | 23 | M |

Venetian Resort & Casino, 3355 Las Vegas Blvd. S. (bet. Flamingo & Spring Mountain Rds.); 702-733-5000; www.venetian.com

☑ Granted, you'll float "through a crowded, brightly lit mall" while "gawked at by hundreds of strangers" at the Venetian, but the gondoliers are "charming and witty", it's "a real bargain compared with Venice" and you get to "ride canals without garbage"; the boats "sell out fast, especially for private trips", so "get tickets early", expect "long lines" and "get over the fact that there's a motor in the gondola", because your "kids will enjoy" this "cheesy" adventure.

Hoover Dam ☺ | 18 | 26 | 21 | 20 | I |

US Hwy. 93, SE of Las Vegas, Boulder City; 702-597-5970; 866-291-8687; www.usbr.gov/lc/hooverdam

■ "Lots of concrete", to say the least – an "awe-inspiring" "triumph of engineering" clogging up the Colorado River 45 minutes from Sin

City, this "wonder of the modern world" "marvels" older kids, teens and especially parents, who "don't believe how small they all feel standing next to it"; younger visitors "fidget" on the "educational" "hard-hat tour" and during "informative films", though they "like that they can say 'dam' all day and not get in trouble"; be forewarned: "post-9/11 concerns have limited access" to just "about the only real thing around Vegas."

Imperial Palace Auto Collection ☺ | 12 | 22 | 17 | 16 | I |

Imperial Palace, 3535 Las Vegas Blvd. S. (bet. Flamingo & Spring Mountain Rds.); 702-731-3311; www.autocollections.com

☑ "If you like classic and collectible cars", grab the "free admission" "coupons in the tourist guides in your hotel" and zoom to the Imperial Palace to rev your engines over this "regularly changing" assortment of "chrome and shine"; but you might want to bring your checkbook because all the wheels here are "for sale"; still, though "memories of autos of yesteryear" are "fun for the older crowd", these Dusenbergs and Studebakers "can be boring for young children or anyone not into historical vehicles", as proven by the Child Appeal rating above.

Lied Discovery Children's Museum ☺☺ | 26 | 17 | 20 | 22 | I |

833 Las Vegas Blvd. N. (bet. Bonanza Rd. & Washington Ave.); 702-382-3445; www.ldcm.org

■ It's "a bit far from the Strip", but it's no lie that this "marvelous" museum is "a great place to take little children", especially "when everyone needs some downtime" from Vegas overload; "kids can be kids" with "imaginative, hands-on" exhibits, which are "especially geared toward preschoolers" in the Desert Discovery area; head here for a "short" but "sweet" couple of hours at a "bargain price."

Lion Habitat | 25 | 21 | 21 | 19 | $0 |

MGM Grand, 3799 Las Vegas Blvd. S. (Tropicana Ave.); 702-891-1111; www.mgmgrand.com

■ Your cubs will "rooooooar!" with "excitement" when the trainers feed the "big kitties" in the MGM's "cool", "freebie" habitat, if you can claw past the other "gawkers"; otherwise, remember the "king of beasts" only seems so "tame and cute" – and "boring" – because he "sleeps 16 hours a day"; still, the "recorded tour is informative", as is "walking through the clear tunnel with a drooling lion overhead" (it's a "good place to explain biology"); P.S. if you're "saddened" by their "captivity", note that the cats spend most of their time on a spacious ranch.

Madame Tussaud's Las Vegas ☺☺ | 18 | 24 | 23 | 20 | M |

Venetian Resort & Casino, 3355 Las Vegas Blvd. S. (bet. Flamingo & Spring Mountain Rds.); 702-862-7800; www.madame-tussauds.com

☑ "Take your camera" and "get a picture with your favorite celebrity", even if she or he is made out of "wax", at this "enjoyable", self-guided offshoot of the London original where an "excellent selection of figures" feels like a "party with the stars"; "children really get a kick" out of mugging with Shaq or J-Lo "in classic poses", though "kids under 4 may be spooked" by such "lifelike" fakes as that of "local favorite Liberace."

Manhattan Express Roller Coaster ☺ | 23 | 23 | 20 | 18 | M |

New York-New York Hotel, 3790 Las Vegas Blvd. S. (Tropicana Ave.); 702-740-6969; www.nynyhotelcasino.com

☑ "Holy moly!" – leave "weak stomachs", "bad backs", "faint hearts" and kids under 54 inches tall on the ground, "grab your socks" and strap yourself in for a "wild" ride on this "scary" "gut wrencher" "dropping right off the side of New York-New York"; "it shoots you across the 'Big Apple' in a way you never imagined", as the "proximity of the buildings" in the "replica skyline" "makes the coaster feel faster" than it is, while its "bumpy, rickety" "banging" brings back memories of Coney Island's Cyclone for "nostalgic" adults.

Mystic Falls 😊😊

| 22 | 21 | 24 | 21 | $0 |

Sam's Town Hotel, 5111 Boulder Hwy. (Nellis Blvd.); 702-456-7777; www.samstownlv.com

■ "You can hear a wolf howl throughout the casino", calling your pack to the "beautiful", 10-story atrium at Sam's Town on the East Side for the "fab-u-lous", "free" Sunset Stampede "laser light and water show with music and animation" four times a day; the "clever presentation" is "like a mini-Bellagio", but even when the H_2O isn't dancing, it's a "pretty cool place" – "you really feel like you're outdoors" while indoors for a "relaxing" break from the Sin City hubbub.

Pharaoh's Pavillion 😊😊

| 20 | 20 | 21 | 19 | M |

Luxor, 3900 Las Vegas Blvd. S. (Reno Ave.); 702-262-4000; www.luxor.com

☑ With shopping, dining, an arcade and IMAX experiences, this "dark, airy" atrium above Luxor's casino is "fun for older school-age kids, preteens and adults who like simulator rides", while toddlers "love running around all the 'genuine' [not!] artifacts" amid "Tut's tomb replica"; "if you like Egyptology" and aren't too picky about authenticity, you might feel you're on a "real trip back into the wonders" of the Nile, but "egads" – did all those "cheesy gift stores" exist back in 1350 B.C.?

Red Rock Canyon National Conservation Area 😊😊

| 16 | 24 | 17 | 15 | $0 |

Hwy. 159 (off W. Charleston Blvd.); 702-515-5350; www.redrockcanyon.blm.gov

■ "Bring lots of water and snacks" and "leave the glitz behind" at the "anti-Vegas", a "mini–Grand Canyon" "escape from the excesses" "not far from Downtown"; "go at sunset" for "stupendous" views of "beautiful rock formations" and encounters with "begging wild burros" in the "cool" dusk, but "don't expect to find yourself alone in the wilderness" or to find it "easy for strollers to move on the trails"; still, "older kids enjoy the challenge" of "hopping across the boulders", and there's "open space" for little legs to "hike, walk or bike."

Shark Reef 😊😊

| 26 | 24 | 25 | 22 | M |

Mandalay Bay Resort & Casino, 3950 Las Vegas Blvd. S. (Mandalay Bay Rd.); 702-632-4555; www.mandalaybay.com

■ "Sharks and giant sea turtles in the middle of the desert?!" – you bet your rubber boots at Mandalay Bay's "awesome" aquarium; landlubbers have to "schlep" to get to Vegas' overall top-rated attraction in this *Survey*, "but once inside", "walking within the glass-enclosed tunnel makes you feel like you're scuba diving", the "hands-on area is really cool" and the audio tour gives you "lots of fun facts about all the fascinating critters" for an "educational", "visually appealing" "family event" "chock-full of fishies."

Siegfried & Roy's Secret Garden and Dolphin Habitat 😊😊

| 25 | 24 | 25 | 22 | I |

Mirage Hotel & Casino, 3400 Las Vegas Blvd. S. (bet. Flamingo & Spring Mountain Rds.); 702-791-7188; www.themirage.com

■ Via hand-held audio, "Siegfried & Roy tell you about each animal along the path" for a "personal touch" at their "cute, little zoo in the Mirage" Hotel; "what's better than frolicking tiger cubs" amid a "lush", "tropical atmosphere"? – how about frolicking *white* tiger cubs, plus lions, panthers, leopards and elephants?; "you also view dolphins above and below the water", so "stop in when you need serenity" courtesy of a duo that, despite a hiatus from performing following Roy's "tragic mishap", remains fiercely loyal to the "big cats."

Speed ☺   22 | 26 | 18 | 18 | M

Sahara Hotel & Casino, 2535 Las Vegas Blvd. S. (Sahara Ave.);
702-737-2111; 888-696-2121; www.saharavegas.com

☑ A "top-notch ride that goes backward and forward and hits 70 mph" after it blasts off from inside the NASCAR Cafe in the Sahara Hotel, this "smooth, enjoyable" roller coaster is "a little different than the average amusement park ride"; it's "not for the little or the weak of heart", and after an "annoying wait", the thrill "is a little too fast" – "once you start having fun, it's over"; still, "fanatics" pile on, "for sure."

Star Trek: The Experience ☺☺   20 | 24 | 23 | 22 | E

Las Vegas Hilton, 3000 Paradise Rd. (bet. Desert Inn Rd. & Sahara Ave.);
702-697-8700; 888-462-6535; www.startrekexp.com

■ "Bring your imagination and some Dramamine", and let Scotty beam you up on "an amazing adventure" spanning the generations that's "as close to being in a *Star Trek* episode as you can get"; the Hilton's "Trekkie mecca" may "sound like a geekfest, but it's surprisingly entertaining" "to see the memorabilia", visit the bridge of the Enterprise and chomp on a "good Hamborger"; "young ones get a kick out of flying through space" on the "fun 3-D ride", though the "Cyborgs walking around" might be "scary" for them.

Stratosphere Tower & Rides ☺   20 | 23 | 20 | 18 | I

Stratosphere Hotel Tower & Casino, 2000 Las Vegas Blvd. S. (Main St.);
702-380-7777; 800-998-6937; www.stratospherehotel.com

■ Those "afraid of heights" are "hardly able to stand on the observation deck" of this 1,149-ft. tower; "try it once" for "unmatched" views, a meal "at the rotating restaurant", "cool shopping" and, on extra-fee rides like the Big Shot "that shoots you in the air", "the chance to see your life flash before your eyes"; the roller coaster "doesn't go very fast, but how speedy should it be 100 stories up?"; even the elevator is part of "the biggest test of courage in Vegas."

Wet 'n Wild Water Park   27 | 21 | 20 | 18 | E

2601 Las Vegas Blvd. S. (bet. Desert Inn Rd. & Sahara Ave.); 702-765-9700;
www.wetnwildlv.com

■ "Who can't have fun at a water park", especially one right on the Strip?; "there's something for everyone" into swimming here: "good slides" and wet playground equipment offer kids "a decent way to cool off in the heat", while adults "can spend hours" on the "great Lazy River Raft" "enjoying the Vegas sun" and "getting a nice tan"; look for a new splashy surprise ride in 2004.

HOTELS

Ratings: Family Appeal, Rooms, Service, Public Facilities, Cost

	FA	R	S	P	$
	18	23	23	25	$300

Caesars Palace

3570 Las Vegas Blvd. S.; 702-731-7110; 800-634-6661; www.caesars.com;
2418 rooms

☑ The "fabulous" circular Palace pool with lots of fountains is fit for a Roman emperor, and may be the best thing about this slightly "run-down" "slice of old Las Vegas" "located in the center of the strip"; there's "fantastic entertainment for all ages" (including a "terrific magic dinner show"), a "giant talking horse at FAO" Schwarz in the adjacent Forum Shops and a "wonderful spa facility" for moms and dads; but a fussy few feel it's "highly variable", insisting there are better options, so "take your little caesars to another palace."

Mandalay Bay
23 | 24 | 22 | 28 | $259

3950 Las Vegas Blvd. S.; 702-632-7777; 877-632-7000; www.mandalaybay.com; 3200 rooms, 1120 suites

☑ The "wave pool and floating river" "keep families happy for days" at this "very tropical" hotel with the "best swimming complex in Vegas"; little ones "love" the shark display and "riding the waters" at the faux beach, while adults appreciate "beautiful decor", "spacious rooms" and babysitting services so they can "enjoy a fabulous meal at Aureole"; although there's "not a lot" more for kids at this place, they'll "have a blast" if splashing about makes them happy.

MGM Grand
23 | 21 | 20 | 23 | $150

3799 Las Vegas Blvd. S.; 702-891-1111; 800-929-1111; www.mgmgrand.com; 4254 rooms, 751 suites, 29 villas

☑ "Lights! action! – it's all here" at this movie-themed resort where the "lion habitat and the Rainforest Cafe are magnets for children" and "every day there is someone famous performing"; but the less enthralled conclude "the loss of the theme park" it operated on-site "lowers its family appeal, and it's much "too large for those with small children", since "you can get lost trying to find your room", but a "wonderful" pool and "prime location" may make up for that.

Mirage
22 | 22 | 22 | 24 | $499

3400 Las Vegas Blvd. S.; 702-791-7111; 800-929-1111; www.mirage.com; 2770 rooms, 279 suites

■ "Even without Siegfried and Roy, the white tigers are still here" for viewing, which "gives this hotel a real jump on the others", since they're a "main attraction for children"; kids love the Dolphin Habitat and a "pool that's a big hit" as well, plus there's an on-site California Pizza Kitchen, "larger-than-average rooms" and, just outside at sister property Treasure Island, "you can watch the [faux] Volcano erupt."

Paris Las Vegas
18 | 23 | 21 | 23 | $299

3655 Las Vegas Blvd. S.; 702-946-7000; 888-266-5687; www.parislasvegas.com; 2916 rooms, 295 suites

☑ "Youngsters feel like they're in another country" at this French-themed hotel that sports a replica of the Eiffel Tower outside; while some say the rates are "very reasonable", the "buffet is excellent" and there are "awesome shops" and restaurants "for all tastes and sizes", others find this "plastic Paris" "a bit tacky" and "not oriented toward children."

Rio All-Suite
18 | 24 | 22 | 23 | $370

3700 W. Flamingo Rd.; 702-252-7777; 800-752-9746; www.harrahs.com; 2548 suites

☑ The "large suites" featuring refrigerators are "perfect for families" and are "affordable" at this off-the-strip property with "entertainment for all ages"; there's a "vast selection of food", while the Masquerade Village (with free shows seven times a day) and "very colorful decor" appeal to children; but others complain "so much activity that's fun for kids takes place in the casino itself" and you'll have to dodge the time-share sales staff that "hounds you when you walk through the lobby"; N.B. there are plans to complete the world's tallest observation wheel (with luxury orbiting cabins) by July 2005.

Treasure Island
24 | 21 | 20 | 23 | $150

3300 Las Vegas Blvd. S.; 702-894-7111; 800-944-7111; www.treasureisland.com; 2665 rooms, 215 suites

■ Youngsters "love the fantasy" of this pirate-themed spot that's "much more kid-friendly" than other hotels on the Strip, featuring "lots of action" including a live sea battle at the front entrance and an arcade area that keeps little mates "entertained for hours"; there's also a Ben & Jerry's ice cream shop, a Krispy Kreme doughnut outlet and a Starbucks on-site, along with a range of eateries; P.S. if you "spend the dollars and take the family to see Cirque du Soleil's Mystère" show, you won't be disappointed say its fans.

Venetian, The
20 | 28 | 25 | 26 | $250

3355 Las Vegas Blvd. S.; 702-414-1000; 888-293-6423; www.venetian.com; 3036 suites

☑ Parents have mixed views of this "intimidating" Italian-themed palace where "the rooms are the highlight" – "all are suites that sleep six comfortably" and have "two TVs so there's no need to argue over remotes"; while most find the gondola rides and dining under the faux St. Mark's sky "have appeal" and "children enjoy the wax museum" and the living statue people at the Grand Canal shops, others say it "caters more to business types than families", so it's "better suited for preteens", teens and adults.

Top Family-Friendly Hotel Chains in the Area:

Embassy Suites	Marriott
Four Seasons	Residence Inn
Hampton Inn	Ritz-Carlton
Hyatt	Westin

See Hotel Chain reviews, starting on page 256.

RESTAURANTS

Ratings: Family Appeal, Food, Decor, Service, Cost

FA | F | D | S | $

America ◗
23 | 17 | 22 | 19 | M

New York-New York Hotel & Casino, 3790 Las Vegas Blvd. S. (Tropicana Ave.); 702-740-6451; www.arkrestaurants.com

☑ "Huge pop-up book–style maps of the U.S. hanging from the walls and ceilings" "keep the kids occupied" "in this bright, colorful and fun restaurant" in New York-New York serving "good, old American food" from every state that "appeals" to "picky" pip-squeaks 'round the clock; yeah, the grub might be "average", but "the atmosphere makes it special", and "quick service with a smile" for the youngsters means you can get back to the Manhattan Express for another ride lickety-split.

Bellagio Buffet
21 | 25 | 21 | 21 | M

Bellagio Hotel, 3600 Las Vegas Blvd. S. (Flamingo Rd.); 702-693-7111; www.bellagio.com

☑ "Even though it's in a ritzy hotel" (home of the dancing fountains), the Bellagio's "magnificent spread" is "very child-friendly"; the "sophisticated" Eclectic buffet is "constantly being refilled" with a "refined yet approachable" global "bounty" including "lots of kiddie choices", so even though it's "not the most economical" eatery for a family meal in Vegas, it's "worth" the price; your little fressers might not even mind suffering the "excruciating wait" once they get a load of the "huge selection of desserts."

Emeril's New Orleans Fish House
14 | 25 | 22 | 24 | VE

MGM Grand Hotel, 3799 Las Vegas Blvd. S. (Tropicana Ave.); 702-891-7374; www.emerils.com

☑ So, it's "a bit upscale" and "pricey" "for screaming, food-throwing little ones", but if your kids are *Food Network* fans, they'll say "bam!" as often as Fred Flintstone's son at celebri-chef Emeril Lagasse's "fantastic" New Orleans–style seafood house in the MGM; the "spectacular" kitchen and "trademark" synchronized servers are "flexible enough for young ones" while "allowing parents a treat", but it might "be more appropriate with children for lunch when it's not so crowded" – either way, "bribe" your babies into quietude "with one of the delicious desserts."

Harley-Davidson Cafe
21 | 16 | 26 | 20 | M

3725 Las Vegas Blvd. S. (Harmon Ave.); 702-740-4555;
www.harley-davidsoncafe.com
■ Parents with babies born to be wild have an easy ride at this Traditional American faux "biker's den" on the Strip; motorcycles that "make the loops of the restaurant on an overhead track" – plus those "you can actually sit on and take photos of" – "capture the attention" of tiny speedsters "while you wait for your food"; it's "the last place you would think would be good", but "large portions" at decent prices will "pleasantly surprise" you and "keep you coming back for more."

Lake Mead Cruises
– | – | – | – | E

Lake Mead Nat'l Recreation Area, 490-B Horsepower Cove (off I-93), Boulder City; 702-293-6180; www.lakemeadcruises.com
You've taken the Hoover Dam tour – now get a different angle on the engineering marvel during a breakfast or dinner cruise on Lake Mead in a multi-decker *Tom Sawyer*–style paddle wheeler that takes you right up to the man-made landmark, as well as past an extinct volcano, the islands in the middle of the water and several other natural sensations along the Arizona-Nevada border; the Traditional American buffet keeps hungry little sailors sated.

Lotus of Siam
▽ 21 | 28 | 14 | 22 | M

Commercial Ctr., 953 E. Sahara Ave. (bet. Maryland Pkwy. & Paradise Rd.); 702-735-3033
■ "Who cares about decor when the food is this good?" – certainly your kids won't, and neither should you when some of "the best Thai food you've ever had" can be found at "super-reasonable prices" in this "hole-in-the-wall" east of the Strip; the "great staff" is "very helpful in ordering off the menu", and they're "prompt" enough for a quick, "inexpensive" meal with fidgety munchkins, who will probably want to "return just for the coconut ice cream."

Metro Pizza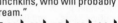
▽ 21 | 23 | 15 | 18 | M

Ellis Island Casino & Brewery, 4178 E. Koval Ln. (Flamingo Rd.); 702-312-5888
1395 E. Tropicana Ave. (Maryland Pkwy.); 702-736-1955
Renaissance Ctr. W., 4001 S. Decatur Blvd. (Flamingo Rd.); 702-362-7896
www.metropizza.com
■ The only place in this grown-up gambling town where the "kids [get] dough to play with" too is this chain of "local joints" flipping "good, quick, hot", "delicious" pies of the "gourmet" variety; not only that, but for an educational meal, it "houses the Pizza Hall of Fame", "featuring a U.S. map on the wall paying homage to the nation's top" 'za palaces.

Mirage Buffet
22 | 21 | 19 | 20 | M

Mirage Hotel, 3400 Las Vegas Blvd. S. (Spring Mountain Rd.); 702-791-7111; www.themirage.com
■ When your brood's bellies are growling, "turn 'em loose at this expansive" pig-out palace, where "a stupendous choice of food for anyone and everyone" awaits at "many optional stations"; the Mirage's "reasonably priced" Continental buffet features "huge peeled shrimp", "great meat choices", "good iced tea" and, often, some of the "best peanut butter cookies you'll ever have"; when everyone's sated, check out Siegfried & Roy's Secret Garden in the hotel.

Mr. Lucky's 24/7

▽ 15	18	18	18	M

Hard Rock Hotel & Casino, 4455 Paradise Rd. (bet. Flamingo Rd. & Harmon Ave.); 702-693-5592; www.hardrockhotel.com

☑ If your adolescents are rolling their eyes at the buffets, bring 'em to the Hard Rock's hipster diner for some good old American coffee shop chow and – if you're lucky, mister – a possible brush with their favorite teenybopper heartthrob of the moment; it's open "all night" for "casino grub" and stargazing, but any time of day it's an "inexpensive place to eat with the kids."

Paradise Garden Buffet

23	20	19	19	M

Flamingo Las Vegas, 3555 Las Vegas Blvd. S. (Flamingo Rd.); 702-733-3282; www.flamingolasvegas.com

■ If your kids suffer from the "eyes-bigger-than-their-stomachs syndrome", don't despair – just flock to the Flamingo, where the "good-value" smorgasbord is "super for kids to pick what and how much they want" from a "charming" Eclectic buffet offering a wide variety of choices; while they chow at one of the "well-spaced tables", children can scope out the "nice view" of the namesake long-legged fowl filling the hotel aviary.

Quark's

23	18	24	20	M

Las Vegas Hilton, 3000 Paradise Rd. (bet. Desert Inn Rd. & Karen Ave.); 702-697-8725; www.startrekexp.com

■ If your family's mission is to eat where lots of Trekkies have eaten before, you're in the right place; an intergalactic gastronomic "adventure for all" in the Hilton's Star Trek attraction, this theme American with a "24th-century atmosphere" is not only a "must for fans" of the show but also "fun all around" for everyone; "what it does, it does extremely well", "from Romulan Ale to Tribble Tenders" – "just watch out for the Klingons!"

Roxy's Diner

▽ 22	17	21	18	I

Stratosphere Hotel & Tower, 2000 Las Vegas Blvd. S. (S. Main St.); 702-383-4834; www.stratlv.com

■ One of the "best cheap cafes in Las Vegas" is "better than those twice the price", particularly when you're traveling with baby bobby-soxers – "toddlers find the bright colors appealing and the '50s music entertaining" at the Stratosphere's retro-themed burger-and-malted joint where the staff lays down doo-wop tunes along with your plates; after digesting, remind yourself you're in the 21st century by catching an elevator that shoots to the top of the tower for a panoramic view of contemporary Vegas.

Sir Galahad's Pub & Prime Rib House

▽ 21	18	19	20	E

Excalibur Hotel, 3850 Las Vegas Blvd. S. (Tropicana Ave.); 702-597-7448; www.excaliburcasino.com

☑ Roast beast "carved tableside inside a castle that's inside a castle" is "nice for kids who like King Arthur" and want to pretend they're a prince or princess; at this "reasonably priced steakhouse" inside Excalibur, there's "good prime rib" and "other standard fare", and while kingly carnivores might find the fare "ordinary", the "interesting atmosphere" pleases runt-sized royalty.

Wild Sage Café

–	–	–	–	E

8991 W. Sahara Ave. (bet. Durango Dr. & Fort Apache Rd.); 702-304-9453 600 E. Warm Springs Rd. (Amigo St.), Henderson; 702-944-7243

A "lucky place for non-gambling food-o-philic" families, Stan Carroll and Laurie Kendrick's "wonderfully anti-Strip" and kid-friendly New American "oasis of excellence" in Green Valley now has a "pretty" West Side sibling serving the same "imaginative comfort food" as the "perennial favorite"; wildly sagacious "low-key" "locals" and touring clans alike "love them" for "grand pork chops", "delicious chicken" and lunch's "generous, unique sandwiches."

RESTAURANT CHAINS

See reviews, starting on page 262.

Ratings: Family Appeal, Food, Decor, Service, Cost

	FA	F	D	S	$

Applebee's

	21	16	17	17	M

Smith's Shopping Ctr., 500 N. Nellis Blvd. (Stewart Ave.); 702-452-7155

Baja Fresh Mexican Grill

	20	22	14	18	I

Mission Ctr., 1380 E. Flamingo Rd. (Maryland Pkwy.); 702-699-8920
Sahara Pavilion, 4760 W. Sahara Ave. (Decatur Blvd.); 702-878-7772
Summerhill Plaza, 7501 W. Lake Mead Blvd. (Buffalo Dr.); 702-838-4100
The Lakes, 8780 W. Charleston Blvd. (bet. Durango Dr. & Rampart Blvd.);
702-948-4043

Benihana

	23	20	18	22	E

Las Vegas Hilton Hotel, 3000 Paradise Rd. (bet. Desert Inn Rd. & Karen Ave.);
702-732-5334

Buca di Beppo 🈂️

	24	19	22	21	M

412 E.Flamingo Rd. (Paradise Rd.); 702-866-2867

California Pizza Kitchen ◗

	21	21	16	19	M

Fashion Show Mall, 3200 Las Vegas Blvd. S. (Fashion Show Ln.); 702-893-1370
Mirage Hotel, 3400 Las Vegas Blvd. S. (Spring Mountain Rd.); 702-791-7357

Chevys Fresh Mex

	23	19	18	18	M

4090 S. Eastern Ave. (Flamingo Rd.); 702-731-6969
6800 W. Sahara Ave. (Rainbow Blvd.); 702-220-4507

Chili's Grill & Bar

	21	19	18	19	M

2011 N. Rainbow Blvd. (Lake Mead Blvd.); 702-638-1482
2520 S. Decatur Blvd. (Sahara Ave.); 702-871-0500
9051 W. Charleston Blvd. (Rampart Blvd.); 702-228-0479

Chuck E. Cheese's 🈂️

	26	10	17	13	I

4175 S. Grand Canyon Dr. (bet. Katie & Twain Aves.); 702-531-8000
7381 W. Lake Mead Blvd. (bet. Buffalo Dr. & Tenaya Way); 702-243-9944

Claim Jumper Restaurant 🈂️

	23	24	22	21	M

1100 S. Ft. Apache Rd. (Charleston Blvd.); 702-243-8751

Hard Rock Cafe ◗

	22	16	26	18	M

4475 Paradise Rd. (Harmon Ave.); 702-733-7625

In-N-Out Burger ⌿

	24	24	13	21	I

4888 Industrial Rd. (W. Tropicana Ave.); 800-786-1000
51 N. Nellis Blvd. (Charleston Blvd.); 800-786-1000
1960 Rock Springs Dr. (Lake Mead Blvd.); 800-786-1000
2900 W. Sahara Ave. (Teddy Dr.); 800-786-1000

Joe's Crab Shack 🈂️

	23	17	21	19	M

1991 N. Rainbow Blvd. (Lake Mead Blvd.); 702-240-6055

Mimi's Cafe 🈂️

	23	21	22	20	M

1121 S. Fort Apache Rd. (Charleston Blvd.); 702-341-0365

Olive Garden ⊠ | 20 | 19 | 18 | 19 | M |
1545 E. Flamingo Rd. (Maryland Pkwy.); 702-735-0082
80 N. Nellis Blvd. (Charleston Blvd.); 702-438-0082
1361 S. Decatur Blvd. (Del Ray Ave.); 702-258-3453
6850 W. Cheyenne Ave. (bet. Hwy. 95 & Rainbow Blvd.); 702-658-2144

Original Pancake House, The ⊠ | 24 | 22 | 12 | 17 | I |
4833 W. Charleston Blvd. (Decatur Blvd.); 702-259-7755
8620 W. Cheyenne Ave. (Durango Dr.); 702-396-8220

Planet Hollywood | 24 | 13 | 24 | 16 | M |
Forum Shops at Caesars Palace, 3500 Las Vegas Blvd. S. (Flamingo Rd.);
702-791-7827

Red Robin ⊠ | 25 | 20 | 19 | 20 | M |
Sahara, 2575 S. Decatur Blvd. (Sahara Ave.); 702-364-1858
7860 W. Tropical Pkwy. (Centennial Center Blvd.); 702-656-0096

Romano's Macaroni Grill | 21 | 21 | 19 | 21 | M |
2001 N. Rainbow Blvd. (Lake Mead Blvd.); 702-648-6688
2400 W. Sahara Ave. (Rancho Dr.); 702-248-9500

T.G.I. Friday's ◐ | 21 | 17 | 18 | 17 | M |
1800 E. Flamingo Rd. (Spencer St.); 702-732-9905
4570 W. Sahara Ave. (bet. Arville St. & Decatur Blvd.); 702-889-1866

Tony Roma's ⊠ | 20 | 21 | 16 | 19 | M |
31900 Las Vegas Blvd. S. (bet. Charleston Blvd. & St. Louis Ave.); 800-386-7867
Reno Sands Hotel, 345 N. Arlington St. (bet. 3rd & 4th Sts.); 775-348-2200

Los Angeles

There's no time of the year that isn't good to visit Los Angeles. Of course, the beaches are best during the warm, dry season between May and October, but the mild winter is a wonderful time to explore the Disney parks, Knott's Berry Farm, Universal Studios and other attractions that are packed in summer. The sprawling landscape and limited public transit make a car a necessity, as tourist favorites are spread far and wide. Traffic can be taxing, but for a true SoCal experience, cruising the Sunset Strip, Hollywood Boulevard, Mulholland Drive and the Pacific Coast Highway are musts. For art fans, there are few better venues than the Getty and MOCA. Stay in pricey Santa Monica for close proximity to the beaches, the Santa Monica Pier and the quirky Venice Boardwalk; Beverly Hills is a central location for prime hotels, restaurants, shopping and stargazing; and Hollywood is . . . well, Hollywood. If you're a theme-park enthusiast, a hotel in Orange County's Anaheim will put you on the doorstep of Disneyland and Disney's California Adventure.

ATTRACTIONS

Ratings: Child Appeal, Adult Appeal, Public Facilities, Service, Cost

| | C | A | P | S | $ |

California Science Center ☺☺ | 28 | 25 | 24 | 21 | $0 |
Exposition Park, 700 State Dr. (Exposition Blvd.); 323-724-3623;
www.casciencectr.org
■ There's "stimulation for bored kids and plenty of exciting action for hyperactive ones" at this "well-planned", "spiffy" "gem" in Exposition

Park, just south of Downtown; with loads of "educational, hands-on" free exhibits and extra-charge attractions including the High Wire Bicycle, Motion-Based Simulator, Cave Climb and IMAX, adults find almost as much appeal as their kids do; "elementary schoolers" will be "entertained without a Game Boy", 'tweens will "use their brains" and "parents will get swept up in everything" during a "thought-provoking" couple of hours.

Central Library ☺☺

| 17 | 24 | 25 | 21 | $0 |

630 W. Fifth St. (Grand Ave.); 213-228-7000; www.lapl.org
■ "Wow!" – there's a "library of dreams" Downtown, a "beautifully refurbished" "art deco" "respite from city life" with "amazing exhibits", "a spectacular garden" and "huge collections" of written works, including "an incredible section just for children"; sure, parents may find more to their liking here, but "if your kid loves books", the "free tours" and "special programs like storytelling, demonstrations and drama" make for an enlightening visit, and in the event of a meltdown, the "cafeteria keeps screaming toddlers at bay."

Descanso Gardens

| 14 | 25 | 21 | 19 | I |

1418 Descanso Dr. (Verdugo Blvd.), La Cañada Flintridge; 818-949-4200; www.descansogardens.org
◨ For a floral "feel of old Southern California", grab the munchkins and stroll the "breathtaking", "inviting" grounds of this La Cañada Flintridge garden "retreat" 20 minutes northeast of Downtown in the San Gabriel foothills, where blissful botanists can't get enough of the "beautiful roses" and "shady camellia forest"; though they "enjoy the train" and the "wide-open spaces", unless you've spawned a brood of "nature lovers", "kids get bored very quickly"; still, a tiptoe through the "gorgeous tulips" "won't take all day."

DISNEYLAND

| 29 | 25 | 26 | 25 | VE |

1313 S. Harbor Blvd. (Ball Rd.), Anaheim; 714-781-4565; www.disneyland.com
■ "Chase your children as they follow Disney characters" around "Walt's original wonderland"; approaching its 50th anniversary, this "cultural icon" (Los Angeles' No. 1 overall attraction and its highest-rated for Child Appeal) paved the way for the mid-century development of Orange Country and is "older than kids, older than parents, but still a hoot"; "powerhouse attractions" include *Peter Pan's Flight* and *Pirates of the Caribbean* plus "dazzling" fireworks, "don't-miss parades" and the "breathtaking *Fantasmic!*" "spectacular", and though it's "crowded" and "astronomically priced", the place has such "timeless appeal", they should dub it "Foreverland"; "use FastPass" and "stay on-site" but be advised Space Mountain is closed until July 2005.

DISNEY'S CALIFORNIA ADVENTURE

| 23 | 23 | 25 | 24 | VE |

1313 S. Harbor Blvd. (Ball Rd.), Anaheim; 714-781-4565; www.disneyland.com
◨ Disneyland's "mini offshoot"-in-progress with a Golden State motif has some "awesome rides", "great theater" and "food that's superior" to its parent, plus "you can drink wine in the park"; "*A Bug's Land* is a huge hit with the sippy-cup crowd", while the "roller coaster is great for adults and teens", as is the *Soarin' Over California* virtual "flying" tour and the new *Tower of Terror*; it "can be done in a half-day", but get the multi-day discount "Park Hopper pass for loads of fun" at both Mouse-y pleasure grounds.

Dodger Stadium ☺

| 21 | 25 | 20 | 17 | E |

1000 Elysian Park Ave. (Stadium Way), Echo Park; 323-224-1448; www.dodgers.com
◨ "Gobble a Dodger Dog" and root, root, root for the home team at this "timeless Southland treasure" north of Downtown in a scenic

Echo setting where "all ages and ethnicities come together"; "slap the sunscreen" on the kiddies and take in a day game or tour, but "keep their ears plugged" during "profanity"-filled "rivalries" with the SF Giants, don't expect a "play area" and "don't bring them on a school night" because you'll need to be an artful Dodger to "get out of the parking lot"; still, the "nosebleed tix can't be beat" for "cheapy" "baseball nirvana."

Farmers Market ☺   14 | 24 | 18 | 19 | $0

6333 W. Third St. (Fairfax Ave.); 323-933-9211; www.farmersmarketla.com
◪ The "funky" "authentic-ness" of "vintage LA" bursts from this "bustling" "crossroads of the edible world" with stalls for "everything from souvenirs to fresh produce" to "almost anything for anyone" to eat on the spot; you "could gain 10 pounds here", if you weren't burning calories trying "to keep track of children", "push a stroller" and "spot celebs" amid the "crowds"; gruff "gourmet" grown-ups "leave the kiddies at home", but others say now that it's "connected by trolley or walkway to the huge, modern" Grove mall, there's "even more reason to make it a family destination."

Getty Center ☺   13 | 28 | 28 | 25 | $0

1200 Getty Center Dr. (Sepulveda Blvd.); 310-440-7300; www.getty.edu
■ The "breathtaking" view from this "world-class" museum/ architectural "wonder" "atop the hills" over the Pacific is the "best freebie in town" (plus $5 for parking); but the visit may be "frustrating for kids" with the exception of the "tram ride up", a "small children's section that holds their attention from 20 minutes to an hour" and a spin through Robert Irwin's spiraling garden; "the docent tours add enjoyment", but the rugrats "need to be quiet" and "not touch", so "run them outside first" on the "spectacular" grounds, or "wait till they're older."

Grauman's Chinese Theatre ☺   15 | 22 | 17 | 13 | I

6925 Hollywood Blvd. (bet. Highland & La Brea Aves.); 323-461-3331
◪ Hollywood's "fossil record" "is at your feet" outside this "kitschy" and "commercial but legendary" "landmark" where "the stars" fall to their knees to press their prints into cement; for a price, "have your picture taken with any number of costumed", unauthorized look-alikes lurking about, or "for a break, go in and see a movie" "on the big screen" or tour "the beautiful, historical" main theater; kvetchy kid critics may give the celluloid celebration two thumbs down, but parents enjoy "seeing if their foot is as big as Ahnuld's", er, the Governor's.

Griffith Park ☺☺   24 | 23 | 18 | 14 | $0

4730 Crystal Springs Dr. (Los Feliz Blvd.); 323-913-4688; www.laparks.org
■ Let your little angels fly "off the leash" in this "expansive treasure" of a park "near the base of the Hollywood Hills" in Los Feliz, a "wonderful mix of train rides, the Zoo, hiking spots, the Griffith Observatory and the Greek Theater – who can ask for more?"; well, junior equestrians can ask for "fantastic pony rides", aspiring Tiger Woodses "love the public golf course" and everyone thrills to the holiday Festival of Lights; best of all, you don't need a pocket of green to enjoy this "oasis of green."

Hollywood Bowl ☺   13 | 27 | 22 | 20 | I

2301 N. Highland Ave. (Cahuenga Blvd.), Hollywood; 323-850-2000; www.hollywoodbowl.org
■ "Summer wouldn't be the same" without "music under the stars" at this "legendary" seasonal Hollywood venue (with "a new acoustical shell for June 2004") in a "wonderful outdoor setting" where you can "bring your own picnic"; miniature concertgoers "get bored" with the "wine-and-cheese crowd" at most events, but "go on a night with

fireworks" and "the right performers", and "it's great for kids", as is the smash-hit daytime SummerSounds festival with "classes to participate in"; P.S. "take the bus" or a nearby hotel shuttle to avoid "insane stacked parking."

Hollywood Wax Museum ☺☺

20	20	18	17	M

6767 Hollywood Blvd. (bet. Highland & Las Palmas Aves.), Hollywood; 323-462-5991; www.hollywoodwax.com

◪ While "it's no Madame Tussaud's" à la London or Vegas, this "cheesy" but "fun experience" "conveniently located" in Hollywood is worth visiting "at least once for a laugh" when "standing with Superman or letting Scotty beam you up"; paraffin-averse parents protest that toddlers "sometimes get afraid" of the "lifelike" "celebrities immortalized in wax", but "movie fans" "10 and up should enjoy" it, as long as they "don't touch anything."

Huntington Library ☺☺

13	27	26	23	M

1151 Oxford Rd. (bet. Euston & Stratford Rds.), San Marino; 626-405-2100; www.huntington.org

■ "Far more than a library", this multifaceted "gem" in "sweet, old" San Marino "has everything": a "fabulous botanical collection matched with great private art" met by "unbelievable books" of "historical importance"; "run the children ragged" amid "mysterious, ghostly cacti", "roses in full bloom" and "sprawling lawns", "bring some bread" for the denizens of "the koi pond in the Japanese garden", and when the whippersnappers have "burned off energy", "set foot inside" where "you'll see the *Blue Boy*" by Gainsborough and can have a reserve-ahead, casual-attire "spectacular afternoon tea."

Japanese American
National Museum ☺

▽ 13	24	24	23	I

369 E. First St. (Central Ave.); 213-625-0414; 800-461-5266; www.janm.org

■ "Thought-provoking exhibits" in a "gorgeous building" in Little Tokyo make this "leading historical and cultural institution" an "important museum" for young history buffs who appreciate more "meaningful" sites; the "friendly, informative" staff and a "great gift shop" ensure that visits are "educational and fun at the same time", though some children may not fully grasp "the hardship of the World War II internees", nor the grace of the museum's "beautiful woodwork and exterior garden."

Knott's Berry Farm

27	22	21	21	E

8039 Beach Blvd. (bet. Crescent & La Palma Aves.), Buena Park; 714-220-5200; www.knotts.com

■ "Lesser known than Disneyland" but "more relaxed" and a "heckuva better value", this Buena Park amusement-fest an hour south of town may not "transport you to Fantasyland", but it's still "a blast" for the "whole family": Camp Snoopy "caters to younger children" with "mini-Ferris wheels and mini-cars", while the many "hair-raising" rides are "terrific" for "teens who prefer thrills"; "you can pan for gold" here, though culinary clans would rather stake claim to "the best fried chicken this side of Dixie!"

La Brea Tar Pits/Page Museum ☺☺

23	22	21	19	I

5801 Wilshire Blvd. (Curson Ave.); 323-857-6311; www.tarpits.org

■ "How cool!" – "millions of years ago, animals were trapped" in these "bubbling pits", and today they're "smack dab" on "glitzy" Miracle Mile, inducing "lots of 'ooh, look at that' and 'eew, that's gross'" moments from "awestruck" kids "who like dinosaurs"; "walk the grounds, read the signs, check out" an "actual Ice Age fossil excavation" and "observe places where a recent eruption has busted up the sidewalk", "all for free", or pay to "travel through time in the small but extremely informative museum"; just "bring nail polish remover – your kids will find tar."

Long Beach Aquarium of the Pacific ☺☺

| 27 | 25 | 25 | 22 | M |

100 Aquarium Way (Shoreline Dr.), Long Beach; 562-590-3100; 888-742-7572; www.aquariumofpacific.org

■ There's "nothing fishy" about "petting a sting ray" or "getting up close and personal with a shark" at Long Beach's "fantastic aquarium" where "they actually let you touch the animals"; "if you're lucky, you'll see a scuba diver play chambermaid" to "exotic" "wonders of the ocean", or one of the "special birds" in the Lorikeet Forest will sit on your head; maybe it's "not as good as" Monterey, but the six-year-old center "continues to improve", and it's a "solid winner" with kids, who might even "cry when they have to leave."

Los Angeles County Museum of Art ☺

| 13 | 26 | 24 | 21 | I |

5905 Wilshire Blvd. (Spaulding Ave.); 323-857-6000; www.lacma.org

☑ "Check out Family Day" every Sunday afternoon when "craft centers for all ages" help little dabblers get in touch with their inner Matisse at this Miracle Mile "hodgepodge of galleries" housing "beautifully presented world-class exhibits" and "marvelous special shows"; despite the "children's programs" and free admission for visitors under 17, it is an "art museum nonetheless", meaning that it's "generally more geared to teens and adults", so "if the kids get bored, the Tar Pits are right next door."

Los Angeles Zoo

| 26 | 21 | 17 | 17 | I |

5333 Zoo Dr. (Crystal Springs Rd.); 323-644-4200; www.lazoo.org

☑ Kids are sure to find friends among the 1,200 animals at this "small, but satisfying zoo" in Griffith Park, north of Downtown; "do your stretches before" embarking, as "lots of hills" "make everyone's feet sore, unless they're lucky enough to ride in a stroller"; though "amazing renovations" with additions like the Red Ape Rain Forest and 2004's sea lion habitat have it "on the upswing", cagey critics who call it "old-school with too much concrete" howl "why not just visit the San Diego Zoo only two hours" to the south instead?

Malibu Lagoon State Beach

| 25 | 25 | 15 | 11 | $0 |

23200 PCH (Serra Rd.), Malibu; 818-880-0350; www.parks.ca.gov

■ Old and young salts comb "the best sights and sounds in LA" from this "hidden beach" where Malibu Creek and ocean meet; tucked between auto and marine traffic, with the Pacific Coast Highway on one side and migrating gray whales on the other, it boasts flower gardens, "wetlands harbor nesting sites for many birds" and rad spots for riding the wild surf; if your brood gets sun-baked, duck inside the historical Adamson House around the corner for a peek at 1930s "celebrity enclave" living; N.B. it's five clams to park your Woody.

Museum of Television & Radio ☺

| 14 | 24 | 26 | 24 | I |

465 N. Beverly Dr. (bet. Brighton Way & Santa Monica Blvd.), Beverly Hills; 310-786-1000; www.mtr.org

☑ "If your idea of fun is to sit inside, this is your place": "a TV lover's paradise" where, for "the suggested contribution", small-screen "addicts" "access thousands of hours of shows from throughout history"; "unless you bring them to a program specifically for them", such as the weekend kids' screenings or radio workshops for announcers 9 and up, there isn't much for munchkins in the Beverly Hills branch of this bicoastal museum, but they'll love the big swivel chairs and individual consoles for *Barney* or *Sesame Street* viewing; N.B. closed Mondays and Tuesdays.

Museum of the American West 😃☺ | 19 | 23 | 24 | 21 | I |

Griffith Park, 4700 Western Heritage Way (Zoo Dr.); 323-667-2000;
www.autrynationalcenter.org

■ To teach your little pardners "how the West was won", blaze a trail to this "handsome" "bit of Americana" "next door to the Zoo" in Griffith Park; an "excellent museum on Southwestern, Native American and frontier heritage", it "has things for toddlers to climb on", "special programs like cowboy movies and singing" and – just like the prairie itself – "lots of open space to run"; "the highlight is sitting on a saddle while watching yourself on screen playing" Gene Autry.

Museum of Tolerance ☺ | 16 | 27 | 26 | 26 | M |

9786 W. Pico Blvd. (bet. Castello Ave. & Roxbury Dr.); 310-553-8403;
800-900-9036; www.museumoftolerance.com

■ "Horror and hope are presented with grace and style" for a "moving experience" at this West LA museum that "should be a required field trip for every youngster in every high school"; it's "too intense for young children", but the "focus on the Holocaust", with "dioramas that bring an awful era to life", as well as interactive, "excellent exhibits" on genocide and racism are "enlightening" "for preteens" and up, no matter how "disturbing" – just "be ready to face some hard questions."

Natural History Museum of Los Angeles County 😃☺ | 25 | 24 | 20 | 19 | I |

Exposition Park, 900 Exposition Blvd. (bet. Figueroa St. & Vermont Ave.);
213-763-3466; www.nhm.org

☑ It's "dinosaurs and more dinosaurs" at this "well-kept" – if "dated" – museum in Exposition Park, just south of Downtown; though the permanent displays "could use some renovation", the "rotating exhibits are excellent" (call ahead for timed tickets), and the family programs are plentiful: if your kid "loves rocks and minerals or is interested in bones and fossils", take the budding paleontologist to the "Discovery Center for some hands-on experience" with artifacts; preteens will be buggin' for the "don't-miss bug zoo", and everyone digs the digestibles at the "outstanding cafe downstairs."

NBC Studios ☺ | 19 | 24 | 22 | 23 | I |

3000 W. Alameda Ave. (Niagara St.), Burbank; 818-840-4444

■ "TV fans flock to this mecca of pop culture" in Burbank for "well-guided tours" "through favorite sets"; "write for tickets in advance" "to get into the taping of a show", and though you'll "still wait outside for hours" with only "fast-food hot dogs" nearby to eat, you're "in the LA sun", so "it's hardly objectionable"; in fact, "it's worth it" to see stars like "Jay [Leno] signing autographs and taking photos with audience members"; younger "children may not be allowed" into some shows.

Petersen Automotive Museum | 20 | 25 | 24 | 21 | I |

6060 Wilshire Blvd. (bet. Fairfax & Orange Grove Aves.); 323-930-2277;
www.petersen.org

■ "Way cool!" cry giddy "gearheads" "sitting in a real race car" and slobbering over the Hot Wheels and the Batmobile during an "absolutely superb" automotive-themed afternoon on Miracle Mile; if "all those shiny vehicles with 'Do Not Touch' signs are enough to drive your son [or daughter] nuts", the interactive Discovery Center, "a whole floor dedicated to child's play", is "aces" for "toddlers and young children"; P.S. "easy parking", seriously.

Rose Bowl ☺ | 14 | 22 | 17 | 15 | E |

1001 Rose Bowl Dr. (bet. Rosemont Ave. & West Dr.), Pasadena;
626-577-3100; www.rosebowlstadium.com

☑ So "parking is horrid" – in the lot, the "sub-standard restroom facilities" and the "cramped" seats – but "the grandaddy of bowls" "is still a thrill", if only for Pasadena's "magnificent mountain views"; plus, the "nice parklands" surrounding this "storied stadium" make it a "great place to slip on the rollerblades", "go jogging" or have a picnic; gridiron fans "love UCLA games during the fall" and the namesake game is "one of the all-time favorites", while consumerist clans clamor for "deals every month at the huge swap meet" on second Sundays.

Santa Monica Pier ☺☺   24 | 20 | 15 | 14 | $0

Colorado Ave. (Palisades Beach Rd.), Santa Monica; 310-458-8900; www.santamonicapier.org

✉ "Rides, arcades, fast food", "fishing", "the usual parade of interesting passerby" and "all the honky-tonk you could want" make up the "carnival atmosphere" at this "cheap, convenient" "kid heaven" jutting into Santa Monica's "dirty" surf; "the Ferris wheel is spectacular" and "street performers add to the excitement", but bag the "family strolling" once "the sun sets over the Pacific", as it "gets seedy" at night; sensory overload? – "walk down to the beach to decompress."

Santa Monica State Beach   24 | 23 | 15 | 12 | $0

1642 Ocean Front Walk (Colorado Ave.), Santa Monica; 310-394-3266

✉ For that "vacation feeling" moments away from bustling Santa Monica, this "wide, sandy" but "crowded" beach may not be "the most beautiful", but with a "boardwalk for bikes, rollerblades" and "people-watching", plus "waves that come in nice and easy", it's popular with families looking to avoid a schlep; sun-worshipers longing for a little more "California dreamin'" "head north" to "cleaner", less-congested sands in Malibu.

Six Flags California ☺   25 | 24 | 20 | 17 | VE

Magic Mountain Pkwy. (off I-5), Valencia; 818-367-5965; www.sixflags.com

■ "Bring your Dramamine" north to Valencia – about 45 minutes from Downtown – where "the best roller coasters anywhere" provide the "ultimate in thrill rides" and "screams"; given the "aggressive" jolts and height requirements of these "mix-masters for the stomach", it's "not for small kids or the faint-hearted", but "teenaged" daredevils jonesing for "high speeds" and "death-defying" drops suffer "insane lines" and mob scenes as "scary" as the contraptions, or else play hookey on a "weekday to avoid the larger crowds."

Staples Center ☺   17 | 25 | 25 | 21 | E

1111 S. Figueroa St. (bet. 11th & 12th Sts.); 213-742-7340; www.staplescenter.com

■ "Every seat is a good seat" Downtown at "one of the top arenas in the nation" "for either sports or concerts" that's "modern" and "cleaner than a hospital"; the "child appeal really depends on the event", but if your kid is into athletics, you can't go wrong with tickets to the "Lakers and Clippers and Kings – oh my!"; "bring lots of cash if you want to eat" – or park – because the "tens of millions of dollars" put into the "glam" building are passed along via high prices at the concessions.

Travel Town   25 | 17 | 14 | 13 | $0
Transportation Museum ☺☺

Griffith Park, 5200 Zoo Dr. (Griffith Park Dr.); 323-662-5874

■ Kids can "climb all over large locomotives", playing "engineer for the day" at this Griffith Park museum, the "be all, end all" for aspiring conductors where you'll "drag your two-year-old kicking and screaming" from the miniature choo-choo ride and the "elaborate train set"; it's an engine of "fun for the little tykes" but probably "boring" for teens, unless they're certified boxcar "buffs"; "bring a lunch" and picnic or barbecue outside because there are only vending machines on the premises.

Universal CityWalk ☺☺

| 21 | 23 | 22 | 19 | $0 |

*1000 Universal Studios Blvd. (off US Hwy. 101), Universal City; 818-622-4455;
800-864-8377; www.citywalkhollywood.com*

☑ This "Main Street on steroids" right outside the same-named studios has "something for everyone", particularly "teens" who can "do a little shopping, eat, catch a movie, watch the dancing water fountain", "hang out" and maybe "meet their first boy- or girlfriend"; it's always "crowded" and the "assault of neon and loud noise is almost painful" for sensitive "chaperones", but "kids love the lights", "cartoon architecture" and "youth-oriented" commerce, while the smorgasbörd of food is a universal "crowd-pleaser" – even if you "spend more on parking than on dinner."

Universal Studios Hollywood ☺

| 27 | 25 | 24 | 22 | E |

*100 Universal City Plaza (off US Hwy. 101), Universal City; 800-864-8377;
www.universalstudioshollywood.com*

■ "Out-of-towners", relax: when the "earthquake shakes you" at this Universal City studio theme park, it's just "movie magic"; "get behind the scenes" on the "entertaining" "if somewhat dated" tour, and if the little ones fidget on the tram – "what child still cares about Woody Woodpecker", after all? – they'll "like the stunt show" and "terrific" rides like Jurassic Park; the VIP Experience offering fuller backlot access makes "you wish you were in front of the camera", but while you're waiting to be discovered, take a spin on the new Revenge of the Mummy roller coaster.

Venice Boardwalk ☺

| 17 | 23 | 13 | 11 | $0 |

*Venice Beach, 1800 Ocean Front Walk (18th Ave.), Venice; 310-399-2775;
www.laparks.org/venice*

☑ The "funky", daily "cultural explosion" at this "classic" California "circus by the sea" along the gritty sand below Santa Monica provides "awesome people-watching", "eclectic" shopping and "kooky" street entertainment – you can find "a guy who can write your name on a grain of rice" or go in for a family "photo-op with a bikini-clad grandma", a "Jimi Hendrix lookalike", "skateboarders" or "lifters at Muscle Beach", but "be prepared to discuss body piercing, alternative lifestyles and pink Mohawks in the car" afterward.

Warner Bros. Studios ☺

| 21 | 25 | 24 | 24 | E |

*4000 Warner Blvd. (Olive Ave.), Burbank; 818-954-1669;
www.wbstudiotour.com*

■ "Walk behind the sets and learn the tricks of the trade" in Burbank on what some studio sleuths say is "the nicest and most thorough" of the "movie world's" tours; "more intimate than Universal", the "well-organized", "in-depth" experience shows you "what's going on that day in the soundstages, recording studios and backlots" of a working institution; the "fabulous" guides "answer anything and tell all they know", and "if you're lucky, you'll see extras" or even a "real star" "walking around" – just note that the "long" journey is better suited to 'tweens than toddlers.

Will Rogers State Historic Park ☺

| 19 | 23 | 20 | 16 | $0 |

*1501 Will Rogers State Park Rd. (Sunset Blvd.), Pacific Palisades;
310-454-8212; www.parks.ca.gov*

■ Pack a "picnic" and "get away from the city" to this "beautiful" Pacific Palisades "oasis", once the ranch of the eponymous cowboy; "if you like hiking", the "trails set in the canyon" are "jewels", particularly on a "clear day", when you can snap this year's holiday card in front of an "expansive" "view of LA or the ocean"; malleteers "go for the polo" on the only regulation field in the county, but film-history buffs will have to wait until late 2004, when Rogers' house re-opens following renovations.

HOTELS

Ratings: Family Appeal, Rooms, Service, Public Facilities, Cost

FA	R	S	P	$

Casa Del Mar, Hotel

21	26	24	23	$380

1910 Ocean Way, Santa Monica; 310-581-5533; 800-898-6999;
www.hotelcasadelmar.com; 129 rooms, 28 suites

■ A "perfect location with the beach just steps out the door" has folks returning to this Santa Monica seaside resort where "splendid service" includes "greetings for the kids", books, teddy bears and "rubber ducks by the bathtub"; parents love the "beautiful surroundings" and proximity to art galleries, museums, tons of stores and the West Coast's oldest pier, while the 22-mile oceanfront bike path keeps active types happy; just 13 miles from Downtown LA, it oozes "old-world charm" at "steep" prices.

Disneyland Hotel

–	–	–	–	$270

1150 Magic Way, Anaheim; 714-956-6425; www.disneyland.com;
925 rooms, 55 suites

Located adjacent to Downtown Disney, this hotel is filled with kid-friendly fun including themed eateries like Hook's Pointe and Goofy's Kitchen, the Fantasy Waters show with synchronized lights and water-jet fountains, remote-controlled jungle cruise boats, an outdoor pool and koi fish ponds; although this large property can get busy with business meetings and events, overall it's a reasonable, convenient spot and offers "Extra Value Days" in which guests receive two free adult admissions to the character breakfasts held at the property.

Disney's Grand Californian

29	25	25	27	$340

1600 S. Disneyland Dr., Anaheim; 714-635-2300; 800-225-2024;
www.disneyland.com; 713 rooms, 38 suites

■ "Quite possibly the best family hotel ever created", this resort "right next to California Adventure" (there's a private entrance for guests) feels like an "old West Coast lodge with modern amenities" and "great perks" for kids including a "fun pool area", bunk beds, cookies at bedtime, "enchanting" fireside stories and a casual restaurant where you can dine with Disney characters; the "outstanding staff" "can't do enough for you", creating a "worry-free stay" "right in the middle of the theme park action."

Fairmont Miramar

▽ 24	23	21	22	$389

101 Wilshire Blvd., Santa Monica; 310-576-7777; 800-441-1414;
www.fairmont.com; 208 rooms, 62 suites, 32 bungalows

■ The "bungalows are superb for families" (with French doors that open to private patios and views of the Pacific) at this "fabulous" hotel across from the beach in Santa Monica; even if "some of the other guests look upon your children with horror", the staff is "wonderful and accommodating" to kids and the "casual", though luxurious, vibe is appreciated; babysitting services are available upon request, should you want to escape for an adult-only outing.

Loews Santa Monica Beach Hotel

23	23	23	24	$265

1700 Ocean Ave., Santa Monica; 310-458-6700; 800-235-6397;
www.loewshotels.com; 321 rooms, 19 suites

■ They "make you feel like family" (theirs, if not yours) at this hotel whose location "right on the beach" "can't be beat" for lapping waters and warm sands; "you can see the Ferris wheel, bikers and skaters from the room", and it's just a few minutes' walk to the Pier; "dogs are permitted", there's a "fabulous pool" and the kids' program includes a game library, welcome kits and other amenities.

Paradise Pier Hotel

 $190

1717 S. Disneyland Dr., Anaheim; 714-956-6425; www.disneyland.com; 347 rooms, 20 suites

Sporting its own entrance to the California Adventure park, this smallest of the Disneyland resorts, located in one tower, offers a rooftop pool and spa, views of the resort, character breakfasts at the on-site restaurants and a beach-themed theater where kids can watch their favorite Disney movies; adults appreciate the Japanese eatery, Yamabuki, and all will love the proximity to major LA attractions.

Park Hyatt

▽ 21 | 25 | 24 | 24 | $345

2151 Ave. of the Stars; 310-277-1234; 800-233-1234; www.hyatt.com; 179 rooms, 187 suites

☑ Rated surprisingly well for families, this "top-notch" hotel goes "above and beyond" for junior, say pleased parents who point to check-in gifts and toiletry kits for kids, refrigerators and rollaway beds on demand and the impressive breakfast buffet; better still, weary adults can relax in the brand-new spa and fitness center, which features private villas for body and beauty treatments.

Renaissance Hollywood

21 | 25 | 21 | 24 | $199

1755 N. Highland Ave., Hollywood; 323-856-1200; 800-468-3571; www.renaissancehotels.com; 604 rooms, 33 suites

☑ A centerpiece of the Hollywood & Highland retail complex with lots of movies and restaurants, this chain outpost has a "good location for families" not far from Grauman's Chinese Theater and the Hollywood Walk of Fame (just don't allow young 'uns to roam off the beaten path in this neighborhood); there's a "great" rooftop pool, "rooms are big enough" to get some space from the kids and child-care services are available when needed, but a few say it's "probably better for teens and preteens."

Ritz-Carlton Marina del Rey

19 | 23 | 23 | 22 | $299

4375 Admiralty Way, Marina del Rey; 310-823-1700; 800-241-3333; www.ritzcarlton.com; 281 rooms, 23 suites

☑ "Be sure to ask for a marina view so the kids can watch the boats come in" at this upscale property not far from LAX Airport with a "great pool" and nice outdoor areas; but although it can be a "fun location" for some, it's "too far from everything" for others who advise "stay at the end of a trip" so you can catch that early flight without too much fuss.

Shutters on the Beach

21 | 26 | 26 | 25 | $405

1 Pico Blvd., Santa Monica; 310-458-0030; 800-334-9000; www.shuttersonthebeach.com; 180 rooms, 12 suites

■ It's "worth breaking the piggy bank" to bunk at this "first-class" hotel "right on the beach" in Santa Monica where "huge rooms" with high-speed Internet access and the "short walk to the Pier's rides and arcades" are "great for the whole family"; it's "hidden away from the crowds" and "very elegant", yet the service is "friendly to kids" and the casual, open-air restaurant, Pedals, has a menu for little ones.

Top Family-Friendly Hotel Chains in the Area:

Embassy Suites	Hyatt
Four Seasons	Marriott
Hampton Inn	Residence Inn
Holiday Inn	Westin
Homewood Suites	

See Hotel Chain reviews, starting on page 256.

RESTAURANTS

Ratings: Family Appeal, Food, Decor, Service, Cost

	FA	F	D	S	$

Alejo's
FA 22 | F 22 | D 9 | S 19 | $ M

*4002 Lincoln Blvd. (bet. Maxella Ave. & Washington Blvd.), Marina del Rey;
310-822-0095*
8343 Lincoln Blvd. (84th St.), Westchester; 310-670-6677

■ "Garlic lovers of all ages" love this Marina del Rey Italian that
offers "healthy portions at reasonable prices" in "relaxed" digs;
despite "not much ambiance" and "long lines" on weekends, most
agree it's "worth the wait", especially since the "accommodating"
staff will "work with you" to mollify any "picky eaters" in your party.

Art's Deli
22 | 22 | 14 | 20 | M

*12224 Ventura Blvd. (bet. Laurelgrove & Vantage Aves.), Studio City;
818-762-1221*

☑ After a romp through Universal Studios, schlep the family to this
Studio City deli known for its "huge menu" of "classic" items that
"will please everyone"; ok, it's "not New York" and may be somewhat
"overpriced", but the sandwiches are big enough to "easily feed two"
and the "casual atmosphere" is "definitely family-friendly" – and
besides, "where else can you introduce the kids to kishkas?"

Back on the Beach
26 | 16 | 19 | 15 | M

*445 PCH (California Blvd.), Santa Monica; 310-393-8282;
www.backonthebeach.com*

☑ "Eat with your feet in the sand" at this "fun" Santa Monican "right
on the beach", where the "salty air" and "Pacific Ocean vistas" add
up to a "home-run family destination"; though the Americana menu is
"ok, not great", and the "service a bit slow for dining with little ones",
the mood's so "comfortable" that you can't help but be "relaxed" here.

Cafe '50s ●
25 | 17 | 22 | 18 | I

838 Lincoln Blvd. (Lake St.), Venice; 310-399-1955 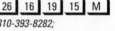
11623 Santa Monica Blvd. (bet. Barry & Federal Aves.), West LA; 310-479-1955
4609 Van Nuys Blvd. (Hortense St.), Sherman Oaks; 818-906-1955
www.cafe50s.com

■ "Kids of all ages" dig this "high-energy" diner chain with "retro" '50s
decor that will "keep the little ones' attention" while "bringing back old
memories" for their elders; the food may be "unremarkable" (be ready
to "forgo your diet"), but the prices are reasonable and the "noisy,
happening" atmosphere works well for large groups or birthday parties.

C & O Trattoria
25 | 23 | 20 | 23 | M

31 Washington Blvd. (Pacific Ave.), Marina del Rey; 310-823-9491
3016 Washington Blvd. (Thatcher Ave.), Marina del Rey; 310-301-7278
www.cotrattoria.com

■ "Family-style eating" alfresco is the name of the game at this
"popular" Marina del Rey Italian near the Venice Pier where the
"portions are enormous", the staff "energetic" and the mood "lively";
child-friendly diversions include "creating your own tablecloth" design
via crayon and "singing along to 'That's Amore'"; weary parents are
relieved that "it's so noisy that no one notices your loud kids."

Cole's P.E. Buffet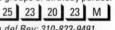
– | – | – | – | I

*Pacific Electric Bldg., 118 E. Sixth St. (bet. Los Angeles & Main Sts.);
213-622-4090; www.colespebuffet.com*

A "classic LA experience" and a "must" for tourists, this "scenic",
"old-world" Downtown Traditional American (circa 1908) offers a "taste

of history – and the dust to prove it"; kids like that it has appeared in more than 400 films and TV shows, and adults will appreciate the friendly prices, just "stay with the French dip" sandwich that "can't be beat" – "you'll be glad you did."

Gladstone's Malibu | 22 | 18 | 20 | 17 | E |

17300 PCH (Sunset Blvd.), Pacific Palisades; 310-573-0212; www.gladstones.com

☑ Given the "generally high noise level" and "casual", "peanut-shells-on-the-floor" ambiance, parents needn't be nervous about anchoring their kids at this Malibu seafooder best known for its "beautiful beachfront location"; too bad that the "wait for an inside table can be grueling" and the fin fare is only "decent" ("big portions do not equal good food"), though many call it a "must-see for vacationers" and reserve it for the "next time the relatives are in town."

Islands | 26 | 19 | 21 | 20 | I |

350 S. Beverly Dr. (Olympic Blvd.), Beverly Hills; 310-556-1624
101 E. Orange Grove Ave. (N. 1st St.), Burbank; 818-566-7744
3200 Sepulveda Blvd. (bet. 30th & 33rd Sts.), Manhattan Beach; 310-546-4456
3533 E. Foothill Blvd. (Rosemead Blvd.), Pasadena; 626-351-6543
www.islandsrestaurants.com

■ "Overdone" island-themed decor, televised "surfing competitions" and an "energetic" atmosphere keep "restless toddlers" entertained at this "kid-oriented" archipelago of "casual" eateries scattered all over LA; grown-ups report the "consistent", Hawaiian-style menu is both "dependable" and "affordable", the staff is "patient" and "quick", and the "loud" sound levels "drown out misbehaving children."

Johnny Rebs' Southern Roadhouse | 25 | 22 | 17 | 20 | M |

4663 Long Beach Blvd. (bet. 46th & 47th Sts.), Long Beach; 562-423-7327; www.johnnyrebs.com

■ "Large families" like this "always busy", "true Southern" joint in Long Beach where you can "toss peanut shells on the floor" and "hear chickens singing on the restroom loudspeakers"; it's a "perfect place to take a child" hankering for "tasty, fried" eats, with a "friendly" staff and an outdoor patio to boot.

Kay 'n Dave's | 26 | 21 | 19 | 25 | M |

15246 Sunset Blvd. (bet. Monument St. & Swarthmore Ave.), Pacific Palisades; 310-459-8118
262 26th St. (San Vicente Blvd.), Santa Monica; 310-260-1355

■ Even though the walls are "decorated with kids' art", these "funky" Mexican cantinas in Santa Monica and the Palisades are "cool enough for teenagers" (and "fresh and healthy enough" for grown-ups); the "friendly" staff will gladly "modify a variety of dishes" for younger palates, while the "cheery", "family-friendly" vibe works well for smaller fry who "don't have a volume control."

Mel's Drive-In ◐ | 22 | 16 | 18 | 16 | I |

1650 N. Highland Ave. (Hollywood Blvd.), Hollywood; 323-465-2111
8585 Sunset Blvd. (La Cienega Blvd.), West Hollywood; 310-854-7200
14846 Ventura Blvd. (Kester Ave.), Sherman Oaks; 818-990-6357
www.melsdrive-in.com

☑ The "convenience factor" is everything at this trio of "dependable", "*American Graffiti*"–ish eateries, though some say for "restaurants with family appeal", they seem to "cater more to late-night singles"; still, "kids get the feel of the '50s" thanks to its "spiffy, classic-car" food wrappers, even if present-day parents deplore the "ordinary" grub and "low-end diner" setups.

Miceli's
_ | _ | _ | _ | M

1646 N. Las Palmas St. (Hollywood Blvd.), Hollywood; 323-466-3438
3655 Cahuenga Blvd. W. (Regal Pl.), Universal City; 323-851-3345
www.micelis1949.com
Little ones enjoy the "singing waiters" at this "campy" Italian duo in Hollywood and Universal City that's "fun, fun, fun for families" with "red-and-white checkerboard tablecloths" and "Chianti bottle decorations"; many come for the "atmosphere" rather than the "hit-or-miss cooking", but parents with hungry tykes in tow will be glad there are so many "affordable menu choices" of "basic" red-sauce fare.

Philippe the Original ☞
_ | _ | _ | _ | I

1001 N. Alameda St. (Ord St.); 213-628-3781; www.philippes.com
An "amazing cross section of Angelenos" comes to this self-serve LA landmark" (circa 1908) to "dine at a shrine" to the French dip (purportedly its birthplace), where the "awesome" signature sandwich is served in a "period" room with "sawdust on the floors" that's comfortable for kids; with the stadium so close by, if you hold off on eating those Dodger dogs, you can grab a bite here after the game instead, just don't let little ones near the house mustard – it can "hurt your insides from your nose to your toes."

Pig, The
_ | _ | _ | _ | M

612 N. La Brea Ave. (Melrose Ave.); 323-935-1116;
www.thepigcatering.com
"This little piggy goes wee-wee-wee all the way into your stomach" gush groupies of this "cute" "Memphis-style BBQ" in La Brea run by chef Daly Thompson and wife/pastry chef Liz, where families can pig out on "down-home style ribs", "fabulous brisket and chicken wings"; but for youngsters, it's really all about the "desserts as huge as the entrees", judging from the cheers when they see the "fantastic apple rumble-crumble" and the double-fudge brownie.

Reel Inn
22 | 21 | 18 | 14 | M

18661 PCH (Topanga Canyon Rd.), Malibu; 310-456-8221
■ The "paper-plates-and-sawdust" crowd feels right at home at this "charming" but admittedly "rattletrap shack" in Malibu where "fresh, tasty seafood", self-service and "childproof, picnic-style seating" make for "adequate but not spectacular" meals; given the very "casual atmosphere", "other tables won't mind a wandering toddler", though hopefully the "children will be engrossed by the saltwater aquarium" and not get too rambunctious.

Spago
_ | _ | _ | _ | VE

176 N. Cañon Dr. (Wilshire Blvd.), Beverly Hills; 310-385-0880;
www.wolfgangpuck.com
A "classic" that's "constantly evolving", this Beverly Hills "flagship of the Wolfgang Puck empire" offers a taste of "LA glamour and Californian cuisine"; "even a nobody is made to feel like a somebody" at this "power hangout", and if the young 'uns turn up their nose when you "go for the foie gras three ways" and other "inventive" dishes from chef Lee Hefter, they'll get on board after they eye pastry chef Sherry Yard's "amazing" desserts.

Uncle Bill's Pancake House
26 | 26 | 16 | 21 | I

1305 Highland Ave. (13th St.), Manhattan Beach; 310-545-5177
■ "Come early" or be prepared for a "long weekend wait" at this Manhattan Beach breakfast "favorite", the "perfect way to start the day" thanks to its "to-die-for" menu of "stick-to-your-ribs" classics; the "portions are huge" and "reasonably priced", so get in line and make sure to "request outside seating for a gorgeous ocean view."

RESTAURANT CHAINS

See reviews, starting on page 262.

Ratings: Family Appeal, Food, Decor, Service, Cost

	FA	F	D	S	$
Baja Fresh Mexican Grill Ⓢ	20	22	14	18	I

5757 Wilshire Blvd. (Courtyard Pl.); 323-549-9080
6333 Sunset Blvd. (Vine St.), Hollywood; 323-464-5505
720 Wilshire Blvd. (7th St.), Santa Monica; 310-393-9313
245 Main St. (bet. Marine St. & Rose Ave.), Venice; 310-392-3452

Bubba Gump Shrimp Co. Ⓢ	24	18	23	20	M

87 Aquarium Way (W. Shoreline Rd.), Long Beach; 562-437-2434

Buca di Beppo	24	19	22	21	M

1442 Second St. (bet. Broadway & Santa Monica Blvd.), Santa Monica;
310-587-2782
Universal CityWalk, 1000 Universal Studios Blvd. (off US Hwy. 101),
Universal City; 818-509-9463

Chili's Grill & Bar Ⓢ	21	19	18	19	M

1056 Westwood Blvd. (bet. Kinross & Weyburn Aves.); 310-481-2228

Chuck E. Cheese's Ⓢ	26	10	17	13	I

6885 La Tijera Blvd. (Centinela Ave.); 310-337-0497
930 N. San Fernando Blvd. (bet. E. Burbank Blvd. & Delaware Rd.),
Burbank; 818-841-3453

Fuddrucker's Ⓢ	24	20	15	16	I

221 N. San Fernando Rd. (Orange Grove Ave.), Burbank; 818-848-4856
3883 E. Foothills Blvd. (Michillinda Ave.), Pasadena; 626-351-8958
Sherman Oaks Galleria, 15301 Ventura Blvd. (Sepulveda Ave.),
Sherman Oaks; 818-995-4552

Johnny Rockets ◖	25	17	20	18	I

Farmer's Mkt., 6333 W. Third St. (Fairfax Ave.); 323-937-2093
474 N. Beverly Dr. (Little Santa Monica Blvd.), Beverly Hills;
310-271-2222
6801 Hollywood Blvd. (Highland Ave.), Hollywood; 323-465-4456
1322 Third St. Promenade (bet. Arizona Ave. & Santa Monica Blvd.),
Santa Monica; 310-394-6362

Maggiano's Little Italy	22	22	21	22	M

The Grove at Farmer's Mkt., 189 The Grove Dr. (Fairfax Ave.);
323-965-9665
The Promenade at Woodland Hills, 6100 N. Topanga Canyon Blvd.
(bet. Erwin & Oxnard Sts.), Woodland Hills; 818-887-3777

Mimi's Cafe	23	21	22	20	M

2925 Los Feliz Blvd. (bet. Revere & Seneca Aves.); 323-668-1715
1240 N. Euclid Ave. (W. Romneya Dr.), Anaheim; 714-535-1552
1400 S. Harbor Blvd. (S. Manchester Ave.), Anaheim; 714-956-2223
6670 E. PCH (N. Studebaker Rd.), Long Beach; 562-596-0831

Old Spaghetti Factory, The	25	20	22	20	I

5939 Sunset Blvd. (Tamarind Ave.); 323-469-7149 Ⓢ
110 E. Santa Fe Ave. (S. Harbor Blvd.), Fullerton; 714-526-6801

Olive Garden	20	19	18	19	M

936 Westwood Blvd. (Weyburn Ave.), West LA; 310-824-7588

On the Border
Mexican Grill & Cantina ⌧ | 20 | 19 | 19 | 18 | M |
6081 Center Dr. (Sepulveda Blvd.); 310-665-0994

Original Pancake House, The ⌿ | 24 | 22 | 12 | 17 | I |
1418 E. Lincoln Ave. (bet. East St. & State College Blvd.), Anaheim;
714-535-9815

Rainforest Cafe ⌧ | 27 | 16 | 27 | 18 | M |
1515 S. Disneyland Dr. (Katella Ave.), Anaheim; 714-772-0413

T.G.I. Friday's ⌧ | 21 | 17 | 18 | 17 | M |
6721 La Tijera Blvd. (S. La Cienega Blvd.); 310-337-1143

Tony Roma's ⌧ | 20 | 21 | 16 | 19 | M |
1640 S. Harbor Blvd. (bet. I-5 & Katella Ave.), Anaheim; 714-520-0200
246 S. Lake Ave. (bet. Cordova St. & Del Mar Blvd.), Pasadena; 626-405-0612

Miami

*There's much more to Miami than its palm trees and miles of beaches,
and that includes plenty to do even in the steamy summer off-season.
From fine art and history museums, four professional sports teams and a
sizzling nightlife to kid-pleasing airboat rides, performing dolphins and
water activities, there's something for every age group – all in a vibrant
subtropical setting rich in Latin and Caribbean influences. Among
Greater Miami's 31 municipalities are lively Coconut Grove and elegant
Coral Gables; glitzy tourist-centric Miami Beach and the art deco district
South Beach are on a thin barrier island across Biscayne Bay. On the
mainland, visitors find a more urban atmosphere and attractions such as
the Miami Museum of Science & Space Transit Planetarium and the
Miami Metro Zoo. For $1.25, you can ride the public, elevated Metrorail;
the Downtown Metromover, making a 4.4-mile city loop, is free. You'll
need a car for most travel beyond the city center, but with the Keys to the
south, the Everglades to the west and Boca Raton, Ft. Lauderdale and
Palm Beach to the north, there are lots of places that are worth the drive.*

ATTRACTIONS

Ratings: Child Appeal, Adult Appeal, Public Facilities, Service, Cost

	C	A	P	S	$

Actor's Playhouse at the | 18 | 23 | 20 | 21 | M |
Miracle Theater ☺
280 Miracle Mile (bet. Ponce de Leon Blvd. & Salzedo St.), Coral Gables;
305-444-9293; www.actorsplayhouse.org
☑ Parents applaud the "quality" shows at this "old theater" in Coral
Gables, especially on a rainy Saturday afternoon, when young
audiences can cheer productions like *Rumplestiltskin* and *Hansel &
Gretel*; even though there's "a lot of theater that appeals to children",
critics charge "it's a long way from Broadway" and the facility is
"mediocre"; N.B. check schedules for kid-friendly performances.

American Airlines Arena ☺ | 17 | 23 | 22 | 18 | E |
601 Biscayne Blvd. (NE 6th & 8th Sts.); 786-777-1000; www.aaarena.com
☑ It seems like "everyone takes a limo" to this "fan-friendly" facility
"right on the bay", the place to catch acts from the Harlem Globetrotters
to Britney Spears; though critics caution "it's a bit too large for the
kiddies, with seats up too high", grown-ups laud the "great acoustics"

and "multiple entertainment possibilities", especially since it's near Bayside Marketplace – "only in Miami can you combine a waterfront lounge, a Cuban disco and an arena."

Barnacle State Historic Site ☺ | ▽ 16 | 24 | 21 | 21 | I |

3485 Main Hwy. (Charles Ave.), Coconut Grove; 305-448-9445;
www.floridastateparks.org/thebarnacle

■ "Nestled in the heart of Coconut Grove", this "fascinating restored house" – the oldest residence in Miami-Dade County in its original location – "is history made fun" for school-age and older kids, and "it's a great place for a picnic"; but adults probably get more enjoyment than their offspring on the tours, offered four times daily, that explore how yacht designer Ralph Middleton Munroe, his wife and two children lived back in 1891, when their one-story bungalow was built on a limestone ridge by Biscayne Bay.

Bill Baggs Cape | 23 | 24 | 19 | 18 | I |
Florida State Recreational Area ☺☺

1200 S. Crandon Blvd., Key Biscayne; 305-361-5811;
www.floridastateparks.org/capeflorida

☑ "A must-see for anyone who loves nature", "one of the finest state parks" draws big "weekend crowds" for sun, surf and the scene after climbing109 steps to the lighthouse to "enjoy" the bird's-eye view of the "gorgeous beach"; the stairs may be tough for toddlers, but older children can watch the short movie, then tour the keeper's quarters; bring a picnic or feast on the cafe's fresh seafood.

CocoWalk ☺ | 13 | 23 | 20 | 17 | $0 |

3015 Grand Ave. (Virginia St.), Coconut Grove; 305-444-0777;
www.cocowalk.com

☑ A "three-story shopping and eating mecca", this vertical "break from South Beach", where families can cool off, grab lunch and catch a movie inside the AMC 16 Theater, has a "good vibe", at least for "young adults, teens and big kids who like Hooters"; magicians, clowns, street artists and live music are distractions for young 'uns, but with the "shop-till-they-drop" vibe and the "crazy nightlife", it has more adult appeal, of course.

Crandon Park | 26 | 26 | 18 | 13 | I |

4000 Crandon Blvd., Key Biscayne; 305-361-5421

■ Many laud this "awesome" two-mile outdoor recreational area as "the most attractive beach in Miami", a "terrific" "spot for all ages" with an offshore sandbar that protects against strong currents and "an excellent public park"; it also has golf, tennis, biking, Rollerblading and, for small children, an amusement area with a playground, merry-go-round and splash fountain.

Everglades Alligator Farm | 24 | 21 | 15 | 17 | M |

40351 SW 192nd Ave. (Palm Dr.), Florida City; 305-247-2628;
www.everglades.com

■ Get up close and personal with 3,000 alligators at this "super cool" real working gator farm just outside Everglades National Park, where the whole family will find "tons of fun"; daily feedings, alligator wrestling and "informative" snake and unusual animal shows are part of the experience, and kids can take the "neat" 'River of Grass' airboat tour that's "almost like a ride."

Everglades National Park | 24 | 26 | 17 | 19 | I |

40001 State Rd. 9336 (Ingraham Hwy.), Homestead; 305-242-7700;
www.nps.gov/ever

■ "Breathtaking views" "engulf every visitor" at this "spectacular" "national park treasure"; "kids love" the "unique" view of large wading birds, fish, turtles, alligators and crocodiles (it's the only place in the world where crocs and gators exist side by side), and everyone gets a glimpse into "how Florida looked before condos"; so "grab the bug spray" and explore by car, bike, motorboat, canoe or, on the northern border, the Shark Valley "tram tour" (main entrance near Homestead and Florida City); N.B. join ranger-led walks, talks and campfire programs during cooler months.

Fairchild Tropical Garden

| 15 | 25 | 23 | 21 | I |

10901 Old Cutler Rd. (Snapper Creek Rd.), Coral Gables; 305-667-1651; www.fairchildgarden.org

■ The "fantastic" 83-acre "tropical garden" may be too "serene" for most children, but others "will love running around the open areas", exploring a rain forest, "exquisite" plant life, the sunken garden and, "if lucky", smelling the "rare bloom" Mr. Stinky (a titan arum); set your own admission fee on the first Wednesday of every month, then wander along paths or take a narrated tram tour.

Haulover Beach Park

| 17 | 22 | 16 | 12 | I |

10800 Collins Ave. (Harbour Way), Miami Beach; 305-947-3525; www.miamidade.gov/parks

◪ This stretch of seaside "between the Atlantic Ocean and Biscayne Bay" in Miami Beach gets attention for its designated "clothing optional" quarter-mile segment at the north end, but turn south for the "typical" "family beach" and kite park where kids "love" flying creations of all shapes and sizes (bring your own or buy them here); there are also volleyball, boat rentals, fishing and picnic areas.

Holocaust Memorial ☺

| 13 | 27 | 24 | 20 | $0 |

1933-1945 Meridian Ave. (19th St.), Miami Beach; 305-538-1663; www.holocaustmmb.org

■ A "powerful and moving tribute" to the "millions of victims lost in the Holocaust", this "tastefully done", "thought-provoking" "tribute" is "contemplative and elegant" though "heart-wrenching", and an "educational" "opportunity to discuss oppression" "with children ages 8 and up"; allow about an hour to visit the monument with its photographic mural, "outdoor sculpture garden", memorial wall and dome of contemplation, but you might want to think twice before bringing younger kids.

Lincoln Road Mall ☺

| 13 | 26 | 22 | 19 | $0 |

Lincoln Rd. (bet. Alton Rd. & Washington Ave.), Miami Beach; 888-766-4264

■ "Food, fun and fabulous people-watching" give this "hip" pedestrian-only "open-air mall", "filled with shops, cafes and theaters" in Miami Beach, a "great vibe", especially for reviewers who rate it higher for Adult Appeal than Child Appeal; "hot evening dining and clubbing" is a big draw at night, but by day the movieplex, street performers and "strolling outdoors" can amuse the kids while parents "browse boutiques"; on Sundays, there's an "open market" selling "everything from flowers to antiques."

Matheson Hammock Park ☺☺

| 25 | 22 | 19 | 17 | I |

9610 Old Cutler Rd. (Kendall Dr.), Coral Gables; 305-665-5475

■ "Absolutely the best beach for toddlers and young kids", this "heavenly" Coral Gables lagoon is a "well-kept secret" offering "the best views of Downtown Miami", boating facilities, fishing, biking, walking trails and a "shallow atoll that's especially attractive to young children", though "insect repellant is a must"; there are charcoal grills (in the park about a mile from the beach) for outdoor cooking, or you can retreat to "classy" Red Fish Grill in a historic coral rock building right on the sand.

Miami Children's Museum

| – | – | – | – | M |

980 MacArthur Cswy. (Watson Island); 305-373-5437;
www.miamichildrensmuseum.org
Kids enter this museum, which moved to a new location on Watson Island last year, through a three-story cone, then visit an educational mock bank, grocery, music studio, art gallery, cruise ship, vet's office and fire truck; they also climb through a two-story sandcastle and learn about caring for animals at Pet Central; preschoolers can do activities with mom or dad, and olders kids can learn about Florida's Everglades and seashore; N.B. there's a sub shop on-site.

Miami Metro Zoo

| 28 | 24 | 23 | 21 | M |

12400 SW 152nd St. (124th Ave.); 305-251-0400; www.miamimetrozoo.com
■ "Your kids won't want to leave" Miami's top-rated attraction – a "huge array" of animals and exhibits, from the rare white tigers and Aviary Wings of Asia (with fossil digs) to the "awesome" children's zoo where toddlers pet Vietnamese pot-bellied pigs and Polish hens; tykes can ride the Wildlife Conservation Carousel and observe hissing cockroaches and bearded dragons, while air-conditioned monorails and a sprinkler system help beat the heat – no wonder it also garners the highest Child Appeal score in the city; even though it's about 22 miles southwest of Downtown Miami, "it's worth the trip."

Miami Museum of Science & Planetarium

| 26 | 23 | 22 | 24 | M |

3280 S. Miami Ave. (SE 32nd Rd.), Coconut Grove; 305-854-4247;
www.miamisci.org
■ From astronomy to zoology, this Coconut Grove museum is one of the area's prime kid-pleasing attractions, packed with "lots of hands-on stuff" in traveling and permanent exhibits where visitors can spend hours exploring Indiana Jones–style jungles and ruins or learn why things bounce; cosmic capers amuse young visitors, while older ones like laser light shows, science demos and planetarium presentations and all ages fawn over the birds of prey at the Wildlife Center.

Miami Seaquarium

| 26 | 21 | 16 | 17 | E |

4400 Rickenbacker Cswy. (Arthur Lamb Jr. Rd.); 305-361-5705;
www.miamiseaquarium.com
☑ "Kids love" former TV star Flipper "and friends" at this "fun" longtime attraction on Biscayne Bay presenting "splashy shows" including Lolita the killer whale, "below-ground aquarium views" of "divers feeding fish", shark channels and crocodile flats; updates include a renovated manatee exhibit and a new two-story pirate ship playground firing water cannons; N.B. ask about the two-hour Water and Dolphin Exploration – children at least 52 inches tall can swim with these friendly mammals.

Parrot Jungle Island

| – | – | – | – | E |

1111 Parrot Jungle Trail (MacArthur Cswy.); 305-258-6453;
www.parrotjungle.com
Scarlet macaws, Bengal tigers, Malaysian bear cats, a 22-ft. python and a 20-ft. crocodile (said to be the largest in North America) are among the 3,000 animals and 500 plant species found in the new home of this nearly 70-year-old South Florida attraction, which last year moved from the suburbs to an island between Miami and South Beach; there's a petting zoo, picnic area, trails, aviaries, a new primate exhibit and a musical review, and the cafe overlooks a lake with pink flamingos.

Pro Player Stadium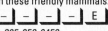

| 21 | 24 | 22 | 17 | E |

2269 Dan Marino Blvd. (NW 27th Ave.); 305-623-6100;
www.proplayerstadium.com
☑ Fans are mixed on this stadium, saying it's "a great football arena", but "bad for baseball" ("if only the Dolphins could play as well as the

Marlins do"); there are occasional monster truck shows and concerts, plus "very interactive" Sportstown activities for all ages that open a few hours before game times, but it's "not the most sophisticated" facility around and you'll have a "hellacious time parking" in the "expensive" lots; still, they earn points for serving arepas and for the "amazing club seats" with "carving stations" – just "bring lots of money" here.

Venetian Pool 😊😊

| 26 | 24 | 23 | 18 | I |

2701 De Soto Blvd. (Granada Blvd.), Coral Gables; 305-460-5356; www.venetianpool.com

■ Kids relish this "enchanting oasis" in Coral Gables, a "unique swimming hole" formed from a coral rock quarry in 1923; the 820,000-gallon pool, filled daily with spring water, features two waterfalls, caves "to hide out in and explore" and "beautiful" grottos, all guarded by "strict" lifeguards (children must be at least 38 inches tall and three years old to enter); P.S. the nearby Biltmore Hotel is a good place to "stay a night", "dine in high fashion" at Palme d'Or or "play golf."

Vizcaya Museum and Gardens ☺

| 13 | 26 | 24 | 22 | M |

3251 S. Miami Ave. (SE 32nd Rd.), Coconut Grove; 305-250-9133; www.vizcayamuseum.com

☑ This "stunning" Italian Renaissance–style villa, built as the winter residence of industrialist James Deering, offers a glimpse into "how people lived" at the time; though it's "not on the top" of family travelers' lists since it's boring for most kids and "you can't bring strollers inside the house", adults find the 34-room mansion furnished with antiques and art from the 15th to 19th centuries "absolutely gorgeous", and older kids might just enjoy the "well-manicured" gardens with "fantastic" views of Biscayne Bay; P.S. "many will recognize it as a frequently used movie location."

HOTELS

Ratings: Family Appeal, Rooms, Service, Public Facilities, Cost

| FA | R | S | P | $ |

Biltmore Hotel, The

| 20 | 21 | 25 | 26 | $339 |

1200 Anastasia Ave., Coral Gables; 305-445-1926; 800-727-1926; www.biltmorehotel.com; 241 rooms, 39 suites

☑ With "the largest swimming pool in the continental U.S.", this "somewhat business-oriented" Coral Gables hotel, six miles from Miami Airport, starts out with an "advantage" for kids who love splashing around for hours; while they may not appreciate the "wonderful 1920s ambiance" or the design (meant to emulate a Seville Renaissance cathedral), they'll like the "fabulous" Sunday brunch, and their parents will appreciate the on-site golf; just be warned, it's a "little stuffy" for a few who find young and old "need to be well-behaved" here.

Doral Golf Resort & Spa

| 19 | 20 | 22 | 23 | $325 |

4400 NW 87th Ave.; 305-592-2000; 800-713-6725; www.doralresort.com; 493 rooms, 200 suites

☑ If you've got golfers in the family, "this is your place" with its "world-famous" courses delighting duffers young and old; children like the "great" Blue Lagoon water park with "plenty of shaded areas for babies and toddlers" and the Camp Doral kids program with "excellent" activities, while adults appreciate the "very nice" spa and "accommodating" service; still, it's a "long drive to the beach" or zoo and some find it "too expensive", so stay here only if you need "rest and relaxation."

Fontainebleau Hilton Resort
$\boxed{\text{—} \; \text{—} \; \text{—} \; \text{—} \; \$279}$

4441 Collins Ave.; 305-538-2000; 800-445-8667;
www.fontainebleauhilton.com; 876 rooms, 50 suites

When it added a $5-million water park, complete with a 100-ft.-long Cookie the Octopus cement sea creature, a lazy river raft ride and a spiral slide, this veteran property got a lot more kid-friendly; but parents appreciate the lush greenery, cascading waterfalls, poolside cabanas overlooking the ocean, children's menus and babysitting services; South Beach is two miles down the boardwalk.

Loews Miami Beach
$\boxed{22 \; 23 \; 24 \; 24 \; \$369}$

1601 Collins Ave., Miami Beach; 305-604-1601; 800-235-6397;
www.loewshotels.com; 739 rooms, 51 suites

■ With a staff that's "extremely helpful to parents" ("they'd probably change a diaper if you asked"), this "beautiful" hotel "has everything for everyone" gush guests, and "you can even bring your pet" – "now this is the way a family hotel should be"; "from packages to amenities" to that "awesome" beachfront pool, they're "prepared for and welcome kids", and it's all "in the heart of South Beach", where you can "walk everywhere – no car seats needed."

Ritz-Carlton Coconut Grove
$\boxed{\nabla \; 22 \; 27 \; 29 \; 26 \; \$305}$

3300 SW 27th Ave., Coconut Grove; 305-644-4680; 800-241-3333;
www.ritzcarlton.com; 58 rooms, 57 suites

■ "What can you say?" this is a "classy hotel" for tiny tykes and adults alike, and its location in Coconut Grove within walking distance of CocoWalk and five minutes from Vizcaya Museum is perfect for families; the Italian Renaissance design features a cascading courtyard waterfall, while "exceptional service" makes it "worth the splurge"; P.S. mom or dad should book a four-hands massage at the on-site spa.

Ritz-Carlton Key Biscayne
$\boxed{27 \; 26 \; 26 \; 27 \; \$409}$

455 Grand Bay Dr., Key Biscayne; 305-365-4500; 800-241-3333;
www.ritzcarlton.com; 365 rooms, 37 suites

■ They "really make families feel welcome" say fans who give this luxury outpost high ratings when it comes to small-fry friendliness, reporting it "a notch above the rest"; the "perfect setting" "right on the beach", "outstanding facilities" including a stunning S-shaped pool, "great entertainment", an afternoon Teddy bear tea and a Ritz Kids program with supervised activities mean there's "plenty" for youngsters to do, and adults "love the tennis, spa" and restaurants; indeed, it's "hard to beat" this one for a South Florida vacation.

Sonesta Beach Resort Key Biscayne
$\boxed{25 \; 23 \; 22 \; 22 \; \$295}$

350 Ocean Dr., Key Biscayne; 305-361-2021; 800-766-3782;
www.sonesta.com; 293 rooms, 12 suites

■ Sometimes you just need a "solid family resort"; with an "excellent kids' program", Just Us, featuring a "wonderful staff" that supervises activities, crafts and beach outings for ages 5–13 (there's a separate program for those aged 3–4), this is one such place; active types can visit the tennis center, rollerblade, rent electric-powered Segway transporters, bikes and kayaks or go snorkeling, while the 10,000-sq.-ft. spa provides pampering by appointment; N.B. nearby attractions include CocoWalk, the Museum of Science and the Seaquarium.

Top Family-Friendly Hotel Chains in the Area:

Embassy Suites	Homewood Suites
Four Seasons	Hyatt
Hampton Inn	Marriott
Holiday Inn	Residence Inn

See Hotel Chain reviews, starting on page 256.

RESTAURANTS

Ratings: Family Appeal, Food, Decor, Service, Cost

FA	F	D	S	$

Archie's Gourmet Pizza

▽ 24	21	20	21	M

166 Giralda Ave. (Ponce de Leon Blvd.), Coral Gables; 305-444-1557 ☽
Winn-Dixie Shopping Ctr., 600 Crandon Blvd. (Sunrise Dr.), Key Biscayne;
305-365-5911

■ "When your babysitter cancels", take the gang to these twin pizzerias with "perfect family atmospheres" and "excellent thin-crust" pies; fans call them the "end of the 'best pizza' debate", while parents breathe a sigh of relief: the "kids were happy and so were we."

Beverly Hills Cafe

–	–	–	–	M

Cypress Village Shopping Ctr., 7321 Miami Lakes Dr. (Miami Lakeway),
Miami Lakes; 305-558-8201
1559 Sunset Dr. (56th Ave.), South Miami; 305-666-6618
www.thebeverlyhillscafe.com

"Big portions" plus "moderate prices" equal "faithful customers" at this Traditional American chain where kids can chomp into burgers, "fabulous rolls", "spectacular salads" and other "standouts" on the "diverse menu"; even if "the staff could be more attentive" and the decor's "dated", they're "reliable" for a quick sit-down family meal.

Big Cheese

–	–	–	–	I

8080 SW 67th Ave. (US 1), South Miami; 305-662-6855;
www.bigcheesemiami.com

There's "always a line" at this "grungy Italian", "crowded" with families who can't get enough of the "huge" slices of "cheesy" pizza and rolls "drowning in chopped garlic and oil"; your preteens and teens will feel right at home amid the "noise", and with the Hurricanes motif, they may get an early yearning for the University of Miami.

Big Pink ☽

25	21	19	19	M

157 Collins Ave. (2nd St.), Miami Beach; 305-532-4700;
www.bigpinkrestaurant.com

■ "Just about everything you could want is on the menu" of this "bountiful" diner that's "one of the best family-oriented restaurants on South Beach"; its "inexpensive" comfort food with a twist (i.e. "daily TV dinner specials served on metal trays") arrives in "huge portions", and even better, it's an "easy atmosphere for children" and parents – the "kids can make lots of noise and no one will care."

Bongos Cuban Café

–	–	–	–	E

American Airlines Arena, 601 Biscayne Blvd. (NE 8th St.); 786-777-2100;
www.bongoscubancafe.com

An "eye-catching setting" and ownership by Gloria and Emilio Estefan make this "lively" Downtown Miami "hot spot" filled with tourists a good choice for families with teens; although some find the "overpriced Cuban cuisine" humdrum ("if you want authentic, eat in Little Havana"), there's "great music and dancing on weekends."

Cafe Sambal

▽ 15	26	28	23	E

Mandarin Oriental Hotel, 500 Brickell Key Dr. (SE 8th St.); 305-913-8251;
www.mandarinoriental.com

◩ A "cool waterfall" matches the elegance of the food and service at Azul's "less expensive" sibling in the Mandarin Oriental, this waterfront Pan-Asian with dining overlooking Biscayne Bay; it has added a sushi and sake bar but also takes care of young visitors with crayons, games and a children's menu.

La Carreta

| 23 | 20 | 15 | 17 | M |

Miami Int'l Airport, concourse D; 305-871-3003
10633 NW 12th St. (NW 107th Ave.); 305-463-9778
3632 SW Eighth St. (36th Ave.); 305-444-7501
12 Crandon Blvd. (Harbor Dr.), Key Biscayne; 305-365-1177
◪ "Fantastic deals" can be had at this chain of Cuban restaurants offering "large portions" of grub that ranges from "basic" to "superior" at mostly "moderate" tabs; "fast service" keeps the kiddies from getting impatient, while the "hokey" decor provides some distraction.

Las Culebrinas

| ▽ 23 | 27 | 21 | 24 | M |

4700 W. Flagler St. (47th Ave.); 305-445-2337
2890 SW 27th Ave. (Coconut Ave.), Coconut Grove; 305-448-4090
■ "Bring a big appetite", because the "portions are huge" at these "excellent" Cuban-Spanish venues in Downtown Miami and Coconut Grove; "low prices and good service" make it easy for families to enjoy "great selections" that are "well worth the money."

Los Ranchos

| 20 | 23 | 19 | 20 | M |

Bayside Mktpl., 401 Biscayne Blvd. (bet. NE 4th & 5th Sts.); 305-375-8188
Holiday Plaza, 125 SW 107th Ave. (Flagler St.); 305-221-9367
Cocowalk, 3015 Grand Ave. (Virginia St.), Coconut Grove; 305-461-8222
2728 Ponce de Leon Blvd. (bet. Almeria & Sevilla Aves.), Coral Gables; 305-446-0050
www.losranchossteakhouse.com
◪ "Kids won't leave hungry" at this Nicaraguan steakhouse chain where beef lovers chow down on "excellent" churrasco and "great sauces"; though it's not cheap, it's a "good value for the money", and the staff will "always accommodate extended family and friends."

News Cafe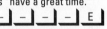

| – | – | – | – | M |

800 Ocean Dr. (8th St.), Miami Beach; 305-538-6397; www.newscafe.com
If "location is everything", then "it doesn't get much better" than Mark Soyka's "busy" "landmark" diner where all of SoBe watches the "Ocean Drive spectacle"; the food's "good" enough for little tykes and "reasonable" for parents with a hungry brood; though some say it's "where tourist meets trap", most families "have a great time."

Nikki Beach

| – | – | – | – | E |

Penrod's, 1 Ocean Dr. (1st St.), Miami Beach; 305-538-1231;
www.nikkibeach.com
Whether it evokes "Rio", the "South of France" or a "Pacific Island fantasy", this South Beach paradise in the Penrod's complex offers a quintessential "scene"; your kids will enjoy dining "on the sand under the coconut trees" or in "lit-up teepees", and even though "no one comes for the food", the Eclectic fare is surprisingly "good."

RESTAURANT CHAINS

See reviews, starting on page 262.

Ratings: Family Appeal, Food, Decor, Service, Cost

FA	F	D	S	$

| 21 | 16 | 17 | 17 | M |

Applebee's
Cutler Ridge Mall, 20405 S. Dixie Hwy. (S. 211th St.); 786-293-9406
9815 NW 41st St. (Doral Blvd.); 305-716-4942

| 20 | 22 | 14 | 18 | I |

Baja Fresh Mexican Grill
1010 S. Miami Ave. (bet. 9th & 10th Sts.); 305-523-2393 ⊠
220 Miracle Mile (S. Douglas Rd.), Coral Gables; 305-442-9596

Benihana | 23 | 20 | 18 | 22 | E |
Dadeland Mall, 8727 S. Dixie Hwy. (N. Kendall Dr.); 305-665-0044
1665 NE 79th St. Cswy. (E. Treasure Bay Dr.), North Bay Village; 305-866-2768

Bubba Gump Shrimp Co. | 24 | 18 | 23 | 20 | M |
401 Biscayne Blvd. (NE 5th St.); 305-379-8866

California Pizza Kitchen | 21 | 21 | 16 | 19 | M |
Miami Int'l Airport, concourse east, 2nd level; 305-876-7238

Chevys Fresh Mex 🅱 | 23 | 19 | 18 | 18 | M |
8191 NW 12th St. (82nd Ave.); 305-392-2883

Chili's Grill & Bar 🅱 | 21 | 19 | 18 | 19 | M |
8696 NW 13th Terr. (Galloway Rd.); 305-471-8178
19905 Biscayne Blvd. (199th St.), Aventura; 305-682-9898
11900 SW 88th St. (117th Ave.), Kendall; 305-596-5025
5705 NW 173rd Dr. (NW 57th Ave.), Miami Lakes; 305-821-5699

Chuck E. Cheese's 🅱 | 26 | 10 | 17 | 13 | I |
20335 Biscayne Blvd. (NE 203rd St.); 305-936-0002
8515 Pines Blvd. (NW 86th Ave.), Pembroke Pines; 954-437-8178

Dave & Buster's 🅱 | 26 | 16 | 21 | 17 | M |
Dolphin Mall, 11481 NW 12th St. (111th St.); 305-468-1555

Fuddrucker's 🅱 | 24 | 20 | 15 | 16 | I |
7800 SW 104th St. (S. Dixie Hwy.); 305-274-1228
1555 Washington Ave. (16th St.), Miami Beach; 305-538-4330
17985 Biscayne Blvd. (bet. NE 179th & 180th Sts.), Miami Beach; 305-933-3572

Hard Rock Cafe | 22 | 16 | 26 | 18 | M |
Bayside Mktpl., 401 Biscayne Blvd. (NE 5th St.); 305-377-3110

Joe's Crab Shack | 23 | 17 | 21 | 19 | M |
4402 N. University Dr. (44th St.), Lauderhill; 954-749-2722

Johnny Rockets 🅱 | 25 | 17 | 20 | 18 | I |
Aventura Mall, 19501 Biscayne Blvd. (William Lehman Cswy.); 305-682-7979
728 Ocean Dr. (bet. 7th & 8th Sts.); 305-538-2115
3036 Grand Ave. (McFarlane Rd.), Coconut Grove; 305-444-1000
1025 Lincoln Rd. (bet. Lenox & Michigan Aves.), Miami Beach; 305-531-6585

LongHorn Steakhouse 🅱 | 21 | 21 | 19 | 21 | M |
15135 N. Kendall Dr. (151st Ave.); 305-383-9955
1630 NW 87th Ave. (bet. 15th & 17th Sts.); 305-477-4122

Olive Garden 🅱 | 20 | 19 | 18 | 19 | M |
8201 W. Flagler St. (82nd Ave.); 305-266-5000
18101 Biscayne Blvd. (180th St.), Aventura; 305-935-5742
Pembroke Lakes Mall, 11425 Pines Blvd. (Hiatus Rd.), Pembroke Pines; 954-432-5529

On the Border
Mexican Grill & Cantina 🅱 | 20 | 19 | 19 | 18 | M |
12295 SW 88th St. (Kendall Dr.), Kendall; 305-275-3255
16375 Biscayne Blvd. (165th Terr.), North Miami; 305-945-6449
12100 Pines Blvd. (Flamingo Rd.), Pembroke Pines; 954-437-3787

Original Pancake House, The ☒ | 24 | 22 | 12 | 17 | I |
9901 NW 41st St. (99th Ave.); 786-507-0564
11510 SW 72nd St. (117th Ave.); 305-274-9215

Roadhouse Grill | 20 | 18 | 16 | 18 | M |
12599 Biscayne Blvd. (NE 126th St.), North Miami; 305-893-7433

Romano's Macaroni Grill | 21 | 21 | 19 | 21 | M |
8700 NW 18th Terr. (Galloway Rd.); 305-477-6676
12100 SW 88th St. (SW 123rd Ave.), Kendall; 305-270-0621
16395 Biscayne Blvd. (163rd St.), North Miami Beach; 305-945-7990

Ryan's Family Steakhouse ☒ | 24 | 17 | 12 | 16 | I |
3125 Columbia Blvd. (Ronald McNair Way), Titusville; 321-385-2780

T.G.I. Friday's ☒ | 21 | 17 | 18 | 17 | M |
11401 NW 12th St. (NW 107th Ave.); 305-470-9885
500 Ocean Dr. (5th St.), Miami Beach; 305-673-8443

Tony Roma's | 20 | 21 | 16 | 19 | M |
6728 Main St. (67th Ave.), Miami Lakes; 305-558-7427

New Orleans

Once Spanish, then French, New Orleans still has a reputation – more than 200 years after the U.S. acquired it in the Louisiana Purchase – as the most European of America's cities. That's why many tourists never leave the picturesque French Quarter, with its latticed balconies and devotion to haute cuisine, cold drinks and hot jazz. But the Crescent City – which stretches along the riverfront between the Mississippi and Lake Pontchartrain, embracing everything from Kenner on the west to Chalmette ("da Parish") on the east – is more complex than that. Ride a streetcar Uptown (upriver) along St. Charles Avenue or Magazine Street to see the arty restored Warehouse District, the genteel Garden District, Uptown's university area (Tulane, Loyola and Xavier) and Audubon Park's golf course and zoo. Or take the recently reinstated trolley from Downtown (downriver) to City Park, where kids will swarm over the Storyland playground and Hines Carousel Gardens. Streetcars cost $1.25 or $1.50 per ride and may spare you the aggravation of auto rental. Note that the nonstop revelry of the Big Easy's famous Mardi Gras is probably too crazy – and racy – for youngsters; instead, let the good times roll during the other winter months via a carriage ride through the Quarter or City Park's Yuletide Celebration in the Oaks. If you can take the heat (75 degrees or so, with 85 percent humidity), don't miss JazzFest in late spring.

ATTRACTIONS

Ratings: Child Appeal, Adult Appeal, Public Facilities, Service, Cost

| C | A | P | S | $ |

AUDUBON AQUARIUM OF THE AMERICAS | 28 | 26 | 26 | 23 | M |
1 Canal St. (Convention Center Blvd.); 504-581-4629; 800-774-7394;
www.auduboninstitute.org
■ "You'll wish you were a fish when you visit" this Mississippi "riverfront" "treasure", an "impressive aquarium" that's rated the city's top attraction and "one of the few good places to take kids" in New Orleans (especially on "a rainy or scorchingly hot day"); the "regional"

"ecosystem displays" feature "lots of unusual marine life" including jellyfish, "amazing white alligators" and "the coolest frog exhibit ever", plus the staff's "Southern hospitality can't be beat"; P.S. it's within walking distance of the French Quarter, so head "to Jackson Square for beignets at Café Du Monde afterward."

Audubon Park

| 22 | 25 | 20 | 17 | $0 |

6500 St. Charles Ave. (bet. Calhoun & Walnut Sts.); 800-672-6124; www.auduboninstitute.org

■ "Take a streetcar to the entrance", then "feed the ducks", go "cycling or roller-blading" – or "just relax and picnic" among the "stately" "300-year-old live oaks" in this "Uptown haven", a "refreshing, pastoral" "getaway" that's a "nice change of pace from Bourbon Street hoopla"; there are "lots of jungle gyms for the kids" throughout this vast expanse (which also encompasses a zoo), plus "great festivals", but correspondents caution "don't go after dark."

Audubon Zoo ☺☺

| 28 | 26 | 24 | 21 | M |

6500 Magazine St. (Exposition Blvd.); 504-861-2537; 866-487-2966; www.auduboninstitute.org

■ "Double your pleasure" by taking a riverboat to this "outstanding" "natural habitat" zoo where flamingos greet you at the entrance; "kids will love" exploring the new treehouse on Monkey Hill, "the highest point in New Orleans", and then rolling down the slope and splashing in its wading pools, or taking a whirl on the Endangered Species carousel; "adults will enjoy the Cajun-style food at the Louisiana Swamp", an "informative" bayou section complete with albino alligators ("watch them feeding!"); P.S. "take advantage of the discount on the zoo-cruise-aquarium circuit."

Cabildo ☺

| 14 | 24 | 23 | 21 | I |

701 Chartres St. (St. Peter St.); 504-568-6968; lsm.crt.state.la.us

☑ "History, history, history" is the focus at this "impressive" colonnaded building on Jackson Square, the site where the Louisiana Purchase was signed in 1803; it's now an "educational" museum with "excellent tour guides" and "interesting" artifacts from Colonial times through the Reconstruction; kids of a particular bent "will like the lock of Andrew Jackson's hair" and Napoleon's death mask, but others will "find this place a bore"; N.B. nearby are two historic dwellings, also museums: the 1850 House and Madame John's Legacy.

Chalmette Battlefield & National Cemetery ☺

| 16 | 22 | 18 | 18 | $0 |

8606 W St. Bernard Hwy (Jean Lafitte Pkwy.); 504-281-0510; www.nps.gov/jela

■ Part of Jean Lafitte National Historical Park, this field six miles southeast of the city is where the War of 1812's Battle of New Orleans was "fought and won" in 1815 "after the peace treaty was already signed"; history buffs can go "see reenactments" every January to find out "all they want to know", while others will prefer the visitor center's 15-minute orientation; if you "get here by paddle-wheeler" from Downtown, "kids will love" it and you'll get an "informative" and "reflective" round trip "at a reasonable rate."

City Park

| 22 | 23 | 19 | 16 | $0 |

1 Palm Dr. (Marconi Dr.); 504-482-4888; www.neworleanscitypark.com

■ "Sprawling oaks draped with moss shelter quaint playgrounds" at this "absolutely beautiful" 1,500-acre refuge; sporty sorts can partake of four golf courses, tennis courts or "pedal boats in the lagoons", nature lovers can hike, tour botanical gardens and encounter "lots of ducks to feed", and those who want to "have a lazy afternoon" can "fish in the ponds" or picnic; Celebration in the Oaks, a "spectacular holiday lights show", is a "must-see."

French Market ☻☺

| 13 | 24 | 16 | 18 | $0 |

1008 N. Peters St. (St. Phillip St.); 504-522-2621; www.frenchmarket.org

☑ Have "breakfast in heaven" (chicory cafe au lait and donut-like beignets) at this 200-year-old French Quarter marketplace that's also a "mesmerizing" "feast for the eyes, nose and ears": the open-air "shops, kiosks and farmer's stalls" sell "an astounding variety" of goods ("feather masks", "alligator heads", "fresh meat and handbags" plus "every variety of hot sauce known to man"); little ones "will love" the "roving mimes and musicians" and preteens will find "plenty to spend allowance money on" – but the "tourist" throngs do make it "difficult to maneuver a stroller."

Hermann-Grima House ☺

| ▽ 12 | 25 | 22 | 23 | I |

820 St. Louis St. (bet. Bourbon & Dauphine Sts.); 504-525-5661; www.hgghh.org

■ "Older children and adults" are most likely to appreciate this carefully restored 1831 Federal mansion, a "beautiful example of old New Orleans" "in the middle of the Vieux Carré"; equipped to resemble the home of a prosperous 19th-century Creole family, it features "nice antiques", "a stable and [the only outdoor] working kitchen" in the French Quarter; "great historical insight" can be yours via an "interesting" guided tour, but canny correspondents caution this casa's "not for young kids"; N.B. closed weekends.

Hines Carousel Gardens ☻☺

| 28 | 20 | 22 | 19 | I |

City Park, 1 Palm Dr. (Marconi Dr.); 504-482-4888; www.neworleanscitypark.com

■ Tourists "should find" this "hidden treasure", a City Park Shangri-la that's a "great place for children to be children and for adults to be children"; named for its "beautifully restored" 1906 wooden carousel, it also boasts a miniature Ferris wheel, roller coaster, antique bumper cars and tot-sized trains that tour the park; it's "particularly enchanting" during the holiday-season Celebration in the Oaks, when sparkling lights and ornaments "transform it into a virtual fairyland"; P.S. it's cash-only, and insiders advise it's "cheaper to purchase the armband for unlimited rides."

Louisiana Children's Museum

| 29 | 21 | 26 | 25 | I |

420 Julia St. (bet. Magazine & Tchoupitoulas Sts.); 504-523-1357; www.lcm.org

■ "Imaginations young and old" can "run wild" at this "innovative" Warehouse District museum, a "top-notch" "place to explore and pretend" that's been voted the city's No. 1 for Child Appeal (and the top-rated children's museum in this *Survey*); among the 100-plus "educational, fun exhibits" that "capture everyone's attention" are scientific adventures and social studies (piloting a tugboat, anchoring the news); meanwhile, in First Adventures toddlers climb through a maze or build with blocks – and believe it or not, "even the grown-ups will love playing and learning" here; N.B. multi-day passes available.

Memorial Hall/ Confederate Museum ☺

| ▽ 13 | 24 | 18 | 22 | I |

929 Camp St. (bet. Andrew Higgins Dr. & St. Joseph St.); 504-523-4522; www.confederatemuseum.com

■ An "absolute must for Civil War buffs", this 1891 Lee Circle landmark stuffed with "one of the largest collections of Confederate artifacts in the U.S." contains a "fabulous" array of "impressive" memorabilia (battle flags, uniforms, period guns and swords, vintage photographs); an exhibit of CSA president Jefferson Davis' effects includes his top hat, cane, saddle, Bible and a crown of thorns given to him by Pope Pius IX; given this repository's "no-glitz", "just-the-facts" approach, surveyors suggest a stop here is "best for older children and adults."

Musee Conti Wax Museum 😃😊 | 20 | 20 | 18 | 20 | I |

917 Conti St. (Dauphine St.); 504-525-2605; 800-233-5405;
www.get-waxed.com

☑ Significant scenes from the Big Easy's 300-year history are "brought to life" by 154 life-size wax figures (Napoleon, 19th-century boxers, Louis Armstrong) at this French Quarter paraffin palace; partisans praise the place as a "fun, quick history lesson" and point out "kids will love the monster section"; critics counter "are you kidding?", calling it "amateurish", "hokey" and "dull" and claiming "if you've ever been to Madame Tussaud's you'll have difficulty not chuckling" at the Haunted Dungeon.

National D-Day Museum 😊 | 16 | 29 | 27 | 27 | I |

945 Magazine St. (bet. Andrew Higgins Dr. & St. Joseph St.); 504-527-6012;
www.ddaymuseum.org

■ "Thank you, Stephen Ambrose", salute admirers of the World War II historian who founded this "fascinating" and "profoundly moving" museum that spotlights all 17 D-Day invasions in Europe and the Pacific; it "sucks you right in" and "brings the reality of war home" via "expert use of multimedia" ("enthralling personal accounts", "great documentary video", artifacts, photos); reviewers report it's "not to be rushed", so allow two to three hours at this "learning site" near Lee Circle – and note that this "intense subject matter" is obviously "not for young children."

New Orleans Botanical Garden | 16 | 24 | 24 | 22 | I |

City Park, 1 Palm Dr. (Marconi Dr.); 504-483-9386;
www.neworleanscitypark.com

■ Another of City Park's "beautiful areas", this "well-kept garden" provides "lots to look at and learn about, even for someone who is not interested in horticulture"; with its art deco design, "wonderful statues" and hundreds of tropical and subtropical flora set amid majestic live oaks, it's "very New Orleans" ("you know you're not in Kansas"), because "any time of year" it provides adults with a "fragrant" "respite" and kids with "lots of room to roam around"; N.B. no bikes, skates or skateboards.

New Orleans Museum of Art 😊 | 14 | 26 | 24 | 23 | M |
(aka NOMA)

City Park, 1 Collins Diboll Circle (Esplanade Ave.); 504-488-2631;
www.noma.org

■ "You'll find out Fabergé made much more than eggs" thanks to the unusually varied, "surprisingly good collection" at the heart of this "beautiful museum in a beautiful [City Park] setting"; modern-art mavens "love the new sculpture garden" (50 pieces on display in a five-acre landscape), while parents point out that "children will enjoy the exploration of art" at weekend family workshops where the whole clan can be creative together; P.S. be sure to keep an eye out for "wonderful traveling exhibits."

Old Mint 😊 | 16 | 23 | 20 | 18 | I |

400 Esplanade Ave. (N. Peters St.); 504-568-6968; 800-568-6968;
lsm.crt.state.la.us

■ Not just for numismatists, this 1835 coinery – which churned out cash for the U.S. (and, briefly, Confederate) government till 1909 – now serves as an "old-fashioned museum" of money; the French Quarter quarters also house "intriguing artifacts and illustrations of Louisiana history", especially the development of jazz (there's audio of vintage broadcasts); it's generally "geared toward adults who love history", though, so kids may find it a tad "dry"; P.S. timesavers suggest you "ride the ferry to get there" because sometimes "parking can be problematic."

Presbytere/Mardi Gras Museum ☺☺

▽ | 15 | 23 | 20 | 19 | I |

751 Chartres St. (St. Anne St.); 504-568-6968; lsm.crt.state.la.us
■ "To experience Carnival" "without having to come during the season", party people prance on over to this Mardi Gras "must-see", located in a Jackson Square edifice that once housed Capuchin monks; kids will "enjoy the flamboyant costumes and Dixieland music", while "adults appreciate learning" "how the city's various ethnic and social groups celebrate in their own slightly twisted ways"; you can join in via computerized photo ops and a 15-song jukebox – but be careful: you may glimpse "a few displays of the fabled flashing for trinkets"; N.B. closed Mondays.

Six Flags New Orleans

| 28 | 18 | 22 | 17 | M |

12301 Lake Forest Blvd. (Paris Rd.); 504-253-8100; www.sixflags.com
■ Of course "the kids will love it", but even adults adjudge the amusement park formerly known as Jazzland "much better since Six Flags took over"; among the playland's newest rides are a SpongeBob SquarePants simulator and a Batman roller coaster, plus there are arcades, live musical shows and thrills for tiny tykes in the Looney Tunes Adventures section; still, some sunstrokers sigh for more "shady escapes" where folks can "stay cool in the heat of the summer."

Storyland ☺☺

| 26 | 14 | 18 | 16 | I |

City Park, 1 Palm Dr. (Marconi Dr.); 504-482-4888;
www.neworleanscitypark.com
◪ "Kids are attracted to this" City Park "fantasyland" "like bees to honey" because it offers far more than the "typical swings and slides"; in 26 scenes constructed decades ago by Mardi Gras float builders, "you can sail aboard Captain Hook's pirate ship" or "hide out in a whale's mouth" with Pinocchio; little ones also like the "great puppet shows" and crafts in the Mother Goose Circle, but some grown-ups grouse the grounds "could use some updating"; N.B. no food service.

Woldenberg Riverfront Park

| 18 | 23 | 18 | 14 | $0 |

Canal St. to Esplanade Ave.; 800-672-6124
■ "Spend a lazy afternoon" "relaxing and reflecting" at this 14-acre waterside park overlooking the river; "buy a muffaletta" nearby for a perfect NO-style picnic, then stroll on the Moon Walk, a French Quarter promenade, "watch ships navigate" the "mighty Mississippi" ("the best free show in town") and "listen to the nearby steamboat music"; however, concerned contributors counsel "use caution at night", citing "too many grifters."

HOTELS

Ratings: Family Appeal, Rooms, Service, Public Facilities, Cost

| FA | R | S | P | $ |

Embassy Suites

| – | – | – | – | $255 |

315 Julia St.; 504-525-1993; 800-362-2779; www.embassysuites.com
Located in the Arts & Warehouse District, this all-suite hotel is one block from the Louisiana Children's Museum and two blocks to Mississippi River attractions; families like the daily made-to-order breakfasts and evening cocktails included in the rate, and the outdoor, heated lap pool, whirlpool and sundeck are further enticements; the new, more upscale Lofts property, in a renovated turn-of-the-century building adjacent to the hotel, is completely smoke-free and features exposed brick and designer furnishings; N.B. special packages include tickets to area attractions.

Fairmont New Orleans

| 18 | 21 | 22 | 21 | $309 |

123 Baronne St.; 504-529-7111; 800-441-1414; www.fairmont.com;
615 rooms, 85 suites

☑ This "excellent historic hotel" with "spacious rooms" is "especially family-friendly during the holidays" when "the lobby becomes a winter wonderland" and all the "decorations are wonderful"; other amenities include an outdoor heated pool, a fitness center and two tennis courts, and it's a block and a half away from the French Quarter.

Ritz-Carlton New Orleans

| 19 | 26 | 27 | 26 | $419 |

921 Canal St.; 504-524-1331; 800-241-3333; www.ritzcarlton.com;
393 rooms, 112 suites

☑ As long as your kids have manners, they'll be "kings" at this luxury outpost full of "class and charm"; the staff "spoils you so much" that even though it's "not a super-kid-oriented hotel", they're always "extremely accommodating" to toddlers and older children; located just on the edge of the French Quarter, it's near the Audubon Aquarium of the Americas and offers day-trips to historic plantations and the bayou swamps; N.B. the adjacent Iberville Suites, also run by Ritz-Carlton, offers spacious units for families.

Windsor Court Hotel

| 20 | 28 | 28 | 26 | $350 |

300 Gravier St.; 504-523-6000; 800-262-2662; www.windsorcourthotel.com;
324 suites

■ The "monster suites are worth every penny" especially for "toddlers who need room to run", say reviewers who relish this "old-world" facility that's "not as stuffy as you think" situated "near attractions" such as the Aquarium and Riverwalk; the "pampering" staff "treats kids like royalty", "going out of its way to be friendly", and there's an impressive pool; but a few wallet-watchers warn you "might have to sell the crown jewels to afford the rates" and they "expect children to be proper"; N.B. its New Orleans Grill is "top-notch."

Wyndham at Canal Place

| 20 | 24 | 23 | 24 | $194 |

100 Rue Iberville; 504-566-7006; 800-822-4200; www.wyndham.com;
398 rooms, 40 suites

☑ You'll be "as close as you can get to wherever you want to go" ("a car is not necessary) in this "heart-of-the-city" spot near restaurants, upscale shopping at Canal Place and galleries; there's an "upbeat family atmosphere" that's especially "good for older kids" and plenty of bookable walking tours to enjoy (try the 'Ghosts and Spirits' one) as well as demonstrations of New Orleans cooking; it's also got "the best river view" so children can "watch the passing ships and barges."

Top Family-Friendly Hotel Chains in the Area:

Hampton Inn	Hyatt
Holiday Inn	Marriott
Homewood Suites	Residence Inn

See Hotel Chain reviews, starting on page 256.

RESTAURANTS

Ratings: Family Appeal, Food, Decor, Service, Cost

FA	F	D	S	$
–	–	–	–	E

Brennan's

417 Royal St. (bet. Conti & St. Louis Sts.); 504-525-9711;
www.brennansneworleans.com

"Brunch has become an art form" – and a "splurge" – at this Creole–Classic French "institution", the "epitome of everything New Orleans", with "sublime food" (e.g. "knee-weakening" bananas Foster and breakfast crêpes that tots find tasty), "amiable", "attentive" servers and a "labyrinth" of "genteel" rooms ("explore – you'll need the exercise"); seen-it-alls shrug, though, that it's "famous for being famous", calling it "too high-priced, too crowded, too touristy."

Bud's Broiler ⊖

2338 Banks St. (S. Miro St.); 504-821-3022
500 City Park Ave. (Conti St.); 504-486-2559
6325 Elysian Fields Ave. (Robert E. Lee Blvd.); 504-282-6696
2008 Clearview Pkwy. (W. Napoleon Ave.), Metairie; 504-889-2837
■ A "New Orleans tradition for decades", this local chain has Crescent Citians calling its chargrilled patties the "best burgers within 100 miles" (some like them "covered in chili", others "with cheddar cheese and hickory sauce"); it's a "great place for a family nibble" but be prepared for spartan surroundings that are sometimes "greasy."

Café Du Monde ❶⊖

French Market, 800 Decatur St. (St. Ann St.); 504-587-0833;
www.cafedumonde.com
"Starbucks who?" ask aficionados of the thick, dark chicory coffee ("no wussy lattes here") at this "busy, crazy", round-the-clock French Market "icon", where the whole family will flip for the signature "heaven-sent" beignets covered in an "avalanche of powdered sugar" ("don't wear black!"); at "3 PM or 3 AM" the Jackson Square tableau makes for the "best people-watching on the planet", so devotees grab a chair and overlook the "sticky tables" and "slow, sometimes abrupt" service.

Commander's Palace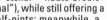

1403 Washington Ave. (Coliseum St.); 504-899-8221;
www.commanderspalace.com
This Garden District "celebration place" is considered by many the "unrivaled crown jewel" in the Crescent City's culinary coronet; it preserves the "essence of New Orleans" in "stellar" "haute Creole cuisine" (Sunday's jazz brunch is "phenomenal"), while still offering a few entrées familiar enough for hungry half-pints; meanwhile, a "near-psychic" staff and "venerable" surroundings convince most that this "classic" still "deserves its reputation" – though a few fret that the "granddaddy" has "lost a step."

Deanie's Seafood

841 Iberville St. (bet. Bourbon & Dauphine Sts.); 504-581-1316
1713 Lake Ave. (Live Oak St.), Metairie; 504-834-1225
www.deanies.com
■ Set sail for "a seafood feast" at this popular pair in the French Quarter and Bucktown "near Lake Pontchartrain"; "extra-large portions" and "great prices" make these fin finds "fine for families", but since neither takes reservations, "be prepared for a long wait" at prime times.

Emeril's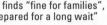

800 Tchoupitoulas St. (Julia St.); 504-528-9393; www.emerils.com
"Don't hate it because of Emeril's overexposure", urge Lagasse loyalists who assert that his Warehouse District "flagship" eatery still serves up "stellar" Contemporary Louisiana cuisine that's "exquisitely presented" by a "coordinated" contingent of "eager waiters"; the recently revamped, modern room has a "trendy" feel, though "with no sound insulation" it can get "objectionably noisy" (at least rambunctious kids are a non-issue); given the "max-out-the-credit-card" prices, many maintain the celeb chef owes "more attention to his namesake restaurant."

Five Happiness
20	25	21	21	M

3605 S. Carrollton Ave. (Palm St.); 504-482-3935
■ "A Cajun two-step above the average Chinese", this Carrollton venerable offers up "tasty, reasonable" classics in a large, gold-and-red-lacquered room decorated with "large tables and the obligatory fish tank" ("kids like to look at it"); no one needs too much distraction, however, since the "service is prompt and friendly."

Franky & Johnny's
21	20	11	16	M

321 Arabella St. (Tchoupitoulas St.); 504-899-9146
☑ "Family and friends meet on a regular basis" at this Uptown old-timer, which has served Cajun-style seafood ("don't bother with anything other than the po' boys, fried oysters or boiled crawfish") at "closely spaced" picnic tables since 1942; "be forewarned", however, that the "pretty gritty" digs leave much to be desired.

Hansen's Sno-Bliz ⌿
–	–	–	–	I

4801 Tchoupitoulas St. (bet. Bordeaux & Lyons Sts.); 504-891-9788
On "hot summer afternoons", devotees "make the pilgrimage" to 92-year-old Ernest Hansen's "family-run" Uptown sno-ball shack, a six-decade "legend" that combines the "softest ice in the world" and "incredible flavors" into the "platonic ideal" of this "heavenly" confection; parents who loved these treats as children want to share the experience with their own offspring, so lines for this "real New Orleans experience" tend to stretch "out the door" ("expect to wait and wait"); P.S. hours of operation are "very limited", so "call" first.

Louisiana Pizza Kitchen
21	19	15	17	M

95 French Market Pl. (Barracks St.); 504-522-9500
615 S. Carrollton Ave. (St. Charles Ave.); 504-866-5900
2112 Belle Chasse Hwy. (Wall Blvd.), Gretna; 504-433-5800
☑ Some "kids may be put off by the nontraditional pizzas" (roasted garlic, smoked salmon) served at this "easy, casual" trio scattered in "good locations" around town, but not to worry – the pastas and other Italian staples also on hand are sure to "be appreciated"; prices that won't "break the bank" will be too.

Popeyes ●
20	18	8	13	I

621 Canal St. (Exchange Pl.); 504-561-1021
4041 Magazine St. (Marengo St.); 504-895-8608
1243 St. Charles Ave. (bet. Clio & Erato Sts.); 504-522-1362
www.popeyes.com
■ Locals "love dat chicken" "served with unmatched red beans, rice and a buttermilk biscuit" at this bawn-in-N'Awlins franchise; no surprise, the decor is less than eye-popping and "locations make the difference" servicewise; but "when you want something" "in a fast-food motif", "you can't go wrong with" this "consistent" chain.

R & O's
23	21	7	17	M

216 Hammond Hwy. (bet. Carrollton & Lake Aves.), Metairie; 504-831-1248
■ Ranging from "perfect seafood" to "great po' boys" to "excellent pizza", "there's something for everyone on the menu" of this large, "laid-back" Metairie "joint" where "every waitress calls you 'hon'"; the variety of offerings "makes it perfect for picky eaters", and if you've got "noisy kids, no problem" – "everyone in here is yelling to be heard, no matter how old they are."

Rocky's Gourmet Pizzeria
▽ 23	19	18	19	I

3222 Magazine St. (bet. Harmony & Pleasant Sts.); 504-891-5152
2701 Airline Hwy. (S. Labarre Rd.), Metairie; 504-833-1288
■ A "good, easy meal" of pizza with innovative toppings and "cracker"-thin crusts (white or whole wheat – your choice) keeps this pair of pie

purveyors rockin' in the Garden District and Metairie; Monday and Tuesday eves are especially good times to "bring the kids", given the two-for-one deals; however, the flour really flies at Airline Highway Saturday night, when young 'uns can make their own.

Semolina International Pasta   21 | 21 | 19 | 19 | M

3226 Magazine St. (Louisiana Ave.); 504-895-4260
5080 Pontchartrain Blvd. (I-10); 504-486-5581
Oakwood Shopping Ctr., 197-139B Westbank Expwy. (Terry Pkwy.), Gretna; 504-361-8293
Clearview Mall, 4436 Veterans Memorial Blvd. (Clearview Pkwy.), Metairie; 504-454-7930
www.semolina.com

■ "When the kids must have spaghetti but the parents are sick of it", use your noodle and head for this "reliable pasta" chain, whose "varied menu" of Eclectic entries from all over the globe (particularly "adored: the macaroni-and-cheese-cake") offer "plenty of choices for everyone", along with "alcohol for mom and dad"; the "portions are big", the "prices are decent", and best of all, the scene's "loud enough so that you don't feel your children are disrupting other diners."

Uglesich's 🖼🍴   – | – | – | – | M

1238 Baronne St. (Erato St.); 504-523-8571; www.uglesichs.com
"Please don't retire this year, Anthony", beseech acolytes who adore Mr. U's 80-year-old lunch-only "culinary mecca", a Garden District "monument to New Orleans eating" where the "sublime" "renditions of Cajun-Creole staples" "beat the pants off" the competition; disciples "dream of being spoon-fed shrimp Uggie 24 hours a day" and "would fight Mike Tyson for the BBQ oysters", while families can feast on kid-friendly foodstuffs like top-notch po' boys accompanied by french fries; as a result, "limos" regularly "pull up outside" this "ramshackle", "decrepit" seafooder; note to parents of hungry youngsters: the wait can be "mind-numbing."

Zea Cafe   21 | 22 | 21 | 21 | M

1655 Hickory Ave. (Citrus Rd.), Harahan; 504-738-0799
Esplanade, 1401 W. Esplanade Ave. (Arizona Ave.), Kenner; 504-468-7733
4450 Veterans Memorial Blvd. (Clearview Pkwy.), Metairie; 504-780-9090
■ Perhaps it "doesn't cater to the kiddies" specifically, but this chainlet is still a "good place to take the family", given the Eclectic array of grilled items, including "excellent ribs" and "rotisserie chicken", plus sweet-potato pudding for dessert; each has a distinctly different ambiance, and the Metairie location contains a microbrewery as well.

RESTAURANT CHAINS

See reviews, starting on page 262.

Ratings: Family Appeal, Food, Decor, Service, Cost

	FA	F	D	S	$
Applebee's	21	16	17	17	M
4005 General DeGaulle Dr. (Holiday Dr.); 504-361-9700					
Bubba Gump Shrimp Co.	24	18	23	20	M
429 Decatur St. (Conti St.); 504-522-5800					
Chuck E. Cheese's	26	10	17	13	I
3701 General DeGaulle Dr. (Macarthur Blvd.); 504-367-1214					
Hard Rock Cafe	22	16	26	18	M
418 N. Peters St. (St. Louis St.); 504-529-5617					

Joe's Crab Shack	23	17	21	19	M

8000 Lakeshore Dr. (Canal Blvd.); 504-283-1010

T.G.I. Friday's 🗷	21	17	18	17	M

132 Royal St. (Canal St.); 504-523-4401

New York City

Urban jungle? Fuhgeddaboudit. Now FBI-certified as the nation's safest large city, NYC is famously hustle-bustle, but it's much more navigable than it might seem: The central island of Manhattan, reached by eight spectacular bridges and best viewed from the water, is mostly a straightforward, walkable grid. As Frank Sinatra sang, the Bronx – home of the Zoo and Yankee Stadium – is up; the Battery – jumping-off point for the Statue of Liberty and Ellis Island – is down. Flanking the always lovely Central Park are the East and West Sides, where all those fancy New Yorkers reside. Uptown, you'll find Harlem; Midtown (including Times Square) is where most of the tourist attractions, major stores and restaurants, and Broadway theaters cluster; head Downtown for Greenwich Village, SoHo, Little Italy, Chinatown and Lower Manhattan, the site of Wall Street, Trinity Church, the South Street Seaport and, sadly, the former World Trade Center site. See it all or head for the outer boroughs – Brooklyn, Queens, the Bronx and Staten Island – via 24/7 subways and buses at $2 per ride; kids under six travel free. Yellow cabs carry up to four people for one metered fare, while the no-charge Staten Island Ferry is the best bargain in town. (Try to stay car-free; parking is scarce and costly and driving is infuriating.) When to come? A Yuletide visit thrills children with elaborate Fifth Avenue window displays, Rockefeller Center's towering tree and Radio City's Christmas Spectacular, but for the best results, bite the Big Apple in springtime when Central Park blooms, or in the golden days of Indian summer when there are so many free outdoor activities. You'll never see it all, not even if you move there.

ATTRACTIONS

Ratings: Child Appeal, Adult Appeal, Public Facilities, Service, Cost

	C	A	P	S	$
AMERICAN MUSEUM OF NATURAL HISTORY	27	27	25	21	M

Central Park W. (79th St.), Manhattan; 212-769-5000; www.amnh.org
■ It's no surprise this Upper West Side "champion" is ranked the No. 1 overall attraction in New York in this Survey, with high ratings in both Child and Adult Appeal; it has 132 million "astounding" artifacts spanning everything "from evolution to planets", a "new Hayden Planetarium that rocks", wildlife dioramas that are "like capsule safaris" and an "awe-inspiring" dinosaur collection that "your kids will never forget"; there's also an IMAX theater, a Discovery Room for ages five–12 and convenient subway access; you can literally "spend days and days here and even your most impatient teenager will never get bored" (take the one-hour guided tour to hit some main areas quickly).

American Museum of the Moving Image ☺☺	19	26	20	21	I

35th Ave. (36th St.), Queens; 718-784-0077; www.ammi.org
■ "Get ready for your close-up" at this "little-known gem" in Astoria that "traces the history of television, movies" and digital media through

"equipment and memorabilia"; a "paradise" for preteens, "teens with a TV addiction" and "adult couch potatoes" who enjoy "great interactive displays" in sound editing, blue-screen technology and animation, "it's definitely worth" the 25-minute subway ride from midtown Manhattan, even if some say "kids won't get 80 percent" of the references; N.B. call for info on film screenings at the on-site theater.

Battery Park   16 | 22 | 15 | 12 | $0

bordered by Battery Pl., State & Whitehall Sts., Manhattan; 212-267-9700; www.bpcparks.org

■ With "fabulous views" of the Statue of Liberty and a great vantage point for "watching the boats", this park at the southern tip of the island is more a "starting point" than a destination, offering an "escape from the bustle of the lower Manhattan" Financial District; "stroll along the esplanade", visit the former site of cannons that guarded the city, then take a short walk to the "moving 9/11 site" or to the ferries for a visit to Ellis Island and Lady Liberty; though a few find "too many annoying vendors" as well as "homeless sleepers", it's not a bad place for "spring-afternoon people-watching."

BRONX ZOO   29 | 26 | 23 | 20 | M

Boston Rd. (bet. Bronx Park S. & 180th St.), Bronx; 718-367-1010; www.bronxzoo.com

■ "It's "hard to believe you're in the Bronx" when you visit this "huge", "spectacular" 265-acre "oasis of creatures great and small", the largest urban wildlife park in the U.S.; it's always "an amazing adventure" for "kids of all ages", who can come close to roughly 4,000 animals, including lowland gorillas, snow leopards and Chinese alligators; there's an express bus from Manhattan if you'd rather not drive, but "bring your walking shoes" and strollers because "it's like a marathon", and in the zoo's naturalistic settings, you're liable to "spend as much time hunting" for animals to look at as our ancestors spent hunting them; couple this with the Botanic Garden for a full-day trip.

Brooklyn Botanic Garden   17 | 26 | 23 | 19 | I

1000 Washington Ave. (Montgomery St.), Brooklyn; 718-623-7200; www.bbg.org

☑ "Yes, a tree does grow here" – in fact, this "serene", "enchanted garden" of 52 acres near Prospect Park has a veritable forest, including a fragrant plaza of magnolias, a "bonsai collection to die for", blooming springtime "cherry trees that make you feel like you're in Kyoto", lots of roses and an "excellent" hands-on Discovery Garden for your younger kids; those who "jump on the noisy subway" for a trip to this "quiet haven" ask "why isn't this place packed?"

Brooklyn Children's Museum   27 | 20 | 21 | 20 | I

145 Brooklyn Ave. (St. Marks Ave.), Brooklyn; 718-735-4400; www.brooklynkids.org

■ The world's first children's museum is still one of the best, say fans of this "outer-borough gem" in Crown Heights, consisting of nine galleries with plenty of "hands-on fun" "for the under-10 set"; there's the new Animal Outpost, featuring a 17-ft. python, and a Totally Tots area with "learning experiences" for toddlers and lots of toys and puzzles; though some say it's "out-of-the-way" and they'd "like to see more updates", others find it "perfect for the youngsters" (but not teens); N.B. open Wednesday-Sunday, with free admission before noon on weekends.

Brooklyn Museum 😊😊   15 | 26 | 22 | 19 | I

200 Eastern Pkwy. (Washington Ave), Brooklyn; 718-638-5000; www.brooklynmuseum.org

■ "A source of pride for Brooklyn", this "stunning" beaux arts building with a spiffy, modern $63-million glass front is a 15-minute subway ride from Times Square; the second-largest museum in NYC, it houses "one of the finest Egyptian collections in the world" as well as "excellent" Asian and Decorative Arts departments; the "Native American display fascinates the children", and because this "too-often overlooked gem" is "never crowded" your kids can get pretty close to the exhibits; P.S. "combine it with a trip to the Botanic Garden."

Cathedral of St. John the Divine ☺ | 11 | 25 | 21 | 18 | $0

1047 Amsterdam Ave. (bet. 111th & 112th Sts.), Manhattan; 212-316-7490; www.stjohndivine.org

■ "Who would have thought the largest Gothic cathedral in the world would be found in New York City"? – this "architectural marvel", begun in 1892 (but still far from finished), can be reached via a convenient subway ride to the Upper West Side that "takes you back to old-world Europe"; you can "pop a pacifier in your kiddie's mouth and enjoy the quiet splendor" and stained glass aplenty, head to a "Sunday service that has been called the greatest show in town" or get tickets to a recital or concert in this "acoustic gem", but "dress warm in winter, 'cause baby, it's cold inside"; N.B. get a quick bite around the corner at Tom's Diner, made famous by *Seinfeld*.

CENTRAL PARK | 25 | 27 | 20 | 15 | $0

59th to 110th Sts., 5th Ave. to Central Park West, Manhattan; 212-360-3456; www.centralpark.org

■ "Ya gotta go" to this "little piece of heaven smack-dab in the middle of Manhattan", an "843-acre paradise" created 150 years ago from the designs of Frederick Law Olmsted; it's "hard to believe you're in New York" when you're "escaping" on the miles of tranquil trails (truly impressive in spring and "golden" fall), riding on the carousel, skating at Wollman Rink, boating on the pond or just picnicking on the "sprawling" Great Lawn; there are lots of free activities in the summer (Philharmonic concerts, Shakespeare in the Park, Summerstage performances) and when it's time for a bite, head to Tavern on the Green, the Boathouse or a good ol' hot dog vendor – it's truly a "haven in the middle of Stressville", yet on weekends, a stroll here is as exciting as the circus.

CENTRAL PARK WILDLIFE CENTER | 27 | 22 | 20 | 18 | I

Central Park, 830 Fifth Ave. (64th St.), Manhattan; 212-439-6500; www.centralparkzoo.com

■ "Just the right size for little legs", this five-acre wildlife center on the east side of Central Park is a nifty diversion for younger kids because "what it lacks in size it makes up for in charm"; penguins and polar bears fascinate children, the daily sea lion feedings are always a "blast" and the Tisch Children's Zoo includes a petting area, an enchanted forest and theaters with daily kiddie shows; so while it's "no substitute" for the bigger Bronx bastion, this "manageable" "treasure" can be seen "end to end in under an hour."

Chelsea Piers ☺☺ | 23 | 25 | 25 | 20 | $0

West Side Hwy. (bet. 17th & 24th Sts.), Manhattan; 212-336-6666; www.chelseapiers.com

■ Thirty acres and four piers on the bank of the Hudson River are chock-full of "everything under the sun for active fun", a "phenomenal" "entertainment and sports center" with "activities from A to Z" – baseball, bowling, ice skating, rock climbing, tennis and even a driving range overlooking the river; though the complex is most fun for teens and adults, there is a preschool gym for the under-three set, plus a fanciful dog run, good dining facilities and lots of free onlooker options like watching gymnasts do triple flips; just remember to bring enough bills because it's "pricey" to participate; N.B. exercise junkies should note that there's a bicycle/jogging/walking path along the water past this place.

Children's Museum of Manhattan 😊😊

| 26 | 16 | 19 | 19 | I |

Tisch Building, 212 W. 83rd St. (bet. Amsterdam Ave. & B'way), Manhattan; 212-721-1234; www.cmom.org

■ "Little ones under six" "won't want to leave" this "fun Upper West Side museum that's "ideal" for toddlers on rainy days; it has "dozens and dozens of activities, books, slides and ladders", sing-alongs, an art room and a "little area for water play in the summer"; "there aren't too many places like this in Manhattan" – so it can get "overcrowded", and "older kids get bored quickly."

Circle Line Sightseeing Cruises

| 20 | 24 | 17 | 17 | E |

Pier 83, 42nd St. (12th Ave.), Manhattan; 212-563-3200; www.circleline42.com

■ For "an illuminating way to see parts of Manhattan you'd never otherwise view" hop aboard this "classic New York sightseeing" vehicle at 42nd Street and the Hudson; "eye-popping" views and "wry, close-to-stand-up-comedy" commentary ensue as you sail by landmarks like the Statue of Liberty, the Brooklyn Bridge and the Cloisters; pick a "nice, clear day" in summer ("it's brutal in cold weather") and choose the "shorter" two-hour tour since the three-hour one can be "tedious for children"; overall, this is one time when "going around in circles is recommended."

Cloisters 😊

| 12 | 26 | 22 | 19 | I |

Fort Tryon Park, Margaret Corbin Dr. (bet. 190th St. & West Side Hwy.), Manhattan; 212-923-3700; www.metmuseum.org

☑ If you really "love medieval stuff", then "take the A train way up to this hidden museum", a "refuge" "tucked into Fort Tryon Park" with Middle Ages "treasures beyond the imagination" (check out the famous Unicorn Tapestries 'cause they alone are "worth the trip", particularly for older children); even young kids can appreciate this "fairy-tale castle" with its impressive views "above the broad and beautiful Hudson River", so take a few hours and play out the fantasy; as ratings indicate, this half-day adventure is far more appealing to parents than to their kids.

Coney Island Boardwalk 😊😊

| 22 | 20 | 13 | 11 | $0 |

Surf Ave. (Atlantic Shore), Brooklyn; 718-372-5159; www.coneyisland.com

■ "Nostalgia rules the day" at this beach setting, once the location of the world's largest amusement park, that's still worth the long subway ride in summer for "honky-tonk amusements" like the "classic [wooden] Cyclone" roller coaster, the Wonder Wheel and the old-style Circus Sideshow with oddities galore; though it now has "only a shadow of its former glory" and the area can get "pretty sketchy", kids "like the games and rides" and you can "taste history" at the original Nathan's hot dog stand before heading to Key Span Park for a ball game or to the "outstanding" New York Aquarium.

Ellis Island Immigration Museum 😊😊

| 15 | 27 | 23 | 21 | $0 |

Ellis Island (New York Harbor), Manhattan; 212-363-3206; www.ellisisland.com

☑ "Feel the ghosts of immigrants past" at this "true museum of America", a "touching tribute" to the 12 million who passed through here from 1892 to 1954; there's "no place else so many can walk in the same steps that their parents, grandparents or great-grandparents once did", learning "how the different cultures came together" to create the patchwork of New York and the country; older children and preteens are "fascinated" by the interactive displays that let you "look up your ancestors", and younger "kids love the ferry ride" from Battery Park, though little ones may not grasp the spot's significance.

Empire State Building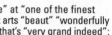

| 23 | 25 | 20 | 17 | M |

350 Fifth Ave. (bet. 33rd & 34th Sts.), Manhattan; 212-736-3100;
www.esbnyc.com

■ For the "world's greatest view" head to the 86th floor of Midtown's "classic American icon", an art deco triumph "that defines skyscraper" and is now the tallest tower in Manhattan; on a "clear day or night" you can see a "breathtaking" panorama of three states that's so "terrific" even locals visit; tiny tots "may become impatient" waiting in the "killer lines on weekends and around holidays" though, so "go early" or simply take the New York Skyride, a thrilling, if "cheesy for adults", simulated aerial tour of the city within the building's theater; grandparents can't help picturing *King Kong* or recalling Cary Grant and Deborah Kerr in *An Affair To Remember.*

Grand Central Terminal

| 13 | 22 | 22 | 17 | $0 |

Lexington Ave. (bet. 42nd & 44th Sts.), Manhattan; 212-340-2210;
www.grandcentralterminal.com

■ "See how beautiful a train station can be" at "one of the finest indoor public spaces in America", this beaux arts "beaut" "wonderfully restored" to its original 1913 grandeur – and that's "very grand indeed"; "most people are amazed by the expanse", so start with the "free tours" offered every Wednesday and Friday, then check out the "specialty shops and high-end eateries" on three levels, the "amazing food market", the "breathtaking" "constellations on the 125-ft. ceiling", the holiday light show and the 'whisper corner' next to the Oyster Bar that's "very cool for kids", who can hear each other talking softly from quite a distance – just "avoid rush hours" or you'll "be stampeded"; as ratings show, tiny tots may consider this simply a yawning space.

Guggenheim Museum

| 12 | 26 | 25 | 21 | I |

(aka Solomon R. Guggenheim Museum)

1071 Fifth Ave. (bet. 88th & 89th Sts.), Manhattan; 212-423-3500;
www.guggenheim.org

☑ "A piece of art in itself", this Upper East Side Frank Lloyd Wright design is a "great structure" designed around a "giant spiral" ramp; while most adults "go for the art", a collection of "mostly 20th-century" works that are admittedly "not everyone's cup of tea", there aren't many kids that would appreciate this museum except as a great skateboard run; if you go, "just start at the top and work your way down" because it's "less tiring" that way, and keep in mind that its appeal to youngsters "wholly depends on the exhibits of the day"; P.S. although "strollers are not allowed", they do offer "free baby backpacks."

Hudson River Park

| – | – | – | – | $0 |

Hudson River (bet. Battery Pl. & 59th St.), Manhattan; 212-791-2530;
917-661-8777; www.hudsonriverpark.org

Now that Manhattan's West Side waterfront is all spruced up, it's the place to be for walking the pooch, running, biking, rollerblading, sunbathing and sunset-viewing; the five-mile stretch of paved footpath, piers and lawns along the Hudson from Battery Park to 59th Street (including Chelsea Piers) is the site of activities ranging from playground romping, historic ship touring, fishing and miniature golf to kayaking, volleyball, radical skateboarding and trapeze lessons, plus a full seasonal roster of alfresco flicks, concerts, theater, dancing and other events; who knew New York City was so outdoorsy?

Intrepid Sea, Air & Space Museum

| 25 | 25 | 20 | 19 | M |

Pier 86, 46th St. (12th Ave.), Manhattan; 212-245-0072;
www.intrepidmuseum.org

■ "It's all about airplanes at this floating museum" on a "giant aircraft carrier" (circa 1943) on the Hudson west of Times Square; "chock-full of aviation history from George Bush Sr.'s plane to an actual Concorde" plus a submarine and a destroyer, it's a stop that's "fun for salts both young and old" with "loads of interactive exhibits for the kids" including a virtual plane ride; P.S. "it's one of the few places to see the rare SR-71 Blackbird up close."

Lincoln Center ☺

| 12 | 27 | 26 | 23 | M |

Columbus Ave. (bet. 62nd & 66th Sts.), Manhattan; 212-875-5000; www.lincolncenter.org

☑ "The cultural capital of the U.S.", home to "world-class dance, opera, orchestras and Shakespeare all in the same complex", this "elegant" center is made up of several "stately" buildings; stop for a rest and a photo at the "gorgeous fountains" in the plaza, "one of the most beautifully designed squares in the world" and a "great place to let kids blow off some steam"; there are "lots of cultural performances" for youngsters, like the Little People Orchestra, the Big Apple Circus, and Jazz for Young People, and in the summer free outdoor concerts are held at Damrosch Park next door; still, as our ratings indicate, it's much more appealing to parents than to their offspring.

Lower East Side Tenement Museum ☺☺

| 16 | 26 | 17 | 21 | I |

90 Orchard St. (Broome St.), Manhattan; 212-431-0233; 212-431-0714; www.tenement.org

☑ For a "unique and fascinating" "history of early immigrants", tour this 1863 "preserved tenement" on the Lower East Side's Orchard Street, containing recreated apartments of three families from the 1870s, 1910s and 1930s; "even younger kids will be fascinated by how life was lived", and there's a "costumed "tour especially geared to children"; N.B. when you're down in the area, grab lunch at Katz's Deli on East Houston Street, an attraction of its own since 1888 and the site of a certain well-known scene in *When Harry Met Sally.*

Macy's ☺☺

| 12 | 21 | 18 | 16 | $0 |

151 W. 34th St. (Broadway), Manhattan; 212-695-4400; 800-343-0121; www.macys.com

☑ Some claim the world's biggest department store, a 10-minute walk south from the Theater District, is "still a miracle on 34th Street", with an "incredible selection", from mattresses to muffin pans; it's the place to go during the holidays – "their Santa Land is the best anywhere" and the annual spring flower display at Easter time is a sight to behold; but grinches gripe this "zoo" is "too crowded for strollers" – "if you're from farm country, it's heaven", but if you live in a city it's "hardly an attraction", especially for young children.

Madame Tussaud's New York ☺☺

| 23 | 25 | 23 | 20 | E |

234 W. 42nd St. (bet. 7th & 8th Aves.), Manhattan; 800-246-8872; www.nycwax.com

☑ Visitors "wax eloquent" about the "amazingly lifelike", "extensive display" of "all their favorite celebs" (some 200 of them, from Charlie Chaplin to Oprah Winfrey) in this five-floor Times Square museum; it's "not appropriate for toddlers" and "can even be scary for some young kids", but preteens and teens will like "rubbing shoulders with the world's bigwigs" and "taking pictures next to the figures"; others say this "tacky tourist paradise" is "not as good as the London version" and the "cost for a family of four is outrageous."

Madison Square Garden ☺☺

| 20 | 23 | 20 | 17 | E |

Seventh Ave. (bet. 31st & 33rd Sts.), Manhattan; 212-465-6741; www.madisonsquaregarden.com

■ "There's nothing like catching the circus or the Knicks" (or a Rangers game) at this "most exciting arena in the world" located "above

Penn Station" and a few blocks from Macy's; there are so many family events held here, from *Sesame Street* shows to *Dora the Explorer* productions that you should "find out what's going on before you come" or else go on the one-hour "goose bump"–inducing "behind-the-scenes tour"; "there's nowhere else like" this slice of "real New York" – "now if only they could fill it with a winning team."

METROPOLITAN MUSEUM OF ART 😊☺

| 17 | 29 | 27 | 24 | I |

1000 Fifth Ave. (82nd St.), Manhattan; 212-535-7710; www.metmuseum.org

■ A "lifetime of visits is not enough" to see everything at this "world-class" spot that is itself a "masterpiece"; with the "greatest permanent collection in the world" (two million works), this Upper East Sider is a "feast for the eyes" and has "something for everyone"; boys especially like "the exhibit of armor and weapons from early times", girls go for the historic costumes, and all appreciate the Egyptian mummy collection and the roof garden; pick up a scavenger-hunt map for older kids and "watch for special exhibits" – but no matter who you are, "don't try to do it all in one day."

Museum of Modern Art ☺
(aka MOMA)

| 12 | 26 | 22 | 20 | I |

33rd St. (Queens Blvd.), Queens; 212-708-9400; www.moma.org

◪ The "best modern art anywhere" is living in its temporary home in a Long Island City former Swingline staple factory; while it houses "some of MOMA's greatest hits" plus impressive temporary exhibits from the collection of 100,000-plus artworks, some still "aren't sure it's worth the trek out to the middle of nowhere" on the 7 train ("wait until it returns to Manhattan" in 2005) and there's not much that will appeal to little ones except "unique gifts" in the on-site shop.

Museum of Television & Radio ☺

| 19 | 25 | 24 | 23 | I |

25 W. 52nd St. (bet. 5th & 6th Aves.), Manhattan; 212-621-6600; www.mtr.org

■ A "boob-tuber's fantasy", this "fantastic little gem nobody knows about" in a "great location in Midtown" off Fifth Avenue is an ideal place to "be entertained while learning about the history of radio and television"; you can "watch almost any program ever recorded" from an "impressive collection of old sitcoms, ads and cartoons" and attend daily screenings, plus there are "special children's-themed exhibits" that are "great for a rainy day" – it's just "too bad they don't let you wear your pj's."

Museum of the City of New York 😊☺

| 17 | 24 | 19 | 20 | I |

1220 Fifth Ave. (103rd St.), Manhattan; 212-534-1672; www.mcny.org

■ Families can spend a few hours at this "quirky", "unheralded" site on the Upper East Side that celebrates the city's history with a vast collection of artifacts and "surprisingly top-notch" displays, including incredible photographic archives; "kids will especially like the exhibit of old toys" – more than 10,000 specimens stretching back to New York's founding in the 17th century – and "wonderful dollhouses", but you'd better "avoid this museum on weekdays" when schoolchildren swarm; P.S. for a delightful respite in summer, go "see Central Park's Conservatory Gardens across the street" when you're done.

National Museum of the American Indian 😊☺

| 19 | 22 | 20 | 18 | $0 |

George Gustav Heye Ctr., 1 Bowling Green (Whitehall St.), Manhattan; 212-514-3700; www.nmai.si.edu

■ "One of the best-kept secrets in New York" is "in a beautiful beaux arts" building that was formerly the Customs House near Battery Park – a free facility containing a "fantastic American Indian collection" (all on one floor) detailing the history of the country's earliest residents, as well as contemporary artifacts that appeal to "children of school age and older"; you can combine this easily with a visit to the Statue of Liberty, the South Street Seaport or Wall Street.

New York Aquarium   27 | 23 | 18 | 17 | M

Surf Ave. (W. 8th St.), Brooklyn; 718-265-3474; www.nyaquarium.com
☑ It may be a "haul to get to" this Coney Island location, but the "low-tech", "very quaint" setup with more than 8,000 animals is a "wonderful place to explore with kids"; they'll love the enormous shark tank, the "walruses who kiss visitors through the glass", "great dolphin, seal, sea lion and beluga whale shows throughout the day" and "stingray and jellyfish exhibits"; though fussy types feel it "needs a facelift", you can "combine it with a stroll down the boardwalk" and a Nathan's hot dog at the chain's nearby original location.

New York Botanical Garden ☺☺   18 | 26 | 23 | 20 | I

200th St. (Kazimiroff Blvd.), Bronx; 718-817-8700; www.nybg.org
■ It's "hard to find a more beautiful retreat in the metropolis" than this "oasis in the Bronx", "conveniently located across the street from a Metro-North commuter stop" (take a train from Grand Central Station); the 48 gardens displayed in 250 "beautifully landscaped" acres are a "jewel to behold", especially in spring and fall, with "outdoor trails", original forest, a "wonderful children's garden" that has a "rock-climbing area" and an "outstanding" train show at Christmastime set in a heated Victorian glass pavilion (visit when there's snow outside and you'll feel like you're in the Amazon); just be sure to "bring a stroller for toddlers due to the long walks involved."

New York City Fire Museum   24 | 22 | 18 | 20 | I

278 Spring St. (bet. Varick & Hudson Sts.), Manhattan; 212-691-1303; www.nycfiremuseum.org
■ Future firemen "love" this renovated 1904 "attractive old firehouse", a "delightful surprise tucked away" in TriBeCa a few blocks from Hudson River Park; an "awesome tribute to the men and women who dedicated their lives to saving yours", the "limited collection" features historic material from the 18th century to the present, and is staffed by retired members of the Fire Department; "truck-obsessed" tots to teens can get up close to the real red thing.

New York Hall of Science ☺☺   26 | 22 | 21 | 19 | I

Flushing Meadows Park, 47-01 111th St. (bet. 47th & 48th Aves.), Queens; 718-699-0005; www.nyhallsci.org
☑ For the "scientist in all of us", this distinctive "leftover World's Fair building" houses a "fantastic" "interactive museum" that's "fun for all ages"; four floors are packed with "hands-on, cool", "creative" exhibits that explore "how science is applied in real life", as well as two replica space rockets; the "outdoor science playground" is "always a hit with kids", but its location near Shea Stadium means it's out of the way unless you want to catch a Mets game afterward.

New York Public Library,   12 | 24 | 24 | 21 | $0
Humanities and Social Sciences ☺

Fifth Ave. (42nd St.), Manhattan; 212-930-0830; www.nypl.org
■ "The mother of all libraries", this "spectacular beaux arts structure" built in 1911 is a "monument to human achievement", a "wonderful resource for everything from obscure research to art to children's books" as well as a map room holding treasures from the 16th century and an airy, "awe-inspiring" main reading area; although the Child Appeal rating confirms that it's more "kid-friendly than kid-fun" and the "shhh policy" is tough on "restless" tykes, don't leave these "hallowed halls" without showing them the "original *Winnie the Pooh*

in the children's library" and letting them "pet Patience and Fortitude", the landmark's outdoor stone lions.

New York Transit Museum 😊😊   24 | 24 | 19 | 18 | I

Boerum Pl. (Schermerhorn St.), Brooklyn; 718-694-1600; www.mta.nyc.ny.us/mta/museum
■ Take a "trip back in time" when you "descend into this 1936 out-of-commission subway station" in Brooklyn Heights to "experience New York's entire mass-transit history" (dating back to 1900); "recently reopened after renovations", the U.S.'s largest museum devoted to urban transit has "lots of engaging kids' activities", several "vintage trains" ("sitting in the old cars is great") and other "really fine" exhibits that display "how city-ites traveled" during the past 100 years.

Prospect Park   22 | 22 | 16 | 13 | $0

bordered by Flatbush, Ocean & Parkside Aves., Brooklyn; 718-965-8999; www.prospectpark.org
■ "Central Park's little brother" in Brooklyn is a 526-acre "green refuge with playgrounds, ponds, ballfields", a Revolutionary-period historic house, an Audubon center and tennis courts that some maintain is "more elegant", "less crowded and more manageable" than Manhattan's; younger kids will love the "fun and different" zoo and the 1912 carousel, while older ones enjoy the "horseback riding at Kensington Stables", skating at the rink or rowing on the 60-acre lake; though it's an "integral part of life" in this borough, tourists find it's worth it "only if you're nearby or going there for an event."

Radio City Music Hall 😊😊   23 | 25 | 25 | 22 | M

1260 Sixth Ave. (50th St.), Manhattan; 212-247-4777; www.radiocity.com
■ "All Americans should see" this 1932 "grand, glorious and gaudy" art deco hall in Rockefeller Center "at least once in their lives", since it's a "classic New York venue" with "phenomenal acoustics" and "not a bad seat" among the 2,000 in the house; the setting is "consistently magical" for young and old, so take the kids to the "spellbinding" Rockettes' Christmas Spectacular or on one of the backstage tours – "that's all it takes to get hooked."

Riverside Park   20 | 21 | 15 | 9 | $0

Riverside Dr. (bet. 68th & 155th Sts.), Manhattan; 212-408-0264
■ A "beautiful narrow park" along the West Side, this "hidden pleasure" is definitely "more manageable than Central Park" even though it was designed by the same architect; it has a "great view of the Hudson" (though the proximity to the West Side Highway means it's often "noisy") and kids can "watch sailboats", "paddle a kayak", hit the "great trails for hiking" or stake a claim at one of the "small playgrounds"; tiny tots consider the hippos at 90th Street a "treasure", while just about everyone is impressed by Riverside Church, an "incredible Gothic jewel" at 490 Riverside Drive, or Grant's Tomb a block north.

Rockefeller Center   21 | 24 | 21 | 17 | M

47th to 51st Sts. (bet. 5th & 7th Aves.), Manhattan; 212-632-3975; www.rockefellercenter.com
■ Best known as the "quintessential holiday attraction", this six-block area boasts a "magical", "giant" Christmas tree each December and "fantastic" ice skating in winter, but it's also "great any time of year" for the "subterranean" shopping complex, the NBC Experience store and tour, the "beautiful landscaping" and restaurants where you can "enjoy eating outside"; plus if you're there "early in the morning, you may be able to catch a glimpse of co-anchors Katie Couric and Matt Lauer on the *Today* show" through its glass windows or meet Al Roker when he comes outside to check on the weather.

Shea Stadium 🐶☺

| 23 | 22 | 14 | 14 | E |

123-01 Roosevelt Ave. (123rd St.), Queens; 718-507-6387; www.mets.com
☑ Meet the Mets – or at least, greet them – at this Flushing arena
that's "a great place to take the kids" for the "excitement of a live
game" ("when the home team wins, watch out – the stadium actually
shakes"); okay, Yankee boosters call it "second-rate", but when Mr.
Met starts firing free T-shirts into the crowd and the planes from
LaGuardia roar overhead, you can't help feeling this is baseball like it
oughta be; N.B. check schedules for concerts and other events.

Skyscraper Museum, The

| – | – | – | – | I |

39 Battery Pl. (Little West St.), Manhattan; 212-968-1961; www.skyscraper.org
Documenting the skyline is a tall order, but after a post-9/11 delay, this
small museum newly ensconced in Battery Park is at the top of its
game with an exhibition on vertical NYC; building buffs stretch their
knowledge through a long look at photos and arcana, and if short
attention spans tire, at least kids can stare at themselves ad infinitum
in the polished steel which lines the space to heighten the illusion of,
um, height; these folks also curate the former World Trade Center site.

South Street Seaport/Museum

| 19 | 22 | 20 | 17 | I |

Visitor Ctr., 12 Fulton St. (bet. Front and South Sts.), Manhattan;
212-748-8600; www.southstseaport.org
■ "New York's own little bit of Fisherman's Wharf" allows fanatics to
experience "maritime history" on the East River; the 12-square-block
landmarked area, dating from the 17th century, has "surprisingly good
food", "upscale shops", "galleries in old wharfside buildings", "quaint
cobblestone streets", a museum with "military appeal", "tours of old
sailboats", street vendors and entertainers and an "unobstructed view
of New York's three downtown bridges"; though jaded mateys may call
it a "tourist trap", most feel it's "fun on holidays and summer weekends."

Staten Island Ferry

| 23 | 23 | 14 | 13 | $0 |

1 South St. (Whitehall St.), Manhattan; 718-727-2508; www.siferry.com
☑ "Who says you can't get somethin' for nothin'?"; you can if you head
to the Battery and hop aboard the "best free cruise in the world", a
great way "to see some of the sights of the city on the cheap" and get
"a break from a day of furious" walking; in fact, it's "the perfect place
to take impressive photos of the Manhattan skyline" and see the
Statue of Liberty up close without waiting in line; but critics cry "what
a dump" and warn that you avoid rush hour unless you want "to rub
shoulders with" too many "real New Yorkers."

Statue of Liberty

| 24 | 27 | 19 | 18 | $0 |

Liberty Island (New York Harbor), Manhattan; 212-363-3200; www.nps.gov/stli
☑ "Closed to the public" since September 2001, this "symbol of our
country", "shining" tall in the Harbor, is set to reopen its base museum
(with a new glass viewing ceiling) by summer 2004; while you won't
be able to climb to the top, you can go up 16 stories to an observation
deck; "kids love the boat ride over" from Battery Park, and everyone
finds "standing in her shadow humbling"; bear in mind, this can turn
out to be a full-day trip with "horribly long lines", so think about
riding by on the Staten Island Ferry instead; N.B. admission to the statue
is free, but the boat costs $10 for adults, $4 for kids.

St. Patrick's Cathedral 🐶☺

| 13 | 25 | 22 | 18 | $0 |

14 E. 51st St. (bet. 5th & Madison Aves.), Manhattan; 212-753-2261
■ "As awe-inspiring and reverential as any of the 15th-century
churches in Europe", this largest Catholic cathedral in the country is
"a place of calm in the frantic city" with its "magnificent stained-glass
windows", "beautiful altar and woodwork" and "amazing" organ;
though it may be "too holy and solemn for a noisy two-year-old because

any scream is magnified in the cavernous space", it's often crowded and even "too touristy" for some, especially near the front entrance; N.B. its Fifth Avenue location is right near Rockefeller Center.

TIMES SQUARE ☺

| 19 | 24 | 16 | 12 | $0 |

W. 42nd St. to W. 47th St. (Broadway), Manhattan; 212-768-1560; www.timessquarebid.org

■ "It's certainly bright lights, big city" at the "center of the world" – a Midtown neighborhood that's "overwhelming, tacky and absolutely mad – but that's part of the charm"; with "wonderful theater, shopping and restaurants" as well as "blinking lights, animated advertisements", news tickers, giant TV screens, a huge Toys "R" Us and a frenetic ESPN Zone, it's all a manic, "family-friendly" fun time; even if locals call it "tourist-idiot central", it's "much safer" than in years past, just "hold on tight to your children's hands" since it's "like rush hour 24/7."

Toys "R" Us ☺☺

| 29 | 18 | 21 | 19 | $0 |

1514 Broadway (44th St.), Manhattan; 800-869-7787; www.toysrustimessquare.com

■ "Even the Grinch would love going here", a "megastore" in Times Square that will make you think you "made a wrong turn and ended up in Santa's workshop", with a "three-story Ferris wheel" you can ride for free, an "animatronic" "giant growling dinosaur", a "4,000-sq.-ft. Barbie dollhouse", "Lego replicas of Manhattan's famous buildings" and a "spectacular giraffe" – no wonder it's voted No. 1 for Child Appeal in New York in our *Survey;* just "reserve your ride" on the wheel as soon as you get in, and "watch your wallet"; N.B. parents may find this a strain, judging by our scores, but kids are pleased every time.

United Nations ☺☺

| 13 | 23 | 21 | 19 | M |

First Ave. (46th St.), Manhattan; 212-963-8687; www.un.org

☑ Older kids might like the "fascinating" tour conducted in "nearly any language" from Arabic to Swedish at this "hot seat of international relations", the sleek headquarters "where the world meets"; but there's "high security" and "no entertaining" slant so it can be "boring for younger children" and a "bit dry" for elders as well; "try to eat in the Delegates Dining Room with its great East River views" to overcome the "disappointment" in a site that "could be so much more."

USTA National Tennis Center ☺☺

| 15 | 26 | 25 | 19 | E |

Flushing Meadows-Corona Park (Roosevelt Ave.), Queens; 718-760-6200; www.usta.com

☑ "Home to some of the world's best tennis", this "top-notch stadium" reached from Manhattan by the 7 train can be a "great destination" – whether you're there during the two weeks of the U.S. Open (late summer) or the rest of the year to hit some balls and dream; if you're around for the big tourny, pint-size players will "love the early rounds at the small courts" and you can take advantage of "Arthur Ashe Kids' Day festivities"; but with the price of tickets and food, you may have to "take out that second mortgage before spending a day" here.

World Trade Center Site

| 11 | 23 | 10 | 9 | $0 |

Liberty St. (Church St.), Manhattan; 212-484-1222 (NYC & Co.)

☑ The notion of out-of-towners gazing at the hole where the Twin Towers once stood sparks sharp debate among surveyors; some say a trip downtown to this "Pearl Harbor of the 21st century" is a "must" in order to "pay respects to those lost", so adults who "feel compelled to see" this "moving", "emotional" site take the opportunity to "educate children" "10 and up" and "teens who understand the tragedy" about its "historical significance"; others counter "who needs to be reminded?" – this "heartbreaking and depressing" "place of grief and horror" is "not a place to gawk" – and are offended by

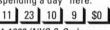

"ghoulish" vendors selling "tacky baseball caps" and "tourists taking toothy smiling pictures" by the pit; if you do go, "make your visit an introspective one" and "be prepared to cry."

YANKEE STADIUM ☺☺

25	27	19	16	E

50 E 161st St. (River Ave.), Bronx; 718-293-4300; www.yankees.com
■ "The house that Ruth built" in the 1920s is a veritable "cathedral" to the sport, a "grand arena" with "history" dripping from every pore and "the place to introduce a kid to baseball"; it may be in a "crumbling" neighborhood (be careful where you park), but if you "get there early" you can visit Monument Park behind center for a tribute to all the great Yankees of old (the view from the field "gives anyone chills"); though grumps "give a Bronx cheer to the extortion-priced hot dogs", "if you don't love this place you either hate the game or you're from Boston."

HOTELS

Ratings: Family Appeal, Rooms, Service, Public Facilities, Cost

FA	R	S	P	$

DoubleTree Guest Suites

24	21	20	19	$319

1568 Broadway, Manhattan; 212-719-1600; 800-222-8733;
www.nyc.doubletreehotels.com; 460 suites
■ "Step out to shows, restaurants and action" at this "wonderfully located" all-suite property with reasonable rates "right in the heart of Times Square"; children like it because the staff is "friendly", there's a "great breakfast buffet" and "they always have warm cookies when you check in"; rooms feature refrigerators, separate living areas and "good views from high floors"; there's an on-site kids' room with video games, but with so much to visit outside – including the nearby Toys "R" Us with its own Ferris wheel – they won't be inside very long; N.B. Circle Line sightseeing tours leave from the pier a few avenues west.

Embassy Suites Hotel

25	23	21	20	$379

102 North End Ave., Manhattan; 212-945-0100; 800-362-2779;
www.newyorkcity.embsuites.com; 463 suites
☑ If you want proximity to the Statue of Liberty and Ellis Island, head to this "relatively inexpensive" Downtown spot where the "suites make it especially appealing" because you can stay together in one room "with privacy"; "free breakfasts offer good value" and "kids love the playground at Battery Park" next door; while it's "not convenient" to Midtown attractions and it "can get costly" cabbing it uptown, most say they "can't imagine a better place for families"; N.B. some rooms have beautiful views of Lady Liberty.

Hilton Times Square

20	21	21	20	$399

234 W. 42nd St., Manhattan; 212-840-8222; 877-946-8357; www.hilton.com;
429 rooms, 15 suites
■ You "can't get a better location" say satisfied sightseers of this "mid-range hotel" with "excellent public transportation access" near Fifth Avenue shopping, Madame Tussaud's Wax Museum, Radio City Music Hall and Rockefeller Center; it's just a "quick walk to Times Square", and the "rooms are large" as well, but be warned: "if you don't like hustle and bustle", this busy, "noisy" spot, which hosts conventions and business meetings, is not for you.

Library Hotel

23	25	26	23	$315

299 Madison Ave., Manhattan; 212-983-4500; 877-793-7323;
www.libraryhotel.com; 52 rooms, 8 suites
■ "If the family is into reading, this is the place" say bookworms wowed by the "very clever" "high concept" at this Midtown hotel

where each of the 10 floors is named for a Dewey Decimal System category (e.g., history, philosophy, poetry) and you "sleep among" a collection of hardcovers (ask for your child's favorites); there are "lovely common spaces" and it's just one block from Grand Central Terminal and its subway connections to all parts of town; N.B. rates include a daily continental breakfast and evening wine and cheese.

Marriott Marquis

21 | **19** | **19** | **20** | **$379**

1535 Broadway, Manhattan; 212-398-1900; 800-228-9290; www.marriott.com; 1896 rooms, 50 suites

■ For "the ultimate" "big-city experience", head to this "way-big" Times Square outpost "in the middle of everything" with a "stunning atrium", "huge glass elevators that kids love" and a "rotating restaurant with wonderful views" on top; sure, the lobby's pretty "crowded" and "noisy", but "it's great having a [Broadway] theater right inside your hotel", as well as a "multitude of restaurants" inside and out; N.B. walk across the street to the TKTS booth for half-price show tickets.

New York Marriott at the Brooklyn Bridge

17 | **23** | **23** | **22** | **$199**

333 Adams St., Brooklyn; 718-246-7000; 800-228-9290; www.marriott.com; 355 rooms, 21 suites

■ It's "much more affordable than staying in Manhattan" say fans of this "great find over the bridge" that has "easy access" to the main island via mass transit or a "quick cab ride" (five minutes to the South Street Seaport and lower Manhattan); there's a "nice pool and gym" and even if the hotel doesn't particularly cater to kids, "the atmosphere welcomes them"; plus it's just a few miles from great Brooklyn sights like the Children's Museum and the Botanical Garden.

Plaza, The

21 | **23** | **25** | **24** | **$344**

768 Fifth Ave., Manhattan; 212-759-3000; 800-759-3000; www.fairmont.com; 805 rooms, 96 suites

◪ "Every girl needs to be Eloise at least once" say parents, referring to the character from the children's book series who stayed at this "elegant" "landmark" that offers "adventures both inside and out"; the "holiday decorations can't be beat" and "kids enjoy the views of the horse-drawn carriages" across the street at Central Park (it's also close to great Fifth Avenue shopping); sure, there are lots of tourists gawking in the lobby and the "rooms are not very large", but the majority love the "tattered pomp of it all."

Renaissance

▽ **23** | **25** | **25** | **24** | **$279**

714 Seventh Ave., Manhattan; 212-765-7676; 800-468-3571; www.renaissancehotels.com; 300 rooms, 5 suites

■ "With a view of Times Square that's worth every penny", this hotel is easy to find thanks to its huge outdoor signature clock towering over the area; there's "great concierge service" that will help you score tickets to Broadway shows playing within walking distance, and it's a 10-minute stroll down to Macy's and Herald Square; rooms have high-speed Internet connections, complimentary coffee and refrigerators upon request, and you earn Marriott Rewards points for future upgrades and free rooms.

RIHGA Royal

21 | **26** | **24** | **23** | **$495**

151 W. 54th St., Manhattan; 212-307-5000; 800-937-5454; www.marriott.com; 500 suites

◪ Fans of this JW Marriott "undiscovered gem" find the "all-suite" concept "perfect for families" because the "ultra-comfortable" rooms (all measuring at least 500 square feet) provide plenty of space "so your kids can sleep in the bedroom while you and your spouse watch TV" or enjoy in-room dining from top restaurant Halcyon in the living area; it's "not too exciting" for children otherwise, but the "top few floors have magnificent views of Central Park", where little ones can enjoy many activities.

Ritz-Carlton Battery Park

| 21 | 26 | 27 | 26 | $500 |

2 West St., Manhattan; 212-344-0800; 800-241-3333; www.ritzcarlton.com; 254 rooms, 44 suites

☑ It's "worth every penny" say fans of this ritzy Downtown spot that's "a little out of the way" for Midtown sightseeing, but is in close proximity to Battery Park, Ellis Island and the National Museum of the American Indian; rooms with feather beds and marble bathrooms "wow" most visitors who say "it's a thrill using in-room telescopes" for an "unbelievable view" of the Statue of Liberty, while the staff "really goes out of its way to make kids feel welcome"; N.B. its Midtown sister property is located on Central Park South.

Trump International Hotel & Tower

| 22 | 25 | 24 | 27 | $595 |

1 Central Park W., Manhattan; 212-299-1000; 888-448-7867; www.trumpintl.com; 47 rooms, 120 suites

☑ The "Donald reigns supreme" at this parkside property that appeals more to parents than to kids, but still "offers the best service and facilities in the city"; just steps from the new Time Warner Center with its upscale retail shops and restaurants, and several blocks from Lincoln Center, it has "hard-to-beat views of Central Park" from large rooms and suites with Euro-style kitchens (fridges can be pre-stocked with child-friendly snacks); it may be a "bit cold" for fun-loving folks, but the on-site New French restaurant Jean Georges is one of the best in Manhattan.

Top Family-Friendly Hotel Chains in the Area:

Four Seasons	Hyatt
Hampton Inn	Westin
Holiday Inn	

See Hotel Chain reviews, starting on page 256.

RESTAURANTS

Ratings: Family Appeal, Food, Decor, Service, Cost

| FA | F | D | S | $ |

America

| 23 | 18 | 19 | 17 | M |

9 E. 18th St. (bet. B'way & 5th Ave.), Manhattan; 212-505-2110; www.arkrestaurants.com

☑ This "safe bet" in the Flatiron District is "extremely spacious by NYC standards" yet so "loud, loud, loud" that "you'll never worry about your kids making too much noise"; the "fun", "Americana-themed" decor echoes the wide-open, "affordably priced" menu offering "everything on the planet", so even though it's "conventional, cafeteria-like food" served at a "slow" pace, at least there's always "something for even the pickiest eater."

Barking Dog

| 22 | 20 | 19 | 20 | M |

150 E. 34th St. (bet. Lexington & 3rd Aves.), Manhattan; 212-871-3900
1678 Third Ave. (94th St.), Manhattan; 212-831-1800 ☞
1453 York Ave. (77th St.), Manhattan; 212-861-3600 ☞

■ "After a long day chasing the kids, kick back and rest your barking dogs" at this "down-to-earth", canine-themed East Side threesome offering "wholesome" comfort food at "reasonable" tabs in "low-key" surroundings; even better, "Fido can tag along too", provided you sit and stay outside.

Brooklyn Diner USA ◑

| 19 | 18 | 17 | 17 | M |

212 W. 57th St. (bet. B'way & 7th Ave.), Manhattan; 212-977-2280;
www.brooklyndiner.com

☑ There's "something for all ages and all palates" at this Midtown "upscale diner" that's "nostalgic for adults and fun for kids"; sure, the grub's "pricey" for what it is, the quarters are "tight" and you can "expect to wait in line", but all is forgiven after a bite of "NY's biggest hot dog" – it's "humongous enough for three to share."

Bubby's

| 24 | 22 | 18 | 20 | M |

120 Hudson St. (N. Moore St.), Manhattan; 212-219-0666
1 Main St. (bet. Plymouth & Water Sts.), Brooklyn; 718-222-0666
www.bubbys.com

■ "Families with diverse tastes" like the menus at these "Maclaren stroller"–laden "favorites" in TriBeCa and Brooklyn because they offer "surprisingly sophisticated" American fare yet "nothing's too spicy or weird for the kids"; despite enticements like a "friendly" staff, balloons and an atmosphere reminiscent of "grandma's" house, be aware that "insane" weekend waits can make for "cranky" toddlers.

Carmine's

| 24 | 22 | 18 | 20 | E |

2450 Broadway (bet. 90th & 91st Sts.), Manhattan; 212-362-2200
200 W. 44th St. (bet. B'way & 8th Ave.), Manhattan; 212-221-3800
www.carminesnyc.com

■ "Even the baby should wear loose pants" to these "crowd-pleasing red-sauce palaces" famed for serving family-style Italian eats with "tons of garlic" in portions large enough to "feed an army"; since they're also celebrated as being "good value for the money", you should "expect to wait, wait, wait for your table", though the "boisterous" atmosphere is so "chaotic" that no one will notice if someone in your party "throws a fit"; N.B. the Times Square outpost has recently added a second floor, doubling its capacity.

Carnegie Deli ◑⇭

| – | – | – | – | M |

854 Seventh Ave. (55th St.), Manhattan; 212-757-2245;
www.carnegiedeli.com

To experience "NY between two slices of bread", try this Midtown deli "legend" where you sit "shoulder-to-shoulder" with "tourists", "showbiz hangers-on" and wide-eyed kids fascinated by its "platinum standard" of pastrami, pickles and cheesecake; the "enormous sandwiches" may come via "surly" waiters, but that's "part of the charm", especially when you see Soon-Yi and Woody treated the same way as you.

Comfort Diner

| 21 | 20 | 15 | 18 | M |

214 E. 45th St. (bet. 2nd & 3rd Aves.), Manhattan; 212-867-4555
25 W. 23rd St. (bet. 5th & 6th Aves.), Manhattan; 212-741-1010

■ The "name says it all" at this "50s-style" diner mini-chain dishing out a "large selection" of "hearty, homey" comfort chow that appeals to "kids of all ages"; assets like "big booths", a "friendly staff" and a "fun atmosphere" (replete with "oldies music") make them "solid" options for breakfast, lunch or dinner.

Cowgirl

| 21 | 19 | 22 | 18 | M |

519 Hudson St. (10th St.), Manhattan; 212-633-1133

■ A "circus" for Buffalo Bills and Calamity Janes, this "ranch-themed" West Village Tex-Mex spot features lots of "knickknacks for little eyes to look at" (don't miss the "barbed wire collection") as well as time-tested favorites like macaroni 'n' cheese and the regional delicacy Frito pie; though the "staff has a high tolerance for kids", many tenderfeet report it's "only family-friendly at lunch" – "later in the evening, it turns into a bar."

Dallas BBQ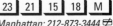

| 20 | 17 | 11 | 16 | M |

132 Second Ave. (St. Marks Pl.), Manhattan; 212-777-5574
1265 Third Ave. (bet. 72nd & 73rd Sts.), Manhattan; 212-772-9393
21 University Pl. (8th St.), Manhattan; 212-674-4450
27 W. 72nd St. (bet. Columbus Ave. & CPW), Manhattan; 212-873-2004
www.bbqnyc.com

■ "Large families who don't want to break the bank" make a beeline for this BBQ chain known for "huge", "finger-friendly" servings of "serviceable vittles" at "oh-so-cheap" tabs; though the "quantity-not-quality" approach and "cattle-call" atmospheres are turnoffs, at least they're "spacious" enough to let the "kids run around" while you drain an "aquarium-size margarita."

EJ's Luncheonette

| 23 | 21 | 15 | 18 | M |

447 Amsterdam Ave. (bet. 81st & 82nd Sts.), Manhattan; 212-873-3444
432 Sixth Ave. (bet. 9th & 10th Sts.), Manhattan; 212-473-5555
1271 Third Ave. (73rd St.), Manhattan; 212-472-0600

■ Brace yourself for the "stroller brigade out in force" at these "fast-paced", "old-style diners" that welcome kiddies with "open arms" (there's "no attitude" when you request "extra spoons after all six have been dropped on the floor"); grown-ups get happy with "ample" menus of "better-than-average" grub, although downsides include "long" weekend waits, "squished" seating and "somewhat loud" acoustics.

Golden Unicorn

| – | – | – | – | M |

18 E. Broadway, 3rd fl. (Catherine St.), Manhattan; 212-941-0911

If you're trying to expose your finicky little eater to more than just chicken nuggets, it's no myth that this busy dim sum palace upstairs in Chinatown is golden for grazing on a wide variety of steamed buns, dumplings and other Asian delicacies; the servers can chat with you in English and explain the dizzying parade of pushcart dishes, but rise early for weekend brunch because the joint gets jammed.

Jackson Hole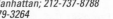

| 21 | 20 | 13 | 17 | M |

517 Columbus Ave. (85th St.), Manhattan; 212-362-5177
232 E. 64th St. (bet. 2nd & 3rd Aves.), Manhattan; 212-371-7187
1611 Second Ave. (bet. 83rd & 84th Sts.), Manhattan; 212-737-8788
521 Third Ave. (35th St.), Manhattan; 212-679-3264

■ "Big, sloppy burgers" (just "the way they should be") are the draw at these "convenient", "cholesterol-city" outposts offering "enough on the menu" to please "even that discriminating seven-year-old food critic"; so ignore the "cramped" setups and the "inevitable mess", and remind yourself that "kids are always happy" here.

John's Pizzeria ●

| 24 | 24 | 15 | 18 | M |

278 Bleecker St. (bet. 6th & 7th Aves.), Manhattan; 212-243-1680
408 E. 64th St. (bet. 1st & York Aves.), Manhattan; 212-935-2895
260 W. 44th St. (bet. B'way & 8th Ave.), Manhattan; 212-391-7560

■ You "can't go wrong bringing the family" to this burgeoning pizzeria chainlet where some of "New York's best" thin-crust pies emerge from wood ovens (a word to the wise: "they don't serve by the slice" – "you have to order a whole one"); the favorite branch may be the Times Square outpost, "set in a beautiful old church", where "kids can be kids" and "roam around when ants-in-the-pants hits."

Katz's Delicatessen

| – | – | – | – | M |

205 E. Houston St. (Ludlow St.), Manhattan; 212-254-2246

"Pastrami or corned beef?" – the big question at this huge Jewish deli "avatar of the old days" before "cholesterol" and "cardiac" ("oy") entered the vocabulary; given cured meat piled so "high" that it'll "make you cry", nobody minds the "cranky countermen" or "bleak setting" – consider it an education for your brood in the joys of "nosh-talgia"; N.B. the location is great for lunch after a visit to the Lower East Side Tenement Museum.

La Mela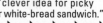

23 | 20 | 13 | 22 | E

167 Mulberry St. (bet. Broome & Grand Sts.), Manhattan; 212-431-9493
■ Since there's "no menu", there are "no fights about what to eat" at this Little Italy family-style joint where the "baby-loving staff" will "make the kids feel like part of *la famiglia*"; though there's not much decor in this "crowded, loud" spot, there's plenty of "reasonable" fare ("start Atkins tomorrow") as well as "authenticity for the tourists."

Mars 2112

26 | 10 | 25 | 16 | M

1633 Broadway (51st St.), Manhattan; 212-582-2112; www.mars2112.com
☑ "Children will have a blast" at this "well-executed" Theater District theme spot, an "out-of-this-world" experience that begins with a "really cool" spaceship ride to a "dark" restaurant populated by "roaming Martians"; sure, the "appeal wears off quickly" and the "barely edible" food is "not recognizable as any cuisine on Earth", but "kids don't care", especially with a room of video games to try out after dinner.

Mickey Mantle's ◑

21 | 15 | 22 | 18 | E

42 Central Park S. (bet. 5th & 6th Aves.), Manhattan; 212-688-7777
☑ A destination for "sports fans" and "adults who never grew up", this Central Park South shrine to No. 7 has more "baseball paraphernalia" than "Cooperstown" (forget the "pedestrian", "Icky Mantle's" grub); though it's "almost affordable in a high-priced location", some wonder "do kids even know who the Mick was anymore?"

Peanut Butter & Co.

25 | 20 | 16 | 19 | I

240 Sullivan St. (bet. Bleecker & W. 3rd Sts.), Manhattan; 212-677-3995; www.ilovepeanutbutter.com
■ A "fun place to take a kid (or a kid at heart)", this Greenwich Villager is a "must-try" for its novelty concept, a "sticky" specialty menu devoted to "peanut butter–inspired creations"; though the digs are "small" and the service "slow", this "cross between a day-care center and a nostalgic time trip" is still a "clever idea for picky children" – they'll even "cut the crusts off your white-bread sandwich."

Popover Cafe

22 | 22 | 19 | 19 | M

551 Amsterdam Ave. (bet. 86th & 87th Sts.), Manhattan; 212-595-8555; www.popovercafe.com
■ "Amazing popovers" with flavored butters and "adorable" "stuffed bears all over the place" are the draws at this "warm and fuzzy" Upper West Sider, a "homey", "happy" spot that "lives up to the hype", provided you stick to the signature dish (the "other selections are just average"); since weekend brunch can be a "madhouse" with "long, annoying waits", smart parents "bring the kids during off hours."

Ruby Foo's ◑

20 | 22 | 24 | 20 | E

1626 Broadway (49th St.), Manhattan; 212-489-5600
2182 Broadway (77th St.), Manhattan; 212-724-6700
www.brguestrestaurants.com
■ "Over-the-top", "theatrical" decor "keeps youngsters entertained" at these twin Pan-Asian palaces on the West Side where "everything's served family-style" and prices are "relatively reasonable"; true, the rather "exotic" offerings are "not for picky eaters", but the "lively atmosphere" and "friendly staff" are ample distractions.

Serendipity 3 ◑

26 | 22 | 23 | 18 | M

225 E. 60th St. (bet. 2nd & 3rd Aves.), Manhattan; 212-838-3531; www.serendipity3.com
■ When you want to treat your kids to a "sugar rush", this "one-and-only" "New York City institution" (now 50 years old) is known for its

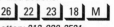

"out-of-this-world desserts", especially that "signature frozen hot chocolate" that can "stop any diet in its tracks"; there are also unique children's gifts at the "cluttered" toy shop at the entrance, but since service is "slow" and the space "tight", either "make reservations, get there when it opens" or be prepared for a "horribly long wait."

Tavern on the Green

| _ | _ | _ | _ | VE |

Central Park W. (bet. 66th & 67th Sts.), Manhattan; 212-873-3200;
www.tavernonthegreen.com
"Everyone's inner child" finds this Central Park "fantasyland" an "enchanting" experience, from the "convivial" garden to the "gorgeous Crystal Room"; even if a few feel the American food is "expensive for the quality" and the decor is too reminiscent of "Elvis's bedroom", its "evergreen appeal" charms everybody from "hardened NYers" to "tourists" with families in tow.

Tony's Di Napoli

| 24 | 22 | 17 | 21 | E |

1606 Second Ave. (83rd St.), Manhattan; 212-861-8686
147 W. 43rd St. (bet. B'way & 6th Ave.), Manhattan; 212-221-0100
www.tonysdinapoli.com
■ "Welcome alternatives to Carmine's" – they're "easier to get into" – these "family-style" purveyors of "hungry man–size platters" of Italian grub please parents as well as kids, since no one has to "compromise their taste buds" (just be in the mood to "eat large"); besides offering "terrific bang for the buck", they're also "loud enough to drown out any unruly child."

Two Boots

| 21 | 21 | 15 | 17 | I |

74 Bleecker St. (B'way), Manhattan; 212-777-1033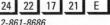
Grand Central, lower level (42nd St. & Lexington Ave.), Manhattan;
212-557-7992
30 Rockefeller Plaza, downstairs (bet. 49th & 50th Sts.), Manhattan;
212-332-8800 🅂
201 W. 11th St. (7th Ave. S.), Manhattan; 212-633-9096 ●
www.twoboots.com
■ "They're lovely to children" at this pizzeria chainlet, supplying "dough to play with" as well as coloring books and crayons (the Brooklyn outpost even sports a "windowed platform to observe the kitchen"); though "your kid will have plenty of company here", some say the "nontraditional" toppings may be "too exotic for a young palate."

Virgil's Real BBQ

| _ | _ | _ | _ | M |

152 W. 44th St. (bet. B'way & 6th Ave.), Manhattan; 212-921-9494;
www.virgilsbbq.com
"Bring your appetite" and "stretch pants" to this Times Square joint serving "surprisingly authentic" BBQ that "goes straight to your arteries"; despite throngs of "tourists" and "long" waits to get in, decor that's "more Disney than down-home" will thrill the kiddies.

RESTAURANT CHAINS

See reviews, starting on page 262.

Ratings: Family Appeal, Food, Decor, Service, Cost

| FA | F | D | S | $ |

Applebee's

| 21 | 16 | 17 | 17 | M |

234 W. 42nd St. (bet. Eighth Ave. & Broadway), Manhattan; 212-391-7414
205 W. 50th St. (Broadway), Manhattan; 212-262-2400
World Financial Ctr., 102 North End Ave. (bet. Murray & Vesey Sts.),
Manhattan; 212-945-3277

Benihana | 23 | 20 | 18 | 22 | E
120 E. 56th St. (bet. Lexington & Park Aves.), Manhattan; 212-593-1627
47 W. 56th St. (bet. 5th & 6th Aves.), Manhattan; 212-581-0930

Bubba Gump Shrimp Co. ☒ | 24 | 18 | 23 | 20 | M
1501 Broadway (bet. 43rd & 44th Sts.), Manhattan; 212-391-7100

California Pizza Kitchen | 21 | 21 | 16 | 19 | M
201 E. 60th St. (bet. 2nd & 3rd Aves.), Manhattan; 212-755-7773

Chevys Fresh Mex ☒ | 23 | 19 | 18 | 18 | M
102 North End Ave. (Vesey St.), Manhattan; 212-786-1111
243 W. 42nd St. (bet. 7th & 8th Aves.), Manhattan; 212-302-4010

Chuck E. Cheese's ☒ | 26 | 10 | 17 | 13 | I
34-19 48th St. (Northern Blvd.), Queens; 718-728-3600

Hard Rock Cafe ◑ | 22 | 16 | 26 | 18 | M
221 W. 57th St. (bet. B'way & 7th Ave.), Manhattan; 212-489-6565

Johnny Rockets ◑ | 25 | 17 | 20 | 18 | I
42 E. Eighth St. (bet. B'way & University Pl.), Manhattan; 212-253-8175

Olive Garden ☒ | 20 | 19 | 18 | 19 | M
696 Sixth Ave. (22nd St.), Manhattan; 212-255-1240
201 W. 47th St. (bet. B'way & 7th Ave.), Manhattan; 212-333-3254

Planet Hollywood ◑ | 24 | 13 | 24 | 16 | M
1540 Broadway (45th St.), Manhattan; 212-333-7827

T.G.I. Friday's | 21 | 17 | 18 | 17 | M
196 Broadway (bet. Fulton & John Sts.), Manhattan; 212-240-1280
1552 Broadway (46th St.), Manhattan; 212-944-7352 ◑
47 E. 42nd St. (bet. Madison & Vanderbilt Aves.), Manhattan; 212-681-8458
604 Fifth Ave. (bet. 48th & 49th Sts.), Manhattan; 212-767-8335

Uno Chicago Grill ◑ | 20 | 18 | 15 | 16 | M
432 Columbus Ave. (81st St.), Manhattan; 212-595-4700
391 Sixth Ave. (bet. 8th St. & Waverly Pl.), Manhattan; 212-242-5230
South Street Seaport, 89 South St. (Pier 17), Manhattan; 212-791-7999
37-11 35th Ave. (38th St.), Queens; 718-706-8800

Orlando

Once a sleepy little citrus-farming community, Orlando sprang to Technicolor life in 1971 with the opening of Walt Disney World. Thirty-plus years later, this reliably sunny city is one of the world's top tourist destinations, thanks to its unparalleled assemblage of theme parks. Walt Disney World alone now has four – Magic Kingdom, Epcot, Disney-MGM Studios and Animal Kingdom – plus two water parks, two miniature-golf courses, nearly 20 lodging facilities, a dining/entertainment complex and much more. Universal Orlando offers up another two, Universal Studios and Islands of Adventure, while the SeaWorld folks also run Discovery Cove. Meanwhile, countless family-oriented enterprises survive off the parks' overflow. Go-cart operators, oddity museums, haunted-house attractions and child-friendly dinner theaters crowd the tourist corridors in the city's southwest section, where nearly every restaurant has a kids' menu. Visitors can take shuttle buses back and forth from most hotels to the major theme parks, but those looking to explore farther afield (the Kennedy Space

Center and Cape Canaveral to the east, or the Ocala National Forest to the north) should rent a car. In fact, rentals are often more convenient and less expensive in Orlando than elsewhere; they may be included in money-saving package deals with accommodations and tickets.

ATTRACTIONS

Ratings: Child Appeal, Adult Appeal, Public Facilities, Service, Cost

C	A	P	S	$

BLIZZARD BEACH ☺

28	26	26	24	E

Walt Disney World, 1500 W. Buena Vista Dr. (Osceola Pkwy.); 407-824-4321; www.disneyworld.com

■ Adults tolerate "standing in line half-naked and damp all day" so that their offspring can enjoy this "cool" Disney water park, one that simulates "a blizzard in 80-degree weather"; "what a feeling" – "swimming in melted snow", "what a scream" – plunging down "the fastest, wettest slide ever", "what a blast" – "sucking in your gut and joining the kids" in "the meandering river with tubes"; just "get there early to claim a beach chair", and don't expect "much choice" for dining here; instead, head to one of the many top-shelf restaurants throughout Disney World and its surroundings.

DISCOVERY COVE ☺☺

27	28	27	27	VE

Central Florida Pkwy. (bet. International & Sea World Drs.); 877-434-7268; www.discoverycove.com

■ Just a couple of miles northeast of Walt Disney World, a "once-in-a-lifetime experience" awaits at this *Survey's* top water park (adjacent to big brother SeaWorld); though swimmers must be six or older to realize the "fantasy" of frolicking with "playful" "kissing" dolphins (the "main attraction"), this "day-long treat" is "enjoyed by all ages", since visitors can "interact with stingrays" and "other creatures of the sea", not to mention "beautiful birds in the aviary"; yes, it's "expensive", but "everything is included" – from the "awesome eats" to the keepsake photograph; N.B. rates vary significantly by season.

DISNEY-MGM STUDIOS ☺

25	27	27	26	VE

Walt Disney World, 3111 World Dr. (Epcot Center Dr.); 407-824-4321; www.disneyworld.com

◪ "Dreams become reality" as you "live out your favorite movies" and TV shows at this theme park "for film buffs and media-savvy" older kids who "get a kick out of" "thrills" such as the "unpredictable" *Twilight Zone* Tower of Terror elevator "drop-p-p-p-p", plus "educational" features like "the animation studios and back-lot tour" and the new *Who Wants To Be A Millionaire* attraction, all of which you can "see in one day"; however, beyond characters "to meet and greet" and "spectacular shows" featuring the likes of the Little Mermaid, there's "not as much appeal for toddlers."

DISNEY'S ANIMAL KINGDOM ☺

26	25	26	26	VE

Walt Disney World, Osceola Pkwy.; 407-824-4321; www.disneyworld.com

◪ "Who would've thought anyone could combine a theme park with a natural reserve?" – well, "Diz has", with "wonderful shows, exciting rides" and "breathtaking" "animal encounters" perfect for a full day; "digging for fossils", visiting the petting zoo, "cracking up" at *A Bug's Life* performers and singing along to the "incredible" *Festival of the Lion King* are "excellent" for toddlers; "don't come here for thrills and spills" with pre-teen daredevils, but do take the "outstanding" safari (in the "cooler" "early morning" to avoid the "disappointment" of sleeping critters); an overnight stay at the adjacent Lodge, with "night visions" of the fauna, makes the experience even more "authentic."

DISNEY'S TYPHOON LAGOON PARK ☺😊

| 28 | 26 | 26 | 25 | E |

Walt Disney World (bet. Buena Vista & Epcot Center Drs.); 407-824-4321; www.disneyworld.com

■ The popularity of this "laid-back" sloshfest "for all sizes, ages and physical abilities" proves kids really like to get wet; "toddlers have the great" Ketchakiddie Creek to themselves, and parents can "veg out in the cool water" of the Lazy River while their courageous older children enjoy "snorkeling with sharks", "boogie-boarding and fast water slides"; plan to spend the day, but "bring sunscreen, a picnic lunch" (to supplement limited dining options) and your own towels to avoid the dollar-per rental charge "on top of the hefty entrance fee."

EPCOT

| 20 | 28 | 27 | 27 | VE |

Walt Disney World, 1320 Ave. of the Stars (Epcot Center Dr.); 407-824-4321; www.disneyworld.com

☑ "Take two days" to explore Disney's most "education-minded" and "sophisticated" park, where families find "hands-on" exhibits, enjoy "high-octane thrill rides" and "see other countries without leaving ours" at the 11 World Showcase pavilions where there are "genuine" ethnic foods ("finally, an adult can get a decent meal") and "mini-shows in every corner"; though some find it all a little "dated", it's "mom and dad's favorite" (it gets much higher ratings for Adult Appeal than for Child Appeal) and older kids can "have so much fun they don't know they're learning stuff"; there are also "dancing fountains" and character encounters for the littlest ones; P.S. "the new Space ride makes you think you're on your way to Mars."

Gatorland

| 24 | 21 | 17 | 20 | M |

14501 S. Orange Blossom Trail (Cypress Crossing Dr.); 407-855-5496; 800-393-5297; www.gatorland.com

☑ Get "amazing views" of "gators, gators and more gators" performing, eating and just resting at this "kitschy but fun", "grimy but authentic", "Old-Florida park", a "low-tech alternative" that bills itself as the 'Alligator Capital of the World'; spend an afternoon enjoying "beautiful walks" along planked trails and taking in oddly interesting offerings, including a show "toddlers and young children enjoy" that gets the dangerous creatures "jumping"; while most find it "well worth the money", a humorous handful "can't help thinking what a great pocketbook one of these would make."

ISLANDS OF ADVENTURE

| 26 | 27 | 26 | 24 | VE |

Universal Studios, 1000 Universal Studios Plaza (Vineland Rd.); 407-363-8000; 800-711-0080; themeparks.universalstudios.com

☑ "Not for the faint-hearted", Universal's newer theme park is a piece of "vibrantly colored" "eye candy" "for daredevils" with enough "stupendous", "technologically advanced" thrills to deem it "roller-coaster heaven"; "the Spiderman ride rocks" and "the Hulk cannot be beat" for preteens and up, while the diaper set is satisfied with the "whimsical" Seuss Landing for Cat-in-the-Hat–themed fun; a handful of harsh critics croak it "doesn't compare" to Disney's parks and there "aren't enough attractions to fill a whole day", but Hard Rock and Portofino Bay hotel guests appreciate the express passes that let them "cut every line."

Kennedy Space Center Visitor Complex ☺

| 22 | 27 | 24 | 22 | E |

Kennedy Space Ctr., State Rd. 405 (Kennedy Pkwy.), Cocoa Beach; 321-449-4444; www.kennedyspacecenter.com

■ "Blast off" at this "out-of-this-world" day-long attraction an hour east of Orlando, where older kids and parents take a "mesmerizing" bus tour of NASA's space program, visiting the Apollo center, meandering through a "display of ships and rockets", experiencing a "re-creation of lift-off", ogling a "real mission-control room" and maybe even "meeting an astronaut" or "seeing a space shuttle on the launch pad"; while "bored" brats whine it "feels like a school field trip", most older kids and their parents depart declaring they're "proud to be an American."

MAGIC KINGDOM

29 | 26 | 27 | 27 | VE

Walt Disney World, N. World Dr. (Magic Kingdom Dr.); 407-824-4321; www.disneyworld.com

■ It's all pure "magic" at this undisputed crown jewel in Disney's 35,000-acre empire (encompassing four theme parks, two water wonderlands and more than 20 hotels), thanks to fireworks, parades, shows, rides and meals with Mickey that "bring out the kid in everyone"; "no matter how many times you go", there's always more to do, eat and explore at this *Survey's* No. 1 rated attraction overall, so you'll "need two days to really see" everything; shrewd use of the free FastPass system helps transport you more quickly around the "happiest place on earth"; N.B. guests at all on-site lodgings can enter an hour early on Sunday and Thursday.

Orlando Museum of Art

▽ 13 | 25 | 26 | 22 | M

2416 N. Mills Ave. (E. Princeton St.); 407-896-4231; www.omart.org

■ Culture buffs make a beeline downtown to this "quiet", "small and creative" gallery that's "getting better all the time" with a "wonderful variety of shows" and creations from all over the world that change regularly; true, your tots would probably rather spend another day with the Disney folks than come here, but all little museum mavens get activity bags with things "to do as they view the art" and "learn about shapes, colors, people, etc."; just "check the event calendar" in advance "to make it worth your time and money" – not everything in Orlando has big round ears attached.

Orlando Science Center ☺

25 | 23 | 25 | 24 | M

777 E. Princeton St. (Camden Rd.); 407-514-2000; www.osc.org

■ Downtown Orlando's "first-class" exploratorium is packed with "great hands-on exhibits" for "children of all ages", demonstrating how the human body, energy, Florida's ecosystem, film special effects and laser beams work, among other things; the smallest scientists will process faux orange juice at KidsTown, while pre-teen would-be astronomers find the planetarium laser show the star attraction; yup, "it's a place to take kids", and although it can be "humdrum for adults" they like visiting an Orlando attraction with so much educational appeal.

Ripley's Believe It or Not! Odditorium

20 | 20 | 19 | 18 | M

8201 International Dr. (W. Sand Lake Rd.); 407-363-4418; www.ripleysorlando.com

☑ Enter a lopsided building "made to look as if it's falling" into a Florida sinkhole and you'll find a world of "quirky" oddities such as a shrunken head, a life-size 1907 Rolls Royce replica made of more than one million matchsticks and an actual piece of the Berlin Wall, plus brain teasers, optical illusions, a tilted room and a statue of the world's tallest man; while it's "too weird" for some, it's "a fun way to spend a couple of hours" and adults will surely appreciate a mosaic of Van Gogh made of 3,000 postcards.

Scenic Boat Tour

17 | 26 | 18 | 23 | I

Winter Park, 312 E. Morse Blvd. (N. Interlachen Ave.); 407-644-4056; www.scenicboattours.com

■ Board an 18-passenger pontoon to "ogle homes where the other half live" in "lovely" seven-lake Winter Park and listen to a "running commentary" about "rich people's real estate"; you'll pass Rollins College, "the alma mater of Mr. Rogers", glide through canals, and spot cranes, alligators, cypress trees and semi-tropical flowers; this one's more heavily suited to adults, but teens and 'tweens will enjoy seeing comedian Carrot Top's home (littler ones may find the sail "long and slow").

SEAWORLD ORLANDO   28 | 26 | 24 | 23 | VE |

7007 Sea World Dr. (Central Florida Pkwy.); 407-351-3600; 800-423-8368; www.seaworld.com

■ Decidedly "laid-back" compared to its theme-park neighbors – even with its "upscale" new waterfront retail, restaurant and entertainment area – everyone "from age one to 100" can make a full day of visiting this salute to sea life; "you can never get enough of Shamu" (the new nighttime show "rocks") and kids get to "feed the dolphins and fish", "pet the stingrays", "have dinner next to the shark tank" at a fine-dining restaurant and view so many "entertaining" attractions they "may want to take up marine biology" afterward; two roller coasters "keep teens from dozing", while a nifty playground embraces the preschool set.

UNIVERSAL STUDIOS   25 | 26 | 25 | 23 | VE |

1000 Universal Studios Plaza (Vineland Rd.); 407-363-8000; 800-711-0080; www.universalorlando.com

■ "Film buffs are in paradise" at this Hollywood-themed park where "rides are so life-like they magically transport you into the movies" where you spend time with *Shrek*, zip *Back to the Future* and phone home to *E.T.*; the park is mostly geared for kids "seven and older" and their parents – there are "a few high-test rides for adrenaline junkies" – but toddlers are tickled by the Nickelodeon area, the Barney show and the Curious George and Fievel playgrounds.

Wet 'n Wild   28 | 23 | 21 | 20 | E |

6200 International Dr. (Universal Blvd.); 407-351-1800; 800-992-9453; www.wetnwildorlando.com

■ Splash aboard a wide assortment of "sparkling" water rides and slides for some "great wet fun" at this festive I-Drive water park that offers plenty of "relief from the Florida sun"; "adults discover their inner child" (who may "feel the black-and-blue marks for a couple of days"), older children and teens who meet various height restrictions will find even more "enjoyment" and tots can frolic in shallow play areas like the mushroom-shaped fountain and a castle-themed section; if you "spend a day", "a great time can be had by all."

HOTELS

Ratings: Family Appeal, Rooms, Service, Public Facilities, Cost

	FA	R	S	P	$

Disney's Animal Kingdom Lodge   29 | 25 | 26 | 28 | $324 |

2901 Osceola Pkwy., Lake Buena Vista; 407-938-3000; www.disneyworld.com; 1274 rooms, 19 suites

■ You'll be "up to your earlobes in African wildlife" when you stay at this "breathtaking" resort on the grounds of the Animal Kingdom park, especially if you're lucky enough to "wake up in the morning and see giraffes, zebras and other mammals grazing before your eyes" (kids become "so captivated" it's tough getting them out of the room); Disney character visits, lots of activities and a "fabulous pool and playground" have tots smiling, while the buffet restaurant is a dream for parents with finicky eaters in tow; it's all an "A+" at this "coolest" of the themed hotels.

Disney's Beach Club Resort

| 28 | 24 | 26 | 28 | $449 |

1800 Epcot Resorts Blvd., Lake Buena Vista; 407-934-8000;
www.disneyworld.com; 520 rooms, 56 suites

■ It's all about Stormalong Bay, the "amazing" three-acre mini-water-park "work of art" (with slides and a "unique sand-bottomed pool" that's a "child's dream") at this seaside-themed resort "a short walk from Epcot"; you can "hop on the Monorail to visit Mickey and friends" at the Magic Kingdom, then be "swept back to the beaches of the Caribbean" when you stay here, getting "the best of both worlds"; "the villas are a good value", and the staff "makes last-minute reservations for all events and restaurants"; N.B. proximity to the Boardwalk means lots of evening options.

Disney's Boardwalk Inn

| 27 | 25 | 26 | 27 | $449 |

2101 N. Epcot Resorts Blvd., Lake Buena Vista; 407-939-5100;
www.disneyworld.com; 372 rooms, 383 resort homes

■ "Step back in time to the Atlantic City (or Coney Island) of long ago" when you stay at this "unique Disney blast from the past" located on the Boardwalk among shops, eateries and nightlife, and within walking distance of Epcot and MGM (though "not as convenient to the Magic Kingdom"); the "clown pool with huge waterslide keeps younger kids busy for hours" and the "villas are an excellent setup for families" since "having a kitchen takes so much stress out of your trip"; just make sure your room is near the elevator or "you could end up having to walk quite some distance to get in and out"; N.B. it may have more appeal for preteens.

Disney's Grand Floridian Resort & Spa

| 26 | 27 | 27 | 28 | $514 |

4401 Floridian Way, Lake Buena Vista; 407-824-2421; www.disneyworld.com;
867 rooms, 25 suites

■ "If you can afford the high price" of this "elegant" Victorian-style resort, you'll get "fun" for the kids (character breakfasts, mouse-shaped water-car rentals for "zipping around the Seven Seas lagoon", singing groups in the lobby) and hassle-free amenities (Monorail right to the Magic Kingdom next door) without sacrificing "adult ambiance" and pampering (there's a "superb" spa on-site); the "accommodating chefs will prepare special meals", there's a kiddie pool where "even the smallest toddler can play" and the decor is more subdued than other resort properties – "what more could you ask for?"

Disney's Polynesian Resort

| 27 | 23 | 25 | 25 | $404 |

1600 Seven Seas Dr., Lake Buena Vista; 407-824-2000; www.disneyworld.com;
847 rooms, 6 suites

◿ It's "like going to the islands with Mickey and the gang" at this Polynesian-themed property with luau dinners, "lush grounds" and a waterfall pool with a volcano; try to get a room that features a "view of Cinderella's castle" and the fireworks, and expect that your mouseketeers "won't want to leave the Neverland kids' club" when it's time to hop on the Monorail to the parks; just be prepared to "suffer from Disney overload" amid all this "outdated", "very '70s-ish" decor ("looks like the set for the Brady Bunch trip to Hawaii") that's "still as hokey as when you were a kid."

Disney's Wilderness Lodge

| 29 | 24 | 26 | 28 | $324 |

901 Timberline Dr., Lake Buena Vista; 407-824-3200; www.disneyworld.com;
700 rooms, 27 suites

■ If you want to "take a break from all the Disney" characters, head to this "lovely 'Yosemite' hotel" that feels like a part of "the great Northwest" (the "woodsy" grounds feature Douglas firs and a geyser) with an "eye-popping lobby", expansive fireplaces and timber ceilings; the "rooms are a little small" but you can "ask for bunk beds" and kids will love "the towel-animals left on the pillows each night"; the "only drawback" is that it's farther from the parks, but children enjoy taking a boat to the Magic Kingdom.

Disney's Yacht Club Resort
27 | 25 | 26 | 28 | $449

1700 Epcot Resorts Blvd., Lake Buena Vista; 407-934-7000; www.disneyworld.com; 610 rooms, 11 suites

■ Folks who want a "little more elegance than the Beach Club resort" drop anchor here for the "high-class" yacht theme, "proximity to Epcot" ("you can see its nightly *Illuminations* light show from some rooms") and access to "one of the best swimming areas in Disney" – the Stormalong Bay mini water park with its "unusual" sand-bottom pool; the staff is "top-notch" and it's a "fun Monorail ride everywhere" you want to go, so even if it's "got the feel of an old Ivy League club" it will still "delight the kids."

Hard Rock Hotel Orlando
27 | 26 | 24 | 28 | $269

5800 Universal Blvd.; 407-503-2000; 800-232-7827; www.universalorlando.com/hardrock; 621 rooms, 29 suites

■ It's an "easy boat ride" to Universal Studios Orlando from this rockin' resort, where guests receive "express passes to the two parks so they can bypass lines"; there are "swimming diapers available" at the 12,000-sq.-ft. pool, which has a sand beach, an "excellent slide" and an underwater stereo, and its cabanas are "perfect" for allowing little ones to nap while adults enjoy the sun; with so much "great memorabilia" and music, it's "better for preteens" ("good luck explaining the Rolling Stones to your four-year-old"), but the Camp Lil' Rock activity center will have tots smiling too.

Hyatt Regency Grand Cypress
25 | 24 | 25 | 27 | $410

1 Grand Cypress Blvd.; 407-239-1234; 800-233-1234; www.hyatt.com; 676 rooms, 74 suites

■ The "best off-Disney option" may very well be this "large-scale resort" with "exotic birds in the lobby" and "lush grounds" that have "everything from swimming pools with grottos, caves and waterfalls to a white-sand beachfront"; there's a playground for kids, a Camp Hyatt program of supervised children's activities, a "can't-be-beat" swimming pool (along with "lots of shady areas for strollers") and breathtaking "views from the top floor of the nightly Magic Kingdom fireworks"; adults can enjoy "fabulous" on-site golf and "excellent restaurants", and "full-size cribs with their own sheets and receiving blankets" are provided for infants.

Portofino Bay Hotel at Universal Orlando Resort
24 | 27 | 24 | 27 | $309

5601 Universal Blvd.; 407-503-1000; 800-232-7827; www.universalorlando.com/portofino; 705 rooms, 45 suites

◪ With "easy access" to Universal Studios Orlando (guests gain early admission and can bypass lines with an express pass), "palatial rooms for even the most luggage-laden families" and an on-site health club and spa, some find this "beautiful" "re-creation of a European resort town" a good choice; others complain "it's not exactly Italy" with those "painted façades", the service is "lacking" and it's probably better for mom and dad than the children, even though kids "really enjoy" the waterslide and pool.

Top Family-Friendly Hotel Chains in the Area:

Embassy Suites	Marriott
Hampton Inn	Residence Inn
Holiday Inn	Ritz-Carlton
Homewood Suites	Westin

See Hotel Chain reviews, starting on page 256.

RESTAURANTS

Ratings: Family Appeal, Food, Decor, Service, Cost

FA	F	D	S	$

Artist Point

–	–	–	–	E

Disney's Wilderness Lodge, 901 Timberline Dr. (Wilderness Way), Lake Buena Vista; 407-824-1081; www.disneyworld.com

Sample "great Pacific Northwest food without the rain" at this "rustic but refined" Wilderness Lodge "jewel" "nestled in the pines"; owing to "myriad little diners running around", this Mouse house can get "as noisy as a theme-park ride", but the parents of those happy campers say the "gorgeous faux-wilderness setting" makes you "feel like you're in Yellowstone", as "knowledgeable" servers bring you "still-sizzling", "best-smelling" cedar-plank salmon, "buffalo steak not to be missed" and "outstanding" regional wines.

Boma

25	26	28	27	E

Disney's Animal Kingdom Lodge, 2901 Osceola Pkwy. (Sherbert Rd.), Lake Buena Vista; 407-938-4722; www.disneyworld.com

■ "Knowledgeable, friendly" staffers guide explorers through this African-themed "buffet on steroids" in Disney's Animal Kingdom Lodge; designed to look like an open-air marketplace, it "makes exotic food friendly" – adding a "whole slew of flavors" (tamarind, curry) to an "incredible variety" of dishes – enabling diners to "experiment without straying too far outside their comfort zones"; of course, kids can still get faves like mac 'n'cheese too.

California Grill

19	27	26	25	E

Disney's Contemporary Resort, 4600 N. World Dr., Lake Buena Vista; 407-824-1576; www.disneyworld.com

This hotel Californian is "no Mickey Mouse" joint, say smitten surveyors; local hotshot toque John State serves up "delectable" cuisine (including "great" pork tenderloin) that "sensuously melts in your mouth", "enthusiastic" staffers "really know the menu" and there are 31 on-site sommeliers to oversee 100 by-the-glass offerings; for the little mouseketeers, views of the Magic Kingdom's nightly fireworks are "spectacular", which often gives rise to a "boisterous" atmosphere that makes some respondents feel like they're "sitting in a nursery school."

Chef Mickey's

29	21	23	25	M

Disney's Contemporary Resort, 4600 N. World Dr., Lake Buena Vista; 407-824-1520; www.disneyworld.com

■ "Mickey sure knows how to serve up the fun" when he and the cartoon corps at Disney's Contemporary Resort dress in chef's whites and lead the crowd in "napkin-waving", then greet youngsters and sign autographs; while you have to wonder about "Goofy being a chef", the "standard buffet fare" is "actually very good"; "tot-size stations" are tops, "and the "make-your-own-dessert bar" is "a kid's dream."

Cinderella's Royal Table

28	20	27	25	M

Magic Kingdom, 1365 N. Monorail Way, Lake Buena Vista; 407-824-2222; www.disneyworld.com

☑ "If you have a daughter, you have no choice" – it's "the ultimate for every little girl" to breakfast "like royalty" with the glass-slipper gal and her fairy godmother at Cinderella's Castle; the "astounding decor", "walking characters and views of the Magic Kingdom make this place worth a visit" even though most diners find the food "pricey" and just "so-so"; N.B. reservations are a must.

 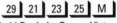

Crystal Palace, The

| 28 | 22 | 23 | 24 | M |

Magic Kingdom, Lake Buena Vista; 407-824-6517; www.disneyworld.com

■ There's 'hunny' and much more at this "exciting" buffet with Winnie the Pooh, Tigger and their friends from the Hundred-Acre Wood, who "dance in the middle of the restaurant" and "pose happily for pictures", making a meal here an "absolute must" for the pre-K set; furthermore, this airy Victorian eatery "smack-dab in the Magic Kingdom" boasts "something for everyone" among its "extensive", "surprisingly good" offerings.

Disney's Spirit of Aloha Dinner Show 🖫

| 27 | 18 | 25 | 22 | VE |

Disney's Polynesian Resort, 1600 Seven Seas Dr., Lake Buena Vista; 407-939-3463; www.disneyworld.com

☑ "Do it for the show, not the food", suggest surveyors who've seen this Hawaiian-style luau at Disney's Polynesian Resort where "very entertaining dancers" put on a "fun" and "kitschy" production ("great for little girls who want to hula" and "boys who want to see fire" being twirled); preschoolers may find it "a little long", though, and feedback on the family-style dinner ranges from "high-quality" to "not that great."

Emeril's Restaurant Orlando

| 16 | 27 | 24 | 27 | VE |

Universal Studios CityWalk, 6000 Universal Blvd. (Vineland Rd.); 407-224-2424; www.emerils.com

☑ While "a more casual place might be better" for smaller tykes, "there is something for everyone" in the family to enjoy on the menu of Emeril Lagasse's Universal CityWalk cradle of Creole cooking, "worth every penny" and "artfully presented on colorful dishes" by a "staff that pays special attention to the tiny critics"; if some call it "loud", others point out that at least "you don't have to worry about using your indoor voices."

50's Prime Time Cafe

| 28 | 20 | 27 | 25 | M |

MGM Studios, 424 Perimeter Rd., Lake Buena Vista; 407-939-3463; www.disneyworld.com

■ You're practically "at the Cleavers' house" at this "whimsical" '50s-sitcom-themed Disney-MGM Studios grubspot; guests gather in "kitschy" Formica kitchens and waitresses "ham up the homage" to decades past by "yelling at you to keep your elbows off the table" and "eat your veggies"; in fact, the servers "really make this place" with their "energy" and "silliness", though the "retro" comfort food is "straightforward and pretty good."

Flame Tree Barbecue

| 22 | 22 | 18 | 20 | I |

Disney's Animal Kingdom (World Dr.), Lake Buena Vista; 407-938-2236; www.disneyworld.com

☑ Within the imitation African savanna of Disney's Animal Kingdom, this "above-average" counter-service restaurant is a "great place to rest and enjoy" large portions of "delicious" ribs and chicken, or to get a "fast" meal before scoping out the Tree of Life and the surrounding trails; its tiered outdoor seating area overlooks the Discovery River and the park beyond, so you can plan your safari while scarfing your sandwich.

Flying Fish Café

| 19 | 25 | 25 | 24 | E |

Disney's BoardWalk Inn, 2101 N. Epcot Resorts Blvd. (Buena Vista Dr.), Lake Buena Vista; 407-939-3463; www.disneyworld.com

■ "For adults who need good grown-up food but want the kids to join them", this "classy and eclectic", "mainly seafood" Contemporary American set amid the "pleasant distraction" of Disney's BoardWalk Inn fills the bill; while tots and teens are kept entertained "watching the chefs in the open kitchen", their grown-up companions are

 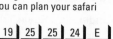

equally enthralled by "some of the best food and service in town" amid "nifty" surroundings.

Jimmy Buffett's Margaritaville Cafe

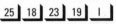

23 | 21 | 25 | 20 | M

Universal Studios (Turkey Lane Rd.); 407-224-2155; www.margaritaville.com

☑ "Parrotheads unite" to enjoy a "cheeseburger in paradise" – or "great sandwiches" – at Universal CityWalk's "energetic" tribute to the Caribbean; the joint "has fun written all over it" (an "erupting volcano of margaritas", a balloon artist on stilts) and the "music is terrific", leading to a lively scene that's well "suited to older children"; party poopers protest the "food is abysmal" and – unkindest cut – the "margs are below average."

Jungle Jim's

25 | 18 | 23 | 19 | I

Crossroads Plaza, 12501 State Rd. 535, Lake Buena Vista; 407-827-1257; www.jungle-jims.com

■ Trek out of the theme-park jungle and into this safari-themed watering hole, full of foliage and faux fauna along with live tropical birds; toddlers "love all the animals that decorate the restaurant", not to mention the live baby tigers who show up on Sundays, and parents can savor nearly two dozen creative and "reasonably priced" beef, chicken or veggie burgers along with colorful tropical cocktails.

Kona Cafe

21 | 24 | 20 | 24 | M

Disney's Polynesian Resort, 1600 Seven Seas Dr. (World Dr.), Lake Buena Vista; 407-824-1158; www.disneyworld.com

☑ Say aloha to the South Seas at an "open, contemporary", Asian-inflected eatery within Disney's Polynesian Resort; fans flock here for a menu of trusted staples (chicken, prime rib) enhanced by Pacific specialties (macadamia nuts, Kona coffee), and "chocolate art works" for dessert; it's best for "on-the-go food" with older kids, since young 'uns face a kiddie menu that's "not very extensive."

Liberty Tree Tavern ⊠

26 | 21 | 23 | 24 | M

Magic Kingdom, Lake Buena Vista; 407-939-3463; www.disneyworld.com

☑ "Don't wait until November" to have "a traditional Thanksgiving meal" at the Magic Kingdom's Colonial inn; no matter what time of year it is, you can patriotically partake of "plentiful but ordinary" "mainstream American" fare served family-style amid a "historical atmosphere"; over supper, Minnie, Pluto and their pals, dressed in tricorn hats and demure dresses, will come join you in the 18th century.

1900 Park Fare

27 | 22 | 24 | 25 | M

Disney's Grand Floridian Resort & Spa, 4401 Grand Floridian Way, Lake Buena Vista; 407-939-3463; www.disneyworld.com

■ It's a jolly holiday with Mary Poppins at this carousel-themed smorgasbord in Disney's "divine", Victorian-style Grand Floridian Resort & Spa; at "one of the best character brunches around", poppets can pose for photos with the practically perfect English nanny (plus Alice in Wonderland, Pooh and others); as a bonus, the food is "bountiful and fresh" and the atmosphere "relatively relaxing."

Wolfgang Puck Cafe

18 | 21 | 18 | 19 | E

Downtown Disney West Side, 1482 E. Buena Vista Dr. (Hotel Plaza Blvd.), Lake Buena Vista; 407-938-9653; www.wolfgangpuck.com

☑ It's "not quite Spago, but what is?" observe patrons of this Downtown Disney casual Californian with the same celebrity chef; still, it offers "the best pizza this side of the Atlantic", "super-fresh sushi" and, for the small-fry, "eclectic yet safe" entrées; the decor is "cool" and "colorful", but be prepared for "slow" service – and "bring earplugs."

RESTAURANT CHAINS

See reviews, starting on page 262.

Ratings: Family Appeal, Food, Decor, Service, Cost

	FA	F	D	S	$

Applebee's — 21 | 16 | 17 | 17 | M
12103 Collegiate Way (Alafaya Trail); 407-282-2055
7055 County Rd. 46-A (Rinehart Rd.), Lake Mary; 407-444-9930 ☒
298 Southhall Ln. (W. Maitland Blvd.), Maitland; 407-838-3585

Benihana ☒ — 23 | 20 | 18 | 22 | E
Walt Disney Resort Hilton, 1751 Hotel Plaza Blvd. (Buena Vista Dr.);
407-827-4865

Buca di Beppo ☒ — 24 | 19 | 22 | 21 | M
Florida Mall, 8001 S. Orange Blossom Trail (Bee Line Expwy.);
407-859-7844

California Pizza Kitchen ☒ — 21 | 21 | 16 | 19 | M
4200 Conroy Rd. (Millenia Blvd.); 407-248-7887
695 N. Alafaya Trail (bet. Hwy. 408 & Waterford Lakes Pkwy.); 407-384-5689
8001 S. Orange Blossom Trail (Sand Lake Rd.); 407-854-5741

Chevys Fresh Mex ☒ — 23 | 19 | 18 | 18 | M
12547 State Rd. 535 (Palm Pkwy.), Lake Buena Vista; 407-827-1052

Chili's Grill & Bar ☒ — 21 | 19 | 18 | 19 | M
12181 E. Colonial Dr. (bet. Alafaya Trail & Challenger Pkwy.); 407-384-6622
8002 Golden Sky Ln. (Sand Lake Rd.); 407-857-9909
7021 International Dr. (Carrier Dr.); 407-352-7618
6949 S. Semoran Blvd. (Hazeltine National Dr.); 407-859-3234

Chuck E. Cheese's ☒ — 26 | 10 | 17 | 13 | I
7419 International Dr. (Rte. 482); 407-351-3368
7456 W. Colonial Dr. (Dorscher Rd.); 407-521-5997
541 W. Hwy 436 (Spring Oaks Blvd.), Altamonte Springs; 407-788-0122

Don Pablo's ☒ — 20 | 19 | 18 | 18 | I
8717 International Dr. (Austrian Ct.); 407-354-1345
4645 S. Semoran Blvd. (Bee Line Expy.); 407-208-0801
900 State Rd. 436 (Hibiscus Rd.); 407-834-4421
11400 University Blvd. (Rouse Rd.); 407-208-1828

Hard Rock Cafe ☒ — 22 | 16 | 26 | 18 | M
6050 Universal Blvd. (off Kirkman Rd.); 407-351-7625

Joe's Crab Shack ☒ — 23 | 17 | 21 | 19 | M
12124 S. Apopka Vineland Rd. (Vinnings Way Blvd.); 407-465-1895
4601 S. Semoran Blvd. (bet. Gatlin & Pershing Aves.); 407-658-9299
4659 W. First St. (off Hwy. 46), Sanford; 407-323-0934

Johnny Rockets ☒ — 25 | 17 | 20 | 18 | I
9101 International Dr. (Samoan Ct.); 407-903-0762
Mall at Millenia, 4200 Conroy Rd. (off I-4); 407-903-1006
551 N. Alafaya Trail (Hwy. 408); 407-381-9010

LongHorn Steakhouse ☒ — 21 | 21 | 19 | 21 | M
309 N. Alafaya Trail (Hwy. 408); 407-482-2100
12901 S. Orange Blossom Trail (Deerfield Blvd.); 407-854-5400
7365 W. Colonial Dr. (bet. Dorscher & Hiawasse Rds.); 407-296-5950

Medieval Times 🗷   29 | 14 | 25 | 19 | E
4510 W. Vine St. (bet. Four Winds Blvd. & Oren Brown Rd.), Kissimmee

Olive Garden 🗷   20 | 19 | 18 | 19 | M
4101 Conroy Rd. (Millenia Blvd.); 407-345-8331
8984 International Dr. (Samoan Ct.); 407-264-0420
1555 Sand Lake Rd. (S. Orange Blossom Trail); 407-851-0344
300 W. State Rd. 436 (off I-4), Altamonte Springs; 407-862-0378

Outback Steakhouse 🗷   20 | 22 | 18 | 20 | M
8195 Vineland Ave. (bet. Lake St. & Rte. 535); 407-477-0098

Planet Hollywood 🗷   24 | 13 | 24 | 16 | M
Downtown Disney, 1506 E. Buena Vista Dr. (World Dr.); 407-827-7827

Rainforest Cafe 🗷   27 | 16 | 27 | 18 | M
Downtown Disney Mktpl., 1800 E. Buena Vista Dr. (World Dr.),
Lake Buena Vista; 407-827-8500
Disney's Animal Kingdom, 505 N. Rainforest Rd. , Lake Buena Vista;
407-938-9100

Roadhouse Grill 🗷   20 | 18 | 16 | 18 | M
2881 S. Orange Ave. (bet. Michigan St. & Pineloch Ave.); 407-481-2991
4155 W. Vine St. (Hoagland Blvd.), Kissimmee; 407-932-4401
2300 W. State Rd. 434 (bet. Montgomery Rd. & I-4), Longwood; 407-682-5065

Romano's Macaroni Grill 🗷   21 | 21 | 19 | 21 | M
315 N. Alafaya Trail (Hwy. 408); 407-658-0109
12148 S. Apopka-Vineland Rd. (Palm Pkwy.), Lake Buena Vista; 407-239-6676

Ryan's Family Steakhouse 🗷   24 | 17 | 12 | 16 | I
1754 Econlockhatchee Trail (Hwy. 50); 407-381-0595

T.G.I. Friday's 🗷   21 | 17 | 18 | 17 | M
5933 Caravan Ct. (Major Blvd.); 407-903-0338
6424 Carrier Dr. (Canada Ave.); 407-345-8822
8955 International Dr. (bet. Rte. 528 & W. Sand Lake Rd.); 407-903-9556
4151 Millenia Blvd. (Conroy Rd.); 407-352-7540

Tony Roma's 🗷   20 | 21 | 16 | 19 | M
8560 International Dr. (bet. Hwys. 482 & 528); 407-248-0094
7015 S. Semoran Blvd. (off Hwy. 528); 407-857-7244
11674 University Blvd. (Rouse Rd.); 407-207-3010
12167 S. Apopka Vineland Rd. (Rte. 535), Lake Buena Vista;
407-239-8040

Uno Chicago Grill 🗷   20 | 18 | 15 | 16 | M
Crossroads Shopping Ctr., 12553 State Rd. (off Hwy. 4); 407-827-1212
4120 E. Colonial Dr. (off Bennett Rd.); 407-895-7404
8250 International Dr. (off W. Sand Lake Rd.); 407-351-8667
11633 University Blvd. (bet. N. Alafaya Trail & Rouse Rd.); 407-207-1740

Philadelphia/Lancaster

There's a lot to love about the City of Brotherly Love. Start with the location, on the Delaware and Schuylkill Rivers halfway between New York City and Washington, Pennsylvania Dutch country and the New Jersey shore. Philly is a summer city – think soft pretzels with mustard, Italian ices and the 4th of July – but any season works for a visit to this former capital of the U.S. The family-friendly Historic

District, on the eastern side of Center City, includes the new National Constitution Center, Independence Visitors' Center and Liberty Bell Pavilion on Independence Mall. Colonial attractions, including the Betsy Ross House, can be covered in a day on foot. Or by duck – Ride the Ducks, an amphibious bus line, includes a scenic splash in the Delaware. The city's purple "Phlash" bus ($10 per family per day) links the district with the Ben Franklin Parkway, home to the Philadelphia Museum of Art (as in Rocky), Franklin Institute, Academy of Natural Sciences and Please Touch Museum. Another don't-miss for local flavor is the Reading Terminal Market, where you can taste the rich mélange of ethnicities that make up this metropolis. To venture outside the city to Valley Forge, Gettysburg, Longwood Gardens, Sesame Place or Hersheypark, you'll need a car.

ATTRACTIONS

Ratings: Child Appeal, Adult Appeal, Public Facilities, Service, Cost

C	A	P	S	$

Academy of Natural Sciences ☺☺ | 26 | 23 | 22 | 21 | M |

1900 Ben Franklin Pkwy. (N. 20th St.), Philadelphia; 215-299-1000; www.acnatsci.org

■ No "bones" about it: to those who "dig" all things prehistoric, this "intimate" "cornerstone" of the Parkway's Museum Row is one of "the best dinosaur museums anywhere"; "children love the fantastic worlds brought to life" when they "feast their eyes upon scenes" depicting "terrific stuffed animals", and science buffs of "all ages" "treasure" the "informed staff's" "very entertaining scheduled shows and talks", the IMAX and "cool" "hands-on opportunities", especially "digging for fossils", "petting" live animals and flitting around the "don't-miss" butterfly garden.

Betsy Ross House ☺☺ | 17 | 21 | 17 | 18 | $0 |

239 Arch St. (bet. 2nd & 3rd Sts.), Philadelphia; 215-686-1252; www.betsyrosshouse.org

☑ "Don't forget to duck" while taking a "step back" to 1777 inside the "tiny" Old City "colonial" said to have housed America's "best-known" "seamstress", the avowed creator of 'Old Glory'; "little girls can envision themselves living" amid the period artifacts, particularly in summer when the "cute courtyard" fills with "amusing actors in costume"; this "in-and-out" tour of "the history of the flag" won't "break the bank", though "accessibility can be an issue", as only the gift shop is "stroller-friendly."

Brandywine Battlefield ☺ | 14 | 21 | 17 | 15 | $0 |

Creek Rd. (Rte. 1), Chadds Ford; 610-459-3342; www.ushistory.org/brandywine

☑ "Let the kids run wild" while you enjoy a "quiet picnic" with the ghosts of Washington, Lafayette and Howe at this Revolutionary War battlefield "on the way to the Wyeth Museum" that's now a "serene" spot for a "short hike" in "autumn" in Chadds Ford, 30 miles from Center City; "defeat"-ists who call it "a big field with an old tree" and "nothing to teach" might have missed the museum and generals' headquarters that make it "worth" a "quick stop" off Route 1 to contemplate the "sacrifices that were made."

Christ Church ☺ | 12 | 24 | 21 | 21 | $0 |

20 N. American St. (2nd St.), Philadelphia; 215-922-1695; www.christchurchphila.org

☑ The "spiritual home to many Founding Fathers" "remains the quintessential Colonial church", a "terrific" example of Old City's "early American architecture"; children may "delight in sitting in Betsy Ross' seat" and "looking for" the home of the rodential "main character" in Robert Lawson's book, *Ben and Me,* as "every cranny is a possible mouse hole", but plan a brief trip to accommodate short attention spans; "high school students don't find it too appealing" either, except perhaps "during the Fringe Festival" in September when it hosts "wonderful performances"; P.S. its cemetery, "Benjamin Franklin's final resting place", is located a few blocks away at the intersection of 5th and Arch Streets.

Crayola Factory ☺☺   28 | 20 | 23 | 22 | M
30 Centre Sq. (bet. Northhampton & 3rd Sts.), Easton; 610-515-8000; www.crayola.com/factory
✓ "It's not really a factory", but "crafty" young kids and pre-teens "adore" getting "colorful" and "creative" with innumerable crayons at this "hands-on" "indoor theme park" 80 miles north where the Lehigh and Delaware Rivers meet, "even if it does seem like a big commercial for Crayola" ("no shortage of opportunities to try and buy"); while young Picassos "can take home lots of [art] projects", "there's not as much to do with toddlers", and it's "noisy" and "hectic" in summer; N.B. entrance fees also get you admission to the National Canal Museum upstairs.

Eastern State Penitentiary Historic Site ☺   18 | 25 | 17 | 18 | I
2124 Fairmount Ave. (21st St.), Philadelphia; 215-236-3300; www.easternstate.org
■ "Get scared out of your wits" at this "one-of-a-kind site" near the Art Museum, the "spooky" remains of the nation's first penitentiary, built in 1829 and once home to Al Capone and to "Willie Sutton who escaped" by tunneling out; the doors are unlocked for "historically interesting", "ghoulish tours" for "curious" jailbirds seven years old and up (Wednesdays through Sundays, April to November), but go around Halloween "when they turn the place into a haunted house" that "makes you scream"; after a "morbid" spin through the joint, your kids "won't break the law – ever."

Edgar Allan Poe National Historic Site ☺   ▽ 13 | 23 | 18 | 20 | $0
532 N. Seventh St. (Spring Garden St.), Philadelphia; 215-597-8780; www.nps.gov/edal
■ Literary types are raven about the "great tour" that ushers you through the restored house occupied by the master of the macabre from 1838 to 1844; a tell-tale sign of an "inspiring" visit: "spooked" kids "checking out that black bird" statue at the entrance will "begin reading" *'The Fall of the House of Usher'* and other Poe classics as soon as they hit the library inside; it's closed Monday and Tuesday, and the neighborhood itself, about 10 minutes north of Center City, can get a bit creepy at dusk.

Fairmount Park   21 | 23 | 18 | 14 | $0
4231 N. Concourse Dr. (Memorial Hall Dr.), Philadelphia; 215-685-0000; www.phila.gov/fairpark
■ There's "all you need" for "an amazing introduction to Philadelphia" at this "extremely large" and "beautiful" "getaway"; with "lots of ball fields" and "unmanicured grass" meandering westward from the Ben Franklin Parkway, it's "a fantastic place to fish, bike, hike, picnic or do any other outdoor activity", as well as indoor touring of "loads of historic houses"; partake of "everything from horseback riding to rowing", "feed the ducks with the little ones" and enjoy an "amazing variety of vistas" along the "picturesque" Schuylkill; just note that it's "safer before dark."

Franklin Institute Science Museum ☺

| 28 | 26 | 25 | 22 | M |

222 N. 20th St. (bet. Race & Winter Sts.), Philadelphia; 215-448-1200; 800-285-0684; www.fi.edu

■ "Wanna be a scientist? – "borrow a kid for an excuse" to visit this "rainy-day" "treasure" on the Parkway for "world-class" "geeky fun" with "hands-on learning that brings physics, astronomy and medicine to life"; "wear comfy shoes" to "catch up with the young ones" racing from "driving the locomotive" to the "great planetarium", and to "dodge" "buses full of children" on school days; P.S. if your pulse quickens at the thought of "walking through the beating heart", note that the "giant replica" is closed for renovations until fall 2004.

Gardens at Morris Arboretum, The

| 16 | 26 | 24 | 22 | I |

100 Northwestern Ave. (Andorra Rd.), Philadelphia; 215-247-5777; www.morrisarboretum.org

■ "A pleasant way to spend an afternoon" – "especially if you like trees" – is "to have a picnic" at this "immaculately maintained", "breathtakingly gorgeous" Chestnut Hill arboretum; it's "more fun for a romantic stroll" than it is for kids' activities, but summer's "outdoor" "miniature train collection" and other "amazing special exhibits", with "lots of room to run, make up for the lack of neon and loud noises" – the rascals might not even suspect that they're getting an "education."

HERSHEYPARK

| 29 | 25 | 25 | 24 | E |

100 W. Hersheypark Dr. (Park Ave.), Hershey; 800-437-7439; www.hersheypa.com

■ Less than 15 miles from the state capital of Harrisburg and 95 miles from Philadelphia, the "smell of chocolate permeating the air" and the "Kiss[-shaped] streetlights" signal the "special treat" awaiting at this "beautiful and unbelievably clean park" voted Philly's No. 1 attraction in this *Survey*; the resort boasts a mix of activities "to please the whole family" for days – toddlers enjoy the "beautiful merry-go-round", older children "love the water rides and roller coasters" (not to mention the "free candy at the end" of the simulated factory tour), grown-ups "ahhh"-preciate "getting pampered" at the nearby spa and all value the "great food", "wonderful service" and "terrific" accommodations at its affiliated hotels; note that the amusements are open only during summer, Christmas and Halloween seasons.

Independence National Historical Park ☺☺

| 21 | 26 | 23 | 22 | $0 |

143 S. Third St. (Chestnut St.), Philadelphia; 215-597-8974; www.nps.gov/inde

■ "No visit to Philadelphia is complete without a stop" "where it all began" on the streets of Old City, where "history books come alive" ("eat your heart out, Boston") and the sights and sounds are "amazing", "important" and "free"; America's "Founding Fathers" didn't have to put up with "post 9/11 construction barriers" and "horrendous" "summer lines" for timed tickets, but even though 21st-century adults and children do, they can "relish" a "beautifully done visitors' center", "informative guides" and "costumed characters" at Independence Hall, "the birthplace of the Constitution and home of the Liberty Bell."

Independence Seaport Museum ☺

| 19 | 22 | 21 | 20 | I |

211 S. Columbus Blvd. (Walnut St.), Philadelphia; 215-925-5439; www.phillyseaport.org

■ "What's more fun than running around old boats?" – there's a "sea" of "interesting" stuff to see at this maritime museum "out of the way" on Penn's Landing, where "marine nuts in the family" can "batten down the hatches" for a "sub and battleship self-tour" that covers the years from "masted days to nuclear power"; even if the seafaring life is naut your style, many think it still "merits a quick visit."

Italian Market
`11` `24` `15` `19` `$0`

Ninth St. (bet. Christian & Federal Sts.), Philadelphia; 215-965-7676; www.phillyitalianmarket.com

◪ "Yo" – the nation's largest open-air marketplace, where Rocky Balboa trained, is "not for the weak or meek", but it is the "shopping destination" when you want "multi-ethnic" South Philly "realness"; "foodies" brave the "seedy" "hustle and bustle" along the crowded streets in search of "all the bad things you aren't supposed to eat" ("whole pigs" from "the friendliest man covered in blood you will ever meet"), along with the "cheapest fruits and vegetables" around; note that "kids run out of interest" quickly unless they are "really into olive oil and pasta."

Longwood Gardens ⊕☺
`16` `27` `26` `24` `M`

Rte. 1, south of Philadelphia, Kennett Square; 610-388-1000; www.longwoodgardens.org

■ "Run wild" through the "manicured grounds" and greenhouses of Pierre DuPont's "horticultural tour de force" in the Brandywine Valley, a "respite from the city" 45 minutes south out Rte. 1; "overwhelming fountain displays" and "memorable" flora in "each season" are "visions to behold" and there's "always something going on", but little sprouts especially dig summer's many activities or the "spectacular end-of-year" light show, and they "really enjoy the Children's Garden, which is under reconstruction" until 2006; "when it's finished, this should rate very high" for tiny greenthumbs.

National Constitution Center ☺
`21` `27` `27` `25` `I`

Independence Mall, 525 Arch St. (bet. 5th and 6th Sts.), Philadelphia; 215-409-6600; 866-917-1787; www.constitutioncenter.org

■ We the people think you'll "learn more than in any history class" about "one of our country's most sacred documents" at Independence Mall's "clean, well-lit" new museum that "doesn't shy away from controversy"; if you'd like to try your hand at running the country, get "sworn in as president" yourself as part of an "interactive" experience that's particularly "enthralling" for "older kids and adults"; the multimedia show, a "fascinating reminder of what it means to be a citizen", "brings tears to the eyes."

New Jersey State Aquarium
`27` `22` `22` `19` `M`

1 Riverside Dr. (Federal St.), Camden, NJ; 856-365-3300; 800-616-5297; www.njaquarium.org

◪ Now that "most of the gray New Jersey fish" are out to sea, "there's some great stuff" left in "the outside garden, the seal and penguin exhibits, the tanks themselves and the fantastic feature shows" with divers at this "bit of civility" across the Delaware in Camden; "take the ferry" from Penn's Landing and wade through schools of "screaming kids" to ogle the beautiful "collection of underwater creatures" and even "pet the sharks and stingrays"; it's "not as impressive as Baltimore's" National Aquarium, but it sure is a lot closer.

Philadelphia Museum of Art
`15` `28` `26` `23` `M`

Ben Franklin Pkwy. (26th St.), Philadelphia; 215-763-8100; www.philamuseum.org

■ After your little chicks fly up "the famous steps Rocky ran", "take them inside" Philly's "top-notch" art museum "for some culture" in this "user-friendly" setting "guards won't yell" if tiny, temperamental artists "throw their toys" next to "world-class" works ranging "from ancient Greek sculptures" to a "Dada collection that's the best of the movement"; "take it in small doses" on "free-entrance Sunday mornings", "visiting the armor, the Japanese tea room and temples", and kids might not "want to escape."

Philadelphia Zoo

| 28 | 24 | 20 | 19 | M |

3400 W. Girard Ave. (N. 34th St.), Philadelphia; 215-243-1100; www.philadelphiazoo.org

☑ "Nothing can beat" "cavorting" at this "magical" "escape" "for young ones learning their animals" 15 minutes from Center City's "hustle and bustle" in Fairmount Park; it's "compact" enough to "explore" the "fun Treehouse", petting area, elephant rides and tethered ZooBalloon for "awesome views of the city" "and be done before the afternoon nap"; just "pack a lunch" to avoid "expensive, limited" concessions, and remember that despite a facelift and efforts to reach out to the community, "America's first zoo" is as "long in the tooth" as its eldest equine residents.

Please Touch Museum ☺☺

| 29 | 18 | 23 | 22 | M |

210 N. 21st St. (bet. Race & Spring Sts.), Philadelphia; 215-963-0667; www.pleasetouchmuseum.org

■ The lower "single-digit crowd" "has a blast" getting "sensory overload" indoors and outdoors at this "completely hands-on" "fantasy playland" off the Parkway; "once they grasp the concept" "that they are *supposed* to touch", little "thinkers" are "only limited by their imagination" as they trip from mock grocery store to faux farm to pretend television station; grown-ups might want to "bring a book" while rugrats "run around", but it's always a kick to watch "yuppie parents" fawn over their "budding geniuses."

Sesame Place ☺

| 29 | 16 | 21 | 19 | E |

100 Sesame Rd. (Oxford Valley Rd.), Langhorne; 215-752-7070; www.sesameplace.com

☑ "My three-year-old got over her fear of characters here, 'nuff said" attest parents of shy tots "spending the day playing with" "Cookie Monster, Telly and the whole gang" at *Sesame Street*'s "miniature Disneyland" half an hour up I-95; "children wear adults out" "getting drenched", "grooving on Big Bird" and waiting in "torturous" weekend "lines" at Philly's No. 1 for Child Appeal in this *Survey*; tips: "get a locker to keep dry clothes in", reserve dinner with the fuzzy stars and splurge for a "private meet-and-greet session" to tickle Elmo without having to "jockey for position."

Six Flags Great Adventure

| 28 | 24 | 20 | 17 | VE |

Rte. 537 (off I-195), Jackson, NJ; 732-928-1821; www.sixflags.com

☑ "From a huge, drive-thru wild animal park" where the creatures "come right up to your vehicle" to kiddie rides, amphitheater shows, "cutting-edge", "stand-up roller coasters" "for preteens and adults tall enough" and the water park, "there's definitely something for everyone" at this "big-name" amusement park 25 miles north of Philadelphia on the Jersey Turnpike; keep in mind, however, that "it's expensive, summer traffic is horrid", their "service record is spotty" and "weekend lines are so long that you forget what ride you're waiting for."

University Museum of Archaeology and Anthropology

| 16 | 26 | 22 | 18 | I |

3260 South St. (Spruce St.), Philadelphia; 215-898-4000; www.museum.upenn.edu

■ Mummies and daddies with an "*Indiana Jones* fantasy" bring their little explorers to excavate for the "interesting stuff" that "the University of Pennsylvania has amassed" at its "astounding" archaeological museum in West Philly; the "breathtaking building highlighted by the magnificent Chinese rotunda" is a "treasure chest" "if your interests run to Egyptology" and the study of other "fabulous" antiquities, though "they don't give the feeling that they really want children wandering the halls", particularly during ongoing renovations; N.B. closed Sundays in summer.

Valley Forge ☺

| 19 | 25 | 21 | 20 | I |

Rte. 23 (N. Gulph Rd.), Valley Forge; 610-783-1077; www.nps.gov/vafo

■ "Feel history" at this "national shrine"/"glorious" park 20 minutes west out the Schuykill Expressway, where there are "more deer than people" but the humans include "great tour guides and reenactors"; visit the "small, nice museum", take the "enlightening" driving loop and let your kids exercise their "freedom to wander" amid the "remnants of the Revolutionary War encampment"; "go in January to understand the sacrifices" that Washington's troops made (they "picked the worst time of the year to visit" but "would've been better fed if they had gone to the malls next door").

Wachovia Center ☺☺
(fka First Union Center)

| 21 | 26 | 25 | 21 | E |

3601 S. Broad St. (Pattison Ave.), Philadelphia; 215-336-3600; www.comcast-spectacor.com

☑ "If you love hockey, basketball, rock concerts" and kiddie shows, this "great new stadium" is a winner for the Flyers, the Sixers, David Bowie and *Disney on Ice*; activities for junior sports fans include face painting, balloon animals and bobblehead giveaways; still, acrophobes are "terrified" by "steep rows" "far from the action", and foodies are frightened by the concessions' "expensive" "junk" – "don't come hungry", or "prepare to shell it out for popcorn" at South Philly's "best place to get a $10 cotton candy."

Winterthur & Enchanted Woods ☺☺

| 13 | 28 | 27 | 25 | M |

Rte. 52 (Old Kennett Rd.), Winterthur, DE; 302-888-4600; www.winterthur.org

■ Savor "the fruits of capitalism", if only for an afternoon, at the "palatial" DuPont estate 30 miles south of Philadelphia on I-95 near Wilmington; "the docents are knowledgeable" about "how the rich and famous lived", the "outstanding period rooms'" "lavish" "antiques are the best quality" and the "glorious" grounds "are as wonderful as the family china"; the littlest visitors can "play in the midst of the fairy ring" in the Enchanted Woods, paw the goods in the Touch-It Room and take a family-friendly lunchtime tour; N.B. closed Mondays.

HOTELS

Ratings: Family Appeal, Rooms, Service, Public Facilities, Cost

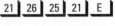

	FA	R	S	P	$

Four Seasons Philadelphia

| 23 | 28 | 29 | 28 | $320 |

1 Logan Sq., Philadelphia; 215-963-1500; 866-516-1100; www.fourseasons.com; 260 rooms, 104 suites

■ "For a kid coming to the big city, what's not to like" about this "upscale" hotel that offers arriving youngsters "a red wagon of toys" to choose from and "special attention" wherever they are?; rooms have child-sized bathrobes and Playstation, and room service "will bring popcorn served in an origami plate" and "milk and cookies at bedtime"; it's no surprise "there are too many families" here, "there's nowhere better to keep tots entertained and mom and dad pampered at the same time", and be a few minutes' walk to the Franklin Institute Science Museum and the Please Touch Museum.

Hershey, The Hotel

| – | – | – | – | $329 |

100 Hotel Rd., Hershey; 717-533-2171; 800-437-7439; www.hersheypa.com; 235 rooms, 27 suites, 1 houses

Wake up to a chocolatey breeze at this historic hotel at Hersheypark, where sweet tooths savor the unlimited candy bars at the front desk and there's an extensive spa and fitness center to work them off; other attractions include carriage rides and a Cocoa Kids Club that offers supervised daytime and nighttime activities from May to Labor Day, for an added daily fee; N.B. the adjacent Hershey Highmeadow Campground allows for a more rustic, less expensive resort getaway.

Marriott Philadelphia ⬜ 18 | 18 | 19 | 19 | $159

1201 Market St., Philadelphia; 215-625-2900; 888-236-2424; www.marriott.com; 1332 rooms, 76 suites

◪ With a "central location", this chainster less than a mile from the Liberty Bell, Independence National Historic Park and the Betsy Ross House is a "solid choice" with an "accommodating staff" that is "not fazed by children", providing cribs and other necessities for infants; "rooms are not large" but it's a "nice value" for the convenience.

Omni Hotel at Independence Park ⬜ 22 | 23 | 22 | 22 | $250

401 Chestnut St., Philadelphia; 215-925-0000; 800-843-6664; www.omnihotels.com; 147 rooms, 3 suites

◼ "If you're looking to take the little ones on a historical tour of Philadelphia", you can't beat this "gem" "across the street from Independence Park", "right in the heart of the historic district" and within walking distance of many South Street restaurants; "rooms and service are excellent", the Omni Kids Program offers special amenities and you can take carriage rides from right outside the hotel.

Ritz-Carlton, Philadelphia ⬜ 20 | 24 | 25 | 25 | $299

10 Ave. of the Arts, Philadelphia; 215-523-8000; 800-241-3333; www.ritzcarlton.com; 297 rooms, 32 suites, 1 penthouse

◪ The "exceptional" staff exudes "the same warm feeling to parties of five as it does to parties of two" say folks who flock to this "expensive" Center City property, set in a "centrally located", historic bank building with a "splendid interior" designed as a replica of Rome's Pantheon; it's admittedly "a little stuffy" for tots and more business-oriented than family-focused, but it's "always friendly to kids", and when adults want to hit the spa or the Rotunda bar, there's babysitting available.

Sheraton Society Hill ⬜ 22 | 20 | 20 | 21 | $179

1 Dock St., Philadelphia; 215-238-6000; 888-625-5144; www.sheraton.com; 352 rooms, 13 suites

◪ "Ask for a river view" at this reasonably priced spot with a "good location for walking" (Independence National Historic Park is four blocks away) and a "knowledgeable concierge" who'll help you chart your course; adjoining rooms and proximity to cruises boost family appeal, and an indoor kids' pool is appreciated on rainy days.

Top Family-Friendly Hotel Chains in the Area:

Embassy Suites	Hyatt
Hampton Inn	Residence Inn
Holiday Inn	Westin
Homewood Suites	

See Hotel Chain reviews, starting on page 256.

RESTAURANTS

Ratings: Family Appeal, Food, Decor, Service, Cost

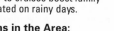

FA	F	D	S	$

Blue in Green ⊅ ▽ 21 | 21 | 12 | 19 | I

719 Sansom St. (bet. 7th & 8th Sts.), Philadelphia; 215-923-6883

◼ Before touring the Historic District, join its "trendy" 21st-century denizens for "down-home comfort food", "awesome breakfasts" and

$8 prix-fixe brunches at this "perennial" "neighborhoody" American "favorite" on Jewelers' Row; "bringing the kids lets you try more cool dishes", including "mixed blueberry pancakes" ("the best" in town, say some) and "great salads for moms" who, after window-shopping nearby, may develop a craving for baguettes of a sparkly nature; N.B. no reservations.

City Tavern

| 19 | 20 | 25 | 21 | E |

138 S. Second St. (Walnut St.), Philadelphia; 215-413-1443; www.citytavern.com

◪ If not quite "revolutionary", chef Walter Staib's re-created Colonial dishes do offer "a taste of history" at this "tourist-stop" inn (circa 1773) in Old City, where "costumed servers" and "small candlelit rooms" make you feel you're "dining with Franklin and Washington"; many think it's a decent "period piece" "if your little girl is into American Girl dolls", but others opine it's "pricey" and perhaps "a little too fancy" for finicky youngsters.

El Azteca ⊠

| 20 | 20 | 14 | 18 | M |

714 Chestnut St. (bet. 7th & 8th Sts.), Philadelphia; 215-733-0895; www.elazteca2go.com

◪ *Amigos pequeños* "find renditions of their favorite Taco Bell"–esque "standards" just blocks from that other Bell (the one named 'Liberty') at this "casual" BYO Mexican on Washington Square in Center City; "the decor is poor, parking is tight, but for the quality and quantity of the meal" (and all the margarita fixin's they provide) served in a "chaotic" environment "that can handle all of the noise a family can drum up", "what better place is there to take the kids?"

Fountain Restaurant

| 15 | 29 | 29 | 29 | VE |

Four Seasons Philadelphia, 1 Logan Sq. (bet. Ben Franklin Pkwy. & 18th St.), Philadelphia; 215-963-1500; www.fourseasons.com

◪ "Philly's best for food, service and decor" is also "very good with children, since it's in a hotel" – and what a hotel it is: spitting distance from Museum Row, the Four Seasons is "elegant" as can be, and so is its New French dining room; dinner is "too formal for most children", but try it for Sunday brunch, when kids eat half-price; "our seven-year-old daughter got crayons, a coloring book, a balloon and SpongeBob tableware" says one parent attesting to "special treatment" for the whole family.

Geno's Steaks ⊅

| – | – | – | – | I |

Italian Mkt., 1219 S. Ninth St. (Passyunk Ave.), Philadelphia; 215-389-0659; www.genossteaks.com

"Assume the position to avoid staining shirt", fasten a bib on junior and "take a bite" of the indi-geno-us "savory" "soul food" at this 24/7 South Philly cheese-steak stand where "you'd better know how to order, or be mocked"; whether it's better than the competition across the street is open to debate – it might come down to "which line is shorter" – but most agree it's a "must-do for tourist" families.

Italian Bistro

| 23 | 18 | 19 | 20 | M |

211 S. Broad St. (bet. Locust & Walnut Sts.), Philadelphia; 215-731-0700; www.italianbistro.com

■ "Just what you and your kids need!" – "a big pasta dinner" to "please even the fussiest eaters" at a "child-friendly" mini-chainster in a "great locale" smack in the middle of the Avenue of the Arts (not far from Independence National Historical Park); "tables are large and suitable for families", "there's much to look at on the walls to keep the young ones' attention", and the "warm" servers treat you right, all at a "nice price"; just "reserve ahead" as, otherwise, "waits can be awhile."

Jim's Steaks ⌐| 20 | 22 | 10 | 15 | I |
400 South St. (4th St.), Philadelphia; 215-928-1911;
www.jimssteaks.com
■ "Two blocks away, you can smell the meat" grilling at this "landmark" cheese-steak palace, the "quintessential" "get 'em in, get 'em out" Philly "joint" on the South Street strip, where "devotees" line up "around the block" to watch "cooks put together their sandwiches" (locals order it "with", i.e. plus onions and Cheez Whiz), with a "nice, cold Coors Light" on the side for grown-ups; "seating is practically nonexistent" amid the "'50s" checked tile and "celebrity pics", so take 'em back to the hotel to "eat in peace."

Jones | – | – | – | – | M |
700 Chestnut St. (7th St.), Philadelphia; 215-223-5663;
www.jones-restaurant.com
High-concept king Stephen Starr's new kid-friendly, comfort-food haven in the Historic District merits wows all around, from the youngest diners to the oldest, for its retro-chic decor that merges Howard Johnson's orangey interior with *The Brady Bunch*'s den and an alpine ski lodge and for its ever-chipper servers; the homespun American menu is particularly popular with brunching families, but unless you want to buy earplugs for your little Bobby or Cindy, avoid weekend nights when the DJ lays down high-decibel grooves.

Marathon Grill | 19 | 19 | 14 | 18 | M |
1339 Chestnut St. (Juniper St.), Philadelphia; 215-561-4460
Commerce Sq., 2001 Market St. (bet. 20th & 21st Sts.), Philadelphia;
215-568-7766 Ⓢ
1818 Market St. (19th St.), Philadelphia; 215-561-1818 Ⓢ
121 S. 16th St. (Sansom St.), Philadelphia; 215-569-3278
www.marathongrill.com
■ "Adults find tasty sandwiches" and among "the best salads in the city", "while kids thrill to delicious desserts and some great burgers and fries" at this New American deli chainlet dotting Center City; the setting might be a bit "industrial", but it's "casual" enough that "families feel comfortable" "grabbing a quick bite" here, particularly when little hands and big are giving "two thumbs up for the smoothies"; N.B. if you're traveling by train to the suburbs, there's also an outlet in Suburban Station.

Pat's King of Steaks ⌐| – | – | – | – | I |
1237 E. Passyunk Ave. (9th St.), Philadelphia; 215-468-1546;
www.patskingofsteaks.com
When you and your kids find yourselves with "cheese running down your arms" at the possible "ground zero of the cheese-steak universe", and the "pigeons are cleaning up after you", you know you're enjoying the "quintessential Philadelphia" feast of "gooey, greasy, yummy junk food with attitude" at this 24-hour South Philly stand; whether the king deserves its self-bestowed crown is a hot debate, however, with insurgents insisting it's "not all it's cracked up to be."

Pietro's Coal Oven Pizzeria | 25 | 21 | 18 | 21 | M |
121 South St. (bet. Front & 2nd Sts.), Philadelphia; 215-733-0675
1714 Walnut St. (bet. 17th & 18th Sts.), Philadelphia; 215-735-8090
www.pietrospizza.com
■ The "yummy", "gourmet" pizzas and "family-style pastas" "can't be beat" crow carb-loaders about these "very spacious" Italians that "accommodate large parties" near Rittenhouse Square in Center City and on South Street not far from the Seaport Museum; "the prices won't kill you" and a "quick, nice" staff that's "great" with munchkins won't want to kill your kids, even if they're busy as can be in a place where you should "expect long waits during peak hours."

Reading Terminal Market ⑤ | 24 | 24 | 15 | 17 | I |

51 N. 12th St. (Arch St.), Philadelphia; 215-922-2317;
www.readingterminalmarket.org

■ "Philly's culinary heartbeat" pumps with "choices, choices, choices" at this indoor "playground" for "eat-on-the-go" families located next to the Convention Center; a "farmer's market to suit today's times", it offers "anything you could want", "from noodles to pretzels" to Bassetts ice cream to "delicious" Pennsylvania Dutch dishes served by "fully dressed Amish folk"; "have fun chasing your kids" amid "food stands of all types", and don't worry – "it's noisy enough that no one will notice your screamer"; just "be aggressive" about grabbing seating, particularly on Saturdays.

Rose Tattoo Cafe ⑤ | – | – | – | – | E |

1847 Callowhill St. (19th St.), Philadelphia; 215-569-8939;
www.rosetattoocafe.com

"Still awesome after all these years", this "all-time favorite" New American is the place to get a bite after attending a kid's program at the nearby Free Library; its "New Orleans-style atmosphere really puts you in the mood" for a "superb" meal "with your sweetie" and your offspring; even the tiniest diners agree that the balcony "overlooking the garden" "is the place to be" – it's so "beautiful" "you'll feel like you're eating in a greenhouse."

RESTAURANT CHAINS

See reviews, starting on page 262.

Ratings: Family Appeal, Food, Decor, Service, Cost

	FA	F	D	S	$
Applebee's	21	16	17	17	M
7650 City Line Ave. (77th St.), Philadelphia; 215-477-3397					
Bertucci's	23	20	17	19	M
1515 Locust St. (bet. 15th & 16th Sts.), Philadelphia; 215-731-1400					
Oxford Valley Mall, 675 Middletown Blvd. (off Lincoln Hwy.), Langhorne; 215-752-9200					
Buca di Beppo	24	19	22	21	M
258 S. 15th St. (bet. Latimer & Spruce Sts.), Philadelphia; 215-545-2818					
California Pizza Kitchen	21	21	16	19	M
King of Prussia Mall, 470 Mall Blvd. (DeKalb Pike), King of Prussia; 610-337-1500					
Chili's Grill & Bar	21	19	18	19	M
3801 Chestnut St. (Rte. 13), Philadelphia; 215-222-7322 ⑤					
1239 Filbert St. (bet. 12th & 13th Sts.), Philadelphia; 215-569-0850 ⑤					
739 W. Dekalb Pike (202 Rt and Golf Rd.), King of Prussia; 610-992-0899					
Dave & Buster's	26	16	21	17	M
Pier 19 N., 325 N. Columbus Blvd. (bet. Callowhill & Spring Garden Sts.), Philadelphia; 215-413-1951					
Don Pablo's	20	19	18	18	I
Oxford Valley Mall, 2763 E. Lincoln Hwy. (N. Oxford Valley Rd.), Langhorne; 215-269-4976					
Hard Rock Cafe	22	16	26	18	M
1113-31 Market St. (12th St.), Philadelphia; 215-238-1000					

Johnny Rockets ☒ | 25 | 17 | 20 | 18 | I
443 South St. (5th St.), Philadelphia; 215-829-9222

Maggiano's Little Italy | 22 | 22 | 21 | 22 | M
1201 Filbert St. (12th St.), Philadelphia; 215-567-2020
King of Prussia Mall, 205 Mall Blvd. (Gulph Rd.), King of Prussia;
610-992-3333

Olive Garden ☒ | 20 | 19 | 18 | 19 | M
1346 Chestnut St. (Broad St.), Philadelphia; 215-546-7950

Red Robin ☒ | 25 | 20 | 19 | 20 | M
621 Park Ave. (off Hershey Park Dr.), Hershey; 717-520-1776

T.G.I. Friday's ☒ | 21 | 17 | 18 | 17 | M
1776 Ben Franklin Pkwy. (N. 18th St.), Philadelphia; 215-665-8443
4000 City Line Ave. (Presidential Blvd.), Philadelphia; 215-878-7070
160 N. Gulph Rd., Suite 2103 (W. DeKalb Pike), King of Prussia; 610-768-9340

Uno Chicago Grill ☒ | 20 | 18 | 15 | 16 | M
198 N. Buckstown Rd. (Sesame Pl.), Langhorne; 215-741-6100
509-511 S. 2nd St. (bet. Lombard & South Sts.), Philadelphia; 215-592-0400

Phoenix/Scottsdale

It's not called the Valley of the Sun for nothing. With well over 300 clear, bright days a year, central Arizona offers hiking, biking and plenty of other outdoor activities, and ultraclean, ever-growing Phoenix is at the heart of it all. Glorious during the early spring, when desert flora bloom, and in the late fall when mild temperatures entice explorers out to native ruins or the city's enormous parks, it's even bearable during the summer due to low humidity and cool nights. Getting around to see and do things, however, will require a car; fortunately, the city's layout is easy to navigate. Spinelike Central Avenue is the north-south dividing line; numbered avenues parallel it to the west, numbered streets to the east. Intersecting them all are east-west streets named after U.S. Presidents, with Washington, Jefferson and other Founding Fathers closest to the city center. If you're staying Downtown, remember the convenient, free DASH (Downtown Area Shuttle) that connects such attractions as America West Arena, Bank One Ballpark, the State Capitol and the Arizona Science Center. Be sure to try some of the city's terrific Mexican food. And if you're going farther afield, bear in mind that it's about four hours to Grand Canyon National Park and five to the Petrified Forest.

ATTRACTIONS

Ratings: Child Appeal, Adult Appeal, Public Facilities, Service, Cost

	C	A	P	S	$

America West Arena ☺ | 17 | 23 | 23 | 18 | I
201 E. Jefferson St. (bet. 1st & 3rd Sts.), Phoenix; 602-379-2000;
www.americawestarena.com
■ Whether Pavarotti is singing or the Phoenix Suns are surging up and down the court, this "gargantuan" downtown venue, "modern in every respect", makes an exciting "playground" for "enthusiastic fans" who appreciate "good views" ("even from the rafters"), a "great selection of concessions" and "easy-in-and-out" auto access; however, even admirers admit that there's "not much for [young] kids

unless the circus is in town", while "big-bucks" tariffs on snacks and parking can make an evening here "a little pricey for an entire family."

Arizona Science Center ☺

600 E. Washington St. (bet 5th & 7th Sts.), Phoenix; 602-716-2000; www.azscience.org

■ More than 300 "hands-on exhibits" keep kids "excitedly running from room to room" at this "excellent science museum", which disciples deem "one of the best around" thanks to "interesting mini-lectures" about topics like astronomy and engineering, a digital planetarium and a giant five-story movie screen for "educational" films on ecology and biology; this pedagogical play place is best for "older kids" (who "can spend the entire day here") and "informative and fun for adults too" – meanwhile, toddlers can explore their own "separate area" or romp around in the "wide-open spaces."

Bank One Ballpark ☺

401 E. Jefferson St. (S. 4th St.), Phoenix; 602-462-6000; www.bankoneballpark.com

■ All agree that this "comfortable", "completely modern" "home of the championship Diamondbacks – aka "the BOB" – is "awesome"; though the "good views from every seat", "play area for restless kids" and "nice variety of shops and concessions" are "memorable", it's the "nifty retractable dome" (an "incredible engineering job"), the "unique swimming pool in right field", and the arena-wide air-conditioning that make this "fabulous stadium" the city's No. 1 attraction in this *Survey* and "the coolest place in the Phoenix summertime."

Casa Grande Ruins National Monument ☺

1100 N. Ruins Dr. (bet. Kenworthy Rd. & Arizona Blvd.), Coolidge; 520-723-3172; www.nps.gov/cagr

■ Named by the Spanish missionaries who found it in the 1600s, this "impressive" four-story "ruin in the desert", built by the Hohokam some 300 years earlier, provides a "fascinating" glimpse of "native lifestyle" and "ancient history"; still, as "nicely presented" as the ranger-guided tours, 20-minute video and archaeological replicas may be, voters note that it's "way out of the way" (an hour southeast of Phoenix) and unless you "go on a cool day", kids may "suffer from the heat"; N.B. special events during November (Native American Month).

Castles N' Coasters ☺☺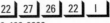

9445 Metro Pkwy. E. (29th Ave.), Phoenix; 602-997-7575; www.castlesncoasters.com

■ You'll "have a good time" with kids and tweens at this "fun" local amusement park near Metro Center Mall that's home to a Ferris wheel, a "nice" 300-game arcade, bumper cars and boats, gas-powered go-carts, two roller coasters and four mini-golf courses; no, it's "not exactly Disneyland" (meaning it's "small"), but for that reason, "you don't get long lines", and "tired parents can sit down" yet keep an eye on youngsters who jump onto the thrill machines "over and over"; N.B. visitors can buy all-day passes or pay per ride.

Desert Botanical Garden ☺

1201 N. Galvin Pkwy. (bet. Scottsdale Rd. & 64th St.), Phoenix; 480-941-1225; www.dbg.org

■ "If this is the first time your family is visiting a desert climate", spend a "pleasant afternoon" at this "extremely mellow" yet "informative" "cactus heaven" "smack in the middle of town"; augmented by free guided tours, the site (part of Papago Park) demonstrates Arizona's "varied, vibrant" and "complex" native flora and offers a "true education on desert animal life"; surveyors suggest the "fabulous butterfly pavilion" (open annually Feb.-May), where hundreds of fluttering insects hover around your head, is most likely to ensure that children won't "get bored quickly."

Heard Museum ☺

| 17 | 27 | 24 | 23 | I |

2301 Central Ave. (W. Encanto Blvd.), Phoenix; 602-252-8848
34505 N. Scottsdale Rd. (E. Carefree Hwy.), Scottsdale; 480-488-9817
www.heard.org

■ "There's always more to see and learn", marvel mavens about this "unusual" "gem" with its "wide-ranging" exhibits about Native American culture, "remarkable collection of Southwestern art", and "wonderful kachina dolls"; "excellent docents enrich the experience", meaning that kids "should remain interested for at least two hours" – especially if they're making crafts or taking in music and dance performances – while grown-ups can easily "leave a wad of cash" in the gift shop "purchasing work by local artists"; N.B. the Scottsdale location is smaller.

McCormick-Stillman Railroad Park ☺

| 29 | 18 | 23 | 22 | I |

7301 E. Indian Bend Rd. (N. Scottsdale Rd.), Scottsdale; 480-312-2312;
www.therailroadpark.com

■ A toot-toot-tootin' good time is had by train "enthusiasts of all ages" at this "clean, well-maintained" and "shady" 30-acre expanse in Scottsdale, what with its rail-car museum, model choo-choos, and "gracious", "knowledgeable volunteers" ("many of them former railroad employees" who love "sharing a good story"); an "excellent" narrow-gauge mini-locomotive is augmented by a vintage carousel, two playgrounds stocked with a "huge variety of slides and climbing apparatus" and "plenty of room to roam, climb and explore"; the result: Phoenix's "best park for kids", voted No. 1 in the city for Child Appeal in this *Survey*; N.B. closed Mondays and Tuesdays.

Old Town Scottsdale ☺

| 12 | 22 | 19 | 19 | $0 |

E. Main St. (bet. Scottsdale Rd. & Brown Ave.), Scottsdale; 480-421-1004
☑ Scottsdale's original downtown, a faux-adobe complex of "art galleries, jewelry stores and tourist junk shops" – with stock "ranging from cowboy chic to the downright tacky" – "beats a big mall" for "souvenir hunting", say surveyors who like to "browse and taste the flavor of the Old West"; however, cynics sniff the retailers "all look the same after about two cowboy steps", so "kid appeal" is limited – in short, "don't plan on spending the day here"; P.S. free daytime trolleys help make up for the "lack of parking."

Out of Africa Wildlife Park ☺☺

| – | – | – | – | M |

9736 N. Fort McDowell Rd. (off N. Beeline Hwy.), Sedona; 480-837-7779;
www.outofafricapark.com

This exotic preserve, northeast of Scottsdale near Fountain Hills, is neither a zoo nor a circus – but it does feature wild animals living in the open and doing what comes naturally; visitors can also watch lions, tigers, panthers, bears and wolves in nine unrehearsed shows that are both entertaining and educational (e.g., Tiger Splash, Big Cat Feeding, Wildlife Safari, Giant Python and Reptile Show); note that picnics are prohibited, but there's an onsite cafe offering food all day long.

Papago Park ☺

| ▽ 21 | 23 | 19 | 14 | $0 |

625 N. Galvin Pkwy. (E. McDowell Rd.), Phoenix; 602-256-3220;
www.phoenix.gov/parks

■ "For midweek fun", "play nine holes" on the public golf course or "take off for an adventure" hiking or biking the "extensive trails" in this 1,200-acre "stretch of desert in the middle of the city"; the terracotta-colored buttes are "great for rock climbing", while the "oasis pond" (for fishing or duck feeding) surrounded by "plenty of covered picnic ramadas [shelters]" is perfect for "relaxing" with the family; don't miss the geological/archaeological curiosity Hole in the Rock; P.S. "bring lots of water; there are no shops and few fountains."

Phoenix Central Library ☺☺

▽ 21 | 25 | 26 | 25 | $0

1221 N. Central Ave. (Culver St.), Phoenix; 602-262-4636; www.phoenixpubliclibrary.org

■ At this "beautifully designed", "huge facility" (aka the Burton Barr), visitors can avail themselves of nearly one million books, plus much more: "architecture buffs" will find the building (designed by local luminary Will Bruder) "fascinating" "inside and out", and moms and dads can share afternoon storytime with preschoolers in the 10,000-sq.-ft. children's section, or take in cultural programs at the Serious Confetti Family Festivals; meanwhile, weary tourists passing near this "excellent downtown location" consider the enormous fifth-floor reading room a "nice refuge from the summer's midday heat."

Phoenix Zoo ☺☺

27 | 24 | 22 | 21 | I

455 N. Galvin Pkwy. (Van Buren St.), Phoenix; 602-273-1341; www.phoenixzoo.org

■ Lots of locals "can't get enough" of Papago Park's "clean, modern", "wonderful zoo"; this "fun, friendly place" offers "plenty of diversions" just for children (an "open wallaby exhibit", a petting zoo/farmyard with "multiple play areas", song-and-game-fests for preschoolers) plus activities for the whole family (camping, bike-riding, guided tours of the animal hospital); when "it gets real hot in the summer", "do a tram tour" – or come during the cooler winter months for the "amazing ZooLights", a "must-see at Christmastime"; N.B. the free-range Monkey Village will open in fall 2004.

Scottsdale Museum of Contemporary Art ☺

▽ 14 | 24 | 24 | 23 | I

7380 E. Second St. (N. Civic Center Blvd.), Scottsdale; 480-994-2787; www.scottsdalearts.org

■ A former movie theater cleverly renovated by award-winning architect Will Bruder, this "wonderful" five-gallery museum features "fantastic exhibits" of modern and contemporary art, architecture and design in a "beautiful setting"; it's a "pleasant place to spend" a few hours, say supporters, thanks to docent-led tours and hands-on art classes for toddlers, and for sculpture lovers James Turrell's "beautiful" Knight Rise "alone is worth the trip" (it's best viewed "at twilight", so plan accordingly).

Slide Rock State Park ☺

– | – | – | – | I

6871 N. Hwy. 89A (Oak Creek), Sedona; 928-282-3034 ; www.pr.state.az.us

When the mercury climbs, Phoenicians head north (about 125 miles) to this former homestead and apple orchard, where they take the plunge into its namesake natural waterslide, a slippery, 30-ft.-long sandstone chute hollowed out by the icy waters of Oak Creek; whether you fish from the steep cliffs, picnic in the wide-open spaces or simply splash around in the always-cold creek, this pleasant park is literally and figuratively an ideal place to chill.

South Mountain Park ☺

▽ 20 | 25 | 15 | 13 | $0

10919 S. Central Ave. (Mineral Rd.), Phoenix; 602-495-0222; www.ci.phoenix.az.us/parks

■ As the largest city park in the country (more than 16,000 acres), this vast yet convenient expanse offers 58 miles of "great" trails ideal for hikers, cyclists and equestrians; "the many ridges of South Mountain" afford "breathtaking views of Phoenix" and its "beautiful sunsets", as well as sightings of such indigenous critters as geckos, jackrabbits, coyotes and diamondbacks; to nab a picnic spot under the shady "ramadas [shelters] for family gatherings", you'll need to get there early, because the place's "popularity makes parking a challenge."

HOTELS

Ratings: Family Appeal, Rooms, Service, Public Facilities, Cost

	FA	R	S	P	$

Fairmont Scottsdale Princess
| 26 | 26 | 25 | 27 | $499 |

7575 E. Princess Dr., Scottsdale; 480-585-4848; 800-344-4758; www.fairmont.com; 458 rooms, 2 suites, 72 villas, 119 casitas

■ The "waterslide keeps the kids entertained for hours" while parents "sip cocktails by the pool" at this "ultimate" pink palace in the desert, where "mist machines are perfect" relief from the blistering summer heat; "great facilities for all ages" include "beautiful grounds for romping" and "lots of games for families: basketball, ping-pong, lawn bowling, etc."; it may be "sprawling" and pricey, but at least the individual "spacious casitas" grant adults some privacy.

JW Marriott Camelback Inn
| 26 | 27 | 26 | 27 | $460 |

5402 E. Lincoln Dr., Scottsdale; 480-948-1700; 800-242-2635; www.camelbackinn.com; 426 casitas, 27 suites

■ Have "a blast with the kids" at this "unbeatable" Scottsdale resort where there's "lots to do" – "adults can golf, hit the spa" (recently renovated) or play tennis, "children can swim" in three pools and all can explore the area by jeep, white-water raft and even hot-air balloon; there are "turn-down treats" each night and the seasonal 'Hopalong College' gets kids biking, creating art and enjoying ice-cream socials; "you feel like you're at your own private" property here, which adds up to a "very relaxing" time for all.

JW Marriott Desert Ridge Resort & Spa
| 25 | 24 | 25 | 28 | $560 |

5350 E. Marriott Dr., Phoenix; 480-293-5000; 800-835-6206; www.jwdesertridgeresort.com; 869 rooms, 81 suites

☑ While some consider this "more of a convention hotel than a family one", with such a "terrific" pool – more like a "water park" – featuring four acres of the wet stuff, a lazy river and whirlpools, it's got plenty of appeal for the little ones; nearby desert trails challenge young hikers, while adults appreciate the Nick Faldo–designed Wild Fire Golf Club and the Revive Spa (outdoor treatments available).

Phoenician, The
| 23 | 26 | 26 | 28 | $255 |

6000 E. Camelback Rd., Scottsdale; 480-941-8200; 800-888-8234; www.thephoenician.com; 464 rooms, 54 suites, 115 casitas, 7 villas

☑ They've "got the Midas touch when it comes to service" proclaim parents patronizing this "magnificent facility" where the staffers "understand that kids are not small adults" and they'll bring "a crib with amenities like bumpers, adorable baby sheets and stuffed animals" to your room or cabana; the waterslide "is a hit" with older children and the "beautiful view of Camelback Mountain" appeals to all; but fussy folks find "too much marble" and "no kid-oriented restaurants" (save for the poolside bites), concluding it may be "too nice for families."

Pointe Hilton Squaw Peak
| 28 | 21 | 20 | 25 | $239 |

7677 N. 16th St., Phoenix; 602-997-2626; 800-876-4683; www.pointehilton.com; 133 casitas, 430 suites

■ The "fabulous" Coyote Camp kids' club for ages 4 to 12 and a mini water park of pools, lazy river and winding slides at the Hole-in-the-

Wall River Ranch have kids "begging to come back" to this Spanish-Mediterranean-style resort; youngsters "love the Western-themed restaurant" and it's "worth upgrading" to a two-bedroom casita for lots of space; all in all, most families have an "outstanding" time here.

Pointe Hilton Tapatio Cliffs   22 | 20 | 19 | 21 | $219

11111 N. Seventh St., Phoenix; 602-866-7500; 800-876-4683;
www.hilton.com; 585 suites

☑ Kids "love the big slide and pool", especially for those 100-plus-degree summer days, at this rambling property (note: "very hilly without sidewalks, so it's hard to manage that stroller"); "all the rooms are suites", a boon for families, and miles of nearby scenic trails mean more opportunity for exercise; but nitpickers note the "dated" decor, maintaining it's "not nearly as nice as the Squaw Peak" property, 10 minutes away.

Pointe South Mountain   27 | 24 | 24 | 27 | $325

7777 South Pointe Pkwy., Phoenix; 602-438-9000; 866-267-1321;
www.pointesouthmountain.com; 640 suites

■ There's lots of "family fun" at this all-suite property that last year added a $12-million water venue with an active river run, wave pool and three waterslides – a "blast" for the kids; "they even have a sand volleyball court", ping-pong, shuffleboard and two children's clubs (one for ages 4 and under, and the other for 5 to 12-year-olds) and there's a free shuttle to Arizona Mills mall with hundreds of shops, "fun restaurants and a late-night Krispy Kreme"; P.S. adults will be impressed with the huge work-out facility and the resort's extensive Phantom Hills Golf Club.

Top Family-Friendly Hotel Chains in the Area:

Embassy Suites	Hyatt
Four Seasons	Marriott
Hampton Inn	Residence Inn
Holiday Inn	Ritz-Carlton
Homewood Suites	Westin

See Hotel Chain reviews, starting on page 256.

RESTAURANTS

Ratings: Family Appeal, Food, Decor, Service, Cost

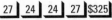

FA	F	D	S	$

Chompies   19 | 23 | 14 | 21 | I

Greenway Park Plaza, 3202 E. Greenway Rd. (N. 32nd St.), Phoenix;
602-971-8010
Mercado Del Rancho, 9301 E. Shea Blvd. (N. 92nd St.), Scottsdale;
480-860-0475
1160 E. University Dr. (S. Terrace Rd.), Tempe; 480-557-0700

■ Ex–New Yorkers find a "taste of home" at these "loud, fun and friendly" Jewish delis, which "rank with the greatest anywhere" thanks to a menu that "appeals to everyone" and "huge portions" that will even satisfy "big kids"; as a bonus, the bakery turns out fresh bagels daily when you're in the mood for "one of the best breakfasts going"; N.B. kids eat free on Tuesdays.

5 & Diner   25 | 19 | 21 | 20 | I

5220 N. 16th St. (Coulter St.), Phoenix; 602-264-5220
12802 N. Tatum Blvd. (Cactus St.), Phoenix; 602-996-0033
20216 N. 27th Ave. (Hwy. 101), Phoenix; 623-869-9311

■ Surveyors swear "you can't go wrong" at these "retro", "nostalgia"-packed diners where '50s memorabilia, table jukes and American chow make for "casual" grazing "geared to families"; so ignore those "guilt feelings" about "greasy burgers" and "yummy shakes" and just remember that "meals served in a cardboard '57 Chevy" "always work for kids."

Houston's

| 16 | 24 | 20 | 22 | M |

Camelback Esplanade, 2425 E. Camelback Rd. (24th St.), Phoenix; 602-957-9700

6113 N. Scottsdale Rd. (bet. E. Lincoln & E. McDonald Drs.), Scottsdale; 480-922-7775

☑ "Utterly consistent", these "safe bets" are an "excellent value" for moms, pops and tots in search of "solid" American food, including the "best spinach dip in the universe", "yum-yum" soups and salads and "juicy burgers"; insiders know to "go at off-hours" when the "team-server approach" makes for a "well-oiled machine", while detractors dismiss what they call its "unremarkable" "chain food" and complain about the "hurried" atmosphere.

Pei Wei Asian Diner

| ▽ 17 | 23 | 21 | 22 | I |

742 E. Glendale Ave. (7th St.), Phoenix; 602-707-0049

4340 E. Indian School Rd. (44th St.), Phoenix; 602-956-2300

7131 W. Ray Rd. (54th St.), Chandler; 480-940-3800

8787 N. Scottsdale Rd. (Double Tree Ranch Rd.), Scottsdale; 480-365-6000

www.peiwei.com

■ Pei-sans are willing to "stand in line" for "reasonably priced", "reasonably healthy" and "very tasty" Pan-Asian cuisine at this chain of "modern" quick-serve operations, where bold colors and smart design raise the experience a notch above the competition; although dishes like kung pao chicken and Hoisin Explosion are "good for families with older children", "young kids won't find much to love on the spice-heavy menu."

Pinnacle Peak Patio

| 29 | 19 | 27 | 21 | M |

10426 E. Jomax Rd. (bet. Alma School & Pinnacle Peak Pkwys.), Scottsdale; 480-615-1113; www.pppatio.com

■ "Everyone goes" to this humongous, rustic North Scottsdale institution as much for the "sawdust on the floor" and "neckties hanging from the ceiling" (snipped from the necks of greenhorns who have dressed for dinner) as for the mesquite-broiled steaks; although "older kids will like the live country music", smaller fry settle for their own special menu and, of course, the gift shop.

Pizzeria Bianco

| – | – | – | – | M |

Heritage Sq., 623 E. Adams St. (7th St.), Phoenix; 602-258-8300

Anointed "the patron saint of pizza" by legions of pie partisans, chef-owner Chris Bianco makes the "best wood-fired pizzas in town" – "hands down" – thanks to his relentless "focus" on "good, simple" ingredients and "attention to quality"; of course, this "historic" "little brick building Downtown is always busy", but young and old alike find that the "freshness" of his handmade mozzarella alone makes it "well worth the wait."

Rustler's Rooste

| ▽ 24 | 18 | 21 | 18 | M |

7777 S. Pointe Pkwy. W. (Baseline Rd. & I-10), Phoenix; 602-431-6474; www.rustlersrooste.com

■ "Don't look for something light on the menu" at this sawdust-floored cowboy themer that serves grilled chicken, ribs and steaks to city slickers who dig its "great views" of Phoenix and its "live country music"; children are entertained by roaming magicians, storytellers and balloon people, as well as a giant slide that dumps them in the middle of it all.

RESTAURANT CHAINS

See reviews, starting on page 262.

Ratings: Family Appeal, Food, Decor, Service, Cost

	FA	F	D	S	$

Applebee's
| | 21 | 16 | 17 | 17 | M |
2547 N. 44th St. (E. Thomas Rd.), Phoenix; 602-952-0033

Baja Fresh Mexican Grill ⬛
| | 20 | 22 | 14 | 18 | I |
1615 E. Camelback Rd. (16th St.), Phoenix; 602-263-0110
3923 E. Thomas Rd. (bet. 39th & 40th Sts.), Phoenix; 602-914-9000
10810 N. Tatum Blvd. (E. Shea Blvd.), Phoenix; 602-569-8600
14858 N. Frank Lloyd Wright Pkwy. (Thompson Peak Pkwy.),
Scottsdale; 480-614-0338

Benihana ⬛
| | 23 | 20 | 18 | 22 | E |
16403 N. Scottsdale Rd. (Bell Rd.), Scottsdale; 480-444-0068

Buca di Beppo ⬛
| | 24 | 19 | 22 | 21 | M |
3828 N. Scottsdale Rd. (E. 1st St.), Scottsdale; 480-949-6622

California Pizza Kitchen ⬛
| | 21 | 21 | 16 | 19 | M |
Biltmore Fashion Park, 2400 E. Camelback Rd. (24th St.), Phoenix;
602-553-8382
Desert Ridge Mktpl., 21001 N. Tatum Blvd. (Deer Valley Rd.), Phoenix;
480-473-3336
10100 Scottsdale Rd. (bet. Gold Dust & Mountain View Rds.), Scottsdale;
480-596-8300

Cheesecake Factory ⬛
| | 21 | 23 | 21 | 20 | M |
Biltmore Fashion Park, 2402 E. Camelback Rd. (24th St.), Phoenix;
602-778-6501
Kierland Commons, 15230 N. Scottsdale Rd. (bet. Greenway Pkwy. &
Kierland Blvd.), Scottsdale; 480-607-0083

Chevys Fresh Mex ⬛
| | 23 | 19 | 18 | 18 | M |
2650 E. Camelback Rd. (N. 26th St.), Phoenix; 602-955-6677

Chili's Grill & Bar ⬛
| | 21 | 19 | 18 | 19 | M |
2057 E. Camelback Rd. (N. 20th St.), Phoenix; 602-955-1195

Chuck E. Cheese's ⬛
| | 26 | 10 | 17 | 13 | I |
Biltmore Fashion Park, 8039 N. 35th Ave. (Northern Ave.), Phoenix;
602-973-1945
4825-16 E. Warner Rd. (48th St.), Phoenix; 480-705-5205
8890 E. Indian Bend Rd. (N. Pima Rd.), Scottsdale; 480-951-1991

Claim Jumper Restaurant ⬛
| | 23 | 24 | 22 | 21 | M |
Deer Valley Towne Ctr., 3603 W. Aqua Fria Blvd. (31st Ave.), Phoenix;
623-581-8595
7000 E. Shea Blvd. (Scottsdale Rd.), Scottsdale; 480-951-6111

Fuddrucker's ⬛
| | 24 | 20 | 15 | 16 | I |
8941 Black Canyon Hwy. (Dunlap Ave.), Phoenix; 602-870-1111
7145 Indian School Rd. (Scottsdale Rd.), Scottsdale;
480-946-9916

Hard Rock Cafe ⬛
| | 22 | 16 | 26 | 18 | M |
3 S. Second St. (Jefferson St.), Phoenix; 602-261-7625

In-N-Out Burger ⊉ | 24 | 24 | 13 | 21 | I |
21001 N. Tatum Blvd. (Deer Valley Rd.), Phoenix; 800-786-1000
19407 N. 27th Ave. (Yorkshire Dr.), Phoenix; 800-786-1000
7467 E. Frank Lloyd Wright Blvd. (Scottsdale Rd.), Scottsdale; 800-786-1000

Johnny Rockets ⑤ | 25 | 17 | 20 | 18 | I |
7014 Camelback Rd. (Goldwater Blvd.), Scottsdale; 480-423-1505

Mimi's Cafe ⑤ | 23 | 21 | 22 | 20 | M |
4901 E. Ray Rd. (bet. 48th & 50th Sts.), Phoenix; 480-705-4811
Metro Ctr., 10214 N. Metro Pkwy. W. (off N. 31st Ave.), Phoenix; 602-997-1299
21001 N. Tatum Blvd. (E. Deer Valley Rd.), Phoenix; 480-419-5006
8980 E. Shea Blvd. (bet. Hwy. 101 & 90th St.), Scottsdale; 480-451-6763

Olive Garden ⑤ | 20 | 19 | 18 | 19 | M |
Metro Ctr., 10223 N. Metro Pkwy. E. (Rte. 17), Phoenix; 602-943-4573
2626 N. 75th Ave. (Thomas Rd.), Phoenix; 623-849-6533
4868 E. Cactus Rd. (bet. 48th St. & Paradise Village Pkwy.), Scottsdale; 602-494-4327
3380 N. Scottsdale Rd. (Osburn Rd.), Scottsdale; 480-874-0212

On the Border | 20 | 19 | 19 | 18 | M |
Mexican Grill & Cantina ⑤
5005 E. Ray Rd. (50th St.), Phoenix; 480-705-5454
21001 N. Tatum Blvd. (E. Deer Valley Rd.), Phoenix; 480-473-3168

Original Pancake House, The ⑤ | 24 | 22 | 12 | 17 | I |
402 E. Greenway Pkwy. (bet. 3rd & 7th Sts.), Phoenix; 602-896-9805
6840 E. Camelback Rd. (68th St.), Scottsdale; 480-946-4902

Outback Steakhouse ⑤ | 20 | 22 | 18 | 20 | M |
4715 E. Cactus Rd. (Tatum Blvd.), Phoenix; 602-494-3902
9801 N. Black Canyon Hwy. (bet. Dunlap & Peoria Aves.), Phoenix; 602-943-2226
2820 N. 75th Ave. (Thomas Rd.), Phoenix; 623-873-1945
4180 N. Drinkwater Blvd. (bet. 6th Ave. & Indian School Rd.), Scottsdale; 480-424-6810

Red Robin ⑤ | 25 | 20 | 19 | 20 | M |
7000 E. Mayo Blvd. (Scottsdale Rd.), Phoenix; 480-513-4220
8970 E. Shea Blvd. (Hwy. 101), Scottsdale; 480-661-7114

Romano's Macaroni Grill ⑤ | 21 | 21 | 19 | 21 | M |
5035 E. Ray Rd. (50th St.), Phoenix; 480-705-5661
21001 N. Tatum Blvd. (E. Deer Valley Rd.), Phoenix; 480-538-8755
2949 W. Agua Fria Frwy. (bet. Behrend & Yorkshire Drs.), Phoenix; 623-580-8681
7245 E. Gold Dust Ave. (Scottsdale Rd.), Scottsdale; 480-596-6676

Ruby's ⑤ | 24 | 19 | 20 | 19 | I |
7014 E. Camelback Rd. (Goldwater Blvd.), Scottsdale; 480-425-7829

T.G.I. Friday's ⑤ | 21 | 17 | 18 | 17 | M |
21001 N. Tatum Blvd. (Mayo Blvd.), Phoenix; 480-538-1945
401 E. Jefferson Blvd. (S. 4th St.), Phoenix; 602-462-3506
11025 N. Black Canyon Hwy. (N. 25th Ave.), Phoenix; 602-861-1577
7435 E. Frank Lloyd Wright Blvd. (N. Scottsdale Rd.), Scottsdale; 480-348-2445

Uno Chicago Grill ⑤ | 20 | 18 | 15 | 16 | M |
14850 N. Northsight Blvd. (Raintree Blvd.), Phoenix; 480-922-7200
455 N. Third St. (bet. Fillmore & Van Buren Sts.), Phoenix; 602-253-3355

San Diego

If you were designing a city just for families, it might look a lot like San Diego. This laid-back metropolis is packed with kid-friendly attractions, from the famous Zoo and Wild Animal Park to Sea World and Legoland. Balboa Park, the city's green oasis, houses the Zoo, plus more museums (the Fleet Science Center, the Aerospace Museum, the Mingei International and many others) than you could see in several visits; the 33 beaches of San Diego County total more than 70 miles of sun, sand and surf. Like many California cities, this one sprawls, so you'll need a car; you can orient yourself by taking the 59-Mile Scenic Drive, which loops past landmarks like the Embarcadero, Point Loma (perfect for winter whale-watching), the Cabrillo National Monument, La Jolla and the Victorian-style Gaslamp District. Take a ferry from the harbor to Coronado Island and its enormous, picturesque hotel (where Some Like It Hot *was filmed in 1958), or travel a half hour south by car or local trolley to taste the tacos in Tijuana. Whenever you come and wherever you go, you'll be fine in just a sweater: Temps are mild year-round, and the little rain that falls tends to do so in winter.*

ATTRACTIONS

Ratings: Child Appeal, Adult Appeal, Public Facilities, Service, Cost

C	A	P	S	$

Balboa Park
23	27	24	19	$0

1549 El Prado (Park Blvd.); 619-239-0512; www.balboapark.org

■ "You could spend a week and still not see everything" in this "remarkable" downtown "oasis" that some say is "comparable to the Smithsonian in DC", with 15 "wonderful" museums and the "famous zoo"; the Hall of Champions, the puppet theater, the Aerospace Museum and the "free concerts" at the "outdoor organ" are "more kid-friendly than some other" attractions, but all enjoy the "gorgeous palm trees" and street musicians that turn this urban "gem" into "one of the great city parks."

Birch Aquarium at Scripps
26	25	24	23	M

2300 Expedition Way (N. Torrey Pines Rd.), La Jolla; 858-534-3474; aquarium.ucsd.edu

☑ "If you don't want to deal with the lines at SeaWorld", this "small but excellent aquarium" may be "just the right size", particularly for wee walkers; "children always enjoy" the "fascinating" "hands-on displays" – they can "touch a sea cucumber" or "take a simulated deep-sea dive" – and the "crowds are never overwhelming"; it may not be the "most exciting" attraction in town, but it's a "slower-paced family activity", with a striking "setting overlooking the ocean" "in beautiful La Jolla."

Cabrillo National Monument
15	24	16	16	I

1800 Cabrillo Memorial Dr. (Hwy. 209); 619-557-5450; www.nps.gov/cabr

☑ "On a clear day", the "panoramic views" "of San Diego harbor and the ocean" are "absolutely magnificent" from this "always windy" peninsula where, in 1542, Juan Rodriguez Cabrillo came ashore with the first European expedition to land on the West Coast; the "modern, informative visitor center" and "knowledgeable rangers" help you learn "about the history of this spot", but younger kids just appreciate "lots of room to run around" because there's "not much" else for them to do; P.S. "don't bother if it's foggy."

Coronado Island

| – | – | – | – | $0 |

Visitor Ctr., 1100 Orange Ave. (C Ave.), Coronado; 619-437-8788;
www.coronadovisitors.com
This city-on-a-peninsula across the bridge from Downtown makes an
entertaining excursion for kids; you can rent bikes, surreys (pedal
carriages), and in-line skates to tool around the 15 miles of mostly flat
paths, or hang out at one of the beaches or playgrounds; an assortment
of restaurants and shops rounds out the attractions; N.B. the Hotel
del Coronado offers sports and spa activities just for teens.

Knott's Soak City USA

| ∇ 29 | 22 | 23 | 18 | E |

2052 Entertainment Circle (Heritage Rd.), Chula Vista; 619-661-7373;
www.knotts.com
■ "Get ready to get wet" at this "family adventure" in Chula Vista that's
modeled after 1950s San Diego (with surf woodies and longboards) –
a "good place to cool down in the summertime"; "older kids love"
the waterslides, of course, and there are "offerings for every age",
including a separate area for those "too young for the bigger" rides;
compared to similar attractions, it's "reasonably priced" say wallet-
watchers, so most "would go back."

La Jolla Cove Beach

| – | – | – | – | $0 |

1100 Coast Blvd. (Girard Ave.), La Jolla; 619-221-8900;
www.lajollaportal.com/jollacove
Nearly hidden between sandstone cliffs, this small beach is a short
walk from downtown La Jolla; though the water is rarely warm, the
sheltered cove is a kid-friendly swimming spot, and adventurous
youngsters can explore the tide pools and mini-caves nearby; above
the cove is a grassy park (with rest rooms), and nearby is Seal Rock,
where you can watch seals and sea lions cavort and sun themselves
during much of the year.

Legoland California ☺☻

| 29 | 20 | 26 | 24 | VE |

1 Legoland Dr. (Cannon Rd.), Carlsbad; 760-918-5346; 877-534-6526;
www.legoland.com
■ If they build it, kids will come – nearly "everything is made of Legos
(except the toilets)" in this "child's dream", a kinder, gentler theme
park that earns an "A+" from the "eight and under" set and San Diego's
No. 1 rating for Child Appeal in this *Survey*; the wildly "imaginative"
designers have "done amazing things" – the "scale-model cities" and
"replicas of well-known monuments" are "a must-see" – and parents
appreciate that this "sparkling-clean" facility "offers creativity" along
with "interactive rides"; jaded juniors find it "a little tame", but this
"unique" amusement center has enough "charm" for budding builders.

Maritime Museum

| 22 | 27 | 22 | 21 | I |

1492 N. Harbor Dr. (W. Ash St.); 619-234-9153; www.sdmaritime.com
■ "Sailing history comes alive" when miniature mateys "climb aboard"
the "great collection of old-time vessels" at this "hands-on museum"
tended by "volunteer docents" who are "boat nuts – and it shows"; a
highlight for little hands is the Star of India, a majestic 1863 sailing
ship that's a "symbol of San Diego's" maritime heritage where the
"hard wooden beds will make anyone appreciate even the worst
motel experience"; film buffs will note that the ship featured in *Master
and Commander* is here; N.B. watch for special family days, with
free admission for those under 12.

Mingei International Museum

| ∇ 12 | 24 | 23 | 21 | I |

Balboa Park, 1439 El Prado (Plaza de Panama); 619-239-0003;
www.mingei.org
◪ If you're "interested in arts and crafts", reviewers "recommend"
the "outstanding collections" in this Balboa Park gallery, one of the

many "fine museums in" this urban green space; depending on the exhibit, "the kids might actually enjoy" the multicultural folk art or the periodic special events (puppet shows, concerts); though a visit here makes a "wonderful afternoon" for adults, some parents posit it's "boring for little ones."

Old Town San Diego State Historic Park

| 16 | 22 | 19 | 18 | $0 |

San Diego Ave. (Twiggs St.); 619-220-5422; www.parks.ca.gov

☑ "From mariachi bands to haunted houses to candle-making demos", this "lively" urban state park mixes "local history", a "taste of Mexican culture" and "kitschy shopping", which suits small sorts just fine; if you want to "feel like you're back in the Wild West", "tour the schoolhouse" and other "old adobe buildings", then stop for a "hot handmade tortilla"; detractors dis the whole area as "too commercial and touristy" with "better traditional food found elsewhere", and say there's "little for small children to do – except complain."

PETCO Park

| – | – | – | – | E |

100 Park Blvd. (bet. 7th & 10th Aves.); 888-697-2373; www.padres.com

The new home of the San Diego Padres, this 40,000-plus-seat major league ballpark is set to open for the 2004 baseball season; located downtown near the Gaslamp Quarter, it boasts views of the bay, the skyline and Balboa Park and is within walking distance of several trolley lines; plans call for a full-service restaurant as well.

Reuben H. Fleet Science Center

| 28 | 26 | 25 | 22 | I |

Balboa Park, 1875 El Prado (Park Blvd.); 619-238-1233; www.rhfleet.org

■ "Perhaps the best argument that science can be fun" is this "first-rate discovery center" in Balboa Park for "inquisitive minds" of every age; it's filled with "neat-o experiments" and other "hands-on demonstrations" that "keep kids and adults alike utterly absorbed", plus a planetarium and IMAX theater showing "first-rate movies"; it may "not be as extensive" as similar facilities in other cities, but youngsters sure "go crazy" at this "excellent" "learning adventure."

San Diego Aerospace Museum

| 23 | 25 | 22 | 20 | I |

Balboa Park, 2001 Pan American Plaza (Park Blvd.); 619-234-8291; www.aerospacemuseum.org

■ Puny pilot wanna-bes cruise to this Balboa Park museum "run by dedicated volunteers", including former flyboys with "a wealth of historical knowledge"; a "must-see for aviation enthusiasts", it "may not be the biggest or best" of the genre, but there are more than 70 artifacts on view, ranging from "great vintage" planes to an "excellent aircraft carrier exhibit", with displays that mix technical information and "fun" (check out the cool motion simulator); you "can see almost everything in one visit" and still have time for other attractions.

SAN DIEGO WILD ANIMAL PARK

| 28 | 27 | 25 | 24 | E |

15500 San Pasqual Valley Rd. (off I-78), Escondido; 760-747-8702; www.wildanimalpark.org

■ It's not just the "long drive" to Escondido (40 minutes northeast of the city) that makes the San Diego Zoo's "fantastic free-range" counterpart "like a trip out of the country" – watching "animals run free in vast areas" is "the closest you get to an African [or Asian] safari without leaving North America"; plan a full day for this "hilly" and "encyclopedic" spot that requires lots of walking, or, on summer days, visit during "cooler" evening hours to avoid the midday heat; in addition, there are "kids' programs, like camping" (reserve in advance), and shutterbugs can splurge "for a photo caravan."

SAN DIEGO ZOO
| 29 | 27 | 26 | 24 | E |

2920 Zoo Dr. (Park Blvd.); 619-234-3153; www.sandiegozoo.org

■ "Happy animals" make for one of the "world's most amazing zoos", just north of downtown San Diego in Balboa Park where "natural settings" affirm "a profound concern for the welfare" of a "huge variety" of inhabitants; that SoCal sun gets "really hot" in summer, so "pack water", "take the bus tour to see large" creatures and "save the walking" "up and down hills" "for close views of elusive cats, playful otters" and the "panda cub" Mei Sheng; "there's so much to see" at this place, voted the city's No. 1 attraction in this *Survey,* that you should "allow two full days"; take toddlers to the "outstanding" children's area for "educational shows and hands-on activities"; there's even fine dining, at Albert's next to the Gorilla Tropics.

SEAWORLD
| 28 | 26 | 25 | 23 | VE |

500 SeaWorld Dr. (W. Mission Bay Dr.); 619-226-3901; www.seaworld.com

■ "Plan to get wet", courtesy of the "always-popular Shamu", who's "still flipping" at this "outstanding" aquarium owned by the Anheuser-Busch "beer barons" and set on "lovely grounds" drenched in SoCal "sunshine and ocean air"; dine next to the celebrity orca's tank, and enjoy "exciting rides", "interactive" feeding areas and "delightful exhibits" of "beautiful marine animals"; with "so much to see and do", it's a "fun, educational" "all-day excursion" "for all ages" and the backstage tour is "well worth" the "extra money"; use the all-inclusive CityPass for SeaWorld, the Zoo, Disneyland, Disney's California Adventure and Knott's Berry Farm to save some simoleons.

HOTELS

Ratings: Family Appeal, Rooms, Service, Public Facilities, Cost

	FA	R	S	P	$

del Coronado, Hotel
| 26 | 21 | 24 | 25 | $300 |

1500 Orange Ave., Coronado; 619-435-6611; 800-582-2595; www.hoteldel.com; 600 rooms, 7 cottages, 1 houses

☑ Maybe tykes won't appreciate the "quirky Victorian charm that oozes from every corner" of this "old-world" "classic" where the movie *Some Like It Hot* was filmed, but the "ocean and huge pool have a big appeal" and the "great Sunday brunch" gets their attention too; a "helpful" staff "provides all the necessary equipment to make traveling with an infant comfortable" from cribs to "swim diapers at the pool", so even if a few find it "lives off its name and location" (near SeaWorld, the San Diego Zoo and Balboa Park), most say it's "made for families"; P.S. for "lots of history", get a room in the original building.

Four Seasons Aviara
| 25 | 28 | 28 | 28 | $400 |

7100 Four Seasons Point, Carlsbad; 760-603-6800; 800-332-3442; www.fourseasons.com; 285 rooms, 44 suites

■ There's "everything you could want at a family hotel" say seasoned travelers about this "fancy" – "albeit expensive" – resort that offers "special treatment for babies, including toiletries and their names spelled out in alphabet bath sponges"; with "beautiful grounds", "top-notch", "kid-friendly" food (youngsters think they've "found heaven" when they see the "personalized cookies") and an outstanding spa, everyone is happy here – and it's just five minutes from Legoland.

Hilton San Diego Resort
| 25 | 19 | 18 | 23 | $299 |

1775 E. Mission Bay Dr.; 619-276-4010; 800-774-1500; www.hilton.com; 337 rooms, 20 suites

■ You "can't go wrong" at this waterfront resort on Mission Bay, where "you're right on the beach" and there are plenty of children's activities in a supervised kids' club, as well as a video arcade, a playground, water sports and a "wading pool that's perfect for little ones"; the "unpretentious staff tries hard" and the rooms are "large and comfortable"; N.B. it's just two-and-a-half miles west of SeaWorld and four miles south of Old Town State Historic Park.

Loews Coronado Bay Resort

| 22 | 23 | 23 | 24 | $325 |

4000 Coronado Bay Rd., Coronado; 619-424-4000; 800-235-6397; www.loewshotels.com; 438 rooms, 17 suites

■ Set on a 15-acre private peninsula, this "very family-oriented property" where even your pets are welcome draws raves for having "its own beach", an "incredible brunch" and "plenty of activities" (the 'Loews Loves Kids' program includes a game-lending library, special gifts for children under 10 and supervised recreation); "they'll give you a safety kit for the room" and tots get coloring books and crayons in the restaurants; the only qualm is it's "a bit removed from town", so you "must have a car to go anywhere"; N.B. a new 10,000-sq.-ft. spa recently opened.

Marriott Coronado Island

| ▽ 24 | 23 | 23 | 26 | $269 |

2000 Second St., Coronado; 619-435-3000; 800-228-9290; www.marriott.com; 273 rooms, 27 suites

■ "Over the bridge from downtown San Diego", this "quiet enclave with views of the ships" is a "great place to spend a long weekend with the family"; located in "a fun area for bike riding", it also has a nearby beach, an on-site pool, a full-service spa and babysitting services; "just a ferry ride to the city" and "close to golf, shops and tennis", it's a more relaxing option for many visitors.

Marriott San Diego & Marina

| 21 | 21 | 21 | 24 | $350 |

333 W. Harbor Dr.; 619-234-1500; 800-228-9290; www.marriott.com; 1305 rooms, 55 suites

■ "It's an easy walk to the Seaport Village of shops and restaurants" from this pet-friendly bayside hotel with "panoramic views" of the water and an outdoor pool and spa on-site; "children enjoy riding bikes around the harbor" and both the San Diego Zoo and Balboa Park are just a mile-and-a-half away; N.B. for the more adventurous, Tijuana, Mexico, is an 18-mile drive.

Top Family-Friendly Hotel Chains in the Area:

Embassy Suites	Hyatt
Hampton Inn	Residence Inn
Holiday Inn	Westin

See Hotel Chain reviews, starting on page 256.

RESTAURANTS

Ratings: Family Appeal, Food, Decor, Service, Cost

| FA | F | D | S | $ |

Anthony's Fish Grotto

| 22 | 21 | 18 | 20 | M |

7081 Clairemont Mesa Blvd. (I-805); 858-244-0228
1360 N. Harbor Dr. (Ash St.); 619-232-5103
Rio Vista Ctr., 8660 San Diego Dr. (Friars Rd. & Qualcomm Way.); 619-291-1547
215 W. Bay Blvd. (E St.), Chula Vista; 619-425-4200
www.gofishanthonys.com

☑ "Everyone feels welcome" at this "San Diego institution", a mini-chain that's been shelling out "fresh" seafood at "reasonable prices" since 1946; though some carp about "noisy" environs and "hit-or-miss" meals, overall it's "excellent for families or groups"; P.S. insiders "stick with the original location down at the waterfront."

Corvette Diner

| 28 | 20 | 27 | 23 | I |

*3946 Fifth Ave. (bet. University Ave & Washington St.); 619-542-1001;
www.cohnrestaurants.com*

■ Rock 'n' roll will never die at this Hillcrest "blast from the past", a
"hoppin'" '50s-style diner, where "wacky waitresses" in poodle skirts
dish out "basic" all-American grub with lotsa "sassy" attitude; "hold
onto your wigs" – it can get "loud", but at least there's "no need to
worry about your screaming children."

Delicias

| – | – | – | – | VE |

6106 Paseo Delicias (La Granada), Rancho Santa Fe; 858-756-8000

"The name says it all" at this Californian that, despite a little "ambient
noise", makes an "excellent hideaway" in horsey Rancho Santa Fe;
equipped with "a menu for every mood" ("fabulous lobster bisque",
"wonderful" wood-fired-oven pizza), it's fit for a family feast "served
superbly" in a "charming bungalow" brightened by "wonderful flowers"
(especially in the "small garden"); if "it ain't cheap", especially when
you're feeding hungry youngsters, at least it's a "good value."

D.Z. Akin's

| 22 | 23 | 15 | 22 | M |

6930 Alvarado Rd. (bet. I-8 & 70th St.); 619-265-0218

■ "It's not New York" exactly, but locals hankering for East Coast deli
fare insist that the "home-cooked" dishes on the "lengthy menu" of
this "family-friendly" spot are "as close as San Diego has come so
far"; bargain hunters note the servings are so "plentiful" that there's
"enough food on one plate to feed four."

Emerald Chinese
Seafood Restaurant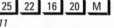

| ▽ 22 | 23 | 17 | 18 | M |

*Pacific Gateway Plaza, 3709 Convoy St. (Aero Dr.); 858-565-6888;
www.emeraldrestaurant.com*

■ Although maybe not "better than SeaWorld", this family-style
Chinese seafooder in Kearny Mesa does provide live "fish on display"
that "kids love to look at" as well as "delicious" dim sum for grown-ups;
in order to get your young 'uns to sample the more exotic menu items,
experienced parents suggest you "just tell them everything is chicken."

Filippi's Pizza Grotto

| 25 | 22 | 16 | 20 | M |

10330 Friars Rd. (Riverdale St.); 619-281-3511
962 Garnet Ave. (Cass St.); 858-483-6222
1747 India St. (Date St.); 619-232-5095
5353 Kearny Villa Rd. (Clairemont Mesa Blvd.); 858-279-7240
www.realcheesepizza.com

◪ There's "good grub for the whole clan" at this "homestyle" Italian
pizzeria chain offering "plenty of choices" that are "priced just right";
aficionados say the quality "depends on which one you go to", though
all share "funky", "Chianti-bottles-hanging-from-the-ceiling" decor.

Ghirardelli's Soda Fountain

| 28 | 23 | 24 | 20 | I |

643 Fifth Ave. (Market St.); 619-234-2449; www.ghirardelli.com

■ Reward your family with a "special treat" at this "old-school soda
shop", a "family favorite" in the heart of the Gaslamp Quarter cloned
from the San Francisco–based chocolate company; "great sundaes"
with all the "requisite gooey toppings" make up the menu, and it gets
bonus points for being handy to San Diego's new ballpark.

Hodad's

| ▽ 20 | 21 | 18 | 19 | I |

5010 Newport Ave. (bet. Abbott & Bacon Sts.); 619-224-4623

■ "Take the kids to the beach, then sit" in a VW bus-turned-booth to
eat lunch, say surfmeisters stoked about this "great joint" in Ocean
Beach that serves "some of the best burgers around"; the "very
juicy" patties are also "messy", so daddy-os and mommy-os direct

"use plenty of napkins" and don't fret about decorum; toddlers can hone alphabet skills by "reading the license plates" all over the walls.

Old Town Mexican Cafe

| 22 | 23 | 20 | 21 | M |

2489 San Diego Ave. (Harney St.); 619-297-4330

☑ A "must for Mexican food" when you're in Old Town, this "authentic" south-of-the-border specialist is a "lively" cantina where you can "watch tortillas being made in the front window" or listen to a festive mariachi band; on the downside, however, the "always crowded" conditions and long waits to get in "can truly try your patience."

Parallel 33 ⌧

| – | – | – | – | E |

741 W. Washington St. (Falcon St.); 619-260-0033; www.parallel33sd.com

Teach the kids geography over dinner – with the help of a menu full of eatables "from the 33rd Parallel [which intersects San Diego as it circles the globe]", a "novel idea" that qualifies this "slightly exotic" Hillcrest eatery as a "leader in high-quality fusion" food; along with the "unique and inspired" "multicultural" Eclectic fare, the "calm, lovely decor" lures a young, Uptown crowd for "friendly service", a "fun bar" scene and moderate prices.

Sammy's Woodfired Pizza

| 21 | 19 | 14 | 18 | M |

565 Pearl St. (Draper Ave.), La Jolla; 858-456-5222
Costa Verde, 8650 Genesee Ave. (bet. La Jolla Vlg. & Nobel Drs.); 858-404-9898
Horton Plaza, 770 Fourth Ave. (F St.); 619-230-8888
Park in the Valley, 1620 Camino de La Reina (Mission Center Rd.); 619-298-8222
www.sammyspizza.com

☑ Purveyor of the "best original wood-fired pizza in San Diego", this homegrown chain garners "long lines" for its "traditional" and "designer" pies, "unique chopped salads" and trademark "messy sundaes" ("a sinful delight" that'll motivate kids to clean their plates); the "servers tend to be young, so service may vary", and since it's "a casual, family favorite", "the atmosphere is seriously lacking for evening dining" – but "if you're hungry", "it's never a letdown."

Via Italia Trattoria

| – | – | – | – | M |

Clairemont Town Sq., 4705A Clairemont Dr. (Clairemont Mezza Blvd.); 858-274-9732; www.viaitaliapizzeria.com

"The food is so darn good" at this "hidden gem" in Clairemont with a wide-ranging menu that offers "the best Italian value in San Diego"; kids won't mind the "mall location" as a backdrop for artful pizzas and "great pasta dishes", and though service may be "hit or miss", "you'll be glad when you find" this "great local place" that "defines the dinner-and-a-movie concept", since the multiplex "is right next door."

RESTAURANT CHAINS

See reviews, starting on page 262.

Ratings: Family Appeal, Food, Decor, Service, Cost

| FA | F | D | S | $ |

Applebee's

| 21 | 16 | 17 | 17 | M |

7677 Balboa Ave. (Ruffner St.); 858-569-4590
9480 E. Mira Mesa Blvd. (Westview Pkwy.); 858-578-8280

Baja Fresh Mexican Grill ⌧

| 20 | 22 | 14 | 18 | I |

145 Broadway (2nd Ave.); 619-702-2252
845 Camino De La Reina (Mission Center Rd.); 619-295-1122
3737 Murphy Canyon Rd. (Aero Dr.); 858-277-5700
120 W. Washington St. (1st Ave.); 619-497-1000

Buca di Beppo ⑤ | 24 | 19 | 22 | 21 | M |
705 Sixth Ave. (G St.); 619-233-7272
10749 Westview Pkwy. (Mira Mesa Blvd.); 858-536-2822

Cheesecake Factory ⑤ | 21 | 23 | 21 | 20 | M |
Fashion Valley Mall, 7067 Friars Rd. (Ulric St.); 619-683-2800

Chevys Fresh Mex ⑤ | 23 | 19 | 18 | 18 | M |
1202 Camino Del Rio N. (Mission Center Rd.); 619-297-5667
11630 Carmel Mountain Rd. (Rancho Carmel Dr.); 858-675-9292

Chili's Grill & Bar ⑤ | 21 | 19 | 18 | 19 | M |
4252 Camino Del Rio N. (Fairmont Ave.); 619-280-7996
5969 Lusk Blvd. (Mira Mesa Blvd.); 858-457-5962
10184 Scripps Poway Pkwy. (Scripps Highland Dr.);
858-566-2096
3494 Sports Arena Blvd. (Camino Del Rio); 619-223-1107

Chuck E. Cheese's ⑤ | 26 | 10 | 17 | 13 | I |
3146 Sports Arena Blvd. (Camino Del Rio); 619-523-4385

Dave & Buster's ⑤ | 26 | 16 | 21 | 17 | M |
2931 Camino Del Rio N. (off I-8 & I-805); 619-280-7115

Fuddrucker's ⑤ | 24 | 20 | 15 | 16 | I |
8285 Mira Mesa Blvd. (Camino Ruiz); 858-693-3916
340 Third Ave. (K St.), Chula Vista; 619-420-4881

Hard Rock Cafe ⑤ | 22 | 16 | 26 | 18 | M |
801 Fourth Ave. (F St.); 619-615-7625

In-N-Out Burger ⊭ | 24 | 24 | 13 | 21 | I |
2910 Damon Ave. (Mission Bay Rd.); 800-786-1000
3102 Sports Arena Blvd. (Rosecrans St.); 800-786-1000

Joe's Crab Shack ⑤ | 23 | 17 | 21 | 19 | M |
7610 Hazard Center Dr. (Frazee Rd.); 619-260-1111
4325 Ocean Blvd. (Pacific Beach Dr.); 858-274-3474

Old Spaghetti Factory, The ⑤ | 25 | 20 | 22 | 20 | I |
275 Fifth Ave. (K St.); 619-233-4323

Olive Garden ⑤ | 20 | 19 | 18 | 19 | M |
11555 Carmel Mountain Rd. (Rancho Carmel Dr.); 858-485-9873
3215 Sports Arena Blvd. (Camino Del Rio); 619-226-2124
585 I St. (Broadway), Chula Vista; 619-498-1717

On the Border Mexican | 20 | 19 | 19 | 18 | M |
Grill & Cantina ⑤
1770 Camino De La Reina (Camino Del Este); 619-209-3700
10789 Westview Pkwy. (Mira Mesa Blvd.); 858-530-1130

Original Pancake | 24 | 22 | 12 | 17 | I |
House, The ⑤
3906 Convoy St. (off I-805 & Hwy. 163); 858-565-1740

Outback Steakhouse ⑤ | 20 | 22 | 18 | 20 | M |
1640 Camino Del Rio N. (bet. Camino Del Este & Mission Center Rd.);
619-294-8998
4196 Clairemont Mesa Blvd. (bet. Clairemont Dr. & Genesse Ave.);
858-274-6283

	C	A	P	S	$

Red Robin ⑤ — 25 | 20 | 19 | 20 | M
Del Mar, 12865 El Camino Real (Del Mar Heights Rd.); 858-793-0445
University Towne Centre Mall, 4373 La Jolla Village Dr. (Genesse Ave.);
858-450-0343

Romano's Macaroni Grill ⑤ — 21 | 21 | 19 | 21 | M
202 East Via Rancho Pkwy. (I-15), Escondido; 760-741-6309

Ruby's ⑤ — 24 | 19 | 20 | 19 | I
1640 Camino del Rio N. (bet. Mission Center Rd. & Texas St.); 619-294-7829
5630 Paseo del Norte (off I-5), Carlsbad; 760-931-7829

T.G.I. Friday's ⑤ — 21 | 17 | 18 | 17 | M
403 Camino Del Rio S. (off Hwy. 8); 619-297-8443
11650 Carmel Mountain Rd. (Rancho Carmel Dr.); 858-675-7047
743 Fifth Ave. (bet. F & G Sts.); 619-234-4393
8801 Villa La Jolla Dr. (Nobel Dr.), La Jolla; 858-455-0880

Tony Roma's ⑤ — 20 | 21 | 16 | 19 | M
4110 Mission Blvd. (Pacific Beach Dr.); 858-272-7427

Uno Chicago Grill ⑤ — 20 | 18 | 15 | 16 | M
Fashion Valley Mall, 7007 Friars Rd. (off Rte. 163); 619-298-1866
4465 Mission Blvd. (Hornblend St.); 858-483-4143
Chula Vista Sq., 555 Broadway, Suite 1076 (bet. H & I Sts.), Chula Vista;
619-420-8660

San Francisco

Though chilly coastal fog means you'll sometimes need a sweater even in sunny spring and fall, San Franciscans live outdoors. Golden Gate Park from the Pacific to the Haight, Crissy Field at the foot of the Golden Gate Bridge, Muir Woods across the Bridge, Alcatraz and Angel Islands in the bay, and Berkeley's Tilden Park offer meadows, forests, windblown beaches and magnificent vistas. On clear days, the view astounds from all over this hilly, colorful Victorian town, particularly up corkscrewing Lombard Street or atop Coit Tower. Stroll through Chinatown, arty North Beach, the Latin-flavored Mission, hippie Haight-Ashbury and the gay Castro for up-close glimpses of SF's bohemian spirit. Taxis are pricey, but the city's signature transport, the cable car, offers premium sightseeing for $3 (try the Powell-Hyde line to Fisherman's Wharf or the California Street line up and over Nob Hill). You can also opt for MUNI buses and the Bay Area Rapid Transit, known as BART, which runs east across the Bay Bridge to the warm weather of Oakland and beyond. To travel north to Napa and Sonoma's wine country or south to Monterey and Carmel, you'll need a car. Remember to pull the emergency brake really hard when parking on the city's steep streets!

ATTRACTIONS

Ratings: Child Appeal, Adult Appeal, Public Facilities, Service, Cost

	C	A	P	S	$

ALCATRAZ ISLAND ☺ — 19 | 26 | 18 | 19 | M
Blue & Gold Fleet Ferries, Pier 41 (Jefferson St.); 415-561-4900;
www.nps.gov/alcatraz
■ There's no escaping that "it's super-touristy" – and "brrrr!", "it's a chilly", "windy" ferry ride to get there – but this "notorious prison"

"where infamous criminals like Al Capone were held" "enthralls pre-teens" and adults alike; the "creepy" but "fascinating" audio tour, "complete with bars clanging, prisoners yelling" and a chance to "get locked in solitary", helps older ones "imagine being stuck in these cold, gray surroundings with a fairy-tale view of beautiful SF beyond arms' length"; P.S. as the Child Appeal rating suggests, "leave young kids on the mainland", pack snacks and jackets, and "book online in advance."

Angel Island State Park ☺ | 19 | 24 | 16 | 15 | M |
Blue & Gold Fleet Ferries, Pier 41 (Jefferson St.); 415-435-1915;
www.angelisland.org
■ For a heavenly "one-day getaway from civilization", "pack a lunch" and hop a ferry to this "treasure in the middle of the bay"; "younger children enjoy the shorter trails" or "tram tours that visit army sites from the Civil War to the Cold War" as well as the former "immigration station", "school-age kids, teens and parents" "hike to the top" of Mt. Livermore for "million-dollar" views, and the ride over is "magical" "for the whole family"; it's also "great for easy mountain biking" (rentable seasonally) and "kayak tours around the island."

Aquarium of the Bay ☺☺ | 25 | 21 | 20 | 19 | M |
Pier 39, Embarcadero St. (Beach St.); 415-623-5300;
www.aquariumofthebay.com
☑ "Watch out – a shark might swim by above your head" as the "moving floor takes you through the underwater tunnel" simulating "the bottom of the bay" at this "well-managed, nicely designed" aquarium on Pier 39; at the "small" facility, "oohing and ahhing kids" literally get a "close-up feel" of life in the water, courtesy of the creatures in the "interactive tidal pool"; still, old salts say "go to the Steinhart Aquarium when its regular building reopens [in 2008] or travel down to Monterey Bay" for a deep-sea dive that's "worth the admission."

Bay Area Discovery Museum | – | – | – | – | I |
Fort Baker, 557 McReynolds Rd. (Bunker Rd.), Sausalito; 415-339-3900;
www.badm.org
Crawlers and early walkers are hot for Tot Spots, the indoor/outdoor tactile discovery center at this ever-expanding, hands-on feast of a kids' museum just over the Golden Gate Bridge in Sausalito's restored Fort Baker; grade-schoolers are agog at the array of traveling science, environmental and media exhibitions, permanent interactive laboratory, drop-in arts studio and music, dance and lit workshops; spend a few hours chasing your miniature genius around, and then refuel afterwards at the cafe or picnic areas overlooking the bay.

Cable Car Museum ☺ | 20 | 23 | 18 | 17 | $0 |
1201 Mason St. (Washington St.); 415-474-1887;
www.cablecarmuseum.com
☑ "If your children (including the one you're married to) are interested in trains and trolleys", a "quick stop" of "not more than 30 minutes" at this "charming museum" reveals "the inner workings" and "history of the city's most famous transportation system"; the "cable spooling" around the "large spinning wheels is a sight to behold", and "best of all, it's free" – that is, except for the "gift shop's great array of souvenirs"; PS. for the full experience, "hop aboard a cable car" to get there.

Cartoon Art Museum ☺ | 18 | 24 | 17 | 18 | I |
655 Mission St. (bet. New Montgomery & 3rd Sts.); 415-227-8666;
www.cartoonart.org
■ "If you're into cartoon art, you'll be in heaven" at "this tiny" but "great museum" featuring an eclectic comics collection that's "all over the map, from R. Crumb to Charlie Schultz" (whose endowment helped established its residence near SoMa's Yerba Buena Gardens);

although it's "a little off the beaten path", it's "fun", "informative and insightful" "for all ages" ("check the appropriateness of the current exhibit" as there could be "too many politically based" artworks for young children).

Chabot Space & Science Center ☺ | 25 | 24 | 24 | 21 | M |
10000 Skyline Blvd. (Joaquin Miller Rd.), Oakland; 510-336-7300; www.chabotspace.org

■ "Space rules" at Oakland's "excellent planetarium"/"cosmic" museum, a "universe" of "scientific" "amusement" that even your teenagers will enjoy; like the Red Planet in the Mars Encounter, it's "tricky getting there", but it's "worth the trip over the Bay Bridge" "to view the wonders of the sky" while your tots "play in the Discovery Room"; the "IMAX is [locals'] reason for repeat visits", but even if you don't spring for the mega-movie's extra fee, it's "the place to be during meteor showers" on weekend nights when exhibits are closed since a "look through the huge telescopes" is free.

Coit Tower ☺ | 15 | 23 | 14 | 12 | I |
1 Telegraph Hill Blvd. (Kerney St.); 415-362-0808; www.coittower.org

☑ "On a clear day" "you can see forever" from this "landmark" tower perched at the "top of Telegraph Hill"; "if you need to wear out the kids", "huff up the hill" on the "beautiful garden-lined steps", or simply catch the "bus that takes you right to it", avoiding the "nightmare parking"; either way, "you'll be rewarded" with "spectacular WPA murals" inside and "fantastic" "bird's-eye" "views of the city and the bay" outside; there's "not much to entertain children", but they'll "enjoy the elevator ride" to the observation deck.

Crissy Field ☺ | 22 | 24 | 21 | 17 | $0 |
Presidio, N. of Mason St.; 415-561-7690; www.crissyfield.org

■ "Bundle up" and "recharge the batteries" with an "afternoon" picnic at "San Francisco's newest natural recreation area" in the Presidio; it's a "fantastic bayside" park with "restored wetlands" and room for "runners, walkers", bikers, "strollers and dogs" "to roam", "fly kites", "ogle sailboats in the Marina" and "turbo-fast windsurfers" or "build sand castles" at the "wading beach", with "the Golden Gate Bridge so close, you can almost touch it"; the Crissy Field Center runs ecologically oriented programs and a healthy cafe/bookstore that's open Wednesday–Sunday.

Exploratorium ☺ | 29 | 25 | 24 | 22 | M |
Palace of Fine Arts, 3601 Lyon St. (Jefferson St.); 415-561-0360; www.exploratorium.edu

■ "Children won't even know they're learning" while pawing the "overwhelming display of hands-on activities" at the Palace of Fine Arts' "funky" but "amazing" science museum, garnering SF's highest rating for Child Appeal in this *Survey*; from "the ever-popular cow's-eye dissection" to the Tactile Dome (a reserve-ahead, extra-fee "maze of rooms and tunnels" "for crawling around in the dark and feeling for stuff"), it "turns kids into thinkers and adults into kids"; it's "a bit overstimulating for the very young", but pack snacks and bring your "older ones" for "at least half a day."

Fisherman's Wharf ☺ | 20 | 21 | 17 | 16 | $0 |
Embarcadero St. (bet. Ghirardelli Square & Pier 39); 415-956-3493; www.fishermanswharf.org

☑ Once a working waterfront, this is "now SF's best-known tourist trap" with "overpriced seafood restaurants" and "tacky souvenir shops"; sure, there are "cool tall ships to board" here, but "the best part is the bit you don't pay for": street performers, "great Golden Gate views" and "barking sea lions on Pier 39", all enjoyed while

eating a "yummy" sourdough bowl of chowder and a "delicious" Ghirardelli Square ice cream sundae; P.S. it's also "the departure spot" for the boat to Alcatraz and the cable car.

Fort Point ☺

| 18 | 23 | 15 | 15 | $0 |

Long Ave. & Marine Dr. (Rte. 101); 415-556-1693; www.nps.gov/fopo

☑ "Let your imagination of the old army days run wild" "through narrow staircases, darkened nooks and viewing areas at the top" of this "cool" Civil War fort, open weekends "in a breathtaking setting under the Golden Gate, with water crashing against rocks"; "little ones" "may get bored", but take your "school-age kids", listen to "docents who love to tell tales", "be there when the cannon is fired" and "combine it with a walk across the Bridge" or to Fort Point Pier to "watch the windsurfers" – just "dress warmly."

GOLDEN GATE BRIDGE ☺

| 20 | 26 | 16 | 12 | I |

San Francisco Bay; 415-921-5858; www.goldengate.org

☑ "The most famous bridge in the world", the city's "iconic landmark" is an "engineering marvel" "must-see" for "any trip to SF"; older kids and adults "brave the winds" to "walk or bike across" for "goosebump"-inducing views ("when the fog's not obscuring them") and a visit to "quaint Sausalito" across the bay; easier, especially with "little children": "drive it" and "snap" the "mandatory vacation photo" from parking lots at either end, as "the narrow walkway" "with cars racing by" is "colder", "louder and longer than you think."

Golden Gate Park

| 24 | 26 | 20 | 16 | $0 |

bordered by Fulton St., Great Hwy., Lincoln Way & Stanyan St.; 415-831-2700; www.parks.sfgov.org

■ "You could spend days" at this "mammoth" park stretching "from the Haight to the Pacific" and brimming with "any activity" imaginable: "visit the buffalo", "take a boat trip on Stow Lake, view the museums, look at the windmill, go horseback riding, play bocce ball", ride the "fabulous, inexpensive antique carousel", romp at the "excellent playground", let your teens go biking, "expose younger kids to flowers more exotic than the dandelions in your backyard" at the botanical gardens and let them "burn off energy" amid "meadows, woods" and "ocean beaches"; just "be sure to enter with a good map."

Japanese Tea Garden ☺

| 15 | 24 | 22 | 20 | I |

Golden Gate Park, Martin Luther King Jr. Dr. (off 9th Ave.); 415-752-4227

☑ "Magnificent gardens" and a "delightful Japanese tea house" "overlooking" a waterfall make this "small" yet "lovely" "oasis in Golden Gate Park" a place for parents to "soak in" the Zen "ambiance", particularly during early spring "cherry blossom season"; however, "kids old enough to scamper" across the "not-for-strollers" terrain "will be enchanted" "winding around the narrow paths" past pagodas and koi ponds and "climbing the round wishing bridge"; though the "snacks may be unusual" for them, they'll also enjoy a "tea party" "served by women in traditional attire."

Lawrence Hall of Science ☺

| 25 | 23 | 23 | 20 | I |

1 Centennial Dr. (Bancroft Way), Berkeley; 510-642-5132; www.lawrencehallofscience.org

☑ "Unquestionably the best view of the Bay Area you can find while perched atop a fiberglass whale" awaits at this modest museum and planetarium in the Berkeley hills that offers "science displays and hands-on activities tailored to interest kids and adults" alike, including a "fun exhibit on earthquakes"; the adjacent Outdoor Science Park is "great on sunny days", but there's a "somewhat limited number of things to see" and it's "not near anything else", so families short on time find it "not worth the drive" from the city.

Metreon

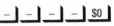

101 Fourth St. (Mission St.); 415-369-6000; www.metreon.com
Sony's entertainment juggernaut next to Yerba Buena Gardens offers hours of indoor fun for all ages; adults shop till they drop and catch flicks on 15 screens; older kids flock to the IMAX, the state-of-the-art arcade Portal One and the Action Theatre showing Japan-style animated features, while tots go nuts over _Where the Wild Things Are_, a Maurice Sendak–inspired interactive exhibit (open Friday–Monday only); the ethnically diverse food court dishes up enjoyable edibles for every appetite; N.B. entering the mall itself is free, but attractions cost extra.

Muir Woods National Monument

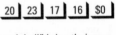

Hwy. 101 (Hwy.1/Muir Woods exit), Mill Valley; 415-388-2595; www.nps.gov/muwo
■ "Wow, Daddy – big trees"; even a toddler appreciates the "magnificence" of the "towering", ancient redwoods in this "mystical" grove over the Golden Gate Bridge; the "self-guided" "main trail is paved, flat and easy" for a "multigenerational one-to two-hour hike" amid "tiny ferns and miniature flowers under a monster, virgin canopy", while a "full day's" trek will "take you to the sea"; "putting short-lived human history in perspective", the "majestic" "giants" are particularly "humbling" once you realize that protected specimens like these might be "the only ones standing in the 22nd century."

Musée Mécanique ☺

Pier 45 (end of Taylor St.); 415-346-2000
■ "Baby boomers" "nostalgic" for "ancient pinball" bring their own babies to bang on a "one-of-a-kind collection of coin-operated vintage amusements from the early 20th century" on through Atari at this "whimsical", "old-time arcade" that's been relocated to Pier 45 in Fisherman's Wharf; admission is free, but you and your "fascinated kid" will feed "rolls of quarters" into "favorites" from "old penny movies", "fortune teller mannequins and test-your-grip machines" "taken from carnivals and boardwalks" to "video games à la Pac-Man" – it's a "kick-ass" "blast from the past."

Palace of Fine Arts ☺

3301 Lyon St. (Bay St.); 415-750-3600
☑ After glimpsing the future at the Exploratorium, you can "step back in time" at the adjacent "architecturally gorgeous" replica of Bernard Maybeck's faux "ancient ruins", a structure built for the 1915 Pan-American International Exposition; incorporating a theater but no actual art, the "stunning" lakeside colonnade and rotunda make for a "romantic stroll" for mom and dad, but since it's "one of San Francisco's most picturesque places" it's "cluttered with wedding photographers", "swans and ducks" – "kids may be amused" feeding the fowl, but "it's difficult to picnic" amid "blowing bridal gowns" and "molted feathers."

Randall Museum

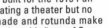

Corona Hts. Park, 199 Museum Way (Roosevelt Way); 415-554-9600; www.randallmuseum.org
Perched on a hilltop in Corona Heights Park with spectacular skyline views, this small kids' museum brims with free activities; in addition to hosting educational exhibits, performances and visiting programs such as Bug Day, it's home to more than 50 species of rescued wildlife available for pawing; pony up $5 to bring your kid on a Saturday when special arts and science workshops are going full force, and track down the Golden Gate Model Railroad Club's trains, rounding the bend in the basement.

San Francisco Museum of Modern Art ☺ (aka SFMoMA)

| 12 | 27 | 27 | 22 | M |

151 Third St. (bet. Howard & Mission Sts); 415-357-4000; www.sfmoma.org

◩ "A good place to introduce" "budding artists" to modern works is this "fantastically lit, striped granite" museum "housing a diverse permanent collection" and "outstanding traveling exhibits"; "there's always something to spark the mind", including "interactive" stuff, and the top-floor "see-through catwalk by itself makes a visit worthwhile", as do the "excellent cafeteria" and "cool gift shop"; "older kids, especially teens, are more often interested" in its Warhols and Beardens, but if "bored" little ones are "tagging along", at least it's "across the street" from "other Yerba Buena Gardens attractions."

San Francisco Zoo ☺

| 28 | 23 | 20 | 19 | I |

1 Zoo Rd. (Skyline Blvd.); 415-753-7080; www.sfzoo.org

◩ "Bring a sweater, pack a picnic and you're set" for a "half day" at SF's "evolving" zoo where the critters "jump up and down for you", "as the location near the ocean provides a cool climate" to keep them "animated"; "recent and upcoming improvements" include the "(literally) howling good" Lemur Forest and "the new African Savanna, due to open in spring 2004", and as the "engaging staff" will tell you, "don't miss the wildcat feeding" at 2 PM, the "little puffer train", the restored "wooden carousel" or the "excellent" children's petting area.

SBC PARK

| 26 | 28 | 28 | 22 | E |

24 Willie Mays Plaza (bet. 2nd & 3rd Sts.); 415-972-2000; www.sfgiants.com

■ "Keep your fingers crossed" for a "home run into McCovey Cove" at this "magical stadium" – this *Survey*'s top-rated ball park and the city's No. 1 attraction – where the "captivating" bay setting makes the national pastime "even more fun to watch"; contrary to expectations, it's not just for games, since kids "enjoy the huge Coke-bottle slide", "softball on the mini-diamond" or having their photos made into a Giants baseball card, while parents relish "creative" eats including sushi, bratwurst, fish tacos and "world-famous garlic fries"; it may be "pricey and sometimes hard to get into" for a game or other event, but it's a great addition to a day of SF sightseeing, and you can "take a tour" if there's nothing specific scheduled.

Six Flags Marine World

| 28 | 21 | 20 | 17 | VE |

2001 Marine World Pkwy. (Broadway St.), Vallejo; 707-643-6722; www.sixflags.com

■ "Animal lovers and roller-coaster fanatics" mingle at this "SoCal-style amusement park in NoCal", 30 miles northeast of SF in Vallejo; "the emphasis has switched" recently from the roar of the wild to the roar of "looping rides", "changing the atmosphere from low-key family spot to teenage hangout", particularly on "crazy summer weekends"; still, it's "a blast" for everything from older kids' "thrill" machines and little contraptions "catering to toddlers" to feedable giraffes and "typical dolphin shows"; P.S. you'll "enjoy it more" if you zip here in the high-speed ferry from Fisherman's Wharf.

Tilden Regional Park

| 23 | 25 | 19 | 15 | $0 |

600 Canon Dr. (Grizzley Peak Blvd.), Berkeley; 510-525-2233; www.ebparks.org

■ Berkeley's "huge", "hidden" park with "breathtaking views" of the "whole Bay Area" is "scattered" with "treasures", including a demonstration farm where children can pet and feed animals, a pony ride, a "lovingly restored carousel and steam trains", "magnificent botanical gardens" chock-full of Californian flora, a "nice lake for swimming", a "gorgeous public golf course", "miles of easy-to-medium hiking trails" in the redwoods and "picnic areas everywhere"; if one of your brood is four-legged, don't "dare let Rover roam", as the "patrol is quick to hand out tickets" for the leash-less.

USS Pampanito ☺

| 24 | 25 | 19 | 19 | I |

Pier 45 (The Embarcadero); 415-775-1943; www.maritime.org
■ "For WWII buffs, no trip to SF is complete unless you step foot on" this "cool submarine" museum, a restored Navy ship set "in the water" at Fisherman's Wharf; while its "cramped" quarters are "not for claustrophobes" or "little kids", "preteens and up enjoy" "rocking the vessel" on a "fascinating", "self-guided tour" illuminating "the workings" of a "Balao-class" vessel and the city's "marine history."

Yerba Buena Gardens

| 18 | 22 | 20 | 15 | $0 |

Third St. (bet. Folsom & Market Sts.); 415-247-6500; www.yerbabuena.org
■ "There's something for everyone" around this "lovely oasis" near SFMoMA: a "great playground" and "antique carousel", a "bowling alley and ice-skating rink", Metreon and the interactive Zeum and Yerba Buena Museum for "cutting-edge theater, dance" and art; there are "several eating places" too, so get "take-out lunch" and scope the "passersby", the "Japanese men and women doing their stretches" and the "birds bathing" by the "MLK memorial waterfall" in this "beautiful place to daydream" "in the middle of the city."

HOTELS

Ratings: Family Appeal, Rooms, Service, Public Facilities, Cost

FA	R	S	P	$
▽ 20	22	22	22	$269

Argonaut Hotel-Fisherman's Wharf

495 Jefferson St.; 415-563-0800; 866-415-2800; www.argonauthotel.com; 239 rooms, 13 suites
■ With "one of the best locations for a family in San Fran", this nautical-themed Kimpton hotel in a 1907 building draws hip parents who appreciate the high design and views of the Golden Gate Bridge, San Francisco Bay and Coit Tower; "even though the hotel is somewhat adult-oriented", tot-toting types trill "yippee – it's on flat ground and easy to push a stroller when you venture outside"; the "excellent staff" helps ease any trip and it's close to Fisherman's Wharf, the boat to Alcatraz and the Exploratorium.

Claremont Resort

| 19 | 19 | 21 | 23 | $280 |

41 Tunnel Rd., Berkeley; 510-843-3000; 800-551-7266; www.claremontresort.com; 279 rooms, 10 suites
◩ The "family will find plenty of activities to keep them busy" at this Berkeley property with "awesome views" of the water, a kids' program, a "beautiful pool" and room-service options for children; it's "a little inconvenient for visiting the city", but it's a "good jumping-off point for trips to Yosemite" and adults can indulge in "expensive spa treatments."

Four Seasons San Francisco

| 19 | 27 | 28 | 28 | $469 |

757 Market St.; 415-633-3000; 800-332-3442; www.fourseasons.com; 231 rooms, 46 suites
◩ The "amazing service" at this "magnificent" property "well located for shopping in Union Square" includes "knowing your children's names" and providing full-size cribs, diapers, baby shampoo and anything else you might need; "the beds are so comfortable you'll want to sleep a little longer" before taking a few minutes' walk to Yerba Buena Gardens and the Cartoon Art Museum; while a couple of critics carp "this is not the place to bring boisterous children", others reply "you can always count" on Four Seasons to treat everyone right.

Holiday Inn Vallejo

| – | – | – | – | $159 |

1000 Fairgrounds Dr., Vallejo; 707-644-1200; 800-465-4329;
www.holiday-inn.com; 168 rooms, 2 suites
If you want to avoid the 30-mile drive back to San Francisco after a
visit to Six Flags Marine World, you can head to the park's official
hotel just across the street, where they're prepared for families with
a pet-friendly policy, cribs, laundry facilities, an on-site restaurant
open for breakfast and dinner, an outdoor heated pool and, at certain
times, discounts to the park; completely remodeled a few years ago,
it's 10 minutes from the Napa Valley wine country and there's a ferry
directly to San Francisco.

Hotel del Sol

| – | – | – | – | $159 |

3100 Webster St.; 415-921-5520; 877-433-5765; www.thehoteldelsol.com;
47 rooms, 10 suites
In the heart of the Marina District, this affordable boutique spot
features California beach-house decor with bright, cheerful colors,
and offers complimentary daily coffee and continental breakfast
poolside as well as free kites, beach balls and sunglasses for kids;
children under 12 years old stay free, and it's a short walk to the
Golden Gate Bridge and Fort Point.

Hyatt Regency

| 18 | 19 | 19 | 22 | $169 |

5 Embarcadero Ctr.; 415-788-1234; 800-233-1234; www.hyatt.com;
760 rooms, 45 suites
☑ With an ideal location "right in the center of everything" on the
Embarcadero waterfront within five minutes of Fisherman's Wharf,
this chain outpost is "close to many kid-friendly attractions"; pay
extra for the rooms with "wonderful views" of the Bay Bridge and let
children enjoy the glass elevators all the way up; the "hotel itself is
just ok" say discriminating types, and the "food and beverages are
not so great", but there are plenty of eateries nearby.

Ritz-Carlton, The

| 19 | 27 | 28 | 25 | $360 |

600 Stockton St.; 415-296-7465; 800-241-3333; www.ritzcarlton.com;
294 rooms, 100 suites, 42 suites
☑ The "hike up the hill may be a bit much for kids" headed for this
luxury outpost atop Nob Hill, but "the rooms are perfect for a family
of four" and the Ritz Kids program keeps the tots busy for hours on end;
"superb service" from a "friendly and accommodating staff" means
"they'll even print out a list of children's activities taking place in
the city during your stay", and you can hop onto the cable car across
the street for easy transport; a few admit the "formal environment"
is a "little stuffy", but nannies who come along sure "feel welcome"
with their own 'Survival Kits.'

Westin St. Francis, The

| 20 | 21 | 23 | 22 | $409 |

335 Powell St.; 415-397-7000; 888-625-5144; www.westin.com;
1130 rooms, 65 suites
☑ You'll feel like you're in "the nerve center of the city" at this "old
favorite" "in the middle of Union Square" where the "great fancy non-
alcoholic drinks in the lobby" and the "glass elevators with fabulous
views" make it "a really good spot for children"; while some say it's
"too adult-oriented" with all the major conventions going on and the
lack of a pool, others disagree, citing all the usual Westin Kids–program
amenities and a location that "can't be beat."

Top Family-Friendly Hotel Chains in the Area:

Embassy Suites	Marriott
Hampton Inn	Residence Inn
Homewood Suites	

See Hotel Chain reviews, starting on page 256.

RESTAURANTS

Ratings: Family Appeal, Food, Decor, Service, Cost

	FA	F	D	S	$

Alioto's
| | 19 | 18 | 19 | 19 | E |

8 Fisherman's Wharf (bet. Jefferson & Taylor Sts.); 415-673-0183; www.aliotos.com

☑ "Kids seem to love" the Sicilian food at this Fisherman's Wharf Italian with a "great" waterfront location and Bay views; though fusspots look past the fresh seafood and call it a "tourist trap" that's "fake, fake, fake", others find a "reasonably priced" place to "watch the fog come in."

A. Sabella's
| | 19 | 21 | 20 | 21 | E |

2766 Taylor St. (Jefferson St.); 415-771-6775; www.asabellas.com

■ Still owned by the original family's descendants, this 83-year-old Fisherman's Wharf "classic" has "*Jetsons*-like light fixtures that fascinate children" and "great crab" and other seafood that's "enjoyable" for adults; hometowners may howl that it's "very touristy with prices to match", but visitors appreciate "attentive" service and the kind of "straightforward food" that kids can love – oh, and it's got "a nice view" too.

Barney's Gourmet Hamburger
| | 25 | 22 | 14 | 17 | I |

3344 Steiner St. (bet. Chestnut & Lombard Sts.); 415-563-0307
4138 24th St. (Castro St.); 415-282-7770
1600 Shattuck Ave. (Cedar St.), Berkeley; 510-849-2827
1591 Solano Ave. (Ordway St.), Berkeley; 510-526-8185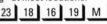
www.barneyshamburgers.com

☑ "Awesome burgers" (from "standard to California-esque" to "avec or sans meat") are the calling cards of this "well-priced" Bay Area chainlet; though service can be "erratic", this "tried-and-true favorite" compensates with "crayons and puzzle place mats" to "distract the kids" as well as "nice outdoor patio seating" at most locations.

Capp's Corner
| | 23 | 18 | 16 | 19 | M |

1600 Powell St. (Green St.); 415-989-2589; www.cappscorner.com

■ Harkening back to "another era", this "down-home", longtime North Beach Italian has remained popular thanks to a "huge, family-style" menu of Italian-American classics and "friendly waiters"; although the "funky" decor ("mostly autographs and black-and-white photos of the famous who have dined here") will be "lost on the kids", this "fun original" is "well located" near many San Francisco tourist attractions, including Fisherman's Wharf.

Fog City Diner
| | – | – | – | – | E |

1300 Battery St. (The Embarcadero); 415-982-2000; www.fogcitydiner.com

"Don't let the diner tag" or art deco "railway car" exterior "fool you" – you're more apt to order a Bloody Mary than a beer at this perpetually packed, "upscale" Embarcadero eatery that, to many a child's delight, specializes in Americana dining, albeit with a "gourmet" twist ("macaroni and Gouda cheese"); even if sometimes the "servers are in a fog" from waiting on so many tourists, the place remains a real San Francisco "treat."

Isobune
| | – | – | – | – | M |

Kintetsu Shopping Ctr., 1737 Post St. (bet. Laguna & Webster Sts.); 415-563-1030

Renowned for its circular sushi bar ringed by a narrow moat, this inexpensive Nipponese sequestered in the Japantown shopping center keeps kids (and adults) transfixed as tiny boats bearing the fresh fish float by for your inspection; sure, there may be fresher, fancier fish elsewhere, but noveltywise, this one's hard to beat.

Mama's on Washington Square ⊭ | 24 | 26 | 18 | 20 | M |

1701 Stockton St. (Filbert St.); 415-362-6421

◪ "Amazing breakfasts" "for all ages" at "budget" tabs add up to "big crowds" at this North Beach coffee shop/bakery located just off Washington Square; the "only downside" if you have children in tow – "long weekend waits" – leads experienced parents to suggest "tag-teaming" it: "one adult stands in line while the other watches the kids run around in the park" nearby.

Max's | – | – | – | – | M |

1 California St. (Market St.); 415-781-6297 ⊠
311 Third St. (Folsom St.); 415-546-6297
Union Sq., 398 Geary St. (Mason St.); 415-646-8600
601 Van Ness Ave. (Golden Gate Ave.); 415-771-7301
www.maxsworld.com

Big is beautiful at this mini-empire of Bay Area diners famed for their groaning portions of respectable New York–style deli fare along the lines of towering pastrami sandwiches, gargantuan chocolate malts and Coney Island–size slices of cheesecake; it's moderately priced, but the fanatically frugal can easily share entrées or opt for half portions when ordering for smaller tykes; N.B. the waiters belt out opera and show tunes between courses at the Opera Cafe locations.

Mel's Drive-In ◗ | 26 | 16 | 19 | 17 | M |

3355 Geary Blvd. (bet. Beaumont & Parker Aves.); 415-387-2255
2165 Lombard St. (Steiner St.); 415-921-2867
801 Mission St. (4th St.); 415-227-4477
Richelieu Hotel, 1050 Van Ness Ave. (Geary St.); 415-292-6357
www.melsdrive-in.com

◪ Small fry have "fun, fun, fun" at these "bustling", "reinvented drive-ins", a salute to "nuclear family dining in the '50s" complete with jukeboxes at each table and "nothing too daring on the menu"; they're "great for kids because they're already noisy" (with "meal boxes shaped like cars to please the under-10" set), though some oldsters complain about "uneven" food and "not much service."

Mo's | ▽ 21 | 23 | 14 | 15 | I |

1322 Grant Ave. (bet. Green & Vallejo Sts.); 415-788-3779
Yerba Buena Gardens, 772 Folsom St. (bet. 3rd & 4th Sts.);
415-957-3779

▮ This "excellent" pair of patty providers are contenders for the title of "best burger in San Francisco", with locations that are both family destinations: the South of Market outpost boasts proximity to Moscone Center and the Yerba Buena Gardens, while the North Beach branch gives you an inside look at how they "cook on lava grills."

Pasta Pomodoro | 22 | 18 | 15 | 18 | M |

2304 Market St. (16th St.); 415-558-8123
1865 Post St. (Fillmore St.); 415-674-1826
655 Union St. (Columbus Ave.); 415-399-0300
1875 Union St. (Laguna St.); 415-771-7900
www.pastapomodoro.com

◪ "Families on a budget" looking for something "quick and easy" ask "what's not to love?" about this "efficient", "reliable" Italian chain known for "dependability"; though foodies say it's a "hit-or-miss" affair that's "not what you come to San Francisco to experience", at least there's "enough noise to make your kids blend in" and "there's always a pasta the children will like" – in short, it "gets the job done."

Savor | 23 | 24 | 21 | 21 | M |
3913 24th St. (bet. Noe & Sanchez Sts.); 415-282-0344
■ Although it "doesn't scream 'bring your kids'", this attractive Mediterranean restaurant in residential Noe Valley does accommodate little ones while still appealing to adults with its combination of "awesome breakfasts", "wonderful crêpes" and a "fun neighborhood" to explore afterwards; in addition, "service is kind" and the atmosphere is "comfortable", and "if you have a kid who likes to run around, request a table outside."

Scoma's | 19 | 21 | 19 | 20 | E |
Pier 47, 1 Al Scoma Way (bet. Jefferson & Jones Sts.); 415-771-4383; www.scomas.com
588 Bridgeway (Princess St.), Sausalito; 415-332-9551; www.scomassausalito.com
☑ "So what if it's touristy?" ask unapologetic fans of these "good ol' classic" fish houses where "long waits" are rewarded with "simply prepared seafood" that even kids will like (plus adults love the "stunning views" of the Bay at the Pierside locale); sure, it's an "institution" say those not so satisfied, but "unfortunately most institutions aren't known for their exceptional food."

RESTAURANT CHAINS

See reviews, starting on page 262.

Ratings: Family Appeal, Food, Decor, Service, Cost

	FA	F	D	S	$
Baja Fresh Mexican Grill	20	22	14	18	I

30 Fremont St. (bet. Market & Mission Sts.); 415-369-9760 ☒
2237 Shattuck Ave. (Kittredge St.), Berkeley; 510-548-4444

Benihana	23	20	18	22	E

1737 Post St. (Webster St.); 415-563-4844

Bubba Gump Shrimp Co.	24	18	23	20	M

Pier 39 (The Embarcadero); 415-781-4867

Buca di Beppo	24	19	22	21	M

855 Howard St. (bet. 4th & 5th Sts.); 415-543-7673

Cheesecake Factory ☒	21	23	21	20	M

Macy's, 251 Geary St., 8th fl. (bet. Powell & Stockton Sts.); 415-391-4444

Chevys Fresh Mex	23	19	18	18	M

2 Embarcadero Ctr. (bet. Davis & Front Sts.); 415-391-2323
201 Third St. (Howard St.); 415-543-8060
Stonestown Galleria, 3251 20th Ave. (bet. Buckingham Way & Winston Dr.); 415-665-8705
590 Van Ness Ave. (Golden Gate Ave.); 415-621-8200

Fuddrucker's ☒	24	20	15	16	I

685 Beach St. (Hyde St.); 415-351-0125

In-N-Out Burger ⌿	24	24	13	21	I

333 Jefferson St. (bet. Jones & Leavenworth Sts.); 800-786-1000

Joe's Crab Shack	23	17	21	19	M

245 Jefferson St. (bet. Jones & Taylor Sts.); 415-673-2266

Johnny Rockets | 25 | 17 | 20 | 18 | I
2201 Chestnut St. (Pierce St.); 415-931-6258
1946 Fillmore St. (Pine St.); 415-776-9878
Fisherman's Wharf, 81 Jefferson St. (Mason St.); 415-693-9120

Old Spaghetti Factory, The | 25 | 20 | 22 | 20 | I
Jack London Sq., 62 Webster St. (Embarcadero), Oakland; 510-893-0222

Olive Garden ⊠ | 20 | 19 | 18 | 19 | M
Stonestown Galleria, 3251 20th Ave. (bet. Buckingham Way &
Winston Dr.); 415-661-6770

Outback Steakhouse | 20 | 22 | 18 | 20 | M
196 Donahue St. (Drake Ave.), Sausalito; 415-331-6193

Rainforest Cafe | 27 | 16 | 27 | 18 | M
Wax Museum Bldg., 145 Jefferson St. (bet. Mason & Taylor Sts.); 415-440-5610

T.G.I. Friday's ⊠ | 21 | 17 | 18 | 17 | M
450 Water St. (Broadway), Oakland; 510-451-3834

Tony Roma's ⊠ | 20 | 21 | 16 | 19 | M
2 Embarcadero Ctr. (bet. Davis & Sacramento Sts.); 415-374-2733
Jack London Sq., 55 Washington St. (Water St.), Oakland; 510-271-1818

Uno Chicago Grill | 20 | 18 | 15 | 16 | M
2200 Lombard St. (Steiner St.); 415-563-3144
Jack London Sq., 499 Embarcadero W. (bet. Broadway & Washington St.),
Oakland; 510-251-8667⊠

Seattle

They call Seattle the Emerald City, a tribute to the deep green and blue
of its forest-mountain-sea scenery (the product of 36 inches of annual
rainfall). Ferryboats ply the waters, taking commuters and visitors to
islands dotting the Puget Sound. The heart of this laid-back town
offers a wide range of museums – from Northwest culture to rock 'n'
roll – as well as the state-of-the-art ballpark Safeco Field, the iconic
Space Needle from the 1962 World's Fair, phenomenal aeronautical
displays at the Museum of Flight, tasty treats at Pike Place Market
and, of course, plenty of coffee (Starbucks originated here). Seattle's
two other great companies are Boeing and Microsoft; you can tour
the former's factory in Everett. There's a mass transit Metro bus
system (the best bet for visitors is the $5-per-day unlimited pass), but
if you hoof it, beware: Jaywalkers often get tickets. Try to make time
to rent a car and explore the old-growth trees and other features of
vast Olympic National Park on the Washington peninsula, one of the
nation's few temperate-climate rain forests.

ATTRACTIONS

Ratings: Child Appeal, Adult Appeal, Public Facilities, Service, Cost

	C	A	P	S	$
Burke Museum ☺	▽ 19	23	22	21	I

Univ. of Washington, NE 45th St. (17th Ave.); 206-543-5590;
www.washington.edu/burkemuseum
■ Older kids and adults are charmed by this "small gem of a museum"
on the University of Washington campus with "excellent regional

Native American artifacts" such as totem poles, volcanoes, dinosaurs and other exhibits with "links to the Northwest's" natural history and culture, plus "first-class visiting exhibitions"; the first-floor cafe, a "favorite student hangout", serves sandwiches, salads and pastries, along with coffee in many forms, natch; N.B. free admission on the first Thursday of the month.

Children's Museum, The ☺☺

| 28 | 19 | 23 | 21 | I |

Seattle Ctr., 305 Harrison St. (5th Ave.); 206-441-1768;
www.thechildrensmuseum.org

■ Experts explain you can expect "good imaginative fun" thanks to the "excellent technology, ecology and cultural exhibits" plus "rotating art projects" on display at this Seattle Center museum; there's "lots to do and redo", and it's all "easy to manage in an afternoon", so it's a "fantastic" "hit" with preschoolers and "can't be beat for toddlers"; the Discovery Bay area in particular – a terrific "space for tiny tots" to enjoy hands-on nautical pastimes – "should not be missed."

Chittenden Locks

| 21 | 24 | 16 | 15 | $0 |

(aka Ballard Locks)
3015 NW 54th St. (32nd Ave.); 206-783-7059;
www.nws.usace.army.mil/opdiv/lwsc

■ "How perfectly maritime", observe onlookers of the "nautical activity" and wildlife at this "fascinating" destination seven miles from downtown; families can"spread a blanket on the hill and watch" the "pleasure craft and working boats" "move between Puget Sound and Lake Union" via the locks (like "a visit to the Panama Canal, without the expense"), and if you "go between July and September" you can see migratory salmon ("twice the size of the toddler next to you") "jumping up the fish ladder" – "enormous fun."

Experience Music Project

| 19 | 25 | 25 | 22 | E |

325 Fifth Ave. N. (Broad St.); 206-367-5483; www.emplive.com

■ "The wanna-be rock star or any serious fan" will groove on this Seattle Center "interactive monument" to twanging guitars and danceable backbeats, perhaps the best place in town for your teens; anchored by an "excellent" exhibit on "hometown boy Jimi Hendrix" and full of "fascinating" "'60s and '70s memorabilia", it appeals to adults – "whether brought up on blues, the British Invasion or grunge" – and is also "wonderful" "for kids eight and up" who can "have their own jam session" or "sing in a studio"; there's discord over Frank Gehry's "sculptural building", though – is it a "psychedelic" "masterpiece" or "hideously ugly?"

Klondike Gold Rush
National Historic Park

| 17 | 23 | 20 | 22 | $0 |

117 S. Main St. (1st Ave.); 206-553-7220; www.nps.gov/klse

■ This "tiny park is really" an "educational" "pocket museum" in the Pioneer Square area; it offers a "child's first look at the Alaska Gold Rush" with "fun old photos and a pool to pan for gold" as well as a Junior Ranger program for kids six to 12; the "great" rangers are "full of interesting stories" that give a "glimpse of Seattle's wild heritage" and help you understand how this land stampede "put the city on the map."

Marymoor Park

| 21 | 23 | 19 | 14 | $0 |

6046 W. Lake Sammamish Pkwy. NE (Marymoor Way), Redmond;
206-205-8751; 800-325-6165 ext. 53661; www.metrokc.gov/parks

■ A "fantastic" one-square-mile "family park", this is the "best place on the east side to burn off Fido's, the kids' and your energy", with its "wide-open places to run, hike and bike", a "nice playground" (with rocking dinosaur), 45-ft. "climbing rock" and 40 "excellent" acres where you can "let your dog run off-leash"; watch "cycle races in the velodrome" and folks "flying radio-controlled model planes" or take in an "awesome summer concert series"; P.S. it's "near the Red Hook Brewery" (minors allowed).

Monorail ☺

23	18	16	16	I

Seattle Ctr. to Westlake Ctr. (across from Space Needle); 206-905-2600; www.seattlemonorail.com

☑ "See the city from a different vantage point" on this "landmark" from the 1962 World's Fair, a "quiet" yet "zippy trip" "connecting the Seattle Center (Space Needle) to downtown (Westlake Center)" and zooming right "through the EMP"; "the younger you are, the cooler it is" – which means it's "always fun for the kids", who "love flying above all that traffic" ("a friendly driver" may even "let them honk the horn"); seen-it-alls shrug the one-mile, two-minute ride is "nothing to get excited about" ("overrated", "pointless" and "too short").

Museum of Flight ☺

24	26	24	22	M

9404 E. Marginal Way S. (94th Pl.); 206-764-5720; www.museumofflight.org

■ "Cooooooollll" coo aviation aficionados who affirm this "world-class" collection of "modern and vintage aircraft" "next to King County Airport" is "on a par with the Smithsonian"; "plan several hours" so you can "see planes take off and land", "tour a decommissioned Concorde", "sit in a couple of cockpits" or try a "fun flight simulator"; school-age kids can be pilots or air-traffic controllers in the Flight Zone, do "hands-on craft projects" and ramble through the Red Barn, the "original Boeing building", and teenagers get a charge too, but "the very young probably won't last long here."

Olympic National Park

22	28	21	19	I

3002 Mt. Angeles Rd. (Heart o' the Hills Rd.), Port Angeles; 360-452-4501; www.nps.gov/olym

■ It's "a bit of a drive" (about three hours from Seattle) but "spectacular ocean and mountain scenery" await at this "vast", "gorgeous" wilderness, a "jewel of nature" that "offers endless exploring opportunities for everyone from the novice to the experienced adventurer"; "Hurricane Ridge on a clear day" yields "breathtaking views", Lake Crescent is "splendid", the Hoh Rain Forest is a "primeval, amazing place" and there are "whales, marmots, deer" and glaciers to boot; at the "great visitors' centers", youngsters can take part in a variety of educational programs and activities.

Pacific Science Center

29	25	24	23	M

Seattle Ctr., 200 Second Ave. N. (John St.); 206-443-2001; www.pacsci.org

■ "A winner for the whole family" and voted this *Survey*'s No. 1 for Child Appeal in Seattle by surveyors, this "venerable" Seattle Center museum has "wide appeal" thanks to "excellent hands-on exhibits" that "keep all ages entertained all day": "dig with heavy machinery, pull the pulleys, make huge bubbles"; "fabulous" "old favorites" include the "beautiful butterfly house" ("a spring/summer fix in the winter"), a "don't-miss IMAX" and the "great toddler area" at Kids Works, while "ever-changing" special exhibits make it "fun to come back over and over again"; N.B. there are weather-protected tables for brown-baggers.

Pike Place Market

17	26	19	20	$0

Pike Pl. (bet. Pike & Virginia Sts.); 206-682-7453; www.pikeplacemarket.org

■ "Locals and tourists alike flock" to this "stimulating" "shopping mecca", a "quintessential Seattle experience" with "hustle, bustle", "gorgeous flowers", "salmon-tossing" fishmongers, "local produce merchants" and "a variety of fun foods to sample", often at "unbeatable prices"; "grab a bag of hot mini donuts" and "visit the first Starbucks", then "spend all day wandering" through or just enjoy the "summer street performers" and "magnificent bay views"; practiced parents point out, though, that on crowded weekends there's "no room for strollers" and young children "might be bored."

SAFECO FIELD ☺☺

| 24 | 28 | 28 | 23 | E |

1250 First Ave. S. (Bet. Atlantic St. & Royal Brougham Way); 206-346-4001; www.seattlemariners.com

■ Home to the Mariners since 1999, this "sparkling", "state-of-the-art" stadium, just south of downtown, boasts a "brilliant design", "wonderful city views" and a Puget Sound backdrop; expect "a wide selection of delicious food" (microbrews, espresso, garlic fries, hot dogs, even sushi), "a kids' [play] area", "bathrooms everywhere" and "not a bad seat in the house" – voted the city's No. 1 attraction in this *Survey,* it's considered by some "the most fan-friendly ballpark in the country"; "best of all", the "sliding roof guarantees" "no rainouts."

Seattle Aquarium

| 27 | 24 | 21 | 22 | M |

1483 Alaskan Way (off Rte. 99); 206-386-4320; www.seattleaquarium.org

☑ At this "great facility" "near the Pike Place Market", "kids of all ages will delight" in the "fish tanks, octopus, sea otters and hands-on tide pool exhibits"; fin fans favor its "easy-to-view" displays that are "part indoors, part outdoors – good for any weather", and say "it's small enough to not wear you out", with a "friendly and informative staff"; scourgers scold it's "uninspiring" and "could be better" for such a "fish-dependent city"; P.S. there's an IMAX theater next door, so "be sure to get the combo tickets."

Space Needle ☺☺

| 23 | 23 | 21 | 19 | I |

Seattle Ctr., 400 Broad St. (bet. Broad and John Sts.); 206-443-2111; 800-937-9582; www.spaceneedle.com

■ Another "leftover from the 1962 World's Fair", this "Seattle classic" provides a "perfect orientation to the city"; "kids will love the elevator ride up" 520 feet to the observation deck, with its "jaw-dropping" "360-degree view" ("wait for a clear day, if you've got that much time"); below, a "just plain cool" revolving restaurant serves "pricey but good food", and at the base an amusement park with "rides and cotton candy" awaits; wallet-watchers warn, however, that with the extra attractions here, it's "typically overpriced"; N.B. six-attraction discount tickets available.

Washington Park Arboretum

| 16 | 25 | 18 | 15 | $0 |

2300 Arboretum Dr. E. (Lake Washington Blvd.); 206-543-8800

■ It's just five miles from downtown, but this "jewel" of a park is nevertheless a "complete escape from the urban surroundings" of the Emerald City; its 230 "lovely" acres of "towering trees and flowering shrubs" make a "great place for a long walk" or a picnic "with the kids"; lovers of "azaleas and rhodies" suggest "see the blooms in April and May", but it's also a "beautiful place to wander in the fall" – and the formal "Japanese gardens are a must."

Woodland Park Zoo

| 29 | 26 | 24 | 22 | M |

(aka WPZ)

601 N. 59th St. (Evanston Ave.); 206-684-4800; www.zoo.org

■ "If I were an animal, that's where I'd want to live", say fauna fanciers of the "top-notch", "realistic habitats" at this "gem of a zoo" about five miles from downtown; be sure to "bring your walking shoes" and "push a stroller", because the "nicely laid-out" property is expansive ("it never feels crowded"), incorporating a "good family farm area for little kids" and "lots of open grassy spaces for picnics"; tipsters also tout the ZooTunes "summer family music concerts" on the North Meadow.

HOTELS

Ratings: Family Appeal, Rooms, Service, Public Facilities, Cost

	FA	R	S	P	$

Edgewater, The
	20	21	20	22	$270

Pier 67, 2411 Alaskan Way; 206-728-7000; 800-624-0670; www.edgewaterhotel.com; 230 rooms, 4 suites

☑ For a port-side feel, families head to this hotel with a "waterfront location that can't be beat", just a "quick walk to the Seattle Aquarium"; rooms have river-rock fireplaces and handcrafted pine furnishings, but make sure to "request one with a water view" since the vistas of Puget Sound and the Olympic Mountains are the highlight here; while a few feel it's a "bit of a walk" to other attractions, it's "worth the extra money" to watch the ships roll in and out; N.B. music fans will note that the Beatles stayed here 40 years ago.

Fairmont Olympic
	23	25	27	26	$355

411 University St.; 206-621-1700; 800-821-8106; www.fairmont.com; 234 rooms, 216 suites

☑ Parents are split over this former Four Seasons, a centrally located "grand old hotel" that still exudes a "formal atmosphere": some say "the pool is a real attraction" and their children "are treated like royalty", finding themselves "right at home" with "milk and chocolate chip cookies upon arrival", while others "can't see kids being happy" here since it's "geared toward business travelers."

Grand Hyatt Seattle
	17	26	23	26	$260

721 Pine St.; 206-774-1234; 800-223-1234; www.hyatt.com; 312 rooms, 113 suites

■ The "spacious rooms" with oversized bathrooms and a "child-friendly" Cheesecake Factory restaurant make this hotel a "fabulous" place to stay, and it doesn't hurt that FAO Schwarz toy store is across the street and Pike Place Market is within walking distance; not only is it generally "excellent for business travelers", it's also "highly recommended" for anyone who enjoys "quality service" and views of the Olympic and Cascade Mountains.

Inn at the Market
	▽ 17	24	23	19	$260

86 Pine St.; 206-443-3600; 800-446-4484; www.innatthemarket.com; 60 rooms, 10 suites

☑ It's all about location at this "quaint facility" that's "in the thick of things", cutting down on traveling hassles since you can "walk to everything" and it's "right at Pike Place Market"; there's a rooftop deck and a courtyard, and though it's "not particularly appealing for children", there are warm apple cider at the front desk, "great attached restaurants" and a "comfortable" vibe.

Westin Seattle, The
	20	23	22	23	$325

1900 Fifth Ave.; 206-728-1000; 888-625-5144; www.westin.com; 857 rooms, 34 suites

■ With "heavenly cribs – *real* cribs with bumpers and blankets", as well as proximity to the monorail, numerous restaurants and Pike Place, this Westin wins over parents "traveling with babies and toddlers"; there are such "fantastic views" of the lake and the sound, "topped only by the fabulous beds", that some "never want to leave" – though when they do they can "borrow a stroller for the duration" of their stay.

Top Family-Friendly Hotel Chains in the Area:

Embassy Suites	Hyatt
Hampton Inn	Marriott
Holiday Inn	Residence Inn
Homewood Suites	

See Hotel Chain reviews, starting on page 256.

RESTAURANTS

Ratings: Family Appeal, Food, Decor, Service, Cost

FA	F	D	S	$

Cafe Nola

–	–	–	–	M

101 Winslow Way E. (Madison Ave.), Bainbridge Island; 206-842-3822; www.cafenola.com
Boat-crazy little buoys and gulls will love the ferry ride to this "charming little cafe" in Winslow, possibly the "best on Bainbridge Island" thanks to its "innovative", "excellent" New American cuisine employing "fresh" local ingredients at "reasonable prices"; P.S. check out the "homestyle" weekend brunch, bound to appeal to all ages.

Cucina! Cucina!

25	19	19	21	M

901 Fairview Ave. N. (Eastlake & Mercer Sts.); 206-447-2782
Bellevue Pl., 800 Bellevue Way NE (8th St.), Bellevue; 425-637-1177
Redmond Town Ctr., 16499 NE 74th St. (Redmond Way), Redmond;
425-558-2200
www.cucinacucina.com
■ "Light, bright and family-friendly", this all-over-town Italian chain is "good for kids of all ages" thanks to a something-for-everyone philosophy: before dinner, "parents can sip Chianti" while youngsters get "pizza dough to play with", and everyone can "draw on the butcher-paper tablecloths with crayons" while perusing the "excellent variety" of dishes on the menu.

Elliott's Oyster House

22	25	21	24	E

1201 Alaskan Way (Seneca St.); 206-623-4340; www.elliottsoysterhouse.com
■ Great "views of the bustling waterfront" keep young folks entertained at this Elliott Bay seafooder with "great family appeal" derived from its friendly, calming setting as well as "service and food beyond expectations"; it may "look touristy" but locals are also lured in by the "very good fish" and fresh-shucked oysters.

Etta's Seafood

–	–	–	–	E

2020 Western Ave. (bet. Lenora & Virginia Sts.); 206-443-6000;
www.tomdouglas.com
"After the hustle-and-bustle of the Pike Place Market" builds an appetite, "locals know" to take the family to this Tom Douglas–owned "gem" for "inventive" "NW seafood at its best", from the "fabulous brunch" menu's "delightful eggs Benedict with crab" to the signature "melt-in-your-mouth salmon" to the side dishes ("even the veggies are divine"); never mind if at times it seems "overrun by tourists" – its windows overlooking the "Western Avenue crowds" make the place prime for "people-watching."

5 Spot ◗

22	20	20	21	M

1502 Queen Anne Ave. N. (Galer St.); 206-285-7768; www.chowfoods.com
■ There's "terrific food at reasonable prices" at this "consistent" American at the top of Queen Anne that "feels like a new place every three months" owing to its "ever-changing regional themes"; it's "easy to enjoy your meal with your children" since there are a "great kids' menu" and "high chairs aplenty."

Ivar's Acres of Clams ⌂

| 25 | 22 | 19 | 19 | M |

Pier 54, 1001 Alaskan Way (Madison St.); 206-624-6852; www.ivars.net
■ "Right on the waterfront", this "real Seattle" seafooder offers "plenty of kid-friendly items" on its "Diver Dan mask–shaped menu" (a "nice touch"); it's an "original" with "terrific clam chowder" and overall "good value", and "you can sit outside when the weather is warm" and let the children "feed the seagulls french fries."

Kidd Valley

| 24 | 20 | 13 | 18 | I |

135 15th Ave. E. (bet. Denny Way & John St.); 206-328-8133
4910 Green Lake Way N. (Stone Way); 206-547-0121
Northgate Mall, 418 Northgate Way (bet. 3rd & 5th Aves.); 206-306-9516
5502 25th Ave. NE (55th St.); 206-522-0890
www.kiddvalley.com
■ This "great" clan of burger houses is a Seattle family "staple" since the service is "fast" and the "kid-size meals with toys" are big hits with small fry; their parents love the "excellent prices" and "sensational shakes", and not incidentally, the seasonal "Walla Walla onion rings are the best!"

Macrina Bakery & Cafe

| – | – | – | – | I |

2408 First Ave. (Battery St.); 206-448-4032
615 W. McGraw St. (6th Ave. W.); 206-283-5900
www.macrinabakery.com
It's "worth blowing every diet known to man" to get a taste of the "fabulous" breads, pastries and other baked goods that are "pure bliss" at these beloved Belltown-Queen Anne bakeries ("when I die, I hope heaven is filled with their lemon tarts"); kids love the sweet treats, naturally, and all savor the famously "spectacular" "weekend brunch" (First Ave.); both locations also make "superb" lunch places.

Pagliacci Pizza

| 22 | 25 | 15 | 21 | I |

426 Broadway (Harrison St.); 206-324-0730
550 Queen Anne Ave. N. (Mercer St.); 206-285-1232
4529 University Way NE (bet. 45th & 47th Sts.); 206-632-0421
www.pagliacci.com
■ They make a "darn fine pie" at this "fabulous" troupe of pizzerias that might be "more expensive than the chains but are worth it" for their "gourmet", "out-of-the-ordinary" toppings; they're "no-brainers" for "kids from eight months to 80 years", who are more than happy to settle for takeout from the no-seating outlets.

Ray's Boathouse

| – | – | – | – | E |

6049 Seaview Ave. NW (Market St.); 206-789-3770; www.rays.com
"Always tops" for all ages, this "old-school" Shilshole "institution" is among the "best places for visitors to get their fill of really good salmon" and other "fantastic" seafood prepared with "classic NW" touches while taking in a "million-dollar view over Puget Sound to the Olympic Mountains"; also contributing to the "pleasurable experience" here is a "voluminous wine list" offering myriad "domestic and import choices" for oenophiles.

Shuckers

| – | – | – | – | E |

The Fairmount, 411 University St. (4th Ave.); 206-621-1984
With a long, carved wooden bar, pressed-tin ceiling and paneled alcoves, this 79-seater in the Fairmont Olympic Hotel is a charming "place for a cozy little family dinner"; it's a best bet for bivalves, of course, along with salmon and other fin fare and a range of local microbrews, but there's also "a wonderful children's menu" (one parent reports a young daughter who "loves their milkshakes with her clam chowder"); if the weather cooperates, try to nab one of the few outdoor tables.

SkyCity at the Needle   25 | 19 | 25 | 20 | E
Space Needle, 400 Broad St. (John St.); 206-905-2111;
www.spaceneedle.com
■ For an "elevating experience", look no further than this revolver atop the Space Needle that offers "magnificent" panoramas of the "rest of the world"; even though "food is secondary" here ("you're paying for the view"), fans say it's "surprisingly good for such a touristy place" and while the Pacific Northwest cuisine is "geared toward adult tastes", the restaurant does offer a children's menu.

RESTAURANT CHAINS

See reviews, starting on page 262.

Ratings: Family Appeal, Food, Decor, Service, Cost

	FA	F	D	S	$

Baja Fresh Mexican Grill ☒   20 | 22 | 14 | 18 | I
601 N. 34th St. (Freemont Ave. N.); 206-545-1101

Benihana ☒   23 | 20 | 18 | 22 | E
1200 Fifth Ave. (Seneca St.); 206-682-4686

Buca di Beppo ☒   24 | 19 | 22 | 21 | M
701 Ninth Ave., N. (W. Broad St.); 206-244-2288

California Pizza Kitchen ☒   21 | 21 | 16 | 19 | M
Northgate Mall, 401 NE Northgate Way (bet. 3rd & 5th Aves.); 206-367-4445

Claim Jumper Restaurant   23 | 24 | 22 | 21 | M
Redmond Town Ctr., 7210 164th Ave. NE (Bear Creek Pkwy.), Redmond;
425-885-1273

Johnny Rockets ☒   25 | 17 | 20 | 18 | I
University Village Mall, 2710 NE University Village (25th Ave.);
206-522-4483
600 Pine St. (6th Ave.); 206-749-9803

Old Spaghetti Factory, The ☒   25 | 20 | 22 | 20 | I
2801 Elliott Ave. (Clay St.); 206-441-7724

Olive Garden ☒   20 | 19 | 18 | 19 | M
300 NE Northgate Way (3rd Ave.); 206-363-7250

Outback Steakhouse ☒   20 | 22 | 18 | 20 | M
701 Westlake Ave. N. (Broad St.); 206-262-0326

Rainforest Cafe ☒   27 | 16 | 27 | 18 | M
290 Southcenter Mall (Klickitat Dr.), Tukwila; 206-248-8882

Red Robin   25 | 20 | 19 | 20 | M
Pier 55, 1101 Alaskan Way (Spring St.); 206-623-1942

Ruby's ☒   24 | 19 | 20 | 19 | I
16501 NE 74th St. (bet. 164th & 165th Aves.), Redmond; 425-861-7829

T.G.I. Friday's ☒   21 | 17 | 18 | 17 | M
1001 Fairview Ave., No. 3100 (Ward St.); 206-621-7290

Tony Roma's ☒   20 | 21 | 16 | 19 | M
543 Northgate Way (5th Ave.); 206-367-8384

St. Louis

To 19th-century Easterners, St. Louis was the gateway to the West – as commemorated by the 630-ft. signature Gateway Arch on the bank of the Mississippi River – but nowadays, travelers are just as likely to be arriving from California or Colorado. For them, this compact riverport city serves as an introduction to the East, thanks to its red-brick houses, cobblestone streets and continental flourishes. No matter where they're from, visitors can get their bearings by starting at the Arch: To its north lies historic Laclede's Landing, now home to swanky nightclubs and hip restaurants; abutting the Arch to the west is Downtown, the site of the Cardinals' Busch Stadium. The Metrolink light rail can whisk you from one to the other for $1.25 (children 5–12 travel for half). Just south of the Arch is the historic Anheuser-Busch brewery (the famous Clydesdales are stabled on-site); farther south are kid faves Grant's Farm, Purina Farms and the Magic House. West of Downtown you'll find elegant Lafayette Square, fun-filled Forest Park (site of the top-notch Zoo, the Science Center and the History Museum) and Washington University. And if you're truly channeling the area's pioneer spirit, journey upriver to Mark Twain's Hannibal or southwest for an Ozark overnight (replete with lots of country music) in Branson.

ATTRACTIONS

Ratings: Child Appeal, Adult Appeal, Public Facilities, Service, Cost

	C	A	P	S	$

Busch Stadium

	22	26	19	20	E

250 Stadium Plaza (bet. Spruce & Walnut Sts.); 314-421-3060; www.stlcardinals.com
◪ "Whether you're a baseball fan or not", Cardinals supporters "are among the friendliest in the major leagues", which helps make a trip to this 1960s park with its "small-town feel" a "fun" "summer outing for the entire family" – though "kids may be 'bushed' after a couple of hours"; unfortunately, like an aging pitcher, this "familiar relic" is "still striking from a distance, but showing its wrinkles up close" – and "soon to be a thing of the past" (it'll be "replaced in 2006").

Butterfly House

	25	25	26	23	I

Faust Park, 15193 Olive Blvd. (Appalachian Trail.), Chesterfield; 636-530-0076; www.butterflyhouse.org
■ "Get up close" to "thousands of butterflies in every color" as you take a "magical", "tropical nature walk" through the "rain forest–like interior" of this "relaxing", almost "meditative" pavilion; it's "especially delightful in winter" – "in the humid summertime", the "torrid" heat can be "too much like St. Louis outdoors" – and it's "fabulous for all ages", though "if your child is afraid of things that fly, don't go"; P.S. the Faust Park location in suburban Chesterfield is also home to "a wonderful indoor carousel" and "interesting" historical homes that illustrate life for the area's early settlers.

City Museum ☺

	28	23	25	23	I

701 N. 15th St. (Washington Ave.); 314-231-2489; www.citymuseum.org
■ With "trains to ride, tunnels to explore, boats to float and circus acts to learn", this "creative" children's museum downtown is "unlike anything anywhere"; an "old warehouse converted into a hands-on learning facility", this "totally whacked-out, goofy trip" "takes play to another dimension" and "appeals" not only to "kids of all ages" but also to "adults with any Peter Pan spirit"; "be prepared to crawl through weird spaces" and have some "wild, wonderful" "fun."

Gateway Arch, The ☺ | 23 | 26 | 22 | 20 | I |

Jefferson National Expansion Memorial, 50 S. Leonor K. Sullivan Blvd. (bet. Poplar St. & Washington Ave.); 314-655-1700; 877-982-1410; www.gatewayarch.com

■ "Take a ride to the top of the Midwest" in architect Eero Saarinen's "graceful" "engineering masterpiece" on the Mississippi riverfront; "you feel like George Jetson" in the "teeny" "elevator capsules" like "ratcheting egg pods" (they're "not for the claustrophobic"), but your reward is "fantastic views across Missouri and Illinois"; "be sure to see" the "amazing" "movie on how the Arch was built", and if you haven't "booked your tickets online", "get here early" or you'll have to "endure long lines"; P.S. there's a "marvelous Museum of Westward Expansion" downstairs.

GRANT'S FARM | 27 | 25 | 27 | 26 | I |

10501 Gravois Rd. (Grant Rd.); 314-843-1700; www.grantsfarm.com

■ For a "relaxing, pastoral" "getaway", try this "super family venue", a "beautifully maintained property" owned and operated by Anheuser-Busch with "something for everyone" to enjoy; tour General Ulysses S. Grant's cabin, take the tots to the "cute petting zoo" in the Tier Garten, ride the "excellent tram" through open terrain to "view antelope, deer and other grazing animals" and "don't miss" those "world-famous Clydesdale horses"; not only is admission to this "wonderful attraction" free, but so is the "beer that adults can sample"; N.B. closed November–March.

Magic House, The ☺ | 30 | 22 | 26 | 23 | I |

(aka St. Louis Children's Museum)
516 S. Kirkwood Rd. (Woodbine Ave.); 314-822-8900; www.magichouse.com

■ Garnering the highest Child Appeal score of any attraction in the country in this *Survey,* this "safe environment" "with hands-on exhibits sure to fascinate all ages" is "one of the best children's museums in the U.S." and a "must-do" "favorite" for locals and visitors alike; it "makes science fun" via "imaginative activities", and there's "a special toddler area" to appeal to the littlest ones; it's "perfect on a rainy day", but "try to go at an off time" when it's less "crowded" and "noisy."

Mark Twain | ▽ | 18 | 21 | 15 | 18 | I |
Boyhood Home and Museum

208 Hill St. (Main St.), Hannibal; 573-221-9010; www.marktwainmuseum.org

☑ "See all the places you remember from the books about Tom and Huck" – from Becky Thatcher's house to Grant's drugstore – when you explore this collection of historic homes and museums that "brings to life the stories of Samuel Clemens"; "it's interesting and educational" "for Mark Twain fans" and "helps introduce" kids (and their parents) to his "life and writings"; it's "a long drive" (about 120 miles) from St. Louis to Hannibal, however, and this destination is "not a wild fun time for very young children."

Mark Twain Cave and Annex | ▽ | 22 | 23 | 18 | 20 | M |

7097 County Rd. 453 (Hwy. 79), Hannibal; 573-221-1656; www.marktwaincave.com

☑ If you or your children "love Mark Twain's" books, "you'll love this cave and the stories" the guides tell – especially if the family "reads up on Tom Sawyer and others before your trip"; not only is it a refreshing, "informative" stop on a hot day (perhaps when "you're visiting Hannibal for other reasons"), but it's also "cool due to the author's cachet"; P.S. "better caves exist" elsewhere in Missouri – the "Cave State" has more than 5,500 caverns.

Mississippi River Boat Tour ▽ 21 | 21 | 20 | 18 | I

Gateway Arch Riverboats, 50 S. Leonor K. Sullivan Blvd. (Washington Ave.); 314-621-4040; 800-878-7411; www.gatewayarchriverboats.com

☑ "If you want to say that you've cruised the Mississippi", a riverboat ride can be a "perfect way to end the day", whether it's part of a sightseeing trip in the city, where cruises "give a historical perspective on the St. Louis riverfront" as well as "great views of the Gateway Arch", or while exploring Mark Twain country in Hannibal; at night some of the excursions "are on gambling boats", though, so families may prefer morning or afternoon departures.

Missouri Botanical Garden 16 | 28 | 28 | 24 | I

4344 Shaw Blvd. (Tower Grove Ave.); 314-577-5100; 800-642-8842; www.mobot.org

■ "Stop and smell the roses" indeed – the "wonderful fragrances and spectacular colors" of "every imaginable type of plant and climate" make this "incredibly beautiful" 79-acre "oasis" a "St. Louis treasure", "no matter the season"; here at one of "the oldest botanical gardens in the U.S." (founded 1859), children "like feeding the massive koi in the Japanese garden", "going through the space-age-looking" geodesic hothouse with its "amazing, gargantuan specimens" or just "running around"; "families bring picnics" to enjoy the "summer jazz festivals."

Missouri History Museum 16 | 24 | 26 | 23 | $0

Forest Park, 5700 Lindell Blvd. (De Baliviere Ave.); 314-746-4599; www.mohistory.org

■ A "wide variety of exhibits" and "interesting educational and cultural programs" "are put together with great intelligence" at this "informative" Forest Park museum that's "excellent for the history buff"; from Lewis & Clark to African-American traditions to baseball artifacts, the displays focus on not only Missouri's past but also American and Western themes; the "beautiful" Jefferson Memorial Building constructed with proceeds from the 1904 World's Fair is worth a look, and the Emerson Center's top-floor "restaurant has one of the best Sunday brunches in town."

Museum of Transportation 24 | 23 | 18 | 18 | I

3015 Barrett Station Rd. (Big Bend Rd.); 314-965-7998; www.museumoftransport.org

■ With "planes, trains, and automobiles" "galore" (and "big boats" too), both "kids and transportation enthusiasts" "love this place"; little ones may prefer to stay outdoors, where they can "walk and climb" on the "huge collection" of vehicles, while "adults can read the great historical information" or "take a self-guided tour"; though some surveyors say "the facility could be improved", admirers of this downtown "must-do" insist that "railroad fans" will "go nuts" here.

Museum of Westward Expansion 21 | 25 | 24 | 21 | $0

11 N. Fourth St. (bet. Chestnut & Market Sts.); 314-655-1700; www.nps.gov/jeff

■ "As part of a visit" to the Gateway Arch or as a "place to spend a day" on its own, this "wonderful" museum showcases "the history of the West" and the pioneer days; respondents recommend the "nicely done" "visuals of Lewis & Clark and their trip down the Missouri River", though kids may be more excited about the stuffed grizzly, covered wagons and Native American tipis; since lots of folks "kill time here" "while waiting" for a ride to the top, it's "always crowded."

Purina Farms ☺ ▽ 26 | 19 | 22 | 23 | $0

Visitor Ctr., 200 Checkerboard Dr. (County Rd. MM), Gray Summit; 314-982-3232; www.purinafarms.com

■ "For the littlest kids", this "field trip extraordinaire" 45 miles from St. Louis "can't be beat" for a "morning or afternoon" of entertainment;

they can explore the "workings of a farm" and enjoy "animals everywhere", especially in the barns and in the "delightful" "hands-on" petting area; adults may consider "all the food statistics interesting" (it's run by a pet-chow company, after all), but for the biggest thrills, "be sure to visit when you can see a canine agility performance" in the dog obedience center.

Silver Dollar City
| 26 | 24 | 24 | 25 | VE |

399 Indian Point Rd. (Crows Nest Trail), Branson; 800-475-9370; www.silverdollarcity.com

☑ "Part of the Branson experience", this "down-home" theme park "in the beautiful hills of the Ozarks" is "one of the most family-friendly" around; in a "well-maintained" environment run by "genuinely helpful workers", there are "wholesome shows" and "wild rides" for the kids, while "adults enjoy" the "top-of-the-line craftsmen and women" who "show you the old-time trades"; sure, it's "a tad old-fashioned", even "kinda hokey" ("the antithesis of Six Flags or Disney"), and mutinous modernists maintain that this "quaint" spot is just "another two-bit roadside attraction."

Six Flags St. Louis
| 28 | 22 | 21 | 20 | VE |

4900 Six Flags Rd. (Eureka Rd.), Eureka; 636-938-4800; www.sixflags.com

☑ "If you like being turned inside out and upside down" – and most kids certainly do – don't miss this "summer classic", a "Midwest Disney" that's actually a "double park, one with rides and another with water" attractions; "full of fun" "for all ages" and run by "friendly employees", it's "ok for an extra day on a visit to St. Louis", though detractors who dub it "ungodly expensive" dismiss it with "seen one, seen 'em all."

St. Louis Art Museum 😊
| 12 | 27 | 27 | 25 | M |

Forest Park, 1 Fine Arts Dr. (S. Skinker Blvd.); 314-721-0072; www.slam.org

☑ Sometimes "on a weekday, you can be alone with a Rembrandt" in this "well-run museum" that showcases "art from many periods" and genres; "originally built for the 1904 World's Fair", this "majestic building" in a "beautiful" Forest Park setting "still carries the grandeur" of that era; aside from the Sunday afternoon art-making sessions for the whole family, the facility is probably best "for older kids", but the permanent collections are "free for all" (and admission to special exhibits is waived on Fridays), so what have you got to lose?

ST. LOUIS SCIENCE CENTER
| 28 | 25 | 26 | 24 | $0 |

Forest Park, 5050 Oakland Ave. (S. Kingshighway Blvd.); 314-289-4400; www.slsc.org

■ It's "nothing less than awesome" rave respondents about this "high-energy", "hands-on" "learning facility" with loads of "cool stuff" that keeps both adults and kids "entertained for the entire day"; children especially "love the radar guns" "aimed at the cars below" on I-64, though everything from the "awe-inspiring planetarium" and IMAX theater to the "biological science exhibits" and "giant dinosaurs" earns praise; like other Forest Park attractions, it's free, so the only challenge is "so much to do, so little time"; N.B. renovations are in the works for 2004-05.

ST. LOUIS ZOO
| 29 | 28 | 27 | 24 | I |

1 Government Dr. (S. Skinker Blvd.); 314-781-0900; 800-966-8877; www.stlzoo.org

■ Coastal dwellers are sometimes surprised to find that St. Louis boasts "one of the premier zoos in the U.S.", voted the nation's No. 1 animal park in this *Survey* (and the No. 1 attraction in St. Louis); not only is this "wonderful facility" in Forest Park "a great way for families to spend an entire day", but "constant improvements" mean there's "always something new" to love each time you visit (the "excellent Penguin & Puffin Coast exhibit" is already "very popular"); helpful hint: though general "admission is free (a huge plus)", parking isn't, so "get there early" and stash your wheels on the street.

HOTELS

Ratings: Family Appeal, Rooms, Service, Public Facilities, Cost

	FA	R	S	P	$

Embassy Suites
St. Louis Downtown

	FA	R	S	P	$
▽	21	21	16	18	$229

901 N. First St.; 314-241-4200; 800-362-2779; www.embassysuites.com; 297 suites

☑ The "indoor pool is always packed with kids" at this all-suite Laclede's Landing chainster that offers cribs, high chairs and special menus for children; it's got a "great location" less than a half-mile from the Gateway Arch and 15 blocks from Busch Stadium, but some lament that "service problems exist" here.

Hyatt Regency

FA	R	S	P	$
23	20	21	23	$199

1 St. Louis Union Station; 314-231-1234; 800-233-1234; www.hyatt.com; 518 rooms, 21 suites

■ The "location inside the restored Union Station means there's plenty for children to see and do" among the festive shops and restaurants when they stay at this "beautiful hotel" with a grand lobby that makes you "feel like you're going back in time"; "check out the paddle boats on the man-made lake", walk to Busch Stadium for a baseball game or take convenient rail links to the St. Louis Zoo and a host of other kid-friendly attractions.

Pointe Royal Resort

FA	R	S	P	$
–	–	–	–	$119

158A Pointe Royale Dr., Branson; 800-962-4710; www.pointeroyale.com; 225 condos

If you're headed to Branson (four hours from St. Louis) to take in Silver Dollar City or the many other attractions in the area, this nearby condominium golf resort offers an affordable option for families; one-, two- and three-bedroom units feature fully equipped kitchens, separate living and dining areas, a private patio or deck, and views of the course greens or the Ozark Mountains; it also offers entertainment packages for nearby shows and sites.

Renaissance Grand Hotel

	FA	R	S	P	$
▽	18	25	25	23	$229

800 Washington Ave.; 314-621-9600; 800-468-3571; www.renaissancehotels.com; 875 rooms, 43 suites

■ The "service has a 'how-can-I-help-you attitude'" at this newish property with a "magnificent Sunday brunch" that's great for kids and adults alike; although it's primarily a business spot, adjacent to the convention center, little folks will like swimming in the indoor pool as well as taking tours on the nearby riverboats.

Yogi Bear's Jellystone Park

FA	R	S	P	$
–	–	–	–	$83

I-44, exit 261, Eureka; 800-861-3020; www.eurekajellystone.com; 30 cabins, 30 cottages

Just a half-mile from Six Flags St. Louis, this family-themed resort offers cottages with kitchens and outdoor grills, one-room camping cabins or rental tents for a rougher experience; tons of activities keep the little cubs content: character appearances by Yogi Bear, scavenger hunts, water-balloon volleyball, s'mores roasts, mini-golf, hiking and train rides; at certain times of year guests receive free tickets to Six Flags when they book a minimum number of nights.

Top Family-Friendly Hotel Chains in the Area:

Hampton Inn   Residence Inn
Holiday Inn   Ritz-Carlton
Homewood Suites   Westin
Marriott

See Hotel Chain reviews, starting on page 256.

RESTAURANTS

Ratings: Family Appeal, Food, Decor, Service, Cost

FA	F	D	S	$

Big Sky Cafe

| 14 | 26 | 25 | 23 | M |

*47 S. Old Orchard Ave. (Frisco Ave.), Webster Groves; 314-962-5757;
www.bigskycafe.net*

☑ A stylish "little" spot in Webster Groves, this cafe decked out
in bright primary colors has a "great atmosphere" for little ones,
"especially in warm weather" when you can sit "out on the patio"; the
"eclectic" American fare – new takes on comfort food favorites –
earns high marks (don't miss the "great" garlic mashed potatoes), but
still some say it "may be a little too fancy for young children."

Charlie Gitto's

| 15 | 22 | 22 | 20 | M |

207 N. Sixth St. (Pine St.); 314-436-2828; www.charliegittos.com

■ Diners "feel like they're in a neighborhood restaurant in the Bronx"
at this "St. Louis fixture", a comfortably "historic" Italian eatery that's
convenient to Busch Stadium and the Edward Jones Dome downtown;
adorned with baseball memorabilia, it gets busy "before a game",
but the "helpful" staff get you in and out "fast"; N.B. they're open
Sundays when the Cardinals or Rams are playing.

Crown Candy Kitchen

| 28 | 22 | 20 | 18 | I |

1401 St. Louis Ave. (14th St.); 314-621-9650; www.crowncandykitchen.com

☑ To show your "kids the way things used to be", take them to this
"old-time soda fountain" and candy shop downtown – a "family-
run" "classic" that "hasn't changed in over 90 years", from the
vintage jukebox to the chocolate phosphates; while the place serves
sandwiches and other diner fare (but no burgers), tiny sweet-tooths
will love to "gorge on the greatest malts and other ice cream creations";
however, natives note that at night the neighborhood can be "quite
dodgy" "for the unsuspecting tourist."

Cunetto House of Pasta

| – | – | – | – | M |

5453 Magnolia Ave. (Southwest Ave.); 314-781-1135; www.cunetto.com

"So much awesome pasta, so little time" could be the motto at this
"family-owned" "king of the Hill" where fans of "Italian comfort food"
gather to "truly savor" "high-dollar tastes for medium-dollar cost";
"Pavarotti may find" the "massive" portions reasonable, but all but
the largest broods will "need a doggy bag" to take home what little
tummies can't hold; lunch reservations are accepted, but they're
"unheard-of" for dinner, so "get there early", otherwise "your feet
may grow roots due to the long wait."

LuLu

| – | – | – | – | M |

8224 Olive Blvd. (82nd Blvd.), University City; 314-997-3108

The "friendly" girl in University City's mushrooming "multicultural"
restaurant strip is "a 10" declare disciples who make tracks for "terrific"
"Chinese cooking" and "dim sum that has to be the best buy on the
planet"; the "interesting menu" is so "big and complicated" it's like
"reading a Russian novel" and the "staff doesn't speak much English",

so tell the kids that for once, it's polite to point to what you want on the menu.

Pat's Bar & Grill

| – | – | – | – | I |

6400 Oakland Ave. (Tamm Dr.); 314-647-6553

"A true Dogtown neighborhood establishment" "near the St. Louis Zoo" and Turtle Park, this "always packed", "fun hangout", now owned by longtime bartender Joe Finn, may be the "best-kept secret" for American "comfort food"; "all ages" adore the "hearty portions" of tot-pleasing "great fried chicken", and for once you can "leave stuffed to the gills, with money left in your pocket."

St. Louis Bread

| 24 | 24 | 19 | 21 | I |

(aka Panera Bread Company)
9922 Kennerly Rd. (Tesson Ferry Rd.); 314-843-9900
4651 Maryland Ave. (Euclid St.); 314-367-7636
3114 S. Grand Blvd. (Arsenal St.); 314-772-5300
www.stlouisbread.com

☑ The St. Louis incarnation of the national Panera Bread Company, this "cute chain" is popular with families "for breakfast, lunch, dinner or a little snack during the day" thanks to its "mostly self-serve", "laid-back atmosphere" and surprisingly "creative" sandwiches, soups and salads – they make "wonderful grilled panini for grown-ups" – plus bakery goods, served at "palatable prices"; they even have "PB&J for those picky" half-pints.

Super Smokers Bar-B-Que

| 22 | 23 | 13 | 18 | I |

10012 Manchester Rd. (Sappington Rd.), Glendale; 314-966-8910;
www.supersmokers.com

■ Roll up your sleeves and dive into some of the "best barbecue east of Kansas City" at this local rib "joint" where finger-lickers find that the "rustic decor" and "affordable prices" "free you to dig into" the hearty plates of grub; service is "cafeteria-style, so kids don't have to wait long", and along with several suburban locations, there's a game-day-only outlet at Busch Stadium.

RESTAURANT CHAINS

See reviews, starting on page 262.

Ratings: Family Appeal, Food, Decor, Service, Cost

	FA	F	D	S	$
Applebee's	21	16	17	17	M

4680 Chippewa St. (S. Kingshighway Blvd.); 314-352-3700
1836 W. Hwy. 76 (Truman Dr.), Branson; 417-336-5053

	FA	F	D	S	$
California Pizza Kitchen ⊠	21	21	16	19	M

St. Louis Int'l Airport, East Terminal, 10701 Natural Bridge Rd. (off I-70);
314-426-6317

	FA	F	D	S	$
Cheesecake Factory ⊠	21	23	21	20	M

St. Louis Galleria, 1062 Brentwood Blvd. (off Hwy. 40); 314-721-0505

	FA	F	D	S	$
Chevys Fresh Mex ⊠	23	19	18	18	M

158 Crestwood Plaza (Sappington Rd.); 314-968-8485
9119 Olive Blvd. (bet. Hilltop Dr. & Price Rd.); 314-997-3700

	FA	F	D	S	$
Chili's Grill & Bar ⊠	21	19	18	19	M

St. Louis Airport, Terminal 1, 10701 Natural Bridge Rd. (off I-70);
314-429-3400
955 Chesterfield Ctr. (Fontaine Rd.), Chesterfield; 636-530-9525

Chuck E. Cheese's ⊠ | 26 | 10 | 17 | 13 | I |
South County Ctr., 720 South County Center Way (Union Rd.); 314-487-7317
2805 Target Dr. (off Hwy. 20); 314-741-8001

Dave & Buster's ⊠ | 26 | 16 | 21 | 17 | M |
13857 Riverport Dr. (I-70), Maryland Heights; 314-209-8015

Fuddrucker's ⊠ | 24 | 20 | 15 | 16 | I |
10752 Sunset Plaza (Watson Rd.); 314-966-3833

Hard Rock Cafe ⊠ | 22 | 16 | 26 | 18 | M |
1820 Market St. (St. Louis Union Station); 314-621-7625

Max & Erma's ⊠ | 22 | 20 | 19 | 21 | I |
316 Market St. (S. Memorial Dr.); 314-621-5815

O'Charley's ⊠ | 22 | 21 | 18 | 18 | I |
4130 Rusty Rd. (off S. Lindbergh Blvd.); 314-845-8200
17276 Chesterfield Airport Rd. (Boone's Crossing St.), Chesterfield;
636-519-0661

Old Spaghetti Factory, The ⊠ | 25 | 20 | 22 | 20 | I |
727 N. First St. (bet. Lucas Ave. & Morgan St.); 314-621-0276

Olive Garden ⊠ | 20 | 19 | 18 | 19 | M |
3790 Country Music Blvd. (Little Petes Rd.), Branson; 417-337-5811

Outback Steakhouse ⊠ | 20 | 22 | 18 | 20 | M |
5240 S. Lindbergh Blvd. (Baptist Church Rd.); 314-843-0777

Red Robin ⊠ | 25 | 20 | 19 | 20 | M |
17308 Chesterfield Airport Rd. (Boone's Crossing St.), Chesterfield;
636-733-0066

Romano's Macaroni Grill ⊠ | 21 | 21 | 19 | 21 | M |
1 South County Center Way (Lindbergh Blvd.); 314-487-9070
963 Chesterfield Ctr. (off Clarkson Rd.), Chesterfield; 636-532-2227

T.G.I. Friday's ⊠ | 21 | 17 | 18 | 17 | M |
529 Chestnut St. (6th St.); 314-241-8443
5262 S. Lindbergh Blvd. (bet. Baptist Church Rd. & Hackberry Dr.);
314-849-4556

Uno Chicago Grill ⊠ | 20 | 18 | 15 | 16 | M |
15525 Olive Blvd. (Chesterfield Pkwy.), Chesterfield; 636-530-9119

Washington, DC

The U.S. capital, laid out in quadrants along the Potomac River between Maryland and Virginia, is a study in monumental marble. Most of the attractions are federal government buildings or Smithsonian museums located in the northwest section (NW) along the National Mall, a 2.5-mile lawn with the U.S. Capitol to the east, the Lincoln Memorial and river to the west and the Washington Monument rising in the middle. The White House is a few blocks due north of the monument. Most of these places are free, but popular demand and heightened security can make entering slow going. Arrive early, reserve or, in some cases, get tickets through your Congress member. Driving is a hassle, and cab fares, priced by zone, add up – but the clean, efficient Metro transit system runs near most major sights and into the city from the airport. (Visitors with cars can park at an outlying station and take the Metro in.) Even more convenient is the Tourmobile (ticket booths are located at Arlington National Cemetery, the Washington Monument and Union Station), which makes 25 stops at various sites. The ride is lovely in the evening when the Mall is spectacularly lit. In daylight, DC is also magical in spring when cherry blossoms hang like cotton candy over the Tidal Basin and along Georgetown's romantic 18th-century streets.

ATTRACTIONS

Ratings: Child Appeal, Adult Appeal, Public Facilities, Service, Cost

C	A	P	S	$

Arlington National Cemetery ☺

11	26	21	19	$0

Memorial Dr. (Washington Blvd.), Arlington, VA; 703-607-8000; www.arlingtoncemetery.org

☑ "Moving" and "inspirational", this "national treasure" across the Potomac is the "sacred ground" in which at least one person from every American war is buried – 220,000 in all – amidst a "beautiful location" with "scenic walkways and hidden paths"; whether you're contemplating JFK's eternal flame, witnessing the "fascinating changing of the guard at the Tomb of the Unknown Soldier" or taking in an "authentic view of 19th-century life" at the Custis Lee Mansion, it's a "stirring" place for more mature children to "learn about history", even though everything but "the tram ride" may be "boring" for younger kids.

Bureau of Engraving and Printing ☺

23	25	19	18	$0

14th St., SW (C St.); 202-874-3019; www.moneyfactory.com

■ "Prove to the family that money doesn't grow on trees" at the U.S. currency plant south of the Mall; "older children find it fascinating" to see the moolah "roll off the presses" and peruse "different monetary units that have been printed over time"; March–August you must make early-morning, in-person reservations for the "informative" tour, and "tight security" may keep you waiting in line; "the fun gift shop" sells "gotta-have" "bags of shredded currency" and "sheets of uncut bills" – "if only they gave away free samples."

Capital Children's Museum

–	–	–	–	I

800 3rd St., NE (H St.); 202-675-4120; www.ccm.org

Not far from Union Station, this institute just for tykes has kept little eyes, ears, hands and minds occupied for more than a quarter-century; permanent exhibits take kids through concocting in a chemistry lab, driving a big city bus, adventures in cartoonland, a visit to a Japanese home and a Mexican holiday, plus there are special science and art workshops daily; N.B. closed Mondays, except during summer.

Dumbarton Oaks

12	24	21	17	I

1703 32nd St., NW (R St.); 202-339-6401; www.doaks.org

☑ Flower-loving families view the flora ("stunning" "formal gardens") and the fauna ("young policy wonks in love") at this "hidden gem in Georgetown", "a breath of fresh air in the DC pressure cooker"; the estate is "especially beautiful in spring when the daffodils are blooming", and is crowned with a Federal-style mansion housing a "lesser-known" museum/library that showcases Byzantine and pre-Columbian art; note: our ratings indicate it's much more popular among adults than their kids, "there is little to speak of in the gift shop or facilities" and "stairs are everywhere", so it's only "good for children who can walk."

Ford's Theatre and | 16 | 24 | 19 | 19 | $0
Lincoln Museum ☺

511 10th St., NW (E St.); 202-426-6924; www.nps.gov/foth

☑ "It gives you a shiver" to tour the Downtown site "where Lincoln was shot", a "step back" in time for kids who are old enough to appreciate "the meeting of theater and history"; while tour guides provide a "moving description" of what Honest Abe "meant to this country", the "basement exhibits" are "most interesting" and "across the street" "you can still see his blood on the pillow"; after "attending a play" here, "make a beeline for the presidential box upstairs" – otherwise you'll "stand in line forever to see it."

Franklin D. Roosevelt Memorial | 15 | 25 | 20 | 15 | $0

National Mall, 900 Ohio Dr., SW (West Basin Dr.); 202-426-6841;
www.nps.gov/fdrm

■ "Let your young kids run around" the "fountains, pools", waterfalls and "rocks to play on" while you "reflect" at "one of the city's least discovered, most beautiful" and "human-scale" memorials, a "thought-provoking" "tribute" to "FDR's astounding" presidency and to "the populace" during "trying times in U.S. history"; set on the Tidal Basin with "views of the Potomac", it might "move you to tears", particularly during spring cherry-blossom season and when lit up at night; just note it's a "long walk from the Metro."

Freer and Arthur M. Sackler | 12 | 26 | 24 | 22 | $0
Galleries of Art ☺☺

1050 Independence Ave., SW (12 St.); 202-633-4880; www.asia.si.edu

■ The Smithsonian's tandem "hidden gems" buried beneath the Mall, these free "sister" galleries are "wonderful for an introduction" to "Eastern and Eastern-themed art" combined with a "pilgrimage to the Whistler" galleries; "exquisite" works from around the world are presented on a "pleasantly human scale", and if the museums are "of no interest to small children", the Peacock Room will impress school-age kids, and the "interactive", "family-oriented" weekend workshops "educate" "in fun, innovative ways."

George Washington | 13 | 20 | 19 | 18 | $0
Masonic National Memorial, The ☺☺

101 Callahan Dr. (Duke St.), Alexandria, VA; 703-683-2007;
www.gwmemorial.org

☑ In Alexandria across the Potomac is a sparkling-white 333-foot building dedicated to the Father of Our Country, who was a Mason; "take time for a tour" to see a larger-than-life bronze statue of Washington and a "very interesting mini-museum with memorabilia" including his family Bible, swords and trunk; your clan will also be rewarded with a "spectacular view of the DC area" from the observation deck; N.B. there's "not much" for most younger children, though older ones can learn some interesting facts about the first president.

Hirshhorn Museum & | 14 | 26 | 22 | 19 | $0
Sculpture Garden, The ☺☺

Independence Ave. (7th St., SW); 202-357-2700; www.hirshhorn.si.edu

☑ It's "often overlooked, since Air & Space is next door", but parents "in favor of mixing art with a place to run around" say the Smithsonian's "great", "circular" "repository of 20th-century art" at least has the potential to "amuse kids" with its "whimsical sculptures" and its "very Zen" garden ("an excellent place to relax"); the "more interesting pieces" inside "inspire conversation" and "participation", as do the guided family tours and the Improv Art Room's activities for junior Jasper Johnses; just note that some creations are "a little racy" for naive eyes.

International Spy Museum, The ☺☺

| 24 | 26 | 24 | 21 | M |

800 F St., NW (8th St.); 202-393-7798

■ "Fans of *Harriet the Spy* to James Bond" "six years old and up" "find themselves immersed in the spy world" at this "way-cool museum" near Chinatown; despite "pricey" tickets it often gets "packed" by visitors who "assume an identity before entering" as part of the "interactive" look at the history of espionage; you can also gain intelligence from more than 600 "neat artifacts" and "actual devices used to snoop during wartime" and complete the mission by staking out the kid-friendly gift shop.

Jefferson Memorial ☺☺

| 17 | 25 | 20 | 16 | $0 |

900 Ohio Dr., SW (East Basin Dr.); 202-426-6841; www.nps.gov/thje

■ It may be a "hike to get to" but this "inspiring", "graceful" colonnaded tribute to the author of the Declaration of Independence and third U.S. president is in "one of the most beautiful locations on the Tidal Basin"; "especially at night" or "when the cherry blossoms are in bloom", the "majestic memorial" containing a statue of Jefferson evinces a "grandeur" "befitting the great democratic mind"; school-age children can "read the quotes to appreciate" the "brilliant American" while toddlers "burn off energy" in the "open, park-like space."

John F. Kennedy Center for the Performing Arts, The ☺☺

| 14 | 25 | 25 | 21 | $0 |

2700 F St., NW (Rock Creek Pkwy.); 202-467-4600; www.kennedy-center.org

■ Though primarily for adults, the "nation's center for the performing arts" offers a "great variety of world-class" plays, music and dance, including some "very good family programs"; "even if you're not seeing a show", it's "interesting" for a free tour of the "high-ceilinged corridors full of flags", the main theaters, the enormous bronze "bust of Kennedy", the "spectacular views from the top terrace" and "every night at 6 PM", "fine free entertainment" on the Millennium stage, kept "short for short attention spans."

Korean War Veterans Memorial ☺

| 15 | 25 | 18 | 13 | $0 |

900 Ohio Dr., SW (Daniel French Dr.); 202-426-6841; www.nps.gov/kowa

■ With an "innovative design" that "gives life to the forgotten war" of the early 1950s, this "small yet moving" memorial on the Mall makes for a "tearjerker" for older adults, an "educational" experience for teens and a "temptation" for little ones who'll want "to run through the rows of oversized soldiers"; "seeing all those names is overwhelming", and the "haunting" phalanx of "surreal" statues gives you the "feeling of being in the trenches."

Lincoln Memorial ☺☺

| 20 | 26 | 19 | 16 | $0 |

National Mall, 900 Ohio Dr., SW (23rd St.); 202-426-6841; www.nps.gov/linc

■ "Honest Abe would be proud" to see this "magnificent temple of liberty" and "famous site of MLK Jr.'s 'I Have A Dream' speech"; built on the Mall in the ancient Greek style and anchored by the seated, "gigantic president" statue seemingly enjoying the "breathtaking" view of the Washington Monument, its walls are inscribed with "excerpts from his speeches", including the Gettysburg Address; while the "beautiful memorial" will "bring history alive" for preteens, young kids just "love running up and down the steps."

Mount Vernon

| 21 | 27 | 23 | 23 | M |

3200 George Washington Memorial Pkwy. (Mt. Vernon Memorial Hwy.), Alexandria, VA; 703-780-2000; www.mountvernon.org

■ For an "interesting look" at George and Martha and "insight into the lives of their slaves", take the troops about 10 miles south to this "beautiful site on the Potomac" where you can "step back into the 18th century" and enjoy this "well-restored" historic "treasure" that was the Washingtons' home for 45 years; young children may "snooze" during the "long-winded" house tour, but "take a stroller" and "wear comfy shoes" because "you easily could spend a full day" exploring the pastures, herb garden and "great animal farm."

NATIONAL AIR & SPACE MUSEUM

| 28 | 28 | 26 | 23 | $0 |

National Mall, Independence Ave. (4th St., SW); 202-357-2700; www.nasm.si.edu

■ "A spectacular display" of an industry that went "from a few hundred feet" of flight "to landing on the moon in 66 years" is the mission of this *Survey*'s top science museum and the No. 1 DC attraction; "not to be missed", the Smithsonian's aviation branch is "packed" with everything from Charles Lindbergh's 'Spirit of St. Louis' to a space vessel you can walk through"; while the main branch can keep your family engaged for hours with all the "inanimate objects that come to roaring life", there's also a new annex at Dulles Airport where the *Enterprise* shuttle and the *Enola Gay* are housed.

National Arboretum

| 15 | 24 | 21 | 19 | $0 |

3501 New York Ave., NE (South Dakota Ave.); 202-245-2726; www.usna.usda.gov

■ It "gets very little attention from tourists", but this "tropical paradise in the middle of urban DC" 10 minutes northeast of the Capitol is a "fabulous spot to indulge in the beauty of nature", with "hundreds of botanical and floral species to admire" including an "unforgettable bonsai collection"; "miles of roads for walking and biking" and "great places to picnic, run and play" amid "hillside after hillside of explosions of color" make for "one of the prettiest" locations for "mom and dad to decompress [and the kids to play] after a long day."

National Archives ☺

| 16 | 25 | 21 | 20 | $0 |

700 Pennsylvania Ave., NW (7th St.); 202-501-5000; 1-866-272-6272; www.archives.gov

☑ The "chance to see, inches before your eyes, the very documents that changed the world forever" – namely the Declaration of Independence, the Constitution and the Bill of Rights – makes this newly remodeled building on Pennsylvania Avenue "one of the most moving places in the capital", especially for "school-age children who can understand their significance"; adults "searching for their roots shouldn't miss the research rooms" with "everything from ship passenger lists to census records" – just "catch it on a weekday, as weekends are mobbed."

National Gallery of Art, The ☺

| 14 | 28 | 27 | 23 | $0 |

401 Constitution Ave., NW (4th St.); 202-842-6691; www.nga.gov

☑ Although "some of the most treasured art in the world" is "displayed in a top-flight manner" at this "good use of our tax money", children 12 and under will have a limited tolerance for this Mall museum; the "East and West Wing bring together" a "trove" for "artistically reflective adolescents" and adults (get the "great audio tape for children"); when the little ones "get bored", take them to the "moving sidewalk and fountain" or the "ice rink in the sculpture garden" in winter, and have a nosh at the "excellent" cafeteria.

National Geographic Museum at Explorers Hall ☺☺

| 22 | 23 | 21 | 20 | $0 |

1145 17th St., NW (M St.); 202-857-7588; www.nationalgeographic.com/explorer

☑ It's the magazine brought to life, "just like the *National Geographic* TV specials", at this "relatively small" Downtown museum presenting "intriguing" displays on diverse subjects from dinosaurs to robots, all "touch-friendly" and in a "perfectly manageable size"; it's likely to be "very absorbing for kids and preteens", but it's hard to "compare to the Smithsonian's free museums all over town" unless you're truly interested in the exhibitions currently showing.

National Museum of African Art
| 18 | 25 | 24 | 22 | $0 |

950 Independence Ave., SW (9th St.); 202-633-4600; www.nmafa.si.edu

■ Located on the Mall in "spectacular" lodgings, the Smithsonian's "tribute to Africa" is filled with a "fascinating" collection of "rare treasures" from all over the continent; running the gamut from ancient to modern times, it includes prehistoric ceramics and tools to centuries-old musical instruments to contemporary paintings; there's "lots to learn and lots to look at", but bear in mind that it's better suited to older kids.

National Museum of American History
| 25 | 27 | 24 | 22 | $0 |

14th St., NW (Constitution Ave.); 202-357-2700; www.americanhistory.si.edu

■ "Thank God for the Smithsonian for preserving these cherished moments" – with "Fonzie's jacket in the same building as Revolutionary War memorabilia", this museum on the Mall covers U.S. history from the political to the "industrial, scientific and social", "appealing to all generations" with three floors filled with "American artifacts"; "where else can you see Dorothy's ruby slippers", "Julia Child's entire kitchen", "the original star-spangled banner, Archie Bunker's chair and Kermit the Frog" "all in one place?"; plus the Hands-on History Room and Science Center are "interactive" enough to engage kids of all ages.

National Museum of Natural History
| 27 | 27 | 25 | 23 | $0 |

10th St., NW (Constitution Ave.); 202-633-1000; www.mnh.si.edu

■ The "beauty of the universe is on display" via more than 124 million "animal, vegetable and mineral" items at the Smithsonian's "grand dame", the world's most-visited museum; "wanna-be princesses" "'try on' royal tiaras" via "their reflections in the glass cases" of the gem room (home of the Hope Diamond), while itty-bitty entomologists "hold caterpillars", "crawl through the termite hill" or watch hungry "tarantulas at feeding time"; the renovated "mammal family reunion" "is fabulous", and kids into the "big stuff" say "one word: dinosaur."

National Postal Museum
| 18 | 20 | 21 | 20 | $0 |

2 Massachusetts Ave., NE (N. Capitol St. NW); 202-633-1000; www.postalmuseum.si.edu

☑ "Who ever knew that mail could be so interesting?" – this "small", "uncrowded" archive housing rare stamps and money in an old post office near Union Station can be downright "cool"; philatelists and "older kids, more than younger ones, will enjoy" "seeing the Pony Express", plus "collecting stamps, mailing someone a special letter" and other "hands-on stuff" like "sending a postcard and tracking its voyage"; still, a few critics relay this message: the place "needs a lot more exhibits" and "has potential for improvement, just like the postal service."

National Zoological Park
| 28 | 26 | 20 | 19 | $0 |

3001 Connecticut Ave., NW (Cathedral Ave.); 202-673-4800; www.nationalzoo.si.edu

☑ There are 2,600 animals at this free "world-class zoo" in Cleveland Park – voted No. 1 for Child Appeal in the city by our surveyors – but "the pandas are [still] the stars"; "the elephants are a big draw" too, particularly since baby Kandula was born in 2001; the "bat cave and Amazon exhibits are definite must-sees", as are the orangutans that "climb overhead in the open", and "don't forget the reptile house and free-flight aviary"; it's "easy to get to by Metro" but even so, the "place has problems" pout parents pointing at "shabby", "outdated exhibits", "long lines for refreshments" and paths "too hilly for younger kids."

Old Town Alexandria ☺

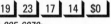

Visitors Ctr., 221 King St. (bet. Lee & Fairfax Sts.), Alexandria, VA; 703-838-4200; 888-738-2764

■ "See what Washington was truly like" in the 18th century on the "quaint" side of the Potomac, with "cobblestone sidewalks", "lovely old townhouses" and "history-filled buildings" like Christ Church, where Washington worshipped; let the kids decide what to do first: view the "artists at work" in the Torpedo Factory (a "real find"), take the "fun ghost walking tours", cruise the "charming" waterfront "with all of the performers" or catch one of the "tour boats leaving almost hourly" – there are also "great restaurants and shops" for you.

Rock Creek Park

| 19 | 23 | 17 | 14 | $0 |

3545 Williamsburg Ln., NW (Porter St.); 202-895-6070; www.nps.gov/rocr

■ "Take a picnic" to "DC's answer to Central Park", a "beautiful" "urban escape" with "miles of hiking trails" amid "hills and streams" "where you can see deer, foxes and other wildlife"; "take the little ones to the equestrian center", "try the Nature Center to see live animals" up close, "visit the small planetarium", and check out Peirce Barn where children can don 19th-century-style clothing and play with toys from that era; "on Sundays, Beach Drive is closed from Maryland to the zoo, allowing runners, bikers and rollerbladers to peacefully coexist"; N.B. this is no place to be after dark.

Supreme Court ☺

| 10 | 24 | 22 | 18 | $0 |

1 First St., NE (E. Capitol St.); 202-479-3000; www.supremecourtus.gov

◪ In this "imposing edifice" "where major decisions of our country are made", you can watch a film, take a "great tour", dine in the "best public cafeteria in town", and when court's not in session, "don't miss the talk" in "the great courtroom, one of the most impressive ever"; if the judges are in, "hearing oral arguments in cases that have a profound impact on every citizen's life is a moving experience", but not literally – you "have to keep quiet and still", which makes it "a treat" only for "older kids" and a mystery for younger ones.

Tidal Basin

| 19 | 23 | 15 | 12 | $0 |

bordered by Independence Ave. & Maine Ave.; 202-484-0206

■ For families who have "overdosed on history", the "lovely", "stroller-friendly" grounds around this "huge" artificial inlet with "spectacular" views of the "Jefferson, FDR and Washington monuments" is the place to be, especially in the spring "when the cherry trees are blossoming" so "spectacularly"; in summer it's "hot as a pistol", but you can "rent a boat and paddle about" or unleash the "kids who love to run around and cool their toes"; "take a picnic and a toy sailboat and lose yourself for a couple of hours."

Union Station ☺☺

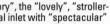

50 Massachusetts Ave., NE (Columbus Circle); 202-289-1908; www.unionstationdc.com

◪ A "magnificent structure", this "grand" "old station" near the Capitol has been handsomely restored and now serves as a "working, busy" transport hub as well as a "surprisingly spectacular place for a meal and window-shopping" amid the "hustle and bustle" on two concourse levels; in general there's "not much for kids to do unless they are into trains or the food court", but there are movie theaters "set in old tunnels" and a "great toy choo-choo exhibit" at Christmas, and most "little ones are enthralled by the subway's long escalators."

United States Botanical Garden | 18 | 26 | 23 | 21 | $0 |

245 First St., NE (Constitution Ave.); 202-225-8333; www.usbg.gov

■ It's "calm amidst the craziness of the DC Mall" at this "newly renovated" "oasis", a "beautiful facility at the steps of the Capitol" holding a glass-domed "national greenhouse" jam-packed with "interesting and exotic plants and flowers", including a "great desert garden as well as a rainforest"; it's "delightful on a cold winter's day" for a "brief visit", but while "some family programs are offered", if your child is not an amateur botanist, he or she is likely to "get bored fast."

United States Capitol ☺☺ | 21 | 27 | 23 | 21 | $0 |

Capitol Hill (east end of National Mall); 202-224-3121; www.aoc.gov

■ "It's hard not to get chills walking" beneath "the roof in the main rotunda" of this "symbol of democracy", an "incredible American building" "where history is made daily" by our elected officials; "seeing how our government works" is an "inspiration for all ages", particularly "school-age and up"; "call your representative beforehand to schedule an appointment for a staff-led tour and maybe a photo with your member of Congress" – without such prearrangement it's "nearly impossible" to "get a visitor's pass" to "sit in the gallery."

U.S. Holocaust Memorial Museum ☺ | 14 | 28 | 27 | 25 | $0 |

100 Raoul Wallenberg Pl., SW (Independence Ave.); 202-488-0400; www.ushmm.org

◪ This "emotionally wrenching", "powerful" and "brutal depiction of the Holocaust",the top-rated memorial in this *Survey*, is an "unforgettable", "phenomenal museum" on the Mall that "should be a required visit for all of humanity"; most of the exhibits are "too graphic and upsetting for younger kids", however, so steer them to the "tastefully and effectively done" Daniel's Story, suitable for ages seven and up, which "discusses the Shoah from a child's point of view", and be sure to "brief them on what to expect."

Vietnam Veterans Memorial ☺ | 12 | 27 | 20 | 16 | $0 |

23rd St., NW (Constitution Ave.); 202-634-1568; www.nps.gov/vive

◪ Maya Lin's "architectural masterpiece" "set a precedent for the use of modern art" in monuments and is "probably the most effective war memorial ever conceived"; a visit to the "dignified" and "solemn" black slab of granite sinking into the ground of the Mall is "heart-wrenching" when you read, etched into its face, the 58,000-plus "names of those brave soldiers that lost their lives" in Vietnam; "kids will not grasp the significance, but teens and adults will", so "bring Kleenex."

Washington Monument ☺☺ | 22 | 23 | 18 | 16 | $0 |

15th St., NW (Madison Dr.); 202-426-6840; www.nps.gov/wash

■ It's "not the most exciting monument in DC", but this "majestic" obelisk rising from the Mall is a "must-see on anyone's trip" because the "history and interior of it are fascinating", the "ride up and down in the elevator is informative" and the "sky-high view", albeit through "very small windows", is "spectacular"; get "advance tickets" or "go early" so you don't have to "wait in line for hours."

Washington National Cathedral ☺ | 13 | 25 | 24 | 21 | $0 |

3101 Wisconsin Ave., NW (Massachusetts Ave.); 202-537-6200; www.cathedral.org

■ To see "a piece of old Europe in America", hop on the Metro to Tenleytown for this "out-of-the-way" cathedral, an "amazing piece of architecture" with "beautiful stained-glass windows, flying buttresses and centuries-old tapestries"; even though this is a solemn place hosting "ecumenical services" "from all over the world", "kids enjoy going up in the tower to look down on the city" and like to "check out all the gargoyles" (there's one "running a movie camera, another wearing a Darth Vader helmet and another that looks like Snoopy").

White House ☺☺

| 23 | 27 | 23 | 20 | $0 |

1600 Pennsylvania Ave., NW (bet. 15th & 17th Sts.); 202-619-7222; www.whitehouse.gov

■ "Come see America's house" – it's "smaller than you imagined" for the place from which "the free world is run" but not surprisingly, gets the highest rating among government buildings in this *Survey*; "kids are thrilled to see where the president lives", but if you don't "get a ticket from your Congress member" six months in advance, you'll be stuck outside the front gate with the "protesters"; even with an in, the "tour is too short – you'll see more watching *The West Wing*" – but the nearby Visitor Center provides "excellent" insight.

HOTELS

Ratings: Family Appeal, Rooms, Service, Public Facilities, Cost

FA	R	S	P	$

Embassy Suites Old Town

| – | – | – | – | $239 |

1900 Diagonal Rd., Alexandria, VA; 703-684-5900; 800-362-2779; www.embassysuites.com; 268 suites

Located in historic Old Town Alexandria and across from the Metro and Amtrak stations, this all-suite family-pleaser is well situated for visiting the charming town's shops and restaurants, as well as getting to attractions such as George Washington National Masonic Monument and Mount Vernon (DC is just over the Memorial Bridge); suites with coffeemakers, microwaves, refrigerators and pull-out beds provide plenty of space; N.B. there are several other Embassy Suites in DC.

Fairmont Washington, The

| ∇ 22 | 28 | 28 | 27 | $149 |

(fka Monarch Hotel)

2401 M St., NW; 202-429-2400; 800-444-1414; www.fairmont.com; 415 rooms, 30 suites

■ "Kids are definitely appreciated" at this West End hotel near Georgetown, receiving "welcome kits at check-in" before heading to their "spacious, well-decorated rooms"; there's an indoor swimming pool and health club, and a "high-end brunch" that's "well worth it"; all in all, it's "simply a great hotel" that's "utterly unappreciated by the mass audience" according to its loyal fans.

Four Seasons

| 20 | 27 | 28 | 26 | $480 |

2800 Pennsylvania Ave., NW; 202-342-0444; 800-332-3442; www.fourseasons.com; 206 rooms, 51 suites

☑ "Toddlers are greeted by name and given presents" at this "top-notch" Georgetown property with a fine-honed "attention to detail" that means you can get "whatever you want or need"; there's a "great Sunday brunch" and an indoor pool, and the "location is amazing" (head to the Waterfront Park for a picnic before touring this charming area); still, despite the "luxury", a few families find "the rooms are small."

Grand Hyatt Washington

| 21 | 22 | 21 | 22 | $370 |

1000 H St., NW; 202-582-1234; 800-233-1234; www.hyatt.com; 850 rooms, 38 suites

■ Even though there are "always several conventions going on here", it's "excellent for any traveler, whether on vacation or business" since "the White House is within walking distance" and there's a subway connection right here for "easy access to other attractions"; the "indoor pond entertains the kids" and the hotel provides cribs; though some insist they "won't stay anywhere else in DC", just be warned that it gets "deserted late at night" in this area.

JW Marriott Hotel

| 19 | 19 | 19 | 20 | $309 |

1331 Pennsylvania Ave., NW; 202-393-2000; 800-228-9290; www.marriott.com; 704 rooms, 34 suites

☑ The "convenient location" "within walking distance of all the attractions" (e.g. the White House and the museums on the National Mall) makes this a "fantastic home base for sightseeing", since you "don't have to have a car"; there's an "adjacent shopping center with family restaurants", an indoor pool and a nearby theater, and Rock Creek Park is a half-mile away, but despite "predictable, consistent" service, a few find it's "not a sparkling hotel" and say there could be more amenities on-site for kids.

Loews L'Enfant Plaza Hotel

| 21 | 21 | 20 | 20 | $329 |

480 L'Enfant Plaza; 202-484-1000; 800-235-6397; www.loewshotels.com; 348 rooms, 22 suites

■ If you're headed to the museums on the Mall (the National Air & Space is particularly popular with kids), this property has "the best location in Washington", within a few minutes' walk of the main hot spots; there are "good kids' meals and buffets", a "goody bag upon check-in" for little ones and a "small dog-run facility" for the family friend; though it's near the Metro lines for easy transport, you may not want to leave the area, especially in springtime when you can see the famed cherry blossoms or go boating on the Potomac.

Park Hyatt

| 22 | 26 | 27 | 26 | $450 |

1201 24th St., NW; 202-789-1234; 800-633-7313; www.hyatt.com; 92 rooms, 131 suites

☑ "Bring the family, even the pooch" profess patrons of this "best family hotel for hitting Georgetown"; there are an "amazing" restaurant, an indoor pool, "spacious rooms" and "service that's beyond the call of duty"; it's "not particularly convenient to other tourist attractions", however, but some say the more sedate and "classy" atmosphere compensates; N.B. portable twin beds, cribs and refrigerators are provided upon request.

Top Family-Friendly Hotel Chains in the Area:

Hampton Inn	Marriott
Holiday Inn	Residence Inn
Homewood Suites	Ritz-Carlton
Hyatt	Westin

See Hotel Chain reviews, starting on page 256.

RESTAURANTS

Ratings: Family Appeal, Food, Decor, Service, Cost

| FA | F | D | S | $ |

Austin Grill

| 21 | 18 | 17 | 18 | M |

750 E St., NW (bet. 7th & 8th Sts.); 202-393-3776
2404 Wisconsin Ave., NW (bet. Calvert St. & Observatory Ln.); 202-337-8080
801 King St. (Columbus St.), Alexandria, VA; 703-684-8969
www.austingrill.com

■ This "family-friendly Tex-Mex" chain makes a "special effort to please" all generations – there's "coloring for the kids and margaritas for mom and dad", plus "plenty" of "decent chow" ("great kid food",

15 different salsas) served up by "helpful", "friendly" waiters; the "fun-filled atmosphere" is "noisy enough to drown out a toddler", meaning parents can relax and dig in.

Cactus Cantina

| 23 | 20 | 19 | 18 | M |

3300 Wisconsin Ave., NW (Macomb St.); 202-686-7222;
www.cactuscantina.com

■ It's a tossup as to what youngsters like more, this Tex-Mexer's "chugging tortilla machine" ("great entertainment") or its Old West–themed mini-museum, but either way, this Northwest DC hitching post has a "very kid-friendly" atmosphere, plus "excellent food" ("lots of choices"), "big tables" and a "lively and crowded" vibe; dinnertime waits can be "much too long", though, so "go early."

Cafe Deluxe

| 21 | 21 | 19 | 20 | M |

3228 Wisconsin Ave., NW (Macomb St.); 202-686-2233
4910 Elm St. (Woodmont Ave.), Bethesda, MD; 301-656-3131
1800 International Dr. (Greensboro Dr.), McLean, VA; 703-761-0600
www.cafedeluxe.com

■ "Not all kids live for French fries" – and at this "quasi-fancy" local trio (with "just enough of an urban feel to make you feel like you haven't given in to a kiddie restaurant"), there are "lots of choices" for everyone; the "large portions" of "good homestyle food" (meatloaf, mashed potatoes) provided by "knowledgeable waiters" amid a "bustling" scene make it perfect for "a much-relieved night out"; N.B. no dinner reservations.

Clyde's

| 20 | 21 | 21 | 21 | M |

Georgetown Park Mall, 3236 M St., NW (bet. Prospect St. & Wisconsin Ave.); 202-333-9180
Mark Ctr., 1700 N. Beauregard St. (Seminary Rd.), Alexandria, VA; 703-820-8300
Tysons Corner, 8332 Leesburg Pike (Westpark Dr.), McLean, VA; 703-734-1901
www.clydes.com

■ A "rock-solid", "perennial Washington feedbag", this "all-American" chain of saloon restaurants serves up a "great night and a great burger"; floating model airplanes and a "fun-to-watch ceiling train" that "whistles every time it enters the dining room" contribute to an "upbeat atmosphere" that's well suited to older kids ("not the best for toddlers"); note that after work the Georgetown original fills up with "young, hip professionals" and becomes more of a "classy pub."

Lebanese Taverna

| 17 | 24 | 18 | 21 | M |

(aka Lebanese Taverna Cafe)

2641 Connecticut Ave., NW (bet. Calvert St. & Woodley Rd.); 202-265-8681
Pentagon Row, 1101 S. Joyce St. (Army Navy Dr.), Arlington, VA; 703-415-8681
5900 Washington Blvd. (McKinley Rd.), Arlington, VA; 703-241-8681
Congressional Plaza, 1605 Rockville Pike (Congressional Ln.), Rockville, MD; 301-468-9086
www.lebanesetaverna.com

■ "If you have kids who enjoy new things, they'll have fun trying to pronounce" the names of all the nibbles on the meze platter at this "warm", "family-run" Lebanese mini-chain serving "finger food that adults enjoy as much as youngsters"; "order the group meal that includes multiple appetizers and entrées to spread about the table", and if the littlest ones aren't happy, "just order them some chicken strips and fries" off the children's menu.

Mi Rancho

| – | – | – | – | M |

19725A Germantown Rd. (Middlebrook Rd.), Germantown, MD; 301-515-7480
8701 Ramsey Ave. (Cameron St.), Silver Spring, MD; 301-588-4872

Kids can "watch delicious tortillas being made on the spot" to be "served hot" following "fabulous chips and salsa" and accompanying hefty portions of "tasty" Tex-Mex at these Germantown and Silver Spring cantinas; the "welcoming" staff, "huge outdoor patio", "straightforward American-style" dishes like mesquite-grilled seafood and "lip-smacking margaritas" for mom and pop make it "ideal for families" – even "rowdy" ones.

Noodles & Company

| 23 | 21 | 17 | 21 | I |

3105 Duke St. (N. Quaker Ln.), Alexandria, VA; 703-212-0008
Pentagon Row, 1201 S. Joyce St. (Washington Blvd.), Arlington, VA;
703-418-0001
Main Street Mktpl., 10296 Main St. (Old Lee Hwy.), Fairfax, VA;
703-218-4400
www.noodles.com
■ "Pad Thai for adults, mac 'n' cheese for the kids" and "noodles from all over the world" are on the "tasty menu" at these suburban pasta purveyors that are utterly "family-friendly"; just order a customized entrée at the counter (meat, shrimp, tofu, veggies? downsized for the dinky ones?), then savor an "affordable", "fun", "quick lunch"; if you don't mind the "very high noise level", it's "perfect for families with young children."

Rio Grande Cafe

| 24 | 21 | 20 | 19 | M |

4301 N. Fairfax Dr. (Glebe Rd.), Arlington, VA; 703-528-3131
4870 Bethesda Ave. (Arlington Rd.), Bethesda, MD; 301-656-2981
■ At these "big", "fun" Tex-Mex Arlington and Bethesda eateries, your "kids can go loco and nobody will notice" thanks to the "relaxed, noisy atmosphere"; in addition, you'll find "reliable", "traditional" *comida*, "fascinating" tortilla-making machines and "pleasant", "speedy service" that make the pair "great for large families"; result: they're "always packed", so you may have to "wait to cross the border during peak dining times."

Tara Thai

| 18 | 22 | 22 | 20 | M |

4001 Fairfax Dr. (bet. Quincy & Randolph Sts.), Arlington, VA;
703-908-4999
4828 Bethesda Ave. (bet. Arlington Rd. & Woodmont Ave.), Bethesda,
MD; 301-657-0488
7501E Leesburg Pike (Pimmit Dr.), Falls Church, VA; 703-506-9788
12071 Rockville Pike (Montrose Rd.), Rockville, MD; 301-231-9899
■ The "friendly" staff at this "consistent" Siamese chain is "always attentive to little ones", so "if you can get the kids to eat Thai food, it's a great, inexpensive place to go" for "child-friendly chicken satay and cashew chicken, as well as spring rolls"; if your brood is "unwilling to experiment", at least the "cool underwater theme" will give them "lots to look at."

Tony Cheng's

| – | – | – | – | M |

619 H St., NW (bet. 6th & 7th Sts.); 202-842-8669
Grab a "large, round table" for your clan, jump into the "buffet line", "stuff your bowls with fresh meat and produce", select your seasonings and let the wok chefs work their stir-fry magic" for "outstanding Mongolian BBQ" at this "kids' favorite" "novelty" "institution" in Chinatown; it's "great entertainment", but for a less "touristy" experience, "head upstairs to the seafood restaurant" for "rare items" and "yummy dim sum."

2 Amys

| 21 | 25 | 17 | 20 | M |

3715 Macomb St., NW (Wisconsin Ave.); 202-885-5700
■ A labor of love from Obelisk's Peter Pastan, this simple, bright eatery near Wisconsin Avenue earns the "vote for best pizza in DC" with "varied and wonderful" wood-fired Neapolitan pies that are "gourmet" (toppings include rapini, capers, anchovies) and truly

authentic; a "loud atmosphere" and a patio "make it easy to bring kids", so it's not surprising that despite its "rather sterile environment", it's "mobbed by young families."

RESTAURANT CHAINS

See reviews, starting on page 262.

Ratings: Family Appeal, Food, Decor, Service, Cost

	FA	F	D	S	$

Applebee's — 21 | 16 | 17 | 17 | M
6310 Richmond Hwy. (S. Kings Hwy.), Alexandria, VA;
703-768-1636

Baja Fresh Mexican Grill ⊠ — 20 | 22 | 14 | 18 | I
1990 K St., NW (20th St.); 202-293-0110
1333 New Hampshire Ave., NW (O St.); 202-835-0570
3231 Duke St. (Quaker Ln.), Alexandria, VA; 703-823-2888
1101 Joyce St. (Hwy. 395), Arlington, VA; 703-414-8211

Benihana ⊠ — 23 | 20 | 18 | 22 | E
3222 M St., NW (Wisconsin Ave.); 202-333-1001

Bertucci's ⊠ — 23 | 20 | 17 | 19 | M
Dupont Circle, 1218-1220 Connecticut Ave., NW (bet. M & N Sts.);
202-463-7733
2000 Pennsylvania Ave., NW (20th St.); 202-296-2600
Old Town, 725-727 King St. (Washington St.), Alexandria, VA;
703-548-8500
Market Common, 2700-2800 Clarendon Blvd. (Fairfax Dr.), Arlington, VA;
703-528-9177

Buca di Beppo ⊠ — 24 | 19 | 22 | 21 | M
1825 Connecticut Ave., NW (Florida Ave.); 202-232-8466

California Pizza Kitchen ⊠ — 21 | 21 | 16 | 19 | M
1260 Connecticut Ave., NW (bet. M & N Sts.); 202-331-4020
Reagan Nat'l Airport, National Hall ; 703-417-1647
Fashion Centre at Pentagon City, 1201 S. Hayes St. (12th St.),
Arlington, VA; 703-412-4900

Chevys Fresh Mex ⊠ — 23 | 19 | 18 | 18 | M
Fashion Centre at Pentagon City, 1201 S. Hayes St. (12th St.),
Arlington, VA; 703-413-8700
4238 Wilson Blvd. (Stuart St.), Arlington, VA; 703-516-9020

Chili's Grill & Bar ⊠ — 21 | 19 | 18 | 19 | M
6250 Inter Parcel Rd. (Manchester Blvd.), Alexandria, VA;
703-922-5100
320 23rd St. (Jefferson Davis Hwy.), Arlington, VA; 703-418-2333

Chuck E. Cheese's ⊠ — 26 | 10 | 17 | 13 | I
6303 Richmond Hwy. (S. Kings Hwy.), Alexandria, VA;
703-660-6800

Fuddrucker's ⊠ — 24 | 20 | 15 | 16 | I
1216 18th St., NW (Jefferson Pl.); 202-659-1660
734 Seventh St., NW (bet. G & H Sts.); 202-628-3380

Hard Rock Cafe ⊠ — 22 | 16 | 26 | 18 | M
999 E St., NW (10th St.); 202-737-7625

Johnny Rockets ☒   25 | 17 | 20 | 18 | I
3131 M St., NW (bet. 31st St. & Wisconsin Ave.); 202-333-7994
Union Station, 50 Massachusetts Ave., NE (bet. F & 1st Sts.); 202-289-6969
Fashion Centre at Pentagon City, 1100 S. Hayes St. (bet. Army Navy Dr. &
12th St.), Arlington, VA; 703-415-3510

Maggiano's Little Italy   22 | 22 | 21 | 22 | M
5333 Wisconsin Ave., NW (Western Ave.); 202-966-5500

Outback Steakhouse ☒   20 | 22 | 18 | 20 | M
6804 Richmond Hwy. (bet. Memorial St. & Schooley Dr.), Alexandria, VA;
703-768-1063
4821 N. First St. (Park St.), Arlington, VA; 703-527-0063

Romano's Macaroni Grill ☒   21 | 21 | 19 | 21 | M
5925 Kingstowne Towne Ctr. (Springfield Pkwy.), Alexandria, VA;
703-719-9082
671 N. Glebe Rd. (Wilson Blvd.), Arlington, VA; 703-248-0000

T.G.I. Friday's ☒   21 | 17 | 18 | 17 | M
2100 Pennsylvania Ave., NW (21st St.); 202-872-4344
4650 King St. (28th St.), Alexandria, VA; 703-931-4100

Uno Chicago Grill ☒   20 | 18 | 15 | 16 | M
3211 M St., NW (Wisconsin Ave.); 202-965-6333
Union Station, 50 Massachusetts Ave., NE (bet. F & 1st Sts.); 202-842-0438

Other Notable Attractions

Ratings: Child Appeal, Adult Appeal, Public Facilities, Service, Cost

Acadia National Park
| – | – | – | – | M |

Rte. 233, near Eagle Lake, Bar Harbor, ME; 207-288-3338; www.nps.gov/acad
From the tippy-top of its granite mountains to its salty ocean shores, this national treasure spilling out on the craggy Atlantic seaboard showcases Maine's natural riches; open all year long for snowmobiling, snowshoeing and ski touring in the cold months and swimming, boating, fishing, hiking and biking when it's warm, the park (less than 50 miles from Bangor and about 280 from Boston) boasts two campgrounds, a historical museum on Little Cranberry Island and visitors' centers; mostly May–October, ranger programs run the gamut from boat cruises to tidal walks to stargazing jaunts to powwows with native critters.

Adirondack State Park
| – | – | – | – | $0 |

Paul Smiths Visitor Ctr., Rte. 30 (Jenkins Mountain Rd.), Paul Smiths, NY; 518-327-3000; www.apa.state.ny.us
Six million forested mountain acres in upstate New York, this wooded wonderland boasts year-round family fun: snowshoe and cross-country ski during winter, fish and view wildflowers in spring, hike and swim in summer and check out the gorgeous fall foliage; Newcomb (112 miles north of Albany) and Paul Smiths (about 160 miles northwest of the capital) have visitors' centers that house exhibits for little hands to paw, plus a butterfly facility at the latter; they also run nature programs like teach-ins on bears, meet-and-greets with birds of prey, and maple-tapping sessions, and the pleasant folks can tell you where to camp, lodge and eat in the park.

Busch Gardens
| 28 | 27 | 24 | 22 | VE |

1 Busch Gardens Blvd. (Hwy. 64), Williamsburg, VA; 800-343-7946; www.buschgardens.com
■ With its "close proximity to Colonial Williamsburg" (three miles) and to Richmond, Norfolk and Virginia Beach (about 50 miles from each), this "first-class", Euro-themed, Anheuser-Busch–funded playland is "arguably the most scenic theme park" in the country, with a "lush, green" setting and "lots of shade"; "super-friendly employees are in costume", and the "plentiful activities" include just the "right combination of thrill rides and little kids' attractions" such as "awesome roller coasters", a "fantastic circus show" and "fabulous animal-feeding" opportunities; a faint few fret "lines can be long" and the sheer size of the place is "overwhelming."

CEDAR POINT ☺
| 27 | 28 | 26 | 24 | VE |

1 Cedar Point Dr. (Lake Erie), Sandusky, OH; 419-627-2350; www.cedarpoint.com
■ "One of the roller coaster capitals of the world", the top-rated amusement park in our *Survey,* midway between Cleveland and Toledo on the shores of Lake Erie, anchors an area flush with nature preserves, nautical villages and small coastal islands; it has "some of the country's largest" "lunch-churning thrills" and equilibrium-rattling rides (there are a few that "children on the shorter side can't do") as well as revues and a Riviera-like setting that's a "beautiful distraction" "as you're plummeting toward the earth at 90 miles per hour."

Colonial Williamsburg
| 23 | 28 | 26 | 25 | E |

1 Visitor Center Dr. (Rte. 132), Williamsburg, VA; 800-447-8679; www.colonialwilliamsburg.org
☑ An hour northwest of Virginia Beach, this "picturesque" "living history" village near Jamestown and Yorktown was restored by the Rockefeller family and is rated the top historic attraction in our *Survey;* it provides a "look back at prerevolutionary Virginia" with

"costumed guides who walk the streets, work in the shops" and "help you understand the lives of Colonial Americans"; you can view parades and mock battles, eat at historic taverns and watch chocolate being made from cocoa beans; "steer clear of building tours", though, because "youngsters will get bored"; N.B. it gets "pricey", especially if you stay at the nearby Williamsburg Inn.

GRAND CANYON NATIONAL PARK ☺
24 | 29 | 22 | 22 | M

South Rim, Hwy. 64, Grand Canyon, AZ; 928-638-7888; www.nps.gov/grca
■ It's "a big hole – but what a hole!" exclaim enthusiasts over this "spectacular beyond belief" "geological wonder" just 80 miles from Flagstaff, Arizona, where "gazing at the view is a spiritual experience" and "each rim is breathtaking in its own way"; take an "overnight mule ride to the inner canyon" or a "rafting trip down the river" and "stay in one of the cabins" (but "don't expect luxury"); bear in mind hiking this attraction is "not for toddlers" since there are "not enough fences" and it's "a long way down"; P.S. the "less hectic" northern edge (roughly 210 miles northwest of Flagstaff) is only open May–October.

Grand Teton National Park
21 | 28 | 22 | 21 | M

Moose Visitor Ctr., Teton Park Rd. (Hwy. 390), Moose, WY; 307-739-3300; www.nps.gov/grte
■ Just north of Jackson Hole, Wyoming and 50 miles south of "better-known Yellowstone" ("great views, same animals, less crowds"), this "stunning" "America the Beautiful" destination contains "some of God's best work" – "mountains rising majestically from the plains" and "abundant wildlife" roaming free; to appreciate the "grandeur", "get out of your car" to "rent canoes, hike", "take a raft ride" or swim, and don't miss the "great ranger programs for kids"; surveyors also swoon for "the lavish Jenny Lake Lodge" and urge "bring extra memory cards for the camera."

L.L. Bean Flagship Store
– | – | – | – | $0

95 Main St. (Bow St.), Freeport, ME; 877-552-3268; www.llbean.com
Here it is: ground zero for preppy apparel, open 24/7 near the Freeport outlets for duck boots, chinos and fleece pullovers; that's not all the store (a 20-minute drive northeast of Portland) has to offer: little ones line up to tackle its small rock climbing wall, junior naturalists study the pond's live trout and the taxidermy specimens that dot the sprawling layout, and parents load up on neat equipment for that camping trip with the kids, popping next door to make like Davey Crockett and test out the fishing and hunting goods.

Mackinac Island State Historic Parks
– | – | – | – | M

Visitors' Ctr., Huron St. (Fort St.), Mackinac Island, MI; 231-436-4100; www.mackinacparks.com
Encompassing a reconstructed fur-trading village, an 18th-century mill and the old Straits lighthouse on the mainland, plus the nature trails, fort and historic downtown of Mackinac Island, this Lake Huron park (about 320 miles northwest of Detroit) lures families for educational and outdoor recreation; cars are verboten on the isle – accessible by air or by ferry from Mackinaw City or St. Ignace – so rent bikes or hop a buggy to tour a landscape of forests, beaches, wind-carved limestone, bluff cottages, fine old lodges like the Grand Hotel, and Victorian harbor streets; in winter, travel by cross-country ski or horse-drawn sleigh.

MONTEREY BAY AQUARIUM ☺
29 | 28 | 27 | 25 | M

886 Cannery Row (David Ave.), Monterey, CA; 831-648-4800; www.mbayaq.org
■ "One would have to be a very cold fish not to love" the "best aquarium" in our *Survey*; "beautifully set" on California's "rocky"

coast within 30 miles of Big Sur and Carmel (and near historic locale Cannery Row), it's a favorite for a "fantastic family outing" thanks to "stunning exhibits" ranging from touch pools for toddlers to "big shark tanks"; with so much to enjoy, your biggest challenge may be "getting the children away from the sea otters to see the rest" of the "fabulous" displays; N.B. just outside, you can watch sea lions, whales and other ocean dwellers swimming in their natural habitat.

Mt. Rushmore
`– | – | – | – | I`

Hwy. 244 (Iron Mountain Rd.), Keystone, SD; 605-574-2523; www.nps.gov/moru

Talk about face time – that's what you get, gazing at the four towering visages of George Washington, Thomas Jefferson, Theodore Roosevelt and Abraham Lincoln carved into this South Dakota mountainside 25 miles from Rapid City; interactive exhibits, construction photos and a short film illustrate how sculptor Gutzon Borglum undertook the 16-year process, walking trails let you see the results from many different perspectives, and kids can learn more about the park from special junior-ranger booklets; plan to spend at least two hours (don't miss the evening lighting ceremony) – then take a trip to neighboring Black Hills National Forest, the Crazy Horse monument-in-progress (17 miles away) or Badlands National Park (85 miles).

Niagara Falls
`25 | 28 | 21 | 20 | $0`

Robert Moses Pkwy. (Prospect St.), Niagara Falls, NY; 800-338-7890; www.niagara-usa.com

☑ You'll get "a rush" when viewing this "natural wonder of the world" just outside Buffalo that "casts a spell over everyone" who's "misted by the spray" and hears "the thunder of the Horseshoe Falls"; "walk underneath and see" the deluge come down above you or "take the [Maid of the Mist] boat ride" ("no barrels required"); for a "better view", "cross the bridge to the Canadian side", though purists protest that "kitschy attractions" there make the area "too commercialized."

Outer Banks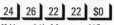
`24 | 26 | 22 | 22 | $0`

Visitors Bureau, 1 Visitors Center Circle (off Hwy. 64), Manteo, NC; 800-446-6262; www.outerbanks.org

■ "East Coast beaches don't get any better than" the "picturesque" "white" shores on this strip of narrow islands southeast of Norfolk, Virginia that buffer the North Carolina coast – but what makes them "ideal" for a trip with "toddlers and young children" is that "from Currituck to Ocracoke" (Blackbeard's former hideout), there's "something for everyone"; drive "the main drag" for "mini-golf and family restaurants galore", get a lift at the "informative Wright Brothers site in Kitty Hawk", enjoy "great kite-flying" at Jockey's Ridge State Park near Nags Head or soak up the sun at the "pristine" National Seashore in the south; there's one thing this area's not, though: "a nightlife scene."

Petrified Forest National Park
`18 | 23 | 16 | 16 | I`

I-40 (I-180), Petrified Forest National Park, AZ; 928-524-6228; www.nps.gov/pefo

☑ This "mind-boggling" 93,533-acre expanse full of "thousands of fossilized tree trunks" with "mineral deposits that make rainbow hues" – plus the multicolored mesas of the Painted Desert – is "like another world" (though it's actually just 75 miles or so northwest of Gallup, New Mexico); paleontologically predisposed people point out the "spectacular" rock formations are "pretty darn cool", making for an "interesting half-day adventure" as you motor along the park's 28-mile road or hike its short and easy trails; still, despite amenities like a visitors' center, picnic areas and "very educational ranger walks", dubious dads and moms deem that it's "not worth" the "boring drive" since "most children", especially the littlest ones, won't "appreciate the complexity or the beauty" of the place.

Temple Square   15 | 24 | 24 | 25 | $0

North Visitors' Ctr., 50 W. North Temple St. (N. Main St.),
Salt Lake City, UT; 801-240-1245

◪ If you're interested in "the history of the Mormon religion", this 10-acre downtown quadrangle containing the Salt Lake Temple is an "inspiring place"; "take a free walking tour" of the "beautifully landscaped" grounds, "catch an organ concert" at the domed Tabernacle (home of the famous choir) or stop into the "informative" visitors' center; some say "go at Christmas", while others feel it's a "must-see in the summer with its acres of flowers" – either way, there's "not a lot for kids to do."

YELLOWSTONE NATIONAL PARK   27 | 29 | 23 | 22 | I

West Entrance, Rte. 20 (Yellowstone Ave.), West Yellowstone, MT;
307-344-7381; www.nps.gov/yell

■ "Electrifying even to the MTV generation", the nation's "first and still greatest" national park showcases "America in all its natural splendor"; this "wonderland" (about 50 miles west of Cody, Wyoming and about 320 miles north of Salt Lake City) "blows you away" with its geysers, waterfalls, lakes and forests, and since there are so "many things to see besides Old Faithful – "grizzlies and bison and wolves . . . oh my!" – "you need three days" to take it all in; "be prepared to entertain the kids in the car" on the way and to encounter "bothersome" summer tourist throngs, though you can avoid them by scheduling your trip for mid-May–early June.

YOSEMITE NATIONAL PARK   27 | 29 | 23 | 22 | M

Arch Rock entrance, Hwy. 140 W. (El Portal Rd.), Yosemite National Park, CA;
209-372-0200; www.nps.gov/yose

■ Just 200 miles east of SF, this "unparalleled" "magnificence" is a "heaven on earth" to its adherents who've rated it the No. 1 national park in our *Survey*; "take a guided tour of the valley floor", see "unbelievably huge redwoods" and "go horseback riding, river rafting and hiking"; "even the most jaded kids will love" this "total immersion in nature" since they "can run, jump and explore" all day long; lodging options range "from camping to the posh Ahwahnee Hotel" – a "must for lunch after a big hike" even if you don't stay there.

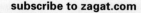

Hotel Chains

Top by Family Appeal

26 Residence Inn by Marriott
Embassy Suites
24 Four Seasons
Homewood Suites
22 Marriott
Holiday Inn
Ritz-Carlton
Hampton Inn
Westin
Hyatt

Ratings: Family Appeal, Rooms, Service, Public Facilities, Cost

Amerisuites
21 | 20 | 18 | 19 | I

800-833-1516; www.amerisuites.com

☑ "Unless you're into sleeping next to your kids on vacation", the "surprisingly large suites" of this "affordable" 230-strong outfit are "indispensable" for families; they do a "good job on the basics" here, from "useful in-room items such as refrigerators and microwaves" to "a very nice breakfast buffet with a complimentary *USA Today*", but picky parents would like units "to have more division between the living room and bedroom and maybe a second TV for the children."

Best Western
19 | 16 | 17 | 16 | I

800-780-7234; www.bestwestern.com

☑ Though "you won't find anything fancy" here, "easy access and many locations to choose from in family destinations" make this "inexpensive" chain with 2,184 U.S. properties "user-friendly" for folks with small fry; still, "wildly inconsistent" quality means your hotel might be "great", with amenities including a gratis, "quite tasty breakfast" and an indoor/outdoor pool ("a hit with everyone after a long drive"), or it might just seem like a wrong turn.

Comfort Inn
21 | 18 | 17 | 18 | I

877-424-6423; www.comfortinn.com

☑ "'Comfort' says it all" for this "standard family stop"; these 3,000 hotels "conveniently" dotting the country are "not fancy, but when you want a soft bed at night", a pool (often indoors) "to keep the kids busy" and "a good [free] breakfast, this is it" for "budget travel" – they also "almost always allow pets"; still, "rooms are on the small side", and "different locations vary greatly": some are "more tired than you are" when you arrive.

Courtyard by Marriott
21 | 21 | 19 | 20 | M

800-321-2211; www.marriott.com/courtyard

■ At the "good-value" family wagon in Marriott's "fleet of brands", there's "lots of space" "in the living room–style lobby" and "video games and a pool to keep preteens busy so you don't have to go anywhere the day after traveling"; when you are ready to see the sights, these 508 U.S. properties are "convenient to the highway" in "good touring locations", and the "free breakfasts give the kick factor" needed to get your group in gear.

Crowne Plaza
19 | 22 | 19 | 21 | M

800-227-6963; www.crowneplaza.com

■ "Comfortable for parents" who, unlike at more chichi hotels, "don't have to worry about the noise their kids may make", these 93 "vacation-destination hotels" are "usually centered in tourist cities" or "resort settings" near "lots of sightseeing" for the whole family; "clean, bright and well-run" with "great pool facilities", the chain is "a small step above the average."

DoubleTree

21 | 21 | 20 | 21 | M

800-222-8733; www.doubletree.com

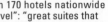 "Kids love the chocolate chip cookies" at this 160-strong Hilton brand offering a range of "affordable" hotels from "plush to plebeian", mostly "located near attractions"; it's "more child-friendly than other properties where the rooms are pretty small" – the "comfy" all-suite "oases" present "an excellent way for a family to travel together and not drive each other nuts."

Embassy Suites

26 | 24 | 21 | 23 | M

800-362-2779; www.embassysuites.com

■ "A mom must have built this" outfit with 170 hotels nationwide offering an "excellent solution for family travel": "great suites that help parents stay sane and let kids have fun" while "two rooms with two TVs means everyone's happy"; the "dining table, microwave and mini-fridge are helpful" and "washing machines are available" for use while the little ones take advantage of indoor pools, game rooms and organized activities; the free "breakfast is a hit with children", and the happy hour pleases adults.

Fairfield Inn by Marriott

20 | 17 | 17 | 17 | I

800-228-2800; www.marriott.com/fairfieldinn

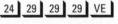 "Dependable and affordable", Marriott's "no-frills" "road-trip hotel" chain's 480 facilities deliver "adequate rooms", a "free breakfast that exceeds expectations" and "service with a smile" "in good locations" at "bargain prices" "for families on a budget"; one tip: "be sure to reserve in advance for any needed extras, like a portable crib."

Fairmont

22 | 26 | 26 | 25 | E

800-441-1414; www.fairmont.com

■ "Parents shouldn't suffer just because they're traveling with children" seems to be the idea behind the "incredible service and attention to kids" at these 16 "routinely elegant" U.S. hotels and resorts providing family-friendly packages that include "top facilities" and "luxurious amenities" "without breaking the bank"; all this plus "super food" "makes everyone feel at home" or rather, wish that home was really this good.

Four Seasons

24 | 29 | 29 | 29 | VE

800-332-3442; www.fourseasons.com

■ Super "luxe but also kid-friendly", these 24 "top-notch" U.S. locations employ staffs that "dote on children just as they do adults"; "cookies and milk magically appear, as do child-size terry robes", "cribs with all bath and diaper amenities", "pint-size slippers" and "adorable gifts" for tots are the norm; "they even have age-appropriate activities", "optional baby-proofing" and "sitters for parents who want to spend an evening on the town"; "you'll pay a pretty penny for it", but your whole family will be pleasantly "spoiled" – as in "spoiled!"

Hampton Inn

22 | 20 | 21 | 20 | M

800-426-7866; www.hamptoninn.com

■ Even when your "kids are keyed up from being in the car all day", the "friendly" staff at this "service-oriented" chain is "very hospitable"; the rooms, including some "suites suited for families", are "average in amenities and decor", but they're "always clean" and "comfortable" "at a reasonable price"; the "expanded continental breakfast includes healthy choices" to nourish growing bodies, and the 1,000 U.S. locations "seem to always have pools" for the amusement of your tadpoles.

Hilton

| 19 | 21 | 20 | 21 | E |

800-445-8667; www.hilton.com

☑ "Huge beds" in "comfortable rooms", "many amenities and usually good restaurants" make these 231 U.S. locales "reliably nice" for a stay; "if the Hilton is a resort" or a "lovely Garden Inn", "the experience will be very positive" for the little ones; otherwise, the "standard", "stuffy" hotels have a business edge and are "more tolerant of, than welcoming to, children" – "besides the pools, there are not a lot of family-oriented things."

Holiday Inn

| 22 | 17 | 18 | 18 | M |

800-465-4329; www.holiday-inn.com

☑ "If you don't want to spend a lot", "a good stop" "while driving" with a hungry "toddler in tow" should be one of these 1,500 U.S. properties ("you can't beat free food for kids" under 12 years old); the staff is "knowledgeable and friendly", some locations have "great pools", the rooms are "ok, if nothing spectacular", and part of the appeal is that "there are a lot of families, so children can play with one another"; "you usually get what you pay for" even if sometimes "the quality is uneven."

Homewood Suites

| 24 | 22 | 18 | 20 | M |

800-225-5466; www.homewood-suites.com

■ As the name suggests, this "long-stay chain" with 120 U.S. hotels sports suites that are "a lot like home" with "great kitchens", "well-furnished sitting areas" and "doors you can shut"; a "real breakfast", the manager's weekday evening buffet, "tea and coffee round-the-clock" and a 24-hour on-site convenience store "contribute to the family fun"; computer-savvy types look forward to the addition of high-speed Internet access.

Hyatt

| 22 | 22 | 22 | 24 | E |

800-223-1234; www.hyatt.com

■ While many of its city "hotels are more suited to business travelers", this group includes some "very family-friendly" hotels "catering to kids" among its 122 properties; Camp Hyatt is one of the "best-managed children's programs" around, staffed by "cheery" folks "willing to go the extra mile" to help little ones "feel like they are really on vacation", so this "consistently good, if consistently pricey"; option is almost always "first tier."

La Quinta

| 19 | 18 | 16 | 16 | M |

800-531-5900; www.lq.com

☑ "The family pet is accepted [almost] everywhere" in this "relaxed", chain with 330 links "conveniently located" in major destinations; if you don't expect more than "clean", "bare-bones" digs and a "free, reasonably diverse breakfast served early" then you, your "younger kids" and Fido will "have a great stay" at a "very good value."

Loews

| ▽ 22 | 24 | 22 | 24 | E |

800-235-6397; www.loewshotels.com

■ You may "see as many dogs as kids" at these 18 "outstanding", "welcoming places for the whole family, including well-behaved pets" of every feline and canine breed; this group "really has its act together": "lots of fun programs" and "special children's gift bags are big hits" with small fry, while "excellent service, large and beautiful rooms" and (best of all) free stays for young 'uns 18 and under make parents "big fans."

Marriott Hotels & Resorts

| 22 | 23 | 23 | 23 | E |

800-228-9290; www.marriott.com

☑ "Seemingly everywhere", this brand (with 279 spots in the U.S. alone) is "definitely a favorite for the teen and preteen age groups", with "well-maintained pools" and "activities to keep them busy" in many locations, and a staff "not intimidated by children" – or pets in some places; however, the "level of amenities, styling and maintenance varies immensely", with not enough "kid-friendly restaurants."

Omni
▽ 20 | 23 | 21 | 22 | E

800-843-6664; www.omnihotels.com

■ "How can you beat being greeted with a loot bag full of candy and toys at check-in" at this chain of 37 U.S. hotels with a "unique kids' program"?; add to that "lists of nearby attractions", fine "restaurants that serve toddlers with a smile", a suitcase filled with stuff to play with, in-room video games, free high-speed Internet access and a designated children's Web site, and you've got "a good choice for family travel."

Park Hyatt
▽ 21 | 27 | 28 | 27 | VE

800-223-1234; www.park.hyatt.com

■ "Service seems significantly better than at a regular Hyatt" when you check into one of these eight "luxurious" hotels; they may be "more oriented to business travelers", but under the new Kidscierge program, the staff delivers "personal touches" to younger guests, including discounts for area attractions, cameras, diaries to record the fun and even tours behind the scenes to see how the "upscale" facilities operate; they "can be pricey", but the 50 percent discount on an additional room for the kids makes it more affordable.

Radisson
19 | 19 | 18 | 18 | M

800-333-3333; www.radisson.com

◪ "A port in the storm", this brand offers "inexpensive double-room suites" that are "great" for big broods, especially given specials on weekends and specific outposts where "kids under 12 receive free meals"; though some find the convenient locations "relaxing for a family stay", modernists maintain that at many of its 168 hotels, the "old lady is showing her age."

Residence Inn by Marriott
26 | 24 | 21 | 22 | M

800-331-3131; www.marriott.com/residenceinn

■ The longer you stay, the cheaper each night gets, so settle in and "spread out" in "apartment-style" accommodations at the 382 U.S. properties of this chain, voted No. 1 for Family Appeal in this *Survey*; units run from "large studios with full living rooms" to suites "set up like houses", all with "well-equipped kitchens" that "make traveling more affordable because you aren't forced to eat out" – in fact, a "wonderful breakfast buffet" is included, and they'll even "grocery shop for you" while you and your kids enjoy the pool and recreation facilities.

Ritz-Carlton
22 | 28 | 28 | 28 | VE

800-241-3333; www.ritzcarlton.com

■ "Impeccable service" means "it's nearly impossible to have a bad stay" at these 26 "pampering" spots throughout the nation; "beautiful rooms" with child-proofing available, "children's menus and even gifts make them very desirable for all ages"; if you think "for the price, you might want to save these properties for a romantic getaway" or a business jaunt, think again: with the "great Ritz Kids program" "in full swing at most resort locations, you can relax and enjoy the top-notch spa facilities" and "typically great pools and grounds" while your kids partake of a "variety of activities" without you.

Sheraton
20 | 20 | 20 | 21 | E

800-325-3535; www.sheraton.com

◪ It might be "more for the convention set", but "families have never been a problem" for the 74 well-above-average properties in the

States; the "great frequent-guest program" and "Service Promise guarantee make it a good choice" at an "excellent value", as the "friendly staff" "tries to accommodate needs" like "special meals for children"; at the resort locations, the recreational facilities can be "exceptional", but "the problem is variability" across the brand, with "some great" hotels mixed in with "others that need work."

Westin

22 | 25 | 24 | 25 | E

800-228-3000; www.westin.com

■ "If your name isn't Rockefeller, a great choice" for a "stylish" but "comfortable" stay is this "upper-middle" chain that "knows how to treat families"; at several of the 81 "elegant" properties in the U.S., "kid-friendly touches such as free drinks, children's menus", "fabulous pools with waterslides" and "plenty for 6- to 12-year-olds to do" make for an "enjoyable experience" for the munchkins and "relaxation for the 'rents", "especially at the resorts."

Wyndham

21 | 21 | 20 | 23 | E

800-822-4200; www.wyndham.com

■ The "excellent ByRequest program" at this "classy" lodging group encompassing "older, converted hotels", newer properties and resorts provides "valuable benefits" like "free local and long-distance calls and Internet to keep the kids happy on your laptop"; the 91 facilities are staffed by "knowledgeable" folks with "no attitude", but "luxury comes at a hefty price", so for the best value, try one of the family-oriented packages, which include tickets to local attractions.

Restaurant Chains

Addresses for individual chain locations appear in their Nearest City/Resort section. The top 10 chains include those with 10 locations or more.

Top by Family Appeal

27 Rainforest Cafe
26 Chuck E. Cheese's
       Dave & Buster's
25 Red Robin
       Old Spaghetti Factory
       Johnny Rockets
24 Bubba Gump Shrimp Co.
       Original Pancake House
       Fuddrucker's
       In-N-Out Burger

Ratings: Family Appeal, Food, Decor, Service, Cost

Applebee's
21 | 16 | 17 | 17 | M

888-592-7753; www.applebees.com

☑ Parents "feel very comfortable" bringing children to this "decent" 49-state Traditional American since youngsters can "color with crayons", "be loud and get food on the floor" as they ponder the locally-themed "faux-antique" "tchotchkes on the walls"; partisans point out the "basic" fare at "moderate prices" is "ideal for young, unadventurous taste buds", and staffers will even bring "extra cherries for milkshakes"; pickier people pan "predictable", "bland" fodder that's "kid-friendly but not nutrition-rich", "painfully slow" service and the "smoky bars" positioned "right as you walk in."

Baja Fresh Mexican Grill
20 | 22 | 14 | 18 | I

877-225-2373; www.bajafresh.com

■ This "upscale" Cal-Mex chain is "*muy bueno*" for families, say supporters who savor "generous portions" of "healthy" (lard- and MSG-free), "flavorful" fare that's "fast but not greasy"; "highly customizable" "finger-food" meals in a semi-self-serve setup ("kids go nuts" over the "fun salsa bar") can be had at "reasonable prices", and though there's "no decor to speak of", the "clean and well-kept" spaces are "colorful" with "upbeat Spanish music" and "plenty of high chairs"; in all, it's "a sure bet", especially for hungry tots.

Benihana
23 | 20 | 18 | 22 | E

800-327-3369; www.benihana.com

■ There's "no need for crayons" at this "festive" Japanese grill group that "captivates kids" with its trademark "slicing-and-serving" spectacle: "entertaining cooks" juggle "twirling knives and flaming steak" and send "shrimp flying onto your plate"; indeed, some youngsters "enjoy the preparation more than the eating" and a few adults fret the "theatrics" aren't suitable for toddlers "scared by flames", but most maintain "the only downside" is "kids think they can play with their food too."

Bertucci's
23 | 20 | 17 | 19 | M

800-290-0280; www.bertuccis.com

■ "Pizza is the ultimate in family friendliness", and these East Coast pie-and-pasta pavilions are "delightful for children" who can watch the brick-oven versions being assembled ("it's like a babysitter!") and then "pretend to make their own" with "dough balls for mushing"; "consistently great" slices with "thin, crispy crusts" and "unique" specialty toppings please even adult palates – though "decent" noodle and meat entrees may be "uneven" – and owing to "kind", "patient" staffers and "easy-on-the-wallet" prices, most are willing to tolerate the "long waits."

Bubba Gump Shrimp Co.

| 24 | 18 | 23 | 20 | M |

877-729-4867; www.bubbagump.com

☑ These "colorful and inspiring" ersatz shrimp shacks are packed with "small touches" that appeal to kids, including "paper towels in a bucket" and a "sign that reads 'Stop Forrest'" to make "the server come to you"; as a result, it's "a must for fans of the movie [*Forrest Gump*], but not necessarily of great cuisine", since the vibe is "touristy" and the seafood's just "so-so" – what's more, "with the film now 10 years old", "younger ones might not know" who the place is named for.

Buca di Beppo

| 24 | 19 | 22 | 21 | M |

www.bucadibeppo.com

■ "Gaudy" ("a cross between a shrine and a bordello") yet somehow also "homey", these pastapaloozas dish up "heavy-on-the-garlic" Southern Italian specialties in "enormous" "family-style portions" designed for sharing ("great for those with sextuplets"); party people are partial to the "fun staff" and "rambunctious" setting that's "noisy enough to bring small kids to", though a smattering of parents warn the experience "could be overstimulating" or "overwhelming" for the littlest ones.

California Pizza Kitchen

| 21 | 21 | 16 | 19 | M |

800-275-8255; www.cpk.com

■ There's "a pizza for every family member's tastes" (whether "traditional" or "funky" and "creative") plus "super salads" at this collection of "bright", "innovative" eateries, "one of America's most consistent chains"; what's more, "receptive" servers "go out of their way" to "make kids welcome and keep them occupied" with activity books, then obligingly "don't make you wait for your check" – so even though a few folks figure it's just "mall food with pizzazz" that's become increasingly "pricey", these "sure-bet" Kitchens remain hot.

Cheesecake Factory

| 21 | 23 | 21 | 20 | M |

www.thecheesecakefactory.com

☑ Everything's "mammoth" at this "upscale" American group that overflows with "enchanting, pseudo–Arabian Nights" decor; that's good news to fans who favor its "eye-boggling" "novel" of a menu ("as long as *War and Peace*") with "humongous portions" of "trendy food" and an array of "30-plus cheesecakes"; it's bad news to detractors who dislike "two-hour waits" ("a problem for kids") and wish youngsters could get smaller servings.

Chevys Fresh Mex

| 23 | 19 | 18 | 18 | M |

800-424-3897; www.chevys.com

■ "They welcome kids here" applaud amigos of these "lively and noisy", mostly coastal cantinas that offer balloons, crayons, chips and "dough that's great fun to play with" along with a "tortilla-making machine" to watch "until the food arrives"; culinarily, these "tried-and-true" spots are "solid performers", with "less grease in your enchiladas" and "non-Mexican options for the littlest of picky eaters"; one caveat: "quality varies so much by location."

Chili's Grill & Bar

| 21 | 19 | 18 | 19 | M |

800-983-4637; www.chilis.com

■ "No, it's not gourmet", but the "reliable", "decent food and family atmosphere" make these "affordable" Mexican-American hybrids "good places to stop if you are on the road"; there's a "wide variety" of casual grub (burgers, ribs and wings, "great fajitas", "margaritas to milkshakes"), a "kids' menu that kids like", "rapid drink refills", "unbreakable" crockery, and crayons and games, plus a "noise level suitable to mask a child's squeals"; though nutritional nitpickers moan "oh, my aching arteries", the "long lines" prove this "formula works."

Chuck E. Cheese's

| 26 | 10 | 17 | 13 | I |

www.chuckecheese.com

☑ "Do you really go here for the food?" ask adults attracted to this "kid magnet" for its arcade games, rides, tubes and slides and "robo-critter" "musicians" that keep youngsters "busy and happy" on "rainy Saturday afternoons" till they "wear themselves out"; not surprisingly, discerning diners dis the "limp pizza" ("cardboard smothered in tomato soup") and "grumpy" employees, and caution that the "chaos" can be "deafening", so "wear earplugs" and "bring the Tylenol."

Claim Jumper Restaurant

| 23 | 24 | 22 | 21 | M |

800-949-4538; www.claimjumper.com

■ Miners *and* minors dig this California-based chain whose "great family appeal" derives from the "mountain feel" of its "woodsy" decor (natural rock and timber, corrugated and pressed tin, log chairs), a "fun wait staff" and "oversized portions" of "good old American" vittles; "kids' menus are excellent", and though rotisserie specialties and lots of steak render it "best for carnivores", there's also a "well-stocked salad bar"; P.S. experienced prospectors confide "bring an empty stomach and a full wallet."

Dave & Buster's

| 26 | 16 | 21 | 17 | M |

www.daveandbusters.com

■ "Woo-hoo!" rave respondents about these "video-game parlors on steroids" (i.e. "Chuck E. Cheese's for grown-ups") that are "perfect for families with preteens"; the sites' "carnival-like" arcades encompass hundreds of games, virtual-reality simulators, pool and shuffleboard tables where "you'll spend $100", but at least the "very good" Traditional American fare (pasta, burgers, seafood) comes at "reasonable prices"; note that the scene's likely to be "too much for toddlers" especially with smoke from the "bars everywhere", "long waits for tables" and the "head-splitting" noise level.

Don Pablo's

| 20 | 19 | 18 | 18 | I |

800-372-2567; www.donpablos.com

■ Thanks to "festive decor", "efficient" staffers and a menu that "satisfies even picky" eaters, "toddlers and young children are kept happy" at these "good Tex-Mex" joints; however, parents are more ambivalent: supporters say the south-of-the-border suppers are "surprisingly good" and the vibe "casual enough that you don't have to worry about spilling", while critics call the *comida* "mediocre" and complain about the "noisy, busy" environment.

Fuddrucker's

| 24 | 20 | 15 | 16 | I |

www.fuddruckers.com

■ "Your little carnivores" can "design their own" "great, big, juicy hamburgers" at this "comfortable" "cafeteria-style" chain where patties are "made to order" for patrons who then accessorize them at the "toppings buffet" ("as much cheese as you want!"); meanwhile, the "health-conscious" can get "huge salads", "fish or even an ostrich burger", and the kids' menu includes a free dessert; "prices are a little high" but "worth it" for the "quality", even though doubters may dub the decor "obnoxiously bright" and the service "sometimes lacking."

Hard Rock Cafe

| 22 | 16 | 26 | 18 | M |

www.hardrock.com

☑ If your baby wants to rock 'n' roll, bring him or her to "explore all the decorations" at this "dependable" American burger chain/"music hall of fame"/"cool" gift shop; the tunes might be "too loud" for the tiniest ears, but the "noise will drown out the ruckus kids cause", and if the "little ones can't figure out why mommy is drooling over a dress from Madonna", at least the displays are "updated from time to time"

so maybe there'll be something from Britney or Justin for your preteen to ogle.

In-N-Out Burger
| 24 | 24 | 13 | 21 | I |

www.in-n-out.com

☑ "Mmmmm" – it's "just burgers, fries and shakes, but what burgers, fries and shakes they are": "piping hot", "juicy", "fresh" patties, "delicious" spuds and "really thick" ice-cream drinks "made to order" "have achieved cult status" for this "Cadillac of fast-food" chains; the "lack of variety may be a problem for picky" toddlers but "young children and preteens should be ok", while adolescents and adults "savvy to the off-the-menu slang" simply say "is anything better than a Double-Double Animal Style?"

Joe's Crab Shack
| 23 | 17 | 21 | 19 | M |

800-552-6379; www.joescrabshack.com

■ The only thing crabby is the menu at one of the "funnest" seafood collections on the high seas; "when the loud music starts, the staff claps, dances" and "sings", and it's perfectly acceptable for toddlers to boogie "in the aisles" between the picnic tables and beneath the "junk hanging from the ceiling"; after they get their "crustacean-leg fix", at most locations the little ones can romp in the outdoor playground – "what else could a kid want?"

Johnny Rockets
| 25 | 17 | 20 | 18 | I |

888-856-4669; www.johnnyrockets.com

☑ "As the Beach Boys said", "the whole family" "will have fun, fun, fun" in a "Formica"-and-"vinyl booth" rockin' to the "tableside jukebox" and pretending they're "in an episode of *Happy Days*" at this collection of "'50s replica diners"; the "singing, dancing" waiters and "ketchup smiley faces" "get a reaction out of kids" and the "limited" all-American burger menu is "decent", though some say "grease" isn't just a "nostalgic" movie reference here.

LongHorn Steakhouse
| 21 | 21 | 19 | 21 | M |

www.longhornsteakhouse.com

■ Children can "look at all the animals and pictures on the walls" or "color to their hearts' content" so adults "can enjoy a decent steak" and a "delicious" baked sweet potato at this herd of "heavy-duty Texas-style" cow palaces where the "attentive, friendly staff" will "mortify" your preteen with a special birthday song; between the country music and the celebrations, it's "good and loud, so it's safe if your kids are noisy."

Maggiano's Little Italy
| 22 | 22 | 21 | 22 | M |

www.maggianos.com

■ "When you have a long time to eat and enjoy" a meal, a "great place for a big dinner with the kids and grandparents" (if the adults "check their Atkins handbooks at the door") is one of these "slightly upscale" Italians for "terrific-value" "family-style" meals; "though they don't have kids' menus", there's still "enough variety for every generation", and if they're "noisy", maybe that's because the joints "scream 'yummy pasta'" as loudly as your kids will.

Max & Erma's
| 22 | 20 | 19 | 21 | I |

www.maxandermas.com

■ "Who doesn't love a bathtub full of ice cream?" – you might not when your kid is bouncing off the walls after too many runs to the "make-your-own sundae bar"; if you rein in the progeny's sweet tooth, though, these "average burger" joints are a "safe bet" for a "fast, friendly", "reasonable" meal; there are "plenty of tasty choices on the children's menu", plus crayons, puzzles and "lots of room" to roam while the grown-ups gobble that overloaded signature "best", the Garbage Burger.

Medieval Times
29 | 14 | 25 | 19 | E

888-935-6878; www.medievaltimes.com

■ "There's a show and no manners" required – "what more can a kid ask for" in an enjoyable (k)night?; paper-crowned Arthurs and Gueneveres "make slobs of themselves" "feasting with their fingers" and "stomping their feet" for the "elaborate jousting" in the sawdust-strewn ring at these dinner theaters; the Continental meal is "just to keep you busy between scenes", but if "your hosts are into their roles", the experience is "stellar."

Mimi's Cafe
23 | 21 | 22 | 20 | M

866-566-4647; www.mimiscafe.com

■ "Catering to children" "with French flair", these "midrangers" offer "a wonderful variety" of Franco-American fare that's a "relief to parents of impatient, hungry little mouths"; "they immediately bring out" "a kids' appetizer as you are seated", along with a menu/activity page and crayons, but "the highlight" is the 'worms in dirt': gummy worms on chocolate pudding with cookie crumbs"; "you might even be able to read the Sunday paper" while your toddler "makes a mess" with the dessert.

O'Charley's
22 | 21 | 18 | 18 | I

www.ocharleys.com

☑ "Kids eat free!" – "you can't beat that" say parents who "love" this "good-value" steak spots "for meat and potatoes"; every adult can get meals on the house for up to two children 10 years old or younger, and though the "service can be spotty" and the "decor is uninspired", the "salads are great", and the prime rib? – "yummm!"

Old Spaghetti Factory, The
25 | 20 | 22 | 20 | I

www.osf.com

■ "Spaghetti eating is a relaxed" (if not relaxing) "event" at these "fast, friendly and cheap" Italian eateries offering all-inclusive meals; "heaping portions and vintage" decor including a "trolley car to eat in" and booths made from bed frames are "wonderfully interesting" for kids; parents like that it's so "crowded and loud", "no one notices if your child decides to be vocal" – "just don't put your toddlers in their Sunday best."

Olive Garden
20 | 19 | 18 | 19 | M

800-331-2729; www.olivegarden.com

☑ "Little pasta eaters" can also "scarf down" the "breadsticks and all-you-can-eat soup/salad deal", making these "Americanized Italian" pasta-pleasers "God's gift" to parents "on a budget"; even if staffers do "tend to seat [all] families in the same loud room", "toddlers feel like big kids" amid the "faux"-"fancy" decor, though more sophisticated diners prefer to "find an authentic restaurant rather than endure the basic, uninspired options" here.

On the Border
Mexican Grill & Cantina
20 | 19 | 19 | 18 | M

800-983-4637; www.ontheborder.com

☑ "Any restaurant that immediately serves food helps stave off kids' tantrums", so parents "love" the "bottomless chips" and "free-flowing", "spicy" salsa at "one of the better Mexican chains" for families; "the music, liveliness", "fun-to-watch" tortilla machine and "dessert included in children's meals" help keep *amigos pequeños* happy, and even if the eats are "nothing special", a "decent margarita" might cheer up the big folks.

Original Pancake House, The
24 | 22 | 12 | 17 | I

www.originalpancakehouse.com

☑ "My babies craved these" "light, fluffy pancakes" "in the womb" claim carbohydrate-carrying members of the OPH fan club; the "cheap", "wonderful breakfast menu" includes the namesake "gargantuan" "showstoppers" in all sorts of flavors with a good variety of syrups, plus "surprisingly delicious" "omelets the size of footballs"; the "peak-time waits are a nightmare", "service is slow" and the decor is nonexistent, but these Traditional Americans are "very popular with kids."

Outback Steakhouse
20 | 22 | 18 | 20 | M

www.outback.com

☑ "One of the few places where grown-ups can get a decent steak without leaving the kids behind with a sitter", this Aussie chophouse chain cheers children with a "friendly staff", a "fun atmosphere", "free refills" on drinks and a "bloomin' good Bloomin' Onion" appetizer; it might be "too dark and too loud" with too long a wait for wee ones, but you can "call ahead" for a table, and the "healthy, delicious", "abundant" fare "appeals to preteens."

Planet Hollywood
24 | 13 | 24 | 16 | M

www.planethollywood.com

☑ "No two" of these "family hot spots" "have the same decor", so "children enjoy" the "excitement of seeing the different locations'" "amazing" collections of "movie memorabilia" when they travel; perhaps the Tinseltown-"themed stalwart has lost a bit of its luster over the years ", but props like a "car hanging from the ceiling" still "almost make you forget" that the "overpriced" American grub "is scarier than Freddy Krueger's glove."

Rainforest Cafe
27 | 16 | 27 | 18 | M

800-552-6379; www.rainforestcafe.com

☑ The "animals come alive" – not those on your plate, but the animatronic "elephants, gorillas" and "talking parrots" at these "awesome jungle"-themed joints that garnered the top Decor and Family Appeal ratings for restaurant chains in this *Survey*; at least "there is much for little eyes to gaze at" during the "long wait for seating" for "just ok" American eats, but keep in mind that the "realistic" "rainstorms with thunder can be scary for toddlers and babies" and the gift shop is a fright for your wallet, as your kids "will want everything" in it.

Red Robin
25 | 20 | 19 | 20 | M

www.redrobin.com

■ "Built on the food groups with universal appeal for kids", these "fast-paced" casual eateries with "a large variety" of "fantastic" burgers and "great" "bottomless fries" "specializes in serving families, so they know how to delight" with crayons and balloons, "brightly colored decor", video games and "the big Red Robin" "mascot" "who wanders around" at certain times; "the servers aren't much older than your preschooler", but they are "chipper as hell."

Roadhouse Grill
20 | 18 | 16 | 18 | M

www.roadhousegrill.com

■ "Kids can party" with "the pail of peanuts" on your "plank table", "throwing shells on the floor" "while waiting for their order" at these "nice, casual" steakhouse/rib spots; the atmosphere gets particularly "goofy" on Tuesdays when "children eat free" and "they have a clown" blowing up balloons; for big people, the "hot" "rolls are great, the rest of the food is pretty good" and "the servings are plentiful enough."

Romano's Macaroni Grill
| 21 | 21 | 19 | 21 | M |

800-983-4637; www.macaronigrill.com

■ It's "a kid's dream" to "color on the table", so the "butcher paper" and crayons "keep little minds occupied while adults eat" at this "Americanized Italian"; it's "a far cry from fine dining", but even with finicky tykes, "you can never go wrong with pasta", and picky parents also "love the make-your-own" option for mix-and-match noodles and sauces; the "friendly", "loud atmosphere" and "young" staff that caters to children are also "a real hit" with hungry families.

Ruby's
| 24 | 19 | 20 | 19 | I |

www.rubys.com

■ "The throwback '50s decor has surefire appeal" "for kids of any age" – "just be sure to wear your poodle skirt" so you can really embarrass your preteens while they chew through all-American "favorites" like "loaded cheese fries", "delicious burgers and shakes"; younger children "enjoy the coloring sheet and crayons", and best of all, "no one notices if your kids are loud because so are everyone else's" here.

Ryan's Family Steakhouse
| 24 | 17 | 12 | 16 | I |

www.ryansinc.com

■ "If you're in the all-you-can-eat frame of mind", "the whole family has a great time" at these "typical buffets" where "you can feed lots of people" of all ages "pretty cheaply" (in fact, "little ones under four years old dine free"); the fare may be "ordinary, but kids don't care what they have for dinner" – "it's the dessert bar that appeals to them."

T.G.I. Friday's
| 21 | 17 | 18 | 17 | M |

800-374-3297; www.tgifridays.com

☑ "Cute kids' menus", crayons, place mats to color and sometimes even balloons and Magna Doodles make a meal as much a "happy hour" for children as for "adults getting off work" who are heading for a "huge" cocktail at this "'70s" American family "standby"; the fare is "tired" and "service is either molasses or mercury", but you can "be yourselves and not worry about how the babies act", both the one in the diapers and the one crying in his drink.

Tony Roma's
| 20 | 21 | 16 | 19 | M |

www.tonyromas.com

☑ "Ribs all the way, baby!" say carnivorous clans clamoring for the "finger-lickin' good" specialty of this "popular" BBQ brigade; parents find it "fabulous" that they "automatically bring" a kids' appetizer to "take the edge off for hungry tots", the "messy" meals cheer children who "love to eat with their hands", the rustic, "great onion loaf" reminds grandfolks "of the good ol' days" and you can "buy some sauces to take home", so never mind that grumps grouse the grub's "gone downhill."

Uno Chicago Grill
| 20 | 18 | 15 | 16 | M |

866-600-8667; www.unos.com

☑ "Whole families" of "thick-crust" "addicts" descend upon the original Chicago deep-dish pizza parlors for "rich, filling", "damn tasty" pies that "are not even the same food" as the "thin" kind; the "children's menu has variety and contains activities to do while waiting", but even so, it "takes too long" "for the food to come out, so this may not be the best choice for those with [very] young kids."

Indexes

ATTRACTION TYPES
ATTRACTION SPECIAL FEATURES
HOTEL SPECIAL FEATURES
RESTAURANT CUISINES
RESTAURANT SPECIAL FEATURES

Properties in indexes are followed by nearest major city.

ATTRACTION TYPES

(Attractions are followed by the section name in which their reviews appear.)

Amusement/Theme Parks

Adventuredome, *Las Vegas*
Bud's Go-Karts, *Boston/Cape Cod Area*
Busch Gardens, *Other Notable Attractions*
Castles N' Coasters, *Phoenix/Scottsdale*
Cedar Point, *Other Notable Attractions*
Coney Island, *Cincinnati*
Disneyland, *Los Angeles*
Disney-MGM Studios, *Orlando*
Disney's California Adventure, *Los Angeles*
Epcot, *Orlando*
Hersheypark, *Philadelphia/Lancaster*
Hines Carousel Gardens, *New Orleans*
Islands of Adventure, *Orlando*
Jump On Us Trampoline Fun Hse., *Boston/Cape Cod Area*
Knott's Berry Farm, *Los Angeles*
Legoland California, *San Diego*
Magic Kingdom, *Orlando*
Manhattan Expr. Roller Coaster, *Las Vegas*
Paramount's Kings Island, *Cincinnati*
Sesame Place, *Philadelphia/Lancaster*
Silver Dollar City, *St. Louis*
Six Flags, *New Orleans*
Six Flags, *St. Louis*
Six Flags AstroWorld, *Houston*
Six Flags California, *Los Angeles*
Six Flags Elitch Gardens, *Denver*
Six Flags Great Adventure, *Philadelphia/Lancaster*
Six Flags Marine World, *San Francisco*
Six Flags Over Georgia, *Atlanta*
Speed, *Las Vegas*
Stone Mountain Park, *Atlanta*
Universal Studios, *Orlando*
Universal Studios Hollywood, *Los Angeles*

Aquariums

Aquarium of the Bay, *San Francisco*
Audubon Aqua. of Americas, *New Orleans*
Birch Aquarium at Scripps, *San Diego*
Dallas Aquarium, *Dallas/Ft. Worth*
Downtown Aquarium, *Houston*
John G. Shedd Aquarium, *Chicago*
Long Beach Aquarium of Pacific, *Los Angeles*
Maui Ocean Ctr., *Hawaii*
Miami Seaquarium, *Miami*
Monterey Bay Aquarium, *Other Notable Attractions*
National Aquarium, *Baltimore*
New England Aquarium, *Boston/Cape Cod Area*
New England Aqua./Whale Watch, *Boston/Cape Cod Area*
New Jersey State Aquarium, *Philadelphia/Lancaster*
Newport Aquarium, *Cincinnati*
NY Aquarium, *NYC*
Ocean's Journey, *Denver*
Sea Life Park, *Hawaii*
Seattle Aquarium, *Seattle*
SeaWorld, *Orlando*
SeaWorld, *San Diego*
Shark Reef, *Las Vegas*
Waikiki Aquarium, *Hawaii*
Zooquarium, *Boston/Cape Cod Area*

Ballparks

Ballpark in Arlington, *Dallas/ Ft. Worth*
Bank One Ballpark, *Phoenix/ Scottsdale*
Busch Stadium, *St. Louis*
Camden Yards, *Baltimore*
Coors Field, *Denver*
Dodger Stadium, *Los Angeles*
Fenway Park, *Boston/Cape Cod Area*
Great American Ball Park, *Cincinnati*
Minute Maid Park, *Houston*
PETCO Park, *San Diego*
Pro Player Stadium, *Miami*
Safeco Field, *Seattle*
SBC Park, *San Francisco*
Shea Stadium, *NYC*
Turner Field, *Atlanta*
U.S. Cellular Field, *Chicago*
Wrigley Field, *Chicago*
Yankee Stadium, *NYC*

Beaches

(L=Lake; O=Ocean)
Ala Moana Beach Park, *Hawaii* (O)
Assateague Island Nat'l Seashore, *Baltimore* (O)
Cape Cod Nat'l Seashore, *Boston/Cape Cod Area* (O)
Cedar Point, *Other Notable Attractions* (L)
Coronado Island, *San Diego* (O)
Crandon Park, *Miami* (O)
Ft. Derussy Park, *Hawaii* (O)
Hanauma Bay Nature Preserve, *Hawaii* (O)
Haulover Beach Park, *Miami* (O)
Kaanapali Beach, *Hawaii* (O)
La Jolla Cove Beach, *San Diego* (O)
Mackinac Island State Hist. Parks, *Other Notable Attractions* (L)
Malibu Lagoon State Beach, *Los Angeles* (O)
Matheson Hammock Park, *Miami* (O)
Molokini, *Hawaii* (O)

Outer Banks, *Other Notable Attractions* (O)
Santa Monica Pier, *Los Angeles* (O)
Santa Monica State Beach, *Los Angeles* (O)
Tilden Regional Park, *San Francisco* (L)
Venice Boardwalk, *Los Angeles* (O)
Waikiki Beach, *Hawaii* (O)

Famous Buildings & Locations

(See also Government Buildings, Historic)
Coit Tower, *San Francisco*
Coney Island Boardwalk, *NYC*
Coronado Island, *San Diego*
Eiffel Tower Experience, *Las Vegas*
Empire State Bldg., *NYC*
Fisherman's Wharf, *San Francisco*
Fremont St. Experience, *Las Vegas*
Gateway Arch, *St. Louis*
Getty Center, *Los Angeles*
Grand Central Terminal, *NYC*
Lincoln Road Mall, *Miami*
Mark Twain Boyhood Home, *St. Louis*
Mark Twain Cave, *St. Louis*
Old Town Scottsdale, *Phoenix/ Scottsdale*
Prudential Ctr./Skywalk, *Boston/Cape Cod Area*
Reunion Tower Observation Deck, *Dallas/Ft. Worth*
Rockefeller Center, *NYC*
Sears Tower, *Chicago*
Space Needle, *Seattle*
Times Square, *NYC*
Union Station, *Chicago*
United Nations, *NYC*
Universal CityWalk, *Los Angeles*
Winterthur/Enchanted Woods, *Philadelphia/Lancaster*
World Trade Ctr. Site, *NYC*

Film & Television
American Mus./Moving Image, *NYC*
CNN Ctr., *Atlanta*
Disney-MGM Studios, *Orlando*
Grauman's Chinese Theatre, *Los Angeles*
Lincoln Road Mall, *Miami*
Metreon, *San Francisco*
Movie Studios/Las Colinas, *Dallas/Ft. Worth*
Museum/Television & Radio, *Los Angeles*
Museum/Television & Radio, *NYC*
NBC Studios, *Los Angeles*
Star Trek: The Experience, *Las Vegas*
Universal Studios Hollywood, *Los Angeles*
Warner Bros. Studios, *Los Angeles*

Gardens/Orchards
Arnold Arboretum, *Boston/ Cape Cod Area*
Atlanta Botanical Garden, *Atlanta*
Brooklyn Botanic Garden, *NYC*
Chicago Botanic Garden, *Chicago*
Cincinnati Zoo/Botanical Garden, *Cincinnati*
Dallas Arboretum/Botanical Garden, *Dallas/Ft. Worth*
Denver Botanic Gardens, *Denver*
Descanso Gardens, *Los Angeles*
Desert Botanical Garden, *Phoenix/Scottsdale*
Dumbarton Oaks, *Washington, DC*
Fairchild Tropical Garden, *Miami*
Ft. Worth Botanic Garden, *Dallas/Ft. Worth*
Gardens/Morris Arboretum, *Philadelphia/Lancaster*
Huntington Library, *Los Angeles*
Japanese Tea Garden, *San Francisco*
Krohn Conservatory, *Cincinnati*
Longwood Gardens, *Philadelphia/Lancaster*
Marymoor Park, *Seattle*
Missouri Botanical Garden, *St. Louis*
Morton Arboretum, *Chicago*
National Arboretum, *Washington, DC*
New Orleans Botanical Garden, *New Orleans*
NY Botanical Garden, *NYC*
U.S. Botanical Garden, *Washington, DC*
Vizcaya Mus./Gardens, *Miami*
Washington Park Arboretum, *Seattle*
Winterthur/Enchanted Woods, *Philadelphia/Lancaster*

Government Buildings
Bureau of Engraving & Printing, *Washington, DC*
Denver U.S. Mint, *Denver*
Georgia State Capitol, *Atlanta*
National Archives, *Washington, DC*
State Capitol, *Denver*
Supreme Court, *Washington, DC*
U.S. Capitol, *Washington, DC*
White House, *Washington, DC*

Historic
Alcatraz Island, *San Francisco*
Betsy Ross House, *Philadelphia/Lancaster*
Black Heritage Trail, *Boston/ Cape Cod Area*
Brandywine Battlefield, *Philadelphia/Lancaster*
Cabildo, *New Orleans*
Chalmette Battlefield/Nat'l Cemetery, *New Orleans*
Colonial Williamsburg, *Other Notable Attractions*
East. State Penitentiary Hist. Site, *Philadelphia/Lancaster*
Edgar Allan Poe Nat'l Hist. Site, *Philadelphia/Lancaster*

Ford's Theatre/Lincoln Mus., *Washington, DC*

Freedom Trail, *Boston/Cape Cod Area*

George Ranch Hist. Park, *Houston*

Gettysburg Nat'l Military Park, *Baltimore*

Hermann-Grima House, *New Orleans*

Hoover Dam, *Las Vegas*

Independence Nat'l Hist. Park, *Philadelphia/Lancaster*

Iolani Palace, *Hawaii*

Martin Luther King Jr. Birth Home, *Atlanta*

Minute Man Nat'l Hist. Park, *Boston/Cape Cod Area*

Mount Vernon, *Washington, DC*

Old City Park, *Dallas/Ft. Worth*

Old Lahaina Town, *Hawaii*

Old North Church, *Boston/Cape Cod Area*

Old Town Alexandria, *Washington, DC*

Paul Revere House, *Boston/Cape Cod Area*

Presbytere/Mardi Gras Mus., *New Orleans*

San Jacinto Battleground, *Houston*

Statue of Liberty, *NYC*

U.S. Capitol, *Washington, DC*

USS Constellation, *Baltimore*

USS Constitution Mus., *Boston/Cape Cod Area*

Valley Forge, *Philadelphia/Lancaster*

Vizcaya Mus./Gardens, *Miami*

Malls & Shopping

Aloha Flea Mkt., *Hawaii*

American Girl Place, *Chicago*

Arundel Mills, *Baltimore*

CocoWalk, *Miami*

Faneuil Hall/Quincy Mkt., *Boston/Cape Cod Area*

Farmers Mkt., *Los Angeles*

Fremont St. Experience, *Las Vegas*

French Mkt., *New Orleans*

Harvard Square, *Boston/Cape Cod Area*

Italian Mkt., *Philadelphia/Lancaster*

Lincoln Road Mall, *Miami*

L.L. Bean Flagship Store, *Other Notable Attractions*

Macy's, *NYC*

Newport on the Levee, *Cincinnati*

Pike Place Mkt., *Seattle*

Prudential Ctr./Skywalk, *Boston/Cape Cod Area*

16th Street Mall, *Denver*

Toys "R" Us, *NYC*

Underground Atlanta, *Atlanta*

Union Station, *Washington, DC*

West End Mktpl., *Dallas/Ft. Worth*

Monuments & Memorials

Arlington Nat'l Cemetery, *Washington, DC*

Battleship Missouri Memorial, *Hawaii*

Bunker Hill Monument, *Boston/Cape Cod Area*

Chalmette Battlefield/Nat'l Cemetery, *New Orleans*

FDR Memorial, *Washington, DC*

George Wash. Masonic Nat'l Memorial, *Washington, DC*

Holocaust Memorial, *Miami*

Jefferson Memorial, *Washington, DC*

Korean War Veterans Memorial, *Washington, DC*

Lincoln Memorial, *Washington, DC*

Mt. Rushmore, *Other Notable Attractions*

Muir Woods Nat'l Monument, *San Francisco*

San Jacinto Battleground, *Houston*

Sixth Floor Mus./Dealey Plaza, *Dallas/Ft. Worth*

U.S. Holocaust Memorial Museum, *Washington, DC*

Cultural

American Mus./Moving Image, *NYC*

Atlanta History Ctr., *Atlanta*

Baltimore Mus. of Industry, *Baltimore*

Bishop Mus., *Hawaii*

Burke Museum, *Seattle*

Cartoon Art Mus., *San Francisco*

Experience Music Project, *Seattle*

Heard Museum, *Phoenix/Scottsdale*

Hollywood Wax Mus., *Los Angeles*

Internat'l Spy Museum, *Washington, DC*

Japanese Amer. Nat'l Mus., *Los Angeles*

Madame Tussaud's Las Vegas, *Las Vegas*

Madame Tussaud's NY, *NYC*

Michael C. Carlos Mus., *Atlanta*

Musee Conti Wax Mus., *New Orleans*

Museum/American West, *Los Angeles*

Museum/City of NY, *NYC*

Museum/Television & Radio, *Los Angeles*

Museum/Television & Radio, *NYC*

Museum/Tolerance, *Los Angeles*

National Geographic Mus./Explorers Hall, *Washington, DC*

National Mus./American History, *Washington, DC*

National Mus./American Indian, *NYC*

Petersen Automotive Mus., *Los Angeles*

Ripley's Believe It or Not! Odditorium, *Orlando*

Spertus Museum, *Chicago*

Stockyards Collection Mus., *Dallas/Ft. Worth*

Women's Museum, *Dallas/Ft. Worth*

History

Age of Steam Railroad Mus., *Dallas/Ft. Worth*

Atlanta Cyclorama/Civil War Mus., *Atlanta*

Atlanta History Ctr., *Atlanta*

Babe Ruth Birthplace, *Baltimore*

Baltimore Mus. of Industry, *Baltimore*

Bishop Mus., *Hawaii*

Black Heritage Trail, *Boston/Cape Cod Area*

Cabildo, *New Orleans*

Cable Car Mus., *San Francisco*

Chicago Hist. Society, *Chicago*

Cincinnati History Mus., *Cincinnati*

Colorado History Mus., *Denver*

Ellis Island Immigr. Mus., *NYC*

Ford's Theatre/Lincoln Mus., *Washington, DC*

Ft. McHenry, *Baltimore*

Ft. Worth Mus./Science & History, *Dallas/Ft. Worth*

Hawaii Maritime Ctr., *Hawaii*

Holocaust Memorial, *Miami*

Independence Seaport Mus., *Philadelphia/Lancaster*

Intrepid Sea, Air & Space Mus., *NYC*

JFK Library & Mus., *Boston/Cape Cod Area*

King Center, *Atlanta*

Lower E. Side Tenement Mus., *NYC*

Maritime Museum, *San Diego*

Memorial Hall/Confederate Mus., *New Orleans*

Missouri History Mus., *St. Louis*

Musée Mécanique, *San Francisco*

Museum/Flight, *Seattle*

Museum/Tolerance, *Los Angeles*

Museum/Transportation, *St. Louis*

Museum/Westward Expansion, *St. Louis*

National Constitution Ctr., *Philadelphia/Lancaster*

National D-Day Mus., *New Orleans*

National Mus./American History, *Washington, DC*

National Mus./American Indian, *NYC*

National Postal Mus., *Washington, DC*

New England Fire & History Mus., *Boston/Cape Cod Area*

NYC Fire Mus., *NYC*

NY Transit Mus., *NYC*

Old Mint, *New Orleans*

Peabody Museum, *Boston/Cape Cod Area*

Presbytere/Mardi Gras Mus., *New Orleans*

San Diego Aerospace Mus., *San Diego*

Sixth Floor Mus./Dealey Plaza, *Dallas/Ft. Worth*

Skyscraper Museum, *NYC*

Southern Mus./Civil War & Locomotive History, *Atlanta*

South St. Seaport/Mus., *NYC*

Stockyards Collection Mus., *Dallas/Ft. Worth*

University Mus./Archaeol. & Anthrop., *Philadelphia/Lancaster*

U.S. Holocaust Memorial Museum, *Washington, DC*

US Naval Academy, *Baltimore*

USS Constitution Mus., *Boston/Cape Cod Area*

Natural History/Science

Acad. of Natural Sciences, *Philadelphia/Lancaster*

Adler Planetarium/Astronomy Mus., *Chicago*

American Mus./Natural History, *NYC*

Arizona Science Ctr., *Phoenix/Scottsdale*

Burke Museum, *Seattle*

California Science Ctr., *Los Angeles*

Cape Cod Mus./Natural History, *Boston/Cape Cod Area*

Chabot Space/Science Ctr., *San Francisco*

Dallas Mus./Natural History, *Dallas/Ft. Worth*

Denver Mus./Nature & Science, *Denver*

Exploratorium, *San Francisco*

Fernbank Mus. of Natural History/Science, *Atlanta*

Field Mus. of Natural History, *Chicago*

Franklin Inst. Science Mus., *Philadelphia/Lancaster*

Ft. Worth Mus./Science & History, *Dallas/Ft. Worth*

Houston Mus./Natural Science, *Houston*

Intrepid Sea, Air & Space Mus., *NYC*

John P. McGovern Mus./Health, *Houston*

Kennedy Space Ctr., *Orlando*

La Brea Tar Pits/Page Mus., *Los Angeles*

Lawrence Hall of Science, *San Francisco*

Maryland Science Ctr., *Baltimore*

Miami Museum/Science & Planetarium, *Miami*

Museum/Flight, *Seattle*

Museum/Natural Hist. & Science, *Cincinnati*

Museum/Science, *Boston/Cape Cod Area*

Museum/Science & Industry, *Chicago*

National Air & Space Mus., *Washington, DC*

National Geographic Mus./Explorers Hall, *Washington, DC*

National Mus./Natural History, *Washington, DC*

Natural History Mus./LA County, *Los Angeles*

NY Hall of Science, *NYC*

Orlando Science Ctr., *Orlando*

Pacific Science Ctr., *Seattle*

Peggy Notebaert Nature Mus., *Chicago*

Port Discovery, *Baltimore*

Reuben H. Fleet Science Ctr., *San Diego*

Science Place, *Dallas/Ft. Worth*

SciTrek, *Atlanta*

Space Center Houston, *Houston*

St. Louis Science Ctr., *St. Louis*

Natural Sites

(See also Parks)

Assateague Island Nat'l Seashore, *Baltimore*

Cape Poge Wildlife Refuge, *Boston/Cape Cod Area*

Hanauma Bay Nature Preserve, *Hawaii*

Hawaii Nature Ctr./'Iao Valley, *Hawaii*

La Brea Tar Pits/Page Mus., *Los Angeles*

Manoa Falls, *Hawaii*

Muir Woods Nat'l Monument, *San Francisco*

Mystic Falls, *Las Vegas*

Santa Monica State Beach, *Los Angeles*

Parks

Acadia Nat'l Park, *Other Notable Attractions*

Adirondack State Park, *Other Notable Attractions*

Akaka Falls State Park, *Hawaii*

Angel Island State Park, *San Francisco*

Audubon Park, *New Orleans*

Barnacle State Hist. Site, *Miami*

Battery Park, *NYC*

Bill Baggs Cape FL Recreat'l Area, *Miami*

Boston Common, *Boston/Cape Cod Area*

Boston Public Garden, *Boston/Cape Cod Area*

Cabrillo Nat'l Monument, *San Diego*

Casa Grande Ruins Nat'l Monum., *Phoenix/Scottsdale*

Centennial Olympic Park, *Atlanta*

Central Park, *NYC*

City Park, *Denver*

City Park, *New Orleans*

Crandon Park, *Miami*

Crissy Field, *San Francisco*

Everglades Nat'l Park, *Miami*

Fairmount Park, *Philadelphia/Lancaster*

Fair Park, *Dallas/Ft. Worth*

Ft. Derussy Park, *Hawaii*

Ft. McHenry, *Baltimore*

Ft. Point, *San Francisco*

Gateway Arch, *St. Louis*

Golden Gate Park, *San Francisco*

Grand Canyon Nat'l Park, *Other Notable Attractions*

Grand Teton Nat'l Park, *Other Notable Attractions*

Grant Park, *Chicago*

Griffith Park, *Los Angeles*

Haleakala Nat'l Park, *Hawaii*

Hawaii Volcanoes Nat'l Park, *Hawaii*

Hermann Park, *Houston*

Hudson River Park, *NYC*

Independence Nat'l Hist. Park, *Philadelphia/Lancaster*

Klondike Gold Rush Nat'l Hist. Park, *Seattle*

Mackinac Island State Hist. Parks, *Other Notable Attractions*

Malibu Lagoon State Beach, *Los Angeles*

Matheson Hammock Park, *Miami*

McCormick-Stillman Railroad Park, *Phoenix/Scottsdale*

Millennium Park, *Chicago*

Minute Man Nat'l Hist. Park, *Boston/Cape Cod Area*

Mt. Rushmore, *Other Notable Attractions*

Niagara Falls, *Other Notable Attractions*

Old Town San Diego State Hist. Park, *San Diego*

Performing Arts Centers

Planetariums

Religious

Attraction Type Index

Temple Square, *Other Notable Attractions*
Washington Nat'l Cathedral, *Washington, DC*

Spectator Venues
(See also Ballparks, Performing Arts Centers)
American Airlines Arena, *Miami*
American Airlines Ctr., *Dallas/Ft. Worth*
America West Arena, *Phoenix/Scottsdale*
Centennial Olympic Park, *Atlanta*
FleetCenter, *Boston/Cape Cod Area*
Madison Sq. Garden, *NYC*
Reliant Park, *Houston*
Rose Bowl, *Los Angeles*
Soldier Field, *Chicago*
Staples Center, *Los Angeles*
Texas Stadium, *Dallas/Ft. Worth*
USTA Nat'l Tennis Ctr., *NYC*
Wachovia Ctr., *Philadelphia/Lancaster*

Tours
Atlantis Submarine, *Hawaii*
Black Heritage Trail, *Boston/Cape Cod Area*
Circle Line Sightseeing Cruises, *NYC*
CNN Ctr., *Atlanta*
Freedom Trail, *Boston/Cape Cod Area*
Grapevine Vintage Railroad, *Dallas/Ft. Worth*
Lahaina-Kaanapali Sugar Cane Train, *Hawaii*
Mississippi River Boat Tour, *St. Louis*
Monorail, *Seattle*
Scenic Boat Tour, *Orlando*
Staten Island Ferry, *NYC*
World of Coca-Cola Pavillion, *Atlanta*

Water Parks
Beach, The, *Cincinnati*
Blizzard Beach, *Orlando*
Coney Island, *Cincinnati*
Discovery Cove, *Orlando*
Disney's Typhoon Lagoon, *Orlando*
Knott's Soak City, *San Diego*
Six Flags AstroWorld, *Houston*
Six Flags Elitch Gardens, *Denver*
Slide Rock State Park, *Phoenix/Scottsdale*
Splashtown Houston, *Houston*
Venetian Pool, *Miami*
Wet 'n Wild, *Orlando*
Wet 'n Wild Water Park, *Las Vegas*

Zoos/Animal Parks
(See also Aquariums)
Audubon Zoo, *New Orleans*
Baltimore Zoo, *Baltimore*
Bronx Zoo, *NYC*
Brookfield Zoo, *Chicago*
Butterfly House, *St. Louis*
Butterfly Pavilion, *Denver*
Central Park Wildlife Ctr., *NYC*
Chattahoochee Nature Ctr., *Atlanta*
Cincinnati Zoo/Botanical Garden, *Cincinnati*
Dallas Zoo, *Dallas/Ft. Worth*
Denver Zoo, *Denver*
Disney's Animal Kingdom, *Orlando*
Everglades Alligator Farm, *Miami*
Flamingo Wildlife Habitat, *Las Vegas*
Franklin Park Zoo, *Boston/Cape Cod Area*
Ft. Worth Zoo, *Dallas/Ft. Worth*
Gatorland, *Orlando*
Grant's Farm, *St. Louis*
Hanauma Bay Nature Preserve, *Hawaii*
Honolulu Zoo, *Hawaii*
Houston Zoo, *Houston*
Kentucky Horse Park, *Cincinnati*
Lincoln Park Zoo, *Chicago*

Attraction Type Index

ATTRACTION SPECIAL FEATURES

(Indexes list the best of many within each category. Attractions are followed by the section name in which their reviews appear.)

Arcades/Video Games
American Mus./Moving Image, *NYC*
Castles N' Coasters, *Phoenix/Scottsdale*
Cedar Point, *Other Notable Attractions*
Disneyland, *Los Angeles*
GameWorks, *Las Vegas*
Islands of Adventure, *Orlando*
Metreon, *San Francisco*
Musée Mécanique, *San Francisco*
Navy Pier, *Chicago*
Pharaoh's Pavillion, *Las Vegas*
Santa Monica Pier, *Los Angeles*
Six Flags, *New Orleans*
Six Flags AstroWorld, *Houston*
Six Flags Great Adventure, *Philadelphia/Lancaster*
Six Flags Marine World, *San Francisco*
Six Flags Over Georgia, *Atlanta*
Universal Studios, *Orlando*
USS Constitution Mus., *Boston/Cape Cod Area*
Waikiki Beach, *Hawaii*
West End Mktpl., *Dallas/Ft. Worth*

Biking
Angel Island State Park, *San Francisco*
Audubon Park, *New Orleans*
Balboa Park, *San Diego*
Battery Park, *NYC*
Cabrillo Nat'l Monument, *San Diego*
Cape Cod Nat'l Seashore, *Boston/Cape Cod Area*
Central Park, *NYC*
Chelsea Piers, *NYC*
City Park, *Denver*

Fairmount Park, *Philadelphia/Lancaster*
Fisherman's Wharf, *San Francisco*
Grand Canyon Nat'l Park, *Other Notable Attractions*
Grant Park, *Chicago*
Haulover Beach Park, *Miami*
Hudson River Park, *NYC*
Matheson Hammock Park, *Miami*
Papago Park, *Phoenix/Scottsdale*
Phoenix Zoo, *Phoenix/Scottsdale*
Red Rock Canyon, *Las Vegas*
Riverside Park, *NYC*
Rock Creek Park, *Washington, DC*
Rocky Mountain Nat'l Park, *Denver*
South Mountain Park, *Phoenix/Scottsdale*
Tilden Regional Park, *San Francisco*
Venice Boardwalk, *Los Angeles*
White Rock Lake Park, *Dallas/Ft. Worth*
Will Rogers State Hist. Park, *Los Angeles*
Yellowstone Nat'l Park, *Other Notable Attractions*

Educational
(See also Aquariums, Zoos/Animal Parks)
Age of Steam Railroad Mus., *Dallas/Ft. Worth*
Alcatraz Island, *San Francisco*
American Mus./Natural History, *NYC*
American Visionary Art Mus., *Baltimore*
Amon Carter Museum, *Dallas/Ft. Worth*

Attraction Special Feature Index

Attraction Special Feature Index

Travel Town Transport. Mus., *Los Angeles*

Warner Bros. Studios, *Los Angeles*

Women's Museum, *Dallas/ Ft. Worth*

Woodland Park Zoo, *Seattle*

Zooquarium, *Boston/Cape Cod Area*

Full-Service Restaurant

America West Arena, *Phoenix/ Scottsdale*

Art Inst. of Chicago, *Chicago*

Arundel Mills, *Baltimore*

Balboa Park, *San Diego*

Baltimore Mus. of Art, *Baltimore*

Bill Baggs Cape FL Recreat'l Area, *Miami*

Blizzard Beach, *Orlando*

Boston Public Library, *Boston/ Cape Cod Area*

Brandywine Battlefield, *Philadelphia/Lancaster*

Brookfield Zoo, *Chicago*

Cedar Point, *Other Notable Attractions*

Central Park, *NYC*

Chelsea Piers, *NYC*

Chicago Hist. Society, *Chicago*

Cincinnati Art Mus., *Cincinnati*

CocoWalk, *Miami*

Colonial Williamsburg, *Other Notable Attractions*

Coronado Island, *San Diego*

Dallas Mus. of Art, *Dallas/ Ft. Worth*

Disneyland, *Los Angeles*

Disney-MGM Studios, *Orlando*

Disney's Animal Kingdom, *Orlando*

Disney's California Adventure, *Los Angeles*

Disney's Typhoon Lagoon, *Orlando*

Downtown Aquarium, *Houston*

Epcot, *Orlando*

Experience Music Project, *Seattle*

Faneuil Hall/Quincy Mkt., *Boston/Cape Cod Area*

Farmers Mkt., *Los Angeles*

Field Mus. of Natural History, *Chicago*

Fisherman's Wharf, *San Francisco*

Flamingo Wildlife Habitat, *Las Vegas*

FleetCenter, *Boston/Cape Cod Area*

Fremont St. Experience, *Las Vegas*

French Mkt., *New Orleans*

Getty Center, *Los Angeles*

Golden Gate Park, *San Francisco*

Grand Canyon Nat'l Park, *Other Notable Attractions*

Grand Central Terminal, *NYC*

Grant Park, *Chicago*

Hancock Observatory, *Chicago*

Harborplace, *Baltimore*

Hersheypark, *Philadelphia/ Lancaster*

Hudson River Park, *NYC*

Imagine It! Children's Mus., *Atlanta*

Islands of Adventure, *Orlando*

Kennedy Space Ctr., *Orlando*

Legoland California, *San Diego*

Lincoln Ctr., *NYC*

Lincoln Park Zoo, *Chicago*

Lincoln Road Mall, *Miami*

Longwood Gardens, *Philadelphia/Lancaster*

Macy's, *NYC*

Madison Sq. Garden, *NYC*

Magic Kingdom, *Orlando*

Matheson Hammock Park, *Miami*

Maui Ocean Ctr., *Hawaii*

Metropolitan Mus. of Art, *NYC*

Michael C. Carlos Mus., *Atlanta*

Minute Maid Park, *Houston*

Monterey Bay Aquarium, *Other Notable Attractions*

Morton Arboretum, *Chicago*

Morton H. Meyerson Symphony, *Dallas/Ft. Worth*

Attraction Special Feature Index

JFK Ctr./Performing Arts, *Washington, DC*

JFK Library & Mus., *Boston/ Cape Cod Area*

John G. Shedd Aquarium, *Chicago*

Kimbell Art Mus., *Dallas/ Ft. Worth*

Knott's Berry Farm, *Los Angeles*

Knott's Soak City, *San Diego*

Lawrence Hall of Science, *San Francisco*

Long Beach Aquarium of Pacific, *Los Angeles*

Los Angeles County Mus./Art, *Los Angeles*

Los Angeles Zoo, *Los Angeles*

Mark Twain Cave, *St. Louis*

Maryland Science Ctr., *Baltimore*

Marymoor Park, *Seattle*

McCormick-Stillman Railroad Park, *Phoenix/Scottsdale*

Metreon, *San Francisco*

Miami Children's Mus., *Miami*

Miami Metro Zoo, *Miami*

Miami Seaquarium, *Miami*

Minute Man Nat'l Hist. Park, *Boston/Cape Cod Area*

Mississippi River Boat Tour, *St. Louis*

Missouri Botanical Garden, *St. Louis*

Missouri History Mus., *St. Louis*

Mt. Rushmore, *Other Notable Attractions*

Muir Woods Nat'l Monument, *San Francisco*

Museum/American West, *Los Angeles*

Museum/Fine Arts, *Houston*

Museum/Flight, *Seattle*

Museum/Modern Art, *NYC*

Museum/Science, *Boston/Cape Cod Area*

Museum/Science & Industry, *Chicago*

Museum/Tolerance, *Los Angeles*

National Air & Space Mus., *Washington, DC*

National Constitution Ctr., *Philadelphia/Lancaster*

National D-Day Mus., *New Orleans*

National Mus./American History, *Washington, DC*

National Mus./Natural History, *Washington, DC*

National Zoological Park, *Washington, DC*

Natural History Mus./LA County, *Los Angeles*

New England Aquarium, *Boston/Cape Cod Area*

New England Aqua./Whale Watch, *Boston/Cape Cod Area*

New Jersey State Aquarium, *Philadelphia/Lancaster*

New Orleans Botanical Garden, *New Orleans*

New Orleans Mus. of Art, *New Orleans*

Newport Aquarium, *Cincinnati*

NY Aquarium, *NYC*

Ocean's Journey, *Denver*

Ohio Renaissance Festival, *Cincinnati*

Old Town Alexandria, *Washington, DC*

Out of Africa Wildlife Park, *Phoenix/Scottsdale*

Paramount's Kings Island, *Cincinnati*

Petrified Forest National Park, *Other Notable Attractions*

Philadelphia Zoo, *Philadelphia/ Lancaster*

Phoenix Zoo, *Phoenix/ Scottsdale*

Piedmont Park, *Atlanta*

Port Discovery, *Baltimore*

Pro Player Stadium, *Miami*

Prospect Park, *NYC*

Reliant Park, *Houston*

Reuben H. Fleet Science Ctr., *San Diego*

Gift Shop

Attraction Special Feature Index

Guided Tours

Attraction Special Feature Index

National D-Day Mus., *New Orleans*
National Gallery of Art, *Washington, DC*
National Mus./African Art, *Washington, DC*
National Mus./Natural History, *Washington, DC*
NBC Studios, *Los Angeles*
New England Aqua./Whale Watch, *Boston/Cape Cod Area*
New Orleans Mus. of Art, *New Orleans*
Newport Aquarium, *Cincinnati*
Pacific Science Ctr., *Seattle*
Philadelphia Mus. of Art, *Philadelphia/Lancaster*
Polynesian Cultural Ctr., *Hawaii*
Purina Farms, *St. Louis*
Safeco Field, *Seattle*
San Diego Wild Animal Park, *San Diego*
San Diego Zoo, *San Diego*
San Fran Mus. of Modern Art, *San Francisco*
SBC Park, *San Francisco*
SeaWorld, *Orlando*
Shark Reef, *Las Vegas*
Southern Mus./Civil War & Locomotive History, *Atlanta*
Spertus Museum, *Chicago*
St. Louis Art Mus., *St. Louis*
St. Louis Science Ctr., *St. Louis*
Universal Studios, *Orlando*
U.S. Holocaust Memorial Museum, *Washington, DC*
USS Arizona Memorial, *Hawaii*
Warner Bros. Studios, *Los Angeles*
Winterthur/Enchanted Woods, *Philadelphia/Lancaster*
Woodland Park Zoo, *Seattle*
World of Coca-Cola Pavillion, *Atlanta*

Hearing-Impaired Exhibits

Adler Planetarium/Astronomy Mus., *Chicago*
American Airlines Arena, *Miami*

American Mus./Natural History, *NYC*
Art Inst. of Chicago, *Chicago*
Baltimore Mus. of Art, *Baltimore*
Blizzard Beach, *Orlando*
Brookfield Zoo, *Chicago*
Brooklyn Children's Mus., *NYC*
Chabot Space/Science Ctr., *San Francisco*
Disneyland, *Los Angeles*
Disney-MGM Studios, *Orlando*
Disney's Animal Kingdom, *Orlando*
Disney's California Adventure, *Los Angeles*
Disney's Typhoon Lagoon, *Orlando*
Epcot, *Orlando*
Everglades Nat'l Park, *Miami*
Franklin Inst. Science Mus., *Philadelphia/Lancaster*
Ft. McHenry, *Baltimore*
Getty Center, *Los Angeles*
Hanauma Bay Nature Preserve, *Hawaii*
Harold Washington Library, *Chicago*
Hollywood Bowl, *Los Angeles*
Hoover Dam, *Las Vegas*
Internat'l Spy Museum, *Washington, DC*
Islands of Adventure, *Orlando*
JFK Ctr./Performing Arts, *Washington, DC*
Kennedy Space Ctr., *Orlando*
Lincoln Ctr., *NYC*
Los Angeles County Mus./Art, *Los Angeles*
Magic Kingdom, *Orlando*
Missouri History Mus., *St. Louis*
Museum/Modern Art, *NYC*
Museum/Science, *Boston/Cape Cod Area*
Museum/Television & Radio, *Los Angeles*
Museum/Television & Radio, *NYC*
Museum/Tolerance, *Los Angeles*
National Air & Space Mus., *Washington, DC*

Attraction Special Feature Index

National Constitution Ctr., *Philadelphia/Lancaster*
National Gallery of Art, *Washington, DC*
National Mus./African Art, *Washington, DC*
NY Botanical Garden, *NYC*
NY Hall of Science, *NYC*
Paramount's Kings Island, *Cincinnati*
Philadelphia Mus. of Art, *Philadelphia/Lancaster*
Pro Player Stadium, *Miami*
Reuben H. Fleet Science Ctr., *San Diego*
Shark Reef, *Las Vegas*
Siegfried & Roy's Secret Garden/Dolphin, *Las Vegas*
Sixth Floor Mus./Dealey Plaza, *Dallas/Ft. Worth*
Star Trek: The Experience, *Las Vegas*
St. Louis Art Mus., *St. Louis*
St. Louis Science Ctr., *St. Louis*
Symphony Center, *Chicago*
Universal Studios, *Orlando*
U.S. Cellular Field, *Chicago*
Walters Art Mus., *Baltimore*
Washington Nat'l Cathedral, *Washington, DC*

Hiking

Acadia Nat'l Park, *Other Notable Attractions*
Adirondack State Park, *Other Notable Attractions*
Akaka Falls State Park, *Hawaii*
Angel Island State Park, *San Francisco*
Balboa Park, *San Diego*
Cabrillo Nat'l Monument, *San Diego*
Cape Cod Nat'l Seashore, *Boston/Cape Cod Area*
Cape Poge Wildlife Refuge, *Boston/Cape Cod Area*
Fairmount Park, *Philadelphia/Lancaster*

Golden Gate Park, *San Francisco*
Grand Canyon Nat'l Park, *Other Notable Attractions*
Grand Teton Nat'l Park, *Other Notable Attractions*
Griffith Park, *Los Angeles*
Haleakala Nat'l Park, *Hawaii*
Hawaii Volcanoes Nat'l Park, *Hawaii*
Mackinac Island State Hist. Parks, *Other Notable Attractions*
Malibu Lagoon State Beach, *Los Angeles*
Manoa Falls, *Hawaii*
Matheson Hammock Park, *Miami*
Mt. Rushmore, *Other Notable Attractions*
Olympic Nat'l Park, *Seattle*
Papago Park, *Phoenix/Scottsdale*
Petrified Forest National Park, *Other Notable Attractions*
Red Rock Canyon, *Las Vegas*
Rock Creek Park, *Washington, DC*
Rocky Mountain Nat'l Park, *Denver*
Slide Rock State Park, *Phoenix/Scottsdale*
South Mountain Park, *Phoenix/Scottsdale*
Stone Mountain Park, *Atlanta*
Tilden Regional Park, *San Francisco*
Valley Forge, *Philadelphia/Lancaster*
Waimea Canyon State Park, *Hawaii*
White Rock Lake Park, *Dallas/Ft. Worth*
Will Rogers State Hist. Park, *Los Angeles*
Yellowstone Nat'l Park, *Other Notable Attractions*
Yosemite Nat'l Park, *Other Notable Attractions*

Horseback Riding

Cape Cod Nat'l Seashore, *Boston/Cape Cod Area*
Central Park, *NYC*
Grand Canyon Nat'l Park, *Other Notable Attractions*
Griffith Park, *Los Angeles*
Kentucky Horse Park, *Cincinnati*
Papago Park, *Phoenix/ Scottsdale*
Petrified Forest National Park, *Other Notable Attractions*
Philadelphia Zoo, *Philadelphia/ Lancaster*
Prospect Park, *NYC*
Red Rock Canyon, *Las Vegas*
Rock Creek Park, *Washington, DC*
Rocky Mountain Nat'l Park, *Denver*
South Mountain Park, *Phoenix/ Scottsdale*
Waikiki Beach, *Hawaii*
Yosemite Nat'l Park, *Other Notable Attractions*

Ice-Skating

Boston Common, *Boston/Cape Cod Area*
Central Park, *NYC*
Chelsea Piers, *NYC*
Cincinnati Zoo/Botanical Garden, *Cincinnati*
Millennium Park, *Chicago*
Prospect Park, *NYC*
Yerba Buena Gardens, *San Francisco*

IMAX Theaters

Adventuredome, *Las Vegas*
American Mus./Natural History, *NYC*
Audubon Aqua. of Americas, *New Orleans*
California Science Ctr., *Los Angeles*
Cape Cod Children's Mus., *Boston/Cape Cod Area*
Chabot Space/Science Ctr., *San Francisco*
Cincinnati History Mus., *Cincinnati*
Denver Mus./Nature & Science, *Denver*
Fernbank Mus. of Natural History/Science, *Atlanta*
Franklin Inst. Science Mus., *Philadelphia/Lancaster*
Ft. Worth Mus./Science & History, *Dallas/Ft. Worth*
Houston Mus./Natural Science, *Houston*
Islands of Adventure, *Orlando*
Kennedy Space Ctr., *Orlando*
Lawrence Hall of Science, *San Francisco*
Maryland Science Ctr., *Baltimore*
Miami Museum/Science & Planetarium, *Miami*
Museum/Science, *Boston/Cape Cod Area*
Museum/Science & Industry, *Chicago*
National Air & Space Mus., *Washington, DC*
National Mus./Natural History, *Washington, DC*
National Postal Mus., *Washington, DC*
Navy Pier, *Chicago*
Pacific Science Ctr., *Seattle*
Pharaoh's Pavillion, *Las Vegas*
Polynesian Cultural Ctr., *Hawaii*
Reuben H. Fleet Science Ctr., *San Diego*
Robert D. Lindner OMNIMAX, *Cincinnati*
Science Place, *Dallas/Ft. Worth*
Seattle Aquarium, *Seattle*
St. Louis Science Ctr., *St. Louis*
Universal CityWalk, *Los Angeles*
Universal Studios, *Orlando*

Live Entertainment for Kids

(Call attraction for more
information; see also
Amusement/Theme Parks,
Children's Museums,
Performing Arts Centers,
Spectator Venues)

Acad. of Natural Sciences,
    Philadelphia/Lancaster
Alcatraz Island, *San Francisco*
Angel Island State Park, *San
    Francisco*
Atlanta History Ctr., *Atlanta*
Audubon Aqua. of Americas,
    New Orleans
Audubon Zoo, *New Orleans*
Balboa Park, *San Diego*
Baltimore Zoo, *Baltimore*
Battery Park, *NYC*
Beach, The, *Cincinnati*
Betsy Ross House,
    Philadelphia/Lancaster
Birch Aquarium at Scripps, *San
    Diego*
Bronx Zoo, *NYC*
Brookfield Zoo, *Chicago*
Butterfly Pavilion, *Denver*
California Science Ctr., *Los
    Angeles*
Cape Cod Mus./Natural History,
    Boston/Cape Cod Area
Cathedral/St. John the Divine,
    NYC
Central Park, *NYC*
Chicago Hist. Society, *Chicago*
Chittenden Locks, *Seattle*
Christ Church, *Philadelphia/
    Lancaster*
Cincinnati Zoo/Botanical
    Garden, *Cincinnati*
City Park, *New Orleans*
CocoWalk, *Miami*
Colonial Williamsburg, *Other
    Notable Attractions*
Crayola Factory, *Philadelphia/
    Lancaster*
Dallas Mus. of Art, *Dallas/
    Ft. Worth*
Dallas Zoo, *Dallas/Ft. Worth*

Desert Botanical Garden,
    Phoenix/Scottsdale
Discovery Cove, *Orlando*
Disney's Animal Kingdom,
    Orlando
Downtown Aquarium, *Houston*
Ebenezer Baptist Church,
    Atlanta
Everglades Alligator Farm,
    Miami
Exploratorium, *San Francisco*
Fairmount Park, *Philadelphia/
    Lancaster*
Fernbank Mus. of Natural
    History/Science, *Atlanta*
Fisherman's Wharf, *San
    Francisco*
Flamingo Wildlife Habitat, *Las
    Vegas*
Fountains of Bellagio, *Las
    Vegas*
Franklin Inst. Science Mus.,
    Philadelphia/Lancaster
Freer/Arthur M. Sackler
    Galleries, *Washington, DC*
Ft. Point, *San Francisco*
Ft. Worth Zoo, *Dallas/Ft. Worth*
Gardens/Morris Arboretum,
    Philadelphia/Lancaster
Gatorland, *Orlando*
George Ranch Hist. Park,
    Houston
Gettysburg Nat'l Military Park,
    Baltimore
Golden Gate Park, *San
    Francisco*
Grand Central Terminal, *NYC*
Grant's Farm, *St. Louis*
Hawaii Maritime Ctr., *Hawaii*
Honolulu Zoo, *Hawaii*
Houston Zoo, *Houston*
Independence Nat'l Hist. Park,
    Philadelphia/Lancaster
John P. McGovern Mus./Health,
    Houston
Kennedy Space Ctr., *Orlando*
Kentucky Horse Park,
    Cincinnati
Lincoln Road Mall, *Miami*

Attraction Special Feature Index

Lodging On-Site

Adirondack State Park, *Other Notable Attractions*
Adventuredome, *Las Vegas*
Blizzard Beach, *Orlando*
Cedar Point, *Other Notable Attractions*
Colonial Williamsburg, *Other Notable Attractions*
Coronado Island, *San Diego*
Disneyland, *Los Angeles*
Disney-MGM Studios, *Orlando*
Disney's Animal Kingdom, *Orlando*
Disney's California Adventure, *Los Angeles*
Disney's Typhoon Lagoon, *Orlando*
Eiffel Tower Experience, *Las Vegas*
Epcot, *Orlando*
Everglades Nat'l Park, *Miami*
Fisherman's Wharf, *San Francisco*
Flamingo Wildlife Habitat, *Las Vegas*
Grand Canyon Nat'l Park, *Other Notable Attractions*
Haleakala Nat'l Park, *Hawaii*
Hawaii Volcanoes Nat'l Park, *Hawaii*
Hersheypark, *Philadelphia/ Lancaster*
Imperial Palace Auto Collection, *Las Vegas*
Islands of Adventure, *Orlando*
Magic Kingdom, *Orlando*
Mystic Falls, *Las Vegas*
Old Town Scottsdale, *Phoenix/ Scottsdale*
Olympic Nat'l Park, *Seattle*
PETCO Park, *San Diego*
Pharaoh's Pavillion, *Las Vegas*
Reunion Tower Observation Deck, *Dallas/Ft. Worth*
Shark Reef, *Las Vegas*
Siegfried & Roy's Secret Garden/Dolphin, *Las Vegas*
Star Trek: The Experience, *Las Vegas*
Stone Mountain Park, *Atlanta*
Stratosphere Tower/Rides, *Las Vegas*
Times Square, *NYC*
Universal Studios, *Orlando*
Universal Studios Hollywood, *Los Angeles*
Waikiki Beach, *Hawaii*
Wainapanapa State Park, *Hawaii*
Yosemite Nat'l Park, *Other Notable Attractions*

Miniature Golf

Castles N' Coasters, *Phoenix/ Scottsdale*
Cedar Point, *Other Notable Attractions*
Coney Island, *Cincinnati*
Hudson River Park, *NYC*
Navy Pier, *Chicago*
Outer Banks, *Other Notable Attractions*

Offbeat/Funky

Adventuredome, *Las Vegas*
Alcatraz Island, *San Francisco*
American Mus./Moving Image, *NYC*
American Visionary Art Mus., *Baltimore*
Atlanta Cyclorama/Civil War Mus., *Atlanta*
Baltimore Mus. of Industry, *Baltimore*
Bureau of Engraving & Printing, *Washington, DC*
Butterfly Pavilion, *Denver*
Cable Car Mus., *San Francisco*
Cartoon Art Mus., *San Francisco*
City Museum, *St. Louis*
Coney Island Boardwalk, *NYC*
Eiffel Tower Experience, *Las Vegas*
Everglades Alligator Farm, *Miami*
Experience Music Project, *Seattle*

Ford's Theatre/Lincoln Mus., *Washington, DC*

Fremont St. Experience, *Las Vegas*

Gondola Rides/Grand Canal, *Las Vegas*

Hollywood Wax Mus., *Los Angeles*

Internat'l Spy Museum, *Washington, DC*

Lower E. Side Tenement Mus., *NYC*

Madame Tussaud's Las Vegas, *Las Vegas*

Madame Tussaud's NY, *NYC*

Movie Studios/Las Colinas, *Dallas/Ft. Worth*

Musee Conti Wax Mus., *New Orleans*

Musée Mécanique, *San Francisco*

Mystic Falls, *Las Vegas*

Ohio Renaissance Festival, *Cincinnati*

Orange Show Ctr./Visionary Art, *Houston*

Petersen Automotive Mus., *Los Angeles*

Presbytere/Mardi Gras Mus., *New Orleans*

Sixth Floor Mus./Dealey Plaza, *Dallas/Ft. Worth*

Star Trek: The Experience, *Las Vegas*

Venice Boardwalk, *Los Angeles*

World of Coca-Cola Pavillion, *Atlanta*

Outdoor Only

Arnold Arboretum, *Boston/ Cape Cod Area*

Assateague Island Nat'l Seashore, *Baltimore*

Battery Park, *NYC*

Boston Public Garden, *Boston/ Cape Cod Area*

Brandywine Battlefield, *Philadelphia/Lancaster*

Brookfield Zoo, *Chicago*

Centennial Olympic Park, *Atlanta*

Chattahoochee Nature Ctr., *Atlanta*

Descanso Gardens, *Los Angeles*

Freedom Trail, *Boston/Cape Cod Area*

Ft. McHenry, *Baltimore*

Grant Park, *Chicago*

Longwood Gardens, *Philadelphia/Lancaster*

Matheson Hammock Park, *Miami*

Morton Arboretum, *Chicago*

New England Aqua./Whale Watch, *Boston/Cape Cod Area*

New Orleans Botanical Garden, *New Orleans*

Niagara Falls, *Other Notable Attractions*

Venetian Pool, *Miami*

Venice Boardwalk, *Los Angeles*

Waimea Canyon State Park, *Hawaii*

Wainapanapa State Park, *Hawaii*

Wet 'n Wild Water Park, *Las Vegas*

Parties for Kids

Acad. of Natural Sciences, *Philadelphia/Lancaster*

Adventuredome, *Las Vegas*

Age of Steam Railroad Mus., *Dallas/Ft. Worth*

American Visionary Art Mus., *Baltimore*

Aquarium of the Bay, *San Francisco*

Art Inst. of Chicago, *Chicago*

Atlanta Cyclorama/Civil War Mus., *Atlanta*

Audubon Aqua. of Americas, *New Orleans*

Audubon Zoo, *New Orleans*

Bay Area Discovery Mus., *San Francisco*

New Orleans Botanical Garden, *New Orleans*
Newport Aquarium, *Cincinnati*
Newport on the Levee, *Cincinnati*
NY Aquarium, *NYC*
NYC Fire Mus., *NYC*
NY Hall of Science, *NYC*
NY Transit Mus., *NYC*
Ocean's Journey, *Denver*
Ohio Renaissance Festival, *Cincinnati*
Orange Show Ctr./Visionary Art, *Houston*
Pacific Science Ctr., *Seattle*
Parrot Jungle Island, *Miami*
Peabody Museum, *Boston/Cape Cod Area*
Philadelphia Zoo, *Philadelphia/Lancaster*
Please Touch Mus., *Philadelphia/Lancaster*
Reunion Tower Observation Deck, *Dallas/Ft. Worth*
Ripley's Believe It or Not! Odditorium, *Orlando*
SBC Park, *San Francisco*
Sears Tower, *Chicago*
SeaWorld, *Orlando*
Shark Reef, *Las Vegas*
Shea Stadium, *NYC*
Six Flags AstroWorld, *Houston*
Six Flags Great Adventure, *Philadelphia/Lancaster*
Skyscraper Museum, *NYC*
South St. Seaport/Mus., *NYC*
Splashtown Houston, *Houston*
St. Louis Science Ctr., *St. Louis*
Storyland, *New Orleans*
Toys "R" Us, *NYC*
Travel Town Transport. Mus., *Los Angeles*
Universal Studios, *Orlando*
University Mus./Archaeol. & Anthrop., *Philadelphia/Lancaster*
USS Constitution Mus., *Boston/Cape Cod Area*
Wet 'n Wild, *Orlando*
Woodland Park Zoo, *Seattle*
Yankee Stadium, *NYC*
Yerba Buena Gardens, *San Francisco*
Zooquarium, *Boston/Cape Cod Area*

Patriotic

Arlington Nat'l Cemetery, *Washington, DC*
Atlanta Cyclorama/Civil War Mus., *Atlanta*
Atlanta History Ctr., *Atlanta*
Betsy Ross House, *Philadelphia/Lancaster*
Brandywine Battlefield, *Philadelphia/Lancaster*
Cabildo, *New Orleans*
Chalmette Battlefield/Nat'l Cemetery, *New Orleans*
Colorado History Mus., *Denver*
Ellis Island Immigr. Mus., *NYC*
FDR Memorial, *Washington, DC*
Freedom Trail, *Boston/Cape Cod Area*
Ft. McHenry, *Baltimore*
Ft. Point, *San Francisco*
George Wash. Masonic Nat'l Memorial, *Washington, DC*
Independence Nat'l Hist. Park, *Philadelphia/Lancaster*
Intrepid Sea, Air & Space Mus., *NYC*
Jefferson Memorial, *Washington, DC*
Lincoln Memorial, *Washington, DC*
Minute Man Nat'l Hist. Park, *Boston/Cape Cod Area*
Mount Vernon, *Washington, DC*
Museum/American West, *Los Angeles*
National Archives, *Washington, DC*
National Constitution Ctr., *Philadelphia/Lancaster*
Old North Church, *Boston/Cape Cod Area*
Paul Revere House, *Boston/Cape Cod Area*
San Jacinto Battleground, *Houston*

Attraction Special Feature Index

Sixth Floor Mus./Dealey Plaza, *Dallas/Ft. Worth*
Space Center Houston, *Houston*
Statue of Liberty, *NYC*
Supreme Court, *Washington, DC*
U.S. Capitol, *Washington, DC*
US Naval Academy, *Baltimore*
USS Constellation, *Baltimore*
USS Constitution Mus., *Boston/ Cape Cod Area*
USS Pampanito, *San Francisco*
USS Texas, *Houston*
Valley Forge, *Philadelphia/ Lancaster*
Vietnam Veterans Memorial, *Washington, DC*
Washington Monument, *Washington, DC*
White House, *Washington, DC*

Petting Zoos
Audubon Zoo, *New Orleans*
Cedar Point, *Other Notable Attractions*
Dallas Zoo, *Dallas/Ft. Worth*
Fairmount Park, *Philadelphia/ Lancaster*
Ft. Worth Zoo, *Dallas/Ft. Worth*
Gatorland, *Orlando*
Grant's Farm, *St. Louis*
Houston Zoo, *Houston*
Kentucky Horse Park, *Cincinnati*
Miami Metro Zoo, *Miami*
Parrot Jungle Island, *Miami*
Philadelphia Zoo, *Philadelphia/ Lancaster*
Phoenix Zoo, *Phoenix/Scottsdale*
Purina Farms, *St. Louis*
San Diego Zoo, *San Diego*
San Francisco Zoo, *San Francisco*
Zooquarium, *Boston/Cape Cod Area*

Rides
(See also Amusement/Theme Parks, Roller Coasters)
Audubon Zoo, *New Orleans*
Beach, The, *Cincinnati*
Blizzard Beach, *Orlando*

Boston Public Garden, *Boston/ Cape Cod Area*
Central Park, *NYC*
Cincinnati Zoo/Botanical Garden, *Cincinnati*
City Park, *New Orleans*
Crandon Park, *Miami*
Disney's Typhoon Lagoon, *Orlando*
Downtown Aquarium, *Houston*
Eiffel Tower Experience, *Las Vegas*
Everglades Alligator Farm, *Miami*
Everglades Nat'l Park, *Miami*
Fisherman's Wharf, *San Francisco*
Ft. Worth Zoo, *Dallas/Ft. Worth*
Golden Gate Park, *San Francisco*
Hermann Park, *Houston*
Honolulu Zoo, *Hawaii*
Lincoln Park Zoo, *Chicago*
McCormick-Stillman Railroad Park, *Phoenix/Scottsdale*
Miami Children's Mus., *Miami*
Miami Metro Zoo, *Miami*
Navy Pier, *Chicago*
Ohio Renaissance Festival, *Cincinnati*
Old Lahaina Luau, *Hawaii*
Philadelphia Zoo, *Philadelphia/ Lancaster*
Prospect Park, *NYC*
Safeco Field, *Seattle*
San Francisco Zoo, *San Francisco*
South St. Seaport/Mus., *NYC*
Splashtown Houston, *Houston*
Star Trek: The Experience, *Las Vegas*
Stratosphere Tower/Rides, *Las Vegas*
Tilden Regional Park, *San Francisco*
Travel Town Transport. Mus., *Los Angeles*
Wet 'n Wild, *Orlando*
Wet 'n Wild Water Park, *Las Vegas*

Roller Coasters

Busch Gardens, *Other Notable Attractions*
Castles N' Coasters, *Phoenix/ Scottsdale*
Cedar Point, *Other Notable Attractions*
Coney Island, *Cincinnati*
Coney Island Boardwalk, *NYC*
Disney-MGM Studios, *Orlando*
Disney's California Adventure, *Los Angeles*
Hines Carousel Gardens, *New Orleans*
Islands of Adventure, *Orlando*
Knott's Berry Farm, *Los Angeles*
Legoland California, *San Diego*
Magic Kingdom, *Orlando*
Manhattan Expr. Roller Coaster, *Las Vegas*
Paramount's Kings Island, *Cincinnati*
Santa Monica Pier, *Los Angeles*
Six Flags, *New Orleans*
Six Flags AstroWorld, *Houston*
Six Flags California, *Los Angeles*
Six Flags Elitch Gardens, *Denver*
Six Flags Great Adventure, *Philadelphia/Lancaster*
Six Flags Marine World, *San Francisco*
Six Flags Over Georgia, *Atlanta*
Speed, *Las Vegas*
Universal Studios, *Orlando*

Sight-Impaired Exhibits

American Mus./Natural History, *NYC*
Art Inst. of Chicago, *Chicago*
Betsy Ross House, *Philadelphia/Lancaster*
Blizzard Beach, *Orlando*
Brookfield Zoo, *Chicago*
Brooklyn Botanic Garden, *NYC*
Brooklyn Children's Mus., *NYC*
Disneyland, *Los Angeles*
Disney-MGM Studios, *Orlando*
Disney's Animal Kingdom, *Orlando*
Disney's California Adventure, *Los Angeles*
Disney's Typhoon Lagoon, *Orlando*
Epcot, *Orlando*
FDR Memorial, *Washington, DC*
Franklin Inst. Science Mus., *Philadelphia/Lancaster*
Harold Washington Library, *Chicago*
Internat'l Spy Museum, *Washington, DC*
Islands of Adventure, *Orlando*
JFK Ctr./Performing Arts, *Washington, DC*
Kennedy Space Ctr., *Orlando*
Lincoln Ctr., *NYC*
Long Beach Aquarium of Pacific, *Los Angeles*
Los Angeles County Mus./Art, *Los Angeles*
Magic Kingdom, *Orlando*
Mark Twain Boyhood Home, *St. Louis*
Miami Metro Zoo, *Miami*
Missouri Botanical Garden, *St. Louis*
Missouri History Mus., *St. Louis*
Museum/Modern Art, *NYC*
National Air & Space Mus., *Washington, DC*
National Constitution Ctr., *Philadelphia/Lancaster*
National Gallery of Art, *Washington, DC*
NY Aquarium, *NYC*
NY Hall of Science, *NYC*
Philadelphia Mus. of Art, *Philadelphia/Lancaster*
Shark Reef, *Las Vegas*
Star Trek: The Experience, *Las Vegas*
St. Louis Art Mus., *St. Louis*
Symphony Center, *Chicago*
Universal Studios, *Orlando*
U.S. Cellular Field, *Chicago*

Strollers Available

Adventuredome, *Las Vegas*
Amon Carter Museum, *Dallas/Ft. Worth*
Atlanta History Ctr., *Atlanta*
Audubon Zoo, *New Orleans*
Baltimore Zoo, *Baltimore*
Blizzard Beach, *Orlando*
Bronx Zoo, *NYC*
Brookfield Zoo, *Chicago*
Cedar Point, *Other Notable Attractions*
Children's Museum, The, *Boston/Cape Cod Area*
Cincinnati Art Mus., *Cincinnati*
City Museum, *St. Louis*
Coney Island, *Cincinnati*
Dallas Zoo, *Dallas/Ft. Worth*
Desert Botanical Garden, *Phoenix/Scottsdale*
Disneyland, *Los Angeles*
Disney-MGM Studios, *Orlando*
Disney's Animal Kingdom, *Orlando*
Disney's California Adventure, *Los Angeles*
Disney's Typhoon Lagoon, *Orlando*
Epcot, *Orlando*
Fisherman's Wharf, *San Francisco*
Ft. Worth Zoo, *Dallas/Ft. Worth*
Getty Center, *Los Angeles*
Grant's Farm, *St. Louis*
Islands of Adventure, *Orlando*
Kennedy Space Ctr., *Orlando*
Kentucky Horse Park, *Cincinnati*
Knott's Berry Farm, *Los Angeles*
Legoland California, *San Diego*
Lincoln Park Zoo, *Chicago*
Los Angeles Zoo, *Los Angeles*
Magic Kingdom, *Orlando*
Miami Metro Zoo, *Miami*
Miami Seaquarium, *Miami*
Missouri Botanical Garden, *St. Louis*
Museum/American West, *Los Angeles*
Museum/City of NY, *NYC*
National Mus./Natural History, *Washington, DC*
National Zoological Park, *Washington, DC*
Natural History Mus./LA County, *Los Angeles*
Navy Pier, *Chicago*
NY Hall of Science, *NYC*
Paramount's Kings Island, *Cincinnati*
Philadelphia Mus. of Art, *Philadelphia/Lancaster*
Philadelphia Zoo, *Philadelphia/Lancaster*
Prudential Ctr./Skywalk, *Boston/Cape Cod Area*
San Diego Wild Animal Park, *San Diego*
San Diego Zoo, *San Diego*
Seattle Aquarium, *Seattle*
SeaWorld, *Orlando*
SeaWorld, *San Diego*
Sesame Place, *Philadelphia/Lancaster*
Six Flags, *New Orleans*
Six Flags AstroWorld, *Houston*
Six Flags California, *Los Angeles*
Six Flags Elitch Gardens, *Denver*
Six Flags Great Adventure, *Philadelphia/Lancaster*
Six Flags Marine World, *San Francisco*
Six Flags Over Georgia, *Atlanta*
Spertus Museum, *Chicago*
St. Louis Art Mus., *St. Louis*
St. Louis Science Ctr., *St. Louis*
Universal Studios, *Orlando*
Universal Studios Hollywood, *Los Angeles*
Venice Boardwalk, *Los Angeles*
Walters Art Mus., *Baltimore*
Woodland Park Zoo, *Seattle*

Tennis

Chelsea Piers, *NYC*
City Park, *Denver*

Water Sports

Wheelchair-Accessible

Attraction Special Feature Index

Attraction Special Feature Index

Attraction Special Feature Index

Attraction Special Feature Index

New Orleans Mus. of Art, *New Orleans*
Newport Aquarium, *Cincinnati*
Newport on the Levee, *Cincinnati*
Niagara Falls, *Other Notable Attractions*
NY Aquarium, *NYC*
NY Botanical Garden, *NYC*
NYC Fire Mus., *NYC*
NY Hall of Science, *NYC*
NY Public Library, *NYC*
NY Transit Mus., *NYC*
Ocean's Journey, *Denver*
Old Mint, *New Orleans*
Old North Church, *Boston/Cape Cod Area*
Old Town Scottsdale, *Phoenix/Scottsdale*
Orlando Mus. of Art, *Orlando*
Palace of Fine Arts, *San Francisco*
Peabody Museum, *Boston/Cape Cod Area*
Peggy Notebaert Nature Mus., *Chicago*
PETCO Park, *San Diego*
Petrified Forest National Park, *Other Notable Attractions*
Philadelphia Mus. of Art, *Philadelphia/Lancaster*
Philadelphia Zoo, *Philadelphia/Lancaster*
Phoenix Central Library, *Phoenix/Scottsdale*
Phoenix Zoo, *Phoenix/Scottsdale*
Please Touch Mus., *Philadelphia/Lancaster*
Plimoth Plantation, *Boston/Cape Cod Area*
Port Discovery, *Baltimore*
Presbytere/Mardi Gras Mus., *New Orleans*
Pro Player Stadium, *Miami*
Prudential Ctr./Skywalk, *Boston/Cape Cod Area*
Randall Museum, *San Francisco*

Red Rock Canyon, *Las Vegas*
Reliant Park, *Houston*
Reuben H. Fleet Science Ctr., *San Diego*
Reunion Tower Observation Deck, *Dallas/Ft. Worth*
Ripley's Believe It or Not! Odditorium, *Orlando*
Rose Bowl, *Los Angeles*
Safeco Field, *Seattle*
San Diego Wild Animal Park, *San Diego*
San Francisco Zoo, *San Francisco*
San Jacinto Battleground, *Houston*
SBC Park, *San Francisco*
SciTrek, *Atlanta*
Scottsdale Mus./Contemp. Art, *Phoenix/Scottsdale*
Sears Tower, *Chicago*
Seattle Aquarium, *Seattle*
SeaWorld, *Orlando*
SeaWorld, *San Diego*
Sesame Place, *Philadelphia/Lancaster*
Shark Reef, *Las Vegas*
Shea Stadium, *NYC*
Siegfried & Roy's Secret Garden/Dolphin, *Las Vegas*
Six Flags Marine World, *San Francisco*
Six Flags Over Georgia, *Atlanta*
Sixth Floor Mus./Dealey Plaza, *Dallas/Ft. Worth*
Skyscraper Museum, *NYC*
Soldier Field, *Chicago*
Southern Mus./Civil War & Locomotive History, *Atlanta*
South St. Seaport/Mus., *NYC*
Spertus Museum, *Chicago*
Star Trek: The Experience, *Las Vegas*
Statue of Liberty, *NYC*
St. Louis Art Mus., *St. Louis*
St. Louis Science Ctr., *St. Louis*
St. Louis Zoo, *St. Louis*
Stockyards Collection Mus., *Dallas/Ft. Worth*

Attraction Special Feature Index

HOTEL SPECIAL FEATURES

(Indexes list the best of many within each category.
Hotels are followed by the section name in which their
reviews appear.)

Adjoining Rooms

Argonaut Hotel, *San Francisco*
Biltmore Hotel, *Miami*
Boston Harbor, *Boston/Cape Cod Area*
Claremont Resort, *San Francisco*
Disney's Animal Kingdom Lodge, *Orlando*
Disney's Beach Club Resort, *Orlando*
Disney's Boardwalk Inn, *Orlando*
Disney's Wilderness Lodge, *Orlando*
DoubleTree, *NYC*
Edgewater, The, *Seattle*
Embassy Suites, *New Orleans*
Embassy Suites, *NYC*
Embassy Suites Downtown, *St. Louis*
Fairmont, *New Orleans*
Fairmont Kea Lani, *Hawaii*
Fairmont Olympic, *Seattle*
Fairmont Scottsdale Princess, *Phoenix/Scottsdale*
Fairmont Washington, *Washington, DC*
Fontainebleau Hilton, *Miami*
Four Seasons, *Atlanta*
Four Seasons, *Boston/Cape Cod Area*
Four Seasons, *Chicago*
Four Seasons, *Houston*
Four Seasons, *Philadelphia/Lancaster*
Four Seasons, *San Francisco*
Four Seasons, *Washington, DC*
Four Seasons Aviara, *San Diego*
Four Seasons Hualalai, *Hawaii*
Four Seasons/Las Colinas, *Dallas/Ft. Worth*
Grand Hyatt, *Washington, DC*
Grand Wailea Resort, *Hawaii*
Harbor Court, *Baltimore*
Hard Rock Hotel, *Orlando*
Hilton Hawaiian Vlg., *Hawaii*
Hilton Waikoloa Vlg., *Hawaii*
House of Blues, *Chicago*
Houstonian, The, *Houston*
Hyatt Regency, *Baltimore*
Hyatt Regency, *Hawaii*
Hyatt Regency, *San Francisco*
Hyatt Regency Grand Cyp., *Orlando*
JW Marriott, *Houston*
JW Marriott, *Washington, DC*
JW Marriott Desert Ridge, *Phoenix/Scottsdale*
JW Marriott Hotel Lenox, *Atlanta*
Kahala Mandarin Oriental, *Hawaii*
Loews L'Enfant Plaza, *Washington, DC*
Loews Miami Beach, *Miami*
Marriott, *Philadelphia/Lancaster*
Marriott, *San Diego*
Marriott Copley Pl., *Boston/Cape Cod Area*
Marriott Maui, *Hawaii*
MGM Grand, *Las Vegas*
Mirage, *Las Vegas*
Omni Chicago, *Chicago*
Omni Mandalay Hotel, *Dallas/Ft. Worth*
Outrigger Waikiki, *Hawaii*
Peninsula, *Chicago*
Pointe Hilton Squaw Peak, *Phoenix/Scottsdale*
Portofino Bay Hotel/Universal, *Orlando*

Hotel Special Feature Index

Renaissance Harborplace, *Baltimore*
Renaissance Worthington, *Dallas/Ft. Worth*
Ritz-Carlton, *Chicago*
Ritz-Carlton, *New Orleans*
Ritz-Carlton, *San Francisco*
Ritz-Carlton Key Biscayne, *Miami*
Sheraton Hotel & Towers, *Chicago*
Sheraton Society Hill, *Philadelphia/Lancaster*
Treasure Island, *Las Vegas*
Waikoloa Beach Marriott, *Hawaii*
Warwick, The, *Houston*
Westin, *Cincinnati*
Westin Copley Pl., *Boston/Cape Cod Area*
Westin Galleria, *Dallas/Ft. Worth*
Westin Maui, *Hawaii*
Westin Peachtree Plaza, *Atlanta*
Westin River North, *Chicago*
Westin Stonebriar Resort, *Dallas/Ft. Worth*
Westin Tabor Ctr., *Denver*
Windsor Court, *New Orleans*
Wyndham/Canal Pl., *New Orleans*

Arcade/Game Room
Disney's Beach Club Resort, *Orlando*
Disney's Boardwalk Inn, *Orlando*
Disney's Wilderness Lodge, *Orlando*
Disney's Yacht Club Resort, *Orlando*
Four Seasons Hualalai, *Hawaii*
Grand Wailea Resort, *Hawaii*
Hard Rock Hotel, *Orlando*
Hilton, *San Diego*
Kahala Mandarin Oriental, *Hawaii*
Mandalay Bay, *Las Vegas*

Marriott, *San Diego*
Marriott Copley Pl., *Boston/Cape Cod Area*
MGM Grand, *Las Vegas*
Mirage, *Las Vegas*
Portofino Bay Hotel/Universal, *Orlando*
Treasure Island, *Las Vegas*

Attractions On-Site
Caesars Palace, *Las Vegas*
del Coronado, *San Diego*
Disneyland Hotel, *Los Angeles*
Disney's Animal Kingdom Lodge, *Orlando*
Disney's Beach Club Resort, *Orlando*
Disney's Boardwalk Inn, *Orlando*
Disney's Grand Californian, *Los Angeles*
Disney's Grand Floridian, *Orlando*
Disney's Polynesian Resort, *Orlando*
Disney's Yacht Club Resort, *Orlando*
Hard Rock Hotel, *Orlando*
Hilton Hawaiian Vlg., *Hawaii*
Inn at the Market, *Seattle*
Kahala Mandarin Oriental, *Hawaii*
Marriott Marquis, *NYC*
MGM Grand, *Las Vegas*
Mirage, *Las Vegas*
Omni Hotel/Independence Park, *Philadelphia/Lancaster*
Paradise Pier Hotel, *Los Angeles*
Paris Las Vegas, *Las Vegas*
Portofino Bay Hotel/Universal, *Orlando*
Rio All-Suite, *Las Vegas*
Treasure Island, *Las Vegas*
Venetian, The, *Las Vegas*

Babysitting
Argonaut Hotel, *San Francisco*
Biltmore Hotel, *Miami*

Hotel Special Feature Index

Boston Harbor, *Boston/Cape Cod Area*

Claremont Resort, *San Francisco*

del Coronado, *San Diego*

Disney's Animal Kingdom Lodge, *Orlando*

Disney's Beach Club Resort, *Orlando*

Disney's Wilderness Lodge, *Orlando*

Disney's Yacht Club Resort, *Orlando*

DoubleTree, *Chicago*

DoubleTree, *NYC*

Edgewater, The, *Seattle*

Embassy Suites, *New Orleans*

Embassy Suites, *NYC*

Fairmont, *New Orleans*

Fairmont Scottsdale Princess, *Phoenix/Scottsdale*

Fairmont Washington, *Washington, DC*

Fontainebleau Hilton, *Miami*

Four Seasons, *Atlanta*

Four Seasons, *Boston/Cape Cod Area*

Four Seasons, *Chicago*

Four Seasons, *Houston*

Four Seasons, *Philadelphia/Lancaster*

Four Seasons, *San Francisco*

Four Seasons, *Washington, DC*

Four Seasons Aviara, *San Diego*

Four Seasons Hualalai, *Hawaii*

Four Seasons/Las Colinas, *Dallas/Ft. Worth*

Grand Hyatt, *Seattle*

Grand Hyatt, *Washington, DC*

Grand Wailea Resort, *Hawaii*

Hilton Hawaiian Vlg., *Hawaii*

Hilton, *San Diego*

Hilton Waikoloa Vlg., *Hawaii*

Hotel del Sol, *San Francisco*

House of Blues, *Chicago*

Hyatt Regency, *St. Louis*

Hyatt Regency Grand Cyp., *Orlando*

Kahala Mandarin Oriental, *Hawaii*

Loews L'Enfant Plaza, *Washington, DC*

Mandalay Bay, *Las Vegas*

Marriott, *Philadelphia/Lancaster*

Marriott, *San Diego*

Marriott Coronado Isl., *San Diego*

Omni Chicago, *Chicago*

Park Hyatt, *Chicago*

Park Hyatt, *Washington, DC*

Peninsula, *Chicago*

Phoenician, The, *Phoenix/Scottsdale*

Pointe Hilton Squaw Peak, *Phoenix/Scottsdale*

Portofino Bay Hotel/Universal, *Orlando*

Renaissance, *NYC*

Renaissance Grand, *St. Louis*

Renaissance Worthington, *Dallas/Ft. Worth*

Ritz-Carlton, *Chicago*

Ritz-Carlton, *New Orleans*

Ritz-Carlton, *Philadelphia/Lancaster*

Ritz-Carlton Key Biscayne, *Miami*

Sheraton Society Hill, *Philadelphia/Lancaster*

Trump Internat'l, *NYC*

Waikoloa Beach Marriott, *Hawaii*

Westin Maui, *Hawaii*

Westin River North, *Chicago*

Windsor Court, *New Orleans*

Wyndham/Canal Pl., *New Orleans*

Beach Setting
(Ocean or Lake)

Biltmore Hotel, *Miami*

Casa Del Mar, *Los Angeles*

del Coronado, *San Diego*

Disney's Beach Club Resort, *Orlando*

Hotel Special Feature Index

Disney's Grand Californian, *Los Angeles*

Disney's Grand Floridian, *Orlando*

Disney's Polynesian Resort, *Orlando*

Disney's Yacht Club Resort, *Orlando*

Fairmont Kea Lani, *Hawaii*

Fairmont Miramar, *Los Angeles*

Fontainebleau Hilton, *Miami*

Four Seasons Aviara, *San Diego*

Four Seasons Hualalai, *Hawaii*

Grand Wailea Resort, *Hawaii*

Harbor View, *Boston/Cape Cod Area*

Hilton Hawaiian Vlg., *Hawaii*

Hilton, *San Diego*

Hilton Waikoloa Vlg., *Hawaii*

Hyatt Regency, *Hawaii*

JW Marriott Ihilani, *Hawaii*

Kahala Mandarin Oriental, *Hawaii*

Loews Coronado Bay, *San Diego*

Loews Miami Beach, *Miami*

Loews Santa Monica Beach, *Los Angeles*

Mandalay Bay, *Las Vegas*

Marriott Coronado Isl., *San Diego*

Marriott Maui, *Hawaii*

Ocean Edge Resort, *Boston/Cape Cod Area*

Outrigger Waikiki, *Hawaii*

Ritz-Carlton Coconut Grove, *Miami*

Ritz-Carlton Key Biscayne, *Miami*

Ritz-Carlton Marina del Rey, *Los Angeles*

Shutters on the Beach, *Los Angeles*

Waikoloa Beach Marriott, *Hawaii*

Westin Maui, *Hawaii*

Childproof Rooms

Biltmore Hotel, *Miami*

DoubleTree, *NYC*

Fairmont Scottsdale Princess, *Phoenix/Scottsdale*

Four Seasons, *Atlanta*

Four Seasons, *Houston*

Four Seasons, *Philadelphia/Lancaster*

Four Seasons, *San Francisco*

Four Seasons Aviara, *San Diego*

Four Seasons Hualalai, *Hawaii*

Grand Wailea Resort, *Hawaii*

Loews L'Enfant Plaza, *Washington, DC*

Loews Santa Monica Beach, *Los Angeles*

Marriott, *San Diego*

Ritz-Carlton, *Chicago*

Ritz-Carlton, *New Orleans*

Ritz-Carlton, *San Francisco*

Ritz-Carlton Buckhead, *Atlanta*

Ritz-Carlton Key Biscayne, *Miami*

Sheraton Buckhead, *Atlanta*

Cradles/Cribs Available

Argonaut Hotel, *San Francisco*

Biltmore Hotel, *Miami*

Boston Harbor, *Boston/Cape Cod Area*

Brown Palace, *Denver*

Caesars Palace, *Las Vegas*

Chatham Bars Inn, *Boston/Cape Cod Area*

Claremont Resort, *San Francisco*

Disneyland Hotel, *Los Angeles*

Disney's Animal Kingdom Lodge, *Orlando*

Disney's Beach Club Resort, *Orlando*

Disney's Boardwalk Inn, *Orlando*

Disney's Grand Californian, *Los Angeles*

Disney's Wilderness Lodge, *Orlando*

Hotel Special Feature Index

Renaissance Harborplace, *Baltimore*
Renaissance Hollywood, *Los Angeles*
Renaissance Worthington, *Dallas/Ft. Worth*
Rio All-Suite, *Las Vegas*
Ritz-Carlton, *Chicago*
Ritz-Carlton, *New Orleans*
Ritz-Carlton, *Philadelphia/ Lancaster*
Ritz-Carlton, *San Francisco*
Ritz-Carlton Buckhead, *Atlanta*
Ritz-Carlton Key Biscayne, *Miami*
Ritz-Carlton Marina del Rey, *Los Angeles*
Sheraton Buckhead, *Atlanta*
Sheraton Hotel & Towers, *Chicago*
Sheraton Inner Harbor, *Baltimore*
Sheraton Society Hill, *Philadelphia/Lancaster*
Shutters on the Beach, *Los Angeles*
Teatro, Hotel, *Denver*
Treasure Island, *Las Vegas*
Trump Internat'l, *NYC*
Venetian, The, *Las Vegas*
Waikoloa Beach Marriott, *Hawaii*
Westin, *Cincinnati*
Westin, *Seattle*
Westin Copley Pl., *Boston/Cape Cod Area*
Westin Galleria, *Dallas/ Ft. Worth*
Westin Maui, *Hawaii*
Westin Peachtree Plaza, *Atlanta*
Westin River North, *Chicago*
Westin St. Francis, *San Francisco*
Westin Stonebriar Resort, *Dallas/Ft. Worth*
Westin Tabor Ctr., *Denver*

Windsor Court, *New Orleans*
Wyndham/Canal Pl., *New Orleans*

Dramatic Design

Argonaut Hotel, *San Francisco*
Biltmore Hotel, *Miami*
Boston Harbor, *Boston/Cape Cod Area*
Caesars Palace, *Las Vegas*
Disney's Grand Floridian, *Orlando*
Fairmont Kea Lani, *Hawaii*
Grand Wailea Resort, *Hawaii*
Hilton Waikoloa Vlg., *Hawaii*
Hyatt Regency, *San Francisco*
JW Marriott Ihilani, *Hawaii*
Mandalay Bay, *Las Vegas*
MGM Grand, *Las Vegas*
Mirage, *Las Vegas*
Paris Las Vegas, *Las Vegas*
Park Hyatt, *Chicago*
Phoenician, The, *Phoenix/ Scottsdale*
Plaza, The, *NYC*
Portofino Bay Hotel/Universal, *Orlando*
Ritz-Carlton, *Philadelphia/ Lancaster*
Ritz-Carlton Battery Park, *NYC*
Venetian, The, *Las Vegas*

Fishing On-Site

Argonaut Hotel, *San Francisco*
Chatham Bars Inn, *Boston/Cape Cod Area*
del Coronado, *San Diego*
Disney's Grand Floridian, *Orlando*
Disney's Polynesian Resort, *Orlando*
Disney's Yacht Club Resort, *Orlando*
Doral Golf Resort, *Miami*
Edgewater, The, *Seattle*
Fairmont Kea Lani, *Hawaii*
Four Seasons Hualalai, *Hawaii*
Hyatt Regency, *Hawaii*
Ocean Edge Resort, *Boston/ Cape Cod Area*

Hotel Special Feature Index

Fontainebleau Hilton, *Miami*
Four Seasons, *Atlanta*
Four Seasons, *Boston/Cape Cod Area*
Four Seasons, *Chicago*
Four Seasons, *Houston*
Four Seasons, *Philadelphia/Lancaster*
Four Seasons, *San Francisco*
Four Seasons, *Washington, DC*
Four Seasons Aviara, *San Diego*
Four Seasons Hualalai, *Hawaii*
Four Seasons/Las Colinas, *Dallas/Ft. Worth*
Grand Hyatt, *Seattle*
Grand Hyatt, *Washington, DC*
Grand Wailea Resort, *Hawaii*
Harbor Court, *Baltimore*
Hard Rock Hotel, *Orlando*
Hershey, Hotel, *Philadelphia/Lancaster*
Hilton Hawaiian Vlg., *Hawaii*
Hilton, *San Diego*
Hilton Times Sq., *NYC*
Hilton Waikoloa Vlg., *Hawaii*
House of Blues, *Chicago*
Houstonian, The, *Houston*
Hyatt Regency, *Baltimore*
Hyatt Regency, *Hawaii*
Hyatt Regency, *San Francisco*
Hyatt Regency, *St. Louis*
Hyatt Regency Grand Cyp., *Orlando*
JW Marriott, *Houston*
JW Marriott, *Washington, DC*
JW Marriott Camelback Inn, *Phoenix/Scottsdale*
JW Marriott Desert Ridge, *Phoenix/Scottsdale*
JW Marriott Hotel Lenox, *Atlanta*
JW Marriott Ihilani, *Hawaii*
Kahala Mandarin Oriental, *Hawaii*
Library Hotel, *NYC*
Loews Coronado Bay, *San Diego*
Loews L'Enfant Plaza, *Washington, DC*

Loews Miami Beach, *Miami*
Loews Santa Monica Beach, *Los Angeles*
Mandalay Bay, *Las Vegas*
Marriott, *Philadelphia/Lancaster*
Marriott, *San Diego*
Marriott Copley Pl., *Boston/Cape Cod Area*
Marriott Coronado Isl., *San Diego*
Marriott Marquis, *NYC*
Marriott Maui, *Hawaii*
MGM Grand, *Las Vegas*
Millennium Bostonian, *Boston/Cape Cod Area*
Mirage, *Las Vegas*
NY Marriott/Brooklyn Br., *NYC*
Ocean Edge Resort, *Boston/Cape Cod Area*
Omni Chicago, *Chicago*
Omni Hotel/Independence Park, *Philadelphia/Lancaster*
Omni Mandalay Hotel, *Dallas/Ft. Worth*
Outrigger Waikiki, *Hawaii*
Paris Las Vegas, *Las Vegas*
Park Hyatt, *Chicago*
Park Hyatt, *Los Angeles*
Park Hyatt, *Washington, DC*
Peninsula, *Chicago*
Phoenician, The, *Phoenix/Scottsdale*
Plaza, The, *NYC*
Pointe Hilton Squaw Peak, *Phoenix/Scottsdale*
Pointe Hilton Tapatio Cliffs, *Phoenix/Scottsdale*
Pointe South Mountain, *Phoenix/Scottsdale*
Portofino Bay Hotel/Universal, *Orlando*
Renaissance, *NYC*
Renaissance Grand, *St. Louis*
Renaissance Harborplace, *Baltimore*
Renaissance Hollywood, *Los Angeles*

Renaissance Worthington, *Dallas/Ft. Worth*
RIHGA Royal, *NYC*
Rio All-Suite, *Las Vegas*
Ritz-Carlton, *Chicago*
Ritz-Carlton, *New Orleans*
Ritz-Carlton, *Philadelphia/ Lancaster*
Ritz-Carlton, *San Francisco*
Ritz-Carlton Battery Park, *NYC*
Ritz-Carlton Buckhead, *Atlanta*
Ritz-Carlton Coconut Grove, *Miami*
Ritz-Carlton Key Biscayne, *Miami*
Ritz-Carlton Marina del Rey, *Los Angeles*
Sheraton Buckhead, *Atlanta*
Sheraton Hotel & Towers, *Chicago*
Sheraton Inner Harbor, *Baltimore*
Sheraton Society Hill, *Philadelphia/Lancaster*
Shutters on the Beach, *Los Angeles*
Sonesta Beach/Key Biscayne, *Miami*
Teatro, Hotel, *Denver*
Trump Internat'l, *NYC*
Venetian, The, *Las Vegas*
Waikoloa Beach Marriott, *Hawaii*
Warwick, The, *Houston*
Westin, *Cincinnati*
Westin, *Seattle*
Westin Copley Pl., *Boston/Cape Cod Area*
Westin Galleria, *Dallas/ Ft. Worth*
Westin Maui, *Hawaii*
Westin Peachtree Plaza, *Atlanta*
Westin River North, *Chicago*
Westin St. Francis, *San Francisco*
Westin Stonebriar Resort, *Dallas/Ft. Worth*
Westin Tabor Ctr., *Denver*

Windsor Court, *New Orleans*
Wyndham/Canal Pl., *New Orleans*

Historic Interest
Argonaut Hotel, *San Francisco*
Biltmore Hotel, *Miami*
Brown Palace, *Denver*
Casa Del Mar, *Los Angeles*
Chatham Bars Inn, *Boston/Cape Cod Area*
Claremont Resort, *San Francisco*
del Coronado, *San Diego*
Edgewater, The, *Seattle*
Fairmont, *New Orleans*
Fairmont Miramar, *Los Angeles*
Fairmont Olympic, *Seattle*
Fairmont Scottsdale Princess, *Phoenix/Scottsdale*
Harbor View, *Boston/Cape Cod Area*
Hershey, Hotel, *Philadelphia/ Lancaster*
Houstonian, The, *Houston*
Hyatt Regency, *St. Louis*
Inn at the Market, *Seattle*
Millennium Bostonian, *Boston/ Cape Cod Area*
Ocean Edge Resort, *Boston/ Cape Cod Area*
Plaza, The, *NYC*
Renaissance Grand, *St. Louis*
Ritz-Carlton, *New Orleans*
Ritz-Carlton, *Philadelphia/ Lancaster*
Ritz-Carlton, *San Francisco*
Teatro, Hotel, *Denver*
Warwick, The, *Houston*
Westin St. Francis, *San Francisco*

Internet Access
Argonaut Hotel, *San Francisco*
Biltmore Hotel, *Miami*
Boston Harbor, *Boston/Cape Cod Area*
Casa Del Mar, *Los Angeles*
Chatham Bars Inn, *Boston/Cape Cod Area*

Hotel Special Feature Index

Claremont Resort, *San Francisco*
del Coronado, *San Diego*
Disney's Beach Club Resort, *Orlando*
Disney's Boardwalk Inn, *Orlando*
Disney's Wilderness Lodge, *Orlando*
Disney's Yacht Club Resort, *Orlando*
Doral Golf Resort, *Miami*
DoubleTree, *Chicago*
DoubleTree, *NYC*
Edgewater, The, *Seattle*
Embassy Suites, *NYC*
Embassy Suites Downtown, *St. Louis*
Fairmont, *New Orleans*
Fairmont Kea Lani, *Hawaii*
Fairmont Miramar, *Los Angeles*
Fairmont Olympic, *Seattle*
Fairmont Scottsdale Princess, *Phoenix/Scottsdale*
Fairmont Washington, *Washington, DC*
Four Seasons, *Atlanta*
Four Seasons, *Boston/Cape Cod Area*
Four Seasons, *Chicago*
Four Seasons, *Houston*
Four Seasons, *Philadelphia/Lancaster*
Four Seasons, *San Francisco*
Four Seasons, *Washington, DC*
Four Seasons Aviara, *San Diego*
Four Seasons Hualalai, *Hawaii*
Four Seasons/Las Colinas, *Dallas/Ft. Worth*
Grand Hyatt, *Seattle*
Grand Hyatt, *Washington, DC*
Grand Wailea Resort, *Hawaii*
Harbor Court, *Baltimore*
Hard Rock Hotel, *Orlando*
Hershey, Hotel, *Philadelphia/Lancaster*
Hilton, *San Diego*
Hilton Times Sq., *NYC*
Hilton Waikoloa Vlg., *Hawaii*

House of Blues, *Chicago*
Houstonian, The, *Houston*
Hyatt Regency, *Baltimore*
Hyatt Regency, *San Francisco*
Inn at the Market, *Seattle*
JW Marriott, *Houston*
JW Marriott, *Washington, DC*
JW Marriott Camelback Inn, *Phoenix/Scottsdale*
JW Marriott Desert Ridge, *Phoenix/Scottsdale*
Kahala Mandarin Oriental, *Hawaii*
Library Hotel, *NYC*
Loews Coronado Bay, *San Diego*
Marriott, *Philadelphia/Lancaster*
Marriott, *San Diego*
Marriott Copley Pl., *Boston/Cape Cod Area*
Marriott Marquis, *NYC*
Marriott Waterfront, *Baltimore*
MGM Grand, *Las Vegas*
NY Marriott/Brooklyn Br., *NYC*
Ocean Edge Resort, *Boston/Cape Cod Area*
Omni Chicago, *Chicago*
Omni Mandalay Hotel, *Dallas/Ft. Worth*
Outrigger Waikiki, *Hawaii*
Park Hyatt, *Chicago*
Peninsula, *Chicago*
Phoenician, The, *Phoenix/Scottsdale*
Plaza, The, *NYC*
Pointe Hilton Squaw Peak, *Phoenix/Scottsdale*
Pointe Hilton Tapatio Cliffs, *Phoenix/Scottsdale*
Portofino Bay Hotel/Universal, *Orlando*
Renaissance Grand, *St. Louis*
Renaissance Hollywood, *Los Angeles*
Renaissance Worthington, *Dallas/Ft. Worth*
RIHGA Royal, *NYC*
Ritz-Carlton, *Chicago*

Hotel Special Feature Index

Ritz-Carlton, *New Orleans*
Ritz-Carlton, *Philadelphia/ Lancaster*
Ritz-Carlton, *San Francisco*
Ritz-Carlton Battery Park, *NYC*
Ritz-Carlton Buckhead, *Atlanta*
Ritz-Carlton Key Biscayne, *Miami*
Ritz-Carlton Marina del Rey, *Los Angeles*
Sheraton Buckhead, *Atlanta*
Sheraton Hotel & Towers, *Chicago*
Sheraton Inner Harbor, *Baltimore*
Shutters on the Beach, *Los Angeles*
Sonesta Beach/Key Biscayne, *Miami*
Teatro, Hotel, *Denver*
Treasure Island, *Las Vegas*
Trump Internat'l, *NYC*
Venetian, The, *Las Vegas*
Waikoloa Beach Marriott, *Hawaii*
Warwick, The, *Houston*
Westin, *Cincinnati*
Westin, *Seattle*
Westin Copley Pl., *Boston/Cape Cod Area*
Westin Galleria, *Dallas/ Ft. Worth*
Westin Maui, *Hawaii*
Westin Peachtree Plaza, *Atlanta*
Westin River North, *Chicago*
Westin St. Francis, *San Francisco*
Westin Stonebriar Resort, *Dallas/Ft. Worth*
Westin Tabor Ctr., *Denver*
Windsor Court, *New Orleans*
Wyndham/Canal Pl., *New Orleans*

Kitchens
Disney's Boardwalk Inn, *Orlando*
JW Marriott, *Houston*

JW Marriott Camelback Inn, *Phoenix/Scottsdale*
Pointe Royal Resort, *St. Louis*
Trump Internat'l, *NYC*
Yogi Bear's Jellystone Park, *St. Louis*

Live Entertainment for Kids
Claremont Resort, *San Francisco*
del Coronado, *San Diego*
Disney's Animal Kingdom Lodge, *Orlando*
Disney's Polynesian Resort, *Orlando*
Four Seasons Hualalai, *Hawaii*
Hard Rock Hotel, *Orlando*
Hilton Hawaiian Vlg., *Hawaii*
House of Blues, *Chicago*
Hyatt Regency, *Hawaii*
JW Marriott Camelback Inn, *Phoenix/Scottsdale*
MGM Grand, *Las Vegas*
Portofino Bay Hotel/Universal, *Orlando*
Ritz-Carlton, *San Francisco*
Treasure Island, *Las Vegas*
Yogi Bear's Jellystone Park, *St. Louis*

Mountain Setting
Fairmont Scottsdale Princess, *Phoenix/Scottsdale*
JW Marriott Camelback Inn, *Phoenix/Scottsdale*
JW Marriott Desert Ridge, *Phoenix/Scottsdale*
Phoenician, The, *Phoenix/ Scottsdale*
Pointe Hilton Squaw Peak, *Phoenix/Scottsdale*
Pointe Hilton Tapatio Cliffs, *Phoenix/Scottsdale*
Pointe Royal Resort, *St. Louis*
Pointe South Mountain, *Phoenix/Scottsdale*

Nurse/Doctor On-Site
Grand Wailea Resort, *Hawaii*
Hilton Waikoloa Vlg., *Hawaii*

JW Marriott Desert Ridge, *Phoenix/Scottsdale*

Kahala Mandarin Oriental, *Hawaii*

Ritz-Carlton, *New Orleans*

Westin Maui, *Hawaii*

Offbeat/Funky

del Coronado, *San Diego*

Disney's Polynesian Resort, *Orlando*

Disney's Wilderness Lodge, *Orlando*

House of Blues, *Chicago*

Library Hotel, *NYC*

Outrigger Waikiki, *Hawaii*

Rio All-Suite, *Las Vegas*

Teatro, Hotel, *Denver*

Yogi Bear's Jellystone Park, *St. Louis*

Pet-Friendly

Argonaut Hotel, *San Francisco*

Boston Harbor, *Boston/Cape Cod Area*

Brown Palace, *Denver*

Disney's Grand Californian, *Los Angeles*

Disney's Grand Floridian, *Orlando*

Disney's Polynesian Resort, *Orlando*

Edgewater, The, *Seattle*

Embassy Suites, *NYC*

Fairmont, *New Orleans*

Fairmont Miramar, *Los Angeles*

Fairmont Olympic, *Seattle*

Fairmont Scottsdale Princess, *Phoenix/Scottsdale*

Fairmont Washington, *Washington, DC*

Four Seasons, *Atlanta*

Four Seasons, *Boston/Cape Cod Area*

Four Seasons, *Chicago*

Four Seasons, *Houston*

Four Seasons, *Philadelphia/Lancaster*

Four Seasons, *San Francisco*

Four Seasons, *Washington, DC*

Four Seasons Aviara, *San Diego*

Four Seasons Hualalai, *Hawaii*

Four Seasons/Las Colinas, *Dallas/Ft. Worth*

Grand Hyatt, *Seattle*

Hard Rock Hotel, *Orlando*

Hilton Times Sq., *NYC*

Holiday Inn Vallejo, *San Francisco*

House of Blues, *Chicago*

JW Marriott Camelback Inn, *Phoenix/Scottsdale*

JW Marriott Desert Ridge, *Phoenix/Scottsdale*

Loews Coronado Bay, *San Diego*

Loews L'Enfant Plaza, *Washington, DC*

Loews Miami Beach, *Miami*

Loews Santa Monica Beach, *Los Angeles*

Marriott, *San Diego*

Marriott Coronado Isl., *San Diego*

Omni Chicago, *Chicago*

Omni Mandalay Hotel, *Dallas/Ft. Worth*

Park Hyatt, *Chicago*

Park Hyatt, *Washington, DC*

Peninsula, *Chicago*

Portofino Bay Hotel/Universal, *Orlando*

Renaissance, *NYC*

Renaissance Grand, *St. Louis*

Renaissance Worthington, *Dallas/Ft. Worth*

RIHGA Royal, *NYC*

Ritz-Carlton, *Chicago*

Ritz-Carlton, *Philadelphia/Lancaster*

Ritz-Carlton Battery Park, *NYC*

Ritz-Carlton Buckhead, *Atlanta*

Ritz-Carlton Key Biscayne, *Miami*

Teatro, Hotel, *Denver*

Westin, *Cincinnati*

Westin, *Seattle*

Westin Copley Pl., *Boston/Cape Cod Area*

Hotel Special Feature Index

Westin St. Francis, *San Francisco*
Westin Tabor Ctr., *Denver*
Windsor Court, *New Orleans*
Yogi Bear's Jellystone Park, *St. Louis*

Playground
Disney's Animal Kingdom Lodge, *Orlando*
Disney's Beach Club Resort, *Orlando*
Disney's Boardwalk Inn, *Orlando*
Disney's Wilderness Lodge, *Orlando*
Disney's Yacht Club Resort, *Orlando*
Four Seasons Hualalai, *Hawaii*
Grand Wailea Resort, *Hawaii*
Hilton, *San Diego*
Hyatt Regency Grand Cyp., *Orlando*
JW Marriott Ihilani, *Hawaii*
Ocean Edge Resort, *Boston/ Cape Cod Area*
Omni Mandalay Hotel, *Dallas/ Ft. Worth*
Pointe Hilton Squaw Peak, *Phoenix/Scottsdale*
Ritz-Carlton Key Biscayne, *Miami*

Playpens Available
Disneyland Hotel, *Los Angeles*
DoubleTree, *Chicago*
DoubleTree, *NYC*
Embassy Suites, *New Orleans*
Embassy Suites, *NYC*
Fairmont Kea Lani, *Hawaii*
Fairmont Washington, *Washington, DC*
Four Seasons, *Philadelphia/ Lancaster*
Four Seasons Hualalai, *Hawaii*
Grand Hyatt, *Seattle*
Grand Hyatt, *Washington, DC*
Grand Wailea Resort, *Hawaii*
Marriott, *San Diego*
Marriott Marquis, *NYC*

Paradise Pier Hotel, *Los Angeles*
Pointe Hilton Squaw Peak, *Phoenix/Scottsdale*
Trump Internat'l, *NYC*

Programs/ Workshops for Kids
(Call hotel for more information)
Boston Harbor, *Boston/Cape Cod Area*
Chatham Bars Inn, *Boston/Cape Cod Area*
Claremont Resort, *San Francisco*
del Coronado, *San Diego*
Disney's Animal Kingdom Lodge, *Orlando*
Disney's Beach Club Resort, *Orlando*
Disney's Boardwalk Inn, *Orlando*
Disney's Grand Floridian, *Orlando*
Disney's Polynesian Resort, *Orlando*
Disney's Wilderness Lodge, *Orlando*
Disney's Yacht Club Resort, *Orlando*
Doral Golf Resort, *Miami*
DoubleTree, *NYC*
Fairmont Kea Lani, *Hawaii*
Fairmont Olympic, *Seattle*
Fairmont Scottsdale Princess, *Phoenix/Scottsdale*
Four Seasons, *Boston/Cape Cod Area*
Four Seasons Aviara, *San Diego*
Four Seasons Hualalai, *Hawaii*
Four Seasons/Las Colinas, *Dallas/Ft. Worth*
Grand Wailea Resort, *Hawaii*
Hard Rock Hotel, *Orlando*
Hershey, Hotel, *Philadelphia/ Lancaster*
Hilton Hawaiian Vlg., *Hawaii*
Hilton, *San Diego*
Hilton Waikoloa Vlg., *Hawaii*

Houstonian, The, *Houston*
Hyatt Regency, *Hawaii*
Hyatt Regency Grand Cyp.,
  Orlando
JW Marriott Camelback Inn,
  Phoenix/Scottsdale
JW Marriott Desert Ridge,
  Phoenix/Scottsdale
JW Marriott Ihilani, *Hawaii*
Kahala Mandarin Oriental,
  Hawaii
Loews Coronado Bay, *San
  Diego*
Loews L'Enfant Plaza,
  Washington, DC
Loews Miami Beach, *Miami*
Loews Santa Monica Beach,
  Los Angeles
Marriott Maui, *Hawaii*
Ocean Edge Resort, *Boston/
  Cape Cod Area*
Omni Chicago, *Chicago*
Omni Hotel/Independence Park,
  Philadelphia/Lancaster
Omni Mandalay Hotel, *Dallas/
  Ft. Worth*
Park Hyatt, *Washington, DC*
Phoenician, The, *Phoenix/
  Scottsdale*
Plaza, The, *NYC*
Pointe Hilton Squaw Peak,
  Phoenix/Scottsdale
Pointe Hilton Tapatio Cliffs,
  Phoenix/Scottsdale
Pointe South Mountain,
  Phoenix/Scottsdale
Portofino Bay Hotel/Universal,
  Orlando
Renaissance Worthington,
  Dallas/Ft. Worth
Ritz-Carlton, *Chicago*
Ritz-Carlton, *New Orleans*
Ritz-Carlton, *San Francisco*
Ritz-Carlton Key Biscayne,
  Miami
Sonesta Beach/Key Biscayne,
  Miami
Waikoloa Beach Marriott,
  Hawaii

Westin, *Cincinnati*
Westin, *Seattle*
Westin Copley Pl., *Boston/Cape
  Cod Area*
Westin Maui, *Hawaii*
Westin Peachtree Plaza,
  Atlanta
Westin River North, *Chicago*
Westin St. Francis, *San
  Francisco*
Westin Tabor Ctr., *Denver*
Windsor Court, *New Orleans*
Yogi Bear's Jellystone Park,
  St. Louis

Refrigerators

Argonaut Hotel, *San Francisco*
Claremont Resort, *San
  Francisco*
DoubleTree, *NYC*
Edgewater, The, *Seattle*
Embassy Suites, *New Orleans*
Embassy Suites, *NYC*
Embassy Suites Downtown,
  St. Louis
Embassy Suites Lakefront,
  Chicago
Embassy Suites Old Town,
  Washington, DC
Embassy Suites Rivercenter,
  Cincinnati
Fairmont Kea Lani, *Hawaii*
Fairmont Olympic, *Seattle*
Fairmont Washington,
  Washington, DC
Four Seasons, *Philadelphia/
  Lancaster*
Four Seasons, *San Francisco*
Four Seasons Aviara, *San Diego*
Four Seasons Hualalai, *Hawaii*
Harbor View, *Boston/Cape Cod
  Area*
Hard Rock Hotel, *Orlando*
Hilton, *San Diego*
Hilton Waikoloa Vlg., *Hawaii*
Hyatt Regency, *San Francisco*
Inn at the Market, *Seattle*
JW Marriott, *Washington, DC*

JW Marriott Camelback Inn, *Phoenix/Scottsdale*
JW Marriott Desert Ridge, *Phoenix/Scottsdale*
Loews L'Enfant Plaza, *Washington, DC*
Marriott, *Philadelphia/ Lancaster*
Marriott, *San Diego*
MGM Grand, *Las Vegas*
Omni Chicago, *Chicago*
Park Hyatt, *Chicago*
Park Hyatt, *Los Angeles*
Pointe Royal Resort, *St. Louis*
Portofino Bay Hotel/Universal, *Orlando*
Renaissance, *NYC*
Renaissance Worthington, *Dallas/Ft. Worth*
Rio All-Suite, *Las Vegas*
Ritz-Carlton, *New Orleans*
Ritz-Carlton, *San Francisco*
Ritz-Carlton Buckhead, *Atlanta*
Sheraton Buckhead, *Atlanta*
Sheraton Inner Harbor, *Baltimore*
Shutters on the Beach, *Los Angeles*
Trump Internat'l, *NYC*
Waikoloa Beach Marriott, *Hawaii*
Warwick, The, *Houston*
Westin, *Cincinnati*
Westin, *Seattle*
Westin Tabor Ctr., *Denver*
Windsor Court, *New Orleans*
Yogi Bear's Jellystone Park, *St. Louis*

Shopping On-Site
Argonaut Hotel, *San Francisco*
Boston Harbor, *Boston/Cape Cod Area*
Caesars Palace, *Las Vegas*
del Coronado, *San Diego*
Disney's Boardwalk Inn, *Orlando*
Four Seasons Aviara, *San Diego*

Four Seasons/Las Colinas, *Dallas/Ft. Worth*
Grand Wailea Resort, *Hawaii*
Hard Rock Hotel, *Orlando*
Hershey, Hotel, *Philadelphia/ Lancaster*
Hilton Netherland Plaza, *Cincinnati*
Hilton Hawaiian Vlg., *Hawaii*
Hyatt Regency, *Baltimore*
Hyatt Regency, *St. Louis*
JW Marriott, *Washington, DC*
JW Marriott Camelback Inn, *Phoenix/Scottsdale*
JW Marriott Hotel Lenox, *Atlanta*
Loews Santa Monica Beach, *Los Angeles*
Marriott Copley Pl., *Boston/ Cape Cod Area*
Marriott Waterfront, *Baltimore*
MGM Grand, *Las Vegas*
Mirage, *Las Vegas*
Paris Las Vegas, *Las Vegas*
Portofino Bay Hotel/Universal, *Orlando*
Renaissance Harborplace, *Baltimore*
Renaissance Hollywood, *Los Angeles*
Ritz-Carlton Key Biscayne, *Miami*
Sheraton Inner Harbor, *Baltimore*
Treasure Island, *Las Vegas*
Venetian, The, *Las Vegas*
Westin Copley Pl., *Boston/Cape Cod Area*
Westin Galleria, *Dallas/ Ft. Worth*
Westin Peachtree Plaza, *Atlanta*
Westin Tabor Ctr., *Denver*
Wyndham/Canal Pl., *New Orleans*

Spa Treatments
Biltmore Hotel, *Miami*
Boston Harbor, *Boston/Cape Cod Area*

Hotel Special Feature Index

Hotel Special Feature Index

Ritz-Carlton, *New Orleans*
Ritz-Carlton, *Philadelphia/ Lancaster*
Ritz-Carlton, *San Francisco*
Ritz-Carlton Battery Park, *NYC*
Ritz-Carlton Buckhead, *Atlanta*
Ritz-Carlton Coconut Grove, *Miami*
Ritz-Carlton Key Biscayne, *Miami*
Ritz-Carlton Marina del Rey, *Los Angeles*
Sheraton Hotel & Towers, *Chicago*
Shutters on the Beach, *Los Angeles*
Sonesta Beach/Key Biscayne, *Miami*
Teatro, Hotel, *Denver*
Treasure Island, *Las Vegas*
Trump Internat'l, *NYC*
Venetian, The, *Las Vegas*
Waikoloa Beach Marriott, *Hawaii*
Westin Copley Pl., *Boston/Cape Cod Area*
Westin Maui, *Hawaii*
Westin Peachtree Plaza, *Atlanta*
Westin River North, *Chicago*
Westin St. Francis, *San Francisco*
Westin Stonebriar Resort, *Dallas/Ft. Worth*
Windsor Court, *New Orleans*
Wyndham/Canal Pl., *New Orleans*

Strollers Available

Boston Harbor, *Boston/Cape Cod Area*
Doral Golf Resort, *Miami*
Fairmont Scottsdale Princess, *Phoenix/Scottsdale*
Fairmont Washington, *Washington, DC*
Four Seasons, *Chicago*
Four Seasons, *Houston*
Four Seasons Aviara, *San Diego*

Four Seasons/Las Colinas, *Dallas/Ft. Worth*
Hard Rock Hotel, *Orlando*
Hilton Times Sq., *NYC*
Hilton Waikoloa Vlg., *Hawaii*
Hyatt Regency, *Hawaii*
Kahala Mandarin Oriental, *Hawaii*
Loews Miami Beach, *Miami*
Marriott Copley Pl., *Boston/ Cape Cod Area*
Omni Chicago, *Chicago*
Park Hyatt, *Los Angeles*
Portofino Bay Hotel/Universal, *Orlando*
Ritz-Carlton, *Chicago*
Ritz-Carlton Marina del Rey, *Los Angeles*
Sheraton Hotel & Towers, *Chicago*
Trump Internat'l, *NYC*
Venetian, The, *Las Vegas*
Westin Peachtree Plaza, *Atlanta*
Westin St. Francis, *San Francisco*
Westin Tabor Ctr., *Denver*

Swimming Pool for Kids

del Coronado, *San Diego*
Disneyland Hotel, *Los Angeles*
Disney's Animal Kingdom Lodge, *Orlando*
Disney's Beach Club Resort, *Orlando*
Disney's Grand Californian, *Los Angeles*
Disney's Grand Floridian, *Orlando*
Disney's Polynesian Resort, *Orlando*
Disney's Wilderness Lodge, *Orlando*
Doral Golf Resort, *Miami*
Embassy Suites Downtown, *St. Louis*
Fairmont Kea Lani, *Hawaii*
Fontainebleau Hilton, *Miami*
Four Seasons Aviara, *San Diego*

Hotel Special Feature Index

Four Seasons Hualalai, *Hawaii*
Grand Wailea Resort, *Hawaii*
Hard Rock Hotel, *Orlando*
Hershey, Hotel, *Philadelphia/
  Lancaster*
Hilton Hawaiian Vlg., *Hawaii*
Hilton, *San Diego*
Hilton Waikoloa Vlg., *Hawaii*
Hyatt Regency Grand Cyp.,
  Orlando
JW Marriott Camelback Inn,
  Phoenix/Scottsdale
JW Marriott Desert Ridge,
  Phoenix/Scottsdale
Kahala Mandarin Oriental,
  Hawaii
Mandalay Bay, *Las Vegas*
Mirage, *Las Vegas*
Phoenician, The, *Phoenix/
  Scottsdale*
Pointe Hilton Squaw Peak,
  Phoenix/Scottsdale
Pointe Hilton Tapatio Cliffs,
  Phoenix/Scottsdale
Pointe South Mountain,
  Phoenix/Scottsdale
Portofino Bay Hotel/Universal,
  Orlando
Ritz-Carlton Key Biscayne,
  Miami
Waikoloa Beach Marriott,
  Hawaii
Yogi Bear's Jellystone Park,
  St. Louis

Tennis
Biltmore Hotel, *Miami*
Chatham Bars Inn, *Boston/Cape
  Cod Area*
Claremont Resort, *San
  Francisco*
del Coronado, *San Diego*
Disney's Beach Club Resort,
  Orlando
Disney's Boardwalk Inn,
  Orlando
Disney's Grand Floridian,
  Orlando

Disney's Yacht Club Resort,
  Orlando
Doral Golf Resort, *Miami*
Fairmont, *New Orleans*
Fairmont Kea Lani, *Hawaii*
Fairmont Scottsdale Princess,
  Phoenix/Scottsdale
Four Seasons, *Atlanta*
Four Seasons Aviara, *San Diego*
Four Seasons Hualalai, *Hawaii*
Four Seasons/Las Colinas,
  Dallas/Ft. Worth
Harbor Court, *Baltimore*
Harbor View, *Boston/Cape Cod
  Area*
Hershey, Hotel, *Philadelphia/
  Lancaster*
Hilton, *San Diego*
Hilton Waikoloa Vlg., *Hawaii*
Houstonian, The, *Houston*
Hyatt Regency, *Baltimore*
Hyatt Regency, *Hawaii*
Hyatt Regency Grand Cyp.,
  Orlando
JW Marriott Camelback Inn,
  Phoenix/Scottsdale
JW Marriott Desert Ridge,
  Phoenix/Scottsdale
JW Marriott Ihilani, *Hawaii*
Loews Coronado Bay, *San
  Diego*
Marriott, *San Diego*
Marriott Coronado Isl., *San
  Diego*
Marriott Maui, *Hawaii*
Ocean Edge Resort, *Boston/
  Cape Cod Area*
Paris Las Vegas, *Las Vegas*
Park Hyatt, *Los Angeles*
Phoenician, The, *Phoenix/
  Scottsdale*
Pointe Hilton Squaw Peak,
  Phoenix/Scottsdale
Pointe Hilton Tapatio Cliffs,
  Phoenix/Scottsdale
Pointe South Mountain,
  Phoenix/Scottsdale
Renaissance Worthington,
  Dallas/Ft. Worth

Ritz-Carlton Key Biscayne, *Miami*
Ritz-Carlton Marina del Rey, *Los Angeles*
Sonesta Beach/Key Biscayne, *Miami*
Waikoloa Beach Marriott, *Hawaii*
Westin Copley Pl., *Boston/Cape Cod Area*
Westin Maui, *Hawaii*

Video Games in Rooms
Argonaut Hotel, *San Francisco*
Biltmore Hotel, *Miami*
Boston Harbor, *Boston/Cape Cod Area*
Disney's Animal Kingdom Lodge, *Orlando*
DoubleTree, *NYC*
Edgewater, The, *Seattle*
Embassy Suites, *New Orleans*
Embassy Suites, *NYC*
Embassy Suites Downtown, *St. Louis*
Embassy Suites Old Town, *Washington, DC*
Embassy Suites Rivercenter, *Cincinnati*
Fairmont, *New Orleans*
Fairmont Kea Lani, *Hawaii*
Fairmont Olympic, *Seattle*
Fairmont Scottsdale Princess, *Phoenix/Scottsdale*
Four Seasons, *Atlanta*
Four Seasons, *Boston/Cape Cod Area*
Four Seasons, *Chicago*
Four Seasons, *Houston*
Four Seasons, *Philadelphia/Lancaster*
Four Seasons, *San Francisco*
Four Seasons, *Washington, DC*
Four Seasons Aviara, *San Diego*
Four Seasons Hualalai, *Hawaii*
Four Seasons/Las Colinas, *Dallas/Ft. Worth*
Grand Wailea Resort, *Hawaii*
Harbor Court, *Baltimore*

House of Blues, *Chicago*
Houstonian, The, *Houston*
Hyatt Regency Grand Cyp., *Orlando*
Marriott, *San Diego*
Marriott Waterfront, *Baltimore*
Omni Chicago, *Chicago*
Omni Mandalay Hotel, *Dallas/Ft. Worth*
Peninsula, *Chicago*
Renaissance Grand, *St. Louis*
Renaissance Worthington, *Dallas/Ft. Worth*
Ritz-Carlton, *Chicago*
Ritz-Carlton, *New Orleans*
Ritz-Carlton, *San Francisco*
Sheraton Hotel & Towers, *Chicago*
Teatro, Hotel, *Denver*
Trump Internat'l, *NYC*
Westin, *Cincinnati*
Westin River North, *Chicago*
Westin Stonebriar Resort, *Dallas/Ft. Worth*

Water Sports
Argonaut Hotel, *San Francisco*
Chatham Bars Inn, *Boston/Cape Cod Area*
del Coronado, *San Diego*
Disney's Grand Floridian, *Orlando*
Disney's Polynesian Resort, *Orlando*
Disney's Yacht Club Resort, *Orlando*
Doral Golf Resort, *Miami*
Edgewater, The, *Seattle*
Fairmont Kea Lani, *Hawaii*
Four Seasons Hualalai, *Hawaii*
Grand Wailea Resort, *Hawaii*
Harbor View, *Boston/Cape Cod Area*
Hilton Hawaiian Vlg., *Hawaii*
Hilton, *San Diego*
Hilton Waikoloa Vlg., *Hawaii*
Hyatt Regency, *Hawaii*
Hyatt Regency Grand Cyp., *Orlando*

Hotel Special Feature Index

JW Marriott Ihilani, *Hawaii*
Kahala Mandarin Oriental, *Hawaii*
Loews Coronado Bay, *San Diego*
Marriott, *San Diego*
Marriott Maui, *Hawaii*
Ocean Edge Resort, *Boston/ Cape Cod Area*

Ritz-Carlton Key Biscayne, *Miami*
Ritz-Carlton Marina del Rey, *Los Angeles*
Sonesta Beach/Key Biscayne, *Miami*
Waikoloa Beach Marriott, *Hawaii*
Westin Maui, *Hawaii*

RESTAURANT CUISINES

(Restaurants are followed by the section name in which their reviews appear. Restaurants not followed by a section name are Chains, and their reviews appear in the Restaurant Chains section.)

African

Boma, *Orlando*

American (New)

Buckhead Diner, *Atlanta*
Cafe Nola, *Seattle*
Cheesecake Factory
City Cafe, *Baltimore*
Daily Review Café, *Houston*
Flying Fish Café, *Orlando*
Fog City Diner, *San Francisco*
Full Moon, *Boston/Cape Cod Area*
Marathon Grill, *Philadelphia/Lancaster*
Palomino, *Cincinnati*
Rose Tattoo Cafe, *Philadelphia/Lancaster*
Wild Sage Café, *Las Vegas*

American (Traditional)

America, *Las Vegas*
America, *NYC*
American Girl Place, *Chicago*
American Roadhouse, *Atlanta*
Annie's Cafe, *Denver*
Ann Sather, *Chicago*
Applebee's
Aquarium, *Houston*
Back on the Bch., *Los Angeles*
Barking Dog, *NYC*
Baugher's, *Baltimore*
Berghoff, *Chicago*
Beverly Hills Cafe, *Miami*
Big Island Grill, *Hawaii*
Big Pink, *Miami*
Big Sky Cafe, *St. Louis*
Black Dog Tavern, *Boston/Cape Cod Area*
Blue in Green, *Philadelphia/Lancaster*
Brooklyn Diner, *NYC*

Bubba Gump Shrimp Co.
Bubby's, *NYC*
Cafe Deluxe, *Washington, DC*
Cafe '50s, *Los Angeles*
Cafe Hon, *Baltimore*
Chatham Squire, *Boston/Cape Cod Area*
Cheeseburger in Paradise, *Hawaii*
Cheesecake Factory
Chef Mickey's, *Orlando*
Chili's Grill & Bar
Cinderella's Royal Table, *Orlando*
City Tavern, *Philadelphia/Lancaster*
Claim Jumper Rest.
Clyde's, *Washington, DC*
Cole's P.E. Buffet, *Los Angeles*
Comfort Diner, *NYC*
Corvette Diner, *San Diego*
Crown Candy Kitchen, *St. Louis*
Crystal Palace, *Orlando*
Dave & Buster's
EJ's Luncheonette, *NYC*
EZ's, *Dallas/Ft. Worth*
50's Prime Time Cafe, *Orlando*
5 Spot, *Seattle*
Friendly Farm, *Baltimore*
Hard Rock Cafe
Harley-Davidson, *Las Vegas*
Highland Park Pharmacy, *Dallas/Ft. Worth*
Houston's, *Phoenix/Scottsdale*
Islands, *Los Angeles*
Jackson Hole, *NYC*
Johnny Rockets
Jones, *Philadelphia/Lancaster*
Jungle Jim's, *Orlando*
Kidd Valley, *Seattle*
Kona Cafe, *Orlando*

Lake Mead Cruises, *Las Vegas*
Leona's, *Chicago*
Liberty Tree Tavern, *Orlando*
Lou Mitchell's, *Chicago*
Lucile's Stateside Bistro,
  Dallas/Ft. Worth
Mama's on Washington Sq.,
  San Francisco
Mars 2112, *NYC*
Max & Erma's
Medieval Times
Mickey Mantle's, *NYC*
Mick's, *Atlanta*
Mimi's Cafe
Mo's, *San Francisco*
Mr. & Mrs. Bartley's Burger,
  Boston/Cape Cod Area
Mr. Lucky's 24/7, *Las Vegas*
News Cafe, *Miami*
1900 Park Fare, *Orlando*
Original Pancake House
Paradise Garden, *Las Vegas*
Pat's Bar & Grill, *St. Louis*
Pizzeria Uno/Due, *Chicago*
Planet Hollywood
Popeyes, *New Orleans*
Popover Cafe, *NYC*
Quark's, *Las Vegas*
Rainforest Cafe
Red Robin
R.J. Grunts, *Chicago*
Roadhouse Grill
Ruby's
Rustler's Rooste, *Phoenix/
  Scottsdale*
Ryan's Family Steakhse.
Serendipity 3, *NYC*
Skyline Chili, *Cincinnati*
St. Louis Bread, *St. Louis*
Tavern on the Green, *NYC*
Ted's Montana Grill, *Denver*
T.G.I. Friday's
Tony Roma's
Uncle Bill's Pancake, *Los
  Angeles*
Uno Chicago Grill
Varsity, *Atlanta*
White Fence Farm, *Denver*
Zesto Drive In, *Atlanta*

Asian
Betty's Wok & Noodle Diner,
  Boston/Cape Cod Area
Cafe Sambal, *Miami*
Flat Top Grill, *Chicago*
OnJin's Cafe, *Hawaii*
Pei Wei Asian Diner, *Phoenix/
  Scottsdale*
Ruby Foo's, *NYC*
Side Street Inn, *Hawaii*
Trader Vic's, *Atlanta*

Bakeries
Macrina Bakery & Cafe, *Seattle*
Mama's on Washington Sq.,
  San Francisco

Barbecue
Dallas BBQ, *NYC*
Flame Tree BBQ, *Orlando*
Goode Co. Texas BBQ, *Houston*
Johnny Rebs', *Los Angeles*
Montgomery Inn, *Cincinnati*
Pig, The, *Los Angeles*
Sonny Bryan's Smokehse.,
  Dallas/Ft. Worth
Super Smokers BBQ, *St. Louis*
Tony Roma's
Virgil's BBQ, *NYC*

Brazilian
Fogo de Chão, *Atlanta*

Cajun
Emeril's, *Las Vegas*
Franky & Johnny's, *New
  Orleans*
Pappadeaux Seafood, *Atlanta*
Tony Mandola's, *Houston*
Uglesich's, *New Orleans*

Californian
California Grill, *Orlando*
Delicias, *San Diego*
Spago, *Los Angeles*
Wolfgang Puck Cafe, *Orlando*

Cheese Steaks
Geno's Steaks, *Philadelphia/
  Lancaster*
Jim's Steaks, *Philadelphia/
  Lancaster*

Pat's King of Steaks, *Philadelphia/Lancaster*
Reading Terminal Mkt., *Philadelphia/Lancaster*

Chinese
(* dim sum specialist)
China Pearl, *Boston/Cape Cod Area**
Emerald Chinese Seafood, *San Diego**
Five Happiness, *New Orleans*
Golden Dragon, *Hawaii*
Golden Unicorn, *NYC**
LuLu, *St. Louis*
Tony Cheng's, *Washington, DC*

Coffeehouses
Café Du Monde, *New Orleans*

Coffee Shops/Diners
Annie's Cafe, *Denver*
Big Pink, *Miami*
Blue in Green, *Philadelphia/Lancaster*
Brooklyn Diner, *NYC*
Cafe '50s, *Los Angeles*
Cafe Hon, *Baltimore*
Chick & Ruth's Delly, *Baltimore*
Comfort Diner, *NYC*
Corvette Diner, *San Diego*
Crown Candy Kitchen, *St. Louis*
EJ's Luncheonette, *NYC*
5 & Diner, *Phoenix/Scottsdale*
Johnny Rockets
Lou Mitchell's, *Chicago*
Mama's on Washington Sq., *San Francisco*
Max's, *San Francisco*
Mel's Drive-In, *Los Angeles*
Mel's Drive-In, *San Francisco*
Mr. Lucky's 24/7, *Las Vegas*
News Cafe, *Miami*
Purple Cow, *Dallas/Ft. Worth*
Roxy's Diner, *Las Vegas*
St. Louis Bread, *St. Louis*
Zippy's, *Hawaii*

Contemporary Louisiana
Emeril's, *New Orleans*

Continental
Cinderella's Royal Table, *Orlando*
Fountain Rest., *Philadelphia/Lancaster*
Mirage Buffet, *Las Vegas*
Rose Tattoo Cafe, *Philadelphia/Lancaster*
Trader Vic's, *Atlanta*

Creole
Brennan's, *New Orleans*
Commander's Palace, *New Orleans*
Emeril's, *Las Vegas*
Emeril's Restaurant Orlando, *Orlando*
Pappadeaux Seafood, *Atlanta*
Uglesich's, *New Orleans*

Cuban
Bongos Cuban Café, *Miami*
La Carreta, *Miami*
Las Culebrinas, *Miami*

Delis
Art's Deli, *Los Angeles*
Carnegie Deli, *NYC*
Chompies, *Phoenix/Scottsdale*
D.Z. Akin's, *San Diego*
Katz's Deli, *NYC*
Marathon Grill, *Philadelphia/Lancaster*
Max's, *San Francisco*
Potbelly Sandwich, *Chicago*
Zaidy's, *Denver*

Dessert
Café Du Monde, *New Orleans*
Cafe Hon, *Baltimore*
Café/Pâtisserie Descours, *Houston*
Commander's Palace, *New Orleans*
Crown Candy Kitchen, *St. Louis*
Ghirardelli's Soda Fountain, *San Diego*
Hansen's Sno-Bliz, *New Orleans*
Macrina Bakery & Cafe, *Seattle*
Serendipity 3, *NYC*
Spago, *Los Angeles*

Restaurant Cuisine Index

Eclectic
Bellagio Buffet, *Las Vegas*
California Pizza Kit.
Fire & Ice, *Boston/Cape Cod Area*
foodlife, *Chicago*
John's Place, *Chicago*
Nikki Beach, *Miami*
Noodles & Co., *Washington, DC*
Paradise Garden, *Las Vegas*
Parallel 33, *San Diego*
Reading Terminal Mkt., *Philadelphia/Lancaster*
Semolina Internat'l Pasta, *New Orleans*
Zea Cafe, *New Orleans*

Floribbean
Jimmy Buffett's Margaritaville, *Orlando*

French
Brennan's, *New Orleans*
OnJin's Cafe, *Hawaii*

French (Bistro)
Café/Pâtisserie Descours, *Houston*

French (New)
Fountain Rest., *Philadelphia/Lancaster*

German
Berghoff, *Chicago*

Greek
Samos, *Baltimore*

Hamburgers
Barney's Gourmet Hamburger, *San Francisco*
Beverly Hills Cafe, *Miami*
Big Pink, *Miami*
Bud's Broiler, *New Orleans*
Cheeseburger in Paradise, *Hawaii*
Clyde's, *Washington, DC*
Corvette Diner, *San Diego*
5 & Diner, *Phoenix/Scottsdale*
Fuddrucker's

Goode Co. Hamburgers, *Houston*
Hard Rock Cafe
Hodad's, *San Diego*
In-N-Out Burger
Islands, *Los Angeles*
Jackson Hole, *NYC*
Johnny Rockets
Kidd Valley, *Seattle*
Kincaid's, *Dallas/Ft. Worth*
Mel's Drive-In, *Los Angeles*
Mel's Drive-In, *San Francisco*
Mo's, *San Francisco*
Mr. & Mrs. Bartley's Burger, *Boston/Cape Cod Area*
Planet Hollywood
Quark's, *Las Vegas*
Red Robin
R.J. Grunts, *Chicago*
Roadhouse Grill
Zesto Drive In, *Atlanta*
Zippy's, *Hawaii*

Hawaiian
Disney's Spirit of Aloha, *Orlando*
Hula Grill, *Hawaii*
Islands, *Los Angeles*
Kona Cafe, *Orlando*
Maui Tacos, *Hawaii*
Pineapple Room, *Hawaii*
Roy's Kahana Bar, *Hawaii*

Hot Dogs
Gold Coast Dogs, *Chicago*
Zesto Drive In, *Atlanta*

Ice Cream Parlor
Cafe Hon, *Baltimore*
Ghirardelli's Soda Fountain, *San Diego*
Hansen's Sno-Bliz, *New Orleans*
Highland Park Pharmacy, *Dallas/Ft. Worth*
Purple Cow, *Dallas/Ft. Worth*

Italian
(S=Southern)
Alejo's, *Los Angeles*
Alioto's, *San Francisco* (S)

Artu, *Boston/Cape Cod Area*
Bertucci's
Big Cheese, *Miami*
Buca di Beppo (S)
C & O Trattoria, *Los Angeles* (S)
Capp's Corner, *San Francisco*
Carmine's, *NYC* (S)
Charlie Gitto's, *St. Louis*
Cucina! Cucina!, *Seattle*
Cunetto House of Pasta,
    St. Louis
Filippi's Pizza Grotto, *San Diego*
Italian Bistro, *Philadelphia/*
    Lancaster
John's Pizzeria, *NYC*
La Mela, *NYC*
Leona's, *Chicago* (S)
Louisiana Pizza Kit., *New*
    Orleans
Maggiano's (S)
Metro Pizza, *Las Vegas*
Miceli's, *Los Angeles*
Old Spaghetti Factory
Olive Garden
Pasta Pomodoro, *San Francisco*
Pietro's Coal Oven Pizza,
    Philadelphia/Lancaster
Ristorante Piatti, *Denver*
Rocky's Gourmet Pizza, *New*
    Orleans
Romano's Macaroni Grill
Sabatino's, *Baltimore*
Sammy's Woodfired Pizza, *San*
    Diego
Saucy Noodle, *Denver*
Semolina Internat'l Pasta, *New*
    Orleans
Tony Mandola's, *Houston*
Tony's Di Napoli, *NYC* (S)
2 Amys, *Washington, DC* (S)
Via Italia Trattoria, *San Diego*

Japanese
(* sushi specialist)
Azuma, *Houston*
Benihana
Isobune, *San Francisco**
Sansei Seafood, *Hawaii*
Tokyohana Grill, *Houston**

Lebanese
Lebanese Taverna,
    Washington, DC

Mediterranean
Cucina! Cucina!, *Seattle*
Merriman's Market Café,
    Hawaii
Palomino, *Cincinnati*
Savor, *San Francisco*

Mexican
Baja Fresh Mexican
Casa Bonita, *Denver*
Chevys Fresh Mex
El Azteca, *Philadelphia/Lancaster*
Jalisco, *Atlanta*
Joe T. Garcia's, *Dallas/Ft. Worth*
Kay 'n Dave's, *Los Angeles*
La Familia, *Dallas/Ft. Worth*
Mama Ninfa's, *Houston*
Maui Tacos, *Hawaii*
Nuevo Laredo Cantina, *Atlanta*
Old Town Mexican, *San Diego*
Pico's Mex-Mex, *Houston*
Rio Grande Cafe, *Washington, DC*

New England
Durgin Park, *Boston/Cape Cod*
    Area
Union Oyster House, *Boston/*
    Cape Cod Area

Nicaraguan
Los Ranchos, *Miami*

Nuevo Latino
Betty's Wok & Noodle Diner,
    Boston/Cape Cod Area

Pacific Northwest
Artist Point, *Orlando*
Elliott's Oyster House, *Seattle*
Etta's Seafood, *Seattle*
Ivar's Acres of Clams, *Seattle*
Ray's Boathouse, *Seattle*
SkyCity at the Needle, *Seattle*

Pacific Rim
Haliimaile General Store, *Hawaii*
Mama's Fish House, *Hawaii*

Restaurant Cuisine Index

Pineapple Room, *Hawaii*
Roy's Kahana Bar, *Hawaii*

Pan-Latin
Joy America Cafe, *Baltimore*
La Duni Latin Café, *Dallas/Ft. Worth*

Pizza
Archie's Gourmet Pizza, *Miami*
Bertucci's
Big Cheese, *Miami*
California Pizza Kit.
Chuck E. Cheese's
Dewey's Pizza, *Cincinnati*
Filippi's Pizza Grotto, *San Diego*
John's Pizzeria, *NYC*
La Rosa's, *Cincinnati*
Leona's, *Chicago*
Louisiana Pizza Kit., *New Orleans*
Metro Pizza, *Las Vegas*
Pagliacci Pizza, *Seattle*
Pietro's Coal Oven Pizza, *Philadelphia/Lancaster*
Pizzeria Bianco, *Phoenix/Scottsdale*
Pizzeria Uno/Due, *Chicago*
R & O's, *New Orleans*
Rocky's Gourmet Pizza, *New Orleans*
Sammy's Woodfired Pizza, *San Diego*
Saucy Noodle, *Denver*
Spago, *Los Angeles*
2 Amys, *Washington, DC*
Two Boots, *NYC*
Uno Chicago Grill
Upper Crust, *Boston/Cape Cod Area*

Sandwiches
Art's Deli, *Los Angeles*
Café/Pâtisserie Descours, *Houston*
Carnegie Deli, *NYC*
Geno's Steaks, *Philadelphia/Lancaster*
Jim's Steaks, *Philadelphia/Lancaster*
Katz's Deli, *NYC*
Marathon Grill, *Philadelphia/Lancaster*
Pat's King of Steaks, *Philadelphia/Lancaster*
Peanut Butter & Co., *NYC*
Philippe/Original, *Los Angeles*
Potbelly Sandwich, *Chicago*
Reading Terminal Mkt., *Philadelphia/Lancaster*
Rocky's Gourmet Pizza, *New Orleans*
Uglesich's, *New Orleans*
Zaidy's, *Denver*

Seafood
Alioto's, *San Francisco*
Anthony's Fish Grotto, *San Diego*
Aquarium, *Houston*
A. Sabella's, *San Francisco*
Bubba Gump Shrimp Co.
Cap'n Frosty's, *Boston/Cape Cod Area*
Deanie's Seafood, *New Orleans*
Elliott's Oyster House, *Seattle*
Emeril's, *Las Vegas*
Etta's Seafood, *Seattle*
Flying Fish Café, *Orlando*
Franky & Johnny's, *New Orleans*
Gladstone's Malibu, *Los Angeles*
Ivar's Acres of Clams, *Seattle*
Joe's Crab Shack
Legal Sea Foods, *Boston/Cape Cod Area*
L.P. Steamers, *Baltimore*
Mama's Fish House, *Hawaii*
Pappadeaux Seafood, *Atlanta*
Phillips, *Baltimore*
R & O's, *New Orleans*
Ray's Boathouse, *Seattle*
Reel Inn, *Los Angeles*
S & D Oyster Company, *Dallas/Ft. Worth*
Scoma's, *San Francisco*
Shuckers, *Seattle*
Tony Mandola's, *Houston*

Uglesich's, *New Orleans*
Union Oyster House, *Boston/ Cape Cod Area*

South American
Américas, *Houston*

Southern
Johnny Rebs', *Los Angeles*

Spanish
Las Culebrinas, *Miami*

Steakhouses
Benihana
Fogo de Chão, *Atlanta*
LongHorn Steakhse
Los Ranchos, *Miami*
O'Charley's
Outback Steakhse.
Pinnacle Peak Patio, *Phoenix/ Scottsdale*
Roadhouse Grill
Rustler's Rooste, *Phoenix/ Scottsdale*
Ryan's Family Steakhse.
Sir Galahad's, *Las Vegas*

Ted's Montana Grill, *Denver*
Trail Dust Steak, *Dallas/ Ft. Worth*

Swedish
Ann Sather, *Chicago*

Tex-Mex
Austin Grill, *Washington, DC*
Bubby's, *NYC*
Cactus Cantina, *Washington, DC*
Chili's Grill & Bar
Cowgirl, *NYC*
Don Pablo's
Goode Co. Hamburgers, *Houston*
Jalisco, *Atlanta*
Mama Ninfa's, *Houston*
Mi Rancho, *Washington, DC*
On the Border Mexican Grill
Rio Grande Cafe, *Washington, DC*

Thai
Lotus of Siam, *Las Vegas*
Tara Thai, *Washington, DC*

RESTAURANT SPECIAL FEATURES

(Indexes list the best of many within each category. Restaurants are followed by the section name in which their reviews appear. Those without a section name are chains – their reviews appear in the Restaurant Chains section.)

Breakfast
(See also Hotel Dining)
Archie's Gourmet Pizza, *Miami*
Berghoff, *Chicago*
Café Du Monde, *New Orleans*
Cheesecake Factory
Chompies, *Phoenix/Scottsdale*
Cinderella's Royal Table, *Orlando*
Emerald Chinese Seafood, *San Diego*
foodlife, *Chicago*
Geno's Steaks, *Philadelphia/Lancaster*
Johnny Rockets
La Carreta, *Miami*
Lake Mead Cruises, *Las Vegas*
Lou Mitchell's, *Chicago*
Marathon Grill, *Philadelphia/Lancaster*
Max's, *San Francisco*
Mimi's Cafe
Mo's, *San Francisco*
Pineapple Room, *Hawaii*
Zippy's, *Hawaii*

Brunch
(Check availability)
America, *NYC*
American Girl Place, *Chicago*
American Roadhouse, *Atlanta*
Austin Grill, *Washington, DC*
Barking Dog, *NYC*
Bellagio Buffet, *Las Vegas*
Beverly Hills Cafe, *Miami*
Blue in Green, *Philadelphia/Lancaster*
Brooklyn Diner, *NYC*
Bubby's, *NYC*
Buckhead Diner, *Atlanta*
Cactus Cantina, *Washington, DC*

Cafe Deluxe, *Washington, DC*
Cafe Hon, *Baltimore*
Cafe Nola, *Seattle*
Carnegie Deli, *NYC*
Cheesecake Factory
Chevys Fresh Mex
City Cafe, *Baltimore*
Clyde's, *Washington, DC*
Comfort Diner, *NYC*
Commander's Palace, *New Orleans*
Cowgirl, *NYC*
Crystal Palace, *Orlando*
Daily Review Café, *Houston*
Dave & Buster's
EJ's Luncheonette, *NYC*
Etta's Seafood, *Seattle*
Fire & Ice, *Boston/Cape Cod Area*
Fog City Diner, *San Francisco*
Fountain Rest., *Philadelphia/Lancaster*
Full Moon, *Boston/Cape Cod Area*
Gladstone's Malibu, *Los Angeles*
Jackson Hole, *NYC*
John's Place, *Chicago*
Jones, *Philadelphia/Lancaster*
Joy America Cafe, *Baltimore*
La Duni Latin Café, *Dallas/Ft. Worth*
Legal Sea Foods, *Boston/Cape Cod Area*
Lucile's Stateside Bistro, *Dallas/Ft. Worth*
Macrina Bakery & Cafe, *Seattle*
Maggiano's
Marathon Grill, *Philadelphia/Lancaster*
Medieval Times

Mel's Drive-In, *San Francisco*
Mickey Mantle's, *NYC*
Mimi's Cafe
Mirage Buffet, *Las Vegas*
News Cafe, *Miami*
Nikki Beach, *Miami*
Paradise Garden, *Las Vegas*
Pat's Bar & Grill, *St. Louis*
Peanut Butter & Co., *NYC*
Popover Cafe, *NYC*
Ruby Foo's, *NYC*
Savor, *San Francisco*
SkyCity at the Needle, *Seattle*
Tavern on the Green, *NYC*
Wild Sage Café, *Las Vegas*
Zippy's, *Hawaii*

Buffet
(Check availability)
Bellagio Buffet, *Las Vegas*
Boma, *Orlando*
Cactus Cantina, *Washington, DC*
Cole's P.E. Buffet, *Los Angeles*
Crystal Palace, *Orlando*
Fire & Ice, *Boston/Cape Cod Area*
Flat Top Grill, *Chicago*
Lake Mead Cruises, *Las Vegas*
Leona's, *Chicago*
Lotus of Siam, *Las Vegas*
Maggiano's
Mirage Buffet, *Las Vegas*
1900 Park Fare, *Orlando*
Paradise Garden, *Las Vegas*
Phillips, *Baltimore*
Popeyes, *New Orleans*
Ryan's Family Steakhse.
Tony Cheng's, *Washington, DC*

Children's Menus
Alioto's, *San Francisco*
America, *Las Vegas*
America, *NYC*
American Girl Place, *Chicago*
American Roadhouse, *Atlanta*
Annie's Cafe, *Denver*
Anthony's Fish Grotto, *San Diego*
Applebee's
Aquarium, *Houston*

Archie's Gourmet Pizza, *Miami*
Artist Point, *Orlando*
Art's Deli, *Los Angeles*
A. Sabella's, *San Francisco*
Austin Grill, *Washington, DC*
Back on the Bch., *Los Angeles*
Baja Fresh Mexican
Barney's Gourmet Hamburger, *San Francisco*
Baugher's, *Baltimore*
Benihana
Berghoff, *Chicago*
Bertucci's
Beverly Hills Cafe, *Miami*
Big Cheese, *Miami*
Big Pink, *Miami*
Black Dog Tavern, *Boston/Cape Cod Area*
Blue in Green, *Philadelphia/Lancaster*
Bongos Cuban Café, *Miami*
Brennan's, *New Orleans*
Bubba Gump Shrimp Co.
Bubby's, *NYC*
Buca di Beppo
Cactus Cantina, *Washington, DC*
Cafe Deluxe, *Washington, DC*
Cafe '50s, *Los Angeles*
Cafe Hon, *Baltimore*
Café/Pâtisserie Descours, *Houston*
Cafe Sambal, *Miami*
California Grill, *Orlando*
California Pizza Kit.
C & O Trattoria, *Los Angeles*
Casa Bonita, *Denver*
Chatham Squire, *Boston/Cape Cod Area*
Cheesecake Factory
Chef Mickey's, *Orlando*
Chevys Fresh Mex
Chick & Ruth's Delly, *Baltimore*
Chili's Grill & Bar
Chompies, *Phoenix/Scottsdale*
Cinderella's Royal Table, *Orlando*
City Tavern, *Philadelphia/Lancaster*
Claim Jumper Rest.

Restaurant Special Feature Index

Restaurant Special Feature Index

Restaurant Special Feature Index

Bubby's, *NYC*
Buca di Beppo
Cactus Cantina, *Washington, DC*
Cafe Deluxe, *Washington, DC*
Cafe '50s, *Los Angeles*
Cafe Sambal, *Miami*
California Pizza Kit.
C & O Trattoria, *Los Angeles*
Carmine's, *NYC*
Chatham Squire, *Boston/Cape Cod Area*
Cheeseburger in Paradise, *Hawaii*
Chef Mickey's, *Orlando*
Chevys Fresh Mex
Chili's Grill & Bar
Chompies, *Phoenix/Scottsdale*
City Tavern, *Philadelphia/Lancaster*
Claim Jumper Rest.
Clyde's, *Washington, DC*
Comfort Diner, *NYC*
Cowgirl, *NYC*
Dave & Buster's
Deanie's Seafood, *New Orleans*
D.Z. Akin's, *San Diego*
EJ's Luncheonette, *NYC*
Filippi's Pizza Grotto, *San Diego*
5 & Diner, *Phoenix/Scottsdale*
Friendly Farm, *Baltimore*
Ghirardelli's Soda Fountain, *San Diego*
Gladstone's Malibu, *Los Angeles*
Haliimaile General Store, *Hawaii*
Italian Bistro, *Philadelphia/Lancaster*
Ivar's Acres of Clams, *Seattle*
Johnny Rebs', *Los Angeles*
Johnny Rockets
Joy America Cafe, *Baltimore*
Jungle Jim's, *Orlando*
Kay 'n Dave's, *Los Angeles*
Kidd Valley, *Seattle*
Kona Cafe, *Orlando*
Leona's, *Chicago*
Maggiano's
Mama Ninfa's, *Houston*
Mama's Fish House, *Hawaii*
Mama's on Washington Sq., *San Francisco*
Mel's Drive-In, *Los Angeles*
Mel's Drive-In, *San Francisco*
Merriman's Market Café, *Hawaii*
Mimi's Cafe
Montgomery Inn, *Cincinnati*
On the Border Mexican Grill
Outback Steakhse.
Palomino, *Cincinnati*
Pasta Pomodoro, *San Francisco*
Pico's Mex-Mex, *Houston*
Pinnacle Peak Patio, *Phoenix/Scottsdale*
Pizzeria Uno/Due, *Chicago*
Popeyes, *New Orleans*
Purple Cow, *Dallas/Ft. Worth*
R & O's, *New Orleans*
Ristorante Piatti, *Denver*
R.J. Grunts, *Chicago*
Romano's Macaroni Grill
Rustler's Rooste, *Phoenix/Scottsdale*
Sansei Seafood, *Hawaii*
Saucy Noodle, *Denver*
Savor, *San Francisco*
Semolina Internat'l Pasta, *New Orleans*
SkyCity at the Needle, *Seattle*
Ted's Montana Grill, *Denver*
2 Amys, *Washington, DC*
Uncle Bill's Pancake, *Los Angeles*
Uno Chicago Grill
Zaidy's, *Denver*
Zea Cafe, *New Orleans*

Delivery/Takeout
(D=delivery, T=takeout)
Alejo's, *Los Angeles* (T)
America, *Las Vegas* (T)
America, *NYC* (T)
American Roadhouse, *Atlanta* (T)
Américas, *Houston* (T)
Annie's Cafe, *Denver* (T)
Ann Sather, *Chicago* (T)
Anthony's Fish Grotto, *San Diego* (T)

Restaurant Special Feature Index

Restaurant Special Feature Index

Friendly Farm, *Baltimore* (T)
Fuddrucker's (T)
Full Moon, *Boston/Cape Cod Area* (T)
Geno's Steaks, *Philadelphia/Lancaster* (T)
Ghirardelli's Soda Fountain, *San Diego* (T)
Gladstone's Malibu, *Los Angeles* (T)
Gold Coast Dogs, *Chicago* (T)
Golden Dragon, *Hawaii* (T)
Goode Co. Hamburgers, *Houston* (T)
Goode Co. Texas BBQ, *Houston* (D, T)
Haliimaile General Store, *Hawaii* (T)
Hansen's Sno-Bliz, *New Orleans* (T)
Hard Rock Cafe (T)
Harley-Davidson, *Las Vegas* (T)
Hodad's, *San Diego* (D, T)
Houston's, *Phoenix/Scottsdale* (T)
Hula Grill, *Hawaii* (T)
In-N-Out Burger (T)
Islands, *Los Angeles* (T)
Isobune, *San Francisco* (T)
Italian Bistro, *Philadelphia/Lancaster* (D, T)
Ivar's Acres of Clams, *Seattle* (T)
Jackson Hole, *NYC* (D, T)
Jalisco, *Atlanta* (T)
Jimmy Buffett's Margaritaville, *Orlando* (T)
Jim's Steaks, *Philadelphia/Lancaster* (T)
Joe's Crab Shack (T)
Johnny Rebs', *Los Angeles* (T)
Johnny Rockets (D, T)
John's Pizzeria, *NYC* (D, T)
John's Place, *Chicago* (T)
Jones, *Philadelphia/Lancaster* (T)
Jungle Jim's, *Orlando* (T)
Katz's Deli, *NYC* (D, T)
Kay 'n Dave's, *Los Angeles* (D, T)
Kidd Valley, *Seattle* (T)
Kincaid's, *Dallas/Ft. Worth* (T)
La Carreta, *Miami* (D, T)
La Duni Latin Café, *Dallas/Ft. Worth* (T)

La Mela, *NYC* (T)
La Rosa's, *Cincinnati* (D, T)
Las Culebrinas, *Miami* (T)
Lebanese Taverna, *Washington, DC* (T)
Legal Sea Foods, *Boston/Cape Cod Area* (T)
Leona's, *Chicago* (D, T)
LongHorn Steakhse (T)
Los Ranchos, *Miami* (D, T)
Lotus of Siam, *Las Vegas* (T)
Louisiana Pizza Kit., *New Orleans* (T)
Lou Mitchell's, *Chicago* (D, T)
L.P. Steamers, *Baltimore* (T)
Lucile's Stateside Bistro, *Dallas/Ft. Worth* (T)
LuLu, *St. Louis* (T)
Macrina Bakery & Cafe, *Seattle* (D, T)
Maggiano's (D, T)
Mama Ninfa's, *Houston* (D, T)
Mama's on Washington Sq., *San Francisco* (T)
Marathon Grill, *Philadelphia/Lancaster* (D, T)
Maui Tacos, *Hawaii* (T)
Max's, *San Francisco* (T)
Mel's Drive-In, *Los Angeles* (T)
Mel's Drive-In, *San Francisco* (T)
Metro Pizza, *Las Vegas* (D, T)
Miceli's, *Los Angeles* (D, T)
Mickey Mantle's, *NYC* (T)
Mick's, *Atlanta* (D, T)
Mimi's Cafe (T)
Mi Rancho, *Washington, DC* (T)
Montgomery Inn, *Cincinnati* (T)
Mo's, *San Francisco* (T)
Mr. & Mrs. Bartley's Burger, *Boston/Cape Cod Area* (T)
Mr. Lucky's 24/7, *Las Vegas* (T)
News Cafe, *Miami* (T)
Noodles & Co., *Washington, DC* (T)
Nuevo Laredo Cantina, *Atlanta* (T)
Old Spaghetti Factory (T)
Old Town Mexican, *San Diego* (T)
Olive Garden (T)
OnJin's Cafe, *Hawaii* (T)
On the Border Mexican Grill (T)
Original Pancake House (T)

Restaurant Special Feature Index

Outback Steakhse. (T)
Pagliacci Pizza, *Seattle* (D, T)
Palomino, *Cincinnati* (T)
Pappadeaux Seafood, *Atlanta* (T)
Parallel 33, *San Diego* (T)
Pasta Pomodoro, *San Francisco* (T)
Pat's Bar & Grill, *St. Louis* (T)
Pat's King of Steaks, *Philadelphia/Lancaster* (T)
Peanut Butter & Co., *NYC* (D, T)
Pei Wei Asian Diner, *Phoenix/Scottsdale* (T)
Phillips, *Baltimore* (T)
Pico's Mex-Mex, *Houston* (T)
Pietro's Coal Oven Pizza, *Philadelphia/Lancaster* (T)
Pig, The, *Los Angeles* (T)
Pineapple Room, *Hawaii* (T)
Pinnacle Peak Patio, *Phoenix/Scottsdale* (T)
Pizzeria Uno/Due, *Chicago* (D, T)
Planet Hollywood (T)
Popeyes, *New Orleans* (T)
Popover Cafe, *NYC* (D, T)
Potbelly Sandwich, *Chicago* (D, T)
Purple Cow, *Dallas/Ft. Worth* (D, T)
Quark's, *Las Vegas* (T)
Rainforest Cafe (T)
R & O's, *New Orleans* (T)
Ray's Boathouse, *Seattle* (T)
Reading Terminal Mkt., *Philadelphia/Lancaster* (T)
Reel Inn, *Los Angeles* (T)
Rio Grande Cafe, *Washington, DC* (T)
Ristorante Piatti, *Denver* (T)
R.J. Grunts, *Chicago* (T)
Roadhouse Grill (T)
Rocky's Gourmet Pizza, *New Orleans* (D, T)
Romano's Macaroni Grill (T)
Rose Tattoo Cafe, *Philadelphia/Lancaster* (T)
Roxy's Diner, *Las Vegas* (T)
Ruby Foo's, *NYC* (D, T)
Rustler's Rooste, *Phoenix/Scottsdale* (T)
Sabatino's, *Baltimore* (D, T)
Sammy's Woodfired Pizza, *San Diego* (D, T)

Samos, *Baltimore* (T)
S & D Oyster Company, *Dallas/Ft. Worth* (T)
Sansei Seafood, *Hawaii* (T)
Saucy Noodle, *Denver* (T)
Savor, *San Francisco* (T)
Semolina Internat'l Pasta, *New Orleans* (D, T)
Side Street Inn, *Hawaii* (T)
Skyline Chili, *Cincinnati* (D, T)
Sonny Bryan's Smokehse., *Dallas/Ft. Worth* (D, T)
St. Louis Bread, *St. Louis* (T)
Super Smokers BBQ, *St. Louis* (T)
Tara Thai, *Washington, DC* (T)
Ted's Montana Grill, *Denver* (T)
T.G.I. Friday's (D, T)
Tokyohana Grill, *Houston* (T)
Tony Cheng's, *Washington, DC* (T)
Tony Mandola's, *Houston* (D, T)
Tony Roma's (D, T)
Tony's Di Napoli, *NYC* (D, T)
Trail Dust Steak, *Dallas/Ft. Worth* (T)
2 Amys, *Washington, DC* (T)
Two Boots, *NYC* (D, T)
Uglesich's, *New Orleans* (T)
Uncle Bill's Pancake, *Los Angeles* (T)
Union Oyster House, *Boston/Cape Cod Area* (T)
Uno Chicago Grill (D, T)
Upper Crust, *Boston/Cape Cod Area* (D, T)
Varsity, *Atlanta* (T)
Via Italia Trattoria, *San Diego* (T)
Virgil's BBQ, *NYC* (D, T)
White Fence Farm, *Denver* (T)
Wild Sage Café, *Las Vegas* (D, T)
Zaidy's, *Denver* (D, T)
Zea Cafe, *New Orleans* (D, T)
Zesto Drive In, *Atlanta* (T)
Zippy's, *Hawaii* (T)

Drive-Thru

Big Island Grill, *Hawaii*
In-N-Out Burger
Johnny Rockets
Zesto Drive In, *Atlanta*

Restaurant Special Feature Index

Early-Bird
Barking Dog, *NYC*
Benihana
Carmine's, *NYC*
Chompies, *Phoenix/Scottsdale*
Cucina! Cucina!, *Seattle*
Dallas BBQ, *NYC*
Jungle Jim's, *Orlando*
Mr. Lucky's 24/7, *Las Vegas*

Hotel Dining
America, *Las Vegas*
Artist Point, *Orlando*
Bellagio Buffet, *Las Vegas*
Boma, *Orlando*
Cafe Sambal, *Miami*
California Grill, *Orlando*
Chef Mickey's, *Orlando*
Disney's Spirit of Aloha, *Orlando*
Emeril's, *Las Vegas*
Flying Fish Café, *Orlando*
Fountain Rest., *Philadelphia/Lancaster*
Kona Cafe, *Orlando*
Mel's Drive-In, *San Francisco*
Mirage Buffet, *Las Vegas*
Mr. Lucky's 24/7, *Las Vegas*
1900 Park Fare, *Orlando*
Paradise Garden, *Las Vegas*
Quark's, *Las Vegas*
Roxy's Diner, *Las Vegas*
Shuckers, *Seattle*
Sir Galahad's, *Las Vegas*
Trader Vic's, *Atlanta*

Live Entertainment for Kids
Barney's Gourmet Hamburger, *San Francisco*
Cafe '50s, *Los Angeles*
Casa Bonita, *Denver*
Chef Mickey's, *Orlando*
Chuck E. Cheese's
Dewey's Pizza, *Cincinnati*
Disney's Spirit of Aloha, *Orlando*
EZ's, *Dallas/Ft. Worth*
Jungle Jim's, *Orlando*
Medieval Times
Quark's, *Las Vegas*

Rustler's Rooste, *Phoenix/Scottsdale*
White Fence Farm, *Denver*

Offbeat/Funky
Alejo's, *Los Angeles*
Back on the Bch., *Los Angeles*
Benihana
Boma, *Orlando*
Buca di Beppo
Cafe '50s, *Los Angeles*
Cafe Hon, *Baltimore*
C & O Trattoria, *Los Angeles*
Capp's Corner, *San Francisco*
Chick & Ruth's Delly, *Baltimore*
City Cafe, *Baltimore*
Cowgirl, *NYC*
Crown Candy Kitchen, *St. Louis*
5 Spot, *Seattle*
Flying Fish Café, *Orlando*
Harley-Davidson, *Las Vegas*
Hodad's, *San Diego*
Jones, *Philadelphia/Lancaster*
La Carreta, *Miami*
Maggiano's
Mars 2112, *NYC*
Max's, *San Francisco*
Nikki Beach, *Miami*
Parallel 33, *San Diego*
Peanut Butter & Co., *NYC*
Philippe/Original, *Los Angeles*
Pig, The, *Los Angeles*
Quark's, *Las Vegas*
S & D Oyster Company, *Dallas/Ft. Worth*
Sansei Seafood, *Hawaii*
Side Street Inn, *Hawaii*
Uglesich's, *New Orleans*
Wolfgang Puck Cafe, *Orlando*

Outdoor Dining
(G=garden; P=patio;
S=sidewalk; T=terrace)
American Roadhouse, *Atlanta* (P)
Ann Sather, *Chicago* (P)
Anthony's Fish Grotto, *San Diego* (P)
Aquarium, *Houston* (P)
Archie's Gourmet Pizza, *Miami* (S)
Artist Point, *Orlando* (T)

Restaurant Special Feature Index

Art's Deli, *Los Angeles* (S)

Austin Grill, *Washington, DC* (P)

Back on the Bch., *Los Angeles* (P)

Barking Dog, *NYC* (G, P, S)

Barney's Gourmet Hamburger, *San Francisco* (P)

Beverly Hills Cafe, *Miami* (P)

Big Cheese, *Miami* (P)

Big Pink, *Miami* (P, S)

Big Sky Cafe, *St. Louis* (G, P)

Black Dog Tavern, *Boston/Cape Cod Area* (T)

Bongos Cuban Café, *Miami* (T)

Bubby's, *NYC* (S)

Cactus Cantina, *Washington, DC* (S)

Cafe Deluxe, *Washington, DC* (P, S)

Cafe '50s, *Los Angeles* (P)

Cafe Nola, *Seattle* (P)

Cafe Sambal, *Miami* (P)

C & O Trattoria, *Los Angeles* (P)

Carmine's, *NYC* (S)

Chompies, *Phoenix/Scottsdale* (S)

City Cafe, *Baltimore* (S)

City Tavern, *Philadelphia/Lancaster* (G)

Commander's Palace, *New Orleans* (P)

Cowgirl, *NYC* (S)

Cucina! Cucina!, *Seattle* (P, S, T)

Daily Review Café, *Houston* (G, P)

Dallas BBQ, *NYC* (S)

Delicias, *San Diego* (G)

Disney's Spirit of Aloha, *Orlando* (T)

Durgin Park, *Boston/Cape Cod Area* (P)

EJ's Luncheonette, *NYC* (S)

El Azteca, *Philadelphia/Lancaster* (S)

Elliott's Oyster House, *Seattle* (T)

EZ's, *Dallas/Ft. Worth* (P)

Filippi's Pizza Grotto, *San Diego* (P)

Flame Tree BBQ, *Orlando* (G)

Flat Top Grill, *Chicago* (S)

Fog City Diner, *San Francisco* (S)

Geno's Steaks, *Philadelphia/Lancaster* (S)

Gladstone's Malibu, *Los Angeles* (P)

Gold Coast Dogs, *Chicago* (S)

Golden Dragon, *Hawaii* (G)

Goode Co. Hamburgers, *Houston* (P)

Goode Co. Texas BBQ, *Houston* (P)

Harley-Davidson, *Las Vegas* (P, S)

Houston's, *Phoenix/Scottsdale* (P)

Islands, *Los Angeles* (P)

Jackson Hole, *NYC* (G, S)

Jimmy Buffett's Margaritaville, *Orlando* (P)

Joe T. Garcia's, *Dallas/Ft. Worth* (P)

John's Pizzeria, *NYC* (G)

John's Place, *Chicago* (S)

Joy America Cafe, *Baltimore* (T)

Jungle Jim's, *Orlando* (P)

Kay 'n Dave's, *Los Angeles* (S)

La Carreta, *Miami* (P)

La Duni Latin Café, *Dallas/Ft. Worth* (P)

La Familia, *Dallas/Ft. Worth* (P)

La Mela, *NYC* (G)

Lebanese Taverna, *Washington, DC* (P, S)

Legal Sea Foods, *Boston/Cape Cod Area* (P)

Los Ranchos, *Miami* (T)

Louisiana Pizza Kit., *New Orleans* (S)

Lou Mitchell's, *Chicago* (S)

L.P. Steamers, *Baltimore* (T)

Lucile's Stateside Bistro, *Dallas/Ft. Worth* (P)

Macrina Bakery & Cafe, *Seattle* (S)

Marathon Grill, *Philadelphia/Lancaster* (P, S)

Maui Tacos, *Hawaii* (P)

Max's, *San Francisco* (S)

Mel's Drive-In, *Los Angeles* (P)

Mel's Drive-In, *San Francisco* (S)

Metro Pizza, *Las Vegas* (P)

Miceli's, *Los Angeles* (S)

Mickey Mantle's, *NYC* (S)

Mick's, *Atlanta* (P)

Mi Rancho, *Washington, DC* (P)

Montgomery Inn, *Cincinnati* (P)

Mo's, *San Francisco* (P)

Mr. & Mrs. Bartley's Burger, *Boston/Cape Cod Area* (S)

Restaurant Special Feature Index

Reservations Required

Anthony's Fish Grotto, *San Diego*
Benihana
Betty's Wok & Noodle Diner, *Boston/Cape Cod Area*
Commander's Palace, *New Orleans*
Disney's Spirit of Aloha, *Orlando*
Emeril's, *New Orleans*
Emeril's, *Las Vegas*
Emeril's Restaurant Orlando, *Orlando*
50's Prime Time Cafe, *Orlando*
Fogo de Chão, *Atlanta*
Fountain Rest., *Philadelphia/Lancaster*
Golden Dragon, *Hawaii*
Lake Mead Cruises, *Las Vegas*
Lebanese Taverna, *Washington, DC*
Los Ranchos, *Miami*
Maggiano's
Medieval Times
Montgomery Inn, *Cincinnati*
Rose Tattoo Cafe, *Philadelphia/Lancaster*
Wild Sage Café, *Las Vegas*

Smoke-Free Section

Américas, *Houston*
Austin Grill, *Washington, DC*
Berghoff, *Chicago*
Big Sky Cafe, *St. Louis*
Brennan's, *New Orleans*
Buca di Beppo
Cactus Cantina, *Washington, DC*
Cafe Deluxe, *Washington, DC*
Cheesecake Factory
Chevys Fresh Mex
Claim Jumper Rest.
Commander's Palace, *New Orleans*
Cucina! Cucina!, *Seattle*
Deanie's Seafood, *New Orleans*
Don Pablo's
Elliott's Oyster House, *Seattle*
Emeril's, *New Orleans*
Emeril's, *Las Vegas*

Fire & Ice, *Boston/Cape Cod Area*
5 Spot, *Seattle*
Flat Top Grill, *Chicago*
Fogo de Chão, *Atlanta*
Fountain Rest., *Philadelphia/Lancaster*
Hard Rock Cafe
Jones, *Philadelphia/Lancaster*
Lebanese Taverna, *Washington, DC*
Legal Sea Foods, *Boston/Cape Cod Area*
Maggiano's
Marathon Grill, *Philadelphia/Lancaster*
Mick's, *Atlanta*
Palomino, *Cincinnati*
Pappadeaux Seafood, *Atlanta*
Phillips, *Baltimore*
Pietro's Coal Oven Pizza, *Philadelphia/Lancaster*
Pizzeria Uno/Due, *Chicago*
Planet Hollywood
Red Robin
Rio Grande Cafe, *Washington, DC*
R.J. Grunts, *Chicago*
Sansei Seafood, *Hawaii*
Semolina Internat'l Pasta, *New Orleans*
Tavern on the Green, *NYC*
Tokyohana Grill, *Houston*
Trader Vic's, *Atlanta*
Uno Chicago Grill

Special Events for Kids

American Girl Place, *Chicago*
Buca di Beppo
California Pizza Kit.
Chuck E. Cheese's
Medieval Times
Pizzeria Uno/Due, *Chicago*
Ryan's Family Steakhse.
Uno Chicago Grill

Theme

America, *Las Vegas*
Benihana
Brooklyn Diner, *NYC*
Bubba Gump Shrimp Co.

Restaurant Special Feature Index

Buca di Beppo
Cheesecake Factory
Chuck E. Cheese's
City Tavern, *Philadelphia/ Lancaster*
Dave & Buster's
Fire & Ice, *Boston/Cape Cod Area*
Fogo de Chão, *Atlanta*
Hard Rock Cafe
Harley-Davidson, *Las Vegas*
Joe's Crab Shack
Johnny Rockets
Maggiano's
Mars 2112, *NYC*
Max's, *San Francisco*
Medieval Times
Mickey Mantle's, *NYC*
Old Spaghetti Factory
Parallel 33, *San Diego*
Planet Hollywood
Quark's, *Las Vegas*
Roadhouse Grill
Union Oyster House, *Boston/ Cape Cod Area*
Varsity, *Atlanta*

Valet Parking

Alejo's, *Los Angeles*
America, *Las Vegas*
Américas, *Houston*
Anthony's Fish Grotto, *San Diego*
Archie's Gourmet Pizza, *Miami*
Artist Point, *Orlando*
Art's Deli, *Los Angeles*
Bellagio Buffet, *Las Vegas*
Big Pink, *Miami*
Boma, *Orlando*
Buckhead Diner, *Atlanta*
Cafe Sambal, *Miami*
California Grill, *Orlando*
C & O Trattoria, *Los Angeles*
Clyde's, *Washington, DC*
Commander's Palace, *New Orleans*
Corvette Diner, *San Diego*
Cucina! Cucina!, *Seattle*
Daily Review Café, *Houston*

Disney's Spirit of Aloha, *Orlando*
Elliott's Oyster House, *Seattle*
Emeril's, *New Orleans*
Emeril's, *Las Vegas*
Emeril's Restaurant Orlando, *Orlando*
Flat Top Grill, *Chicago*
Flying Fish Café, *Orlando*
Fogo de Chão, *Atlanta*
Fountain Rest., *Philadelphia/ Lancaster*
Gladstone's Malibu, *Los Angeles*
Golden Dragon, *Hawaii*
Houston's, *Phoenix/Scottsdale*
Jimmy Buffett's Margaritaville, *Orlando*
Jones, *Philadelphia/Lancaster*
Kona Cafe, *Orlando*
La Duni Latin Café, *Dallas/ Ft. Worth*
Las Culebrinas, *Miami*
Los Ranchos, *Miami*
Mama Ninfa's, *Houston*
Mama's Fish House, *Hawaii*
Metro Pizza, *Las Vegas*
Miceli's, *Los Angeles*
Mirage Buffet, *Las Vegas*
Montgomery Inn, *Cincinnati*
Mr. Lucky's 24/7, *Las Vegas*
News Cafe, *Miami*
Nikki Beach, *Miami*
1900 Park Fare, *Orlando*
Phillips, *Baltimore*
Pig, The, *Los Angeles*
Quark's, *Las Vegas*
Reel Inn, *Los Angeles*
Ristorante Piatti, *Denver*
R.J. Grunts, *Chicago*
Roxy's Diner, *Las Vegas*
Sabatino's, *Baltimore*
Sansei Seafood, *Hawaii*
Scoma's, *San Francisco*
Semolina Internat'l Pasta, *New Orleans*
Shuckers, *Seattle*
Sir Galahad's, *Las Vegas*
SkyCity at the Needle, *Seattle*
Spago, *Los Angeles*

Tara Thai, *Washington, DC*
Tavern on the Green, *NYC*
Trader Vic's, *Atlanta*

Views

Alioto's, *San Francisco*
American Girl Place, *Chicago*
Anthony's Fish Grotto, *San Diego*
Aquarium, *Houston*
A. Sabella's, *San Francisco*
Back on the Bch., *Los Angeles*
Black Dog Tavern, *Boston/Cape Cod Area*
Boma, *Orlando*
Bubby's, *NYC*
Cafe Sambal, *Miami*
California Grill, *Orlando*
Cheeseburger in Paradise, *Hawaii*
Cucina! Cucina!, *Seattle*
Elliott's Oyster House, *Seattle*
Flying Fish Café, *Orlando*
Fog City Diner, *San Francisco*
Fountain Rest., *Philadelphia/Lancaster*
Friendly Farm, *Baltimore*
Gladstone's Malibu, *Los Angeles*
Golden Dragon, *Hawaii*
Hula Grill, *Hawaii*
Ivar's Acres of Clams, *Seattle*
Jones, *Philadelphia/Lancaster*
Joy America Cafe, *Baltimore*
Lake Mead Cruises, *Las Vegas*
Legal Sea Foods, *Boston/Cape Cod Area*
Los Ranchos, *Miami*

Louisiana Pizza Kit., *New Orleans*
L.P. Steamers, *Baltimore*
Mama's Fish House, *Hawaii*
Mo's, *San Francisco*
Nikki Beach, *Miami*
Pappadeaux Seafood, *Atlanta*
Pat's Bar & Grill, *St. Louis*
Phillips, *Baltimore*
Pinnacle Peak Patio, *Phoenix/Scottsdale*
Ray's Boathouse, *Seattle*
Reel Inn, *Los Angeles*
Rustler's Rooste, *Phoenix/Scottsdale*
Scoma's, *San Francisco*
SkyCity at the Needle, *Seattle*
Ted's Montana Grill, *Denver*

Waterside

Alioto's, *San Francisco*
Anthony's Fish Grotto, *San Diego*
Artist Point, *Orlando*
Back on the Bch., *Los Angeles*
Black Dog Tavern, *Boston/Cape Cod Area*
Bongos Cuban Café, *Miami*
Cafe Sambal, *Miami*
Cucina! Cucina!, *Seattle*
Gladstone's Malibu, *Los Angeles*
Hula Grill, *Hawaii*
Ivar's Acres of Clams, *Seattle*
Joy America Cafe, *Baltimore*
Los Ranchos, *Miami*
Mama's Fish House, *Hawaii*
Nikki Beach, *Miami*
Scoma's, *San Francisco*

Alphabetical Index
to Attractions

Alphabetical Index to Attractions

Alphabetical Index to Attractions

Alphabetical Index to Attractions

Alphabetical Index to Attractions

Alphabetical Index to Attractions

Alphabetical Index to Attractions

Alphabetical Index to Attractions

Alphabetical Index to Attractions

Alphabetical Index to Attractions

Alphabetical Index to Attractions

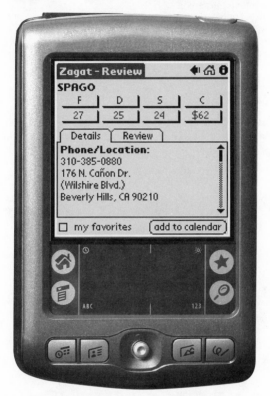